Encyclopedia of Latino Popular Culture

Encyclopedia of Latino Popular Culture

Volume I

A–L

Cordelia Chávez Candelaria
Executive Editor

Arturo J. Aldama
Co-Specialist Editor

Peter J. García
Co-Specialist Editor

Alma Alvarez-Smith
Managing Editor

GREENWOOD PRESS
WESTPORT, CONNECTICUT • LONDON

Library of Congress Cataloging-in-Publication Data

Encyclopedia of Latino popular culture [two volumes] / edited by Cordelia Chávez Candelaria, Peter J. García, and Arturo J. Aldama ; Alma Alvarez-Smith, assistant editor.
p. cm.
Includes bibliographical references and index.
ISBN 0-313-32215-5 (set : alk. paper) — ISBN 0-313-33210-X (v. 1 : alk. paper) — ISBN 0-313-33211-8 (v. 2 : alk. paper)
1. Hispanic Americans—Social life and customs—Encyclopedias. 2. Hispanic Americans—Intellectual life—Encyclopedias. 3. Hispanic Americans and mass media—Encyclopedias. 4. Hispanic American arts—Encyclopedias. 5. Popular culture—United States—Encyclopedias. 6. United States—Civilization—Hispanic influences—Encyclopedias. 7. United States—Ethnic relations—Encyclopedias. I. Candelaria, Cordelia. II. García, Peter J. III. Aldama, Arturo J., 1964–
E184.S75E59 2004
305.868'073'03–dc22 2004047454

British Library Cataloguing in Publication Data is available.

Library of Congress Catalog Card Number: 2004047454
ISBN: 0-313-32215-5 (set)
0-313-33210-X (vol. I)
0-313-33211-8 (vol. II)

First published in 2004

Greenwood Press, 88 Post Road West, Westport, CT 06881
An imprint of Greenwood Publishing Group, Inc.
www.greenwood.com

Printed in the United States of America

The paper used in this book complies with the Permanent Paper Standard issued by the National Information Standards Organization (Z39.48–1984).

10 9 8 7 6 5 4 3 2 1

Advisory Board

Contents

Preface

Popular culture is what people unofficially do, say, value, and practice in everyday life. Art, food, religion, literature, music, entertainment, and a wide variety of other societal activities, customs, and the products they generate constitute popular culture. The *Encyclopedia of Latino Popular Culture* is the first two-volume A-to-Z reference tool devoted to the vast subject of Latina and Latino popular culture. Woven into the fabric of daily experience, pop culture practices and forms of expression help define the varied identities of people collectively and as individual members of their respective identity groups. The editors use *Latina and Latino* interchangeably throughout this encyclopedia, according to the practice of critical cultural studies specialists, with the singular form *Latina/o* and the plural forms *Latinas/Latinos* and *Latinas/os* also employed where appropriate. Occasionally *Hispanic* and *Hispanics* are substituted as equivalent pan-ethnic labels. (See the Introduction and the encyclopedia entry "Race and Ethnicity" for further definition and discussion of descriptive ethnic labeling.)

Researching and compiling this unique project has been exhilarating, demanding, and extremely gratifying to the editors and the extended team of researchers who contributed to the design, research, writing, editing, and all other aspects of its development. The exhilaration and gratification come in part from the amazing variety and compelling fascination of the material. Another part derives from our central purpose: to write the first major reference tool on the vast and engrossing wealth of information about Mexican American, Puerto Rican, Cuban American, and related Latina/o popular cultures in the United States. Motivated by the desire to construct an important general information resource both for the general public and for specialists, the editorial team found that for largely the same reasons the project has been extraordinarily demanding. The vast scope of coverage of this two-volume encyclopedia and its pan–U.S. Latina/o inclusiveness challenged the editorial team at every stage of research—from determining subject definition, ethnic group terminology, time frame, and comparative context to fact-checking, identifying contributors and advisers, and executing the work of writing and editing. Also greatly compounding our editorial challenge was the editors' decision to drive the project to completion on an accelerated schedule to meet the pressing and growing demand from all quarters of the public for a reference work of this type.

Accordingly, by designing this reference tool to fill the current void on the subject of Latina/o popular culture(s) in the United States, the editors sought to build an encyclopedia that would complement existing reference works about the largest ethnic minority population in North America. Our aim is to meet the needs of reference libraries as well as general audiences for research-based, up-to-date information about the wide-ranging hybridity of Latina/o mestizo popular culture(s). Indeed, it is the multiplicity of identities, diverse histories, and continuing growth of the population that explains why we chose to use "culture(*s*)," the combined singular and plural form, when appropriate throughout the two volumes. Our approach captures the cultural similarities among Latinas/os in the United States, while at the same time also acknowledging that there are significant differences both *among* and *within* the subgroups, depending on geography, history, immigrant or nonimmigrant experience, and related features. This multiple subjectivity is often minimized or overlooked in public discourse concerning both American pop culture(s) and contemporary U.S. American society. Although useful reference tools published before 2004 offer research on Latin American history and culture, they are focused by definition for the most part on Central and South American topics and give only spare to minor attention to U.S. Hispanics or to pop culture. Similarly, several helpful Hispanic biographical dictionaries are available, but they include little to no information on pop culture, historical background, or critical cultural studies analysis within which to consider their Latina/o subjects. Thus, to address the gap on current reference tool shelves, this encyclopedia accomplishes the following:

- Focuses on Latinas/os in the United States
- Addresses U.S. Latina/o popular cultural practices and products
- Provides historical context and sociocultural background to illuminate the resurgent popularity of Latina/o popular culture worldwide
- Works within an interdisciplinary critical cultural studies framework to explain the exciting breadth, depth, and multiplicity of the subject
- Meets the immediate needs of broad general audiences for research-based information on Latinas/os generally and on Latina/o pop culture specifically

Of the several informative studies that have been published in the last decade on Hispanics, on Latino life and culture, and on selected areas of Latina/o popular culture, none accomplishes the combined and interrelated objectives enumerated in this two-volume reference.

This project was originally initiated by Greenwood. Arturo J. Aldama and Greenwood editors invited Cordelia Chávez Candelaria to head the enterprise as executive general editor in 2001. Peter J. García's participation was a natural outgrowth of hallway conversations in the Department of Chicana and Chicano Studies (CCS) at Arizona State University in Tempe. As a team, we were reminded repeatedly throughout our collaboration of the immense scope and complex layers of our subject matter, a vastness that can barely be hinted at here. We certainly cannot summarize in a brief preface the many vital topics, themes, theories, viewpoints, resources, and debates that emerged at every step of our compilation as, briefly put, we considered *what to include* and *what to call it*. Everything, from the title itself to the scope and function of the historical chronology and related history entries, raised questions of definition, importance, ideology, and philosophy, and these unavoidably led to other questions regarding theoretical assumptions and their implications. In the Introduction, we summarize the most important aspects of these editorial challenges and conceptual complexities, particularly with respect to matters of socioeconomic class, ethnicity, gender, language, race, sexuality, and related indicators of individual and cultural identities. The Introduction provides an expanded rationale for those users interested in the theoretical premises underlying our decision making and methodology. Suffice it to note at this point that the editors' choices of topics to include were determined by two compelling factors—our title subject and our collective judgment as to what additional conceptual and historical information should be included as a context for the reader's better understanding of the Latina/o pop culture entries. Where our achievement matches our best intention, we gratefully acknowledge the indispensable contributions of our many associates; where the final results fall short, we take full responsibility for the gap or error.

Acknowledgments

The editors wish to express their immense gratitude to the hundreds of individuals who helped in countless ways to compile the information contained within the *Encyclopedia of Latino Popular Culture* and to bring the project to fruition. The contributions of each were indispensable, and we credit each and all of you, even as we take full responsibility for any errors that may remain. We extend special thanks to the Department of Chicana and Chicano Studies (CCS) at Arizona State University (ASU) at Tempe for partial sponsorship through staff and research assistant support, to our CCS colleagues for their outstanding individual contributions and enormous patience as we pushed this project forward, and particularly to CCS Administrative Secretary Alma Alvarez-Smith for her indispensable participation and extraordinary talents, assets that led to her expanded role as Managing Editor for the project.

As well, we extend grateful thanks to Emmanuel Sánchez for his meticulous research assistance and reliable support; to Julie Amparano García, Asunción Benítez-Rush, Barbara Firoozye, Dr. Damarys Lacayo-Salas, Katie Mason, and Laura Slown for efficient editing; to Rajeet Chatterjee for helpful research assistance; to Loyola M. Chávez and Gabriel Higuera for impeccable indexing and general support; and to Vera Galaviz, Jennifer Morehouse, and undergraduate assistants Ana Y. Contreras-Gilbert Celaya and Noémy Martínez for outstanding support within our tight calendar. We acknowledge visiting lecturers Cecilia Aragón, Tlisza Jaurequi, Joyce Lausch, Michelle Martínez, and Dr. Virginia Pesqueira, as well as graduate assistants Lorenzo De La Fuente, James E. García, Socorro Gómez-Barajas, Cristina Muñoz, María Nates, Martha Saavedra, Juan Tanaka, Arthur Valdivia, and Silvia Villota, for enriching the climate in CCS during the press of research and writing. We also thank the ASU students who assisted in the project through classroom workshops on reference tool development and who served as first readers, fact checkers, focus group respondents, preliminary editors, and researchers for draft entries for the project. Thanks, too, to John Wagner, development editor, and Wendi Schnaufer, acquisitions editor, with the Greenwood Publishing Group for their helpful guidance and encouragement, as well as to John Donohue and Westchester Book Services for their meticulous copyediting. With profound gratitude we also thank our families for their simply indispensable support throughout the relentless demands of this project. We greatly appreciate the specific assistance provided by Ronald Beveridge, Dulce Aldama, and Emerson Smith, as well as our respective extended *familias* for their unwavering patience and cheerful encouragement. *¡Mil y muchissimas gracias!*

How to Use This Encyclopedia

There are two main ways to use this reference tool effectively: by starting here in the How to Use This Encyclopedia section or by skipping directly to the Alphabetical List of Entries, arranged A to Z, to locate a person, place, concept, or other term relating to Latina and Latino popular culture and Hispanics in the United States.

Three additional lists provide access to the headword entries by allowing readers to quickly identify related entries. Entries by Subject divides the entries in the two volumes into broad and useful topic categories, such as all entries relating to Folklore, History, Holidays and Fiestas, Music, and Television and Media. Readers can thus more easily trace broad themes and ideas across and through the entries. People by Field of Endeavor categorizes biographical entries by their subject's position, career, or field of expertise or achievement, such as Athletes, Politicians, or Writers. People by Country of Origin or Heritage lists the subjects of biographical entries by the country or culture of their birth or primary identification.

The comprehensive Index at the end of Volume II contains an alphabetical listing of all the headwords, cross-referenced keywords, and other significant terms, names, and concepts defined or discussed within the encyclopedia. As such, the Index offers a second portal of information for those users who do not find the information they are seeking when they check the A-to-Z headwords. For example, although the musical instrument *berimbau* is not a stand-alone headword entry, it is listed in the Index, which refers the user to the entry *Latin American Musical Instruments in the United States, where *berimbau* is defined and discussed in terms of its ethnomusicological role in the Latina/o pop music of the United States. Likewise, Nobel laureate Gabriel García Márquez, as a native and expatriate of

Colombia who writes about his homeland, is not featured in a headword entry; however, a check of the Index for "García Márquez" yields references to the writer in the headword entries *Magic Realism and *Casa de las Américas.

This section describes how the encyclopedia is organized and provides a practical introduction and preliminary context for understanding the substance of the headword entries themselves. Referring to the hundreds of terms defined and explained in these two volumes, the headwords number nearly 500 items. The headwords are supplemented by over 12,000 other keyword references that are listed in the Index and discussed or mentioned in the headword entries. This guide starts with a discussion of the abbreviations and specialized terms used throughout these two volumes. We then outline the editors' recommendations for effective ways to use the encyclopedia.

ACRONYMS, ABBREVIATIONS, AND SPECIALIZED TERMS

An asterisk (*) in front of a word or name signifies a *cross-reference* to a headword entry on that word or name elsewhere in the encyclopedia. Cross-references indicate terms and topics that are related to each other and that would be useful for the user to consult. For example, the headword entry on Academy Award–winning actor Benicio Del Toro contains cross-references to the movies **Traffic*, and **Bread and Roses*, as well as to the entries on Che *Guevara and Mexican actress Salma *Hayek. Each cross-reference is related to Del Toro in some way.

Acronyms and *abbreviations* appear as headwords when the acronym or abbreviation is the best-known identification for the subject. Full names are identified in the body of the headword entry. For example, the acronym MALDEF—for the Mexican American Legal Defense and Education Fund—appears as a headword entry. In other cases, when the subject is best known by a full name, as in the Puerto Rican Legal Defense and Education Fund, the headword entry is listed as such. In general, common abbreviations (e.g., ABC, CBS, CNN, HBO, NBC, NPR, and PBS for media broadcast stations, and CD, DVD, PC, and email for familiar computer and digital formats) are provided in full at time of first appearance. However, when less well known abbreviations are used (like CBO, CCS, LAS, and RCAF), they are immediately identified in parentheses (e.g., community-based organization, Chicana and Chicano Studies, Latin American Studies, and Royal Chicano Air Force, respectively).

To provide background concerning Hispanics in the United States, a detailed Chronology of Latina and Latino history is presented following the Entries of People by Country of Origin or Heritage list in the frontmatter of Volume I of this encyclopedia.

Arranged in thematic categories (Art, Film and Theater, Food, Sports, etc.), a general Bibliography of recommended further readings for readers seeking additional research-based information on Latina and Latino popular culture is found in the back matter to Volume II. For convenience, most headword entries in this encyclopedia also conclude with a listing of recommended further readings that address the specific subject discussed in individual headword entries. By contrast, the general references in the Bibliography provides the editors' recommendations of sources for general research on the theme subject.

Class refers to the interlocked societal factors that explain and contribute to the economic status of people and individuals in society, as well as to socioeconomic stratification or caste systems that historically have defined the degree of power and prestige held by ethnic groups. Socioeconomic class is inextricably linked to other indicators like gender and race and is relevant to the subject of this encyclopedia because popular culture emerges from the totality of Latina and Latino identity, including subalternity and the viability of life options available (or not) to ethnic minority and majority groups of people. As background information to illuminate the headword topic, *class* usually appears in these entries to discuss extremes of wealth or poverty that help explain the origins or history of the headword and its relative popularity within the Latina/o subgroup and to others. For example, in the headword entry *Marielitos, a particular group of Cuban refugees, and in the general theme entry *Immigration, there are several references to economic class and its interrelation to history, political oppression, and socioeconomic status.

Ethnicity and *culture* are often used interchangeably in this encyclopedia because both terms apply to the social context that produces the popular cultural practices, values, human traits, and artifacts that define a given population's distinctiveness. It is important to point out that the ethnic subject and scope of the *Encyclopedia of Latino Popular Culture* focus specifically on Mexican American, Puerto Rican, and Cuban American popular cultures. The twofold rationale for this emphasis is due primarily to demographics and history. These three ethnicities constitute the largest population concentrations of Latinas/os in the United States, with Mexican Americans accounting for over 60 percent of the total, and therefore justify specific focus in a reference tool of this kind. Relatedly, these three Latina/o ethnicities have the longest and most deeply rooted historical connections to the United States, with nearly half of the entire geographical mass of the present United States once bearing the name and flag of México (formerly New Spain). For these positive reasons and also due to space limitations, the encyclopedia focuses on the three largest and historically rooted U.S. American Latina/o groups.

Nevertheless, when necessary, we include a number of entries relating to other ethnicities of the Americas. These additional topics were included to elucidate popular culture generally and certain Latina/o headword topics specifically. For example, the theme entry *Brazilian Popular Music in the

United States and the headword entries on the movie **High Noon* and the art history book **Mixed Blessings: New Art in a Multicultural America* illuminate the Latina/o influences on the cultures of the Americas in a broad pan-ethnic way.

The encyclopedia also includes entries on a number of pop culture celebrities who often have been confused as Mexican, Puerto Rican, or Cuban even though they are not, such as movie stars Raquel *Welch, who is of Bolivian American heritage, and María *Montez, who was born in the Dominican Republic. For a fuller discussion of both the perception and the social construction of racial and ethnic identities, users are referred to the Introduction, to the entry *Race and Ethnicity, to the individual entries on history, and to the Chronology.

Gender frequently is used alongside the identity descriptors—*sexuality* and *sexual orientation*. These interrelated terms refer to physical characteristics and social practices that contribute to individual and social identification as female, male, and related personal identities and sexual orientations. Like "ethnicity" and "class," gender identity is fundamental to and inextricably linked to the social contexts that generate the popular cultural practices, values, human traits, and artifacts that express a culture's uniqueness. The descriptive phrase *Latina and Latino* employed throughout these two volumes offers an immediate lesson on gender inclusivity by denoting gender equality and equivalence in the ethnic identification of Hispanics. This usage reflects the editors' agreement with countless scholars, artists, political activists, and millions of others who use the American English phrase to signal a conscious ideology of gender and sexual equity regardless of traditional patriarchal privilege or grammar conventions. For a fuller discussion of this topic, consult the Introduction and the entries on *gender, Cherríe *Moraga, and John *Rechy.

Latina and Latino refer to the people as well as to their cultural activities and production. Abbreviated forms include *Latina/o* (singular) and *Latinas/Latinos* and *Latinas/os* (plural). These terms are often used interchangeably with *Hispanic* and *Hispanics* to refer to the population subgroups of Mexican Americans, Puerto Ricans, Cuban Americans, and others. The editors' preference for the various forms of Latina/o is congruent with the usage of many scholars and other specialist researchers who choose to emphasize the explicit inclusion of women, which would otherwise be only implicit or overlooked if the traditional linguistic form "Latino" were employed. Although the Spanish-language masculine inflection is linguistic and not necessarily sex or gender specific, the Latina/o form overtly and specifically reflects the uniquely hybrid nature of U.S. American dialects and the interactive bilingual, bicultural everyday influences of American English and American Spanish on pop culture.

Similarly, the preference for *Latinas/os* over *Hispanics* parallels specialist usage to underscore the specific racial inclusion of mestizos (i.e., American

Indian and Spanish hybrids of people and cultures) that is deemphasized in the English-language term *Hispanic*, which focuses on European Spain and Spanish. In addition, many Latinas/os avoid using *Hispanic* because of its emergence in the 1980s among politicians and agencies of the U.S. federal government as a preferred monolithic label to lump all groups together for political expedience. Sociologists and demographers confirm that *Hispanic* was promoted by the U.S. Census Bureau as a means of simplifying its ethnic categories. This practice occurred despite the continuing self-identification by specific ethnicity and/or race by the actual people being counted.

EFFECTIVE WAYS TO USE THIS ENCYCLOPEDIA

To conclude this guide for using the encyclopedia, the editors recommend the following three ways for effective navigation through the abundant research-based information provided.

Users may go directly to the entries, where subjects are listed alphabetically by last name or other identifying headword term. For example, to find information about the musical performer, actor, director, producer, and television star Desi Arnaz, users would look under the headword entry *Arnaz, Desi, where they will find a description of his career. To read more about Arnaz in the encyclopedia, users then may turn to the Index at the end of Volume II for all references to and mentions of Arnaz contained in other headword entries (e.g., *Spanish Caribbean Music).

A second way to use this encyclopedia is to begin by looking for the topic in the Index in Volume II. For instance, to find information about the subject "Theater and Drama," users can locate the term in the Index and under more ethnic-specific headword terms, such as *Theater and Drama—Chican/o and Mexican American and *Theater and Drama—Puerto Rican. These multiple Index subheads and keyword listings alert the user to a range of headword entries and cross-references to related items like *Teatro Campesino and Luis *Valdez. For additional information on these theatrical and dramatic topics for future reference, readers also may consult the Bibliography and look for the thematic topic and specific names related to it.

Advanced researchers are encouraged to use the encyclopedia by beginning with a careful reading of the front matter in Volume I, starting with the Preface and this "How to" guide and continuing through the Introduction. The editors recommend this third approach because it lays out useful historical and theoretical background on Latina and Latino popular culture. In addition, the Introduction provides a summary of the editors' interpretive and theoretical approach to the subject of popular culture itself. Discussing the cultural studies frameworks employed to examine Latinas/os as communities of people and as producers of thriving accumulations of popular culture, the Introduction is designed to reveal the living experiences and vibrant dynamic flux behind the population statistics and the discrete decontextualized bits of information that tend to dominate media accounts of Hispanics. By starting with a thorough review of the front matter, the user of this encyclopedia will be guided to read and comprehend the headword entries from a more informed awareness and a fuller context of Latina and Latino cultural competency.

Introduction

This encyclopedia is meant for everyday use as a resource of handy research-based information about Latina and Latino popular culture(s) for the vast majority of Americans, of any ethnic or national origin, who are not well-acquainted with the many layers and elements of America's Latina and Latino history, heritage, and diverse geographic origins. Aware of the numerous questions and requests for information from the public at large that each of us receives weekly, we targeted a broad audience of students; teachers; scholars; journalists and other media researchers; public policy officials, including law enforcement and health personnel; administrators; artists; performers and other entertainers; and many other general users. Our thinking was to compile a reference tool that would provide the kind of research-based facts and opinions that students and the general public continually ask us about and to include just enough historical and cultural background to illuminate the content as well as to guide interested users to additional research sources as needed.

The widely publicized results of the 2000 U.S. Census stimulated active media and general public interest in Latinas/os. For the first time for many Americans, including a great many Hispanics, the count raised questions about who exactly Latinas/os are ethnically, racially, culturally, and geographically. To help answer these questions and to address hundreds of others that arise from them, the *Encyclopedia of Latino Popular Culture* provides readers with straightforward, basic information about Mexican Americans (also known as Chicanas/Chicanos), Puerto Ricans (also known as Puertorriqueños, Nuyoricans, and Borícua), Cuban Americans, and occasionally, other Latinas and Latinos salient to our central focus. These variously identified peoples of the Americas contributed to the population, civilization, and culture(s) of today's United States of America, and these contributions began long before the 1776 Declaration of Independence and even before the landing on Plymouth Rock in 1620. Thus, we endorse the idea that Chicana playwright and cultural worker Cherríe Moraga expressed in her insightful and provocative 1993 essay "Art in América con Acento": that the United States would be benefited by "a radical transformation of consciousness" achieved by the healthy effects of "the people-of-color population increases." Moraga argues that in this transformed consciousness Latinas and Latinos "will not be just another brown faceless mass hungrily awaiting integration into white America, but that we'll emerge as a mass movement of people to redefine what an 'American' is." Providing reliable research-based information on these varied topics as a means of achieving the common ground implied in Moraga's idea of social transformation is a central purpose of this project.

Another equally important purpose driving the editors' vision and method was to construct the encyclopedia with inside, Latina- and Latino-defined perspectives based on the reality of a bilingual, bicultural lived experience. We bring these perspectives to hundreds of topics ranging from *American Me*, Cinco de Mayo (May 5), and José Feliciano to Jennifer López, MALDEF, the National Council of La Raza (NCLR), and hundreds more from A to Z. Presenting accurate information based on Latina and Latino studies scholarship and actual in-group life experiences helps to answer many questions about who exactly Latinas/os are both as individuals and as members of larger ethnic, racial, cultural, and national groupings, as well as geographical and social contexts. In this approach we were guided by Hungarian philosopher and one of the first modern cultural studies thinkers, György Lukács (1885–1971), who wrote in his 1938 influential essay "Realism in the Balance" that "[g]enuine popular culture [requires] a manifold relationship to every aspect of the life of one's own people," particularly in its development "over the course of history." He also stressed the need for a "critical [i.e., analytical] attitude towards one's own history" as a "necessary consequence of real insight."

In this Introduction, we summarize the most important aspects of the editorial challenges and interrelated complexities that emerged at every step of our investigatory and data-gathering process. Throughout our research, we conceptualized rationales to explain how we decided on *what to include* in the encyclopedia and how to present that information. As noted in the Preface, everything—from the scope of the book to the function of the Chronology—raised questions of definition, salience, importance, and related ideological issues. Inevitably these interrogatories and the dialectic they produced generated more questions and problematized our assumptions and approaches regarding matters of ethnicity, class, gender, language, race, and sexuality. To illustrate some of the challenges that surfaced in compiling research-based information on the vast and complex subject of Latina/o pop culture, we turn to an essay written by Lawrence M. Small, secretary of the internationally prestigious Smithsonian Institution. In "Latino Legacies: The Hispanic Contribution to the Nation's History," published in the *Smithsonian Magazine* in August 2002, Small writes that Americans identified as Latina/Latino "hold the future" of the United States because of their number (approximately 40 million) and youthfulness ("more than 40 percent is under 25 years old"). Small explains that his opinion is also based on the fact that the original "founding heritage of vast regions of this country was Hispanic," and he concludes by emphatically stating that "no account of the [American] past and no understanding of the present can be complete if it does not acknowledge that indelible cultural imprint, which is vivid still and will become even more pronounced in the decades ahead." Despite this recognition of the fundamental importance of the founding Latina/o heritage and its continuing impact on American culture, the Smithsonian, as Small admits, "came late to a formal recognition of the Latino contribution to the history of the nation." He notes that the Smithsonian Center for Latino Initiatives was established "only in 1997," and Latina/o scholars and other advocates know that the center came into being as a result of intense advocacy and pressure from Latina/o policymakers, scholars, and members of the general public.

This attention to the Smithsonian's current thinking and past approach to Latina and Latino groups and cultures underscores some of the obstacles and barriers that have historically faced Latina/o studies scholars and other researchers. On the one hand, the Smithsonian is internationally regarded as one of the premier repositories of American history, heritage, popular culture, and folklore, and the encyclopedia editors agree that it is a positive development for the Institution to have acknowledged in 1997 both America's indispensable Hispanic past and the unignorable impact of that past on America's future. On the other hand, the Smithsonian—like most of its counterparts among public and private academic institutions—is in its infancy in valuing, studying, and appreciating the complexity that forms the vast substance of Latina/o studies. That institutional infancy makes Latina/o studies research especially challenging since it is difficult to locate solid documentary evidence, material artifacts, and related sources of information on the vibrant diversity that comprises the range of Latina and Latino cultural identities and multiple cultural practices.

Despite this slow development and the marginalization of indigenous peoples by what cultural studies scholar Eric Hobsbawm describes in *The Invention of Tradition* as "willful neglect," interdisciplinary research since the 1960s has produced a vast reservoir of research, documentary evidence, theoretical approaches, and sources of knowledge that have begun to repair the damaging consequences of that neglect and the even worse inaccuracies and distortions of traditional Eurocentric gazes. These interdisciplinary fields—for example, women's studies, African American studies, Chicana and Chicano studies, cultural and ethnic studies, and ethnomusicology—in conjunction with the best of received methods and materials, form the scholarly foundation for the *Encyclopedia of Latino Popular Culture in the United States.* Studies such as Arturo Aldama and Naomi Quiñonez's *Decolonial Voices: Chicana/o Cultural Studies in the 21st Century* (2002), Alfred Artéaga's *An Other Tongue: Nation and Ethnicity in the Linguistic Borderlands* (1994), Gary Keller and Cordelia Candelaria's *The Legacy of the Mexican and Spanish-American Wars: Legal, Literary, and Historical Perspectives* (2000), and Walter Mignolo's *Local Histories/Global Designs* (2000) are but four examples of progressive scholarship based on an integration of interdisciplinary frameworks focusing on Latina/o history and culture within a thick sociohistorical context. These and other scholarly research publications in print, digital, and other formats recognize the crucial importance of relying on multiple approaches and disciplines in the research, description, and interpretation of human activities, discourses, and productions.

Appropriately enough, it was as a result of Latina/o studies scholars using this documentary reservoir of interdisciplinary reconstruction and knowledge that institutions like the Smithsonian became conscious of their perpetuation of "part = whole" mythologies received from the dominant canonical tradition. Characterized by a limited worldview and exclusionary methods of research investigation, part = whole thinking occurs whenever a fraction of anything is equated with the entire field, as in the error of confusing a part of the flat earth with the whole universe or of privileging landowning men with the advantages and power accruing from the whole of humankind.

Part of the rationale for drawing research methodologies from a range of fields to approach and interpret Latina/o popular culture is that interdisciplinary studies developed as a means of engaging, explaining, and—importantly—preserving contemporary living cultures marginalized from the dominant elite. Through a combined systematic rigor and curiosity that push the boundaries of academic inquiry, interdisciplinary studies emerged from the practical needs of conducting effective and sensitive fieldwork among peoples outside the ethnographer's culture. Field researchers from linguist Edward Sapir to sociologist W.E.B. Du Bois, from American Indian advocate Helen Hunt Jackson to immigration historian Manuel Gámio, and from folklorist Américo Paredes to medical anthropologist Julián Samora, all learned that reliable ethnography required the rethinking of orthodox theories and conventional ideologies, as well as the need to operate from conceptual frameworks attuned to the basic variability and contingency of people's material lived experiences.

A consequence of the rethinking and concomitant reconceptualizing arising from such vigorous research investigations was the recognition that popular culture—people's living expressive practices and creative forms—encompasses a wide and heterodox range of mutually influencing and interanimating forms and styles. As a result, the attitudes toward popular culture began to shift among scholars and other researchers. Once considered *less than* and *inferior to* the evolved and highly stylized patterns of what was once called and understood as elitist "high" culture, popular culture came to be valued for the shaping multiplicity that it, in fact, is—the dynamic, everyday practices and expressive forms that include food, clothing, language, music, dance, religion, literature (print, spoken, digital, and other forms), theater and ritual performance, geographical influences, and art in all its mediums and performative styles.

Another aspect of the rationale for applying interdisciplinary methodologies to the analysis and interpretation of Latina/o popular culture is the active participation of Latinas and Latinos in the research process in recent decades. When Latinas/os entered the halls of academe and joined the development and debates of scholarly discourses, their research and their life experience led them to challenge vigorously such part = whole mythologies about Hispanics as **La Leyenda Negra* (i.e., the Black Legend) and the deficit model of social science. The deficit model ascribed poverty among the Latina/o population solely to internal cultural limitations, overlooking other societal factors like institutional racism, political disenfranchisement, and deterritorialization (i.e., legalized theft of property) to name several of many examples. The Latina/o contributions to contemporary analytic and interpretive frameworks challenge prior perceptions and current conceptualizations that conceive of Latina/o popular culture and folklore as marginally quaint, exotic, or otherwise outside a dominant mainstream. Scholarly research, ethnographic fieldwork, and artifact collection by, for instance, Afro-Puerto Rican Arturo Alfonso *Schomburg; Cuban Haydée Santamaría, founder of the *Casa de las Américas; and Mexican American folklorist Arthur León Campa helped open a portal to a postcolonialist understanding of Latina/o history, heritage, and popular culture. In *Rethinking Popular Culture* (1991), scholars Chandra Mukerji and Michael Schudson describe this approach as follows:

> [T]he rethinking of popular culture is a commentary on broad intellectual changes initiated by scholars who, in struggling to "see" Western culture without being totally blinded by its assumptions, began to . . . reject the taboos that had kept thinkers away from everyday culture. They bravely redefined the role and value of popular amusements and, in so doing, allowed their thinking and ours to be transformed.

At the same time that attitudes and approaches to grassroots pop culture(s) have broadened to include appreciation and preservation of everydayness, there has also been a keener insight into the reciprocal nature of cultural forms and practices. This interpretation recognizes that just as notions of elite "high" culture are outgrowths from all areas of a people's sociohistorical experiences, so too is popular culture affected by those precedent forms and intellectual traditions. Historians of cultural tradition like Theodor W. Adorno, author of the influential 1947 study *The Culture Industry: Enlightenment as Mass Deception*, explain that human practices were viewed by scholars as part of preset categories of hierarchical levels. The groupings were sorted according to such identifiers as tribal, indigenous, traditional, folk, high standard, bourgeois standard, commercial, mass-mediated, popular, ethnic, mainstream, elite urban, and others. Within this received taxonomy, *popular culture* conventionally was (and in a great many quarters continues to be) perceived as a postindustrial equivalent of folk, ethnic, and/or indigenous patterns and practices defined as normatively "authentic." Accordingly, like folklore, popular culture was considered authentic *because of* its reputed age and *because of* its origin in what were perceived to be archaic grassroots transmission systems (e.g., word of mouth) that were seen as unchanged and untouched by modernity. In music studies, for example, the distinction between high, or classical, and "low" forms (i.e., folk and popular music) is an old one and deeply rooted in the attitudes of music scholars and performing musicians alike. Until the relatively recent advancement of the interdisciplinary field of ethnomusicology, these perspectives dominated music (and other art and culture) studies as the "proper" measure and interpretation of quality.

Understanding of Latina/o pop culture requires consideration of past assumptions that historically led to the marginalization of the arts, crafts, and other cultural forms and practices of grassroots people. This brief review of history is important for a number of reasons, but primarily because of the persistence of many of the old-fashioned negative attitudes even in the twenty-first century, oftentimes without awareness that the attitudes have been taught and learned through reinforced social beliefs and values. Equally important is that the encounter with and appreciation of the eclectic range and vitality of grassroots cultural production often leads to a deeper understanding of the everyday lives of ordinary people as family members, workers, children, and unheralded builders of local communities and, thereby, as anonymous contributors to global achievements.

Four major assumptions help explain the conventional view that dismissed populism and the people's cultural production as unworthy of serious scholarly inquiry. First is the belief that pop culture simply is qualitatively inferior to the conventional styles and standards in vogue with élite trendsetters. Many examples exist, such as that only classical composers like Beethoven, Bach, and Brahms are considered of musical merit, or that the only great masterpieces were written by such early writers as Dante, Shakespeare, and Cervantes. A second rationale for devaluing pop culture is because, by its very nature as living and frequently volatile grassroots activity, it is too new and transient to have passed the test of time that traditional canons require. This standard, according to critical cultural studies scholars, actually reflects a circular logic that equates the "test of time" with the trials and obstructions put forward by members of empowered élites to ensure the exclusion of alternative, folk, dissenting, and other unorthodox forms and practices. These include the dismissal of African American music forms (gospel, jazz, blues, rap, etc.) *until* or *unless* they "cross over" into acceptance by Caucasian producers and audiences, or the dismissal of Spanish-English codeswitching as a literary and discursive idiom *because of* the dominance of a bias in favor of monolingual English in American society. A third assumption posited for undervaluing folk and pop cultures is that they reflect vulgar tastes that often are encouraged by and/or imposed on the masses by empowered economic and political institutions that control and wish to maintain the *status quo*. Representative examples include public events staged by governments (e.g., Roman gladiator circuses and Nazi German parades) to deflect attention from their failures to address poverty, hunger, and other major social problems. The fourth reason is so familiar that it is easy to overlook: habit and tradition. As many folklore and cultural studies theorists have demonstrated through their research, mass consumers of art and entertainment are shaped by an ocean of orthodoxies and manipulated dominant tastes that are difficult to float above or swim out of. Thus, conventional beliefs, customs, and practices remain deeply rooted alongside the grassroots populace's vibrant dynamic flux of experience, change, and experimentation.

The scholarship produced by feminist studies, Chicana/o studies, ethnic studies, and other critical cultural studies discourses in the last half of the twentieth century act as countering voices of dissent against these four and other pejorative assumptions. The acceptance and dissemination of these counter discourses has increased dramatically among scholars, artists, intellectuals, and other challengers of a narrow, monolithic canonical tradition of exclusionary "high" culture. As a result, their exposure and corrections of traditional part = whole mythologies have had positive impact on public discourse, particularly since the 1990 and the 2000 U.S. Census surveys, when the mass public and empowered voices of culture could no longer ignore the fact that the American grain has always been an ethnic and racial mix, and minorities were a central part of the America's cultural foundation. The discourses of women's studies, African American studies, Chicana/o studies, ethnomusicology, and such field-tested foundations of knowledge as art and performance, anthropology, oral history, political science, sociology, and others are the crucial sources for research-based information and knowledge concerning Latinas and Latinos found in this encyclopedia.

It is valuable for users of this encyclopedia to understand five important foundational theories that help explain and justify the elevation of Latina/o pop culture as worthy of scholarly study and general appreciation. To begin, critical cultural studies specialists reject the historical division of the cultural field and peoples into "popular or folk" and "serious or elite" segments and into "low" and "high" standards. These categories are superficial and inadequate to describe the complex and dynamic actuality of people's lives, social communities, historical record, and intersection with economic and political empowerment. As Lukács (1938), Bourdieu (1984), Mukerji and Schudson (1991), and many others have written, the historical record is clear about the fact that people as individuals and nations as collective bodies evolve through active and continuous interaction, mutual influence, and human cross-fertilization. This vertical and horizontal interanimation occurs literally, figuratively, and continually, thereby arguing for a democratic approach to and appreciation of all human cultural activities and resultant forms and thus justifying their worth as topics for scholarly examination.

Second, because the cultural field results from vibrant interactive and interanimating human exchange, "it should be grasped as a whole," as Adorno writes. Such a (w)holistic perspective requires theoretical and methodological frameworks that integrate popular culture research in the equivalently (w)holistic manner accomplished by ethnographic fieldwork and interdisciplinary studies. One cultural aspect, segment, or layer in isolation is not necessarily or essentially more authentic than another in representing *the people*, *the folk*, or *el pueblo* (the community), but all aspects, segments, and layers are mutual and reciprocal influences on one another. Thus, for example, traditional folklore and other people's activities no longer are defined solely as products or symbols of nonurban experience and rural stability, nor are they sited solely within the perceived utopian continuity of pastoral traditions. Recognizing that traditions emerge from continual exchange, interaction, experiential dynamism, and disarray, folk forms and popular culture are equivalent products of people continually seeking to express themselves and their groups through restorative and preservative new rituals, displays, performances, and diverse forms.

A third theoretical rationale for popular culture studies is that they offer a crucially important method of including in scholarly and public discourses the accomplishments of subaltern groups (i.e., women, poor people, ethnic and racial minorities, and other historically colonized, marginalized, or otherwise devalued populations). Popular culture and critical cultural studies offer a space for "talking back," "taking back," and "ticking off" the gaps, errors, and biases of the master myths protected by the dominance of élites and majorities. Consigned to the margins by dominant groups, members of the consciously excluded and ignored peoples have seized marginal space and reclaimed it as the *center* of lived experience that it, in fact, is for them.

Fourth, critical cultural studies approaches to culture are imperative to the study of subalternity. Unlike canonical print-centered traditions, cultural studies frameworks are able to account for the temporal virtuality and resulting alterity caused and influenced by the electronic, transportation, and computerized digital media technologies of the nineteenth, twentieth, and twenty-first centuries. Notions of time and temporality have greatly altered. The "past" as a monolithic *precedent* era no longer holds a defensible sacredness as more *real* or more essentially *knowable* because of a presumed static *past*ness than the present. Futurity and simultaneity have always been affected by memory, but they were radically changed by the dawn of motion pictures, a transformation that has been underscored and essentially reconfigured by the microchip industry and its digitalization of thought, experience, and expression. Inevitably, these changes toward time affect people's social and cultural forms and practices.

Consequently, a fifth rationale for application of critical cultural studies frameworks to Latina/o pop culture is that they are constructed from an enlightened consciousness of *mestizaje* (cultural and racial hybridity) that is imperative for effective analysis and interpretaton. That is, popular culture defines and preserves communities through artistic forms and aesthetic expression transmitted by direct human exchange, including modern technological means and global interchanges. These transfers are inevitably and continually altered and hybridized by the exchange itself and reinforced by collective memory. This is the basis of *mestizaje*. As a metaphor, an evolved *mestizaje* of the Americas recognizes the combined cultural genius and shared bloods of all American peoples as a racial synthesis that simultaneously produces creative interrelated cultural forms and practices that build bridges to common ground and universal humanity.

¿Y que? So what? This homely rhetorical question provides an apt transition to a discussion of what the preceding concepts signify in applied terms. That is, one apt response to the "So what?" question is a summary of the methodological implications on our project of the previously described theoretical assumptions. To begin that summary, we outline some of the conceptual challenges we encountered in applying critical cultural studies frameworks to the vast undertaking of compiling the *Encyclopedia of Latino Popular Culture*. Many of these challenges were linguistic. One such challenge is a direct result of writing in one language, Standard Edited American English (SEAE), about subject matters oftentimes named in other languages, primarily a variety of Standard Spanish and vernacular Spanish idioms (e.g., *caló*) employed by Mexican Americans, Mexican nationals, Puerto Ricans, Nuyoricans, Cuban Americans, Cubans, and others of the diverse ethnic groups comprising the U.S. Latina and Latino population. Consciously writing from a Latina and Latino point of view in SEAE demands a heightened regard for accurate, culturally based translations. We aim throughout the work to inform both monolingual and bilingual users of this encyclopedia, as well as Latinas/os and other ethnically identified readers and nonethnically identified users. A Latina and Latino point of view refers to what the coeditors, as Chicana and Chicano identified scholars, bring to the task as simultaneously *both* observer *and* participant members of the subject matter. A Latina and Latino consciousness (although not solely Chicana/o) also applies to a majority of our Advisory Board and contributors, derived from either or both life experience and specialist training.

Nowhere are the linguistic and cultural challenges more evident than in our use of Latina *and* Latino throughout these volumes. In neat brevity, these usages, along with the combined singular/plural "culture(*s*)," captures the difficulties of accurately naming the project's ethnic subject matter specifically and in a manner most inclusive of *all* its constituent parts—the people, their social practices, and their cultural expressiveness and productions. To begin with, it is generally the case that when asked their ethnicity, most Latinas and Latinos do not specifically refer to themselves as either Latinas or Latinos or Hispanics. Rather, the responses are more precise, often in Spanish, depending on the speaker's origin and native region, for example, Chicano, Mexican, Boricúa, Island Puertorican, Cuban American, and mestiza. We chose "Latina and Latino" over "Hispanic" as the generic label to describe this diversity because the latter emphasizes Spain and Spanish identities, which are significantly less descriptive of the Western Hemisphere's Latin American cultural hybridity, *mestizaje*, of indigenous Native American and European cultural roots. However, whether in Spanish or English, the speaker's self-identification will be explicitly gendered by linguistic inflection or by appearance (Chican*a* or Chican*o*, Cuban*a* or Cuban*o*, etc.). Thus, for reasons of ethnic, racial, and gender precision and inclusivity, we adhered to the practice, which is widespread among specialist researchers, of using both "Latina" and "Latino," abbreviated in actual practice as "Latina/o." This is analogous to specialist and technical precision in other fields that alternate between scientific and lay terminology, depending on the context. Ranging from anthropology and medicine to computerology, theology, and myriad other fields, specialized nomenclature inevitably differs from everyday language.

A related challenge encountered in producing the *Encyclopedia of Latino Popular Culture* concerns the complexities of applying critical culture frameworks with their layered inclusiveness to a large body of material not previously examined in a comprehensive manner. The sheer size and scope of our subject offered daunting bumps and swerves at every point of our compilation, documentation, and conceptual travel. Most of these problems were related to the simplifications and translations necessarily demanded by writing for a broad general audience. Difficulties of coverage and concerns about dilution and overcompression required constant alertness and assessment of the ramifications of using specialized definitions instead of colloquial terms, and vice versa. It is analogous, for instance, to describing Barbie and GI Joe sometimes as "girl and boy dolls" and other times as "anatomically correct representations of hegemonic iconography and socially constructed identities." Both descriptions are conceptually correct, but their functionality as definitions is most effective when appropriately applied.

Nevertheless, within the broad, varied, and challenging conceptual frameworks summarized in this Introduction, it is important to stress that in compiling these two volumes the editors were guided by the following two major principles:

- To ensure the research-based accuracy of information on Latina/o popular culture
- To provide reader/user accessibility and convenience

We placed general audience accessibility alongside research-based integrity as our twofold priorities for the encyclopedia in order to construct a usable and reliable reference tool. Accessibility to general readers refers to *what the average user of this tool wants to know*. Where would s/he look? How much information would s/he need and want? The answers to these queries were determined in a variety of ways, including seeking the guidance of our Advisory Board and our editors at Greenwood, as well as through focus group testing and by soliciting input from outside nonspecialist and specialist readers.

To meet the accessibility imperative, we have presented entries concisely using researched information from published scholarship most often in clear, plain SEAE. Where the demands of research-based integrity collided with that of plainness of language because of the layered complexities and linguistic differences, we have striven to meet both. That is, we use specialist idioms when absolutely needed, providing translations in parentheses or within the immediate context. By *research-based integrity* we mean that every entry and statement of fact in this encyclopedia has been corroborated by at least two different reliable sources—and sometimes by three or more.

Ultimately, we firmly hope that in providing solid, documented information about Latina/o popular culture and heritage, the *Encyclopedia of Latino Popular Culture* will deepen the substance of conversations throughout the world on culture, (trans)nationalism, and representation, to contribute to a genuine narrative of community.

REFERENCES

Adorno, Theodor W. *The Culture Industry: Enlightenment as Mass Deception*. 1947. New York: Routledge, 1990.

Aldama, Arturo, and Naomi Quiñonez, eds. *Decolonial Voices: Chicana/o Cultural Studies in the 21st Century*. Bloomington: Indiana University Press, 2002.

Arrighi, Giovanni. *The Long Twentieth Century*. London: Verso, 1994.

Artéaga, Alfred. *Chicano Poetics: Heterotexts and Hybridities*. New York: Cambridge University Press, 1997.

Artéaga, Alfred, ed. *An Other Tongue: Nation and Ethnicity in the Linguistic Borderlands*. Durham, NC: Duke University Press, 1994.

Baker, Houston. *Blues, Ideology, and Afro-American Literature*. Chicago: University of Chicago Press, 1984.

Bernal, Martha, and George P. Knight, eds. *Ethnic Identity: Formation and Transmission among Hispanics and Other Minorities*. Albany: State University of New York Press, 1993.

Bourdieu, Pierre. *Distinction: A Social Critique of the Judgement of Taste*. Translated by Richard Nice. 1979. London: Routledge and Kegan Paul, 1984. (First published in French.)

Brogan, Jacqueline, and Cordelia Candelaria, eds. *Women Poets of the Americas: Toward a Panamerican Gathering*. Notre Dame, IN: University of Notre Dame Press, 1997.

Candelaria, Cordelia. *Seeking the Perfect Game: Baseball in American Literature*. Westport, CT: Greenwood Press, 1989.

Fanon, Frantz. *The Wretched of the Earth*. Translated by Constance Farrington. New York: Grove Press, 1963.

Giménez, Martha. "The Political Construction of the Hispanic." In *Estudios Chicanos and the Politics of Community*, edited by Cordelia Candelaria and Mary Romero. San Francisco, CA: NACCS, 1989.

Gramsci, Antonio. *Prison Notebooks* (1928). In *The Norton Anthology of Theory and Criticism*, edited by Vincent B. Leitch et al. New York: Norton, 2001.

Hobsbawm, Eric. "*Willful Neglect": The Invention of Tradition*. Cambridge, England: Cambridge University Press, 1983.

Hurston, Zora Neale. "How It Feels to Be Colored Me" (1928). In *The Norton Anthology of American Literature*. 4th ed., edited by Nina Baym et al. New York: Norton, 1994. 2: 1425–1428.

Keller, Gary D., and Cordelia Chávez Candelaria, eds. *The Legacy of the Mexican and Spanish-American Wars: Legal, Literary, and Historical Perspectives*. Tempe, AZ: Bilingual Review Press, 2000.

Langley, Lester D. *The Americas in the Age of Revolution, 1750–1850*. New Haven, CT: Yale University Press, 1996.

Langley, Lester D. *The Banana Men: American Mercenaries and Entrepreneurs in Central America, 1880–1930*. Lexington: University Press of Kentucky, 1995.

Lukács, György. "Realism in the Balance" (1938). In *The Norton Anthology of Theory and Criticism*, edited by Vincent B. Leitch et al. New York: Norton, 2001.

Martí, José. *José Martí: Selected Writings*. Edited and translated by Esther Allen. New York: Penguin Classic, 2002.

Martí, José. *Thoughts on Liberty, Social Justice, Government, Art, and Morality: A Bilingual Anthology/Pensamientos sobre la libertad, la justicia, la política, el arte, y la moral: antología bilingúe*. Compiled by Carlos Ripoll. New York: E. Torres & Sons: Las Américas, 1985.

Mignolo, Walter. *Local Histories/Global Designs*. Princeton, NJ: Princeton University Press, 2000.

Moraga, Cherríe. "Art in América con Acento" (1993). In *Women's Voices from the Borderlands*, edited by Lillian Castillo-Speed. New York: Touchstone, 1995.

Mukerji, Chandra, and Michael Schudson, eds. *Rethinking Popular Culture: Contemporary Perspectives in Cultural Studies*. Berkeley: University of California Press, 1991.

Samora, Julian. *La Raza: Forgotten Americans (Papers in Memory of Charles de Young Elkus)*. Notre Dame, IN: University of Notre Dame Press, 1969.

Samora, Julian, and Patricia Vandel Simon. *A History of the Mexican American People*. 2nd rev. ed. Notre Dame, IN: University of Notre Dame Press, 1993.

Small, Lawrence M. "Latino Legacies: The Hispanic Contribution to the Nation's History." *Smithsonian Magazine* (August 2002). http://www.smithsonianmag.si.edu/smithsonian/issues02aug02/small.html.

Smithsonian Institution Task Force on Latino Issues. *Willful Neglect: The Smithsonian Institution and United States Latinos*. Report of the Smithsonian Task Force on Latino Issues. Washington, DC: Smithsonian Institution, 1988.

Vasconcelos, José. *La raza cósmica (The Cosmic Race)*. Bilingual Spanish/English edition. Edited and translated by Didier T. Jaén. 1925. Los Angeles: Centro de Publicaciones/Department of Chicano Studies, California State University, 1979.

Wallerstein, Immanuel, et al., eds. *Open the Social Sciences*. Palo Alto, CA: Stanford University Press, 1996.

Williams, Raymond. *Marxism and Literature*. New York: Oxford University Press, 1977.

Cordelia Chávez Candelaria, Executive Editor
Co-Specialist Editor for Cultural Studies, History, Literature, Sports

Arturo J. Aldama
Co-Specialist Editor for Art, Film, Media, Cultural Studies

Peter J. García
Co-Specialist Editor for Folklore, Music, Ethnomusicology

Alphabetical List of Entries

Entries by Subject

Actors and Performers

Entries of People by Field of Endeavor

Actors and Performers

Entries of People by Country of Origin or Heritage

Chronology

35,000–12,000 BC — Evidence of human life throughout North America. In Central and South America, the presence of humans is believed to have begun approximately 5,000 to 10,000 years later, but the record is not exact.

10,000–8000 BC — The earliest definitive artifactual record of humans in the Americas is the Clovis culture named for the New Mexico town where the artifacts were found in the 1930s.

5000–1000 BC — Evidence of the Anasazi peoples, ancestors of today's Pueblo Indians, and of the Athabascan peoples, sources of today's Navajo and Apache Indians, exists in the present-day U.S. Southwest. Cultural practices and social traditions (food, language, religion, music, etc.) of these indigenous peoples remain evident among present-day Native Americans, Mexican Americans, and other mestizos (persons of mixed blood).

CE 800–1000 — Settlement of the Greater Antilles (present-day Cuba, Jamaica, Hispaniola [which consists of Haiti and the Dominican Republic], and Puerto Rico) in the Caribbean Sea by the native peoples self-identified as Taino and Guanahatabey (called Arawakan Indians by the Europeans), who are part of the indigenous ancestry of Cuba, Puerto Rico, and other Caribbean peoples. Cultural practices and social traditions of these indigenous peoples remain evident among present-day Native Antilleans, Cubanos, Puertorriqueños, and other mestizos of the region. The natives of today's Cuba called their homeland "Cuba," and those of today's Puerto Rico referred to their homeland as Boriquén (also known as Borinquén or Boriken).

1325 Founding of Tenochtitlán, today's Mexico City, by the Aztecs, also known as the Tenochca and the Mexica peoples who are part of the indigenous ancestry of Mexican Americans.

1400–1423 First known evidence of exploration and settlement of the Americas by the modern Chinese to supplement theories about the presumed migration of prehistoric Asian peoples reputed to have crossed the Bering Strait into North America.

1492 Christopher Columbus, navigator and explorer, aka *Cristoforo Colombo* in Italian and *Cristóbal Colón* in Spanish, began his first of four transatlantic voyages in search of a shorter route to India. His landing in the West Indies historically was referred to as "*the* discovery of the New World," but since the Western Hemisphere had already been discovered by Asians and others, this first landing is more accurately called the first major encounter of Europeans with the native peoples of the "Americas." When he returned to Spain, Columbus took specimens, including several Taino people, from the islands to show at the royal court, and he left a group of forty men behind as a Spanish colony on what he called La Navidad, Hispaniola.

1493–1496 The second of Columbus's four transatlantic voyages that helped strengthen Spain's access to and control of the West Indies. The forty Spaniards left behind at La Navidad disappeared, apparently killed by the Taino residents.

1498–1500 The third of Columbus's transatlantic voyages that began active efforts to Christianize the native peoples through group baptisms into the Roman Catholic Church.

1502–1504 The fourth of the transatlantic voyages of the now ill and politically embattled Columbus who returned to find the Spanish colonies he had started gaining strength. He also completed a difficult trans-Caribbean navigation that many maritime researchers view to be as difficult as his transatlantic crossings.

1519 Spanish conquistador Hernán Cortés travels to Yucatán from the island of Hispaniola to undertake the Conquest of Mesoamerica and the Aztec Empire ruled by Moctecuhzoma.

1521 Fall of Tenochtitlán, present-day Mexico City, and the conquest of the Aztecs by Hernán Cortés. The military takeover of México was completed by 1521 with the help of native allies, including the knowledge and linguistic skills of La Malinche and other tribal leaders (*caciques*).

1531 The reputed miracle on Mount Tepeyac occurred when the Indian Juan Diego reported the appearance of the Virgen de Guadalupe to the bishop.

1542 Exploration of the western coast of México north to present-day Baja California by Juan Rodríguez Cabrillo, which opened up Spanish exploration of the Pacific coast of North America.

1598 Colonial expedition of Juan de Oñate to the northern territories of New Spain, where he began the European colonization of New Mexico and the southwestern territories of today's United States.

1609 Founding of Santa Fe (de San Francisco) in northern New Spain, the present-day state of New Mexico.

1680 Spaniards are driven out of New Mexico and forced to take refuge in Ciudad Juárez by Popé, a Pueblo Indian, in an indigenous rebellion known as the Pueblo Revolt. The bloodless reconquest of New Mexico by the Spaniards occurred in 1692 under the leadership of Diego de Vargas.

1706 Reconquest of New Mexico completed and Spanish settlements spread throughout the Southwest, including the founding of Albuquerque, which led to the stabilization of Spanish colonial authority in northern New Spain.

1718 Founding of the city of San Antonio (de Bexar) in Texas.

1763 The Treaty of Paris ends Spanish conflict with France over the southwestern areas of North America, and Spain gains control of Louisiana.

1769 Colonization of California and establishment of present-day San Diego begins by the Spaniards as a strategy to expel Russian explorers and settlers from the region.

1775 Colonization of Sonora, present-day Arizona, and northern California by Juan Bautista de Anza.

1781 Founding of [Pueblo Nuestra Señora de] Los Angeles [de la Porciúncula] in California.

1810 Led by Father Miguel de Hidalgo y Costilla, his parish villagers in Dolores, México, declare their independence from Spain, following his famous inspirational cry, El Grito de Dolores, on September 16, Día de Independencia (i.e., México's Independence Day).

1821 México gains independence from Spain.

1834 Publication of *El Crepúsculo de la Libertad* (Dawn of Liberty), the first newspaper west of the Mississippi, begins in Santa Fe, New Mexico.

1836 Mexican President General Antonio López de Santa Anna leads a battle into the Alamo in defense of his country's northern territory, Texas. Although victorious at the Alamo, Santa Anna eventually was taken prisoner in San Jacinto by Texan soldiers aided by American support, and he signed the Treaty of Velasco, which established Texas' independence from México.

1836–1846 Border hostilities intensify between México and the Republic of Texas in alliance with the United States and result in the invasion of New Mexico in 1841 by a Texas force aided by American military support. Defeated by Governor Manuel Armíjo's troops, the Texas invaders were taken prisoner and sent to the capital for punishment.

1846 Invoking the Monroe Doctrine and following the principles of Manifest Destiny, U.S. President James Polk declares war on México and assigns General Zachary Taylor to lead the U.S. Army to the Mexican border.

1848 The Treaty of Guadalupe Hidalgo is signed by the United States and México, creating the birth of Mexican America. Along with the Native American and other Latina/o populations, Mexican-origin people are the only citizens and residents of the United States to precede the Anglo Americans in their homelands. This historical fact means that the Mexican and mestizo civilizations, cultures, and way of life that preexisted the Anglo-American takeover were deeply rooted and reinforced by the Mexicans and Mexican Americans who did not perceive a border of separation north or south, since it was geographically and culturally the same homeland.

1851 The U.S. Congress passes the California Land Act, which shifted the legal, political, and economic policies toward land and property from Spanish to English law. Consequently, legal rights to vast amounts of Mexican-owned land were transferred to Anglo Americans through lawful purchase, illegal swindles, violence, litigation, and related land-grabbing tactics in the new state of California, which entered the Union in 1850. Also in 1851, Jean Baptiste Lamy is named Roman Catholic Bishop of New Mexico, Arizona, and Colorado.

1855 Publication of *El Clamor Público* (Public Outcry), the first major newspaper in Los Angeles to protest the land-grabbing policies and abuses of the American hordes arriving to settle the new state from other regions of the United States.

1862 The famous battle between Mexican nationalists led by Benito Juárez and the French soldiers assigned to set up a colony for Napoleon III takes place on May 5, 1862. Resulting in an important victory for México, La Batalla de Puebla (i.e., Battle of Puebla) is celebrated annually on Cinco de Mayo (the 5th of May) as a landmark of national independence from foreign occupation.

1875	California elects its first and still the state's only Mexican American governor, Romualdo Pacheco.
1878	The Ten Years' War in Cuba is brought to an end with the Pact of El Zajón.
1880s	Mutual aid societies, called *mutualistas*, emerge throughout the Southwest (i.e., the former Mexican territories) to protect the rights and safety of the new U.S. citizens, the Mexican Americans, in the face of widespread land fraud, violence, and other racist acts of greed. Las Gorras Blancas (White Caps) were active in New Mexico, the Spanish-American Alliance emerged in Arizona, and diverse other community-based homeland security organizations sprung up throughout the West.
1895	Populist Cuban revolt against foreign domination by Spain. American business interests popularized the Cuban democratic movement in the United States, paving the way for the turn-of-the-century policies that eventually led to the Spanish-American War.
1897–1904	Miguel Antonio Otero II serves as governor of the New Mexico Territory.
1898	The Spanish-American War, the first international conflict to be recorded on film, pitted the United States in support of Cuba's independence movement against Spain, whose monarchy did not want to emancipate one of the last of its distant sugar-, cigar-, and rum-producing territories. Lasting only four months, the war confirmed the United States as an empire as a result of its acquisition of Puerto Rico and the Philippines. It also achieved Cuba's independent status.
1903	The Hay-Bunau-Varilla Treaty is signed by the United States and Panama, allowing the building of the canal, considered a technological wonder, which began construction in 1904 and opened a transoceanic route for East/West trade and traffic.
1905	Using military force, the United States took over the Dominican Republic's customs service, according to President Theodore Roosevelt's administration, to maintain order and prevent regional destabilization in the Caribbean.
1906–1909	The United States dispatches armed forces to Cuba under the Platt Amendment, which President Theodore Roosevelt declared permitted unilateral military action.
1910	The Mexican Revolution begins after a century of political and economic upheaval in México, starting one of the largest mass migrations since 1848 when the Gold Rush spurred the coast-to-coast expansion of the United States.

1910–1912	The United States sends the marines to Nicaragua to protect American business interests and the U.S.-supported government of Conservative president Adolfo Díaz, who ruled until 1917. The United States kept a small military presence there through the administrations of the next two Conservative presidents (Emiliano Chamorro and Diego M. Chamorro).
1912	New Mexico and Arizona enter the Union and become the forty-seventh and forty-eighth states, respectively.
1914–1918	Large numbers of Mexican Americans serve in the U.S. armed forces during World War I, while thousands of Mexican workers migrate en masse to the U.S. Midwest and Northeast to replace American factory, farm, and railroad workers drafted during the war.
1915–1934	The United States installs military forces in Haiti, according to several presidential administrations, to maintain order and prevent regional destabilization in the Caribbean.
1916	Pancho Villa's forces raid the town of Columbus, New Mexico, adding to the revolutionary's fame and legend. Also in 1916 the United States installs an American military government in the Dominican Republic.
1916–1924	The United States again occupies the Dominican Republic, according to several presidential administrations, to maintain order and prevent democratic revolutionary movements from destabilizing the Caribbean.
1917	The Mexican Revolution is officially ended. The U.S. Congress passes the Immigration Act, which includes a head tax for passage into the United States that frequently is waived for Mexicans due to the demand for labor. Also in 1917 the Congress passes the Jones Act, which extends U.S. citizenship to Puerto Rico.
1920s	Self-help and mutual aid societies continue to be formed and expand throughout the decade in Mexican America. In 1921 in response to the heightened xenophobia toward Mexicans and by extension toward Mexican Americans, La Orden de Hijos de America (Order of America's Sons) is organized in San Antonio, Texas. The year 1927 saw the formation of the Confederación de Uniones Obreras Mexicanas (United Mexican Women Workers) in southern California and in 1929 the League of United Latin American Citizens (LULAC) founded in Texas.
1921	In response to public debate about Mexican immigration into the United States, the Congress passes the first of two national origin immigrant quota acts.

1925 The Border Patrol, a federal police force, is created by the U.S. Congress.

1927–1932 The United States sends the marines to Nicaragua to combat Augusto Sandino's revolutionary movement, which, according to U.S. foreign policy, is a necessary Caribbean intervention to maintain order and prevent destabilization of the region.

1930s After many decades of active Mexican American and other Latina and Latino leadership and presence in America's labor movement, several important unions are formed to advocate for fair wages and just treatment of workers. Established in 1926 is the Federation of Agricultural Workers Union of America; in 1933 the Confederación de Uniones de Campesinos y Obreros Mexicanos (Confederated Union of Mexican Farmworkers and Laborers) emerges from the El Monte, California, berry strike; in 1934 La Liga de Habla Española (Spanish-Speaking Workers' League) is formed in Gallup, New Mexico; and in 1938 the San Antonio, Texas, pecan shellers receive national attention for their strike and leader, Emma Tenayuca.

1933 Anastasio Somóza assumes dictatorial power in Nicaragua with the support of the United States. Also in 1933, in a departure from the hostile foreign policy of presidential administrations since James Polk, President Franklin Delano Roosevelt announces a new policy toward the Caribbean, México, and Latin America—his administration's "Good Neighbor Policy."

1940 New Mexico commemorates the Coronado Cuarto Centennial, or 400 years of Spanish and mestizo presence and Native American/European history in North America. By comparison, the American Bicentennial celebration in 1976 marked 200 years of U.S. political history.

1943 Public Law 45 is passed by the U.S. Congress to finance and regulate the Bracero Program. Also in 1943 the so-called Zoot Suit Riots are fomented in California by a xenophobic press.

1952 The United States approves the Commonwealth of Puerto Rico status.

1953 Fidel Castro and his followers stage an ill-fated attack on Cuba's Moncada fortress on July 26, 1953. A key date in the formative years of the Cuban Revolution, the movement became synonymous with the revolution that eventually took power in 1959.

1959 The Cuban Revolution deposed dictator Fulgencio Batista in January and brought Fidel Castro to power with the support of the masses of Cuban people. It eventually produced history's largest migration of Cubans, mostly followers of the U.S.-backed dictator Batista, to the United States.

1960s The period of artistic, literary, and political activism known as the Chicano Renaissance flourishes. It includes such activities as the Viva Kennedy voter registration clubs; the Texas Political Association of Spanish-Speaking Organizations (PASO); the organizing in New Mexico of the Alianza Federal de Mercedes (Confederate Alliance of Land Grants) by Reies López Tijerina; the Crusade for Justice in Denver by Rodolfo "Corky" Gonzáles; and student organizing of the Mexican American Youth Organization (MAYO) in Texas, the United Mexican Americans (UMAS) in Colorado, Brown Berets in Los Angeles, the Movimiento Estudiantil Chicano de Aztlán (MEChA) nationally, the Mexican American Legal Defense and Education Fund (MALDEF), and other groups. The Chicano Renaissance also sees the emergence of bilingual English/Spanish periodicals, presses, literary festivals, mural and art exhibiting, college and community organizing, and the activities collectively known as the Chicano Movement.

1961 Disheartened Cuban exiles in Miami, Florida, get backing from the Central Intelligence Agency for the invasion of Cuba at Playa Girón. Known as the Bay of Pigs fiasco, the failed attack on Castro's socialist government exists as a foreign policy mistake of the President John F. Kennedy administration.

1965 The Immigration and Nationality Act of 1952 was revised by the U.S. Congress to establish the first quotas for immigration to the United States from citizens of other Western Hemisphere countries. Also in 1965 under the leadership of César Chávez, the United Farmworkers union is created as a result of highly publicized strikes and national boycotts, and El Teatro Campesino is founded by playwright Luis Valdez. The United States dispatches troops to the Dominican Republic in 1965 to combat a people's revolutionary movement to achieve democracy.

1967 Consistent with the policy of equal education for all Americans, the U.S. Congress mandates that public schools provide educational programs for children of limited English-speaking ability.

1968 The Olympic Games take place in Mexico City, the first Latin American Olympic venue in history.

1970 Texas activist José Angel Gutiérrez founds the La Raza Unida Party (RUP), the first registered Chicano-identified political party in the country. RUP candidates win elections in Crystal

City, Texas, and run for the state's governorship. Eventually organized in Colorado and California, the RUP faded into the shadows of the two incumbent major American political parties. Also in 1970 journalist Rubén Salazar is fatally hit by a police projectile during public demonstrations in support of the Chicano Moratorium.

1970s Feminists increase calls for women's rights throughout the Latina and Latino communities. In 1971 Chicanas hold a conference in Houston, Texas, in support of fair representation and participation in the Chicano Movement. In 1972 Chicanas in South Bend, Indiana, organize Adelante Mujer (Forward Women), a conference showcasing the roles and accomplishments of women throughout Mexican and Chicana/o history.

1974 Two Mexican American candidates are elected to governorships, Raúl Castro in Arizona and Jerry Apodaca in New Mexico. The first Mexican American archbishop was named to the Santa Fe (New Mexico) diocese, Robert F. Sánchez.

1975 After decades of labor activism and the dedicated work of César Chávez, Dolores Huerta, the United Farmworkers' union, and their supporters, the California Labor Relations Act finally is passed by the state legislature. The legislation brought fieldworkers and some food-processing workers under the protection of fair labor regulations for the first time.

1979 The United States continues its over-a-century-old policy toward the Caribbean and Latin America with continued Central Intelligence Agency (CIA) support of dictatorships and business interests against people's revolutionary movements in Nicaragua, El Salvador, Grenada, and throughout the region.

1980 The Refugee Act is passed by the U.S. Congress, redefining the category of "refugee" for immigration purposes. Media and advertising executives dub the period "The Decade of the Hispanics."

1989 The United States deploys troops to Panama to arrest President Manuel Noriega, a dictator originally installed by the United States earlier in the decade.

2000 The U.S. Census count affirms the growth of the combined Latina/o population to be the largest ethnic minority in North America. Vicente Fox is elected president of México to become the first non–PRI (Partido Revolucionario Institucional [Institutional Revolutionary Party]) Mexican head of state in the country's history. The Elián Gonzalez case dominates headlines in Cuba and the United States. The Fidel Castro government prevails when the boy is returned to his Cuban father over the strenuous objections of his Miami relatives.

2001 Former San Juan mayor and member of the Popular Democratic Party, Sila María Calderón, is inaugurated as Puerto Rico's first woman governor and pledges to continue opposing statehood for the island. Puerto Rican referendum votes for the removal of U.S. naval base from the island of Vieques. President George W. Bush authorizes the base's closure, and troops are removed in 2003.

2002 As part of the war on terrorism since September 11, 2001, the U.S. armed forces incarcerate mostly Muslim prisoners on American military bases in Guantánamo, Cuba. Hispanic American contributions to the U.S. economy continue to increase dramatically, approaching nearly $700 billion worth of buying power nationally and projected to grow to a trillion dollars by 2010.

2003 The number of fatalities continues to increase along the borderlands as hundreds of undocumented immigrants die while trying to cross into the United States in search of work. As of June 16, 2003, more than 1,000 people had died of heat exposure, lack of water, starvation, or suffocation in coyote (smuggler) trucks and trailers during passage north. On July 26, 2003, Cuba celebrates the fiftieth anniversary of the assault by revolutionaries on Mancada army bases that eventually led to the downfall of the U.S.-backed Fulgencio Batista dictatorship and the victory of Fidel *Castro supporters.

2004 As a result primarily of Mexican feminist activism, the international media finally focuses its attention on the over 300 murders of women along the U.S.-México border near El Paso, Texas, and Juarez, Chihuahua. The mass killings of female *maquila* (border factory) workers, prostitutes, and other women date to the early 1990s, but for the most part were ignored by officials on both sides of the border until the victims' families, their advocates, and other supporters called national attention to the *femicidio* (female genocide). President George W. Bush promises Cuban American voters in Florida that he will help accelerate the end of President Fidel Castro's control of Cuba by increasing anti-Castro propaganda, providing more support to dissidents, and suppressing the flow of dollars to the island economy sent to help relatives of Cuban emigres. Over a thousand people die and hundreds of others are reported missing in the Dominican Republic and along the border of Haiti as a result of torrential rains and severe flooding on the island of Hispaniola at the end of May. World governments, relief organizations, and grassroots groups contribute food, water, tools, time, and money to assist the victims. In the Copa América, Brazil beats Argentina in penalty kicks.

Contributors

Ann Aguirre, Independent Scholar, Washington, DC

Arturo J. Aldama, University of Colorado, Boulder

Dulce Aldama, University of Colorado, Boulder

Frederick Luis Aldama, University of Colorado, Boulder

Luis Aldama, Independent Scholar, Galisteo, New Mexico

Alma Alvarez-Smith, Arizona State University, Tempe

Julie Amparano García, Arizona State University, Tempe

Leonora Anzaldúa Burke, Yale University, New Haven, Connecticut

Cecilia Aragón, California State University, San Bernadino

Estevan César Azcona, University of Texas, Austin

Katherine Borland, Ohio State University, Newark

Suzanne Bost, Southern Methodist University, Dallas, Texas

Christina Burbano-Jeffrey, Arizona State University, Tempe

Bernadette Calafell, University of North Carolina, Chapel Hill

William Calvo, Arizona State University, Tempe

Clifford Candelaria, Independent Scholar, Denver, Colorado

Cordelia Chávez Candelaria, Arizona State University, Tempe

Jazmin Chávez, University of Colorado, Boulder

Martha Idalia Chew, Saint Lawrence University, Canton, New York

Robert Chew, Arizona State University, Tempe

Darren Crovitz, Arizona State University, Tempe

Karen Mary Dávalos, Loyola Marymount University, Los Angeles, California

Roman Díaz, Independent Scholar, Bronx, New York

J. Javier Enríquez, Arizona State University, Tempe

Edward Escobar, Arizona State University, Tempe

Gabriel Estrada, University of Arizona, Tucson

Erin M. Fitzgibbons-Rascón, University of Colorado, Boulder

Elizabeth (Lisa) Flores, Grand Canyon University, Phoenix, Arizona

David William Foster, Arizona State University, Tempe

José Gamez, University of North Carolina, Charlotte

Melinda Gandara, University of California, Santa Barbara

Heidi García, Arizona State University, Tempe

James E. García, Arizona State University, Tempe

Peter J. García, Arizona State University, Tempe

Cheryl Greene, Arizona State University, Tempe

Mark Guerrero, Independent Scholar, Palm Springs, California

J. Richard Haefer, Arizona State University, Tempe

Rosa Hamilton, Arizona State University, Tempe

Peter Haney, University of Texas, Austin

Kristie Haro, Arizona State University, Tempe

Juanita Heredia, Northern Arizona University, Flagstaff

Louis M. Holscher, San Jose State University, San Jose, California

Lynn Marie Houston, Southeastern Louisiana University, Hammond

Sydney Hutchinson, Independent Scholar, New York, New York

Joan Koss-Chioino, Georgetown University, Washington, DC

R. Joyce Zamora Lausch, New Mexico State University, Las Cruces, NM

Javier F. León, Tulane University, New Orleans, Louisiana

Iraida H. López, Ramapo College of New Jersey, Mahwah

Yolanda M. López, Independent Scholar, San Francisco, CA

Amelia Maciszewski, University of Pittsburgh, Pittsburgh, Pennsylvania

Lisa Magaña, Arizona State University, Tempe

BJ Manríquez, Texas Tech University, Lubbock

Christina Marín, Arizona State University, Tempe

Christine N. Marín, Arizona State University, Tempe

Katynka Martínez, University of California, San Diego

Louis "Pancho" McFarland, Colorado College, Colorado Springs

Miguel Montiel, Arizona State University, Tempe

Silvia D. Mora, Arizona State University, Tempe

Cristina K. Muñoz, Arizona State University, Tempe

Olga Nájera-Ramírez, University of California, Santa Cruz

Bill Nerricio, San Diego State University, San Diego, California

Jimmy Newmoon Royball, Colorado College, Pueblo

Seth Nolan, Arizona State University, Tempe

Helen Oakley, Open University, East Midlands, United Kingdom

William Orchard, University of Chicago, Chicago, Illinois

Fernando A. Orejuela, Indiana University, Bloomington

Berta Palenzuela Jottar, Williams College, Williamstown, Massachusetts

Daniel Enríque Pérez, Arizona State University, Tempe

Naomi Helena Quiñónez, Independent Scholar, Santa Barbara, California

Armando Quintero, Jr., Arizona State University, Tempe

Shoba S. Rajgopal, University of Colorado, Boulder

Brenda Rascón, Arizona State University, Tempe

Carlos M. Rivera, Davidson College, Davidson, North Carolina

Maythee Rojas, California State University, Long Beach

Brenda Romero, University of Colorado, Boulder

F. Arturo Rosales, Arizona State University, Tempe

Karen Rosales de Wells, Arizona State University, Tempe

Verónica "Roni" Rubio-Bravo, Arizona State University, Tempe

Rebecca Sager, University of Texas, Austin

Mónica Saldaña, Arizona State University, Tempe

Gabriella Sánchez, Arizona State University, Tempe

Trino Sandoval, Arizona State University, Tempe

Miguel A. Segovia, Brown University, Providence, Rhode Island

Marisol Silva, Arizona State University, Tempe

Hope Munro Smith, University of Texas, Austin

Víctor Alejandro Sorell, Chicago State University, Chicago, Illinois

Rose Marie Soto, Arizona State University, Tempe

K. Lynn Stoner, Arizona State University, Tempe

Ned Sublette, Independent Scholar, New York, New York

Deborah Vargas, University of California, Davis

Irene Vega, Arizona State University, Tempe

Santos C. Vega, Independent Scholar, Tempe, Arizona

Ramón Versage, Independent Scholar, Austin, Texas

Kim Villarreal, Arizona State University, Tempe

George Yáñez, Arizona State University, Tempe

Encyclopedia of Latino Popular Culture

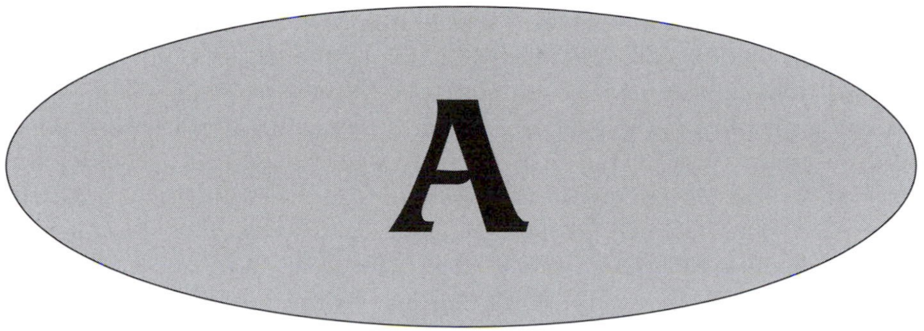

Actors. *See* Stage Performers and Film Actors.

Aguilera, Christina (1980–). Christina María Aguilera was born on December 18, 1980, to parents Fausto and Shelly Aguilera in Staten Island, New York, and is currently one of the most popular Latina pop stars in the United States. Her father, an immigrant from Ecuador, was an officer in the U.S. Army, and her mother, of Irish American descent, was an interpreter of Spanish who met Fausto while studying in New York.

At the age of five, Aguilera's parents divorced, and she relocated with her mother and her older sister, Rachel, to Wexford, Pennsylvania, where her mother's parents resided. As a child, Aguilera developed her musical skills by listening to popular artists such as Whitney Houston, Mariah *Carey, Etta James, Barbra Streisand, and Billie Holiday in a time when "gangsta rap" and "grunge" music were at their height. To cope with her parents' divorce in the mid-1980s, Aguilera memorized and practiced all the songs from the hit musical *The Sound of Music*, and from that point forward, she became intimately involved in music. Close friends and relatives recall the young Aguilera singing into a shampoo bottle, pretending it was a microphone.

Recognizing her talent, Aguilera's mother booked her for public and private events in and around Wexford and, at the age of eight, took her to an audition for the late 1980s television show *Star Search* hosted by Ed McMahon. After passing the local and regional competitions, Aguilera was chosen to appear on the nationally televised competition, where she performed Whitney Houston's hit song "The Greatest Love of All." Aguilera was devastated by her second-place win and returned to Pennsylvania, where she was invited to perform for various events, including professional sporting events for the Steelers (football), the Pirates (baseball), and the Penguins (hockey).

When she was ten years old, Aguilera auditioned for the new version of *The Mickey Mouse Club (MMC)*, which aired on the Disney Channel during the early 1990s. She was chosen as one of the finalists, but due to her age, she was not cast because the producers felt she was too young to fit in with a cast made up primarily of teenagers. Two years after her original audition, Aguilera was invited to a screen test for the *MMC*, and she joined the cast for the second season of the show. Among her fellow "Mouseketeers" were other talented artists, such as Justin Timberlake and J.C. Chasez of 'NSYNC, Britney Spears, Keri Russell (who went on to star in the television show *Felicity*), and actor Ryan Gosling. At the age of twelve, Aguilera was one of the youngest "Mouseketeers" in *MMC* history, and she enjoyed the company of others who shared similar backgrounds. For the two years that she was a member of the *MMC*, she and her mother lived temporarily in Orlando, Florida, where the show was recorded in front of a live audience during the summer months.

When the show was officially canceled, Aguilera hired an agent who got her a contract to perform with Japanese superstar Keizo Nakanishi. Her recording with Nakanishi, "All I Wanna Do," became an instant hit in Japan and opened the doors for a European booking for her to sing at the Golden Stag Festival. Held in Romania, the festival featured prominent artists like Sheryl Crow and Diana Ross performing to an audience of more than 10,000 people. Aguilera won the crowd over when she walked off the stage and performed her song among her audience. Her performance received a standing ovation and ignited determination in Aguilera to become a success in the United States.

In 1998, Disney was in the midst of producing the full-length animated movie *Mulan* and was searching for someone to sing the song titled "Reflection," which was written specifically for the movie and required the female singer to hit a high E-flat, a note few singers can reach successfully. Within forty-eight hours after hearing a cassette tape demo sent by Aguilera's agent, Disney flew Aguilera to Los Angeles to record the song. That same week, Aguilera signed a contract with RCA Records for her own full-length CD titled *Christina Aguilera*. "Reflection" went on to win a Golden Globe Award for "Best Original Song in a Motion Picture." Looking back on that experience, Aguilera has referred to her successful high E-flat note as "the note that changed my life." In 1999, *Christina Aguilera* was elevated to "Platinum" status, and Aguilera's song "Genie in a Bottle" reached the top of *Billboard* charts. "Genie" also reached the Top 10 on MTV's *Total Request Live*. Also that year, Aguilera released a Christmas single of the popular tune titled "The Christmas Song," which also reached the Top 20 on the *Billboard* charts. Her rendition of "The Christmas Song" was the top seller of this song during the 1999 holiday season since Nat King Cole's release, some forty years before.

With her new pop star status, Aguilera was invited for guest appearances on *The Donnie and Marie Show*; *Beverly Hills 90210*; *Macy's Thanksgiving Day Parade*; *Christmas in Washington*, where she performed for former President Bill Clinton and his family, and the European MTV Awards in Ireland in 1999. In January 2000, her song "What a Girl Wants," also from her first album, reached the number-one spot on *Billboard*'s Top 40, making it the first number-one song of the new millennium.

That same year, Aguilera was nominated for "Best New Artist" and "Best Female Pop Vocal Performance" at the 2000 MTV Awards. Up against Macy Grey and former Mouseketeer Britney Spears, Aguilera took home the award for "Best New Artist." She also received the "New Entertainer of the Year" award at the American Latin Media Awards (*ALMA Awards) in April 2000, followed closely by her "Best Latino Album" award for her Spanish album titled *Mi Reflejo*.

Aguilera's discography includes: *Christina Aguilera* (1999), *Mi Reflejo* (2000), *My Kind of Christmas* (2000), and *Stripped* (2002).

Further Reading

Maron, Johanna. *Christina Aguilera: An Unauthorized Biography*. New York: Aladdin, 2000.

J. Javier Enríquez

Airto (1941–). Airto Moreira, known professionally as "Airto," is one of the most influential Afro-Brazilian percussionists in American popular music in the United States. With his wife, singer Flora Purim, Airto created a hybrid form of jazz by combining jazz styles with Afro-Brazilian rhythms including *bossa nova.

Airto was born in the small village of Itaiopolis in southern Brazil and was raised in Curitiba. As a teenager, he was a dance hall musician and singer, playing jazz and other dance music at various nightclubs in Brazil. It was during this time that Airto began to study Afro-Brazilian music, especially the intricate drumming patterns prevalent in this genre. In 1968, his wife moved from Rio de Janeiro to Los Angeles, and Airto soon followed her to the United States. They subsequently moved to New York, where Airto performed with artists such as Reggie Workman, J.J. Johnson, Cedar Walton, and bassist Walter Booker and became well known for his blending of Afro-Brazilian rhythms with the popular jazz and bossa-jazz styles, which were very popular in America's jazz cliques. Airto eventually performed with Cannonball Adderley, Lee Morgan, Paul Desmond, and Joe Zawinul.

Purim came from a well-to-do *family in Rio de Janeiro and was professionally trained in classical and jazz but also performed Afro-Brazilian street music. She began performing with South African singer Miriam Makeba and went on to become a bossa nova singer and big band artist.

Airto is famous for his "unorthodox" use of percussion instruments, as well as his numerous collaborations, recordings, and concerts with an eclectic mix of Latina/o, Anglo-American, and African American artists from throughout the Americas and around the globe. In many of his recordings, Airto used traditional Brazilian instruments like the *berimbau*, as well as unusual instruments that he invented himself. His unique percussion patterns and instrumentation snared him an opportunity to record two cuts with Miles Davis on his album *Bitches' Brew* (1969). The recording, which included keyboardist Joe Zawinul, was influential in the development of the "electric jazz" or "jazz-rock" movement. In addition, his experimental percussion techniques demonstrated on recordings with Chick *Corea helped pave the way for future Afro-Brazilian percussionists such as Dom Um Romão and Guilherme Franco.

After recording with Davis, Airto expanded into music production, generating his first two self-produced albums in 1970 and 1971 under the titles *Natural Feelings* and *Seeds on the Ground*, respectively. Airto also produced other albums with well-known artists like Dizzy Gillespie, Sivuca, Hermeto Pascoal, Ron Carter, and his wife Flora Purim. The texture Airto brought to jazz with his Afro-Brazilian percussion has now become standard in modern jazz music.

He has remained in demand, working, performing, and recording with artists such as Carlos *Santana, Gato Barbieri, Michael Brecker, The Crusaders, Gil Evans, Chicago, Quincy Jones, Herbie Hancock, George Duke, and Paul Simon. Airto has contributed to several movie sound tracks including *The Exorcist*, *Last Tango in Paris*, *King of the Gypsies*, and *Apocalypse Now*. He released his *Homeless* album in 2000.

Airto is a professor in the *Ethnomusicology Department of the University of California, Los Angeles, and divides his time between recording, researching new materials for release, creating new DVD Surround Sound projects, and performing live concerts around the globe.

Further Reading

Roberts, John Storm. *The Latin Tinge: The Impact of Latin American Music on the United States*. 2nd ed. New York: Oxford University Press, 1999.

http://www.airto.com.

J. Javier Enríquez

Alabados. *Alabados* are ancient religious hymns based on the New Testament that lament the passion and crucifixion of Jesus Christ. The Spanish word *alabar* means "to praise" or "to glorify." Beginning with the phrase *alabado sea* (praised be), many *alabados* are often lengthy and contain an indefinite number of verses. Typically performed by La Cofradia de Nuestro Padre Jesús Nazareno, better known as the **penitentes*, *alabados* are commonplace throughout the southwestern United States (e.g., New Mexico, southern Colorado) and México, especially at Lenten rituals in traditional villages. The singing of *alabados*, which are extremely melancholic and sorrowful in melody and style, encourages the active participation of those in attendance. Performed indoors or on the sacred grounds of a *morada* (sacred lodge used as a chapel), *alabados* narrate the story of Christ's life, crucifixion, and passionate death and resurrection. Other *alabado* texts praise the virtues of suffering and penance.

Alabados are also sung as ritual prayers during *novenas de casa* (home rosaries) and other spiritual gatherings and *family/community-based ritual services), during *Vía Crucis* (Stations of the Cross), and as part of religious processions in Catholic parishes. The melodies of *alabados* reveal traces of Middle Eastern musical influence (most likely Moorish and Sephardic), mixed with Iberian medieval plain chant and traces of Pueblo (Tanoan and Keresan) Indian. *Alabados* were introduced to the New World by the Franciscan monks, who used them in converting the native peoples to Christianity. Eventually mixed with New World cultural elements, today's *alabados* are genuine hybrid expressions of the Americas. Many *alabados* have unknown composers; many others were collected, recorded, and transcribed by folklorists during the 1930s and 1940s and continue to fascinate borderlands music historians.

Further Reading

Montaño, Mary. *Tradiciones nuevomexicanas: Hispano Arts and Culture of New Mexico*. Albuquerque: University of New Mexico Press, 2001.

http://www.kuer.org/insidefm90/clarionawardkat.php.

http://memory.loc.gov/ammem/rghtml/rgmusicb.html.

Peter J. García

Alabanzas. *Alabanzas* are ancient Christian religious hymns that praise saints, angels, the Virgin Mary, God, and the Holy Trinity. They are generally sung in such rituals as masses, rosaries, **novenas*, funerals, processions, and wakes. Unlike **alabados*, *alabanzas* are usually performed in major keys and are uplifting and joyful. They are sung by mixed-gender choirs, solo singers, or small groups. *Alabanzas* are typically accompanied by guitars or by *mariachi bands.

Further Reading

Montaño, Mary. *Tradiciones nuevomexicanas: Hispano Arts and Culture of New Mexico*. Albuquerque: University of New Mexico Press, 2001.

Peter J. García

¡Alambrista! Directed by the respected Anglo filmmaker Robert M. Young, *¡Alambrista!* (1977; rerelease 2002) occupies a unique position in American movie history as a product of the late *Chicano Renaissance era. Without the initial exclamation point required by Spanish-language conventions of punctuation, *Alambrista!* was first released in 1977 to a favorable reception among Mexican American intellectuals and other progressives in the United States. Produced by Filmhaus/Bobwin Production, the initial release was shown at the 1980 Denver International Film Festival, where the movie received accolades for its authenticity. Young, who also wrote the script, was lauded for his sensitivity in capturing the abject experience of undocumented workers whose labor produces the food Americans consume. Also contributing to the *film's uniqueness is its rerelease in 2002 with the addition of a musical score composed by anthropologist José B. Cuellar, aka *Dr. Loco, and by Francisco Herrera, Greg Landau, and Tomás Montoya. The music was performed by Dr. Loco's band, Los Tiburones del Norte. The rerelease was produced by Barbara Schulz, Albert Camarillo, David Carrasco, and José B. Cuellar.

Avoiding Hollywood-style simplifications of culture, *¡Alambrista!* portrays Mexicans, immigrants, and Chicanas and Chicanos with documentary intelligence and straightforward respect for the working-class subject matter. The movie presents an "everyman" account of the experience of a Mexican farmer named Roberto (Domingo Ambriz), who leaves his wife and infant to immigrate into the United States without documentation in search of employment. As a hard worker, he hopes to be able to earn enough to return quickly and create a better life for his *family, currently at subsistence poverty level. Through a sequence of low-key episodes, the film captures a visually evocative sense of the lived texture of Roberto's border-crossing experience. The protagonist's disappointments build to a sad ending that suggests a documentary cinema verité effect for the fictional story. Like other films of progressive critique (e.g., the classic **Salt of the Earth*), the original *¡Alambrista!* languished commercially in its first circulation despite its successful screening at the 1980 Denver festival and also despite Young's award-winning respectability as an independent filmmaker. However, it has enjoyed a twenty-first-century revival on college campuses. Besides Ambriz, the cast of *¡Alambrista!* also includes Linda Gillin, Trinidad Silva, Ned Beatty, Salvador Martínez, Jerry Hardin, Julius Harris, Edward James *Olmos, and Dennis Harris.

Further Reading

Cull, Nicholas J., and Davíd Carrasco, eds. *Alambrista and the U.S.-Mexico Border: Film, Music, and Stories of Undocumented Immigrants*. Albuquerque: University of New Mexico Press, 2004.

Hadley-Garcia, George. *Hispanic Hollywood: The Latins in Motion Pictures*. New York: Carol Publishing Group, 1993.

Keller, Gary D. *A Biographical Handbook of Hispanics and United States Film*. Tempe, AZ: Bilingual Press, 1997.

Cordelia Chávez Candelaria

Alamo. The Alamo is the name of a military fort in San Antonio, Texas, where the 1836 historical battle between México and Texas took place. The Alamo serves as an important historical landmark and as a foundational event in the history of Texas, with divergent popular cultural meanings in México and in the United States. The Alamo, as it is known today, was originally named the Misión San Antonio de Valero. It became the "Alamo" in honor of the small town of Álamo de Parras, Coahuila. Many think the Alamo was simply a chapel, but in fact the original structure consisted of many buildings that were grouped in close proximity.

Throughout its history, the Alamo served different functions at different times. In 1724 it served as a mission for converting the native populations and as a base of colonization for Spain. After 1793, the Alamo entered a long period of changing use, often serving as barracks for the Spanish, Mexican, Texan, U.S., and Confederate troops. During the 1810–1820 period of Mexican Independence from Spain it served as a home for both sides of the battle, the royalists and the revolutionaries.

It is the short-lived 1836 battle and twelve-and-a-half-day siege of the Alamo that catapulted the Alamo to its monumental status in Texan, Mexican, and American history. The battle was fought between the Mexican army led by General Santa Anna and those men led by William Travis, who fought to hold the Alamo. The men who died fighting to retain the Alamo have been elevated to a martyr status, and they include such famous icons of American frontier culture as Davy Crockett and James Bowie.

Many believe that the Alamo was a battle between white Texans and Mexicans, but in reality those fighting to hold the Alamo included Mexicans, Texans, Tejanos, Europeans, African American slaves, and southerners from the United States. Davy Crockett, one of the key figures in the battle of the Alamo, was a frontiersman and a member of the Tennessee legislature, who enjoyed creating a rugged image for himself. He supposedly did so by bragging about killing over 100 bears in a year and by calling himself a great "Indian fighter." Some believe that Crockett left for Texas looking for adventure, but others claim he had fled to Texas to avoid criminal charges and federal prosecution. Crockett was one of the defenders of the Alamo, but his death there remains a mystery. Some believe he died fighting, and others say he was captured and executed. Personal accounts in journals and letters state that Crockett was captured and executed by General Santa Anna, the leader of the Mexican forces, after the battle.

James Bowie, another martyr, was a wealthy southerner who came to Texas to take advantage of the land grants that were offered by the Mexican government to help settle Texas. He and his brothers, Rezin P. Bowie and John Bowie, became wealthy from sugar mills and participation in the slave trade. James Bowie left New Orleans in 1821 and headed for San Antonio, where he became a Mexican citizen, converted to Catholicism, and married Úrsula Veramendi, the daughter of Don Juan Martín Veramendi, governor of Coahuila and Texas in 1831. When the siege on the Alamo began, Bowie was told to take whatever men he could to the Alamo and prepare to fight. However, by the time the Mexican army attacked, Bowie was sick in bed with typhoid fever and is said to have died the day the Mexican army entered the complex. William Travis, who was in charge of recruiting men for the Texan Army when he was called in to take all his men to the Alamo, became the famous Texan commander who drew a line in the sand and asked all those that were willing to die for Texas to cross the line over to his side. All but two crossed; one man ran off, and the other man was Bowie, who was too sick with typhoid fever to leave his bed but decided to stay and fight. Travis is also quoted as demanding that Santa Anna surrender and then exclaiming, "Victory or Death!" When no help arrived from Sam Houston, Travis attempted to hold back the Mexican onslaught. He died in battle, as did many others.

General Antonio López de Santa Anna had fought against the royalist army and had joined in the struggle that won México its independence in 1821. Afterward, Santa Anna began a long political career, during which he constantly shifted his allegiance from party to party and found that his fortunes were constantly rising and falling. He found himself leading rebellions against people whom he once had helped into power, such as Agustín de Iturbide, the president at that time, and Vicente Guerrero and Anastacio Bustamente. In 1833, after fighting for power with the vice president, he became president for a brief term lasting to 1836.

Colonel Francisco Duque, General Martín Perfecto de Cos, Colonel José María Romero, Colonel Juan Morales, and Colonel Joaquín Ramírez y Sesma were Santa Anna's most senior officers who led the attack on the Alamo in the early morning of March 6, 1836. All worked together and planned out, with precision, how, when, and where they would attack.

Before the battle at the Alamo, ethnic relations in Texas were becoming hostile. Tension between the incoming southern settlers and the Mexicanos already there led to distrust and violence. Many Mexicanos believed that the large *immigration to the state of Texas in 1821 was a covert operation by the United States to take over the state. Each group began to form initial impressions of each other. To the Mexicans, the Texans were arrogant, aggressive, overbearing, conniving, rude, dishonest, and unreliable. To the American settlers, the Mexicans were lazy, cowardly, jealous, superstitious, immoral, and backward. In 1830 México put a halt to immigration into Texas because the new Texans began outnumbering the original settlers 20,000 to 5,000. After fifteen years of open migration to the state, the Mexican government failed to control the state of Texas, and many began to see hostility among the populations in Texas.

By 1835, the Mexican army and government found it difficult to control the Texan population. The new Texans decided they would form their own army, called the Texan Militia, later to be called the Texan Army. The Texans rebelled against the government of México, and for Santa Anna the culminating point was on October 2, 1835, when Mexican forces entered Gonzáles to retrieve a cannon that had been given to the settlers for protection. The Texas rebels refused to relinquish it and raised a banner that read "Come and take it!" The Mexican forces tried, but the rebels routed them and kept it. Later that year, the Texans gained four ships and created a navy, minimizing the possibility of a blockade or a naval attack by Santa Anna. He would have to attack solely by land.

Santa Anna marched into San Antonio on February 23, 1836, eager to avenge the defeat at Gonzales. Once there, he found that about 180 men, locked up in the fortified mission called the Alamo, would defend the town. The Texan rebels prepared for their death, knowing that they would not survive the attack. When Santa Anna arrived with his troops and surrounded the Alamo, he raised the red flag of "no quarters," meaning that the rebels had to surrender immediately or be executed upon capture. The rebels replied with cannon fire, and the siege began.

The siege lasted thirteen days, but finally on the night of March 5, 1836, Santa Anna read a letter to his troops addressing how they would attack the Alamo. He planned his attack in imitation of Napoleon's tactics. With his troops in columns, Santa Anna stormed the Alamo before dawn in complete silence and darkness. Finally the chords of the *degüello* (beheading) rang out, and the full attack began. The Mexicans advanced and climbed the walls into the Alamo. Once they reached the inside quarters of the building, room-to-room fighting ensued for anywhere from one to five hours. The garrison of the Alamo was completely destroyed, but there were some survivors, mostly women, slaves, and children. The size of the attack force is said to have been anywhere from 1,400 to 8,000 men. Mexican losses were inaccurate at the time, even though Santa Anna claimed that only 70 lives were lost on the Mexican side.

The Mexican army was triumphant, but the victory was short-lived. Sam Houston received word of the battle and vowed revenge on México. On April 21, 1836, Sam Houston and his Texan Army defeated Santa Anna and his forces at the Battle of San Jacinto, and Houston became famous for yelling, "Remember the Alamo!" Santa Anna was captured, and México had lost Texas. Thereafter, Texas became an independent republic and at the end of 1845 was annexed by the United States.

The Alamo in Texas is seen as a shrine to liberty and is referred to as the "Cradle of Texas Liberty." Psychologically, the battle was devastating for the Texans, and it became the breaking point where Texans believed they had to make a stand. The rebels displayed courage in battle, but they also showed that they were not as invincible as they had believed. The Alamo also created remorse against Mexicans for years to come. Prior bitterness against both groups had now intensified. Anglo Texans now felt a bitter hatred toward the Mexicans, and Mexicans felt the same toward them.

For Mexicans the Alamo was seen at first as a great victory of the amazing talents of the Mexican army and cavalry. It was looked at with a sense of pride and prestige, knowing that they had defeated the so-called heroes of Texas such as Bowie, Travis, and above all, Davy Crockett. However, the Alamo later was viewed as humiliating, and Santa Anna was captured in the Battle of San Jacinto. From 1836 to 1846, the shooting wars continued in the Republic of Texas, especially south of the Nueces River. Murder and raids by Texans were matched by México. Because a peace treaty was never negotiated, no boundaries could be fixed. México claimed that the Nueces was the boundary, and Texas claimed that the Rio Grande was the boundary. The zone between the two rivers became a place of bloody guerrilla warfare. These early skirmishes and the resentment that the Alamo caused among Texans and the rest of the United States constituted one of the many factors that finally resulted in U.S. President James K. Polk declaring war against México, a war that lasted from 1846 to 1848 and was concluded by the signing of the *Treaty of Guadalupe Hidalgo. The treaty resulted in the annexation of over half the Mexican territory that included the states in what is now known as the Southwest: Arizona, California, Texas, New Mexico, Colorado, and parts of Kansas.

Further Reading

Gonzáles, Juan. *A History of Latinos in America: Harvest of Empire*. New York: Viking Penguin, 2000.

McWilliams, Carey. *North from México: The Spanish Speaking People of the United States*. Westport, CT: Praeger, 1990.

Ochoa, George. *Atlas of Hispanic-American History*. New York: Checkmark Books, 2001.

Jazmin Chávez

Alba, Jessica (1981–). Actress Jessica Alba was born on April 28, 1981, in Pomona, California. Her father is Mexican American, and her mother is an American of French and Danish descent. Alba became one of the few Latinas in 2000 to star in a prime-time U.S. television series. In the Fox Network science fiction action series *Dark Angel*, which premiered that year, she played a genetically engineered bike messenger named Max Guevara. Alba received People's Choice, Golden Globe, and *ALMA nominations for Best Actress in a Dramatic Series for *Dark Angel*. She has had recurring roles in two other television series—Nickelodeon's *The Secret World of Alex Mac* (1994) and *Flipper* (1995–1996)—and has made guest television appearances in shows such as *Beverly Hills 90210*, *Brooklyn South*, *Oz*, and *Chicago Hope*. Her filmography includes *Idle Hands* (1994), *Never Been Kissed* (1999), *Paranoid* (2000), *The Sleeping Dictionary* (2001), and *Honey* (2003).

Further Reading

http://www.darkangeltheseries.com.

William Orchard

Alfaro, Luis (1957–). A prominent *Chicano spoken-word poet, performance artist, and playwright, Luis Alfaro addresses issues of racism, sexism, poverty, and homophobia in his work dealing primarily with working-class Latina and Latino immigrant communities. In 1997 he received the highly prestigious MacArthur Foundation Genius Grant, which gave him the financial independence to devote himself full-time to his creative work. The following year he won the National Hispanic Playwright Competition for his *film *Chicanismo* (1998). This public recognition and acclaim for the talents of a child of Mexican immigrant farmworkers is all the more remarkable in the context of prior growing-up experiences. He spent his boyhood in the Pico-Union district of central Los Angeles, California, a large enclave of poor Central American and Mexican immigrant families. He later worked as a custodian at the Los Angeles Poverty Department theater where he met Scott Kelman, the theater director who encouraged him to develop his playwrighting and performance skills.

From those humble origins, he eventually met the established playwrights María Irene Fornés (a Cuban American) and Tony Kushner, who influenced his work toward greater expression of his Chicano roots and viewpoint. Alfaro's grassroots upbringing and creativity, combined with his good fortune in meeting influential mentors early in his development, prepared him for the post of resident artist at the Mark Taper Forum in Los Angeles, where he codirects the Latino Theatre initiatives (also called the Latino Playwright Lab) and works with at-risk youth and AIDS patients. Cofounder of three nonprofit arts organizations, he also chaired the Gay Men of Color Consortium as part of his social consciousness–raising agenda. His *Chicanismo* (1998) won the Best Experimental Film at San Antonio's Cine Festival and was nominated for an Emmy. Alfaro has been a visiting artist at the Kennedy Center in Washington, D.C. and continues touring throughout the United States, England, and México as a featured writer and performer.

Further Reading

Coco Muñoz, José, and Coco Fusco. "Corpus Delecti: Performance Art of the Americas." In *Memory Performance: Luis Alfaro's Cuerpo politizado*. New York: Routledge, 2000.

Prieto, Antonio. "Identidades incorporadas: El manejo del estigma en el *Performance Art* de Luis Alfaro." *Chasqui* 26.2 (November 1997): 72–83.

http://www.communications.uci.edu/releases/0971b02.html.

http://www.newdramatists.org/luis_alfaro.htm.

Carlos M. Rivera

Algarín, Miguel (1941–). Miguel Algarín, poet, playwright, author, and scholar, has been called the "poet laureate of Loisaida"—the Spanglish word for New York City's Lower East Side. He was a cofounder of the *Nuyorican Poets Café, where aspiring poets, artists, and performers present their work, as well as one of the founders of the Nuyorican Poetry movement, which provided a platform for Puerto Rican writers to speak out against social, political, and cultural injustice.

Born on September 11, 1941, in Puerto Rico, Algarín arrived with his *family in New York City's East Harlem neighborhood in the early 1950s.

A gifted writer from an early age, Algarín studied at the University of Wisconsin, Madison, and Pennsylvania State University and is a professor emeritus at Rutgers University, where he has taught Shakespeare, creative writing, and ethnic literature for more than thirty years. Algarín has been editor of the Nuyorican Press, a member of the editorial board of Arte Público Press, director of the El Puerto Rican Playwrights/Actors Workshop, and executive director of the Nuyorican Theater Festival.

In addition to the critical acclaim Algarín garnered for his writing, he also has spent much of adult life promoting the creative work of other poets, writers, actors, and musicians, particularly in communities of color. He founded the Nuyorican Poets Café in the early 1970s with poet and playwright Miguel *Piñero. The space helped nurture and develop "slam" poetry, an expressive, freestyle poetic form popularized in America's urban minority communities, and a variety of multicultural and alternative art forms.

In 1975, Algarín and Piñero published *Nuyorican Poetry: An Anthology of Puerto Rican Words and Feelings*. The following year, Algarín translated poet Pablo Neruda's *Songs of Protest* (Morrow, 1976). He has received American Book Awards for *Shameless Hussy* (1981) and *On Call* (1981); for *Time's Now* (1996); and with Bob Holden for *Aloud! Voices from the Nuyorican Poets' Café* (1994), as well as the Larry Leon Hamlin Producer's Award at the 2001 National Black Theater Festival. Algarín's plays include *Olu Clemente: The Philosopher of Baseball* (1973), *Apartment 6-D* (1974), and *The Murder of Pito* (1976).

Futher Reading

"Contemporary Authors Online." *Gale Group*. http://www.galegroup.com.

Kanellos, Nicolas, ed. *Biographical Dictionary of Hispanic Literature in the United States. The Literature of Puerto Ricans, Cuban Americans, and Other Hispanic Writers*. Westport, CT: Greenwood Press, 1989.

Lomelí, Francisco, Nicolás Kanellos, and Claudio Esteva-Fabregat, eds. *Handbook of Hispanic Cultures in the United States: Literature and Art*. Houston, TX: Arte Público Press, 1993.

Meyer, Nicholas E. *Biographical Dictionary of Hispanic Americans*. 2nd ed. New York: Facts on File, 2001.

James E. García

ALMA Awards. The American Latino Media Arts Awards, more commonly known as the ALMA Awards, is the largest and most prestigious Latina/o media and entertainment awards ceremony and television program in the United States. Watched by millions across the country, the ALMA Awards is the only two-hour awards special devoted to Latina and Latina/o performers, other entertainers, and producers aired by the four major English-language networks during prime-time hours. The *National Council of La Raza (NCLR), a Washington, D.C.–based think tank, created the ALMA Awards in 1995 to counter negative stereotyping of Latina/os in entertainment and to promote fair, accurate, and balanced portrayals of Latina/os in television, *film, music, and other media.

NCLR chose the acronym "ALMA," which means "spirit" or "soul" in Spanish, because it both captures the nature of the awards and represents the spirit of the Latina/o people and culture. The ceremony began with only four award categories—Lifetime Achievement, Outstanding Album, Outstanding Television Program, and Emerging Artist of the Year. Since then, the ALMA Awards have expanded to more than twenty-seven different award categories honoring Latina/o performers for their outstanding artistic achievement, impact, and enhancement of the image of Latina/o.

The first recipient of the ALMA Lifetime Achievement Award was veteran actor Ricardo *Montalbán (in 1995). Others recognized with the prestigious honor include actor, dancer, and singer Rita *Moreno (in 1998), and Emilio and Gloria *Estefan (in 1999). ALMA Entertainers of the Year include Jennifer *López (2001), Ricky *Martin (2000), and New Entertainer of the Year Christina *Aguilera (2000). Other actors who have been honored with the highly coveted prize include Antonio Banderas, Cameron *Díaz, Jessica *Alba, Benjamin *Bratt, Edward James *Olmos, Lupe *Ontiveros, and Jimmy *Smits. Musicians include Marc *Anthony, Enrique *Iglesias, Mariah *Carey, and Carlos *Santana.

Further Reading

http://www.almaawards.com/wmspage.cfm?parm1=45.

Julie Amparano García

Almeida, Laurindo (1918–1995). Laurindo Almeida, a classical guitarist from Brazil, helped perpetuate the success of the fusion of *bossa nova and American jazz through the use of an Afro-Brazilian rhythm called the *baião*, a predecessor to the bossa nova style. Almeida was part of Stan Kenton's group, which played bossa-jazz in American ballrooms. In 1953, Almeida was part of a Hollywood-based quartet that played mainly jazz-*baião* music. It was during this time that Almeida and saxophonist-flutist Bud Shank recorded a ten-inch album titled *Brazilliance* (1953), which was important to the development of bossa nova in the United States. In 1959, as the bossa nova sound became integrated into American jazz by artists such as Dizzy Gillespie, João Gilberto, Ella Fitzgerald, Herbie Mann, Johnny *Pacheco, and Willie Bobo, *Brazilliance* was rereleased in the United States.

Further Reading

Roberts, John Storm. *The Latin Tinge: The Impact of Latin American Music on the United States*. 2nd ed. New York: Oxford University Press, 1999.

J. Javier Enríquez

Alomar, Roberto (1968–). Major league baseball player Roberto Velázquez Alomar was born on February 5, 1968, in Ponce, Puerto Rico, and is the son of former major leaguer Santos "Sandy" Alomar, Sr., and

María Angelita Velázquez. Alomar attended Luis Muños Rivera High School in Salinas, Puerto Rico. In February 1985, he signed with the National League (NL) team, the San Diego Padres, for $80,000, and he played for them until they traded him to the American League's (AL) Toronto Blue Jays in 1990. He spent two years in the Padres' minor clubs and joined the major league Padres in 1987 as their second baseman. At age twenty, he became the NL's youngest player and was named Rookie of the Year for batting .266.

At six feet tall and 185 pounds, Alomar had both agility and speed, and though he threw right-handed, behind the plate he could switch-hit. In 1989, he hit .295 and stole forty-two bases. With a busy year in 1991, he had an all-time-high batting average of .474, with forty-one doubles and eleven triples. He ended the 1991 season by playing in an all-star game with his older brother, Sandy Alomar, Jr. In 1992, Roberto Alomar helped the Blue Jays defeat the Atlanta Braves (NL) in the World Series, earning him the Most Valuable Player honors. Roberto Alomar completed his baseball career with the Baltimore Orioles (AL) after they signed him as a free agent in December 1995. In 2004, he was hired by the Arizona Diamondbacks to play second base and inspire the team and fans with his intensity as a player.

Further Reading

http://www.baseball-almanac.com/players/player.php?p=alomaro01.

Kristie Haro

Alonso, María Conchita (1957–). Award-winning model, *film actress, and recording artist María Conchita Alonso was born in Cuba. When she was a child, her *family moved to Venezuela, and she eventually attended schools in France and Switzerland. She began modeling and appearing in television commercials at the age of fourteen, and in 1971, she was named Miss Teenager of the World. In 1975, she represented Venezuela in the Miss World beauty pageant. She later pursued acting in *telenovelas* (soap operas) in Venezuela and also became one of South America's bestselling recording artists.

Driven by her motto "Dare to try new things," Alonso headed for Hollywood in 1982 to establish herself in the movies. She was quickly cast in *Moscow on the Hudson* (1984), playing Robin Williams's girlfriend, and continued to land numerous roles in films such as *Extreme Prejudice* (1987); Dennis Hopper's *Colors* (1988); *Running Man* (1987), with Arnold Schwarzenegger; *Touch and Go Blood* (1986); *Ties* (1987); and *Predator II* (1990). She has also performed on Broadway (e.g., **Kiss of the Spider Woman*) and on U.S. television, starring in a short-lived NBC series *One of the Boys* (1989). Other television credits include the NBC made-for-TV movie *McShayne: Final Roll of the Dice* (1994) and an HBO film *Teamster Boss: The Jackie Presser Story* (1992).

A multitalented entertainer, Alonso received a Grammy Award for Best

Latin Artist in 1985 for her album *María Conchita* and a Grammy Award nomination in 1988 for Best Latin Pop Performance for her single "Otra Mentira Más" (One More Lie). The Sony Pictures Classics Web site lists her album *Imagíname* (Imagine Me) as a Grammy nominee for Best Latin Pop Album in 1993. Her previous four albums, including *O Élla o Yo* (Either Her or Me), were each awarded a Gold Record after selling half a million copies. Her 1991 album *Házme Sentir* (Make Me Feel) received Gold Records in several countries. In 1990, Alonso received the Hispanic Woman of the Year Award from the *Mexican American Opportunity Foundation (MAOF) for her contribution to both the entertainment industry and the Hispanic community.

Further Reading

Keller, Gary D. *A Biographical Handbook of Hispanics and United States Film.* Tempe, AZ: Bilingual Press, 1997.

Tardiff, Joseph C., and L. Mpho Mabunda, eds. *Dictionary of Hispanic Biography.* Detroit, MI: Gale, 1996.

Telgen, Diane, and Jim Kamp, eds. *Latinas! Women of Achievement.* Detroit, MI: Visible Ink Press, 1996.

Unterburger, Amy L., and Jane L. Delgado, eds. *Who's Who among Hispanic Americans 1994–1995.* Detroit, MI: Gale, 1994.

Alma Alvarez-Smith

Alonzo, John A. (1934–2001). Cinematographer and Oscar nominee John A. Alonzo was born in Dallas, Texas, in 1934 and grew up in Guadalajara, México, and Los Angeles, California. He began his professional career as a television cameraman in Dallas before moving to Los Angeles in the late 1950s to try his hand at acting. He landed several small roles in movies such as the classic western *The Magnificent Seven* (1960), *Hand of Death* (1962), and *Invitation to a Gunfighter* (1964). Eventually encouraged to take up cinematography, Alonzo assisted in *Seconds* (1966) before being hired as a cameraman. During his four decades behind the camera, Alonzo was credited with over eighty movies and was nominated for an Oscar in cinematography for the award-winning movie *Chinatown* (1974). He also worked as cinematographer for other critically acclaimed and popular *films such as *Harold and Maude* (1971), *Norma Rae* (1979), *Scarface* (1983), and *Star Trek: Generations* (1994). A significant *Chicano presence in Hollywood film history, Alonzo was one of a small number of Latinos to hold a central role behind the camera on the technical side of film production. He died on March 13, 2001.

Further Reading

http://www.amctv.com/person/detail/0,,2312-1-EST,00.html.

http://www.rottentomatoes.com/p/JohnAAlonzo-1040502/.

Cordelia Chávez Candelaria

Alou Family. One of the most remarkable Latina and Latino contributions to American popular culture in the arena of *sports are those made by the Alou family to major league baseball (MLB). All are generally recognized as outstanding contributors of solid, consistent, and first-rate game performances, with the most noted stars being Felipe, Matty, Jesús, and Moíses. The first three are the sons of Virginia Alou and José Rojas, and the last, Moíses, is their grandson (Felipe's son). The parents were born in the Dominican Republic, a strongly baseball-oriented nation, and their children and grandchildren identify proudly with their Dominican ethnicity. In 1963 the family made sports celebrity history when Felipe, Matty, and Jesús, all playing for the San Francisco Giants, became the first trio of brothers to play on one team.

Felipe Rojas Alou was born on May 12, 1935, in Haina, Dominican Republic. As a youth he was an accomplished all-round athlete and participated in the 1955 Pan American Games, where he set the Dominican record in the javelin throwing competition. Spotted by Horatio Martínez, a successful scout for the Giants, at that time still based in New York. Felipe was signed to a professional contract in 1955 and began playing in the outfield in the club's minor league teams. By 1958 and the Giants' relocation to San Francisco, Felipe was considered strong enough to be moved to the team's main roster, and he contributed to the team's effectiveness in adjusting to the West Coast. In his prime he stood six feet tall and weighed 195 pounds. He played for the Giants until 1969, when he was hired by the Milwaukee Brewers expansion team, playing there until 1974. From there he was hired as a coach for another northern expansion team, the Montreal Expos. His remarkable MLB career was capped in 1992 when he was named manager of the Expos, one of the first Latinos to be so honored, and his continued baseball success led to his being voted Manager of the Year in 1994 by the Associated Press sportswriters. The family scored another first when his son, Moíses, played for the Expos for a short time, giving them another historic first as father/son and manager/player duo.

The second Alou son to make it to the majors was Mateo Rojas Alou, nicknamed Matty, born on December 22, 1938, also in Haina. The middle of the three brothers, Matty is also the smallest, standing five feet nine inches and weighing 160 pounds. Although he was strong enough to be hired to the San Francisco Giants' roster in the early 1960s, Matty began to flourish as a major leaguer when he left the club in 1969 to play for the Pittsburgh Pirates. At the height of his success in 1968, only one player in the majors bested his batting average, and that was fellow Latino and Pirates teammate Roberto *Clemente of Puerto Rico. Matty went on to play for the New York Yankees but gave up his diamond duties with a cumulative total of 1,667 major league games played and a very respectable career batting average of .307 and 1,777 hits. After leaving the Yankees, Matty was hired to scout for the Giants until 2000, when he returned to his birthplace to live.

The third brother, Jesús Maria Rojas Alou, was born in Haina on March 24, 1942, and grew up to be the largest of the offspring at six feet two inches and 195 pounds. Mentored and guided by his older brothers, it did not take long for Jesús to find his place on the San Francisco Giants' roster in 1963. His career was successful, but in the increasingly competitive major leagues, he ended up playing for more teams than his older brothers. In his renowned fifteen consecutive years in the MLB, Jesús played for the Giants, the New York Mets, the Oakland Athletics, and the Houston Astros. Although his overall batting average ended up at .280, he hit a career-high .324 in 1978.

Grandson of patriarchs Virginia and José, Moíses Alou is the son of Felipe, star player and manager. Born in Atlanta, Georgia, on July 3, 1966, Moíses attended Canada College in Redwood City, California, in the 1980s. He grew to outsize his uncle, standing at six feet three inches and weighing 220 pounds. He played for the Montreal Expos in the early 1990s and in 1993 was number three in the Most Valuable Player balloting, despite having to miss part of the season due to a broken leg. Considered an all-around outfielder and accomplished designated hitter, Moíses is credited with being a consistent and disciplined player. In 2004 he was playing for the Chicago Cubs in the role as slugger behind Sammy *Sosa, with a .314 all time batting average, as well as playing left field.

Further Reading

"Baseball Almanac." http://www.baseball-almanac.com/players/player.php?p=aloujeO1html.

Porter, David L., ed. *Biographical Dictionary of American Sports*. Rev. ed. Westport, CT: Greenwood Press, 1995.

Kristie Haro

Alurista (1947–). Alurista (pen name of Alberto B. Urista) is recognized as one of the most important, renowned, and prolific *Chicano poets; in fact, he is considered by many scholars as the poet laureate of Chicano letters for his foundational contributions both as a writer and as an influential Chicano activist over the span of four decades since the 1960s. During the earliest stages of the *Chicano Movement, he was instrumental in making Chicano poetry a vital part of the contemporary American literature of the United States. Literary scholars credit Alurista's *Floricanto en Aztlán* (1971) and *Nationchild Plumaroja* (1972) for helping to initiate the multilingual Chicano literary canon (English, Spanish, Caló, and Nahuatl).

Alurista was born Alberto Baltazar Urista in Mexico City on August 8, 1947, to Baltazar and Ruth Heredia Urista. The oldest of six children, Alurista spent his younger years in the Mexican states of Morelos and Guerrero, until the *family immigrated to the United States when he was thirteen years old. Settling in San Diego, the family encountered a heady period of emerging grassroots activism in California with the student, anti–Vietnam War, and Chicano movements converging and gaining momentum. Inspired creatively and politically by the upsurge of social movements, especially the farmworker and student movements, Alurista, who had started writing poetry and reciting his verses in the second grade, began to write about the experiences of Chicanos. After graduating from high school in 1965, Alurista spent a short while studying business administration at Chapman College in Orange, California, before he transferred to San Diego State College to study religion and later sociology. This exploratory curiosity ultimately directed him to psychology, the major for which he earned both a Bachelor of Arts degree in 1970 and a Master's in 1978. He went on to earn a Ph.D. from the University of California, San Diego, in 1983, writing a dissertation on the novel *The Revolt of the Cockroach People* (1973) written by Chicano author and fellow movement activist Oscar Z. Acosta. Throughout his college studies, Alurista continued to write poetry, and in 1966 he began preparing his compositions for publication. Part of this preparation included creating a pen name for himself, which he did by combining his first name, Alberto, and his surname, Urista; family and friends call him "Beto" in the Spanish tradition of diminutive forms for nicknames.

His first book, *Floricanto en Aztlán* (Flower and Song in Aztlán, 1971), is considered by many literary historians as his most influential collection because the book broke new ground in several ways. It promoted the concept of *Aztlán, the mythical or ancient homeland of the Aztecs, as a unifying metaphor for Mexican Americans as an exalted pre-Columbian root of culture for Chicana and Chicano descendants in the United States. The book also was revolutionary in its use of more than one language, giving rise to—and helping to popularize—multilingualism, particularly in Chicano literature. Fluent in Spanish and English, articulate in Chicano and black dialects, and knowledgeable of Mayan and the Nahuatl language of the Aztecs, Alurista refused to follow his first editor's request that he write it only in English or in Spanish, as was the standard convention of the time. The poet's second collection, *Nationchild Plumaroja* (1972), also received favorable notice when it was published and is regarded as an important extension of his vision. *Nationchild Plumaroja* emphasizes the importance of Chicano identity, employs a bilingual style, and continues to explore the roots of ancient Indian culture. Other noteworthy books include Alurista's next three collections: *Timespace Huracan: Poems, 1972–1975* (1976), *A'nque/Alurista: Acuarelas hechas por Delilah Merriman-Montoyae* (Though Alurista: Watercolors by Delilah Merriman Montoya, 1979), and *Spik in Glyph?* (1981). To an extent overshadowed in the 1980s and 1990s by the emergence of many other Latina and Latino artists, writers, and political activists, Alurista nonetheless continues writing and publishing, for example, *Et tú . . . Raza?* (And you . . . Chicano Community? 1994); *Z Eros* (1995); and *As Our Barrio Turns: Who the Yoke B On?* (2000).

In addition to his poetry, Alurista is known for cofounding *MEChA (Movimiento Estudiantil Chicano de Aztlán [Chicano Student Movement of Aztlán]) in 1967; the Chicano Studies Department at San Diego State in 1968; and the Chicano Studies Center at San Diego State in 1969 while he was a lecturer at San Diego State from 1968 to 1974 and from 1976 to 1979. He also is the founder of *Maize*, a Chicano journal and alternative press for literature and criticism. In the mid-1970s Alurista was the chief organizer of the annual Festival Floricanto, a creative multi-arts event that brought together published and unpublished Chicano authors to read and perform in the Chicano community. Among the poet's honors are a Ford Foundation Fellowship in 1976, a California Art Council creative writing award in 1978, a Writer-in-Residence Professorship at Colorado College in the 1980s, and a Before Columbus American Book Award in 1997 for *Et tú . . . Raza*.

Further Reading

Ginsburg, Judith. "Alurista (Alberto Baltazar Urista)." In *Chicano Writers, First Series*, edited by Francisco A. Lomelí and Carl R. Shirley. Vol. 82 of *Dictionary of Literary Biography*. Detroit, MI: Gale, 1989. 16–23.

Keller, Gary D. "Alurista, Poeta-antropólogo, and the Recuperation of the Chicano Identity." Introduction to *Alurista's Return: Poems Collected and New*, edited by Gary D. Keller. Ypsilanti, MI: Bilingual/Editorial Bilingüe, 1982.

Julie Amparano García

Alvarado, Linda G. (1952–). Linda G. Alvarado, an influential Chicana and a powerful businesswoman, became the first Hispanic in 1991 to own a major baseball franchise, the Colorado Rockies, as part of the Colorado Baseball Partnership. She is the recipient of the Sara Lee Corp.'s Frontrunner Award (1993) and the Revlon Business Woman of the Year Award (1996) and was named one of *Hispanic Magazine*'s "100 most influential Hispanics in America" in 1996. In 1995 President Bill Clinton named her to the Advisory Commission on Educational Excellence for Hispanic Americans.

Alvarado was born in 1952, in Albuquerque, New Mexico. The only girl among six children, Alvarado excelled scholastically and received a scholarship to attend Pomona College in Claremont, California, where she graduated in 1973 with a bachelor's degree in economics. After graduating from college and struggling unsuccessfully to find meaningful employment, she borrowed $2,500 from her parents in 1976 to launch her first business, Alvarado Construction Inc. Alvarado became its chief executive officer in 1978. Alvarado Construction has worked on such projects as the Colorado Convention Center, Denver Bronco Stadium, and the Denver International Airport. Alvarado has served as a corporate director for many companies including 3M Co., Pepsi Bottling Group, Pitney Bowes Inc., Cyprus Amex Minerals, Lennox International, and US West Communications. She is also a member of the Greater Denver Chamber of Commerce, the National Network of Hispanic Women, and the Hispanic Chamber of Commerce.

Further Reading

"President Names Linda Alvarado." http://www.ed.gov/PressReleases/03-1995/html.

http://www.hispaniconline.com/magazine/2002/oct/Business.

Kristie Haro

American G.I. Forum. The American G.I. Forum is an active veterans' organization dedicated to assisting Mexican-American veterans, procuring equal privileges, fostering training and education, and promoting political, social, and economic equality. Founded in 1948 by Hector García, the American G.I. Forum provided support and advocacy for the 500,000 Mexican-American soldiers who fought in World War II for the United States only to return home and find that they were not allowed membership in the veteran advocacy groups that were already in operation. The veterans found a hero in García, who refused to accept the discrimination and injustice that was part of the post–World War II society, and he remains a leader in the Latino civil rights fight.

In 1948, the American G.I. Forum received national coverage in an incident that would go down in history as "The Felix Longoria Affair." Private Felix Longoria was killed while on duty in the military, but when his remains were returned for burial, the only funeral parlor in his hometown of Three Rivers, Texas, would not allow services for a Mexican American. Latinos were incensed at the racism, and his widow turned to García and the American G.I. Forum for assistance. García enlisted the sponsorship of then U.S. Senator Lyndon Baines Johnson, who arranged for Longoria to be interred at Arlington Cemetery. The "Affair" earned the American G.I. Forum respect and forged a long friendship between García and Johnson. Hector García was awarded the Presidential Medal of Freedom in 1984 by President Ronald Reagan. The Presidential Medal of Freedom is the highest award bestowed on a civilian.

The American G.I. Forum continues to provide services and leadership, training, and educational opportunities and advance understanding between different nationalities. It is headquartered in Austin, Texas, with chapters throughout the United States.

Further Reading

http://www.agif.org.

Alma Alvarez-Smith

American Latino Media Arts Awards. *See* ALMA Awards.

American Me. *Chicano actor Edward James *Olmos, known for his 1980s detective role in *Miami Vice*, made his 1992 directorial debut with the epic *American Me*, a *film that charts the evolution of the 1940s Pachuca/o [See Pachucos] youth culture into the violent prison *gangs of the 1980s. The film exposes the processes of criminalization and the cycles of violence that affect the Chicana/o community. This film, which was produced by Olmos and Robert Young, is inspired by a true story. *American Me* follows the life of main character Santana Montoya (Olmos), a young Chicano who becomes the leader of "La eMe" (the Mexican Mafia) behind the gates of Folsom Prison.

Santana was conceived when his mother Esperanza (Vira Montes) was violently raped by white navy sailors on the night of the *Zoot Suit riots in Los Angeles in 1943. Santana grows up in East L.A. ignored by a cold and distant father who sees Santana as a painful reminder of that dreaded night.

Estranged from his parents, Santana finds a place for himself and creates an ad hoc *family by forming a gang (*clica*), along with other alienated Chicanos. His gang affiliation ("la primera," the first) leads him and his cohorts—J.D. (William Forsythe) and big-eyed Mundo (Pepe Serno)—to incarceration in Juvenile Hall. Here the young Santana seals his fate when he murders a potential rapist. As an adult, he is relocated from Juvenile Hall to Folsom State Penitentiary.

Over the eighteen-year period of his incarceration, he becomes the overlord to the Mexican Mafia, "La eMe," and its intricate web of prostitution, drug pushing, and gambling inside and outside the penitentiary walls. After Santana's release in the late 1970s and his failure to reintegrate into society—marked by his violent rape of love interest Julie (Evelina *Fernández)—he realizes that his gang's struggle for territorial and economic dominance is not helping but actively destroying the community. When he returns to prison on a parole violation, transformed by his acquired self-awareness and insight, he disobeys the codes of "La eMe" and is killed by his own prison mates. Director Olmos employs a variety of techniques that include lighting, mise-en-scène, and extended flashback to powerfully breathe life into this story of gang life; moreover, Olmos's bold, no-holds-barred film dares to tell a story that is graphically critical of how racism, criminalization, poverty, and sexism directly contribute to the destruction of the Chicano community. *American Me* was distributed by Universal Pictures.

Further Reading

Keller, Gary D. *A Biographical Handbook of Hispanics and United States Film.* Tempe, AZ: Bilingual Press, 1997.

Frederick Luis Aldama

Americanos: Latino Life in the United States. Directed by Andy Young and Susan Todd, produced by Edward James *Olmos and Nick Athas, and distributed by HBO, *Americanos* (2000) was the winner of the 2000 Sundance Film Festival Documentary Cinematography Award. The documentary explores the contributions made by Latinos to the United States and is part of a larger project conceived and coproduced by Olmos. The full *Americanos* project includes a music CD featuring top Latino musicians, a book presenting photographs by more than thirty award-winning photojournalists, and a touring exhibition highlighting 120 photographs from the book that will travel to thirty-two museums in the United States between 1999 and 2004. The documentary consists of a series of three- to six-minute profiles/segments that focus on themes of *family, community, work, cultural practices, language, ancestry, identity, the arts, music, spirituality, healing, car culture, food, and cultural centers found in the Chicana/o, Puerto Rican, and Cuban American communities. Some of the segments include lowriding (*see* *Lowriders) in the Midwest, the Taco Shop Poets in San Diego, musician Tito *Puente going back to "el barrio" in the Bronx, the *casitas* (little houses) that serve as cultural centers for the Nuyorican/Puerto Rican community in New York, a Hispanic women border patrol agent, *Chicano performance artist El Vez (Elvis), and the Cuban Dr. Joe who cares for the homeless and the poor.

The entire *Americanos* project is committed to showing how religion, culture, language, social conscience, *family, community pride, music, *food, politics, and diverse ethnic heritages intertwine and comprise the daily lives of Latinos in the United States. As such, *Americanos* brings the diverse histories and social practices of Latinos into a forefront that honors the Latina/o communities and challenges the stereotypical ways in which Latinos are seen as noncitizens, ridiculed, and demonized in mainstream society.

Further Reading

http://www.absolutearts.com/artsnews/2000/08/18/27344.html.

William Calvo

Amores Perros. Along with other recent *films like Alfonso Cuarón's **Y Tu Mamá También* (Your Mom Too, 2001) and Carlos Carrera's *The Crime of Padre Amaro* (Father Amaro's Crime, 2002), *Amores Perros* (Love's a Bitch, 2000) signals perhaps the beginning in México of a new era of production of quality films with a large audience appeal both nationally and internationally. *Amores Perros*, the feature debut of director (and producer) Alejandro González Iñárritu, narrates three interwoven tales written by novelist Guillermo Arriaga. The tales are totally autonomous but strongly tied together by one catastrophic event (a car crash), one stultifying emotion (an immoderate love of dogs), and one desperate need (of money and of love). All along, the characters of each separate story cross paths unaware that their individual choices and actions are leading inexorably to an outcome they are jointly but blindly configuring. Indeed, at the end of the story, which is also the beginning of the picture, none of the characters realize that the car accident results from a blind addition of events created separately by each one of them but produced through the agency of dogs.

The film opens with a nerve-wrecking car chase of two young men by thugs shooting guns at them, and the long narrative flashback begins when the car crashes into another vehicle at an intersection. In the back of the pursued car is a bleeding dog that belongs to Octavio's elder brother. Octavio had borrowed the animal hoping that victory in a betting dogfight will allow him to obtain enough money to elope with Susana, his brother's wife. But Octavio's opponent shoots the dog. Octavio knifes his opponent, carries the wounded dog to his car, and takes off, speeding to the fatal intersection. The story of Octavio, his brother, and his sister-in-law is announced by the title "Octavio and Susana."

Another title—"Daniel and Valeria"—leads us into a separate story. Daniel is a wealthy businessman who has left his *family to live with Valeria, his mistress, who works as a model and owns a small dog. To celebrate their moving into a new apartment Valeria gets in her car to go buy some champagne. As she enters an intersection, Octavio and his friend crash into her car, leading to botched surgery on her badly injured leg, then amputation, which results in spending the rest of her life in a wheelchair. Valeria's sense of being trapped in a wheelchair is played out when her little dog gets trapped beneath the floorboards of the apartment. In their frantic search for the animal, Valeria and Daniel lift so many floorboards that the brand-new apartment ends up in ruins. The deterioration of their apartment is a symbolic reflection of the deterioration of their relationship, as Daniel becomes determined to return to his wife.

The third story is also announced by a title—"The Goat and Maru." The Goat is a bearded vagrant named Martín, alias El Chivo (the goat), who left his wife and young daughter, as well as his job as a teacher, to engage in a revolutionary conspiracy that failed and put him in jail for many years. Now a tramp wandering around the city with his handcart and trailed by a pack of scruffy dogs, he has been hired by a businessman to assassinate his partner. He is about to kill the designated man on the street when the two cars we have already seen show up at the intersection and crash. That is, we return to the precise moment of the accident for the third time. But on this occasion we see Martín go to the car to rescue the wounded dog and take both the dog and the money Octavio had won in the dogfight.

The rescued dog recovers from the bullet wound and massacres Martín's other dogs during a brief moment when he is absent. With the loss of his much-loved dogs, Martín is absolutely alone. His daughter Maru, whom he helplessly loves, is also alone, for her mother has just died. Martín had continuously followed and observed Maru at a distance, and at the end of the picture he leaves her a large gift of money under her pillow and a message on her answering machine. We see him walk away determined to start a new life. *Amores Perros* was nominated for a Golden Globe award and was the first Mexican movie in twenty-six years to be nominated for an Oscar for Best Foreign Film in 2000.

Further Reading

http://www.rottentomatoes.com/m/AmoresPerros-1106049/reviews.php.

Luis Aldama

Anaya, Rudolfo A. (1937–). Author of *Bless Me, Última* (1972), his first published novel and the first international bestseller by a *Chicano-identified writer, Rudolfo Alfonso Anaya was recognized for his lifetime achievement in American letters in 2002 with the National Medal of Arts presented by President George W. Bush at the Kennedy Center in Washington, D.C. The award capped over three decades of recognition for Anaya, whose first novel has been canonized by inclusion on high school and college reading lists nationwide. Besides his first novel *Bless Me, Ultima*, his publications include the novels *Heart of Aztlán* (1976), *Tortuga* (1979), *Alburquerque* (1992), and *Zia Summer* (1995), among others, as well as such short fiction as *Cuentos Chicanos* (1980, coedited with Antonio Márquez) and *The Silence of the Llano* (1982), as well as the poem "Elegy on the Death of César *Chávez" (2000). For these and numerous other titles, Anaya has amassed many literary honors including the Premio Quinto Sol (for *Bless Me, Ultima*), the Before Columbus American Book Award, and the PEN Center-West Fiction Award. He also has received plaudits for his dedication to promoting Mexican American writers, including the Excellence in the Humanities Award from the National Endowment for the Humanities (NEH), the New Mexico Governor's Public Service Award, and numerous other awards and citations from education organizations across the country for his role in advancing appreciation for the varieties of Chicana/o and Latina/o literatures.

Anaya was born on October 30, 1937, in the village of Pastura in New Mexico near the town of Santa Rosa east of the state's largest city, Albuquerque. His parents, Martín Anaya and Rafaelita Mares Anaya, like many native New Mexicans, trace their *family's ancestry and cultural roots in the *barrios and borderlands of the present-day United States back many generations prior to 1848 and the *Treaty of Guadalupe Hidalgo. After attending public school in Santa Rosa, his family moved to Albuquerque, where the future author completed his education, eventually earning bachelor's and master's degrees in English from the University of New Mexico (UNM) in 1963 and 1968, respectively. Going on to earn another M.A. in guidance and counselling from UNM in 1972, Anaya's first professional work was as a teacher in the Albuquerque public school system (1963–1970), an experience that has worked its way into his fiction through characterizations of children and adolescents along with his accounts of classroom and schoolyard dramas for a number of his stories. His extended career in higher education began in 1970 when he was named director of counseling at the University of Albuquerque. He also married Patricia Lawless, whom he credits for strongly encouraging him to write about his life experience and pastoral southwestern perspective. In 1974 he joined the English Department at UNM, where he taught American literature until his retirement as professor Emeritus in 1993. He and his wife live in Albuquerque.

This deeply rooted geographical and cultural background in New Mexico is embedded in Anaya's writings and helps explain the American novelist's intense concern for expressing a personal representation of what he perceives as a neglected heritage and folk tradition in the United States, particularly the **mestizaje* of his native state and the surrounding Southwest. His sensibility as a writer is keenly tuned to the indigenous Indian civilizations that preceded the arrival of the Spaniards and other Europeans, and he considers himself as working within the oral storytelling traditions of Native Americans and mestizos in the native languages of his Southwest homeland tribal tongues, Spanish, English, and their hybrids. For these reasons scholars often read his work through the lens of Jungian myth and ethnopoetics. *Bless Me, Ultima*, Anaya's first novel and most celebrated and critically acclaimed work, weaves indigenous myth into its suspenseful plot about a young introspective boy and his *abuela* (grandmother), the title character, and their relationship in a Pastura-like village in late 1940s New Mexico. Continuing his interest in Mexican American family sagas, Anaya's next novel, *Heart of Aztlán* tracks the fictional Clemente Chávez family's move to urban Albuquerque from their pastoral village origins to address issues of diaspora, displacement, workers' rights, and the undermining of *familia* and community. The third in Anaya's trilogy about New Mexican *'*manitos* (literally "little brothers," a diminutive term often used for native *nuevo mejicanos*) is *Tortuga* (Turtle), which the author describes as recounting in part his own boyhood experience with polio. The title symbol represents the protagonist, a Chicano boy trapped in a body cast in a hospital for paralyzed children, whose rite of passage is challenged by other boys, the medical staff (modeled after the Carrie Tingley Hospital in Truth or Consequences, New Mexico), and his poignant adolescent desire for one of the floor aides.

A central part of Anaya's literary project has been his preservation of the wisdom and lore of Chicana/o culture. To achieve this he has retold, translated, and/or represented some of the traditional history and legends of Mexican Americans in the Southwest. These include a treatment titled *The Legend of La Llorona* (1984) about *La Malinche, the Náhuatl slave who became the mistress, guide, and interpreter of the conquistador Hernán Cortés, whom Anaya equates with the source of the *La Llorona legend. Other works are *The Adventures of Juan Chicaspatas* (1985); a personal narrative, *A Chicano in China* (1986); and the detective novels in the style of Tony Hillerman *Albuquerque* (1992) and *Zia Summer* (1995). One of Anaya's more experimental writings is the story "B. Traven Is Alive and Well in Cuernavaca" (1982), which deploys the fragmented narrative style of *magic realism to convey the postmodernistic experience of a Chicano tourist in México. In the late twentieth century, other noteworthy *'manita/o* New Mexicans include: writers Denise *Chávez, Demitria *Martínez, and Nash Candelaria; scholar-writers Erlinda González Berry, Cordelia Candelaria, Enrique Lamadrid, and Arturo Madrid; and documentary filmaker Paul D. *Espinosa, among others.

Although as a stylist and craftsman Anaya is overshadowed in the eyes of some literary scholars by such writers as Sandra *Cisneros, Cherríe *Moraga, Alfredo *Véa, and Helena María *Viramontes, his popularity as the author of the late-twentieth-century classic *Bless Me, Ultima* and his standing as a respected spokesperson for Chicana/o literature and multiculturalism ensure him a position of respect in Latina/o letters.

Further Reading

Candelaria, Cordelia. "On Rudolfo A. Anaya." In *Chicano Literature: A Reader's Encyclopedia*, edited by Julio A. Martínez and Francisco A. Lomelí. Westport, CT: Greenwood Press, 1985.

Candelaria, Cordelia. "Rudolfo Anaya." In *Dictionary of Literary Biography*. Vol. 82, edited by Carl Shirley et al. Columbia, SC: Bruccoli Clark Layman, 1989.

González-T., César A., ed. *Rudolfo A. Anaya: Focus on Criticism*. La Jolla, CA: Lalo Press, 1990.

Márquez, Teresa, Director. *100 Years of Literature in New Mexico: A Literary Discussion with Rudolfo Anaya, John Nichols, and Simon Ortiz*. Moderator: Gabriel Meléndez. Albuquerque: Center of Southwest Research, University of New Mexico, 2001. Videorecording.

Ann Aguirre

Anthony, Marc (1968–). Marc Anthony is an international pop singer, songwriter, actor, and Grammy Award winner who has been called "the reigning king of *salsa." Recording primarily pop music and Latin dance genres in English and Spanish, Anthony incorporates African flute, techno, and dance music sounds with the tropical traditions of salsa. His special sound of music has earned him *Billboard*'s Best New Artist in 1994, Hot Tropical Artist of the Year in 1996, Male Tropical Album of the Year and Hot Latin Track of the Year in 1998, and captured a Grammy Award for Best Tropical Latin Performance for his album *Contra la Corriente* (Against the Current) in 1998.

Born Marco Antonio Muñiz in New York City on September 16, Anthony was raised by his Puerto Rican parents in Spanish Harlem in Manhattan and was the youngest in a *family of five boys and three girls. His mother, Guillermina Muñiz, was a homemaker, while his father, Felipe Muñiz, worked in a hospital and was an amateur guitarist who introduced his son to Latin music superstars Rubén *Blades and Willie *Colón. Named after a famous Mexican vocalist, Anthony began to sing at an early age and often used the family's kitchen table as his performing stage.

He began singing professionally as a teenager, sang backup for The Latin Rascals, and wrote songs in English and Spanish for the boy band called *Menudo. Anthony acknowledges a preference for English-language pop, rock, rap, and dance music, including Jimmy Hendrix and Air Supply. In 1988 he wrote "Boy, I've Been Told" for dance–pop singer Sa-Fire and watched the song become a *Billboard* Hot 100 hit. In the early 1990s, Anthony heard a Spanish-language ballad by Juan Gabriel called "Hasta Que Te Conoci" (Until I Met You), which he arranged as a salsa tune. His performance of that song at a Los Angeles music convention resulted in a wave of publicity that changed his life. He began touring the United States, Latin America, and Puerto Rico, and caught the attention of the music industry.

In 1995, Anthony released the album *Todo a Su Tiempo* (All in Due Time), which won him a Grammy Award nomination in 1996. That year, Anthony also performed his first solo salsa concert at Madison Square Garden, marking the first time a solo salsa artist had sold out the venue.

Anthony albums include *When the Night Is Over* (1991); *Otra Nota* (Another Note, 1993); *Todo a Su Tiempo* (1995); *Contra la Corriente* (1997); *Desde un Principio—From the Beginning* (1999); *Marc Anthony* (1999); and *Mended* (2002). "I Need To Know," the first single on the *Marc Anthony* album, spent eighteen weeks in *Billboard*'s Top 40 and was nominated for a Grammy Award for Best Male Pop Vocal Performance (1999). Anthony's "You Sang to Me" was nominated for a Grammy Award for Best Pop Vocal Performance in 2001.

In addition to his hot musical career, Anthony decided to try his hand at acting in the movie *Hackers* (1995), followed by *Big Night* (1996), *The Substitute* (1996), Martin Scorsese's *Bringing Out the Dead* (1999) (with Salma *Hayek, 2001), and *Man on Fire* (with Denzel Washington, 2004). He made his Broadway debut in Paul Simon's 1998 musical *Capeman*, the first Broadway production to feature Latino actors in the central cast since the 1979 Broadway production of **Zoot Suit* by Luis *Valdez. The show only played for two months, but Anthony earned strong reviews for his starring role as Salvador Algron, a young Puerto Rican man murdered in 1959.

Anthony married former Miss Universe Dayanara Torres on May 9, 2000. He has two children with Torres, Ryan Anthony and Cristian, and a daughter from a previous relationship. After an on-again, off-again marriage, Anthony obtained a divorce from Torres in June 2004, and married singer/actress Jennifer *Lopez five days later.

Further Reading

Deremer, Leigh Ann. *Contemporary Musicians: Profiles of the People in Music*. Vol. 43. Detroit, MI: Gale Research, August 2003.

http://galegroup.com/free_resources/chh/bio/anthony_m.htm.

Marc Anthony Official Web Site. http://www.marcanthonyonline.com.

Torres, John Albert. *Marc Anthony: Real Life Reader Biography*. Bear, DE: Mitchell Lane Publishers, 2001.

James E. García

Antilles. The archipelago of islands in the Caribbean Sea christened by Christopher *Columbus as "Las Indias" (the Indies) when he mistakenly believed he had reached the Orient and India in 1492 came to be known collectively as the Antilles (or Las Antillas to denote the islands situated *before* the mainland, i.e., ante + islas). In modern times, they are usually identified as the West Indies and consist of the Greater Antilles—Cuba, Puerto Rico, Jamaica, and Hispaniola—and the Lesser Antilles—Barbados, Trinidad, and Tobago. The Dutch West Indies located southward toward the coast of

Venezuela are also known as the Netherlands Antilles. Each major island in the archipelago had an original indigenous name prior to the arrival of the Europeans, but for the most part they have been ignored or forgotten in the twentieth century.

Relative to Latina and Latino popular culture in the United States, the Antilles are significant in their geographic importance as the original homeland of Puerto Ricans and Cuban Americans, who are part of the Latina/o diaspora north to the United States. In addition, the variable and multiple names of the Antilles (as in Boriquén, Las Indias, West Indies, San Juan Bautista, Puerto Rico, to name several examples) represents the critical importance of naming and nomenclature for Spanish-speaking descendants of the European Conquest and related hegemonic acts of the history of the Americas. That is, conquered people and their heirs and heritage historically contend with dual and bicultural identities, thereby increasing the significance of ethnic identification among the people. Also pertinent to pop culture is the importance of Puerto Rican, Cuban, and other Caribbean/Antillean people, themes, and sources to *food, language, entertainment, music, *sports, and myriad other forms and practices.

Further Reading

Conrad, James, and John Perivolaris, eds. *The Cultures of the Hispanic Caribbean.* London: Macmillan Caribbean [Warwick University Caribbean Studies], 2000.

Martínez-Fernández, Luis. *Torn between Empires: Economy, Society, and Patterns of Political Thought in the Hispanic Caribbean, 1840–1878.* Athens: University of Georgia Press, 1994.

Cordelia Chávez Candelaria

Anzaldúa, Gloria (1942–2004). Best known for her highly influential book *Borderlands/La Frontera: The New Mestiza* (1987), which was chosen as one of the thirty-eight Best Books of 1987 by the *Library Journal*, Gloria Anzaldúa was a high-profile Chicana lesbian and feminist writer of personal narrative, poetry, historical and political commentary, and fiction. Anzaldúa's *Borderlands/La Frontera* entered a second edition in 1999 and has had an impact on several academic fields and inspired many artists and writers. Her work is a provocative vision of **mestizaje*, or cultural hybridity, that helps diverse audiences understand the conflicting and sometimes violent forces that affect women of color in the United States. Her foundational writings seek to free women from the constrictions of tradition and from limited notions of gender, sexuality, and spirituality within both the *Chicano culture and the majority society.

Born a seventh-generation American on September 26, 1942, to Urbano and Amalia García Anzaldúa, the author grew up in the Rio Grande Valley of south Texas; she grew up after the age of eleven in the border city of Hargill, Texas. Anzaldúa emphatically grounds her theory of borderland consciousness in her personal experience of this region and her memory of her *family's gradual loss of land and their transition to working as sharecroppers and fieldworkers. Motivated both by this borderlands geography and by her personal negotiation of identity as a lesbian Latina, she addresses the ethnic, economic, and gender intersections of marginalization in her major work *Borderlands/La Frontera*. Using a combination of personal narrative, poetry, and essay, Anzaldúa creates a voice that is simultaneously autobiographical and communal. Like the pioneering bilingual poet *Alurista, she challenges English-only constraints by sliding between Spanish, English, Caló, and Náhuatl without translation, forcing English-only readers to grapple with her text and experience the lack of access to language and understanding that many native Spanish speakers, immigrant and sixth or older generation citizens, grapple with daily. Anzaldúa argues that language is crucial to cultural pride and that erasure of this connection to culture by the dominance of the English language is a form of violence.

Like feminist pioneer, borderlands playwright, and fiction writer Estela *Portillo Trambley, Anzaldúa imbues *Borderlands/La Frontera* with a reconceptualization of religion as an earth-based spirituality. Critical of institutionalized religion that confines women to submissive, passive roles, she strives to reclaim spiritually empowered female figures in Mexican history and mythology. Following the lead of Chicana feminists of the 1970s and early 1980s (e.g., Adelaida Del Castillo, Cordelia Candelaria, and Lucha Corpi), she re/presents the history of *La Malinche, the conscripted translator and courtesan of Spanish conquistador Hernán Cortés, as a maligned woman of agency and evolved intelligence. Like other feminists seeking intellectual foremothers, Anzaldúa reclaims Coátlícue, the Aztec mother-goddess who possesses feminine and masculine, as well as generative and destructive traits, as a symbol of powers that have been split over time to the detriment of both men and women.

A crucial voice in the establishment of a Chicana feminist agenda that bridges differences of race, ethnicity, class, and sexual orientation, Anzaldúa coedited with Cherríe *Moraga and Ana *Castillo the groundbreaking *This Bridge Called My Back: Writings by Radical Women of Color* (1981). Reprinted in 1983, *This Bridge Called My Back* was awarded the Before Columbus Foundation American Book Award in 1986. Like the pathbreaking *Frontiers: A Journal of Women Studies* (Summer 1980), which was the first special Chicana issue ever published by a feminist press, *This Bridge Called My Back* contains writings by women of diverse ethnicities, educational backgrounds, sexual orientations, and social class backgrounds and has had watershed impact on late-twentieth-century feminism and perceptions of women of color.

Anzaldúa's collection *Making Face, Making Soul/Haciendo Caras: Creative and Critical Perspectives by Feminists of Color* (1990), for which she was awarded the Lambda Lesbian Small Press Book Award, is evidence of her continuing effort to build solidarity among diverse women of color. A compilation of over seventy selections of creative and theoretical pieces, *Haciendo Caras* addresses issues of sexism, racism, spirituality, multilingualism, and cultural and multiethnic identity. In further recognition of her creative work, she received the 1991 Lesbian Rights Award, as well as the Sappho Award of Distinction in 1992. Her last publication *This Bridge We Call Home: Radical Visions for Transformation* (2002), coedited by Ana Louise Keating, conveys the continued need to move the voices of marginalized women from the ignored margins to the center of consciousness.

Anzaldúa was the only member of her family to pursue higher education, and she received her B.A. in English, art, and secondary education from Pan American University in 1969. She earned an M.A. in English and education from the University of Texas at Austin in 1972. Her classroom experience ranges from preschool and special education settings to university seminars in creative writing, women's studies, and Chicana/o studies. Also a writer of children's literature, she has published three bilingual titles: *Prietita Has a Friend/Prietita tiene un amigo* (1991), *Friends from the Other Side/Amigos del otro lado* (1993), and *Prietita and the Ghost Woman/Prietita y La Llorona* (1996). Anzaldúa passed away unexpectedly on May 15, 2004, due to complications related to diabetes.

Further Reading

Keating, Ana Louis. *Women Reading Women Writing: Self-Invention in Paula Gunn Allen, Gloria Anzaldúa, and Audre Lorde*. Philadelphia: Temple University Press, 1996.

Steele, Cassie Premo. *We Heal from Memory: Sexton, Lorde, Anzaldúa, and the Poetry of Witness*. New York: Palgrave, 2000.

R. Joyce Zamora Lausch

Appropriation and Popular Culture. Implicit in the understanding of appropriation in popular culture studies is the first definition of the word in its strictest sense, which means "to take possession of, without consent and unlawfully." Significantly, the Latin root of *appropriation*, *proprius* and *proprietas*, is the same stem form as that of the word *property*. This linguistic context underscores the significance of appropriation in popular culture studies, for a large number of scholars believe that much of American popular culture, possibly even a majority of it, is adapted and appropriated from the creative property and cultural practices of marginalized peoples. Like the concept of colonialism wherein a more powerful country takes over a smaller, more vulnerable country and exploits that nation's resources, appropriation in essence is about dominance and exploitation for profit.

One of the most famous pop culture examples of this is Elvis Presley, a country singer who adapted his singing and performance style from African American gospel and other race music, as it was called in the pre–civil rights era, to become the world's first rock icon. In turn, Elvis's work and celebrity status were appropriated by agents, recording companies, movie studios, and related business interests, thereby elevating him and them to multimillionaire wealth status. Yet the African American originators of his style and much of his music received little to no recognition, attribution, or financial gain until recent years. In fact, the worldwide cultural studies mapping of the last two decades of the twentieth century in critical interdisciplinary studies are responsible for uncovering and reclaiming the source and influences of Presley's music and his many impersonators, including the *Chicano El Vez. This is one of many widespread forms of cultural appropriation of African American and other subaltern cultures in the United States, especially in music (e.g., the blues, jazz, rhythm and blues, and most recently rap) and spin-off clothing styles.

Historically in the Americas, colonialism and appropriation were part of the conquest of the native peoples from the time of Christopher *Columbus's first arrival. The colonialist appropriation of the Native Americans' lands, agricultural systems, food and cooking methods, villages and cities, and all their other physical, intellectual, and creative properties originated the very notion of human and cultural marginalization in the Western Hemisphere. This dominance and exploitation of indigenous peoples for profit and power continued after the independence revolutions in North, Central, and South America and includes the concepts of American Indian artistic expression (beadwork, silver-smithing, weaving, pottery, and wood carving, etc.); spirituality (the Noble Savage, new age thought, healing, etc.); and the ubiquitous images of Hollywood Indians (savage, dead, sidekicks, etc.).

The same principles and methods of dominant cultural appropriation have occurred with Latina and Latino popular culture(s) as it has with Native American, African American, Asian, and other cultures of color. That is, individuals and/or segments (usually business oriented) of the dominant cultures appropriate aspects of Latina/o culture without consent and without providing the social, cultural, historical, or linguistic context of the original sources. These adaptations often become racist and sexist stereotypes, even though they may have been borrowed with more affirmative or at least benign intentions. For example, the "Latin Lover," the "Sultry Latina," and the "Sleeping Mexican" are media images that can be traced as far back as the silent movie era of the early twentieth century when film pioneer D.W. Griffiths used white actors in brown-face makeup in his highly successful silent movies. Earlier, in the nineteenth century, the Beadle dime novels and syndicated *newspaper serials routinely depicted swarthy Mexicans and Latinos as thieves and murderers.

The appropriation of culture can occur with all aspects of a community's shared activities: its language, food, clothing, music, artwork, religious icons, customs, writing styles, crafts, car design, and related arts and crafts. The appropriation of Latina/o popular culture, most visible in contemporary television marketing campaigns for food and alcohol, deracinate and/or lift out of context certain aspects of Latina/o culture, usually resulting in stereotypes to convey to a mainstream audience a type of Latina/o theme. For example, the highly successful Taco Bell food chain appropriates aspects of the rich and complex Mexican cuisine and turns it into fast-food simulations, and in 2004 Tecate tried to use a blatantly sexist theme to sell its beer, but the strong international outcry from Latinas and others led to the ad's removal. Other examples of appropriation include home furnishings that again take the rich artistry of hand-carved furniture that blends indigenous and Spanish styles and traditions and colorful, hand-painted mason ware and glass and call it Southwest style. Many Hispano residents of New Mexico regard the Anglo colonization of the state capital and the invention of Santa Fe–style cuisine, art, fashion, and architecture in similar terms. Many native Santa Feans claim that Anglos painted the town's walls brown and displaced brown people to mobile home parks and other low-income housing.

Another large area of cultural appropriation that remains largely ignored or denied by mainstream society is western rodeo culture (*see* *Charreada). Most aspects of the contemporary rodeo culture, the competitions, the saddles, roping techniques, bronco riding, etc., come from the Mexican "rodeo" tradition, which means "round-up" in Spanish, that was very popular and part of the frontier lifestyle of what was northern México (California, Texas, New Mexico, Colorado, Arizona, and parts of Wyoming and Kansas) during the nineteenth century. It is important for understanding the underlying cultural (comm)unities of America that the Mexican ranching roots of cowboy and rodeo traditions be recognized.

In music, there has been a history of appropriating aspects of Latin origin dances and rhythms like *mambo (1940s–1960s) and the Brazilian *samba and lambada (1980s) and slowing them to a watered-down mainstream tempo as in the popular 1990s Macarena craze, which featured a Latin rhythm–type of line dancing. The popularity of *salsa and *merengue music among Anglo-musicians and audiences is growing. In addition, it is common to see *tango-influenced music and dance steps in advertising campaigns to convey a type of eroticism and a Latin-flavored hook to the products that are being marketed. The recent popularity of **Rock en Español* and Latin hip-hop shows how Latino artists redefine musical forms from the dominant and other cultures into a hybrid, urban sound that can blend traditional Latin music forms *cumbia, **banda*, *mariachi, and the Jamaican-inspired reggae with blues, rock, punk, and heavy metal. Although the majority of the lyrics are in Spanish and Caló (street slang), some groups like the Mexican-based Molotov and El Gran Silencio use bilingual and bicultural terms and reference points and appeal to Latinas/os in Latin America and in the United States with a growing interest in Western Europe. Manu Chao, a Spanish-origin pioneer of the Latin alternative movement that fuses a variety of Latin and techno music styles, also sings in Spanish, French,

Portuguese, and English. He considers his music a form of paying respect to the working-class musical forms of Latin America, as well as to the immigrant African and Arabic groups in Western Europe.

The fashion industry also takes hand-woven *huipiles* (vests) predominant in Mayan communities in México and Guatemala and mass-produces snippets of *huipiles* into exclusive "haute couture" fashions. Other examples of the fashion industry's appropriation of Latina/o culture, like its appropriation of urban African American hip-hop clothing styles, is the use of tropical-themed clothing like the famous Guayabera shirts popular in Cuba, Veracruz, México, and a staple of working-class Latina/o culture in the United States. Other examples of ongoing appropriation and exchange are the **cholo* and low-riding cultures (*see* Lowriders) and the old English writing styles seen in tattoos and in spray can art. For many in working-class Chicano communities, the clothing, lettering, and car styles are part of preserving ethnic self-definition and cultural history; for many Anglo American youth, it is often part of being hip and urban.

There are also examples of intracultural appropriation that are less dependent on power inequities and consist of "minority" and subaltern cultures borrowing and informing from each other in their own expressions. An example of this is the *Zoot Suit with the large jacket with overstuffed shoulders and overly baggy slacks, which during the 1940s became an icon of Pachuco (*see* *Pachucos) youth culture, African American, and even Filipino youth cultures, and the style eventually traveled to working-class British youth. Part of the appeal of the zoot suit for urban ethnic youth may be that it made them appear bigger than they felt in a society where they are ignored, segregated, and seen as inferior. Spray can and graffiti art, although it has very specific cultural markers in writing styles for Latina/o youth, is another form of cultural expression that has been embraced by African American, Asian, and other urban youth.

Moreover, the human species' need for widespread (trans)migration and trade networking since the earliest history indicates the prevalence and benefit of cultural exchange and cross-cultural adaptation. This fact overturns the notion of pure, rigid, and/or unchanging boundaries between communities of people and, internally, within social classifications. Although **mestizaje* specifically describes the hybrid racial mixture of Spanish, Native American, Asian, and African heritages that identify Latina and Latino peoples in the Americas, it also applies to the admixtures and blends of cultures and cultural inheritance of the people of the United States. The twenty-first century's threshold recognition of cultural hybridity and *mestizaje* as positive values of pluralism and deeply imprinted adaptations of Native American and European cultural roots in the Americas suggests why some observers believe "appropriation" is an anachronistic concept and practice increasingly recognized as retrograde. However, in a globalized society one could argue that all culture is up for grabs and that when food, music, and clothing corporations market international campaigns to appropriate ethnic cultures it is a form of corporate acknowledgment. Until it actually means economic success for impoverished communities, however, and until artisans of the community are credited and paid for their labor, the homogenization and selling of ethnicity will continue to fail to meet the needs of grassroots people and cultures.

Further Reading

Appiah, Kwame Anthony. "Is the Post in Postmodernism the Post in Postcolonial?" *Critical Inquiry* 17 (Winter 1991): 336–357.

Bright, Brenda Jo, and Liza Bakewell, eds. *Looking High and Low: Art and Cultural Identity*. Tucson: University of Arizona Press, 1995.

Chávez, John R. *The Lost Land: The Chicano Image of the Southwest*. Albuquerque: University of New Mexico Press, 1984.

Mazón, Mauricio. *Zootsuit Riots: The Psychology of Symbolic Annihilation*. Austin: University of Texas Press, 1984.

Arturo J. Aldama and Cordelia Chávez Candelaria

Architecture and Urbanism. Even though Latino communities have long-standing roots in many parts of present-day United States, their formal architectural and urban design contributions have been recognized only recently. *Latino architecture and urbanism* is defined here as architectural or urban design created by a member or members of a Latino community that affirms a specific identity and/or sense of place from *within* that community. Historically since 1848, Latino communities have not been in a position to influence the architectural and urban design processes that have shaped the physical landscapes of most U.S. cities or towns. In addition, Latino communities have often suffered from the impact of various forms of political and economic disenfranchisement that have limited the ability of Latino communities to affect change in the constructed environment. One result is that relatively few Latinos have emerged from within formal design professions (i.e., architecture, landscape architecture, urban design, and urban planning).

Despite the fact that few Latinos in the United States have entered into the design professions, Latino communities have had an impact on the physical settings in which they live, and distinct Latino cultural landscapes can be found in cities across the United States. However, because these Latino cultural landscapes usually have not had professional design assistance, Latino communities have often relied on need and their own creativity to transform typical single-family houses, yards, and common public spaces into culturally specific landscapes that constitute distinct neighborhoods. Such cultural landscapes have become the subject of a variety of literary or artistic works, but only recently have Latino communities and their physical settings become subjects of interest for the design disciplines of architecture, landscape architecture, urban design, and urban planning.

Formal recognition of the contemporary impact that Latinos have had upon the architectural and urban character of U.S. *barrios and borderlands appears in a 1991 M.I.T. master's thesis by James Thomas Rojas titled "The Enacted Environment: The Creation of 'Place' by Mexicans and Mexican Americans in East Los Angeles." Rojas documented the transformation of the southern California urban landscape to meet the economic and cultural needs of Mexican and Mexican American groups. For Rojas, East Los Angeles is an *enacted landscape*—a landscape in which the physical shape of the neighborhood is recreated through everyday social activities involving improvised architectural props (such as murals, fences, vendor carts) that are incorporated into the existing urban fabric. It is through informal practices of cultural expression that this multigenerational and recent immigrant Latino community has created a distinctive landscape and sense of place.

Rojas's master's thesis has been widely influential within architectural, urban design, and urban planning circles (particularly in academia), and practitioners, faculty, and students have drawn upon his work as the basis for further research. In this sense, Rojas provided not only a reading of a particular Latino landscape but also a new academic terrain. The importance of this work can be gauged by more recent research into *Chicano Los Angeles. Rodolfo F. Acuña, a Chicano studies scholar whose work has chronicled the history of East Los Angeles, included a section on Chicano urbanism in his recent book *Anything But Mexican: Chicanos in Contemporary Los Angeles* (1996), which draws heavily on the work of Rojas. Other scholars have now taken an interest in Latino cultural landscapes as well: Mike Davis has contributed to the growing literature on Latino social space through the publication of *Magical Urbanism: Latinos Reinvent the US Big City* (2000); Lawrence A. Herzog's *From Aztec to High Tech: Architecture and Landscape across the México–United States Border* (1999) documents Latino landscapes in the American Southwest; and *La Vida Latina en L.A.: Urban Latino Cultures* (1999), edited by Gustavo LeClerc, Raúl Villa, and Michael J. Dear, also adds a new volume to the literature on Latinos in Los Angeles.

While a significant body of literature has emerged focused upon Latino Los Angeles, the impacts of Latino communities upon the architectural and urban landscapes of the United States are not limited to Los Angeles. Monica Ponce de Leon has documented the Cuban American landscapes of Miami in an article titled "Calle Ocho" (Eighth Street) that appeared in the architectural journal *Places: A Quarterly Journal of Environmental Design* (1993). This particular issue of *Places* focused on Latino cultural landscapes in the United States, México, and Cuba. *Places* also recently showcased examples of Puerto Rican *casitas* (small houses) in New York City; the *casita* offers a link to a cultural homeland and simultaneously helps to reaffirm a Latino presence within a new urban space. Other articles focusing on various aspects of Latino physical landscapes have appeared in *Places* in recent years, earning it a reputation as an important outlet for Latino cultural expressions.

These academic accounts are the foundation for projects in the physical realm as well as for ongoing research into Latino cultural landscapes in the United States. The work of the collaborative art and architecture group ADOBE LA (Artists and Designers Opening the Border Edge of Los Angeles) has been featured in exhibits of national importance including *Urban Revisions: Current Projects for the Public Realm* (1994), held at the Museum of Contemporary Art (MOCA) in Los Angeles, and *House Rules* (1996), which was held in 1996 at the Wexner Center for the Arts in Columbus, Ohio. *Urban Revisions* focuses on a number of urban design and planning projects from around the country and addresses a range of social, cultural, economic, ecological, and political concerns. ADOBE LA's contribution highlights the urban transformations found within uniquely Latino cultural landscapes. *House Rules* grapples with the problem of rethinking the American ideal of the single-family detached home. ADOBE LA was invited to participate in this exhibit as part of a team that included urban theorist Margaret Crawford. Their collective effort resulted in an architectural design that documented a typical California suburban bungalow transformed to meet Latino cultural needs. It is significant that these two exhibits were held in major institutions with an expressed interest in architecture and that, in both cases, ADOBE LA's work was presented to a broad audience.

The recent explorations into Latino cultural and physical landscapes highlighted here help to illustrate the importance of space in the cultural politics of contemporary cities and the growing significance of the impact of Latino communities on the national scene. As Latino communities have grown, an audience for publications on Latino design and cultural production has developed as well. Architect and scholar Robert Alexander González, in an effort to meet just such a demand, recently founded the journal *AULA: Architecture and Urbanism in Las Américas*. Additionally, the impact of U.S. Latinos can also be found in a variety of other fields. Literature, for example, has given rise to a growing number of writers whose work is rooted in the Latino urban experience. One example is Raúl Homero Villa's *Barrio-Logos: Space and Place in Urban Chicano Literature and Culture* (2000) illustrates the role that the *barrio has played in the work of many Chicano artists, poets, and writers in his book. Early studies include focusing on the physical spaces of Latino communities.

Further Reading

Acuña, Rodofo A. *Anything But Mexican: Chicanos in Contemporary Los Angeles*. New York: Verso, 1996.

ADOBE LA and Margaret Crawford. "Mi casa es su casa." *Assemblage* 24 (August 1994): 12–19.

Aponte-Parés, Lois. "Casitas: Place and Culture." *Places* 11.1 (Winter 1997): 52–61.

Bond, Evagene H., ed. *La Comunidad: Design, Development, and Self-Determination in Hispanic Communities*. Washington, D.C.: Partners for Livable Places, 1982; grassroots archaeology: Abiquiú, New Mexico; Great Wall of Los Angeles;

tenant-controlled revelopment in Villa Victoria, Boston; Tampa's Ybor City and Miami's Little Havana, Florida.
Davis, Mike. *Magical Urbanism: Latinos Reinvent the US City*. New York: Verso, 2000.
Herzog, Lawrence A. *From Aztec to High Tech: Architecture and Landscape across the México–United States Border*. Baltimore, MD: Johns Hopkins University Press, 1999.
LeClerc, Gustavo, and Ulises Diaz, eds. *Ciudad hibrida/Hybrid City: The Production of Art in "Alien Territory."* Los Angeles, CA: SCI-Arch Public Press, 1998.
LeClerc, Gustavo, Raúl Villa, and Michael J. Dear, eds. *La Vida Latina en L.A.: Urban Latino Cultures*. Thousand Oaks, CA: Sage Publications, 1999.
Ponce de Leon, Monica. "Calle Ocho." *Places: A Quarterly Journal of Environmental Design* 8 (Spring 1993): 23–28.
Rojas, James Thomas. "The Enacted Environment: The Creation of 'Place' by Mexicans and Mexican Americans in East Los Angeles." Master's thesis, Massachusetts Institute of Technology, 1991.
Villa, Raúl Homero. *Barrio-Logos: Space and Place in Urban Chicano Literature and Culture*. Austin: University of Texas Press, 2000.

José Gamez

Arias, Ron (1941–). With a focus on recording the urban *Chicano experience, Ron Arias is a writer whose literary style was inspired by the popular Latin American "Boom" writers of the late twentieth century. Arias entered the annals of important Chicano writers in 1975 when his novel *The Road to Tamazunchale* (1975) won critical acclaim by receiving the top award in fiction from the University of California at Irvine's annual Chicano literary competition. *Road to Tamazunchale* also garnered a National Book Award nomination for its creative treatment of Mexican American experience. Arias is respected for his representation of the varieties of cultural **mestizaje* (the combination of American Indian and Spanish European hybrid forms) through his synthesis of North and South American identities into unique narratives of contemporary U.S. popular culture, including the depiction of border consciousness and transnational experience.

Born in Los Angeles, California, on November 30, 1941, Ronald Francis Arias spent his childhood crisscrossing the United States and Europe because of his stepfather's career in the U.S. Army. Graduating from the American high school in Stuttgart, Germany, in 1959, Arias maintained a penchant for a nomadic lifestyle, often leaving home during the summer months and hitchhiking through Spain, Argentina, Perú, and throughout the United States. Greatly influenced by his parents, Arias's mother was from El Paso, Texas, his father from Juárez, México, and his stepfather from Nogales, Arizona. This geographic and cultural exposure to America's *barrios and borderlands of encounter enters his work in numerous ways. However, he writes that it was an act by his mother that sparked his writing ambition. When hospitalized for a tonsillectomy when he was nine years old, Arias's mother gave him a notepad and told him to record his thoughts and observations while recovering from the surgery. He has been writing ever since, even through his pursuit of a bachelor's degree in Spanish from the University of California, Berkeley. He later obtained a master's in journalism from the University of California, Los Angeles. Despite his college degrees, Arias maintains that his real education took place during his travels and while on assignment writing as a reporter for *newspapers and other periodicals. During this stage of his journalistic career he was caught in combat crossfire in Latin America and encountered such world luminaries as Ernest Hemingway, Jorge Luis Borges, and Indira Gandhi.

These life experiences can be found in the themes and techniques of one of his first stories, "El mago" (The Magician or Wizard), which appeared in *El Grito* in the spring of 1970. For the most part, Arias's writing focuses on ethnic pluralism and the struggle between a free-ranging imagination and a solidly material rationalism. He also worked these themes into his best-known and -acclaimed masterpiece *The Road to Tamazunchale*, on which his prominence rests. The novel recounts old man Fausto Tejada's last week of life. Written in the manner of Latin American *magic realism, the book has a fairy-tale quality as Fausto, a widower and retired encyclopedia salesman living in a Los Angeles barrio, embarks on a magical journey in and out of time, space, and rational consciousness rather than succumbing to death. Even though most of Fausto's travels happen within his mind, the events and encounters of the story are no less vivid. A few of his mental excursions include visits with figures from his past, chats with his deceased wife, an attempt to save illegal immigrants crossing the desert, and a visit to a Hollywood motion picture set where he is mistaken for a Don Quixote–like extra.

In addition to *The Road to Tamazunchale*, Arias has written four other significant pieces of short fiction. In 1976 he published "The Castle" for the *Bilingual Review/Revista Bilingüe*, which chronicles the relationship between Sam, a homeless derelict living in an abandoned unfinished building he calls his castle, and a pensive boy named Carlos, who hasn't seen his prisoner-of-war father in over three years. A carefully developed story of loneliness, friendship, and the persistent affirmation that love provides, "The Castle" effectively combines Arias's familiar literary elements of fantasy, humor, and the struggles of everyday life. The same year saw the publication of "El señor del chivo" (The Goat's Gentleman) for the *Journal of Ethnic Studies*, a tale of a sidewalk vendor of goat-meat tacos in Michoacán, México, and the clever way he balances his homely taco-making existence with animated repartee with his many customers. In the story Arias employs the taco-seller's life as a metaphor for individual and eccentric viewpoints on life and art. In 1977 the *Latin American Literary Review* published Arias's "Chinches," a story of Gabriela, a young schoolteacher who is tired of her life and attempts escape into an alternative that turns out to be nowhere. A common Arias theme is revisited here: hope through some form of escape, whether through memories, imagination, travel, or meanderings through burial caves. The journalist-turned-fictionist went on to transform these basic themes in his short story "The Interview" (*Revista Chicano-Riqueña*, 1974), which he adapted into a play bearing the same name in 1979.

Further Reading

Bruce-Novoa, Juan. "Interview with Ron Arias." *Journal of Ethnic Studies* 3 (Winter 1976): 70–73.

Candelaria, Cordelia. "Ron Arias." In *Chicano Writers, First Series*, edited by Francisco A. Lomelí and Carl R. Shirley. Vol. 82 of *Dictionary of Literary Biography*. Detroit, MI: Bruccoli Clark Layman Book/Gale Group, 1989. 37–44.

Julie Amparano García

Arnaz, Desi (1917–1986). Desi Arnaz, one of the pioneering and better-known Latinos in the entertainment industry, was born Desidero Alberto Arnaz y de Acha III in 1917 in Santiago, Cuba. His father, Desidero Alberto Arnaz II, was a senator and also mayor of Santiago. His mother's name was Lolita. When Desi Arnaz was sixteen, his *family migrated to Miami, Florida, where he serenaded girls with a guitar he bought at a pawnshop for five dollars. His singing and guitar and bongo playing eventually caught the eye of conductor Xavier *Cugat, who took Arnaz into his orchestra. Arnaz later established his own rival band, which received favorable reviews from New York to Miami. In 1939, while playing with his band at New York's nightclub La Conga, he caught the attention of Lorenz Hart and Richard Rogers, who convinced Arnaz to move to Hollywood and try his hand at acting. He made his acting debut in 1940 in *Too Many Girls* opposite comedienne Lucille Ball, whom he married that same year. In 1950, Desi and Lucille cofounded Desilu Productions and approached the television networks about a new situation comedy starring themselves as a husband-wife team. Producers argued that viewers would not accept a sitcom based on a white woman married to a Cuban man. To prove them wrong, Arnaz and Ball put up their own money to make the pilot show and called it *I Love Lucy*. The show was an immediate success, and between 1952 and 1958, it never ranked lower than third place among all programs on the air. The show was on the air until 1960, and it continues in reruns throughout the world.

I Love Lucy was filmed in front of a live audience, which prompted Arnaz to develop the "Three-CameraTechnique." This technique allows for close-ups and long shots and continues to be used today. With the success of *I Love Lucy*, Desilu Productions purchased RKO Studios and began producing other television shows such as *The Untouchables*, *Make Room for Daddy*, and *Our Miss Brooks*. During their twenty-year marriage, Arnaz and Ball had two children: a daughter, Lucie Arnaz, in 1951 and a son, Desi Jr., in 1953. They divorced in 1960, and Arnaz remarried in 1963 to Edith Mack Hirsch, who remained by his side until her death in 1985. He died of lung cancer one year later, in 1986, in Del Mar, California, at the age of sixty-nine.

Desi Arnaz. *Courtesy of Photofest.*

Further Reading

Kanellos, Nicolás, and Cristelia Pérez. *Chronology of Hispanic-American History: From Pre-Columbian Times to the Present*. Detroit, MI: Gale Research, 1995.

Keller, Gary D. *A Biographical Handbook of Hispanics and United States Film*. Tempe, AZ: Bilingual Press, 1997.

Tardiff, Joseph C., and L. Mpho Mabunda, eds. *Dictionary of Hispanic Biography*. Detroit, MI: Gale Research, 1996.

Alma Alvarez-Smith

Art and Artists. *See* Latino Visual Arts.

Asco. In East Los Angeles during the early 1970s, Harry Gamboa, Jr., Gronk, Willie Herrón, and Patssi Valdez formed a group of young *Chicano urban artists—this artistic collective would be known as Asco. Asco (Spanish for "nausea") pushed and challenged the traditional boundaries of didactic Chicano murals and posters of the El Movimiento Chicano (*Chicano Movement). Murals and posters provided a social and "public" space for oppositional narratives and activity; Chicano artists incorporated signs and cultural signifiers that challenged hegemonic mainstream opposition to the rights of full citizenship for Mexican Americans. The Chicano Movement was a largely youth-led struggle begun in the mid-1960s. It represented the largest manifestation of political and social protest by Chicanos, for Chicanos; Asco is important in its production of conceptual and performance art that was a direct response to these artists' urban realities, historical context, and spatial locus. Asco critiqued contemporary Chicano art practices and incorporated conceptual theatrical elements into their public, Los Angeles site–specific interventions. The name Asco, which was taken directly from a critic's comment regarding how their art made him feel, maintained a strong Chicano political consciousness of protest distinct from other Los Angeles–based Chicano artists who utilized their bodies as vehicles for performance art, thereby incorporating and conflating Chicano social activism and Chicana/o cultural production into areas of historic public unrest. Members of Asco documented their work in photographs. Photographs and writings extend the artistic creative expression by documenting a witnessing of the performance art form that remains accessible to us today.

The artists' earliest connections centered on the intellectual and artistic forging of Chicano youth and the social unrest at Garfield High School in East Los Angeles. Garfield High School and other Los Angeles high schools conducted a student walkout on March 5, 1968, that lasted fifteen days; the protest would be known as the 1968 East Los Angeles Blow Outs. Gamboa participated in the organization of the Garfield High School Blowout Committee; his involvement would later target him as a "subversive" in U.S. Senate hearings. Thousands of students, including those that would later become known as Asco, parents, and community activists joined in the demonstration. The students' boycott of classes emptied the high schools. They protested to the Los Angeles School Board with a list of demands highlighting the duplicity of the inequalities they were experiencing in the classroom. These duplicities, such as segregated schools, racial oppression, exceedingly high dropout rates, lack of college guidance counselors, marginalization, and low expectations of Mexican American youth, placed the public educational system on trial.

The Chicano Moratorium, a peaceful 1970 Chicano antiwar demonstration, ended with the Los Angeles Police Department in riot gear and tear gas and the killing of reporter Rubén Salazar on August 29 (*see* Newspapers and Periodicals). The demonstration called to mind and highlighted the extraordinarily disproportionate numbers of Chicanos in the armed forces fighting in Vietnam. Asco responded to these inequities and on December 24, 1971, performed in the midst of holiday shoppers a walking mural titled *Stations of the Cross*. The performance underscored processional Catholic ritual with social protest. Gamboa, Gronk, and Herrón walked in costume along Whittier Boulevard, as Christ carrying a cross, altar boy, and Pontius Pilate. They proceeded to the U.S. Marines' Recruiting Station, and there, after a moment of silence at the last station and blessing of popcorn by Gronk, they left the large fifteen-foot cardboard cross at the station's entrance, blocking the entrance temporarily to any new enlistees. *Stations of the Cross* was an intervention aimed at subversion; even if just for a moment in time, it raised the collective political consciousness, and for that, it has withstood the test of time.

In 1972, Gamboa, Gronk, and Herrón challenged curatorial practices with *Spray Paint LACMA* and the Eurocentric notion of what constitutes "American" art and "American" artists. Gamboa recalls a meeting with a curator of art and being informed that the Los Angeles County Museum of Art (LACMA) did not collect or exhibit Chicano art because Chicanos didn't make "fine art"; they only make "folk art," or were in gangs. Utilizing the museum as their canvas, the three artists spray-painted their names on all the entrances into the museum. Gamboa photographed the piece with Valdez immediately behind their spray-painted names. Their names were whitewashed by the next nightfall and their signatures erased. This daring action was the first Chicano conceptual art for LACMA and served as a wakeup call to Chicano art. The photograph is now part of LACMA's permanent collection.

Asco continued with other important performance pieces—*Walking Mural* (1972), *Día de los Muertos* (1974), and *First Supper* (1974), which like *Stations of the Cross* interjected Catholic ritual practices with unifying activism and Chicano cultural production. Asco artistic production was fluid; in addition to their performances, they created super-8 silent films and No Movie productions (photographic documentation of their activities which captured only a moment in time, with no succeeding or preceding content). The collective challenged the existing lack of representation of Chicanos and interjected resistance that was intentionally volatile and controversial both inside and outside Chicano cultural art practices. Asco came to an end in 1987.

Further Reading

Archives of American Art. Smithsonian Institution. "*Archivos Virtuales*: Papers of Latino and Latin American Artists." Oral history interviews with Harry Gamboa, Jr., Gronk, Willie Herrón, and Patssi Valdez, n.d.

Chavoya, C. Ondine. "Orphas of Modernism: The Performance Art of Asco." In *Corpus Delecti: Performance Art of the Americas*, edited by Coco Fusco. New York: Routledge, 2000.

Gamboa, Harry, Jr. "In the City of Angels, Chameleons, and Phantoms: Asco, a Case Study of Chicano Art in Urban Tones (or Asco Was a Four-Member Word)." In *Chicano Art: Resistance and Affirmation, 1965–1985*, edited by Richard Griswold del Castillo, Teresa McKenna, and Yvonne Yarbro-Bejarano. Los Angeles: Wight Art Gallery/UCLA, 1991.

Melinda Gandara

ASPIRA. ASPIRA is an educational and cultural nonprofit organization dedicated to empowering Puerto Rican and Latino communities through advocacy, education, and leadership development of youth. Founded in 1961 in New York by Antonia *Pantoja and a group of Puerto Rican professionals, ASPIRA takes its name from the Spanish word *aspirar*, which means "to aspire." Seen as an investment in Latino youth, ASPIRA encourages the completion of high school, pursuit of higher education, and working to improve the community by focusing efforts on three key areas: Leadership Development, Educational Access and Careers, and Community Mobilization for Education Excellence. Through these programs and initiatives, ASPIRA is able to provide leadership training, college counseling, financial aid, scholarship programs and assistance, educational advocacy, cultural activities, and opportunities to improve community action projects.

The ASPIRA Youth Leadership Development Program (LDP), the flagship program of the organization, promotes a highly successful intervention model known as the ASPIRA Process. This three-step process teaches youth to Be Aware of the current situation, Analyze the consequences, and Take Action for change. The LDP annually provides approximately ninety students the opportunity to study leadership skills and work with local and national leaders in internships. In addition, over 25,000 students participate annually in over 400 schools through ASPIRA Clubs.

Through the Educational Access and Careers arm of the organization, ASPIRA provides high school and college students experience, motivation, and academic support to pursue careers in health areas that are in dire need of health professionals in a program call the ASPIRA National Health Careers Program. In addition, the Math and Science Academy (MAS) and Community Allies for Smart Access to Math and Science (CASA MAS) provide hands-on activities, mentors, field trips, and academic assistance in math and science education. The initiative contains an after-school enrichment component as well as an alternative school curriculum. The Youth Ventures Entrepreneurship Program is a partnership between Youth Venture and ASPIRA to provide youth the opportunity to develop entrepreneurial skills.

Community mobilization for educational excellence efforts concentrate on three initiatives called Teachers, Organizations, and Parents for Students (TOPS), ASPIRA Parents for Educational Excellence (APEX), and Mobilization for Equity. TOPS is a partnership program that brings teachers and parents together and incorporates activities, child-centered counseling, and mentoring to help students work toward personal and academic goals. APEX trains parents to be informed advocates, who then mobilize others to help improve education in their communities. Mobilization for Equity provides public policy information to help the Latino community understand educational rights and promotes advocacy strategies for change.

ASPIRA is headquartered in Washington, D.C., and has offices in Connecticut, Florida, Illinois, New Jersey, New York, Pennsylvania, and Puerto

Rico. In 2003, ASPIRA claimed the number-two spot in *Hispanic Business Magazine*'s Top 25 National Hispanic Non-Profits list.

Further Reading

http://www.aspira.org.

Alma Alvarez-Smith

Association Football. *See* Soccer.

Auto Sacramental. The *auto sacramental* is a religious (or miracle) play (*auto*, play; *sacramental*, for sacred contexts) used to teach Roman Catholic biblical morality in folk contexts that was brought to the Americas at the time of the Spanish Conquest and continues to be performed throughout the United States, México, the Caribbean, and Latin America today. Most *autos sacramentales* found in the Americas today originated in Spain in medieval times, although some were authored here during colonial times. Some of the ancient plays include the *moresca* (moorish), such as that performed in Brachio, Zacatecas, México, where thousands of people perform. Religious songs were and continue to be integral to the performance of morality plays, although it is notably absent in some, as in the *moresca* of Zacatecas. In Brazil the first autochthonous morality play, *Auto da Pregação Universal*, was performed in 1567. In the province of La Rioja of Argentina, one celebration commemorates events in which, some people believe, the mediation of the baby Jesus made local native Americans submit to Spanish rule.

Expanding the original definition somewhat to accommodate Latin American contexts, *pastorelas* (shepherds plays) and the pantomimed **matachines* danza are *auto sacramentales* that are still performed in the southwestern United States and México. *Pastorelas* are plays that traditionally recounted the shepherds' visit to the newborn Christ child, although in places where they continue as an integral part of folk culture, they often weave social commentary into the core idea of a Nativity procession replete with songs. In New Mexico there still exist a few versions of *Comanchitos*, an indigenized version of the *pastorela* that is preserved among families who can trace their indigenous ancestry. The *matachines* danza uses no spoken text but features a story retold through dance and gesture. The most typical musical accompaniments include guitar and violin in the southwestern United States and among many indigenous groups of north México, and violin and bass drum, or simply one or two bass drums where the violin performance has declined, in many places of north and central México. It is performed among both indigenous and traditional Hispano populations. The Spanish initially introduced the danza as a means of evangelizing the Indians, but today its meaning has changed to conform to local religious concepts that more often than not merge indigenous and Catholic religious ideas. Prior to the Conquest, however, the Spanish considered the *matachines* profane entertainment in religious processions. There is a great deal of evidence that they have the same roots as the English Morris Dance.

Dance drama that might also include narratives are found in various places throughout Latin America, as they are in the Andean region. In Brazil's northeastern region there are three broad categories of dance dramas: the *baile pastoril* (*pastorela*), a Christmas cycle; *chegan̄ças*, recounting Portuguese maritime exploits and battles between Christians and infidels; and *reisados*, cyclic dances associated with Christmas and Epiphany such as the story of the Nativity and the journey of the Wise Men. In Brazil's central and southern areas various genres of dance dramas are termed *ternos*. Like *matachines*, *ternos* are often performed to honor the saints in patronal festivals. All of these Brazilian traditions have their counterparts throughout Latin America in genres such as *Moros y Cristianos* (Moors and Christians) and the like, with musical variation that is typically reflective of the particular ethnic mix of a region. Instrumental accompaniment also varies, although the pipe and tabor configuration is frequently used. The meanings of all aspects of these traditions also vary, reflecting the beliefs of the people who make up the region. Participation is often in fulfillment of a promise for having been granted a favor, *mandamiento*, such as a miraculous cure, by the saint. The Passion Play (*see Penítentes*) is performed at Easter time by both Latino and non-Latino parishioners in many parts of the United States.

Finally, scenes from the Bible are presented on religious floats in parades during saint's day fiestas in México and other parts of Latin America, and although they do not in themselves represent a theatrical tradition, they are seemingly derived from the *auto sacramental*.

Further Reading

Chá, Ercilia Moreno. "Argentina." In *The Garland Encyclopedia of World Music, Volume 2: South America, México, Central America, and the Caribbean*, edited by Dale Olsen and Daniel E. Sheehy. New York: Garland, 1998. 249–272.

Crook, Larry. "Brazil: Northeast Area." In *The Garland Encyclopedia of World Music, Volume 2: South America, México, Central America, and the Caribbean*, edited by Dale Olsen and Daniel E. Sheehy. New York: Garland, 1998. 323–339.

Harris, Max. *Aztecs, Moors, and Christians in México and Spain: Festivals of Reconquest*. Austin: University of Texas Press, 2000.

Heyck, Denis Lynn Daly. "Arsenio Córdova, Interview." In *Barrios and Borderlands, Cultures of Latinos and Latinas in the United States*. New York: Routledge, 1994.

Reily, Suzel Ana. "Brazil: Central and Southern Areas." In *The Garland Encyclopedia of World Music, Volume 2: South America, México, Central America, and the Caribbean*, edited by Dale Olsen and Daniel E. Sheehy. New York: Garland, 1998. 250–271.

Brenda Romero

Ávila, Carlos (1961–). Carlos Ávila, an award-winning writer/director of Latino-themed short *films, television series, and feature films, was born June 26, 1961, in Lima, Peru, and grew up in the Echo Park area of Los Angeles. After receiving his master's of fine arts from the University of California, Los Angeles, School of Theater, Film, and Television, he won the grand prize in 1991 for his short film *Distant Water*, a *Chicano coming-of-age story set during World War II, at the First Film Festival of International Students in Tokyo, Japan. As a result of his success, in 1993 Ávila wrote, directed, and produced the PBS *American Playhouse* television film *La carpa* (the tent) based on a tent theater troupe in California that in 1938 entertained Chicano farm laborers. The success of this PBS film led him to develop a PBS series in 1997 called *Foto Novelas* (photo novels), which loosely follow a comic book and Latin American pulp novel form. Ávila also studied with famed Chicano film director Gregory *Nava. In 2000 he directed his first commercially released feature film about a Chicano boxing family, **Price of Glory*, which stars Jimmy *Smits.

Further Reading

http://www.inmotionmagazine.com/cavila.html.
http://www.premiereweekend.org/bio-avila.html.
http://www.sdlatinofilm.com/trends1.html.

Arturo J. Aldama

Azpiazu, Don (1893–1943). Don Azpiazu gained international prominence for his version of the "Peanut Vendor"—a popular **son* called a *pregones*, which introduced U.S. listeners to an entire battery of Cuban percussion instruments (*see* *Musical Instruments) including maracas, claves, guiros, bongos, congas, and timbales, and became a national dance hit. Azpiazu was born Justo Angel Azpiazu in 1893, in his homeland of Cuba. He emigrated to the United States, where he became a pianist and bandleader, forming his orchestra in 1928. Their big hit, the "Peanut Vendor," derived from Havana street vendors' chants and was adapted from the 1930 recording of the song "El Manisero." Victor Records (which became RCA Victor in 1929) was concerned that the song would sound too foreign for American audiences. Despite this, "El Manisero" remained a popular *rumba for two months, and the Azpiazu Orchestra performed the "Peanut Vendor" in the 1931 movie *Cuban Love Song*. Azpiazu's hit sparked a decade of rumba, and the song was also the first recording of an authentic Cuban dance music that was truly Latin rather than a U.S. pop music hybrid with a Caribbean rhythm or Latin percussion, like the 1920s *tango craze.

American bandleaders like Guy Lombardo were critical of the popularity of the "Peanut Vendor," and its Latin rhythms and instruments remained a challenge to American bandleaders. However, the American public loved it, and the *son* was soon heard at Earl Carroll's Vanities, the Cotton Club, and the Hollywood Restaurant and played by classical orchestras and cellists.

Azpiazu's "Peanut Vendor" was a groundbreaking hit in the United States and brought attention to Latina/o popular music. Genuinely more Latin than anything heard before, Azpiazu's tune also changed the course of American popular music nationwide. Azpiazu's sister-in-law Marion Sunshine was a vaudeville performer who became heavily involved in Latin music and, along with her husband Eusebio Azpiazu, engineered Don's first tour in 1931; she sang the "Peanut Vendor" with the band across the nation. Introducing English lyrics to many Latin songs throughout the 1930s, Sunshine came to be called "The Rumba Lady." The success of the "Peanut Vendor" paved the way for the popularity of further Cuban music in the United States.

Azpiazu's next hit song was "Green Eyes" (1931), which was another recording to cross over into the U.S. popular music scene, and it was also recorded by North American vocalists. Years later it was translated into English and even recorded by Jimmy Dorsey and scores of other American dance bands. Azpiazu's band is regarded as the first group to perform the earliest form of *salsa heard on Broadway with the popular hit "Mama Inez," accompanied by a Cuban dance team performing on stage in the first public rumba ever seen and heard in the United States. Azpiazu's authentic sound is regarded as ensuring that Cuban styles and not just melodies and rhythms would become a major influence in U.S. popular music.

Azpiazu never really benefited from the rumba craze he started. He returned to Cuba in 1932 following a successful European tour. He eventually returned to New York, performing at the Rainbow Room with the Casa Loma Orchestra and then at the Seville Biltmore Hotel. He lost his gig at the Rainbow Room for refusing to stick to Cuban music and leaving the American numbers for the Casa Loma Orchestra.

He also returned in the early 1940s and recorded a version of "Amapola." Regarded as a stubborn man, he insisted on using the front elevators in the clubs and hotels where he performed. Azpiazu was possibly the first Cuban bandleader who included black and white musicians, breaking the race barrier in the United States in 1931. In 1943 he died of a heart attack in Cuba, and his role in introducing Latin popular music to the United States was virtually forgotten, except for the legacy of his son Raúl, a musician who continues to grace the public with a fusion of Latin and American jazz ("Ritmo de Jazz y Mambo en Cláve," 2002).

Further Reading

Clarke, Donald, ed. *The Penguin Encyclopedia of Popular Music*. 2nd ed. New York: Penguin Books, 1998.

Roberts, John Storm. *The Latin Tinge: The Impact of Latin American Music on the United States*. 2nd ed. New York: Oxford University Press, 1999.

Peter J. García

Aztlán. The origin of the people known as the Aztecs and self-identified as Culhua-Mexica is uncertain, but what is known of them and their oral traditions includes the place named Aztlán. Reputed to be their aboriginal homeland in the north, Aztlán is interpreted by modern scholars to refer both to a geographic place of origin (possibly ancient Asia or distinct points along the route) and/or to a mythical genesis site (like Eden and Atlantis). Many scholars attribute the word "Aztec" to the root stem *Aztlán*.

In the 1960s and 1970s Aztlán was reclaimed by *Chicano activists, artists, writers, and other cultural workers as a unifying symbol of pride and cultural nationalism to counter the negative experience caused by the internal colonialism (i.e., class prejudice and institutional racism against Mexicans in the United States), which resulted from the *Treaty of Guadalupe Hidalgo. The 1960s *Chicano Movement adopted Aztlán as a symbol of unity and to demonstrate cultural, temporal, and spatial continuity with the material experience of the peoples of Mesoamerica. For example, in 1967, at a conference in Denver, Colorado, the Plan Espiritual de Aztlán was introduced by poet *Alurista as an aspirational model for the future and enthusiastically endorsed by the conferees. The following year at the University of California at Santa Barbara, a similar but expanded manifesto called El Plan de Santa Barbara was adopted by students and other activists who had gathered to promote Chicano awareness (*see* MEChA). The Plan outlined an agenda for educational and societal reform as a means of political and economic empowerment. In popular culture Aztlán appears in many and varied forms (murals and other artwork, *lowrider cars, t-shirts, etc.) and representations (pre-Columbian images, hieroglyphics, names, human mestizo figures, and political and spiritual renderings).

Like the cultural and political symbol of *Boricúa recovered among Puerto Ricans, Aztlán emphasizes the plural mestizo past of México, Mexican Americans, and the United States. This **mestizaje* simultaneously consists of indigenous Nahua, Culhua-Mexica, and other aboriginal roots, as well as elements from the Spanish, Moorish/Arab, African, slave, and Anglo-American history of conquest and occupation. All make a claim on the Chicana and Chicano imagination as evidenced in such uses of the Aztlán metaphor as poet Alurista's *Floricanto en Aztlán* (1971), the UCLA publication *Aztlán: International Journal of Chicano Studies and Research*, Rudolfo *Anaya's novel *Heart of Aztlán* (1976), Cordelia Candelaria's poem "On Explaining Aztlán to a 'Manita" (1984), George Mariscal's study *Aztlán and Viet Nam: Chicano and Chicana Experiences of the War* (1999), and countless other artistic, literary, and popular culture images of political, spiritual, and cultural significance.

Further Reading

Acuña, Rodolfo. *Occupied America: A History of Chicanos*. 4th ed. New York: Longman, 2000.

Klor de Alva, Jorge. "Aztlán, Borinquen, and Hispanic Nationalism in the United States." In *Aztlán: Essays on the Chicano Homeland*, edited by Rudolfo A. Anaya and Francisco Lomelí. Albuquerque: University of New Mexico Press, 1991.

Cordelia Chávez Candelaria

Baca, Jimmy Santiago (1952–). Jimmy Santiago Baca is a *Chicano ex-convict, poet, and scriptwriter whose honors include the Wallace Stevens Chair at Yale (1989), the National Endowment Poetry Award (1986), the Vogelstein Foundation Award (1987), the National Hispanic Heritage Award (1990), the Berkeley Regents Award (1990), the Pushcart Prize (1988), the Southwest Book Award (1993), the American Book Award (1988), and the International Prize (2001).

Born in 1952, Baca claims Chicano and Apache Indian descendants. By the age of five his father had died, his mother had been murdered by her second husband, and Baca arrived in a New Mexico orphanage, from which he escaped several times before eventually ending up living on the street. At the age of twenty, he was convicted of drug possession (a crime he claims he did not commit) and spent six years in a maximum-security prison in Arizona. Four of his six years were spent in isolation, having received electric shock treatment to reduce his aggression.

Baca revealed to Beth Ann Krier of the *Los Angeles Times* that during his time in prison he decided to teach himself to read and write to understand how to function in the world because he was tired of being "treated like an animal." He explained, "The only way of transcending was through language and understanding. Had I not found the language, I would have been a guerrilla in the mountains. It was language that saved [me]." He began writing poetry and was urged by a fellow inmate to send his work to *Mother Jones* magazine, whose poetry editor was Denise Levertov. She printed his poems and began corresponding with Baca and eventually found a publisher for his first book, *Immigrant in Our Own Land: Poems* (1979).

Baca's semiautobiographical *Martin and Meditations on the South Valley* follows the journey of a "detribalized Apache." In *Black Mesa Poems* (1989), Baca speaks for the disenfranchised who work the fields. In *Working in the Dark* (1992), a collection of essays that won the 1993 Southwest Book Award, Baca confronts the chaotic history of his life. Some of the other works produced by Baca include *Healing Earthquakes* (2001), *C-Train & 13 Mexicans* (2002), *The Importance of a Piece of Paper* (2004), and *Winter Poems Along the Rio Grande* (2004). Baca's movie scripts and productions include **Bound by Honor*, Disney Productions, and *The Lone Wolf—The Story of Pancho *Gonzalez*, HBO Productions.

Further Reading

Baca, Jimmy Santiago. *Martin and Meditations on the South Valley*. Introduction by Denise Levertov. New York: New Directions, 1987.

Balassi, William, John F. Crawford, and Annie E. Eysturoy, eds. *This About Vision: Interviews with Southwestern Writers*. Albuquerque: University of New Mexico Press, 1990.

Meléndez, A. Gabriel. "Jimmy Santiago Baca." In *Chicano Writers*, Second Series, Vol. 122 of *Dictionary of Literary Biography*, edited by Francisco A. Lomelí and Carol R. Shirley. Detroit, MI: Gale Group, 1992. 21–29.

BJ Manríquez

Báez, Joan (1941–). Since the 1960s, folksinger Joan Báez has been an American icon recognized for her musical talent and her political activism on national and global issues of human rights. Báez was born on January 9, 1941, in Staten Island, New York, as Joan Chandos Báez, the middle daughter of Albert Vinicio, a Mexican physicist, and Joan Bridget Báez, a Scottish immigrant. Báez became involved in the *Folklore Revival Movement of the 1950s and 1960s, often appearing in concert with Bob Dylan, and she participated in the first Woodstock concert in upstate New York in 1969. She became politically active in nonviolent protests for civil rights at the side of Martin Luther King, Jr.; she publicly opposed the Vietnam War, and in 1965 she founded an institute for the study of nonviolence. She recorded and popularized the well-known anthem of nonviolent action of the time, "We Shall Overcome." Her music of protest and nonviolence earned her Grammy Award nominations in 1963, 1965, 1969, 1972, 1988, and 1993 and wider international recognition.

In 1974, Báez explored her Latina heritage and released a Spanish-language album, *Gracias a la vida* (Thanks to Life), that features popular folk and protest songs from Latin America. During the 1970s she completed several international tours to Spain, Latin America, and other countries, where she was not always well received due to her political views. In 1980, she received Honorary Doctor of Humane Letters degrees from Antioch University and Rutgers University. She also produced a *film documentary in 1982 titled *There But for Fortune: Joan Báez in Latin America*, which is based on her Latin American tour. She had a strong impact on a Spanish-speaking audience abroad and at home in the United States. During her career,

Báez evolved from a socially conscientious folksinger to a modern feminist transcultural ambassador of peace.

Her selected discography includes *Folksingers 'Round Harvard Square* (1959), *Joan Báez in San Francisco* (1964), *The First Ten Years* (1970), *The Joan Báez Ballad Book* (1972), *Gracias a La Vida* (1974), *Diamonds & Rust* (1975), *Blowin' Away* (1977), *Honest Lullaby* (1979), *Live at Newport* (1996), and *Gone From Danger* (1997).

Further Reading

Báez, Joan. *And a Voice to Sing With: My Story*. New York: Summit, 1987.

Hajdu, David. *Positively 4th Street: The Lives and Times of Joan Baez, Bob Dylan, Mimi Baez Fariña, and Richard Fariña*. New York: Farrar, Giroux & Strauss, 2001.

Telgen, Diane, and Jim Kamp, eds. *¡Latinas!: Women of Achievement*. Detroit, MI: Visible Ink Press, 1996.

Juanita Heredia

Bailando con el Diablo. *Bailando con el Diablo* (Dancing with the Devil) is an urban legend circulating within Mexican American culture, particularly in the Southwest borderlands, intended to warn young women not to disobey their parents, in particular, their mothers. Mothers often tell this tale to their daughters in an effort to dissuade them from fraternizing with strangers, particularly young handsome men.

As the popular legend goes, a young woman disobeys her mother and goes to a dance without receiving permission to attend. A handsome, well-dressed man asks her to dance, and they dance the night away. At around the toll of midnight, the young woman discovers her suitor is not wearing any shoes because he does not have human feet; he has chicken feet or goat's hooves. Upon being discovered, the "handsome man" either vanishes into thin air or runs out the door, leaving an odor of sulfur. The girl subsequently either faints or burns to death, with her remains vanishing into thin air. If the girl remains alive, she will have either a burn on her shoulder or a man's handprint imbedded on her back, symbolizing her devil suitor.

Further Reading

Castro, Rafaela G. *Chicano Folklore: A Guide to the Folktales, Traditions, Rituals, and Religious Practices of Mexican-Americans*. New York: Oxford University Press, 2001.

Armando Quintero, Jr.

Baile. The term *baile* sometimes refers to a certain dance step or, in a different context, to a grand ball. More generally, however, it means a dance party. The *baile*, or local dance party, is one of the most important social traditions among Latinas and Latinos in the United States, a carryover from community-based social festivities dating from New Spain and still popular in contemporary México and the rest of Latin America.

Bailes provide a carnivalesque context for physical activity, choreographic expression, and ethnic solidarity; they may be sexually charged, offering opportunity for flirtation and courtship. At a *baile*, families, friends, relatives, and neighbors interact and enjoy diversions from work, school, and everyday life. They may also engage in class, gender, and ethnic rivalries and aggressive social behavior such as fighting, drunkenness, and lewdness, sometimes even murder—all within a familiar ritualized setting. *Bailes* occur in rural and urban settings and appeal to people across generational, religious, and sexual boundaries.

Further Reading

Castro, Rafaela G. *Chicano Folklore: A Guide to the Folktales, Traditions, Rituals and Religious Practices of Mexican-Americans*. New York: Oxford University Press, 2001.

Lea, Aurora Lucero-White et al., eds. *Folk-Dances of the Spanish Colonials of New Mexico: Recuerdos de la Fiesta*. Santa Fe: Examiner Publishing Co., 1940.

Limón, José E. *Dancing with the Devil: Society and Cultural Poetics in Mexican-American South Texas*. Madison: University of Wisconsin Press, 1994.

Loeffler, Jack et al. *La Música de los Viejitos: Hispano Folk Music of the Río Grande del Norte*. Albuquerque: University of New Mexico Press, 1999.

Peña, Manuel. "Ritual Structure in a Chicano Dance." *Latin American Music Review* 1 (1980): 47–73.

Peter J. García

Baile Folklórico. *Baile folklórico* refers to Mexican folk dances or dances that bear significant Mexican folk influence and are performed generally by professional, semiprofessional, and amateur troupes throughout México and the United States. The basic elements of *folklórico* are dance technique, choreography, costuming, and research. While many *folklórico* shows also contain lyrical examples of *danza, the two are born out of different paradigms with the distinction typically being drawn between the secular (*folklórico*) and the spiritual (danza). Since *folklórico* is a term that describes a developing and dynamic art form, it is important to note that there are within the diaspora of Mexican folk dance many different sects who maintain various views about the true definition, essence, and semantics of *baile folklórico*. Nonetheless, *folklórico* continues to gain popularity in performance and practice across the United States.

Among these differences there are a few distinct commonalities. *Folklórico* presentations and repertoire are based on the specific dance tradition of a given area and/or class of people and that are organized into region and *cuadros*. A *folklórico* show typically includes several *cuadros* and/or regions that are distinguished by a difference in costuming, technique, and musical accompaniment. A *cuadro* is originally a set of four dances that offers a sampling of the distinct dance technique of any given region but may include more or less dances, depending upon the artistic prerogative of the director. A region refers to a geographical area and a set of distinct technique and costuming. Most regions are attributed to the political boundaries of the Mexican States, but some states can contain several distinct regions within them due to a wealth of geographic differences or influences, either indigenous or European that shaped their different social dance customs.

Mexican folk dance as a staged art form began to be popular in the early twentieth century with the native Mexican cultural renaissance that swept the country in conjunction with the Mexican Revolution. Amalia Hernández is recognized throughout México and the world over as being the impetus to the first professional *folklórico* performing company. In fact, her company the Ballet Folklórico Nacional is often recognized as México's foremost company, serving as an ambassador of Mexican *folklore and arts across the world. The rise of the Ballet Folklórico de México proved encouraging to other efforts across México to choreograph and perform Mexican folk material in a formalized manner on stage for entertainment purposes. Additionally, with the new social emphasis on native Mexican culture, many universities dedicated resources to researching and performing dance that reflected their regional histories. Out of this movement rose several choreographers such as Rafael Zamárripa (University of Guadalajara, University of Colima) and Miguel Belez (University of Veracruzana), whose primarily folk-driven choreographies and technical stylings provided a stark contrast to the ballet-driven stylings of Hernández's company.

The two different schools of technique, style, and costuming still cause fervent debate about authenticity, technical merit, and appropriateness for stage. However, the Ballet Folklórico de México embraces a distinct ballet technique as its foundation, placing emphasis on such aspects as open talus movements (pointed toes), ballet forms, and costuming designed to embellish the performance for the audience's sake. Other companies such as those of Belez and Zamárripa have chosen to preserve and develop a greater amount of folk technique that frequently emphasizes closed talus movements, a step style that is more audibly rhythmic, and costuming that is primarily designed to reflect the essence of the folk subject rather than to entertain the audience. There are embellishments in technique, costuming, and choreography in both schools of thought, but the difference between the two personalities of expression is distinct.

Many people like to point to these differences to debate authenticity of content, but academic folklorists agree that once a particular dance has been removed from its original participants and context, then it ceases to be authentic folk material. Even the best-researched performances can only desire to be artistic representations of folk material once they have been placed on the stage. The difference, then, is truly one of artistic style pitting the more abstract "expressionistic" ballet style against a sort of "folk realism."

Folklórico as a growing phenomenon becomes further complicated as it has transcended the U.S.-México border. Since the mid-1960s several companies have been born in the United States. The first generation of companies sprouted mostly in the Southwest and other urban centers where the *Chicano Movement was prevalent. Many *Chicanos sought their own cultural renaissance, as did México during its revolution, and therefore began to participate in cultural activities such as Mexican *folklórico* dance. In some cases, choreographers and dancers were brought into the United States to teach *folklórico*; in others, people were sent to study *folklórico* in México and then returned to teach. The many instructors who found themselves in the United States represented a sizable cross section of the different styles and philosophies of *folklórico* that were still developing in México. Each one of them advocated that their manner of step technique and choreography was the foremost, but in fact there has never been a complete, uniform set of step and choreographic technique compiled and accepted across México. There is some agreement on research methodology that is borrowed from the academic world, but the manner in which researched material may be synthesized and presented on stage is still fervently debated throughout México and the United States.

This debate is complicated by the fact that the prevalence of *folklórico* in the United States occasionally exerts influence on Mexican folk dance. Costuming and research are not as readily available, especially to primary English speakers in the United States, so they will often change or omit important details, but yet they continue to perform under the guises of Mexican *folklórico*, which some believe distorts the perception of Mexican folklore. Mexican *folklórico* purists are further concerned by the many U.S.-based *folklórico* troupes that perform at international dance festivals the world over since they serve as ambassadors of Mexican culture and yet are not from México. Also exacerbating the problem is that some U.S.-based companies do not hesitate to take liberty on the "Hispanic theme" to include a full set of the distinctly Spanish flamenco dance in their performances that are characterized as Mexican *folklórico* shows.

Expanding on that same theme is the debate over whether or not dances that originated in the *U.S.* Hispanic Southwest as a result of Mexican influence should be allowed to appear in a show that is designated as a *Mexican folklórico* show. Correct or not, choreographers continue to insert this material under the flagship label of *folklórico*, thereby exerting influence on the entire genre as lay audiences struggle to understand exactly what *folklórico* encompasses. From coast to coast in the United States one can find *folklórico* companies of vastly diverse quality, philosophy, and technique practicing and performing in venues from street festivals to grand auditoriums, yet few people are familiar with the attributes of quality *folklórico*, due in large part to the dynamic nature of its contents.

The term *folklórico* continues to grow beyond the strict academic criteria that would qualify a given subject as "folk" or "folkloric" and now encompasses all of the aspects of the developing performing art form that appears on stages around the globe. Within loose confines, *folkloristas* continue researching, choreographing, and performing so that they too can make their contribution to the dynamic and developing concept of *baile folklórico.*

Further Reading

Lea, Aurora Lucero-White. *Folk-Dances of the Spanish-Colonials of New Mexico.* Santa Fe, NM: Examiner Publishing Co., 1940. (Music transcribed by Eunice Hauskings. Choregraphy transcribed by Helene Mareau.)

Sedillo, Mela. *Mexican and New Mexican Folkdances.* 2nd ed. Albuquerque: University of New Mexico Press, 1950.

Jimmy Newmoon Royball

Ballad of Gregorio Cortez, The. A **corrido* is a ballad or story song that provides an oral historical report of many different types of events, and *El Corrido de Gregorio Cortez* is probably the most famous *corrido* ever sung. *Corridos* tell a wide range of stories, from personal or social struggles to more contemporary themes, including the drug trade (**narcocorridos*) and the 9–11–2001 terrorist attack on the World Trade Center in New York City, to intercultural and gender conflict. The term *corrido* comes from the Spanish word *correr*, meaning "to run," and these ballads are typically in strophic form, meaning the same melody is used for each strophe or verse of text. The story line of the *corrido* usually begins by giving specific information like the name of the protagonist, the date of the event, and place, then meshes the events into the song and ends with a formal *despedida* or farewell.

The *corrido* is a form of oral history for the Mexican, Chicana/o, and Tejana/o people living throughout the Southwest borderlands. Much scholarship has been completed on *corridos* especially in Texas, and the most famous study was by Texas Mexican folklorist Dr. Americo Paredes, who referred to the period from 1836 to the late 1930s as the "*corrido* century." During this time, there was much violence and conflict between Anglo Americans and Texas Mexicans to report, especially in border towns. The various wars and injustices taking place in México along the border towns of the United States greatly influenced the *corridos* of this time.

"The Ballad of Gregorio Cortez" is a ballad about an ordinary Mexican named Gregorio Cortez who allegedly was accused of selling a stolen horse. Cortez was visited by an Anglo American sheriff who did not speak Spanish. When asked if he sold a horse by the deputy translator, Cortez replied "No, he sold a *yegua* or female horse." The sheriff was killed in what appeared to be a mere accident, and for weeks Cortez evaded the *Texas Rangers throughout the countryside. He was eventually captured and tried, but in 1905, Cortez was found not guilty of the first murder but guilty of a second. Cortez served eight years of the term when he was pardoned. Cortez remains a legendary character in *corridos*. Numerous recordings have been made of "El Corrido de Gregorio Cortez."

In 1982 there was a filmic adaptation of *The Ballad of Gregorio Cortez*, which was directed by Robert M. Young, produced by Moctezuma Esparza, and starred Edward James *Olmos. This classic of *Chicano cinema was adapted by Young, Victor *Villaseñor, Cordelia Candelaria, and others from Américo Paredes's seminal 1970 anthropological study *"With His Pistol in His Hand": A Border Ballad and Its Hero* (1958). The filmmakers received support from the Sundance Institute, Public Broadcasting Service, *the National Council at La Raza and the National Endowment for the Arts. Olmos stars as Gregorio Cortez, who in 1901 kills a sheriff in self-defense as he is about to be arrested in a case of mistaken identity. The *film's focus lies in the mistranslation of the Spanish word for *horse*, which in turn causes a series of events leading to the capture and false incarceration of Cortez. The movie chronicles the eleven-day manhunt for him as he flees from Karnes County, Texas, to the Mexican border and the injustice he faces in the courts afterward. The film differs from Paredes's written text by withholding from a non-Spanish-speaking audience the (mis)translation that sets events in motion. The film portrays Cortez as both victim and folk hero.

Further Reading

Limón, José. *Mexican Ballads, Chicano Poems: History and Influence in Mexican-American Social Poetry*. Berkeley: University of California Press, 1992.

Paredes, Américo. *"With His Pistol in His Hand": A Border Ballad and Its Hero*. Austin: University of Texas Press, 1958.

Wald, Elijah. *Narcocorrido: A Journey into the Music of Drugs, Guns, and Guerrillas*. New York: HarperCollins, 2001.

George Yáñez and William Orchard

Balseros. The homemade rafts called *balsas* constructed by dissatisfied Cubans as a means of transport from their home island to the United States gave rise to the name *balseros* (rafters) by which these particular exiles are known. The dissatisfaction with oppressive government policies and continuing poverty, which produced them, intensified between 1990 and 1994 when everyday life in Cuba became so miserable that thousands of Cubans even began to fear starvation. The island's population felt tremendous pressure to leave in hopes of better lives in the North. On August 5, 1994, the economic pressure swelled to a boiling point, and a spontaneous demonstration broke out in Old Havana. For the first time in his administration, dictator Fidel *Castro publicly stated that he would not use military force to stop anyone wishing to leave the island. Immediately, hundreds of people set out on their homemade *balsas*, and the *balsero* phenomenon entered the popular culture vocabulary.

A great many rafters have perished at sea, and a number of others have made it successfully to land. However, the majority were picked up and detained at the American-controlled Guantánamo Bay Naval Base to stem the tide of evacuees. Nevertheless, over time, approximately 50,000 of the *balsero* detainees were processed and brought to the United States. Among the most famous *balseros* at the turn of the century were the boy, Elián

González, whose mother died in a *balsa* crossing in 1999, and more recently a raft propelled by a 1952 Chevy pickup in July 2003. Part of the ongoing historical flow of Cuba and the United States, the rafters join the long history of hundreds of thousands of Cubans who have emigrated to the United States as political refugees since 1820, when most of Latin America, except Cuba, was emancipated from Spain. Since then the Cuban desire for freedom has led them to persist in their attempt to escape to liberty.

Cordelia Chávez Candelaria

"Bamba, La." *See* "La Bamba."

Bamba, La. *See La Bamba.*

Bandas. The word *banda* simply means "band" in Spanish, and it can refer to any ensemble using brass instruments; however, as a popular music genre it maintains strong symbolic and regional associations with western México, particularly the northern state of Sinaloa. It also has diffused across the border into the southwestern United States and is heard throughout Chicana/o and Mexican communities across the nation today. In México, there are military *bandas* and municipal *bandas*, many types of traditional regional *bandas*, and modern electrified *tecnobandas*. In the United States, *banda* is generally understood to refer to the music of a Sinaloan-style brass band or to *tecnobanda*, its contemporary variant.

In the nineteenth century, Europeans brought brass bands to their colonies around the world. The Mexican brass band was born when México achieved independence in 1821, and it continued to develop throughout the century as various foreign powers came through the country, including the Americans in the 1840s and the French and Austrians in the 1860s. Several types of bands existed to fulfill different functions. First and best known were the large military bands, which were found in all garrison towns. These bands played on board ships and for military affairs as well as at public and private celebrations. Later, cities organized and funded municipal bands to play for public festivities in town squares, a tradition still practiced in many Mexican towns. Informal, smaller bands organized by ordinary civilians without government funding also appeared.

Bandas formed in both cities and rural areas, although there were many differences between the two. Urban *bandas* served the cultured elite by playing a European repertoire from written scores that included concert and opera music as well as dances like *polcas* (polkas), mazurkas, *valses* (waltzes), and *pasodobles* (two-step). In both rural and urban areas, *bandas* were hired to announce events like theater programs, circuses, or bullfights. Rural musicians called their music *música de viento*, wind music, to distinguish it from *música de cuerda* (string music), or the string music of *orquestas*, and they learned their repertoire of traditional and popular songs by ear. Village groups, which were and are often maintained by a single *family over generations, traveled to cities to play at festivals such as those around carnival time or national holidays like May 5 (*Cinco de Mayo) and September 16 (celebrated as Independence Day) (*see* Holidays and Fiestas). They also performed for *fandangos, dances of the lower classes that were viewed with disdain by more elite members of society. Around the turn of the century, *bandas* were contracted by businesses like factories to entertain their workers, and some large companies formed their own brass ensembles.

Unique regional styles of *banda* music developed in many Mexican states, including Sinaloa, Jalisco, Zacatecas, Guanajuato, Morelos, Guerrero, and Oaxaca. In Sinaloa, the instrumentation of the popular *banda* has remained fairly constant since the 1920s. The *banda sinaloense*, also known as *tambora* for its heavy drum sound, is made up of nine to thirteen musicians on a combination of clarinets, cornets or trumpets, valve trombones, saxhorns, tuba, *tarola* (snare drum), and *tambora* (bass drum). It is traditionally a purely instrumental ensemble because vocalists would find it difficult to make themselves heard over such a loud ensemble without amplification. Some musicians in the early to mid-twentieth century were trained at the Escuela Industrial Militar in Culiacán, while others were entirely self-taught. Their repertoire, similar to that of the *mariachis, consisted of regional **sones* and nationally popular songs. Sinaloan *banda* musician Wenceslao Moreno penned "El niño perdido" (The Lost Child), now a standard tune for mariachis as well as *bandas*.

Sinaloan and other regional *bandas* remained purely local art forms, and little was known outside their place of origin until some *bandas* began to participate in the recording industry during the mid-twentieth century. The first *banda sinaloense* recording of four songs was made in 1952 by Los Guamuchileños and was sold as far away as Cuba and Puerto Rico; this record was quickly followed with recordings by Banda El Recodo and others as demand for the style grew. The music reached still wider audiences as a result of the innovations of Don Cruz Lizárraga, Recodo's leader, who outfitted his musicians with uniforms and arranged popular American big band and Mexican *orquesta* music for his group. In the 1960s, Banda la Costeña's director Don Ramón López Alvarado added the newly popularized Colombian *cumbia rhythm to their repertoire. In the 1980s, this same *banda* recorded two hits with Mexican actor/singer Antonio Aguilar.

Though Sinaloan bands like Banda Los Charoles had come north to the Arizona-Sonora border on tour in the early twentieth century, *banda* music was not performed north of the border until much later. Much credit for the music's introduction to and popularization among Mexican American audiences is given to Banda El Recodo, which began touring in California and beyond in the early 1960s. The first Sinaloan-style *banda* in the United States, Banda Mazatlán, formed in the mid-1970s in Los Angeles, where a large number of Sinaloan immigrants lived. Today, several Sinaloan-style *bandas* reside in Los Angeles, and more have been formed in other large American cities such as Phoenix, Arizona. However, *banda* did not gain international popularity until the introduction of a new, electrified style in the early 1990s.

The *tecnobanda* sound was created by Manuel Contreras, manager of the Fonorama studios in Guadalajara, Jalisco. In the mid-1980s he decided to fuse the highly popular *onda grupera* style (soft ballads performed by synthesizer-heavy groups like Los Bukis and Grupo Liberación) with Sinaloan *banda*, paring down the *banda* ensemble to just a few brass instruments filled out with synthesizer, electric bass, vocals, and drum set. The first *tecnobanda* hit was "El Ranchero Chido" by Vaquero's Musical. Other *tecnobandas* soon appeared on the scene; the most successful were two other Jaliscan groups, Banda Machos and Banda Maguey. The new style traveled north and became so popular in Los Angeles, California, that *banda**ranchera* format radio station KLAX ("La Equis") became the number-one station in the city in 1992. A second *banda* format station, KBUE ("Radio Qué Buena"), which also played *norteña* music, went on air in 1995. The Sinaloan bands were also evolving rapidly during this period, keeping up with the new developments. Most added vocalists to their ensembles; they also responded to the popularity of ballad singers like Luis *Miguel by creating a new style, *banda romántica*, to play sentimental songs. Finally, *bandas* incorporated the **corrido* and **narcocorrido* into their repertoire; even Chalino Sánchez, the top *narcocorridista* in Los Angeles in the early 1990s, recorded an album with *banda* accompaniment.

The *tecnobandas* were also responsible for the introduction of a new dance rhythm called **quebradita* or *caballito*, which is actually a very fast cumbia. Mazatlán's Banda el Méxicano bills itself as the creator of the rhythm they term *caballito* (little horse), though other musicians point to "El Ranchero Chido" as the first *quebradita* (little break dance). Regardless, the huge popularity of *tecnobanda* and the *quebradita* rhythm in the U.S.-México border area led to a *banda* dance craze among Mexican American youth. The new style of dance appears to have originated in the American Southwest in the early 1990s and then spread southward. In the Los Angeles area, hundreds of *quebradita* dance clubs formed to practice and compete, with the support of local *banda* radio stations. In other areas, like southern Arizona, competitive clubs were formed by schools and other community organizations. Though some parents were troubled by the dance's sensual movements, most observers saw *quebradita* clubs as a positive phenomenon that kept teenagers away from more destructive influences like *gangs. With its accompanying *vaquero* (cowboy) attire and message of pride in Mexican culture, some saw the dance's popularity as representing a "*banda* movement" that cut across class lines and was accepted both by recent immigrants and by American-born *Chicanos.

In México, *banda* musicians have always had to contend with the problems of social stigma. The music has long been considered vulgar and disreputable, the domain of drunkards, womanizers, and even criminals. But *banda*'s popularity in the United States has given it a new respectability and is having a positive effect in its home country. Long ignored by Mexican scholars, *banda* is finally getting some notice. The *banda* Brígido Santamaría de Tlayacapan, founded in 1875 and still performing, recently won a national prize for outstanding work in the area of Popular Art and Traditions. Pop singer *Thalía recorded with a *banda* in 2001, rock artists Café Tacuba have borrowed from the style, and a *quebradita* *merengue fusion song became popular on New York City radio in early 2003. Though traditionalists decried the flashy *tecnobandas*' innovations and feared the new style was threatening the old with extinction, traditional *banda* is still very much alive in small-town México; in Sinaloa, it can be heard at events such as Culiacán's *feria ganadera* (cattle fair), Mazatlán's February *carnaval*, saint's days, and other celebrations. Also, the popularity of *tecnobanda* has apparently opened the door for a greater interest in the "original" Sinaloan *banda* music among Mexican Americans. It is clear that this music will survive and be enjoyed by many generations to come, not in spite of its embrace of modern technology and musical styles but because of it.

Further Reading

Campos, Rubén M. *El folklore y la música mexicana: Investigaciones acerca de la cultura musical en México (1525–1925)*. Mexico City: Secretaría de Educación Pública, 1928.

Haro, Carlos Manuel, and Steven Loza. "The Evolution of Banda Music and the Current Banda Movement in Los Angeles." In *Selected Reports in Ethnomusicology X: Musical Aesthetics and Multiculturalism in Los Angeles*, edited by Steven Loza. Los Angeles: University of California, 1994.

Simonett, Helena. *Banda: Mexican Musical Life across Borders*. Middletown, CT: Wesleyan University Press, 2001.

Sydney Hutchinson

Barrios and Borderlands. Latina and Latino popular culture manifests itself within specific geographic spaces and has grown out of the vibrant histories and experiences of people rooted in material places. So "where" do Latinas/os reside? An examination of the geography of ethnicity contributes to a better understanding of the genesis and growth of Latina/o communities in the United States, which in turn offers insights into the context that produced or influenced the Mexican American, Puerto Rican, *Cuban American, and other Latina/o popular culture forms and activities. Often it is the popular culture that is created and consumed by *la gente* (the people) that defines the community (*el pueblo*) from which it emerges. Whether in the old barrios of the Bronx, East Los Angeles, or other long-established neighborhoods, or whether in newer immigrant localities of South Carolina, Georgia, or any other recent growth area, Latina/o popular culture helps cultivate and affirm a collective identity.

Likewise, whether on the border between México and the United States or within the broader borderland regions that extend north into the central United States as well as south into the northern rim of Mexican states, the Latina/o population thrives and produces cultural forms and activities that are visible on many levels, including *Architecture and Urbanism and commercial exchange. Through *piñatas hanging in shops, fresh vegetable street markets, *panaderías* (bakeries), the sounds of Spanish and Latin music, murals and other public art examples, *fútbol* (soccer) and similar recreational activities, observances of traditional holidays, and so on, these products and practices reflect an identifiable and culturally distinct people within geographic regions. One of the outgrowths of the border region are communities of *colonias* (shantytowns) that sprout up in peripheral open spaces to house society's poorest workers, many of whom work in **maquilas* (high-speed assembly plants known as "sweat factories"). Some of the *colonia* inhabitants are themselves by-products of the vast *maquiladora* (sweatshop worker) industries, which operate in binational free trade zones throughout the world to exploit low-wage labor pools.

Also part of the border region are agricultural holdings, from small *family farms and ranches to larger haciendas and agribusiness estates, as well as hundreds of villages and towns that spin off from agriculture to provide food processing, meat packing, storage, and related supplies and services. All these *frontera* (border) places and spaces produce their identifiable cultures and have contributed to such popular culture forms as **corridos* (ballad poetry and songs) and *norteño* ("northern" Tex-Mex) music, which have been chronicled in such *films as *The Border*, **¡Alambrista!*, and *Señorita Extraviada* (Young Lady Lost). In addition, many singers (such as *Selena and *Los Lobos) and countless writers (like Rolando *Hinojosa, Estela *Portillo Trambley, and Denise *Chávez) have recorded their interpretations of the border.

Further examination of the geography of Latina/o ethnicity relates to the urban barrio context that has produced and influenced millions of Mexican American, Puerto Rican, Cuban American, and other American popular culture forms and activities. The word *barrio* originally comes from an Arabic expression meaning "open country," and it arrived in the Western Hemisphere with the Spaniards who applied the term to denote a governmental division within a town or city and its adjacent rural regions. In everyday Spanish parlance today the word *barrio* means "neighborhood" or "district," as in *barrio residencial* (residential neighborhood) or *barrio comercial* (business district).

After 1848 and the *Treaty of Guadalupe Hidalgo when the United States took possession of what is now the American Southwest and other regions formerly part of New Spain and México, the meaning of the word began to

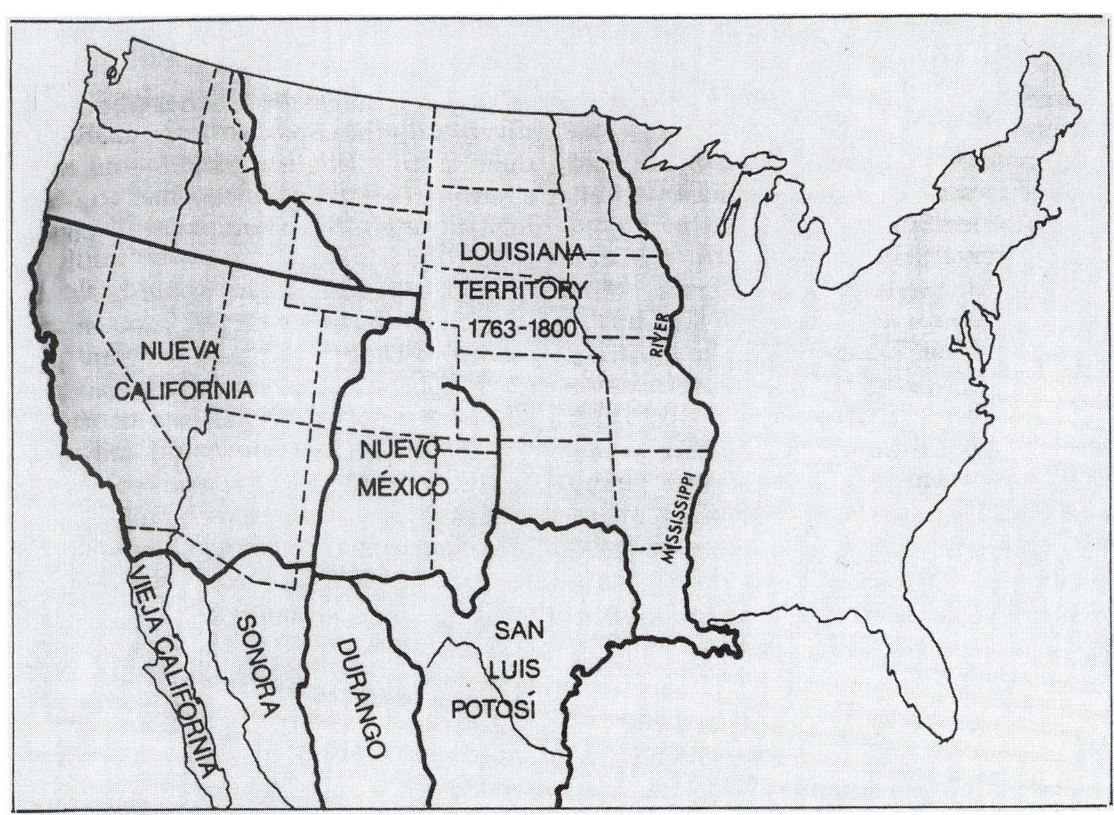

The geography and history of America's Latina/o roots predates the arrival of the English on the Atlantic coast. This map shows northern New Spain in the early 1800s. The region became the Republic of Mexico after 1820. *Courtesy of Cordelia Candelaria.*

evolve to refer to an urban community populated by predominantly Spanish-speaking or Latin-origin people. This connotation survives in common English parlance, particularly among Americans who frequently use *barrio* as an imprecise synonym for "slum," erroneously implying that mainly undocumented immigrants causing high crime rates populate such geographic regions. The 2000 U.S. Census discloses, however, that a significant majority of the people who reside in many of these segregated neighborhoods are actually U.S. citizens with keen concerns for safe communities in which to live.

Like *barrio*, the terms *border* and *borderlands* have multiple meanings and applications. They sometimes are used interchangeably to refer to the binational region and cultures on either side of the 2,000-mile-long political boundary between México and the United States. Many scholars and other researchers, however, typically distinguish between the two terms, describing the border more narrowly as the region immediately adjacent to both sides of the binational political boundary, as in the border cities of Tíjuana, Baja California Norte, and San Diego, California; El Paso, Texas, and Juárez,

Chihuahua; Nogáles, Sonora, and Nogáles, Arizona; and many others. Applied in a broader sense, *borderlands* refers to the regions and cultures that extend northward into the central United States and, to some extent, southward into the northern rim of México. In this sense, it is a more fluid, organic geography, since its identity derives more from the populations that inhabit the borderlands than from the politics that define the border. This usage also recognizes the history of the region, which, like New Spain and México, was once a borderless environment for millions of Mexicans, Mexican Americans, and their Chicana/o descendants.

Historically, north-south migration across the border was not severely restricted because most Mexican immigrants did not stay within the United States permanently, and travel from México was a fluid back-and-forth phenomenon. This open border with two-way traffic and cultural interchanges has defined the north/south frontier since before 1848 and the *Treaty of Guadalupe Hidalgo. The traffic increased with the *Bracero Program, a temporary Mexican guest worker policy approved by both governments, which started in 1942 as part of the World War II effort and continued until 1964. For this reason, one of the most common sentiments heard throughout the barrios and borderlands of the United States is the widespread grassroots popular culture statement, "I didn't cross the border, the border crossed me." This explains why many scholars, policymakers, artists, and activists find it impossible to discuss the Latina/o environments of barrios without discussing borderlands as well, and vice versa. In addition, this understanding of place, politics, and consciousness as interlocking and interanimating gives rise to the idea of comparing the identities that mark the duality of being Mexican American, Cuban American, and any "other" American to the political boundaries that separate nations.

The large metropolitan barrios like East Harlem in New York, East Los Angeles, Little Havana in Miami, and Little Village (Pilsen) in Chicago may be among the most famous in the country, but they are but four of hundreds of others. Among bilingual Latinas and Latinos the term *barrio* usually is used to describe an area distinguished by traditional Latina/o cultural influences. Thus, for many U.S.-México border towns that reflect the influence of Spanish, Mexican, and Chicana/o lifeways (e.g., Brownsville, El Paso, Las Cruces, Nogáles, and San Diego), the entire town is sometimes described as a barrio. Within the boundaries of such border towns and cities, however, the term may carry a distinct socioeconomic connotation mirroring that of the majority English-speaking culture. In such cities, the term *barrio* has come to designate a lower-income, mostly immigrant, and geographically bounded community to most of the town's residents. However, in the case of Laredo, Texas, the population is 94 percent Latina/o, mostly Mexican American and Mexican. By contrast in Laredo and similar towns, the Mexican American middle-class areas often are referred to as simply neighborhoods or housing editions. In that context, the use of the term *barrio* connotes a class-specific and ethnic distinction, demonstrating a cross-cultural adaptation toward the dominant population. San Antonio, Texas, offers another example of a city with a majority Latina/o population where the low-income, working-class area known as West San Antonio is considered a barrio that houses the cultural heart and soul of the city's Mexican American community, while its many other predominantly Mexican American neighborhoods are typically not so designated.

While today's barrios are in part a product of the nation's legacy of discrimination against U.S.-born Latinas/os and Latina/o immigrants, many cultural geographers and other scholars argue that the creation of these largely segregated neighborhoods also had the positive consequences of providing their residents with safe, site-based identities that built ethnic in-group security against prejudice and social alienation. The barrios of the borderlands and beyond offered familiarity and stability in the midst of a surrounding environment of socioeconomic uncertainty and outright racial hostility. In most of the United States, barrios are products of both self-segregation and forced segregation since, until the passage of 1960s federal civil rights legislation against housing discrimination, Latinas/os, like African Americans, were restricted to nonwhite geographic areas of their communities. In some towns, the segregation was accompanied by other prohibitions aimed against Latinos by white-owned restaurants, hotels, movie houses, and other privately owned businesses and often by public facilities like swimming pools and parks as well. The separate facilities included Mexican-only schools, which typically were underfunded and poorly maintained.

At the same time, the barrios of the border towns and eventually of the borderlands north throughout the United States served as familiar destinations for new immigrants from México and Latin America. Barrios in Chicago, Los Angeles, Phoenix, and Houston, for instance, were primary magnets for Mexican immigrants. Likewise, immigrants from Puerto Rico (who are U.S. citizens) and Cuba have continuously replenished their respective communities in New York City, Chicago, and Miami. Since the 1980s, Central American immigrants fleeing the violence of the U.S.-backed civil wars have also found haven in Los Angeles (Pico Rivera), San Francisco (the Mission), Houston, and South Florida. According to scholars, Mexican immigrants arriving in the United States have transitioned from their newfound status as a segregated minority by regarding barrios as welcoming places where they might maintain social continuity through language, *food, and other cultural practices and thereby preserve their cultural identities.

A common misconception of barrio communities is that they are all characterized by low standards of living, including widespread unemployment and elevated crime rates. Some barrios possess these characteristics, but careful research has shown that presumptions about barrio life are often distorted and inaccurate. Refuting the commonly held misperception that people who live in barrios are routinely involved in criminal *gangs, several studies of East Los Angeles between 1978 and 1999 discovered that fewer than 10 percent of the area's residents had any association or direct involvement with gangs. That this finding emerged from "East Los," a proven center of high gang activity, is especially significant since it suggests that barrios in other urban centers with fewer gangs would produce an even smaller percentage of crime associations. Similarly, although official unemployment rates for Latinas/os tend to be high, many of these workers often fall below the measurement statistics because they hold part-time and/or seasonal jobs and are part of the underground employment market (such as construction, restaurant, and landscape work) of day laborers frequently paid in cash. Most important, perhaps, employers normally do not report millions of undocumented laborers in the barrios and borderlands as part of their official workforce.

The existence of barrios and the concurrent lack of access to mainstream institutions often compelled Latinos to create their own social service infrastructure. As a result of the 1848 Treaty of Guadalupe Hidalgo and the Gadsden Purchase, which forced México to cede large regions of what are now modern-day Texas, Arizona, New Mexico, California, Colorado, and parts of Oklahoma, Mexican Americans and Mexican immigrants in the late nineteenth and early twentieth centuries formed *mutualistas* (mutual aid societies). Some of these grassroots community groups ultimately evolved into national Latino social organizations, such as the League of United Latin American Citizens (*LULAC).

Technological developments also played a role in the creation and growth of barrios. Chicano historians argue that the birth of barrios and other largely urban Mexican enclaves across the Southwest happened in part due to the expansion of the railroad system and the development of increasingly sophisticated means of farm irrigation. Mexican laborers, for instance, helped build new rail lines, and the growth of the rail system also made possible the rapid transport of migrant laborers who followed seasonal harvests in Texas, New Mexico, Arizona, and California, as well as agricultural regions of the Midwest and Florida. In many instances, migrant workers settled with their families in established barrios or created new barrios, and later waves of immigrants then expanded and replenished the populations of these communities. Some barrios were established as a result of economic upheaval, natural disaster, or war. As a result of the 1910 Revolution, approximately 750,000 Mexicans fled north across the U.S.-México border to escape the civil war. At the same time, many were recruited to work in the mines, railroad, steel, and agriculture industries. During World War II, Mexicans and other Latin American immigrants came to the United States to fill jobs left vacant by American men and women who had been drafted into the military. In the 1980s, the refugees of the U.S.-backed civil wars in Nicaragua, El Salvador, and Guatemala migrated en masse to Latina/o barrios in Houston, Austin, Los Angeles, San Francisco, Florida, Washington,

D.C., and elsewhere. Other refugees left Central America as a result of earthquakes and hurricanes, which further ravaged the region's economies.

Scholars have noted that contrary to widespread assumptions about the demographic makeup of barrios as a haven for *recíen llegados* (recently arrived), these communities are usually a mixture of immigrant and U.S.-born Latinos. In virtually every instance, the foreign-born constitute a minority of the people living there, since barrios are characterized by substantial and steady influxes of immigrants. Immigrants are generally welcomed to barrios, but in some circumstances U.S.-born Latinos are hostile to these new arrivals—no matter that many of their ancestors arrived in precisely the same manner. In some instances, the roots of this strife have to do with outright prejudice against immigrants, particularly if they are undocumented or of a different national origin. In other cases, U.S.-born Latinos may show antipathy toward the new arrivals based on specific cultural or economic biases. Mexican American construction workers in the Southwest, for instance, complain that nonunionized immigrant workers depress the job market because they work for lower wages than those laborers born in the United States.

Some of the most famous barrios in the United States include East Los Angeles, Pico Rivera, and Logan Heights in Southern California, the Mission District in San Francisco, Little Havana in Miami, East Harlem in New York City, and Little Village/Pilsen in Chicago. Arguably the best-known Mexican American barrio in the United States is East Los Angeles. The vicinity has a long history of multicultural *immigration but has become the single largest predominantly Latina/o community in the nation. Ninety-six percent of East Los Angeles is Latina/o, and 77 percent of the Latina/o population in the community is of Mexican descent, according to the 2000 U.S. Census. Because of California's proximity to México, demographers predict that East Los Angeles will continue to be predominantly Latina/o for decades to come.

The heart of what is today East Los Angeles, *Olvera Street or La Placita, was the location of an eighteenth-century Spanish farming settlement called El Pueblo de Nuestra Señora la Reina de los Ángeles de Porciúncula (The Community of Our Lady of Queen of Angels of Porciúncula). However, before the arrival of the Europeans, the fertile area near the banks of the Los Angeles River was home to Gabrielino Indians for nearly 2,000 years. Other ethnic groups also resided in East Los Angeles. As a result of the 1910 Mexican Revolution, a large influx of Mexican immigrants began to change the neighborhood's dynamics. Until the 1930s, East Los Angeles was the center of the local Jewish community, but after World War II, Jews began to move to neighborhoods on the west side of the city. For a time, the community also was home to a substantial Japanese American population; however, after the Japanese military attack on Pearl Harbor in 1941, they were forcibly removed and sent to internment camps. After the war, most did not return to East Los Angeles.

As the Mexican-origin population in East Los Angeles continued to grow, so did its political and social clout, which culminated in the election of Ed Roybal to the Los Angeles City Council in 1949 and to his eventual election to the U.S. Congress. During the 1960s, East Los Angeles became a hotbed of *Chicano activism. In 1968, more than 30,000 students from five area high schools boycotted classes to protest the poor quality of public education in their communities and through these protests won a series of concessions.

Over the years, East Los Angeles has become a major source of Chicano art and culture. Artists from the community are renowned for their murals presenting social and political statements about their community; and in concert with this activity, artist and activist Judy Baca established a citywide mural program in the 1970s. In the past few decades, East Los Angeles also has become a national center for social, political, and intellectual expression. Although still predominantly Mexican American, the barrio and the surrounding communities have attracted a growing number of Central Americans. The region around East Los Angeles includes other well-known barrios such as Boyle Heights and the nearby cities of Pico Rivera.

The Southern California city of San Diego is home to Barrio Logan, also known as Logan Heights. The community's historical significance is tied to the takeover of what is now known as Chicano Park, which features a cultural arts center made to resemble an Aztec temple. The creation of Chicano Park came out of the community's concerns over decades of neglect by the city. Barrio Logan resident Mario Solís had learned that a substation for the California Highway Patrol was to be built on the site. He helped organize a protest against the construction project in 1970, and residents of Logan Heights marched to the site on April 22, some with shovels, pickaxes, and rakes in hand, and demanded a park be built instead. Their efforts succeeded, and in turn, the park came to symbolize the community's struggle for respect. Inspired by the social and political commentary of México's great twentieth-century muralists, artists from San Diego, Los Angeles, and elsewhere have painted murals in Chicano Park and public art throughout the city in the name of cultural preservation and expression.

Northern California's best-known barrio is the Mission District in San Francisco. For many years, the area was a mix of diverse working-class communities that included Latina/o immigrants, artists, and others. In recent decades, the barrio also has become home to high-tech workers, forcing many lower-income residents to move out as the cost of housing has increased. Nevertheless, the community is regarded as the cultural heart of San Francisco's Latina/o community. Since the 1950s, the Latina/o population there has nearly doubled every ten years. In 2000, about one-third of the city's Latinas and Latinos lived in the Mission District. Today, the community's Latina/o population is a mix of Mexicans, Chicanos, Central Americans, and other Latina/o subgroups, including South American refugees from Chile, Peru, and Argentina. Many of the Central Americans there arrived in the 1980s after escaping the wars of El Salvador, Guatemala, and Nicaragua.

The southside barrio of San Jose, California, is known as ¡Sal Si Puedes! (Get Out If You Can!) a self-deprecating reference to the community's depressing economic conditions. The late civil rights leader César *Chávez lived there before beginning his lifetime commitment to farmworker labor organizing, and he led some of his earliest farmworker support demonstrations in ¡Sal Si Puedes! San Juan Bautista, outside Santa Cruz and near the farmworker capital of Watsonville, California, is home to the *Teatro Campesino (Farmworkers Theater). The group's founder Luis *Valdez still lives in the city and runs the repertory company and movie production there. Valdez founded Teatro Campesino in 1965 as part of the broad effort to support farmworkers and their struggle for union representation. These and other northern California barrios are deeply rooted in the Chicana/o struggle for self-determination, as well as in the shared traditions and heritage of their indigenous and Hispanic roots, that is, its **mestizaje*.

Arizona's barrios include South Phoenix, West Phoenix, Maryvale, and others, as well as Barrio Viejo in Tucson. The Phoenix valley also is home to Guadalupe, a predominantly Mexican American and Yaqui Indian town of approximately 5,000 encircled by Tempe, Chandler, and Phoenix. Guadalupe is a community covering nearly one square mile of property along the southeastern edge of the Phoenix valley, approximately 200 miles north of the Mexican border. A northern Mexican tribe, the Yaquis were, at one point, forcibly relocated by the Mexican government to the Yucatán Peninsula. During the 1910 Revolution, members of the tribe who fought alongside Pancho *Villa were later persecuted. After Villa was defeated, a segment of the Mexican Yaqui population was driven into exile in Arizona, though many remained in the Mexican states of Sonora and Sinaloa.

Barrio Viejo has been home to Tucson's Mexican American community for more than 150 years. Before the Gadsden Purchase, Tucson was part of México, having been settled by the Spaniards in 1775. During the early 1960s, Barrio Viejo was slated for destruction as part of a proposed urban renewal plan. More than 1,200 buildings were to be bulldozed, and 5,000 people, mostly Mexican Americans, were to be relocated. Describing the barrio as a center of dirt, disease, and delinquency, Tucson's mayor at the time actively advocated its razing. Ironically, in the end the neighborhood was rescued by fiscal conservatives who, although unconcerned about the human impact and potential cultural degradation, were staunchly opposed to the use of federal funds on the project. Two years later, eighty acres of the barrio were leveled and more than 1,000 people were evicted. While the neighborhood remains the core of the city's Latina/o community, gentrification and an influx of Anglos and middle-class Latinos are reshaping the barrio's character. The writer Patricia Preciado Martin, a Tucson native, has captured this period of Barrio Viejo's controversial history in her fiction, most notably in her short story "The Ruins" (1992).

Spain's colonization of the modern-day state of New Mexico began in the early 1540s during Francisco Vásquez de Coronado's expedition in search of the Seven Cities of Cíbola. It was part of the northern territory of Nueva España (New Spain) and later of México after independence from Spain in 1820 but was ceded to the United States as part of the terms of the Treaty of Guadalupe Hidalgo in 1848. More than 100 years later, Reies López Tijerina, a grassroots political activist and former evangelist minister, launched a movement to reclaim land and water rights lost by the descendants of Spanish colonists in the decades following the signing of the 1848 treaty. Some historians mark Tijerina's founding of the Alianza Federal, as his land rights organization was called, as one of the seminal events of the 1960s *Chicano Movement. Along with the rural-based organizing efforts of the Farm Workers Union led by César Chávez and Dolores *Huerta and those of the Denver Crusade for Justice led by Rodolfo "Corky" González, Tíjerina's Alianza activities received international press attention in 1968 when New Mexico Governor David Cargo ordered the National Guard to arrest the demonstrators.

One of New Mexico's most celebrated cities is its capital, Santa Fe, which was declared Spain's provincial capital in the colony of New Spain in 1610. It continues to the present as the state capital. The history of Santa Fe, whose name means "holy faith," typifies many southwest borderlands communities in that it presents a vibrant mix of native Indian, Spanish colonial, Mexican mestizo, and Anglo immigrant roots in constant transcultural ebb and flow since their settlement in the sixteenth and seventeenth centuries. Important to the development of the state and later as a Spanish-speaking hub along the trading route called the Santa Fe Trail, Santa Fe is New Mexico's third largest city and a worldwide tourist attraction for its colonial Spanish and Pueblo Indian hybrid layout, its *architecture and public art, its native New Mexican cuisine, and the Santa Fe Opera. As a result, many of the city's original Hispanic and Chicana/o barrios have been displaced by the influx of jetsetters and corporate developers who have bought huge tracts of local real estate for shopping malls, parking lots, expanded streets, and upscale mansions. Nevertheless, because of its strict zoning laws favoring traditional colonial mission and territorial style architecture, Santa Fe continues to have a strong public texture of Spanish/Pueblo/Mexican borderlands external identity. The city's population is about 50 percent Mexican origin and along with its annual fiestas, particularly the burning of El *Zozobra in August, perpetuate the image of a distinctly Hispanic land of enchantment roughly 500 miles north of the Mexican border.

Distinctive Spanish, Pueblo and other Indian, and Mexican influences also permeate the architecture and art of New Mexico's largest city, Albuquerque, home to a population that is about 40 percent of Mexican origin (compared to approximately 45 percent for the state as a whole). The city also contains a number of barrios that trace their origins to *los primeros pobladores* (the first [Spanish] pioneer settlers) such as Old Town, site of San Felipe Church, built in 1706 and one of the oldest continuously functioning colonial structures in North America, and Los Duranes (the Durán family), a barrio originally adjacent to Old Town. Until the last decades of the twentieth century when Interstate Highway 40 was built through the city, Los Duranes contained myriad narrow colonial streets and homes situated on former land grant holdings traceable to the monarchs of Spain. The freeway-divided community has since been sold, rezoned, and transformed by gentrification and commercial development, resulting in the displacement of many Chicana/o families and the economic enhancement of others.

Although not as old as Old Town and Los Duranes, several of Albuquerque's other barrios trace their historic roots to previous centuries. Many of the Río Abajo neighboring villages, including Corrales, Placitas, and Algodones, were invaded by hippies during the 1960s and were later taken over by yuppies in the 1980s. Today many of the older Hispano communities such as Alameda and Bernalillo just north of Albuquerque and Los Lunas and Belén in the south are in danger of further gentrification and urbanization. Barelas in Albuquerque's South Valley along the Rio Grande and Los Griegos in the Northwest Valley, once remnants of previous Spanish/Mexican farms, evolved into urban districts with dense Mexican American populations. As socioeconomic stratification took hold, parts of these barrios became increasingly impoverished, and middle-class flight further depressed conditions. Newer barrios have sprouted up throughout the borderlands, and Albuquerque is no exception as recent Mexican and other Latina/o immigrants move into affordable neighborhoods where spoken Spanish and *comida mexicana* (Mexican food) beckon. At the turn of the century, these newer immigrant areas extend from the old barrios and fan out in all directions to accommodate housing and commercial demands.

Like New Mexico, South Texas reflects a distinctly Mexican borderland culture and heritage. The cultural center of the region's Latina/o influence is San Antonio. Located about 150 miles north of the Rio Grande, the city was founded as a Spanish missionary outpost in 1718 and 50 years later was declared the capital of the Spanish province. In 1813, San Antonio's citizens announced they would back México's war for independence from Spain; and in 1836, Texans too gained their independence from México. The 2000 census found that nearly 60 percent of San Antonio residents are of Mexican origin. Texas is also home to a number of other Latina/o-majority cities, including Laredo, El Paso, and Brownsville, all of which border México at the Rio Grande.

The symbolic heart and soul of the Cuban American community in the United States is the Miami, Florida, barrio known as Little Havana. It is also often the first stop for Cuban exiles. The barrio is a twenty-five-block enclave of Cuban business and residential neighborhoods that more or less flank Eighth Street, known locally as Calle Ocho. Domino Park and Cuban Memorial Boulevard are favorite destinations for celebrations and community and political gatherings. Hialeah, another large South Florida city, also is a home to a major Cuban community. South Florida has also become home to a growing number of Puerto Ricans as well as Mexican and Central American immigrants. The 2000 census found that non-Cuban Latinos are now a majority of Florida's Latina/o population.

New York City's "El Barrio," also known as East Harlem, is the sort of place that sports Puerto Rican flags hanging out of windows or fluttering from car antennas. For decades, it has been the heart of the Puerto Rican community in the United States, though it also has a fast-growing Mexican-origin population. The migration of Puerto Ricans to the United States began around the turn of the twentieth century, but most has occurred since World War II. Puerto Ricans, granted U.S. citizenship as residents of a U.S. commonwealth, are now part of a steady stream of migration back and forth between New York City and the island of Puerto Rico. The New York borough known as the Bronx contains the largest concentration of Puerto Ricans outside of the island commonwealth. In 2000, more than 300,000 Puerto Ricans lived in the borough, along with more than 130,000 people of Dominican descent and nearly 35,000 Mexicans and Mexican Americans. Puerto Ricans are also a major segment of the Manhattan population. El Barrio, an area of East Harlem on the borough's lower eastside, "Loisaida," as Nuyoricans call it, is home to hundreds of thousands of Puerto Ricans.

Since 1970, the proportion of Latinos in New York who are Puerto Rican has declined. In 1970, 68 percent of New York Latinos were Puerto Rican. In 2000, Puerto Ricans made up one-third of New York Latinos. Census data show that nearly 50 percent of Bronx's residents are Latina/o, and they are a growing segment of New York City's population overall. More than 25 percent of New Yorkers were of Latina/o origin in 2000.

Pilsen/Little Village is located on Chicago's Lower Westside. Since the nineteenth century, the area has served as a destination for a number of large immigrant communities from Europe and more recently Latin America. It is home to the second largest urban-based Mexican-origin community in the United States. East Los Angeles is the largest. Eighteenth Street in Pilsen/Little Village, like Olvera Street in Los Angeles, features a wide variety of Latina/o-owned businesses. The barrio also features one of the nation's most prestigious Latina/o cultural arts centers, the Mexican Fine Arts Center Museum, which opened its doors in 1987 (*see* Cultural Centers). As in many Latina/o communities across the country, murals are a common sight in the neighborhood.

Chicago is also home to a substantial Puerto Rican population, which began migrating to the city in significant numbers in the 1950s and 1960s. By 2002, Puerto Ricans in Chicago numbered more than 150,000. The heart of that community is Paseo Boricúa, a seven-block stretch of Division Street between Western and California Streets. U.S. Congressman Luis Gutiérrez is among the city's most prominent Latina/o leaders.

Like other high-growth urban centers, Denver, Colorado, has been transformed by immigration from other states of computer and silicon industry and other white-collar workers. Descendants of the first pioneers and, later, migrant farmworkers originally settled the city's best-known Mexican American barrios. These include Baker on the north side of Denver's industrial factory belt; Cole on the city's east side near the former Stapleton International Airport; the La Alma/Lincoln Park section in the 11th and Osage area and home to West High School; and Rudy Park where the low-income Sun Valley housing projects are located. Denver's oldest slum barrio area, Larimer Street and its immediate environs, euphemistically called "LoDo" (lower downtown), is in the process of reclamation and gentrification. Among the newest emerging barrios is the Federal Street area, which has attracted thousands of new immigrants.

Denver was also another focal point of the 1960s Chicano Movement. Rodolfo "Corky" Gonzáles, a former boxer-turned-grassroots-political-activist, founded the Crusade for Justice in 1966. Gonzáles wrote the extremely popular epic poem and independent film *I Am Joaquín*, which has served as a manifesto of Chicano identity. The community has produced several major local Latina/o organizations, including the Latin American Research and Service Agency, Los Voluntarios, the Denver Service Club, Escuela Tlateloco, the Colorado Committee against Police Brutality, the grassroots theater company Su Teatro, the newspaper *La Voz*, and others.

Just as the word *barrio* has its roots in ancient Arabic culture transmitted to Spain and the Spanish language during the reign of the Moors, the origins of the contemporary use of the word *borderlands* dates back to such classic Mexican American studies as Américo Paredes's *With a Pistol in His Hand* (1958); Carey McWilliams's *North from México* (1968), Rudolfo Acuña's *Occupied America* (1972), with more recent feminist revisions and contributions on borderlands history and thinking from Gloria *Anzaldúa, Vicki Ruiz, Antonia Castañeda, Deena González, Emma Pérez, and Tey Diana Rebolledo, to name a few. These and other researchers greatly affected the thinking of the pathbreaking Chicana and Chicano scholars, artists, and other activists who conceptualize the borderlands as a geopolitical space on the hyphen between the United States and México and as a complex consciousness that engenders a linguistic and cultural mix. The ways that communities and individuals negotiate their identities and cultural expressions across generations and ground them in everyday activities and ceremonial life are inextricably bound to their geography.

Further Reading

Camarillo, Alberto. *Reflections on the Growth of Chicana/o History*. JSRI Occasional Paper #14. Julian Samora Research Institute. East Lansing: Michigan State University, 1999.

Devine, Dave. "Barrio Viejo, Barrio Nuevo." *Tucson Weekly Newspaper*, May 23, 2002.

Gonzales, Manuel G. *Mexicanos: A History of Mexicans in the United States*. Bloomington: Indiana University Press, 1999.

Guerrero, Lucio. "Paseo Boricúa." *Hispanic Magazine*. http://www.hispaniconline.com/magazine/2003/may/Cultura.

Gutiérrez, David G. *Walls and Mirrors: Mexican Americans and Mexican Immigrants and the Politics of Ethnicity*. Berkeley: University of California Press, 1995.

The Handbook of Texas Online. http://www.tsha.utexas.edu/handbook/online.

Haslip-Viera, Gabriel. "The Evolution of the Latino Community in New York City: Early Nineteenth Century to the Present." In *Latinos in New York: Communities in Transition*, edited by Gabriel Haslip-Viera and Sherrie L. Baver. South Bend, IN: University of Notre Dame Press, 1996.

James E. García, Cordelia Chávez Candelaria, and Arturo J. Aldama

Bauzá, Mario (1911–1993). Born in the Cayo Hueso district in Havana, Cuba, on April 28, 1911, Mario Bauzá was one of the outstanding musicians of the swing era and is often regarded as the man who invented *"Latin jazz," although he loathed the phrase. Many Latino musicians performed in African American swing bands of the period, but Bauzá was by far the most influential. Adopted and raised by his godparents and tutored by his godfather, Arturo Andrade, a voice teacher, Bauzá learned music quickly and debuted on clarinet with the Havana Philharmonic at age nine, then became a regular member at age twelve. Bauzá played bass clarinet, oboe, and other reeds and woodwinds until 1932 with various bands, including the Havana Philharmonic in Cuba, and he graduated from the Havana Municipal Conservatory of Music in 1927. He made a brief trip to New York City in 1926, with the orchestra of pianist/composer Antonio María Romeu, to play clarinet on *danzón recordings for RCA. While in New York, he heard live jazz in Harlem, although he had heard jazz recordings on Cuban radio and was inspired to learn to play the alto sax after hearing Paul Whiteman's band. He played saxophone for Noble Sissle's society band and Sam Wooding during 1931–1932 at the Central Park Hotel. Bauzá learned to play trumpet in just two weeks while in New York and made a recording with the Cuban singer Antonio Machin's Cuarteto Machin. Bauzá continued playing trumpet at the Savoy Ballroom with a band called Hi Clark and His Missourians before joining the Chick Webb band as lead trumpeter.

Around this time, in 1936, he returned to Cuba and married Stella Grillo and promised to bring her brother, Machito, to the United States, a promise he fulfilled two years later. In 1938, after five years of playing lead with Webb, Bauzá became musical director for the band and is recognized in part for the discovery of Ella Fitzgerald. He joined the Don Redman band and also played with Fletcher Henderson and Cab Calloway for a short period.

Bauzá is credited with persuading Calloway to hire Dizzy Gillespie (having previously failed to convince Webb to hire him).

In 1941, Bauzá joined the strongly Latin jazz band led by his brother-in-law *Machito. Bauzá played with Machito for the next thirty-five years, often performing with guest jazz greats including Charlie Parker, Cannonball Adderley, Joe Newman, Doc Cheatham, Howard McGhee, and Buddy Rich. As musical director and principal arranger for the Machito band, Bauzá oversaw numerous changes and artistic differences through the 1970s and the international popularity of *salsa. According to Bauzá, the blend of a Cuban rhythm section and repertoire with a trumpet and sax frontline that backed up powerful black swing vocalists took time to be accepted. Once the Latino sound caught on, Machito's band redefined the New York Latin music scene, whose practitioners previously had been white and society-club oriented, as a hot, progressive, black music. The new group opened at the Park Plaza, opposite Panai's Happy Boys, and later performed at the Beachcomber, on Broadway, in the 1950s. Later the band played at La Conga, on 53rd Street between Seventh Avenue and Broadway. Throughout his career, Bauzá included non-Latinos in his horn sections because he wanted jazz-oriented players, and there were few accomplished Latin brass musicians. Bauzá left Machito in 1976 but continued performing and directing his own band, the African-Cuban Jazz Orchestra, appearing regularly in New York. His albums in the 1990s for the Messidor label are some of his best recordings: *My Time Is Now* (1993); *944 Columbus* (1994); and *Messidor's Finest Volume One* (1997). Bauzá died on July 11, 1993, in New York City.

Further Reading

Clarke, Donald, ed. *The Penguin Encyclopedia of Popular Music*. 2nd ed. New York: Penguin Books, 1998.

Peter J. García

Bay of Pigs. The 1961 event known as the Bay of Pigs invasion marked a defining moment in U.S.-Cuba relations and the nature of *Cuban American identity and politics. Thus, any consideration of Latina and Latino popular culture in the United States must take the event into account, for it entered the public consciousness through widespread media coverage, political campaigns, and such pop culture forms as art, *folklore, literature, *film, and song. The invasion of Cuba by the United States took place during the week of April 13–19, 1961, with the land force landing at Playa Girón (the Bay of Pigs) on April 17. Made up of U.S. Central Intelligence Agency (CIA) advisers and Cuban immigrants who considered themselves "exiles" after the *Cuban Revolution, the invaders battled their way to Cuba's Central Highway, expecting to pick up broad support from the local population. Instead, they were met with determined resistance from seaside villagers who kept the CIA-led forces at bay until the Cuban Armed Forces could reach the beachhead. Pinned down by punishing artillery and air fire, the invaders held out until April 19. The expected reinforcements from U.S. military vessels never came, and approximately 100 Cuban American exiles died in the assault and another 1,400 were captured and marched to Havana for a televised trial. After eighteen months of imprisonment, the exiles were released and returned to the United States in exchange for $52,000 in medical, food, and other humanitarian supplies.

The origins of this milestone event in American and world political history go back to the reforms begun by Fidel *Castro's revolutionary government after the 1959 overthrow of U.S.-backed dictator Fulgencio Batista. Castro's assumption of power began a process of continually escalating hostilities with the United States. The vehement nationalism of the new Cuban government included the appropriation of American companies and properties, which prompted the termination of American imports of Cuban sugar. When Cuba requested American oil companies to refine Soviet petroleum, they refused, and Castro's reform government nationalized the refineries. To regain the trade that had been lost from the United States, Cuba opened relations with the USSR (the Soviet Union) in 1960. At first it sold only 10 percent of its sugar to the Soviets, but with the promise of more and larger markets in the future, the sugar exports increased. As a result of this free trade between the two nations, President Dwight D. Eisenhower severed diplomatic ties with Cuba in January 1961; retaining normal ties with the USSR however. With the Cold War raging, the United States would not accept anticapitalist defiance from any country in the Western Hemisphere.

Convinced that Fidel Castro was squarely in the Soviet Union's camp, Eisenhower directed the CIA, under the direction of Allen Dulles, to draw up Operation Zapata, whose aim was to topple Castro and to galvanize what the United States believed to be popular discontent in Cuba against the revolutionary government. Unfortunately, the CIA *over*estimated exile reports of the Cuban people's discontent and *under*estimated Castro's popularity and the weakness of resident opposition groups. These are some of the reasons that many historians think the plan was doomed with fatal flaws from the start.

As early as mid-1960, Cuban exiles had begun training in the Florida Everglades, Guatemala, and Nicaragua, but the plan did not become operational under Eisenhower. The invasion thus was delayed until after John F. Kennedy assumed the presidency in January 1961. Kennedy added a critical new element to the operation: that the United States and his administration not be seen as the instigators of the plot. Thus, strategic air support was withheld from the invasion, and American warships remained offshore, leaving the actual combat to the Cuban exiles. CIA advisers instructed 1,500 exiles in land assault deployment, radio operations, and air raid strikes. The plan was to strike Cuba's south shore east of Trinidad at Playa Girón and to let the world believe that the Cuban military was mutinying and the uprising was entirely the result of internal opposition to Castro. The 1,500 commandos hoped to incite a popular uprising and demonstrate the extent of

Castro's weakness. If Castro proved capable of turning back their assault, the United States promised to rescue the insurgents, and the CIA planners hoped that Kennedy would then commit sufficient U.S. troops to guarantee the overthrow of Castro's regime.

As the flaws of the operation were transparent, the U.S. press exposed American sponsorship of the Bay of Pigs invasion when the first aircraft, posing as a defecting Cuban air force fighter plane, landed in Miami. The phony Cuban insignia could not camouflage the markings of American identification, and the United States was thereby exposed as the architect and underwriter of the operation. On April 13, a bombing mission targeting Cuba's fighter planes was only partially completed, and its single pass had tipped Castro off that the invasion was about to begin. Although Castro did not know immediately where it would start, the advance notice gave him and the Cuban armed forces time to prepare for the attack when it began on April 17 at Playa Girón.

Ultimately the Bay of Pigs fiasco determined the futures of the two young presidents, as well as of the peoples of both nations. Because he did not commit U.S. troops to back up the invading Cuban exiles, Kennedy alienated many of the Cuban American community, who felt betrayed and blamed the betrayal on the Democratic Party. Similarly, because of the hostile action by the United States, Castro's stature was enhanced immeasurably both domestically and internationally. The majority of the Cuban people and much of the world cheered the small nation that had defied and defeated the American Goliath. Cubans found pride in their defiant national identity, and any internal resistance efforts to Castro and his reforms were silenced. Another result of the 1961 Bay of Pigs was that Castro aligned his government even closer to the Soviet Union, eventually permitting the placement of Soviet intercontinental ballistic missiles in Cuba, which provoked the Cuban missile crisis the following year.

The Bay of Pigs invasion defined U.S.-Cuba relations and the evolution of Cuban and Cuban American identities. The U.S. government support for the first wave of exiles produced among them a politically conservative, Republican tilt, while at the same time among progressives it generated further opposition to America's invasive foreign policy. With regard to Latina and Latino popular culture in the United States, the event entered the growing public discourse of and by Cubanos and joined the emergent 1960s lexicon as art, folklore, literature, film, media journalism, music, *sports, and other vital forms. The lingering bitterness resulting from the Bay of Pigs episode also was later to affect public perceptions of the *Marielito immigrants, the Elián *González case, the **Buena Vista Social Club*, and many other late-twentieth-century public events and entertainment celebrities.

Further Reading

Blight, James G., and Peter Kornbluh. *Politics of Illusions: The Bay of Pigs Reexamined*. Boulder, CO: Lynne Reiner, 1998.

Higgins, Trumbull. *The Perfect Failure: Kennedy, Eisenhower, and the CIA at the Bay of Pigs*. New York: Norton, 1987.

Kornbluh, Peter, ed. *Bay of Pigs Declassified: The Secret CIA Report on the Invasion of Cuba*. New York: New Press, 1998.
Rodríguez Cruz, Juan Carlos. *The Bay of Pigs and the CIA*. New York: Ocean Press, 1999.

K. Lynn Stoner

Berrios, Steve. (1945–1996). Born in Manhattan on April 12, 1945, Stephen Berrios Gelly is regarded as one of the most important percussionists in the New York Latina/o popular music scene. His *family left the *barrios of Guayama, Puerto Rico, in the late 1940s and settled in East Harlem. His father, Steve Sr., was a drummer who performed with many of the major Latino bands of the era, including Noro Morales, Miguelito Valdez, and Pupi Campo. Despite economic challenges, Steve was enrolled in trumpet classes in public school and began playing bugle at age eleven. He learned to play modern jazz from his father's records, which included Duke Ellington and Charlie Bird. Two of Berrios's earliest influences were Willie Bobo and Julio Collazo, the legendary master of batá drumming (*see* *Musical Instruments). Berrios learned percussion from Collazo, who also became his spiritual mentor in Santería, an Afro-Cuban spiritual practice. Berrios also studied formally with percussionists Cozy Cole and Willie Kessler but was inspired by the big band drummer Dave Tough, Cliff Leeman, Shadow Wilson, and Generoso Montesino. Berrios is credited with having a unique manner of keeping time and performing breaks through the fusion of Latin and jazz styles.

Berrios met pianist Larry Willis in high school, and the friends developed a lifelong collaboration. By age nineteen, Berrios had a steady gig with the Manhattan hotel band and later joined Mongo Santamaría's band, playing traps and timbales. He was a founding member of the Fort Apache Band in 1981 and remained an active member thereafter. Among percussionists, Berrios is regarded as a master drummer bridging Latin popular music and American jazz with over 300 recordings with greats like Tito *Puente, Paquito D'Rivera, Art Blakely, Max Roach, Michael Brecer, Grover Washington, Hilton Ruiz, and Miriam Makeba.

In 1995, with his newly formed group, Berrios recorded a CD of Santería-based music on Fantasy, *Son Bachéce*. He was also a longtime member of the Larry Willis Trio and recorded at Mapleshade on *Every Rung Goes Higher* (2001). In the late 1990s, Berrios retired from professional music. He died of cancer in New York City on November 11, 1996, but remains a major influence on Latina/o popular musicians.

Further Reading

http://www.mapleshaderecords.com/artists/steve_berrios.html.

Peter J. García

Black Legend. *See La Leyenda Negra.*

Blades, Rubén (1948–). Rubén Blades, an important crossover actor, *salsa musician, onetime presidential candidate in Panama, and a Harvard-trained lawyer, was born in 1948 in Panama City, Panama, to Rubén Dario Blades, Sr., and his wife Anoland Benita. At the age of fifteen, he made his first public appearance as a vocalist for his brother Luis's band, the Saints. He found he had a knack for music and began to write and perform his own songs. While he was gaining popularity in the music scene, he also attended the University of Panama, where he earned a degree in political science. His time at the university allowed him to hone his passion for politics. He left the Saints and moved to New York, where he joined the Willie *Colón combo. For the next five years, Blades toured and collaborated with Colón on several albums. He eventually broke away and created his own group called Seis del Solar. Blades gained notoriety for revolutionizing salsa with his distinctive sounds. His passion for social justice found its way into his music, which unfortunately put him at odds with most of the Latin pop radio stations in Miami because of the overtly political nature of his music. In 1980, his music was banned from many of the radio stations that had previously supported him.

His growing interest in politics led him to take a sabbatical from his music and attend Harvard Law School. While at school, he also got involved in acting and found it much to his liking. When he completed his schooling and returned to music in 1985, Blades continued a very succesful career, garnering six Grammy awards: three for Best Tropical Latin, *Excenas* (1986), *Antecedente* (1988), *La Rosa de los Vientos* (1996); one for Best Latin Pop, *Tiempos* (1999); one for Best World Music, *Mundo* (2002); and a 2003 Latin Grammy award for Best Contemporary Tropical Album, *Mundo*. A versatile artist, Blades also debuted in 1985 as the star of the *film *Crossover Dreams*. Over the next decade or so, Blades continued to hone his artistic skills by acting, writing screenplays, and composing and performing his music. His film acting credits include **The Milagro Beanfield War* (1988), *Disorganized Crime* (1989), *Mo' Better Blues* (1990), *Predator 2* (1990), and *The Two Jakes* (1990), as well as some TV movies such as *Dead Man Out* (1989) on HBO cable network, *The*

Rubén Blades. *Courtesy of Photofest.*

Josephine Baker Story (1990), and *Crazy from the Heart* (1991) on TNT. He won an Emmy Award for Best Actor for his role in *Dead Man Out* and received a nomination for his role in *The Josephine Baker Story.*

In the early 1990s Blades decided to enter politics. In an effort to break the cycle of dictatorial regime and corruption in Panama, he founded an independent party and launched a bid for the presidency in 1993. His fame as an international recording and film star helped him mount a strong fight, but in the end he lost to Ernesto Pérez-Balladares. Saddened by the loss, Blades was able to take solace in the fact that through his efforts the election marked the first time in twenty-six years that Panama did not vote under the shadow of a military dictatorship.

Further Reading

Hadley-Garcia, George. *Hispanic Hollywood: The Latins in Motion Pictures.* New York: Carol Publishing Group, 1993.

Keller, Gary D. *A Biographical Handbook of Hispanics and United States Film.* Tempe, AZ: Bilingual Press, 1997.

Alma Alvarez-Smith

Body Building. In the history of competitive body building, a handful of Latinos have left a memorable mark on the sport and continue to be celebrated. Arguably the first true icon of modern body building was *Cuban American Sergio Oliva, who became known as "the Myth" because of his success in developing his body for competition. The first black athlete to win the International Federation of Bodybuilding's Mr. America, Mr. World, Mr. Universe, and Mr. Olympia titles, Oliva was born in Havana, Cuba, on July 4, 1941. He admits that he used *sports as a means of escape from his country's repressive political system and seized an opportunity to do so as a member of the 1960 Cuban weight-lifting team competing at the Pan-American Games in Kingston, Jamaica. He managed to defect, requested political asylum, and immigrated to the United States. His accomplishments included lifting as much as 1,300 pounds in three Olympic lifts, developing an incredibly massive and proportioned frame despite the limited body-building technology of his era, and winning the most prestigious body-building title, the Olympia, three times. Finally defeated for the Olympia title in 1972, he lost to Arnold Schwarzenegger in a controversial victory that many body-building experts claim might have been racially motivated.

Another body-building star, Lee Labrada, was also born in Havana in 1957 and moved to the United States at the age of two. Labrada competed professionally from the late 1980s to the mid-1990s and is one of only four men in history to finish in one of the top four positions seven years in a row in the distinguished Mr. Olympia competition, a feat that has been equaled only by other legends of the sport (Lee Haney, Dorian Yates, and Arnold Schwarzenegger). Unlike Oliva, Labrada, at five feet six inches, did not become famous for a massive size but for the balanced symmetry, proportion, and muscularity of his physique. Labrada also distinguished himself as an entrepreneur by launching a dietary supplement company, Labrada Nutrition, which he runs as president and chief executive officer, making him a pioneer first Latino in the body-building nutritional foods industry.

Equally important as a pioneering first, Gladys Portuguese, a native of Portugal (date of birth unknown), is acknowledged to be a foremother of competitive body building. She helped pave the way for women's body building and for the rise of the now widely popular women's fitness movement. She first gained notice with her appearance in the 1985 *film *Pumping Iron II: The Women*, a film that altered popular perceptions of what a feminine look or female shape could or should be. Her exotic "dark lady" looks, tone, and feminine physique explain her frequently being confused for a Latina, a marketable appearance that also landed her top modeling jobs for the Weider body-building empire, as well as mainstream women's publications such as *Self*, *Cosmopolitan*, and *Ms. Magazine*. Her muscular but small-framed body appealed to mainstream tastes and traditional concepts of beauty, offering a threshold to publish two books on women's weight training for "shaping perfect proportions" as opposed to hardcore body building. Following the groundbreaking trail of Oliva, Labrada, and Portuguese, a new generation of Latino/a body builders continues making strides in the sport by winning competitions, as well as by being accepted as marketable product endorsers and models in major body-building publications. Two Puerto Rican American brothers, Tito and José Raymond, are gaining international prominence by dominating both the natural and non-drug-tested body-building competition stages.

Further Reading

Webster, David. *Body Building: An Illustrated History*. New York: Arco Publishers, 1982.

Fernando A. Orejuela

Bolero. A bolero is a slow, romantic, and sentimental type of music popular in México and the Caribbean and is characterized by a compound quadruple meter and a habanera rhythm played by the bass instrument. Boleros occupy a prominent place in *mariachi and *tejano repertoires. Originating from the Caribbean, the genre was diffused throughout North and South America in the 1940s and 1950s, mainly through Mexican *films. Agustín Lara, Guty Cadenas, and Juan Gabriel are among the better-known Mexican composers of boleros.

Further Reading

Montaño, Mary. *Tradiciones nuevomexicanas: Hispano Arts and Culture of New Mexico*. Albuquerque: University of New Mexico Press, 2001.

Peter J. García

Bomba. Bomba is an Afro–Puerto Rican music and dance genre with strong cultural connections to other Caribbean genres that are similarly rooted in

Central and West African music and dance traditions. Like many African-derived traditions in the Caribbean, bomba performances incorporate percussion, singing, and dancing, but what is most characteristic of bomba is the dancer's challenge to the lead drummer, who must attempt to synchronize the beat with the dancer's every movement. While bomba today is a vital part of Afro–Puerto Rican community traditions in both Puerto Rico and New York City, it has also been an important musical antecedent of other popular dance musics, including Afro–Puerto Rican *plena, the pan-Carribean genre of *salsa, and even Spanish-language *hip-hop.

Bomba originated possibly as early as the 1600s in Puerto Rico's coastal areas where populations of African descent were concentrated. Bomba was an important communitywide event that would have been performed on many special occasions, including at Catholic saint festivals, end of harvest celebrations, *weddings, christenings, and so on. While some scholars link bomba's origins to the west coast of African (even to a specific Ashanti royal dance dating from the seventeenth century), others have noted the retention of Congolese-style footwork in bomba dancing. Bomba's common cultural link to many other African diasporic traditions in the Caribbean (e.g., Cuban conga, Haitian kongo, Antillean bamboula) was further enhanced by the ongoing *immigration into Puerto Rico of African slaves and freedmen from neighboring islands, particularly from the French Caribbean. Many of the migrants' different drumming, dancing, and singing genres were absorbed into bomba performance (e.g., scholars have evidence of bomba's incorporation of tumbao from Curaçao and vodou from Haiti). Common rhythm patterns and names used in bomba today indicate this shared heritage between Caribbean islands.

Since slavery was not abolished in Puerto Rico until 1873, bomba events served not simply as diversions or to continue veiled African-derived ritual practices, but they also served as important occasions for slaves to gather together and plan uprisings. Government reports from the 1800s show that bomba dances occasionally led to slaves setting sugar cane fields on fire and escaping. For this reason, bomba events were restricted and regulated to minimize the potential that they might lead their enslaved participants to rebellion.

Bomba performances consist of at least two drummers playing conical-shaped drums that traditionally were fabricated out of discarded barrels and covered with a goatskin head secured by pegs. These drums, alternately called *barril* (barrel/cask) or "bomba," were pitched high and low. The lower-pitched bomba, called *buleador* or *sonador* (noisemaker), carries the basic rhythm pattern without variation. The higher-pitched bomba, called *subidor* (bright or strong one) or *repicador* (ringing one), is played by the lead drummer, who improvises rhythms to accompany the movements of the solo dancer. The bomba drums are played with the bare hands as the drums are held upright between the drummer's knees. Other percussion parts may be played by beating *el cuá*—two wooden sticks—on the side of one of the bomba drums, or on a hollow wooden tube, and the lead singer usually plays a *maraca*, a large gourd rattle. There are three main categories of rhythms—*sicá*, *holandés* (Dutch), and *yubá*. The first two are in duple meter (i.e., two-beat groups); the third is in 6/8 (i.e., two three-beat groups). Within each of the categories there are a number of rhythm patterns, called *seises* (literally, sixes) or **sones* (literally, sounds). The *sicá* has the most *sones* (more than twelve different variations) and is the most well known to *salseros* (salsa musicians). Since the *sicá* pattern is the best-known basic bomba rhythm, often *sicá* is simply referred to as "bomba" by *salseros*.

In a street performance context, the drummers are seated and flanked by a large circle of participants who may variously look on, sing, and/or dance. A lead singer typically stands by the drummers and begins by singing the refrain of the song. When the group circled around the drummers begins singing the refrain, the drummers begin to play one of the basic *sones*—rhythms—that accompanies the song. Singing occurs in a call-and-response form: the lead singer sings a verse alone, then is responded to by the larger group singing the fixed refrain. After the soloist has sung a couple of the song's standard verses, she or he can improvise new lyrics and include nonsensical vocables that could allow the solo singer to emphasize the rhythm of the drums and possibly even respond to a dancer's improvised dance movements.

The group flanking the drummers also participates by dancing subtly in place. During the song, dancers will take turns approaching the drummers to dance in the middle of the circle in front of the *subidor* player. When the solo dancer has the drummer's attention, she or he will begin to dance more complicated figures, and the *subidor* player will follow and play a rhythmic approximation of the dancer's improvised movements. The dancer becomes like an orchestra conductor, directing changes in the music through use of gestures. The dancer's movements are a challenge to the drummer to see if he can follow the dancer's improvisations. Even though bomba drummers are typically male, through the influence of their dance, female dancers play an important role in musical creation. During these improvised sections, absolute synchronicity between dancer and drummer is not expected; instead, the beauty of the coordination between the dancer and the drummer is assessed according to how good the dancer's movements make the music sound. The sound of the bomba music is therefore inseparable from the dance. When a dancer's performance is exceptionally inspired, the *subidor* drummer will salute the dancer by tilting his drum onto its side.

Between the incorporation of Puerto Rico into the United States as a commonwealth nation (i.e., colony of the United States) in 1898 and the formation of the Institute of Puerto Rican Culture in 1953, bomba had sufficiently disappeared in its traditional format that it was declared officially to be "folkloric." This decline may be due in part to a persistent social stigma against cultural traditions of African origin that would have caused upwardly mobile Afro–Puerto Ricans to shun bomba. Only in the town of Loíza Aldea did bomba have a continuous tradition of performance; there it was integral to community celebrations such as the annual festival for the patron saint St. James the Apostle. Folkloric versions of bomba were strongly influenced by the Cepeda *family, who set a standard for professionalized, staged bomba performance. The Cepedas also opened a school in Santurce, Puerto Rico, which has been an important place for formal education in bomba performance. Currently run by the founder's eldest son, Modesto Cepeda, classes at La Escuela de Bomba y Plena Don Rafael Cepeda (Don Rafael Cepeda's Bomba and Plena School) are attended primarily by children and youth. In many folkloric presentations of bomba, the performances are highly choreographed, so that what traditionally was an improvisatory dialogue between the *subidor* drummer and solo dancer became predictable and scripted. As well, the staged folkloric performances created boundaries between the audience and performers, inhibiting the traditional interaction and active participation of the "audience."

Bomba rhythms were also carried into commercial music contexts and incorporated in pan-Latin popular music styles. In 1957, the Puerto Rican popular music composer and bandleader Rafael Cortijo brought bomba into a dance band format by using instrumentation typical of jazz orchestras. Cortijo, who came from the town Loíza Aldea, had two especially successful recordings of bomba with singer Ismael Rivera; these were "El Bombón de Elena" (Elena's Chocolate) and "Caballero que Bomba" (Gentleman Who Dances Bomba). In 1974, Cortijo's album *Maquina de Tiempo* (Time Machine) was marketed under the genre label of "salsa." This album is one of the most imaginative *Latin jazz fusions to have been recorded, combining the more Hispanic folk *aguinaldo* (Christmas carol) and Cuban *guaracha* with the more strongly African-derived bomba and plena. Although the album was not a commercial success, its experimental blend of contemporary jazz styles with folk and popular music idioms give the album a notable place in Puerto Rican and salsa music history.

In 1983, the New York–based Puerto Rican group Los Pleneros de la 21 (The Plena Musicians of [Bus Stop] 21) formed, and they included bombas along with their repertoire of plenas. Their 1995 recording *Somos Boricuas* (We Are Puerto Rican) includes two bombas, each of which has both a more traditional section (with only voices and percussion) as well as a section played with melodic and harmonic instruments (like string base, acoustic guitar, and keyboard). More recently, one of Los Pleneros de la 21's lead singers, José Rivera, formed a new band with his brother Ramón, named Amigos de la Plena (Friends of Plena), that blends bomba and plena rhythms with Hispanic–Puerto Rican genres like *seis* and *aguinaldo* and pan-Latin genres like *merengue, salsa, and rap. Their music has been promoted on *Spanish-language radio and television in the New York City area. Yet another band, Viento de Agua (Wind from Water), formed in 1998. Their repertoire consists of fusions of jazz, salsa, rock, and *nueva canción* (literally, new song, a hybrid genre with socially conscious lyrics) with bomba and plena. Their recording *De Puerto Rico al Mundo* (From Puerto Rico to the World, 1998) was a commercial success both in the United States and on the island.

Several highly active bomba musicians and sponsors have also contributed to the revival of bomba in the late twentieth century. In the United States, members of the band Los Pleneros de la 21 run a nonprofit cultural center called the Rincón Criollo (Creole Corner) in the South Bronx, which hosts concerts, community events, and bomba workshops in conjunction with Roberta Singer of City Lore. Important figures in Puerto Rico include the Ayala brothers who have actively performed and hosted bomba events in Loíza Aldea since the 1960s; more recently in the 1990s, Yamil Rios and Juan Usera organized a number of bomba events, which inspired the Cepeda and the Emmanuelli families to host, as in the olden days, informal bomba gatherings. Unlike staged folkloric presentations, these *bombazos*—bomba events—were held in more traditional settings in community centers or on the streets. In 1998 and 1999, bimonthly *bombazos* were being held in the greater San Juan area, and bomba dancing was entering Puerto Rican dance clubs and for the first time ever. Today, *bombazos* can involve more than 500 participants. Since it is impossible for all spectators to be a part of the dance circle at these events, images of dancers soloing in front of the drummers are projected onto large screens for everyone to see. The music has also been adapted into lengthy, continuous suites with no break between individual songs. Once the medley of songs has cycled through the three main rhythm families, the *bombazo* is completed.

Halbert Barton, one of the foremost researchers of contemporary bomba traditions in Puerto Rico, claims that "bomba has provided the foundation, or template, on which Puerto Rican music and dance continue to evolve." Bomba's influence on genres like plena and salsa has been well documented. But many young Puerto Ricans, both in the United States as well as on the island, are not aware of the similarities between bomba and hip-hop—a genre in which Nuyoricans (New York Puerto Ricans) have participated since its beginning in the 1970s. In a 1994 event hosted at Hunter College in New York City, José Rivera of the group Los Pleneros de la 21 described to the audience of young Nuyoricans gathered there the rhythmic resemblances between bomba and hip-hop and the similar experiences of bomba and hip-hop listeners and performers as marginalized, poor, migrant laborers, who—though excluded from so-called mainstream society—express their cultural identity through community performances. Puerto Rican hip-hop also draws upon the poetic language and rhythmic cadences of antecedent song genres like bomba. Some of Puerto Rico's and the United States' top bomba performers, the Emmanuelli brothers, have strong backgrounds in hip-hop and breakdancing. These performers have moved back and forth between New York City and their hometown of Carolina, Puerto Rico, throughout their formative years.

Throughout the twentieth century, bomba musicians like the Emmanuelli brothers, out of economic necessity, often performed other Puerto Rican and pan-Latin popular music genres. These musicians may have brought their knowledge of bomba to those musical engagements, but conversely, they brought rhythms from those other genres back into bomba as well. While some denounce the introduction of popular *Latin rhythms into bomba as an adulteration of tradition, bomba seems to be retaining its original character of accommodating foreign traditions, gleaning influences from the same popular Latin music genres to which it continues contributing. As a result, bomba today is a culturally relevant and thriving tradition in New York City as in Puerto Rico.

Further Reading

Barton, Halbert. "The Challenges of Puerto Rican Bomba." In *Caribbean Dance from Abakuá to Zouk: How Movement Shapes Identity*, edited by Susanna Sloat. Gainesville: University Press of Florida, 2002. 183–198.

Concepción, Alma. "Dance in Puerto Rico: Embodied Meanings." In *Caribbean Dance from Abakuá to Zouk: How Movement Shapes Identity*, edited by Susanna Sloat. Gainesville: University Press of Florida, 2002. 165–175.

Duany, Jorge. "Popular Music in Puerto Rico: Toward an Anthropology of Salsa." In *Salsiology: Afro-Cuban Music and the Evolution of Salsa in New York City*, edited by Vernon Boggs. Westport, CT: Greenwood Press, 1992. 69–89.

Flores, Juan. *From Bomba to Hip-Hop: Puerto Rican Culture and Latino Identity*. New York: Columbia University Press, 2000.

Thompson, Donald. "Puerto Rico." In *New Grove Dictionary of Music and Musicians*, edited by Stanley Sadie. 2nd ed. New York: Grove's Dictionaries, 2001. 583–587.

Vega Drouet, Héctor. "Historical and Ethnological Survey on Probable African Origins of the Puerto Rican Bomba, Including a Description of Santiago Apostol." Ph.D. dissertation, Wesleyan University, 1979.

Vega Drouet, Héctor. "Puerto Rico." In *The Garland Encyclopedia of World Music*, edited by Dale Olsen and Daniel Sheehy. New York: Garland, 1998. 2: 932–941.

Rebecca Sager and Peter J. García

Boricúa, Borinqueño. Boricúa refers to an aboriginal name for the West Indies island of Puerto Rico. Originally inhabited by the native peoples who self-identified as Arawak and who spoke the Taíno language, Boricúa was reclaimed by Puerto Rican activists, artists, writers, and other cultural workers as a unifying symbol of pride and decolonized nationhood in the 1960s and 1970s. By extension, Borinqueño (or, when writing in English, Borinquen) refers to a politically aware Puerto Rican or to ideas and practices that are consciously resistant of the Spanish and U.S. colonialist aspects of Puerto Rico's past. Comparable to the aboriginal myth, cultural metaphor, and political symbol of *Aztlán recovered during the *Chicano Movement, Boricúa is used to emphasize the plural Antillean past of Puerto Rico that is simultaneously indigenous Arawak/Taíno, Spanish conquistador and colonialist,

African slave, and Anglo-American conqueror and occupier. All make a claim on the Puerto Rican/Nuyorican imagination and the Borinquen metaphor allows for a reevaluation of the multiplicity of African, indigenous Caribbean, and even Asian sources of the Puerto Rican material and popular culture realities.

Further Reading

Klor de Alva, Jorge. "Aztlán, Borinquen, and Hispanic Nationalism in the United States." In *Aztlán: Essays on the Chicano Homeland*, edited by Rudolfo A. Anaya and Francisco Lomelí. Albuquerque: University of New Mexico Press, 1991.

Cordelia Chávez Candelaria

"Borinqueña, La." *See* "La Borinqueña."

Born in East L.A. A comedic feature directed by *Chicano comedic actor Cheech *Marín, *Born in East L.A.* was first conceived as a music-video parody of Bruce Springsteen's "Born in the USA," which recasts the lyrics into a story about a Chicano born in the United States who is mistaken as an "illegal alien" and deported to México. In the 1987 full-length *film, the main story line follows Rudy Robles (played by Marín), a Chicano auto mechanic in East Los Angeles who is swept up in an *immigration raid at a local factory but cannot prove his citizenship status because he forgot his wallet. The immigration officers ignore his claims that he "was born in East L.A." and deport him to México. The remainder of the film follows Rudy's travails as he attempts to get back across the border. Through a blend of biting humor and pathos, *Born in East L.A.* sheds light on the issues that Chicanos and Mexican immigrants negotiate both on institutional and daily levels such as racism, biased media perceptions, and unlawful deportations. The film also looks at how Chicanos occupy a cultural border between México and the United States, where they are perceived as foreigners by both México and the United States, a condition that is popularized by the common saying, "Ni de aca, ni de allí" (Neither from here nor from there) in the *barrios and borderlands of experience.

Further Reading

Fregoso, Rosa Linda. *The Bronze Screen: Chicana and Chicano Film Culture*. Minneapolis: University of Minnesota Press, 1993.

Darren Crovitz

Bossa Nova. The bossa nova is a Brazilian musical form developed in Rio de Janeiro in the late 1950s that achieved international popularity for a short time, especially in the United States and in Europe. The term first appeared in 1958 in a newssheet about a concert at the Grupo Universitário Hebraico, although the word *bossa* was used by Brazilian musicians to describe anyone who was different. Musically, bossa nova is a fusion of cool jazz stylistic elements from the West Coast of the United States and of other pop records with Brazilian *salsa rhythms, particularly the *baião*. Often mistaken as Afro-Brazilian, it is sophisticated, developing out of the Brazilian's need to diversify *samba rhythms and also as a reaction against the popular accordion, which had long dominated Brazilian popular music.

The emergence of new songwriters, notably Tom Jobim and the lyricists Vinícius de Moraes and Newton Mendonca, led to the classic bossa nova sound such as that found in the 1958 hit "Chega de Saudade" (That's Enough Nostalgia) by Jobim and Moraes. It was included on an album of the same title in 1958 by Joáo Gilberto. Most bossa nova musicians were white, although Bola Sete (born Djalma de Andrade in Rio), a leading bossa nova guitarist, is an exception. He came to the United States in 1959 and played at the Monterey Jazz Festival with Dizzy Gillespie and produced several original albums with Vince Guaraldi as well as percussionist *Airto (Moreira) and his wife, vocalist Flora Purim. They are among the musicians who introduced Brazilian music to the West Coast. The 1950s hit "The Girl from Ipanema," featuring tenor saxophonist Stan Getz, is another bestselling bossa nova tune, which remains popular today.

Further Reading

Fryer, Peter. *Rhythms of Resistance: African Musical Heritage in Brazil*. London: Pluto Press, 2000.

Perrone, Charles. *Masters of Contemporary Brazilian Song*. Austin: University of Texas Press, 1989.

Perrone, Charles, and Christopher Dunn. *Brazilian Popular Music & Globalization*. Miami: University Press of Florida, 2001.

Vivianna, Hermano. *The Mystery of Samba: Popular Music and National Identity in Brazil*. Charlotte: University of North Carolina Press, 1999.

Peter J. García

Bound by Honor. *Bound by Honor* (1993), a visually powerful and violently raw *film, contributes to the growing genre of films set in East Los Angeles that focus on issues of racism, poverty, violence, *la vida loca* (the crazy life), machismo, brotherhood, and families in the *Chicano community. Directed by Taylor Hackford, *Bound* is a three-hour-long epic story of two Chicano half brothers, Paco (Benjamin *Bratt) and Cruz (Jesse Borrego) and their mixed Anglo-Mexican cousin, Miklos (Damian Chapa), who grow up together in the early 1970s. Paco channels his deep resentment and anger toward the world into a career of law enforcement. After a violent episode that leaves Cruz crippled, he decides to turn to art, hoping to be able to protest racial injustice and paint his way out of the ghetto. The light-skinned (*güero*) Miklos ekes out a place in the Chicano mafia in his zeal to prove his Chicano identity. Paco's career leads to many moments of self-reflection and contradiction—he's incarcerating his own people; Cruz's path leads to self-hatred and drug addiction; Miklos ends up serving time in the state penitentiary.

As the film comes to a close and a *gang war of apocalyptic dimension ensues, the three characters must come to terms with one another's chosen destiny. Director Taylor Hackford chooses to end this visceral detailing of young lives lost in a racist America—where the only options seem to be either to join the armed forces or to join gangs—with a message that affirms the power of reconciliation and strength of community. Moreover, as the film strongly suggests, it is art—film, painting, poetry, fiction—created by those at the social and racial margins that might be able to show us a more harmonious way of coexisting in the world. The film, distributed by Buena Vista Home Entertainment, was produced by Taylor Hackford, Jerry Gershwin, and Jimmy Santiago *Baca, who cowrote the screenplay with Floyd Mutrux. The cast also includes Delroy Lindo and Billy Bob Thornton.

Further Reading

Keller, Gary D. *A Biographical Handbook of Hispanics and United States Film.* Tempe, AZ: Bilingual Press, 1997.

Frederick Luis Aldama

Bracero Program. The Bracero Program, also known as Public Law 45, was a government-sponsored labor program created and implemented jointly by the U.S. and Mexican governments to alleviate the World War II–induced labor shortage in the United States through a managed migration of Mexican workers on a temporary basis. Launched in 1942 during the Franklin D. Roosevelt administration, the program allowed Mexican laborers to come into the United States to work, usually in the agricultural arena, although work sometimes spread to the railroad industry.

Mexican workers were not new to the United States, especially considering that until 1850 the territory that is now Texas, New Mexico, Arizona, and California was actually part of México. Much of the labor in that territory was traditionally performed first by Chinese, then by Japanese, followed by Filipinos and eventually by Mexicans. With the devastation caused by the Mexican Revolution in 1910, unemployment rose in México, leading workers to seek employment in the United States under a variety of auspices resembling the Bracero Program. Travel back and forth across the border was not an issue until 1924 when the Border Patrol was founded, and it became illegal to cross the border without the proper authorization.

In 1942, when many of the men in the United States left to fight in World War II, the United States looked to México for help with the labor shortage, and the Bracero Program was born. The name comes from the Spanish word *brazo*, which means "arm." The men who participated in the Bracero Program migrated from all parts of México to the northern border, where they were screened and selected for jobs in the United States. Many were highly skilled agricultural workers, ranch hands, and miners who found this to be the only alternative to continue to provide for their families. If they passed the screening, they were asked to sign a contract, which laid out the rules and regulations of the program, but since the contracts were in English, most of them did not understand what they were signing. The contracts stipulated working conditions, such as housing, wages, health, and food, although once the *braceros* were in the United States, they were at the mercy of their new employers. Pleased to benefit from the labor and rewards of increased production, the employers welcomed the *braceros*, but racial discrimination and greed abounded, forcing the workers to endure inadequate housing, low wages, long hours, and unfamiliar food.

Despite the drawbacks of the program, *braceros* considered it an improvement over the unemployment situation in México, so they continued to come to the United States in droves. Numbers vary by source, but by most accounts, they arrived annually by the thousands; and at the peak of the program in the late 1950s, the numbers had crept to almost half a million a year. All totaled, it is estimated that approximately 5 million *braceros* participated in the program during its existence, which underwent several iterations and is being discussed in 2004 as a policy option.

Public Law 40, signed by the U.S. Congress in 1947, dictated that the Bracero Program should cease to exist on December 31, 1947, and the *braceros* had to return to México by January 30, 1948. Farmers, faced with the reality that they still needed the labor provided by the *braceros*, turned to their congressmen for assistance and were successful in extending the program through informal agreements until 1951, when the program was reintroduced as Public Law 78, which was renewed every two years until the program officially ended in 1964 when the U.S. economy lagged.

Further Reading

Calavita, Kitty. *Inside the State: The Bracero Program, Immigration, and the I.N.S.* New York: Routledge, 1992.

García, Juan Ramon. *Operation Wetback: The Mass Deportation of Mexican Undocumented Workers in 1954*. Westport, CT: Greenwood Press, 1980.

Gonzales, Manuel G. *Mexicanos: A History of Mexicans in the United States*. Bloomington: Indiana University Press, 1999.

http://www.farmworkers.org.

Alma Alvarez-Smith

Braga, Sonia (1950–). Sonia Braga, a Latina icon in *film and television in the United States and Latin America, was born on June 16, 1950, in Maringá, Paraná, Brazil. At age nineteen, Braga began acting in Brazilian films and *telenovelas* (soap operas), quickly rising to become a major star in her native country. She came to international attention for her portrayal of the title character in *Doña Flor and Her Two Husbands* (1976). Roles in English-language feature films quickly followed. She received Golden Globe nominations for Best Supporting Actress for her work in Hector Babenco's **Kiss*

Sonia Braga. *Courtesy of Photofest.*

of the Spider Woman (1985) and Paul Mazursky's *Moon over Parador* (1988). Among the over twenty films that she has starred in are *The *Milagro Beanfield War* (1988), *The Rookie* (1990), and *Angel Eyes* (2001). She received a Golden Globe nomination in 1994 for Best Actress in a Supporting Role for her work in the American miniseries *The Burning Season*. She was also cast in the PBS drama *American Family* and has appeared in the HBO award-winning hit *Sex and the City*.

Further Reading

Hadley-Garcia, George. *Hispanic Hollywood: The Latins in Motion Pictures*. New York: Carol Publishing Group, 1993.

Keller, Gary D. *A Biographical Handbook of Hispanics and United States Film*. Tempe, AZ: Bilingual Press, 1997.

William Orchard

Bratt, Benjamin (1963–). Award-winning television and *film actor and advocate for Latino and indigenous rights in the Americas, Benjamin Bratt was born to a Quecha-Peruvian mother and a father of German and English descent in San Francisco, California, on December 16, 1963. He graduated in 1986 with his B.F.A. from the University of California at Santa Barbara. Afterward, he attended classes in the master's program at the American Conservatory Theater in San Francisco. Bratt is not the only member of his *family to be drawn to the world of entertainment; his grandfather, George Bratt, was a Broadway actor, and his brother Peter Bratt works as a director. In fact, Peter and Benjamin collaborated together on the 1996 independent movie *Follow Me Home*, a movie about *Chicano and American Indian artists on a road trip to repaint the White House with colors more appropriate to the ethnic diversity of America. Although Bratt's acting career began at the Utah Shakespeare Festival, the first role to bring him widespread public acclaim was as Detective Reynaldo Curtis, whom he played from 1995 to 1999, on the NBC television show *Law and Order*. Bratt's belief that he has a responsibility as a Latino actor to be involved in movies that celebrate Latino culture or that explore the relationship of Hispanic culture to mainstream American culture underlies his participation in such films as **Piñero* (2001), in which he plays the lead role of poet and playwright Miguel Piñero; director Steven Soderbergh's movie **Traffic* (2000), which portrays U.S.-Mexican relations as mediated by aspects of the drug trade; and a movie about Chicano *gang culture, **Bound by Honor/Blood In, Blood Out* (1993).

Other films in which he has played a significant role include: *Chains of Gold* (1991), *Demolition Man* (1993), *Clear and Present Danger* (1994), *The River Wild* (1994), *The Last Producer* (2000), *Miss Congeniality* (2000), *The Next Best Thing* (2000), *Red Planet* (2000), *After the Storm* (2001), and *Abandon* (2002).

While working on the *Piñero* film, Bratt met and fell in love with Talisa Soto, who appeared in the movie as Piñero's girlfriend Sugar. They married in April 2002 and announced the arrival of their first baby daughter, Sophia Rosalinda, in December 2002.

Benjamin Bratt. *Courtesy of Photofest.*

Further Reading

The Advocate. March 5, 2002.
St. James Encyclopedia of Popular Culture. Farmington Hills, MI: Gale Group, 2002.
http://www.eonline.com/Facts/People/0,12,25022,00.html.
http://www.imdb.com/Name?Bratt,+Benjamin.

Lynn Marie Houston

Brazilian Popular Music in the United States. Brazilian popular musics are beloved internationally and recognized as having had a profound cultural impact, especially on the "browning" of U.S. society. As a very broad music genre including several diverse styles, artists, instruments, and recordings, Brazilian music has entertained, informed, and influenced musical audiences and performers both Brazilian and non-Brazilian about Latina/o cultures, aesthetics, nationalism, and the Portuguese language inside the United States and throughout Latin America. Several popular subcategories include *Latin jazz, bossa jazz, and *samba, to mention a few. Brazilian music generally includes a cultural mixture of African, Portuguese, and North American roots. The most striking is the African rhythm and percussion.

When the Portuguese discovered Brazil in the 1500s, they quickly began to colonize it. They used African slave labor as a means of farming and finding gold and other precious metals. The slaves worked in mines, on sugar cane plantations, in sugar mills, and on coffee plantations. When slavery was abolished in 1888, there were so many blacks who stayed in Brazil and established themselves that today Brazil remains the second largest population of African descent in the world. The slaves fused African rhythms and Portuguese language, melody, and harmony to create hybrid styles of Brazilian music.

There are several different types of Brazilian music including: samba, *axé*, *bossa nova, *choro*, *forró*, *tropicalia*, lambada, and *sertanejo*, along with many different folkloric variations. Brazilian music reflects religious events and *holidays throughout the year. Many Brazilians knew the samba as a religious ceremony with music so intertwined with dance and religion that the three were seldom separated. The samba is most popular in Rio de Janeiro during the pre-Lenten ritual ceremonies known as Carnaval. The roots of the samba may be heard in the *batuque*, a type of Afro-Brazilian music that was predominantly composed of percussion, rhythm, and street dancing. After the eradication of slavery in 1888, the samba gained popularity with the now-freed slaves. Although the rhythmic roots of samba date back to African tribes and throughout colonial times during Carnaval, in 1917 the recording "Pelo telefone" (On the Telephone) was the first *samba canção* to actually be regarded as a genuinely Brazilian samba. The golden age of samba occurred during the commodification of Carnaval season and increased popularity through the advent of commercial recordings, radio, and media during the 1930s to 1950s. The samba was beginning to gain acceptance in regions other than that of the *favelas* (shantytowns, ghettos), which were densely populated with poor Afro-Brazilian descendants. *Escolas da samba*, or samba schools, were beginning to gain popularity everywhere. These schools stylized choreographed routines and competed during Carnaval.

Although there were several excellent *sambistas* (samba singers and musicians) of the time, such as Elza Soares, who was considered to be the Queen of Samba in Brazil, the 1930s was the era of another Brazilian bombshell better known as Carmen *Miranda—"The Lady in the Tutti Fruitti Hat," a persona better known among North Americans. Although Brazilians had mixed feelings about Carmen becoming Americanized, North Americans adored her flamboyant and eroticized temperament. Today Carmen Miranda is the inspiration behind the Chiquita banana logo, and the samba is known as a national treasure of Brazil.

Forró music originated in the northeast region of Brazil. *Pagode* entertainment, or informal ball music, incorporated the harmonica, accordion, and the *zabumba* (African drum). This form of music was often called *baião*. This was the frontier music of Brazil.

Choro music was the precursor to Brazilian jazz and bossa nova. *Choro* bands began to emerge as early as the 1870s in Brazil but did not become very popular until after the abolition of slavery. *Choro* music became most popular in Brazil during the 1920s but also made its mark on serious art music by Brazilians, especially by nationalist composer Heitor Villa-Lobos. This type of music was often heard in the small cafés and bistros in Rio de Janeiro and is very similar to that of the traditional New Orleans jazz better known as ragtime. *Choro* music is composed by playing the ukulele or guitar and percussion and is accompanied by a recorder, flute, or a clarinet. This style of music came about when musicians began to bring elements from several different cultures into one type of music. Although the *choro* has little similarity to bossa novas and sambas, it is more similar to European classical music. This was the Brazilian rendition of ballroom dancing, much like waltzes. *Choro* music is mainly instrumental rather than vocal and held strong in Brazil until about the 1950s. The music began to fall out of fashion when bossa nova became popular. For a short time in the 1970s a revival occurred, and the music once again came alive. *Choro* music can still be heard in Brazil today.

The bossa nova came into popularity during the time that *choro* music was very stylish. The bossa nova was a fusion of Brazilian rhythm with American cool-jazz. The lyrics seemed to be more poetic, sung in a soft, sensual voice, which made for a more soothing sound of music. This type of music became popular with the middle class, which was mostly composed of university-educated, urbanized citizens of Brazil. The fusion of samba and jazz created a huge following in both Brazil and the United States. The most popular bossa nova of all time was composer Antônio Carlos Jobim. He was better known as Tom Jobim, and his song was called "Garota do Ipanema" (The Girl from Ipanema). In the United States, Frank Sinatra was so intrigued with the song that he recorded his own rendition of it in 1967. Today the Brazilian sounds of bossa nova are still prevalent in jazz music being played in both Brazil and the United States.

Tropicalia music mixes all kinds of music. This musical genre was a type of pop Brazilian music that encouraged social awareness and creativity. *Tropicalia* music per se lasted only a few years; today, expanded, it is known as *música popular brasileira* (MPB, popular music in Brazil).

"MPB" now describes the popular urbanized music of Brazil. *Tropicalia*, Brazilian rock, and Brazilian pop all fall under the MPB category. Though there are several other styles and genres that fall under MPB, the MPB category is more defined by use of electric instruments and is a way of categorizing the music of the post–bossa nova movement in Brazil.

One of the more recent music crazes in Brazil is the lambada. This music, which originated in Belém, was created as a variation of *forró* and another type of music called *carimbó*. *Carimbó* is the dance music in the Belém region, which is located at the mouth of the Amazon River. This music was mixed with *salsa, *merengue, and reggae, inspiring a style of dance that caught on in the United States during the 1980s.

Other notable music and dance styles are *axé*, which was derived in Bahia and mixes reggae, rock, salsa, samba, merengue, and lambada; *bumba-meu-boi*, which is song and dance that tells the story of the death and resurrection of an ox; *caboclinhos*, which is an indigenous folk dance found in the northeast of Brazil; *congada*, which is a folk dance of African origins; *lundu*, which is a sensuous dance of couples brought by the Bantu tribes of Africa; *fado*, similar to the *lundu*, which is a Portuguese song and dance; *fricote*, which is a danceable mix of samba, reggae, and salsa with the beats of African percussion; *moda de viola*, which is a rural song; *pregãos*, which are the songs or cries of the street vendors; *maxixe*, which is a form of urban dance that originated in Rio de Janeiro; *fandagos, which are adult round dances; *quadrilha*, which is a French square dance; *repentismo*, which is a style of music where two musicians compete with dueling guitars in improvisational verses; *samba breque*, which is a choppy, reggae style of samba; *samba canção*, which is a type of samba that sounds similar to a ballad; *samba terreiro*, which is a samba linked to African religion; *samba enredos*, which are the sambas heard at Carnival; and *samba paulistas*, which are sambas from the state of São Paulo.

Other Musicians and composers who are considered very important in Brazilian popular music include Geraldo Azevedo, Fafá de Belém, Maria Bethánia, João Bosco, Pena Branca, Renato Braz, Chico Burarque do Hollanda, Luis Caldas, Gilberto Gil, Luis Gonzaga, Gozaquinho, Ivan Lins, Sergio Mendes, Vinícius de Moraes, Moraes Moreira, Milton Nascimento, Clara Nunes, Zé Paulo, Elis Regina, Pixinguinho, and Caetano Veloso.

Further Reading

Fryer, Peter. *Rhythms of Resistance: African Musical Heritage in Brazil*. London: Pluto Press, 2000.

Perrone, Charles. *Masters of Contemporary Brazilian Song*. Austin: University of Texas Press, 1989.

Perrone, Charles, and Christopher Dunn. *Brazilian Popular Music & Globalization*. Miami: University Press of Florida, 2001.

Vianna, Hermano. *The Mystery of Samba: Popular Music and National Identity in Brazil*. Chapel Hill: University of North Carolina Press, 1999.

Verónica "Roni" Rubio-Bravo

Bread and Roses. Directed by British social realist filmmaker Ken Loach, *Bread and Roses* (2000), featuring a strong Latino cast and empowering roles for Latinas, charts the struggles of a janitorial service composed mainly of Mexican and Central American immigrants as they try to unionize themselves. The *film is loosely based on an actual janitors' strike that took place in the 1990s in Century City, California, called the "Justice for Janitors" campaign, and was part of the national unionization struggles of service employees. Maya, the central character, played by Pilar *Padilla, comes to Los Angeles from Mexico City to work with her older sister, Rosa, played by Elpidia *Carrillo, cleaning an office building in downtown Los Angeles. The film is made significant by the fact that it shows the exploitation and vulnerability of the Latino immigrant workforce. In particular, it shows the incredible struggles of working-class women to receive equal treatment and equal pay and emphasizes their susceptibility to sexual harassment and coercion as epitomized by the sexist treatment of their ruthless boss played by George *López. Even though the janitors face huge personal risk and sacrifice, their struggles for unionization facilitated by full-time labor organizer Sam (played by Adrien Brody) are successful. The end is bittersweet: for although the workers are able to achieve basic rights like medical benefits, paid overtime, paid holidays, a forty-hour workweek, retirement, and a living wage, Maya is deported.

Further Reading

Scott, A.O. "On the Bumpy Road of a Union Drive" (film review of *Bread and Roses*). *New York Times*, June 1, 2001, sec. E14.

Arturo J. Aldama

Brothers Garcia, The. Set in San Antonio, Texas, and featuring a strong Latino cast, this popular *family-themed television sitcom is about coming of age and sibling rivalries in a large Mexican American family. Following narrative devices that are similar to *Malcolm in the Middle* and *The Wonder Years*, the Garcia family is shown to the audience through the eyes and ears of Larry (played by Alvin Álvarez of Mexican-American heritage), the twin brother of Lorena (played by Vaneza Pitynzki of German Puerto Rican heritage) and the baby of the family. Also like *The Wonder Years* in which there is an adult voice-over, the famed Colombian-American actor and comedian John *Leguizamo provides the voice-over for Larry. The series makes television history by having an English-language sitcom that not only features an all-Latino cast in nonstereotypical roles but also has a strong Latino team of writers and producers. The Nickelodeon series made its debut in July 2000 and is now in its fourth season. Álvarez was nominated in 2001 for an *ALMA Award for Outstanding Actor in a New Television Series. Jeff Valdez, the executive producer of *The Brothers Garcia* and co-chair of SíTV, a Latino-themed production company, was also nominated in 1998 for an

ALMA Award for his commitment to creating bilingual and English-language programming for the Latino community.

Further Reading

www.nick.com/all_nick/tv_supersites/garcia/index.jhtml.
www.sitv.com/brothersgarcia2.htm.

Arturo J. Aldama

Buena Vista Social Club. The *Buena Vista Social Club*, a 1999 documentary on Afro-Cuban music, was awarded the Best Documentary of 1999 by the following associations: New York Film Critics Circle, Los Angeles Critics Association, National Board of Review of Motion Pictures, European Film Academy, and German Film Awards; and it was also nominated for an Oscar by the Academy of Motion Picture Arts and Sciences. The *film was directed by Wim Wenders, produced by Deepak Nayar and Wim Wenders, and distributed by Artisan Entertainment.

Buena Vista Social Club depicts the music scene in Havana through the gaze of blues guitarist Ry Cooder and tells the story of Cooder's trip to Cuba in 1996, where he met and recorded music with Cuban musicians. The film features what is known as **son* music during the big band era of Cuban music of the 1940s and 1950s. Cooder managed to locate some of the key musicians who had played in the Buena Vista Social Club, a multigenerational group of Afro-Cuban musicians. The sound track was recorded into an album—*Buena Vista Social Club*—that won a Grammy in 1997 for Best Tropical Latin Album. As a result of the great popularity of the album, the careers of many of the key musicians were rejuvenated, and many released their own solo albums. These musicians include Compay Segundo, a singer, songwriter, guitarist, and inventor of a seven-string guitar; pianist Rubén González, who had not played the piano for many years prior to the film and subsequently produced two solo albums; Ibrahim Ferrer, the singer known as "The Nat King Cole" of Cuba; guitarist Eliades Ochoa, famous for having constructed his own nine-string guitar; and singer Omara Portuondo, dubbed "The Edith Piaf of Cuba," who performed in many countries with her own orchestra. Segundo and González both passed away in 2003.

The Buena Vista Social Club as a musical and cultural phenomenon has had a far-reaching global impact in the United States, Europe, and Latin America. The resurgence of popularity of the Afro-Cuban *son* has helped boost the Cuban tourist industry and given Cuban music in general a higher profile in the United States and throughout the world.

Further Reading

www.pbs.org/buenavista/film/critical.html.

Helen Oakley

Cabeza de Baca Gilbert, Fabiola (1894–1991). Born May 16, 1894, near Las Vegas, New Mexico, author and educator Fabiola Cabeza de Baca Gilbert dedicated her life to preserving the authenticity and history of native Mexican *foods, culture, and language while staying very involved in her homeland of New Mexico. She was born into a ranching family in La Liendre, New Mexico. The untimely death of her mother caused the four-year-old Cabeza de Baca Gilbert to be raised by her grandparents, Estefanita Delgado Cabeza de Baca and Graciano Cabeza de Baca.

Upon graduating from her high school, Loretto Academy for Girls, Cabeza de Baca Gilbert became a teacher in a rural area a few miles from her father's ranch. She attended New Mexico Normal (now known as New Mexico Highlands University) in Las Vegas, New Mexico, and earned her Bachelor of Arts degree in pedagogy in 1921. Soon after, she ventured to Spain and studied at the Centro de Estudios Históricos in Madrid. In 1929, Cabeza de Baca Gilbert earned a Bachelor of Science degree in home economics from New Mexico College of Agriculture and Mechanic Arts (now known as New Mexico State University) in Las Cruces, New Mexico. Upon earning her degree she served in the Agricultural Extension Service for thirty years as an extension agent teaching people how to prepare traditional foods as well as educating them about the nutritional and cultural value of these foods. These experiences were the motivation for her *food and cookery books, *Historic Cookery* (1956) and *The Good Life* (1949). Cabeza de Baca Gilbert also wrote the book *We Fed Them Cactus* (1954), which incorporates many of her experiences growing up in her *family, at around the same time she served as president of the New Mexico Folklore Society (1955). She also contributed many articles to several New Mexican publications. Retiring in 1959, she continued to lecture and work as a trainer and consultant for the Peace Corps. She helped create an exhibit for the New Mexico Bicentennial Exhibit in 1976, which featured women in New Mexico history. Cabeza de Baca Gilbert passed away at ninety-seven years of age on October 14, 1991.

Further Reading

Castro, Rafaela G. *Chicano Folklore: A Guide to the Folktales, Traditions, Rituals, and Religious Practices of Mexican-Americans*. New York: Oxford University Press, 2001.

"Inventory of the Fabiola Cabeza de Baca Gilbert Papers, 1602–1996." July 2000. http://elibrary.unm.edu/oanm/NmU/nmu1#mss603bc/nmu1#mss603bc_m4.htm.

Peña, Juan José. *The Hispano Round Table of New Mexico*. 2001. http://www.hrtnm.org/2001.html.

Velasco, Juan. "Online Chicano Literature Project." http://www.sscnet.ucla.edu/csrc/webwriters.html#cabeza.

Armando Quintero, Jr.

Calypso. Calypso is a beloved Caribbean popular music heard throughout the United States, especially in larger cosmopolitan urban areas like New York City and Miami. A musical expression originating in the West Indies, most specifically in Trinidad, calypso belongs to a creolized genre with traces of early French musical forms, African stick-fight drumming and singing, and various other influences. It is a highly topical genre, noted for its economy of words, its satire and wit, and its rhythmic syncopation. Associated with carnival time, lively calypso music may be performed on the streets or on stage. In calypso's early period, calypso tents were erected as musical stages featuring singing competitions. Today this music artfully combines poetry, narrative, and oratory through musical performance.

Calypso has been regarded as a form of criticism, a living witty commentary on contemporary life. Its words express deep thought and folk philosophy on simple things. Calypso is also enacted as part of a larger ritual, particularly within the carnival. The local competitions that take place are surrounded by fêtes, dance hall music in clubs and on radio, and large street parades. Likewise, soca, ska, and reggae are also heard throughout the carnival season.

During World War II, U.S. soldiers were based in Trinidad, and many calypso songs mention the greed and moral decadence that accompanied the American presence. One group in particular is the Andrews Sisters who popularized Lord Invader's "Rum and Coca Cola." This tune mentions the havoc that American soldiers played with the lives of the local men, as their women were irresistibly attracted to the free-spending Americans. In this regard calypso has been an indictment of the Americans in Trinidad. Many scholars agree that the oral nature of calypso is precisely what gives it power as a rhetorical form. Many calypso lyrics critique the Americanization and commercialization of Trinidadian society, with mentions of New York City, Brooklyn, and Madison Square Garden as symbols of American consumer culture and power.

One of Trinidad's most popular calypso artists is Sparrow, an artist with remarkable varied vocal ranges who has become internationally famous and performs regularly at Madison Square Garden. Sparrow's calypsos express a keen sensitivity to the needs and cultural conditions of his time and are described as joyful and high-spirited. He does not simply chronicle current events; instead, he revitalizes and updates the major elements of the traditional calypso, dramatizing the stories through song. Sparrow's musical talent is best heard in the flexibility, range, and quality of his voice, as well as his unique speaking quality behind the lyrics. The language is not compromised for musical form or style but takes on its own life and feeling. Sparrow often uses the rhythm and idioms of Trinidadian speech and language, and the meaning of the title becomes more meaningful as the audience is engaged more directly in the performance.

Although many calypso lyrics are serious and critical, the musical style is upbeat and lively. Performed by skillful artists, within the carnivalesque context of ritual, calypso is a living art form and musical expression that critiques, informs, and shapes its audiences and has become a cultural symbol for Caribbean peoples in the United States.

Further Reading

Patton, John H. "Calypso as Rhetorical Performance: Trinidad Carnival." *Latin American Music Review* 15.1 (1994): 55–74.

Rohlerh, Gordon. *Calypso and Society in Pre-Independence Trinidad.* Port of Spain, Trinidad: n.p., 1990.

Rohlerh, Gordon. "Sparrow and the Language of Calypso." *Savacou* 2 (1970): 88–99.

Peter J. García

Camacho, Héctor "Macho" (1967–). Born in Bayamon, Puerto Rico, boxer Héctor Camacho gained notoriety in the early 1980s. He fought his first professional fight in 1980 and his last one in 2001, accumulating seventy-five wins, four losses, one technical draw, and thirty-six knockouts (KOs). In 1983, Camacho, at 130 pounds, won the World Boxing Council (WBC) Junior Lightweight Championship, his first professional title, recording a fifth-round KO of Rafael "Bazooka" Limón. It was Camacho's twenty-second professional fight. He added the WBC Lightweight (135 pounds) title in 1985, with a twelfth-round decision over José Luis Ramírez. Camacho won a decision over Ray Mancini in 1989, for the less prestigious World Boxing Organization Junior Lightweight (140 pounds) title. In 1991, Camacho experienced his first defeat as a professional boxer to Greg Haugen in a disputed decision that the former avenged less than three months later.

The other losses on his record were to three legendary Latinos: Julio César Chávez in 1992, Felix Trinidad in 1994, and Oscar *De La Hoya in 1997. Camacho's son, Héctor Jr., followed in his father's footsteps, took up boxing, and is currently a contender at 140 pounds.

Further Reading

Bunce, Steve, and Bob Mee. *Boxing Greats*. Philadelphia: Courage Books, 1998. http://www.itsmachotime.com.

McGovern, Mike, ed. *The Encyclopedia of Twentieth-Century Athletes*. New York: Facts on File, 2001.

Clifford Candelaria

Canción. The Mexican musical genre heard most often throughout the United States, especially in the Southwest borderlands, the *canción* is a Mexican song form that instead of telling a story reflects an introspective state of emotion such as love, loneliness, sadness, religious feeling, mourning, or gaiety. Its origins may be traced to Spain, but its development throughout México was influenced and stylized most by Italian romantic opera. By the time of the Mexican Revolution (1910–1917), the popularity of the *canción* was declining. Today, the *canción ranchera* is referred to simply as *ranchera* and is often regarded as a Mexican country western song due to its similar tragic thematic content. This genre usually is associated with the many singers who popularized the music throughout the twentieth century, including Pedro Infante, Lucha Reyes, Javier Solís, Miguel Aceves Mejia, Amalia Mendoza, Jorge Negrete, Lucha Villa, and José Alfredo *Jiménez. By far, among this list of performers, composer and singer Jiménez stands out as the most striking, due not only to the numerous hit recordings of his songs but also to the number of artists who have and continue to make hit recordings of his songs and have dedicated entire LPs and concerts to his music. Jiménez first made his musical presence in 1950, and his popularity continued through the next decade as he composed, recorded, and performed hundreds of *cancíon rancheras* that remain as popular as ever even today.

By the end of the eighteenth century, European opera began to affect the music culture of the Americas in profound ways. A 1799 Spanish law forbade the singing of opera in México in any language but Spanish and was finally repealed in 1827, due to the efforts of opera singer Manuel García (1775–1832). García performed in Europe and New York City before touring México. A native of Seville, García adopted Italian for both performance and compositional purposes and soon gained international stature as an opera performer. His efforts encouraged the contracting of Italian opera companies to tour México and perform the latest Italian popular hits, bringing large numbers of Mexicans into contact with the musical styles and artistic tastes of contemporary Europe. Italian musical influence was profoundly regarded as popular music between 1830 and 1850. Italian composers like Rossini, Donizetti, Bellini, and Verdi were international celebrities especially among nineteenth-century Mexicans throughout the Porfirian epoch (between 1880 and 1911, when Porfirio Díaz was president of México).

The Mexican *canción* can designate any type of song, as opposed to an instrumental piece, or it can be used to define specific varieties, such as the *canción romántica*, with its lyrical and sentimental quality in the text and melody. Most *canciones* are in the copla form, but the verse structure tends to vary. The development and diffusion of the *canción mexicana* during the middle of the nineteenth century were most often associated with the musical performances and compositions of the *cancioneros*, itinerant musicians and descendants of the *juglares* of medieval Spain. By 1850 the *canción mexicana* had reached a high degree of musical popularity, and many musicologists regard the second half of the century as the "golden age of Mexican song." By this time, the Mexican song had left the concert hall and opera house and was heard throughout the rural village and city streets. Agricultural fairs in central México served to diffuse the *cancion* throughout the remotest regions of México. Mexican folk simplified the elaborate metric structure of the operatic arias and *cavatinas*, adapting them to more rural tastes and sensibilities.

By the last quarter of the nineteenth century, there were two distinct classes of *canción mexicana*. Under Porfirio Díaz, México as a nation turned toward the United States and Europe for its cultural, economic, and social development. As México entered the twentieth century, the country's national image began to change. Improved transportation and technology brought the urban and rural areas closer than ever before, so that by 1910 when the Mexican Revolution began, all Mexicans began to take pride in *lo mexicano*. The revolution had glorified both peasant and urban proletariats, and the popular music had been regarded with disdain by the mainstream during the Porfiriato. A country music revival occurred in Mexico City's nationalist theater throughout the revolution. The folk songs sung by peasants on the haciendas were now performed by professionally trained singers as interludes between acts. This continued in the following decades but was difficult as the popularity of American jazz, Spanish *zarzuela*, and Argentine *tango rivaled the popularity of Mexican song. The rise in popularity occurred with the development of México's first nationwide radio broadcasting system, XEW, in the 1930s, which also diffused the song across the northern border where Mexican Americans in the Southwest embraced it, as did Latin Americans to the south of México's border. Likewise, the rise to fame of Pedro Infante, Jorge Negrete, and México's beloved **charro* singers who appeared in the early popular cinema further popularized the genre.

Further Reading

Geijerstam, Claes af. *Popular Music in México*. Albuquerque: University of New Mexico Press, 1976.

Gradante, William. "'El Hijo del Pueblo': José Alfredo Jiménez and the Mexican Canción Ranchera." *Latin American Music Review* 3.1 (1982): 36–59.

Mendoza, Vicente T. *La canción mexicana: Ensayo de clasificación y antología*. Mexico City: Universidad Nacional Autónoma de México, 1961.

Peter J. García

Candomblé. *Candomblé*, meaning "house of dance," is an Afro-Brazilian religious practice with West African polytheistic origins that has been transplanted to the United States. Its followers believe in spiritual possession induced by dancing together and call-and-response chanting to highly rhythmic drumming on *atabaque* drums of different sizes. The diverse *candomblé* groups are classified according to their African nation of origin. In Brazil, *candomblé* has millions of followers, and it is becoming a respected mainstream religion even though public performance of its rites was long restricted by government authorities. *Candomblé* is particularly popular among poor black Brazilians, who use *candomblé* worship centers as community meeting houses to provide a variety of social services. Some of the language and drumming rituals practiced in Brazil have been lost in the lands where they originated, and today many African priests come to Brazil to learn them, as do American and European researchers studying the cultural adaptation of indigenous peoples in the face of encroaching *globalization.

Further Reading

Béhague, Gerard. "Afro-Brazilian Traditions." In *The Garland Handbook of Latin American Music*, edited by Dale A. Olsen and Daniel E. Sheehy. New York: Garland, 2000. 272–287.

Peter J. García

Canseco, José (1964–). José Canseco y Capas, who became the first baseball player to hit forty home runs and steal forty bases in one season, was born on July 2, 1964, in Havana, Cuba. He was named the American League's Rookie of the Year in 1986 and Most Valuable Player in 1988. During the 1959 *Cuban Revolution, Canseco's *family fled to Miami. Canseco attended Coral Park High School in Miami until he was drafted by the Oakland A's at age fifteen. At the beginning of his career in the minors, Canseco was accused of being lazy. The pivotal point in Canseco's career came in the spring of 1984, after his mother died. He moved up to a Double-A team and was named Most Valuable Player. The Oakland A's then moved Canseco to their top minor club in Tacoma, Washington, where his batting average was .348.

Canseco spent his first full season in the majors in 1986, where he struck out 175 times but hit 33 home runs and batted in 117 runs. That year, he was voted Rookie of the Year. In Canseco's 1988 season, he openly bragged that he would steal 40 bases and hit 40 home runs. And though he had many skeptics, on September 18 he hit his fortieth home run, and on September 23 he stole his fortieth base. Canseco was the highest-paid contracted player in 1989, with the Oakland A's signing him to a five-year $23.5 million contract. He played for the A's for a decade and then was traded to the Texas Rangers for three players plus cash. After that he played for the Boston Red Sox before being granted free agent status in 1995. As a free agent, the Cuban-born phenom has played for six clubs, commanding multimillion-dollar salaries through the year 2002 with the Tampa Bay Devil Rays. According to his website, Canseconet.com, the superstar who is known for his cocky flamboyance on and off the field tried out for the Los Angeles Dodgers in an open-field walk-on in Vero Beach, Florida, on March 1, 2004. Unsuccessful, Canseco is filling his time since fading out of full-time major league play by competing in golfing, boxing, and other sports-related entertainment venues.

Further Reading

Aaseng, Nathan. *Jose Canseco: Baseball's 40–40 Man.* Minneapolis: Lerner Publications, 1989.

http//www.baseball-almanac.com.

Light, Jonathan Fraser. *The Cultural Encyclopedia of Baseball.* Jefferson, NC: McFarland & Company, 1997.

McGovern, Mike, ed. *The Encyclopedia of Twentieth-Century Athletes.* New York: Facts on File, 2001.

Kristie Haro

Cantinflas (1911–1993). Cantinflas, whose birth name is Mario Moreno Reyes, was one of the best-known Latino comedic *film actors in México and Latin America from the 1930s to the 1970s. He also had huge crossover appeal to U.S. Latina/o audiences, especially in Spanish-language cinema houses. He was born on August 12, 1911, to a large *family in a working-class neighborhood of Mexico City, México.

After working as a circus and rodeo clown, his film career began in 1936, and he appeared in over fifty commercially released films. His enormous success was catapulted by two films that both broke all previously held box office records in México and Latin America, *Ahí está el detalle* (Here's the Point, 1940) and *Ni sangre ni arena* (Neither Blood Nor Sand, 1941). After seeing the movie *Ni sangre ni arena*, Charlie Chaplin commented that Cantinflas was the best comedian alive. In fact, Cantinflas has been called the Charlie Chaplin of México and compared to Buster Keaton for his kinetic dancing, athletic agility, and his high-octane screen presence. In his prolific presence in Mexican film, he almost always played the scrappy working-class hero who would challenge the mores of middle-class and bourgeois society. With regard

Latino comedic film actor Cantinflas entertained audiences internationally for four decades. *Drawing by Edward Joaquin Rodriguez, Photo by Emmanuel Sánchez Carballo.*

to his U.S. films, Cantinflas is best known for his role in *Around the World in 80 Days* (1956), for which he received a Golden Globe Award, and in *Pepe* (1960). Toward the end of his career, he appeared in two Disney films, *The Computer Wore Tennis Shoes* (1970) and *The Strongest Man in the World* (1975).

Despite his success, Moreno never forgot his humble roots. Throughout his career he served as a financial benefactor to humanitarian organizations and to hundreds of individuals and families in need, and he prided himself on being one with the people and not letting fame set him apart from others. In 1988, he received a lifetime achievement award from the Mexican Academy of Cinema. Because of his immense popularity and unique style of speaking rapidly and in fragments, the verb *cantinflear* and the adjective *cantinflesque* have now been adopted into the language of Latina/o popular culture. *Cantinflear* means to talk voluminously without coherence, invert meanings, and speak in innuendoes and speech fragments for comedic effect.

Further Reading

Hadley-Garcia, George. *Hispanic Hollywood: The Latins in Motion Pictures*. New York: Carol Publishing Group, 1993.

Keller, Gary D. *A Biographical Handbook of Hispanics and United States Film*. Tempe, AZ: Bilingual Press, 1997.

Arturo J. Aldama

CARA. Chicano Art: Resistance and Affirmation, 1965–1985, better known as CARA, was a national exhibition of Chicana/*Chicano art that toured ten cities in the United States in the 1990s. Through collaborative efforts of the Wight Art Gallery, on the campus of the University of California at Los Angeles, and the CARA National Advisory Committee, the exhibit opened at the Wight Art Gallery on September 9, 1990, toured through a number of cities, and closed on August 1, 1993, following its showing at the San Antonio Museum of Art in San Antonio, Texas.

The exhibit was composed of ten sections, beginning with a brief historical timeline chronicling the development of Chicana/Chicano artistic expression. Then it covered nine representations of themes associated with El Movimiento, the Chicano civil rights movement of the 1960s and 1970s, and three installations featuring the highly influential collective art groups *Asco, Los Four, and the *Royal Chicano Air Force.

Described as interpretive, the CARA exhibition aimed to illustrate the relationship between a distinct body of artistic work by self-described Chicana/Chicano artists and the Chicano civil rights movement. The CARA exhibition was the first major exhibit featuring Chicana/Chicano artists to receive significant attention from the U.S. press. Although not the first one dedicated to Chicana/Chicano art, the CARA exhibit was significant because it was the first national collaboration between Chicana/Chicano artists and mainstream art institutions. Thus, it marked the first major movement toward self-representation from within Chicano culture. In this sense, its organizers saw the exhibition as an extension of the ongoing efforts of the *Chicano Movement and not simply as a definitive catalog.

The openly ideological stance of the CARA exhibition differed significantly from traditional museum or exhibition practices. By developing a show in which a work of art is not separated from its cultural context, the CARA organizers infused the exhibition with the politics of identity. Traditional museum practices have often attempted to create an appearance of a separation between art and politics. The CARA exhibit actively challenged the idea that museum space could be free from the realm of the political, thereby showing that mainstream museum processes, the processes by which works of art are deemed to be of high quality or of significant cultural value, are themselves not neutral.

Further Reading

Chicano Art: Resistance and Affirmation, 1965–1985. Edited by Richard Griswold del Castillo, Teresa McKenna, and Yvonne Yarbro-Bejarano. Los Angeles: University of California, Los Angeles, 1991.

José Gamez

Cara, Irene (1958–). Performer Irene Cara was born Irene Escalara on March 18, 1958, in New York City. This *Cuban American star of the stage, screen, and recording studio made her Broadway debut at the age of eight in *Maggie Flynn*, a Shirley Jones–Jack Cassidy musical. Her early *film work capitalized on her musical talents. After debuting in the film *Aaron Loves Angela* (1975), she assumed the title role in the cult musical drama *Sparkle* (1976) opposite Philip Michael Thomas. In 1980, she played Coco Hernández, a struggling and ambitious performing arts student, in *Fame*. Cara performed Michael Gore and Dean Pitchford's title song from the film. The song was a Top 10 hit in the United States and won an Academy Award for Best Song in 1981. "Out Here on My Own," another song from the film performed by Cara, was a Top 40 hit. Her performance in *Fame* earned Cara a Golden Globe nomination for Best Actress in a Musical or Comedy and a Grammy nomination for Best New Artist. In 1982 Cara released her own album, *Anyone Can See*. In 1983, she collaborated with Giorgio Moroder and Keith Forsey to compose "Flashdance: What a Feelin'" for the blockbuster movie of the same name. The resulting song earned Cara two Grammy Awards, a Golden Globe Award, and an Academy Award. During this period, Cara also starred in such films as *D.C. Cab* (1983), *City Heat* (1984), and *Busted Up* (1984). These films failed to match the critical and commercial successes of her earlier work. Despite impressive turns in made-for-TV movies such as *Roots: The Next Generation* (1979) and *For Us the Living: The Medgar Evers Story* (1980), Cara's career as an actress stalled. She has done voice work on such animated features as *The Magic Voyage* (1982) and *Happily Ever After* (1990). In 2003, she appeared on *The Disco Ball: A 30-year Celebration* television special.

Further Reading

Keller, Gary D. *A Biographical Handbook of Hispanics and United States Film.* Tempe, AZ: Bilingual Press, 1997.

William Orchard

Carbajal, Michael (1967–). This Phoenix, Arizona–born Chicano boxer came to prominence in the 1988 Summer Olympics in Seoul, South Korea, where he won the silver medal in the 106-pound weight class. Trained as a professional boxer by his brother Danny, Carbajal accumulated a record of forty-nine wins and four losses, with thirty-three knockouts (KOs). He adopted the nickname "Manitas de Piedra" (Little Hands of Stone) after Panamanian boxer Roberto Duran, who was called "Manos de Piedra" (Stone Hands). Carbajal won his first professional title in 1990 with a seventh-round KO of Maungchai Kittikasem in the junior flyweight division (108 pounds). In 1993 Carbajal overcame two knockdowns by Humberto Gonzáles to score a seventh-round KO in what many consider the best fight of that year. He then lost to Gonzáles in a split decision in 1994 and lost another decision to him in the same year. Carbajal regained his title in 1996 with the defeat of Melchor Cob Castro, only to lose it to Mauricio Pastrana in 1997 in a split decision. He retired after another loss in June 1998 but came back in 1999 to win four fights, culminating in an eleventh-round technical knockout of Jorge Arce to win the World Boxing Organization junior flyweight title. Carbajal then retired as champion and currently trains boxers in his Ninth Street Gym in Phoenix.

Clifford Candelaria

Carey, Mariah (1970–). Mariah Carey is an international sensation and superstar in pop music best regarded as a "ghetto fabulous" diva known for her exceptionally broad five-octave tessitura (voice range) and virtuosic vocal technique, recording numerous commercial gold record Top 40 hits in the United States. Her style mixes rhythm and blues, smooth balladry, and *hip-hop in a pop music framework. The rags-to-riches story of this number-one-selling female artist inspires a large body of fans to follow their dreams. The majority of her fan base is teenage and female. Carey's official fan club, called Honey B. Fly, was established in 2003 and allows fans access to everything from early ticket sales to exclusive mobile phone rings.

Carey was born March 27, 1970, in New York, New York, the youngest of three children of Irish and black/Hispanic parents. Her father was Venezuelan and African American, and her mother was the Irish opera singer Patricia Carey. She was raised in an environment of racial tension that contributed to her parents' divorce when she was three years old. Carey's mother performed as an opera singer for the New York City Opera and also worked as a vocal coach. She provided her daughter with input and encouraged her daughter as Mariah's interest in singing grew. She enjoyed singing at talent shows and folk festivals and began composing her own songs in junior high school. In high school she studied voice with professionals in Manhattan. Upon graduating from high school Carey moved to Manhattan and eventually secured a position singing part-time backup vocals for rhythm and blues singer Brenda K. Starr. Through her connections with Starr, she was able to give Sony Music executive Tommy Mottola her demo tape in 1988. Carey recorded her first album, *Mariah Carey*, in 1990, which sold over 6 million copies. The four singles released from this album—"Vision of Love," "Love Takes Time," "Someday," and "I Don't Wanna Cry"—all reached number one on the *Billboard* charts. Carey's self-titled album also earned her Grammy Awards for Best New Artist and Best Pop Female Vocal Performance.

In 1991, Carey released her album *Emotions*. The first single released from this album, "Emotions," topped the charts, making her the first artist in history to have her first five singles hit number one. Up to this time Carey had not yet toured, but she did perform publicly at the 1991 Video Music Awards. In 1992, she recorded her *MTV Unplugged EP*. Her cover of the Jackson Five song "I'll Be There," a duet with Trey Lorenz, from this album hit number one on the *Billboard* charts. Part of the proceeds from the *MTV Unplugged EP* went to charity. In 1993 she released *Music Box*, her third studio album, which achieved high sales of over 25 million copies. This album yielded two more *Billboard* number-one hits. Shortly afterward, Carey toured a few U.S. venues, the last stop of which was New York City's Madison Square Garden. At this closing concert, she dedicated the proceeds from her hit single "Hero" to a fund for families of victims of a shooting on the Long Island Railroad that had occurred a week before. Carey and Tommy Mottola were married in 1993 as well.

In 1994 Carey recorded a remake of "Endless Love" with Luther Vandross that was released on his album. The single reached number three on the Hit 100 charts. Also in 1994 she released *Merry Christmas*, which became the bestselling holiday album ever. During the same year she became the spokesperson for New York's Fresh Air Fund, a charity that provides disadvantaged youth with a summer camp opportunity in Fishkill, New York. In December 1994 Carey performed a benefit concert for the charity that raised over $650,000.

In 1995 she released her sixth album, *Daydream*. The first single from this album debuted at number one on the *Billboard* Hot 100 charts and the *Billboard* Hot R&B charts. With this single, Carey became the first female artist ever to debut one song that topped both of these charts. The success of the *Daydream* album also made her the first female artist ever to have three albums that each sold over 8 million copies. She performed her first world tour in 1995–1996 in support of this album. Every venue for the tour was sold out.

Carey and husband Mottola divorced in 1997. This same year Carey released the album *Butterfly*, which reached gold, platinum, and double platinum record status. The first single from this album, "Honey," debuted at number one, giving Carey the most number-one singles of any female artist thus far.

In 1998 she released a greatest hits album, *#1's*, that included a previously unreleased track, "When You Believe." This track was written for the Disney film *The Prince of Egypt* and was a duet with Whitney Houston. Carey released her next studio album in 1999, titled *Rainbow*, which again achieved chart-topping status. She then became the only artist to have a number-one record each year in the 1990s. As a result of the high level of her success throughout this period, Billboard Music Awards named Carey Artist of the Decade. She also won the title of Best Selling Female Artist of the Millennium at the World Music Awards. By the end of one decade, Carey had released more number-one singles than any recording artist other than the Beatles and Elvis Presley.

Carey won the Horizon Award at the Congressional Foundation Awards in 1999 for her work with and for children. During the same year she also acted in the *film *The Bachelor*. In 2001 Carey starred in the movie *Glitter*. She also performed on the sound track for the film as well as composing some of the music. Sales for the movie and sound track were much lower than expected. Carey experienced a physical and emotional breakdown, which received extensive media attention, during this same year.

In 2002, Carey returned to the fore of popular music with her release of *Charmbracelet*, which by mid-2003 had sold over 3 million copies. She also co-starred in the film *Wisegirls* in 2002 with Mira Sorvino and Melora Walters. This independent film was premiered at the Sundance Film Festival.

The media places virtually no emphasis on Carey's Latin heritage except for her short-lived romantic relationship with singer Luis *Miguel, and neither does the singer involve herself in the Latino community. Carey's heritage as a Latina and the fact that she has achieved unprecedented success in the music industry, however, provide inspiration to aspiring youth of Latino, African American, and Anglo backgrounds, with whom she shares part of her own ethnicity.

Further Reading

Flick, Larry. "Carey Eager to Start a Fresh Chapter." *Billboard* 104 (December 7, 2002): 49, 98.
http://www.azreporter.com/arizona/events/phoenix/mariahcarey.html.
http://www.celebritysun.com/MariahCarey.html.

Christina Burbano-Jeffrey

Carreta de la Muerte. The *Carreta de la Muerte* (Cart of Death) is an oxcart or wheelbarrow used during Holy Week ceremonies and observances in New Mexico. The cart carries a skeleton in black clothing, referred to as Doña Sebastiana. Personifying death, Doña Sebastiana carries a bow and arrow, and it is believed that death will be near to anyone who encounters one of her arrows. Nazario Lopez of Santa Cruz, New Mexico, is credited as being the first to carve the *Carreta de la Muerte* around 1860. An early-twentieth-century rendering of the *carreta* by José Benito Ortega is exhibited at the Museum of International Folk Art in Santa Fe. Variations of the *Carreta de la Muerte* are prevalent in religious and folk art in the southwestern region of the United States. *Carreta de la Muerte* is also the title of Mari Privette Ulmer's 2001 murder mystery novel that takes place in New Mexico.

Further Reading

Castro, Rafaela G. *Chicano Folklore: A Guide to the Folktales, Traditions, Rituals, and Religious Practices of Mexican-Americans.* Oxford: Oxford University Press, 2001.

Armando Quintero, Jr.

Carrillo, Elpidia (1963–). Born in Michoacán, México, Elpidia Carrillo is a prolific actress who has crossed over into U.S. *film and television. Carrillo began her acting career in the late 1970s, appearing in Mexican films such as *Deseos* (1977) and *Pedro Páramo* (1978), based on the now-classic novel by Juan Rulfo. Carrillo's first U.S. film role was costarring with Jack Nicholson in *The Border* (1983), and she was nominated for the Independent Spirit Award in the category of Best Female Lead for her role in Oliver Stone's *Salvador* (1986). She appeared in supporting roles as Veronica in Alan Smithee's *Let's Get Harry* (1986) and as Anna in John McTiernan's *Predator* (1987). In the 1990s, Carrillo played several important roles in U.S.-produced films. In 1995 she played Jimmy *Smits' love interest, Isabel Magana, in Gregory *Nava's **Mi Familia/My Family*. She also continued making guest appearances in TV dramas (such as *Miami Vice* in 1984, *21 Jump Street* in 1987, *ER* in 1994, *The Pretender* in 1996, and *Law and Order* in 1999). Carrillo brings human testament to her role of Rosa in Ken Loach's **Bread and Roses* (2000); Rosa's life is a deeply biting critique of the Latina's struggle to survive in a country where sexism, racism, and economic exploitation intermingle. Carrillo recently played a minor role in Steven Soderbergh's film *Solaris* (2002) and played Hermenegilda in *Tortilla Heaven* (2000). In 2001 she won the Golden Eagle Award in the category of Outstanding Actress in Film for her work in *Bread and Roses*.

Further Reading

Hadley-Garcia, George. *Hispanic Hollywood: The Latins in Motion Pictures*. New York: Carol Publishing Group, 1993.

Keller, Gary D. *A Biographical Handbook of Hispanics and United States Film*. Tempe, AZ: Bilingual Press, 1997.

Luis Aldama

Carter, Lynda (1951–). Best known for her role as "Wonder Woman," actress Lynda Jean Cordova was born on July 24, 1951, in Phoenix, Arizona, to a Mexican-American mother and an Anglo father. She was crowned Miss Arizona and Miss World United States in 1973 before heading to Hollywood to become a movie star known as Lynda Carter. She played the lead role of Diana Prince in the top-rated television series *Wonder Woman* (1976–1979) with Lyle Waggoner. Over the years, she has appeared in nearly forty television and *film projects such as *Bobbie Jo and the Outlaw* (1976), *Hotline* (1982), and *Rita *Hayworth: The Love Prayer in the Dark* (1997). However, none of the projects has been as popular as the *Wonder Woman* series.

Carter prefers to portray women in strong, decision-making roles, as shown by her appearance in the Showtime cable television movie *Red Sneakers* in 2001, in which she played a high school principal, and in the 2002 comedy film *Super Troopers*, in which she played the governor of Vermont. Married to Robert Altman in 1984, Carter volunteers her time and effort to causes that benefit women and children.

Further Reading

Hadley-Garcia, George. *Hispanic Hollywood: The Latins in Motion Pictures*. New York: Carol Publishing Group, 1993.

Keller, Gary D. *A Biographical Handbook of Hispanics and United States Film*. Tempe, AZ: Bilingual Press, 1997.

Arturo J. Aldama

Casa de las Américas. From both national and international perspectives, the Casa de las Américas is the best-known and most prestigious cultural institution in modern-day Cuba. Created in 1959 four months after the *Cuban Revolution that brought Fidel *Castro to power, it originated as a publishing house and information distribution center and quickly became a magnet for attracting the work of intellectuals and artists from all continents.

The Casa de las Américas was founded by Haydée Santamaría, one of the few women directly involved in Castro's revolutionary brigades, and she organized and directed the institution until 1979. In those twenty years she helped build it into both a creative and physical refuge for artists and writers who were being persecuted in their homelands for writings that promoted equality and social justice and that openly criticized political tyranny and military torture. Many were exiled from their countries by Latin American dictators who had supported the tyranny that the Cuban Revolution sought to remove.

The Casa de las Américas is famous as well for its annual award of literary achievement, the much-sought-after Casa de las Américas Prize in Latin American literature. Established as a Latin American counterpart to, for example, England's Booker Award, Sweden's Nobel Prize, and the U.S. Pulitzer Prize for distinguished work, the Casa de las Américas Prize quickly pushed Havana forward on the world stage as a center and supporter of Latin American letters. It also contributed to the international attention to the Latin American "Boom," the major literary renaissance that surfaced in the 1960s and that included the awarding of the Nobel Prize in Literature to Miguel Angel Ásturias (from Guatemala) in 1967, to Pablo Neruda (Chile) in 1971, to Gabriel García Márquez (Colombia) in 1982, and to Octavio *Paz (México) in 1990. Writers who have served as judges for the Casa de las Américas award include such famous luminaries as Ásturias (1899–1974), Aléjo Carpentier (1904–1980), Carlos Fuentes (1928–), Nicolás Guillén (1902–1989), and José Lezama Lima (1939–1976). Among the recipients of the Casa de las Américas Prize are many writers whose work was at first virtually unknown and is now widely read and translated into many languages, like, for example, Jorge Enrique Adoum, José Puig, Roque Dalton, Alfredo Bryce Echenique, *Chicano writer Rolando *Hinojosa, and Antonio Skármeta.

In the forty-five years since the Casa de las Américas Prize was founded, nearly 22,000 contestants have participated, 284 authors have received the award, and 1,097 professional authors have been jurors. In 2000, the Casa de las Américas inaugurated three honorary awards: the José María Argüedas Prize for narrative, the Ezequiél Martínez Estrada Prize for essay writing, and the José Lezama Lima Prize for poetry. Fulfilling a binational agreement, the government of the country of Colombia subsidizes and publishes the books that receive the prize. The 2003 winners are the Argentinian Paola Cristina Yannielli (best novel category), the Cuban Ronaldo Menéndez Plasencia (best short story category), the Cuban Ramón Fajardo Estrada (best nonfiction category), the Brazilian Angela Leite de Souza (special prize for Brazilian literature in poetry), and the *Cuban American Sonia Rivera Valdés (special prize for Hispanic literature in the United States in short story).

Casa de las Américas founder Haydée Santamaría and Melba Hernández were the only women who participated in the formative years of the Cuban

Revolution with Fidel Castro, including being part of the ill-fated attack on the Moncada fortress on July 26, 1953. They were two of a handful of Cuba's female revolutionary leaders to join the future president and his closest associates in other important confrontations that eventually became known as the Movimiento 26 de Julio (26 of July Movement), synonymous with the Cuban Revolution that eventually overthrew dictator Fulgencio Batista in January 1959.

The arc of renown and respect for Santamaría, the Casa, and its prize became tarnished in 1968 with the "Heberto Padilla Affair," an international scandal concerning the persecution by Castro's government of openly gay poet Padilla. As a consequence of the criticisms and concerns lodged by many foreign writers, artists, scientists, and other intellectuals throughout the world, both the Casa de las Américas and its literary awards suffered a severe loss of prestige in local Cuban and global opinion. Adding further intrigue and mystery to the Padilla affair was the fact that he went into exile in March 1980, taking posts at Princeton and New York Universities, and that on the highly symbolic day of July 26 in 1980, Santamaría committed suicide in Havana. Deepening the mystery, shortly after Padilla's acceptance of a writer-in-residence appointment at Auburn University in Alabama, he, too, died in September 2000.

Nevertheless, Santamaría's important cultural legacy remained and was invigorated under its new leadership. Casa de las Américas has been headed since 1980 by Cuban poet and essayist Roberto Fernández Retama, who is best known in the United States for his influential book *Caliban and Other Essays*. In the last two decades, Casa's Center for Literary Studies has continued to award the Casa de las Américas Literary Award, promote Latin American literature and critical studies, organize conferences and postgraduate courses, publish books, and act as consultant to the magazines *Casa de las Américas* and the *Fondo Editorial Casa*. It also maintains the Archivo de la Palabra, an audio archive with the phonographic recordings of more than a thousand writers, politicians, and artists (e.g., Julio Cortázar and José Lezama Lima reading their poems, Eduardo Galeano reading from his *Memories of Fire*, Virgilio Piñera reading his short stories, Violeta Parra singing her songs, and many others), as well as manages the CD label Casa and the publishing house Fondo Editorial Casa. A Caribbean Studies Center, Women Studies Program, Music Department with an annual Casa de las Américas Musicology Award, a Library, Plastic Arts Department, and a Theatre Department that publishes the journal *Conjunto* are also listed on the Casa Web site. After the departure in 1991 of the Soviet military and its substantial financial aid to the Cuban government, Casa de las Américas has struggled to maintain its facilities and staff in the face of the continuing harmful impact of the U.S. economic blockade and Castro's failure to democratize the country.

Further Reading

Fernández Retamar, Roberto. *Caliban and Other Essays*. Translated by Edward Baker. Minneapolis: University of Minnesota Press, 1989.
http://www.casa.cult.cu.
http://www.granma.cu.

Luis Aldama

Cascarones. *Cascarones* is derived from the Spanish term *cascara*, which means "shell," and specifically refers to festive eggshells that are brightly decorated, dyed in brilliant colors, and usually filled with confetti. They are central to holiday games and cultural activities throughout México, Latin America, Spain, and the United States. The egg matter is removed from the shell through a small hole, and the unbroken shell is typically dyed, painted, or decorated and filled with bright and colorful confetti, cologne, perfume, flour, or powder and cracked over an unsuspecting person's head as part of the mischievous activities and fun. The tradition is believed to date back to China where decorated eggs filled with perfume were given as gifts. They were possibly introduced to Europe by Italian explorer Marco Polo, who collected them as part of his travels in Asia. *Cascarones* diffused from Italy to Spain to México and throughout the Caribbean and Latin America.

In México, the tradition was popularized mostly during the early nineteenth century, and there are several written references discussing the use of *cascarones* in California. The French aristocrat Carlotta, wife of Emperor Maximillian, was fascinated with *cascarones* and brought them from Europe to México during the 1860s. Early wedding accounts in California describe a *cascaron* (cascarones is plural for cascaron) filled with cologne in 1826. Accounts describing *fandango games and festivities in California also suggest *cascarones* were filled with flour, ashes, black paint, or cologne during the 1850s when mischievous girls cracked them over the heads of eligible men in attempts to get their attention. *Cascaron* balls were held in Monterey during the 1820s prior to Lent.

The tradition of decorating *cascarones* has continued throughout the *barrios and borderlands in Mexican and Chicana/o communities to the present. They regained popularity across the Southwest, especially in Texas during the 1960s and 1970s as part of the Chicano Movement's cultural revival. Today *cascarones* are used for weddings, fiestas, dances, and almost any *holidays but mostly during Easter festivities. A new technique for *cascaron* decoration has developed in Tucson, Arizona, where the egg is mounted on a rolled-up newspaper and decorated with tissue paper resembling puppets depicting such popular faces as Pancho *Villa, Bill Clinton, Frida *Kahlo, and Mickey Mouse, reminiscent of bobblehead dolls.

Further Reading

Castro, Rafaela G. *Chicano Folklore: A Guide to the Folktales, Traditions, Rituals and Religious Practices of Mexican-Americans*. New York: Oxford University Press, 2001.

Griffith, James S. "Cascarones: A Folk Art in Southern Arizona." *International Folklore Review: Folklore Studies from Overseas* 9 (1993): 34–40.

Martinez, Yleana. "Cracking Cascarones." *Hispanic* (March 1996): 49–50.

Peter J. García

Castañeda, Carlos (c. 1925–1998). Many questions surround the life of the world-famous writer who is best known by his published pseudonym, Carlos Castañeda. Such vital information as his date and place of birth, his name, and the exact date of his death are uncertain. Although his life is shrouded in mystery, Castañeda's books, beginning in 1968 with *The Teachings of Don Juan: A Yaqui Way of Knowledge*, have been stunning successes. Depending on their perspective, many social commentators and cultural studies scholars have credited or cursed *The Teachings of Don Juan* with starting the New Age pop culture movement in self-development through cosmic awareness. The book's surprising popularity created great interest in its author, which only became more intense with the publication of *A Separate Reality: Further Conversations with Don Juan* in 1971 and *Journey to Ixtlán: The Lessons of Don Juan* in 1972. Castañeda's nearly instant celebrity led to a *Time* cover story in March 1973, which in time generated more questions about Castañeda. However, as with other renowned personages with enigmatic biographies (including William Shakespeare, Christopher *Columbus, *Sor Juana, and Vincent van Gogh), the questions and uncertainties about the man have not detracted from Castañeda's success nor from the acclaim bestowed on his work by some critics and millions of readers. In many respects, Castañeda is not unlike other twentieth-century pop culture icons constructed by the media (e.g., Frida *Kahlo, Elvis Presley, and Madonna) whose work cannot be separated from a created persona consciously marketed as such by artist, agent, and mass distributor.

Time reported that the future writer's given name at birth was César Arana, also spelled "Aranha," according to U.S. *immigration records. He is believed to have been born on December 25, 1925, in Cajamarca, Peru, an ancient Inca community in the country's northern mining region. Castañeda's parents were said to be César Arana Burungaray, a jeweler and goldsmith, and his wife, Susan Castañeda Navoa. However, other published accounts based on interviews with the writer after he became famous report his birthdate as 1931 and his birthplace as Brazil. Diligent investigations by scholars, journalists, and fans to trace his biography tend to favor the Peruvian birth and date. His family eventually moved to Lima, the Peruvian capital, where young César is believed to have attended and graduated from the Colegio Nacional de Nuestra Señora de Guadelupe and also to have later studied art in Peru's National School of Fine Arts. However, Castañeda's own account of his past begins with his birth into a family of Italian origin in São Paulo, Brazil, and continues with him growing up in the Brazilian countryside, where he was reared by maternal grandparents who later sent him to school in Argentina. Sources also vary as to when he immigrated to the United States; some say he was a teenager, while others claim he was older or younger. In one version, he is reported to have been placed with foster parents in Los Angeles, to have graduated from Hollywood High School, and then to have studied parapsychology at Los Angeles City College in 1955.

Records show that the enigmatic celebrity, who steadfastly avoided being photographed or interviewed, enrolled at the University of California, Los Angeles, in 1959 to begin his now-famous studies in anthropology. In the same year, he became a naturalized American citizen, taking his mother's surname, Castañeda, as his own. Shortly thereafter, some accounts report that in 1960 he married an American woman fourteen years his senior. The marriage lasted only a few months and officially ended in divorce in 1973. Introduced in the 1970s to American Florinda Donner, Castañeda began a long friendship with her that resulted in their marriage in 1993. It took place after the 1991 publication of Donner's book *Being-in-Dreaming: An Initiation into the Sorcerer's World*, which was about her friendship with the reclusive writer.

Castañeda's legacy to literature and popular culture appears solid, despite the variety of interpretations as to its ultimate meaning and value. Frequently identified as the father of the late-twentieth-century New Age movement in the United States, which continues to thrive on a global scale, Castañeda began research for his first book, *The Teachings of Don Juan*, while working on his doctorate in anthropology at the University of California, Los Angeles. He claimed to have met a Yaqui shaman, whom he called Don Juan Matus, in the late 1960s in Arizona. He wrote that the elder became his teacher and began to enlighten him, in part through the use of drugs and chemical substances, as to the spiritual and physical manipulation of consciousness, space, and time. This experience was the basis for his graduate research and for *The Teachings of Don Juan*, which became an underground success and later a global bestseller. In 1973, after the publication of *A Separate Reality* and *Journey to Ixtlán*, both of which were bestsellers, Castañeda was awarded his Ph.D. Despite their engaging eloquence and compelling plots, the books are often viewed as fictional rather than factual memoirs largely because no one other than Castañeda has ever met or even seen Don Juan Matus. Others point out that the lack of Yaqui language terms and names or other specifically local Arizona evidence weakens the credibility of his writings as documentaries of field ethnography.

Nevertheless, the almost immediate international success of his books is indisputable. This success is often attributed to the convergence of the free speech and antiwar movements, as well as to a growing consciousness among elites of the power of indigenous ethnopoetics, which also helped propel *magic realism into international prominence. Following his remarkable fame as a published writer and his achievement of his doctorate, Castañeda became even more enigmatic and reclusive. In an interview, he stated that he believed any verification of his life by statistics would be like attempting to use science to validate magic. He also was greatly burdened by his fame and by the constant hounding from followers he described as very weird and who pushed the shy man into a hermit's life. In other books, Castañeda wrote about another American Indian teacher, Genaro Flores, of the Mazatec tribe and later about Don Juan's female disciples and guides. These titles include *Tales of Power* (1974), *The Second Ring of Power* (1978), *The Eagle's Gift* (1981), *The Power of Silence: Further Lessons of Don Juan* (1987), *The Art of Dreaming* (1993), *Magical Passes: The Practical Wisdom of the Shamans of Ancient México* (1998), and *The Active Side of Infinity* (1999). Carlos Castañeda died on April 27, 1998, a victim of liver cancer, in his Westwood, California, home, and his cremated ashes were reportedly taken to México. In keeping with the mystery that surrounded his life, his death did not become known until about two months after he died.

Further Reading

De Mille, Richard. *Castañeda's Journey: The Power and the Allegory*. 2nd rev. ed. Santa Barbara, CA: Capra Press, 1976.

De Mille, Richard. *The Don Juan Papers: Further Castañeda Controversies*. Santa Barbara, CA: Ross-Erikson, 1980.

Endrezze, Anita. *Throwing Fire at the Sun, Water at the Moon* [Yaqui beliefs and customs]. Tucson: University of Arizona Press, 2000.

Noel, Daniel C. *Seeing Castañeda: Reactions to the "Don Juan" Writings of Carlos Castañeda*. New York: Putnam, 1976.

Silverman, David. *Reading Castañeda: A Prologue to the Social Sciences*. London: Routledge and Kegan Paul, 1975.

Wallace, Amy. *Sorcerer's Apprentice: My Life with Carlos Castañeda*. Berkeley, CA: Frog Press, distributed by North Atlantic Books, 2003.

Cordelia Chávez Candelaria

Castillo, Ana (1953–). Poet, novelist, artist, and Chicana feminist activist Ana Hernández Del Castillo received an American Book Award from the Before Columbus Foundation in 1986 for her first novel *The Mixquiahuala Letters*; the Carl Sandburg Literary Award in fiction in 1993 for *So Far from God*; and the Gustaves Myers Award in 1995 for her collection of personal essays, *Massacre of the Dreamers*. Her 1996 edited collection of essays, poetry, and fiction on the *Virgin of Guadalupe, *Goddess of the Americas: Writings on the Virgin of Guadalupe*, has received praise for the variety of accomplished writers contributing their perspectives on the patron saint of México, as well as for its range of interpretations of traditional religious teachings. Including writings by such well-known authors as Nobelist

Octavio *Paz, Sandra *Cisneros, Rosario Ferré, Elena Poniatowska, and Richard Rodríguez, *Goddess of the Americas* provides general audiences with the insights of these and other Latina and Latino thinkers on the historical and cultural meanings of the Guadalupe icon.

Born in Chicago, Illinois, on June 15, 1953, to Raymond and Rachel Rocha, Castillo graduated from Jones' Commercial High School and attended Chicago City College before entering Northeastern Illinois University. In 1975 she received a Bachelor of Science degree in art with a minor in secondary education. She taught ethnic studies at Santa Rosa (California) Junior College in 1975–1976 and began professional work as a writer in 1977 when she served as a writer-in-residence for the Illinois Arts Council, a post she held until 1979, the same year she earned a Master of Arts from the University of Chicago in Latin American and Caribbean Studies. Throughout the 1970s while teaching in community colleges in the Chicago and San Francisco areas, she also participated in community organizing on behalf of people of color and advocacy for women's rights. Besides her own creative work in poetry and fiction, one outgrowth of this period was her eventual collaboration in the translation (with Norma Alarcón) of the highly influential book *This Bridge Called My Back* (Esta puente, mi espalda: voces de mujeres tercermundistas en los Estados Unidos), which she and Cherríe *Moraga collaborated on revising in 1988.

Castillo acknowledges that she strives to follow the storytelling tradition of her Mexican heritage and that she wrote her first poems in response to the death of her grandmother. Active in the *Chicano Movement in high school and college, she consciously used her poetry for political expression. Her first published volumes of verse—*Otro Canto* (1977), *Women Are Not Roses* (1984), and *The Invitation* (1986)—voiced an early version of the feminist concerns she would develop later in her thinking under the term "Xicanisma," or a Chicana-identified politics. She articulates these concerns in *Massacre of the Dreamers: Essays on Xicanisma*, published in 1994, which is based on her doctoral research combined with her personal reflections on Chicana experience, history, and the feminist and ethnic studies writings of the late decades of the twentieth century. Her first novel, *The Mixquiahuala Letters* (1986), consists of letters written over a ten-year period between Teresa, a California poet, and her college friend Alicia, a New York artist, and examines the negative reactions of Mexican and Anglo men to the liberal feminism of the 1970s and 1980s. Her next novel, *Sapogonia: An Anti-Romance in 3/8 Meter*, continues this examination of patriarchy, sex, and gender in its narrative of the destructive power of male-female relationships. Her bestselling and widely reviewed novel *So Far from God* is considered by literary scholars to be the first absurdist Chicana novel. Allegorical, satirical, and filled with black humor, *So Far from God* traces the life and misadventures of Sofie and her four daughters as a backdrop for the author's commentary on Chicana and *Chicano *folklore, history, *family relationships, and politics. Her first collection of short stories, *Loverboys* (1996), continues Castillo's exploration of how racial and cultural issues intersect the sexual and psychological dynamics of human relations.

She also has published a collection of poetry, *I Ask the Impossible* (2001); a novel, *Peel My Love Like an Onion* (1999), and a children's book, *My Daughter, My Son, the Eagle, the Dove* (2000). Her other writings include contributions to numerous anthologies such as *The Third Woman: Minority Woman Writers of the United States* (1980); *Cuentos Chicanos* (1984); *Nosotras: Latina Literature Today* (1986); *English con Salsa* (1994); *More Light: Father and Daughter Poems* (1994); *Daughter of the Fifth Sun* (1995); *Latinas* (1995), and *Tasting Life Twice* (1995). Her contributions to periodicals are similarly varied and numerous. Castillo's papers are housed at the University of California, Santa Barbara, where she held a dissertation fellowship in the Chicano Studies Department in 1989–1990. She received a Ph.D. in American studies from the University of Bremen, Germany, in 1991 and in 1995 was honored with a prestigious fellowship from the National Endowment for the Arts for creative writing.

Further Reading

Binder, Wolfgang, ed. *Contemporary Chicano Poetry II: Partial Autobiographies: Interviews with Twenty Chicano Poets.* Erlanger, Germany: Palm & Enke, 1985.

Dictionary of Literary Biography. Vol. 122 of *Chicano Writers.* Detroit: Gale, 1992.

Navarro, Marta A. *Chicana Lesbians: The Girls Our Mothers Warned Us About.* Berkeley, CA: Third Woman, 1991.

BJ Manríquez

Castro, Fidel (1926–). Cuban revolutionary leader Fidel Castro has the remarkable achievement of leading the island nation of Cuba to become the first communist state in the Western Hemisphere. As a political leader, premier, and president of Cuba, Castro has supported revolutionary movements in various Latin American countries and throughout the continent of Africa, and he has become a symbol of revolution worldwide. Depending on the observer's ideology, he is seen as a noble resister in the tradition of David against Goliath and other freedom fighters or as a leftist tyrant motivated by greed for power. Recognized by his trademark army fatigues and common soldier's cap, Castro rose to power meteorically partly because of the Cuban people's distress under right-wing dictator Fulgencio Batista and partly because of his leadership and charisma. For over four decades Castro has managed to evade several attempts on his life by Central Intelligence Agency (CIA) operatives of the United States and by other Cold War ideologues such as many Cuban exiles who are still bitterly resentful of his takeover of the island from Batista.

Fidel Alejandro Castro-Ruiz was born on August 13, 1926, in Mayari on his family's 23,000-acre sugar plantation near Birán, Oriente province in

Fidel Castro. *Courtesy of Photofest.*

Cuba. As a boy he worked on the family plantation and at age six convinced his family to send him to school. He attended two Jesuit institutions, the Colegio Lasalle and the Colegio Dolores, both in Santiago. In 1942, he entered the Colegio Belén, a Jesuit preparatory school in Havana, where he was voted the school's best athlete in 1944. A year after graduation in 1945 Castro entered the University of Havana School of Law, earning a J.D. degree by 1950. As a practicing attorney with two partners in Havana, he frequently devoted his advocacy to helping the poor. He married in 1948, fathered seven children, and was divorced in 1954.

As the son of a wealthy landowner, Castro easily married into one of Cuba's wealthiest, most influential families. With his socioeconomic class status and law degree his future within the comfortable life of the island's affluent oligarchy was assured. However, he was a social rebel and determined to lead a mass movement for progressive change in his country. By the age of twenty-one he had gathered a substantial following of supporters and began preliminary attempts at bringing about social change by nonviolent reforms. For example, he intended to seek a parliamentary seat in the election of 1952, but General Batista staged a military coup d'état, overthrew the government of President Carlos Prio Socarras, and canceled the election.

Castro went to court and charged Batista with violating the constitution, but the oligarch-controlled court rejected Castro's petition. Castro then launched an attack against the military at Moncada Barracks, Santiago de Cuba, on July 26, 1953, leading to his arrest and sentencing to fifteen years in prison. His passionate speech at the trial, "History Will Absolve Me," condemned the regime of Batista and became the basis of his revolutionary manifesto.

He was released from jail in a general amnesty in 1955, and in fear for his life, the young revolutionary went into exile in México and the United States. In México he organized what came to be known as the 26th of July revolutionary movement, and with a group of 82 men, he launched an attack on the north coast of Oriente province on December 2, 1956. Only 12 of the group survived, among them Castro's brother Raúl and his lieutenant, Che *Guevara. The battered survivors retreated to the Sierra Maestra Mountains and from their mountain stronghold began to wage a continuous guerrilla war against the Batista government. Antipathy to the military dictator and a desire for democracy helped Castro's movement grow to over 800 men, and they were able to score victory after victory and win the hearts of many with Castro's dynamic message and his charisma. By 1958, the group of 12 revolutionaries had grown to about 2,000 guerrillas, for the most part young, middle-class men motivated by their desire to redirect their country from the colonialism and tyranny of the past toward a popular democratic rule.

Since 1899 and the conclusion of the Spanish-American War, Cuba had been recognized as an independent republic under U.S. protection. Although the U.S. occupation ended in 1902, the United States continued to hold Cuba under its economic and political control. At the time of Castro's emergence, Cuba was effectively a police state under the dictator Batista with the full support of the United States. American corporations controlled the economy, and Americans operated casinos in an exploitative system of corruption that was ruining the social structure of Cuba. Opponents of this exploitation were murdered without accountability or punishment. It was this U.S.-backed regime of greed and murder that the young Castro gained support from the Cuban masses to help him and his movement overturn.

On May 24, 1958, Batista launched seventeen army battalions against Castro and his supporters. Despite being vastly outnumbered, the revolutionary guerrillas managed to score a series of stunning victories, which were aided by massive desertion and surrenders from Batista's army. On New Year's Day 1959, Batista fled the country, and Castro took over Havana to the hopeful response of crowds cheering the triumphant revolutionaries in their march to the capital. Initially the United States recognized the new government's legitimacy, even though American supporters of Batista were quick to smear the progressive socialism of the *Cuban Revolution as hardcore state communism. To transform the power structure of his country, Castro's administration took control of U.S. investments in banks and industries, among them United Fruit, thereby confirming American suspicions, which were magnified by right-wing Cuban emigrés in Florida. He seized large landholdings, turning them first into cooperative farms and then into Soviet-style state farm collectives. Alarmed, many Cubans especially among the wealthy began to flee the island and seek sanctuary in the United States. Castro established a totalitarian socialist state, with nationalized industry and collectivized agriculture. Historical hindsight suggests that without U.S. government support of a socialist state in the Western Hemisphere and with Castro's emphasis on a new Cuba to benefit the mass working class, Cubans in the small middle and even smaller upper classes suffered significant hardships. As a result, many of them fled to the United States, particularly after Castro confiscated the oil refineries, sugar mills, and electric utilities owned by U.S. corporations in 1960. The U.S. government retaliated by imposing an economic embargo on Cuba.

On April 17, 1961, a force of 1,300 Cuban exiles, supported by the CIA, made an unsuccessful attempt to invade Cuba at a southern coastal area called the *Bay of Pigs. The assumption was that the invasion would inspire the Cuban populace to rise up and overthrow Castro. It was a monumental miscalculation, for the Cuban population supported Castro against the invaders and their U.S. supporters. On January 31, 1961, the United States formally broke relations with Cuba, and Castro immediately turned toward its implacable foe, the USSR, for support. U.S.-Cuban relations continued deteriorating when in 1962 the U.S. government discovered that the Soviet Union was setting up long-range ballistic missiles on Cuban soil with Castro's permission. American President John F. Kennedy instituted a naval blockade of Cuba that lasted until Soviet Premier Nikita Khrushchev agreed to remove the missiles. But Castro continued to remain in power, much to the dismay of the U.S. government. The pope then excommunicated Castro from the Catholic Church, but for Castro, who had already renounced his faith, it was a matter of little consequence. The missile crisis had far greater humiliation for him, and after this event, he jailed, exiled, and even executed opponents as he determined to take his anti-imperialist cause worldwide. He held the title of premier until 1976, when he became president of the Council of State and the Council of Ministers.

The breakup of the Soviet Union at the end of the twentieth century came as a disaster for communist states the world over, and Cuba was no exception. Nevertheless, Fidelismo continues to hold great sway over many of his people, even as the country teeters on the verge of economic catastrophe, thanks to the trade embargo placed on the island by the United States. Despite the embargo, however, Cuba continues to trade with other nations and remains the second most popular tourist destination in the Caribbean. Ironically, its economy continues to be subsidized by large amounts of U.S. currency, estimated at $850 million annually, from *Cuban Americans who send money to their relatives and friends. Nevertheless, Castro has managed to keep the country firmly under his control to this day and has won the reluctant admiration of much of the world despite growing human rights abuses.

To his credit, Castro has succeeded in bringing about 100 percent literacy among his people and has instituted universal health care for all Cubans. He drastically reduced the infant mortality rate for the country and succeeded in making life expectancy in his country close to that of the United States. His supporters point to Cuba's advanced health care as proof of the improvement in the quality of life of the masses; however, his critics claim that his continued leadership is due to coercion and intimidation. Nevertheless, it cannot be denied that, unlike other dictators, Castro has not created a strong personality cult around his persona. Only rarely has his image appeared on postage stamps, one in 1974 and another in 1999, to commemorate the fortieth anniversary of the Cuban Revolution. He also developed organic farming in the country, which was indubitably the result of the loss of Soviet support in agriculture, forcing the country to turn to its own resources. But his human rights record has tarnished his reputation, and critics point to the lack of media freedom in Cuba as a sign of the lack of democracy there. However, supporters claim that the United States continues to wage secret warfare against Cuba, using spies and mercenaries, and that many of the supposed human rights activists are in fact agents of the United States. Moreover, the unpopular government he had replaced—namely, the brutal regime of Batista—had in fact been supported by the United States. Nevertheless, to this day Castro remains a formidable power to reckon with, having continued to exist for over four decades in the very backyard of the United States and despite all attempts to destroy the Cuban Revolution. In 1996, Castro made the following comment to Canadian and American interviewers during a speech to U.S. and Canadian Pastors for Peace: "We have lived through a huge moral fast for over 35 years, a moral fast imposed by those trying to destroy our revolution, those who have tried to starve us to death and hinder any kind of progress in our country."

Further Reading

González-Pando, Miguel. *The Cuban Americans*. Westport, CT: Greenwood Press, 1998.

Stone, Elizabeth. *Women and the Cuban Revolution*. New York: Pathfinder Press, 1982.

Szulc, Tad. *Fidel: A Critical Portrait*. New York: Avon Books, 2000.

http://abcnews.go.com/reference/bios/castro.html.

Shoba S. Rajgopal

Cempasúchil. *Cempasúchil*, also known as a marigold, is a herbaceous plant of Mexican origin. The term comes from the Nahuátl words *cempoalli* (twenty) and *xochitl* (flower). *Cempasúchil* is used to decorate tombs and shrines at occasions honoring the dead in México. The plant was dubbed "twenty flowers" because of the multiple flowers produced by each plant. The use of *cempasúchil* flowers, with their pungent smell and deep orange hue, has become a popular addition to the *Día de los Muertos (All Souls' Day) altars and traditions that have gained wide popularity in the United States.

Gabriella Sánchez

Cerón, Laura (1964–). Laura Cerón, one of the few Latinas to have a recurring role on a prime-time television drama, plays nurse Chuny Márquez on the NBC Emmy award–winning series *ER*. Seen as a role model for Latinas in television, Cerón plays an emergency room nurse who asserts her Latina ethnicity and bilingual skills, thereby reflecting American society's linguistic and cultural pluralism. Cerón was born in México City, México, grew up in Chicago, Illinois, and is actively involved in community service through involvement with the VALE (Voz de la Alianza Latina Estudiantil—Voice of the Latina Student Alliance) Leadership Conference aimed at motivating and promoting leadership among college students. Nominated several times by the American Latino Media Arts (ALMA) for her acting, she received an *ALMA Award Nomination for Outstanding Actress in a Drama Series in 2000. In addition to her television role, her film appearances include *Losing Isaiah* (1995), *The Public Eye* (1992), *The Missing Persons* (1993), **Mi Familia* (1995), *The Big Squeeze* (1996), *Details* (2000), and *King Rikki* (2002).

Brenda Rascón

***César and Rubén*.** A musical written and directed by Ed Begley, Jr., a professional actor with extensive professional credits, *César and Rubén* (also advertised as "The César *Chávez Story") presents a fictionalized account of the title characters, labor and civil rights leader César Chávez and *Los Angeles Times* reporter Rubén Salazar. Produced by Stephen Roseberry, the play premiered at the El Portal *Theater in North Hollywood in March 2003, starring Roberto Alcaraz as Chávez and also Tony D'Arc, Marta Dubois, and Danielle Barbosa.

César and Rubén presents an admiring summary of Chávez's life through a range of music genres, newsreel-type images, and a conversation with another Chicano hero, slain reporter Salazar. The performance mixes humor and drama with its music and dance to tell the story of two men noble who tried to improve their country. Begley, a personal friend of Chávez, describes his motivation to write the script as a labor of love to capture the heroic spirit of nonviolent struggle for better working conditions for hundreds of thousands of migrant farmworkers.

Among the supporters of this monumental endeavor are members of the Chávez *family, the César E. Chávez Foundation, United Farm Workers, Hollywood actors, and elected community leaders. The large supporting cast included Brenda Canela, Charles Dennis, Jeanine Pacheco, Evan Saucedo, Rachelle Carson, Antonio Martínez, Gustavo Rex, and Edward Albert as the character Naylor. The play's musical direction and orchestration was composed by Steve Orich with songs by Rubén *Blades, David Crosby, Peter Gabriel, Enrique *Iglesias, Joni Mitchell, Carlos *Santana, Sting, Carmen Moreno, and Don Henley and sound design by Rick Boot. The choreography was written and directed by Román Vásquez. Diah Wymont was costume designer for the production, with visual effects provided by Stephan Szpak-Fleet and lighting and set design by James Jeremias.

Further Reading

http://www.cesarandruben.com.
http://www.cesarechavezfoundation.org.

Cordelia Chávez Candelaria

Cha cha cha. Cha cha cha refers to a 1950s popular dance craze in Cuba that later took the United States by storm. First introduced to the U.S. audience at a Latin concert at Carnegie Hall on February 20, 1954, its origins point to classically trained violinist, composer, bandleader, and arranger Enrique Jorrín (1925–1987), who began developing the cha cha cha in 1948, probably derived from a final passage or the second section of the *danzón or slower *mambo. The name comes from the shuffling "cha cha cha" sound that the dancers' feet made moving to the new rhythms. Jorrín performed with the Danzonera Arcaño y Sus Maravillas and directed the Orquesta América when he composed "La Engañadora" (The Deceitful Woman) in 1948, which was later recorded in 1953 and soon enjoyed international popularity. The typical instrumentation included strings, piano, bass, congas, timbales, guiro, and flute. Jorrín preferred unison voices rendering a light, bright, and sweet vocal sonority. Orquesta Aragón continues to record in Cuba, as does Fajarda y sus Estrellas, who relocated to New York in the 1960s. In New York City, the big bands emphasized the horn sections, rendering a more unique sound and style. Tito *Puente's covers of Rosendo Ruiz, Jr.'s "Rico Vacilon" (Having a Ball, included on *Dance the Cha Cha Chá*), and Aragón's 1954 "Pare Cochero" (Stop Coachman, included on *Cha Cha Chá for Lovers*), were exquisite compositions. Others include José Curbelo's "El Pescador" (The Fisherman), and *Machito's "El Campesino" (The Peasant; included on *Asia Minor* in the mid-1950s). Dámaso *Pérez Prado's "Cherry Pink and Apple Blossum White" reached number one in the United States for ten weeks in 1955 but was performed as a mambo. Other bands performed it as a cha cha cha. Non-Latino musicians like the Tommy Dorsey Orchestra altered style, making cha cha cha more palatable for American dancers in their 1958 recording "Tea for Two Cha Cha," as did Stan Kenton's album *Viva Kenton*, which included three cha cha chas.

Jorrín eventually relocated to México in 1954 after founding his own orchestra and later returning to Cuba in 1959. He toured Africa and Europe in 1965 and continued performing and recording on Cuba's state label *Areito* through the mid-1980s.

Further Reading

Clarke, Donald, ed. *Penguin Encyclopedia of Popular Music*. 2nd ed. New York: Penguin Books, 1991.

Peter J. García

Charanga. The term *charanga* has a variety of meanings within the context of music. Not only is it the name for a popular style of Cuban music; it also refers to a particular dance, as well as to the dance *orquestas* (orchestras). Developed from *charangas francesas* (French orchestras) of the nineteenth century, and often identified with *danzón, *charanga* is regarded as Cuba's national dance, with the ensembles referred to as *danzoneras* or *charangas*. The dance orchestras typically consist of a lead flute backed by violin, cello, piano, and bass; they also usually include a rhythm section of Afro-Cuban percussion, such as timbales, conga, guiro, and male voices singing in unison.

Influenced by Arsenio Rodríguez's *conjunto*, Antonio Arcaño (1929–1944) introduced the conga to the *charanga*, Later, *charangas* like Orquesta Sensación were formed in 1953 by percussionist Rolando Valdés, who persuaded the retired, infamous sonero legend Abelardo Barroso (1905–1972) to record with his orchestra during the latter part of the decade. Following several important musical tours during the late 1950s by José Fajardo and Orquesta Aragón, New York City's *charanga* heyday actually began in 1960 and was led by Charlie Palmieri's *charanga*, *La Duboney*, with Johnny *Pacheco on flute backed by four violins. Other notable New York City *charanga* artists include flautist, composer, arranger, and producer Lou Pérez (1928–) and Alfredito Valdés (1908–1988).

Charanga's popularity reemerged again during the mid-1970s at the same time as New York City *salsa was also booming. Most bandleaders eventually replaced the strings with a brass section. Among the stylistic changes that occurred during the 1980s was the fusion of *conjunto* trumpets and *tres* with the Colombian *vallenata* accordion style. This hybrid form known as *charanga vallenata* was developed by Roberto Torres, although flautist Nestor Torres is also credited with forging an innovative fusion style. During the mid- to late 1980s, New York City *charangas* underwent a low-key revival under the generic guise of *Latin jazz. *Evolucíonando 96 on RMM* by Los Jovenes del Barrio (Barrio Youth) also experimented with Afro-Cuban styles, jazz, and rhythm and blues (R&B) in recordings produced by *charanga* musician Johnny Almendra (1953–). Throughout his career, Almendra worked with many of the best Latin musicians in the United States and Cuba, such as Tito *Puente and Willie *Colón.

Further Reading

Roberts, John Storm. *The Latin Tinge: The Impact of Latin American Music on the United States*. New York: Oxford University Press, 1979.

Peter J. García

Charreada. The *charreada* is a unique Mexican and Chicana/o equestrian *sport rooted in the cattle ranching culture of colonial México. It remains extremely popular in the Southwest borderlands of the United States where, in the twenty-first century, it is one of the oldest folk customs continuously practiced among Americans in the U.S. Sometimes facilely translated as "rodeo," the *charreada* is a key part of the origin and history of the "American cowboy," which is a staple of U.S. popular culture. During the colonial period, cattle ranching was practiced throughout México, including most of today's southwestern United States, which at that time was still part of México and, before that, part of New Spain. Over time, the skills and techniques employed in cattle ranching activities eventually gave rise to the *charreada* as a seasonal social event featuring competitive games, parades, *food, entertainment, and a variety of riding and roping displays.

Some of the skills and techniques employed in the work of cattle ranching that evolved into the **charro*'s sporting activities include *herraderos* (branding events) and rodeos (roundups). Skilled riding and horsemanship continue to be requirements of the *charreada*. Not until after the Mexican Revolution of 1910 did the *charreada* became institutionalized and sanctioned as the official sport of México. Postrevolutionary México witnessed dramatic growth in its urban population due to the commercialization of agriculture and the move toward industrialization, forcing thousands of Mexicans to migrate out of the countryside into larger cities and even across the border into the United States. The new city dwellers also included an increasing number of displaced cattle ranchers and ranch workers who had reluctantly relocated to the urban centers due to the gradual destruction and disappearance of the haciendas (large estates, plantations). As this segment of urban population grew, they established national *charro* associations to continue to practice, refine, and standardize the *charreada*. The first national *charro* association was established in Mexico City on July 4, 1921, while the Federación Nacional de Charros (National Charros Federation) was instituted on December 16, 1933. To this day the Federación continues to sponsor national meetings to establish and define the rules for all matters concerning participation and competition in *charreadas*.

In the United States, the history and status of the *charreada* have experienced a different development. Long before Anglo-American settlers arrived in the early 1800s, cattle ranching as business and related roping and riding contests as sport were already widely practiced throughout the present-day Southwest. As Anglo-Americans became involved in ranching in the new geographical environment, they learned the cattle trade from the more experienced Mexican vaqueros (cowboys). They not only adopted Mexican technology (equipment, riding methods, technical skills, and related crafts), but they also appropriated the Mexican ranching vocabulary. Many of the terms associated with the cowboy image and culture and with American cattle ranching come directly from Spanish, including *ranch* (*rancho*), *buckaroo* (vaquero), *rodeo* (*rodeo*), *lariat* (*la réata*), *corral* (*corral*), *dallying* (*darle vuelta*), *chaps* (*chaparreras*), and *quirts* (*cuartas*), to name but a few.

Thus, the *charreada* served as a source and immediate precursor of the later American rodeo tradition, but the traditions gradually diverged into distinct forms, related in origin and sharing many elements but vitally different in other ways. One of the main differences between Mexican- and Anglo-American-style rodeo is that in the latter the contests are timed, while in the Mexican rodeo the contests are judged on the grace and elegance with which the skills are executed. Another difference is that participants in professional standardized American-style rodeo usually compete for money, while Mexican *charros* normally compete for trophies. The main difference between the *charreada* and the rodeo is status: historically it has enjoyed greater prestige in México. Supported by a predominantly working-class ethnic population, the official Mexican *charreada* was not formally practiced in the United States until the early 1970s. Before that, *jaripeos*, consisting primarily of informal bull and bronco riding contests, were the only form of Mexican rodeo practiced in the United States. During the *Chicano Movement of the early 1970s, Mexican Americans began searching for ways to reclaim and revitalize their Mexican heritage in the United States. Members of México's Federación Nacional de Charros were invited to help them establish the *charreada* north of the border. Since then, the *charreada* has grown considerably and is currently practiced among Chicanas/os throughout most of the United States. Literally and metaphorically, the *lienzo charro* (rodeo arena) may be seen as a space in which participants practice and/or recoup their history and heritage.

By the twenty-first century, the *charreadas* have become standardized on both sides of the border. Typically held on Sundays, they begin around noontime, open with a *desfile* (parade) featuring all participants in the day's event, before saluting the U.S. and the Mexican flags and the playing of the "Marcha de Zacatecas" (Zacatecas March), which many *charros* consider as México's second national anthem. Throughout the formal event, musical entertainment is provided by a **banda* (a brass and percussive group) or a *mariachi ensemble. The formal competition consists of nine *suertes*, or riding and roping competitive events for men. The nine *suertes* include: (1) *cala*, a reining competition displaying horse control; (2) *piales en el lienzo*, roping a running horse by the hind legs while on horseback; (3) *colas*, bull tailing; (4) *jinete de novillos*, bull riding; (5) *jinete de yeguas*, wild mare riding; (6) *terna*, team bull roping; (7) *manganas a pie*, roping the front legs of a horse while on foot; (8) *manganas a caballo*, roping the front legs of a horse from horseback; and (9) *paso de muerte* (literally "pass of death"), jumping from a bareback running horse to a running wild mare.

A highly masculinized practice, until recently *charreadas* did not allow women to compete in the riding and sporting events. Instead, they were expected to manage food booths, cheer as spectators, serve as queens, and host visitors. However, in 1992, women succeeded in formally instituting the *escaramuza* as the tenth official competitive event. The *escaramuza* is a female precision riding team that displays their equestrian skills through the execution of choreographed patterns in the arena. Riding sidesaddle and dressed in full, lacy skirts, the young women often project an image of "daintiness" that deflects attention away from the rigorous riding skills required to execute the rapid turns, stops, and changes of speed demanded of the choreographed patterns on horseback. Although the *escaramuza* provides women an opportunity to participate more actively, women are still not allowed to compete in the *charreada*'s trick and fancy roping contests.

In addition to the formal events, the *charreada* as a popular culture practice usually features a number of peripheral elements that mark its ethnic history and development. Outside the arena, for example, a thriving food exchange occurs, as Mexican delicacies such as *carnitas* (pork meat), *barbacoa* (Mexican-style barbecue), *elotes* (corn on the cob), and **menudo* (tripe stew), as well as North American imports like popcorn, soft drinks, and beer, attract people to the concessions stands. Amid the lively and constant flow of people circulating between the arena and the food vendors, *conjuntos norteños* (accordion-based ensembles from the border region) perform impromptu serenades and dances. After the parades and competitions conclude, performing artists often continue entertaining the remaining crowds with a variety of talents, often followed by an open-air dance concert.

Thus, as a cultural practice that transcends national boundaries, the *charreada* helps construct a particular conception of Mexican cultural identity by invoking a set of images, landscapes, historical events, symbols, and rituals that represent the shared experiences of a transnational Mexican culture. As a result, for Mexicanos who have been deterritorialized or otherwise displaced from their places of origin, the *charreada* provides a culturally sanctioned space in which Mexicanos can experience themselves as a social body with deep cultural and historical roots in the *barrios and borderlands on both sides of the U.S.-México political boundary.

Further Reading

Islas Escárcega, Leovigildo. *Historical Synthesis of Charrería. El Arte de la Charrería.* Mexico City: Artes de México y del Mundo, 1967.

Le Compte, Mary. "The Hispanic Influence on the History of Rodeo, 1823–1922." *Journal of Sport History* 12 (1985): 21–38.

Nájera-Ramírez, Olga. "Engendering Nationalism: Identity, Discourse, and the Mexican Charro." *Anthropological Quarterly* 67 (1994): 1–14.

Sands, Kathleen Mullen. *Charrería Mexicana: An Equestrian Folk Tradition.* Tucson: University of Arizona Press, 1994.

Olga Nájera-Ramírez

Charro. A *charro* is a Mexican horseman, similar to the American cowboy, distinguished by his unique dress, skills, and implements. The *charro* is a potent symbol of Mexican machismo and masculinity, embodying many personal traits such as honor, virtue, and valor. In Europe, the Spanish word *charro* was a euphemism for a peasant from Salamanca and suggested many connotations such as "rustic," "backward," or "ill bred." In the Americas, *charros* are the vaqueros (cowboys) or New Mexican *ciboleros* (bison hunters), linked by the association of man and beast. Today, Mexican and Chicano horsemen perform their equestrian feats and exhibit their skill and prowess in the **charreada* (rodeo). In the past, they typically worked on the ranches or large haciendas (estates) in colonial México and the Southwest and by the nineteenth century had become symbols of masculinity.

After Mexican independence (1821), President Benito Juarez developed the *rurales* to help establish social order and justice and maintain political control. The *rurales* were a mounted police force that helped curtail the rise of outlaws and bandits, especially in rural areas. They dressed as *charros*, and their image reinforced the strong, skilled, honorable horseman loyal to *family and country. By the end of the Mexican Revolution (1910–1917), the *charro* became a national symbol of masculinity and was becoming a popular character in literature, cinema, and music.

Mexican *mariachi musicians characteristically don the *traje* (suit) and *sombrero* (hat) of the *charro*, having adapted the *charro* attire after appearing in the Mexican cinema. Mexican cinema developed the *charro* genre or western movie beginning in the 1940s, which featured many of México's beloved singing sensations including Pedre Infante, Jorge Negrete, and Miguel Aceves Mejia, to name a few. The singing *cowboy* also became extremely popular in the southwestern United States, performing **ranchera* music and providing an overly romanticized view of rural life on the hacienda. Today the *charro*, either singing or on horseback, remains a highly romanticized and beloved popular symbol of Mexican masculine identity.

Further Reading

Campa, Arturo. *Hispanic Culture in the Southwest.* Norman: University of Oklahoma Press, 1979.

Castro, Rafaela G. *Chicano Folklore: A Guide to the Folktales, Traditions, Rituals, and Religious Practices of Mexican Americans.* Oxford: Oxford University Press, 2000.

Cordelia Chávez Candelaria and Peter J. García

Chávez, César (1927–1993). César Estrada Chávez, a champion of civil rights, is best known for being a grassroots leader and the founder and organizer of the United Farm Workers (UFW) and for his inspirational dedication as an activist for social justice. Through his commitment to the use of nonviolent action, he was able to bring attention to the plight of migrant farmworkers, which ultimately resulted in improved working and living conditions and better wages. Having labored in the fields as a migrant farmworker, Chávez was keenly aware of the injustices the farmworkers suffered at the hands of the growers and corporations who saw them as expendable. The realization that growers were powerful because the workers were weak motivated Chávez to dedicate his life to bringing justice, dignity, and respect to farmworkers.

Born in 1927, Chávez was the second of six children born to Librado Chávez and Juana Estrada Chávez. Raised on a farm near Yuma, Arizona, his father taught him to work hard and stand up for others, while his mother and grandmother instilled in him a deep spiritual faith and kindness. In the late 1930s, when the country was recovering from the stock market crash and the Great Depression, life as Chávez knew it would change forever. Jobs were hard to find, and due to a business deal gone bad, his parents lost their land, and the *family was forced to travel through California seeking work as migrant workers harvesting crops. At the age of ten, this was Chávez's first exposure to the injustices experienced by farmworkers. Migrant farmworkers, most of whom were of Mexican descent, had no permanent homes and traveled to wherever the crops were in season. In return for their hard work, they earned low wages, lived in overcrowded facilities with no bathrooms, running water, or electricity, and were often subjected to major safety and health hazards. Chávez worked in the fields while attending thirty different schools before successfully graduating from eighth grade. This was an unusual and remarkable feat given the tremendous discrimination the migrant children experienced in the school system. Teachers were not sympathetic to the hardships of constant relocation; they did not allow the children to speak Spanish while on school property, and many felt it was a waste of their time to teach migrant children who would soon be moving to another town to work a new harvest. Despite the conflicts and challenges, Chávez graduated and in 1944 joined the U.S. Navy, where he had the opportunity to travel overseas during his four-year tour of duty. Upon his discharge and return to California, he met and married Helen Fabela, a young woman who shared his social concerns. Together, they began the work of improving the lives of farmworkers by teaching them to read and write and helping them become American citizens. Helen became an important partner with Chávez, as well as the mother of his eight children. During this time, Chávez immersed himself in self-education around the use of power and nonviolence, reading books on labor history, social change, St. Francis of Assissi, the life of Mahatma Gandhi, the history of unions, and sacrificing to help others.

In 1952, Chávez went to work for the Community Service Organization, where he registered Latino voters and organized meetings to share information with workers. Initially feeling he was not a good speaker, he spent more time listening to the workers than speaking to them. As his confidence grew, he found his voice and learned that people were listening to him, and they liked his message. At the age of thirty-five, Chávez quit his job and moved his family to Delano, California, where he could concentrate on organizing farmworkers into a union. In 1962, the National Farm Workers Association (NFWA) was formed with Chávez at the helm as president, Dolores *Huerta and Gilbert Padilla as vice presidents, and Antonio Orendáin as secretary treasurer. The organization chose as its symbol a red flag that features a black eagle surrounded by a white circle in the center. The red of the flag symbolizes the sacrifice and hard work necessary to gain justice, the black eagle symbolizes the dark situation they were in, while the white circle symbolizes hope. With their focus on fighting for social justice, they adopted as their official slogan, "Viva La Causa" (Long Live our Cause). The organization would later unite with the Filipino labor union known as the Agricultural Workers Organizing Committee to become the United Farm Workers Organizing Committee (UFWOC) and ultimately the United Farm Workers.

With Chávez leading the cause, workers felt more empowered to stand up for their rights. In 1965, they convinced Chávez that a strike was the only way to get the California wine grape growers to listen to their demands. In 1966, Chávez led a 340-mile march from Delano, California, to Sacramento, California, to bring attention to the strike and solicit support from the public and the governor. The march swelled in size as it made its way toward the capital city, and by the time they reached Stockton, California, the number of marchers had grown to 5,000, convincing the growers that they had to recognize the power behind the union. They agreed to sign the first labor contract ever negotiated between growers and a farmworker's union in the United States. The California table grape growers rejected unionization efforts, so the struggle continued and proved to be a long and bitter dispute that saw Chávez and other union members jailed repeatedly before agreements were signed.

Since lettuce and grapes grown and harvested in California make their way to tables in all parts of the United States, Chávez reasoned that he could bring greater pressure on the growers if he had nationwide support. He expanded his appeal for support beyond California, calling for a nationwide boycott on California table grapes and later on lettuce. He found that there were significant numbers of sympathizers across the United States, who supported the boycotts because they recognized the unjust treatment of the fieldworkers. Throughout the struggle, Chávez remained committed to nonviolence, but with the opposition equally committed to harassing the strikers in the fields, the outbreaks of violence against the union resulted in beatings and some deaths of union strikers. In 1968, Chávez went on the first of three public fasts, in hopes of convincing union members to adhere to nonviolent action. Through the quiet sacrifice of his fasts, he gained spiritual strength, and his fight for justice touched people across the United States. The media covered his fasts, which brought attention to the plight of the farmworkers and garnered support from notable people like Robert Kennedy and civil rights leader Martin Luther King, Jr. By 1970, Chávez's actions proved successful, and the boycott ended when union contracts were signed.

In 1935, when the National Labor Relations Act was passed, workers gained the right to collective bargaining for employment needs. Farmworkers were excluded from this critical act and were not able to participate in collective bargaining until 1975, when they obtained these rights through the help of the UFW. Collective bargaining opened the door for negotiations around issues such as fair wages, safe working conditions, protection from harmful and unhealthy chemicals and pesticides, proper equipment, and provision of clean water and field toilets. As a result of this new negotiating power in 1975 and through Chávez's efforts, the Supreme Court outlawed

Longtime labor leader and UFW founder César Chávez was recognized for his lifetime of service to the nation when Arizona State University became the first university to award him an honorary doctorate in 1992. *Courtesy of the Department of Chicana and Chicano Studies Archive, Arizona State University.*

the short-handled hoe, which was the culprit of thousands of back injuries among farmworkers.

The struggle led by Chávez proved successful by securing collective bargaining and political protection from the National and California Labor Relations Boards. The humble fieldworkers earned higher wages and won human rights that were typically taken for granted by nonmarginalized workers. Before his death in the 1990s, Chávez shifted his attention to boycotts and demonstrations against pesticide use by growers and the industry. Over the years, pesticides had seeped into the water tables, contaminating fresh produce, threatening worker safety, and causing health hazards. Chávez worked tirelessly until his last day, advocating that unjust treatment of farmworkers be eradicated, although the issue of pesticide-related health hazards continues as a labor issue.

In April 1993, while in San Luis, Arizona, to help fight a lawsuit, Chávez died peacefully in his sleep. His funeral was held in Delano, California, and was attended by more than 30,000 mourners from all walks of life and economic classes, who joined in a procession behind his casket for three miles, taking one final march with this humble man who dedicated his life to justice, nonviolence, and service to others.

Chávez was recognized for his tremendous contributions in 1990 when he received the Aguila Award, the highest civilian award presented by the Mexican government, and again in 1992, when he received an honorary doctorate from Arizona State University. In 1994, Helen traveled to Washington, D.C., to receive an award on his behalf when President Bill Clinton posthumously awarded Chávez the Presidential Medal of Freedom Award, the highest honor awarded to civilians in the United States. Since then, some states have declared a holiday in his name, and in 2003 the United Postal Service honored him with a stamp bearing his likeness.

Further Reading

Anaya, Rudolfo A. *Elegy on the Death of César Chávez.* El Paso, TX: Cinco Puntos Press, 2000.

"César Chávez." *Latino Journal.* http://www.asu.edu/clas/hrc/latino/chavez/chavez.intro.html.

Griswold del Castillo, Richard, and Richard A. Garcia. *César Chávez: A Triumph of Spirit.* Norman: University of Oklahoma Press, 1995.

Hachey, Thomas, and Ralph Weber, eds. *American Dissent from Thomas Jefferson to César Chávez: The Rhetoric of Reform and Revolution.* Huntington, NY: R.E. Krieger, 1981.

Matthiessen, Peter. *Sal si puedes: César Chávez and the New American Revolution.* New York: Random House, 1973.

Ross, Fred. *Conquering Goliath: César Chávez at the Beginning.* Foreword by Senator Edward M. Kennedy. Keene, CA: United Farm Workers; distributed by El Taller Grafico, 1989.

http://www.sfsu.edu/967Ececipp/cesar_chavez/chavezhome.htm.

Santos C. Vega and Alma Alvarez-Smith

Chávez, Denise (1948–). A successful Chicana playwright and fiction writer, Denise Chávez is also a poet and actor with professional stage experience. Her novel *Face of an Angel* (1995) received national recognition, winning the Before Columbus American Book Award (1995), and her first book, *The Last of the Menu Girls* (1987), a collection of short stories, attracted favorable critical notice as well as popular attention. Some of the stories from *Last of the Menu Girls* are anthologized in such influential canon setters as *The Norton Anthology of American Literature* (2000). Her other credits include teaching playwriting, drama, acting, and creative writing at the University of Houston, College of Santa Fe; La Compañía de Teatro de Albuquerque; Theater-in-the-Red in Santa Fe; and many others.

Born in Las Cruces, New Mexico, on August 15, 1948, Chávez was reared in a middle-class family of professionals. Her mother was a teacher and her father an attorney. Deeply involved in drama during high school, Chávez received a scholarship to attend New Mexico State University, where she studied with Mark Medoff, author of the successful play *Children of a Lesser God*, and graduated with a bachelor's degree in drama in 1971. She earned a master's in drama from Trinity University in San Antonio, Texas, in 1974 and obtained a master's in creative writing from the University of New Mexico in 1984, where she worked with successful *Chicano writer Rudolfo A. *Anaya. Encouraged by her mentors Medoff and Anaya, Chávez has written more than twenty plays, which she began writing in the 1970s in the tradition and style of Luis *Valdez's *Teatro Campesino. Her plays explore multiple themes intrinsic to Chicano culture, such as lost values and identity, and draw heavily on Chávez's life experience in southern New Mexico. Using humor and bilingualism, she explores themes of feminism and Latino identity, particularly within the context of *family relationships.

Her plays include *Sí, Hay Posada* (Yes, There's Room [in the Inn]), a play produced in 1981 about a Vietnam veteran trying to come to terms with his past; a 1983 production *Hecho en México* (Made in México), which examines the plight of undocumented workers in the United States; and *Plaza* in 1984, which garnered international recognition and was selected for staging at two prestigious, international venues, the Joseph Papp Festival Latino de Nueva York and the Scotland Arts Festival in Edinburgh. Chávez's latest novel *Loving Pedro Infante* (2002) extends the author's fascination with exploring the varieties of *barrios and borderlands experience, as the novel uses flashback, humor, and microcosms of everyday details as a canvas for presenting the way show business icons enter individual lives. She continues to perform, lecture, and teach from her Las Cruces home base.

Further Reading

Rivera, Rowena A. "Denise Chávez." In *Chicano Writers, Second Series*. Vol. 122 of *Dictionary of Literary Biography*, edited by Francisco A. Lomelí and

Carl R. Shirley. Detroit, MI: Gale Group and Bruccoli Clark Layman Book, 1992.
World Literature Today. http://www.ou.edu/worldlit/authors/chavez/chavez.html.

Julie Amparano García

Chávez, Julz (c. 1963–). Julz Chávez is a toy designer and chief creative officer of Get Real Girl, Inc., a line of multiracial action adventure figures. Established in 1999, the Get Real Girl dolls promote self-esteem through a *sports theme, and they allow girls to be their own role models because they come in a variety of races, including biracial.

Chávez was one of eleven children born to migrant farmworkers in Yuma, Arizona. As a child, she had no affinity for the Barbie fashion dolls and longed for dolls that looked like her and her friends, the same motivation that led to the *homies design. After earning her Bachelor of Arts degree in illustration and creative writing at the California College of Arts and Crafts, she accumulated experience and expertise working for toy companies such as Sega, Mattel, and Discovery Toys. In 1995 she went into business for herself and began work creating the sports-themed action figures, which won the Oppenheimer Best Toy Award as well as the Dr. Toy Best Toy of the Year Award in 2001.

Chávez, who sits on the board of directors for The Women's Foundation, has earned several awards for her work, including the Sabre Award for Toys and Games in 2000, *Hispanic Magazine*'s Young Entrepreneur Award in 2001, and the Women's Foundation Ground Breaker Award in 2002. Her life, work, and determination to bring about social change were influenced by her father's cousin, civil rights activist César *Chávez.

Further Reading

http://www.bayarea.com/mld/mercurynews/3729897.htm.

Alma Alvarez-Smith

CHC. *See* Congressional Hispanic Caucus.

Chicana/o Rock and Popular Music in Southern California. Most major *Chicano rock artists have emerged from Southern California and have provided a major source of Latino/a musical entertainment in the United States. To be more specific, most have come from the greater Los Angeles area. The area's enormous population and proximity to the recording industry in Hollywood are two possible reasons. Some artists emigrated to the Los Angeles area from other parts of the country, but the majority are native to the area.

In any survey of Chicano music in general, and particularly Chicano rock, the start begins with the man who is widely considered the "Father of Chicano Music," Lalo *Guerrero. He has also been described by pop singer Linda *Ronstadt as "the first great Chicano musical artist." Born and raised in Tucson, Arizona, Guerrero moved to Los Angeles in 1939, where he recorded virtually his entire catalog, with the exception of many of the children's records he did in Mexico City with Las Ardillitas de Lalo Guerrero. In a career that began in the late 1930s and continued into the twenty-first century, he wrote and recorded over 700 titles, which cover nearly every genre of Latin and American music. Among his composing credits are the classic "Nunca Jamas" (Never Ever), covered by José *Feliciano, Javier Solís, and the Trío Los Panchos, and "Canción Mexicana," recorded by legendary Mexican **ranchera* singers Lucha Reyes and Lola Beltrán. Aside from the Latin forms such as the *ranchera*, *bolero, *cumbia, **corrido*, *cha cha cha, *pachanga, *porro*, *rumba, *samba, *tropical*, and *norteña*, Guerrero also recorded rock and roll, blues, boogie-woogie, swing, and pop ballads, in addition to comedy songs, parodies, and children's music.

In the late 1940s and early 1950s, while an artist for Imperial Records, Guerrero often wrote Spanish-language versions of popular American hits. Some examples are "La Tamalada" (Tamale Feast, "Saturday Night Fish Fry" by Louis Jordan), "Chicas Patas Boogie" (Very Chicano Boogie, "Oh Babe" by Louis Prima), and "Llorar" (Cry, "Cry" by Johnny Ray). He also wrote and recorded his own blues, swing, and rock songs such as "Muy Sabroso Blues" (Very Tasty Blues), "Marijuana Boogie," "El Hombre Gordo" (The Fat Man), and "Se Fue y Me Dejó" (She Left and Abandoned Me). These songs might be considered pre–rock and roll.

Many of Guerrero's songs from his Imperial Records era used an original form of Chicano slang called Caló, which was spoken by pachucos and zoot suiters (*see* Zoot Suit) of the time. He first used Caló in the late 1940s on his recordings with his Trío Imperial. He later utilized it with his band Lalo Guerrero y sus Cinco Lobos. It was with this band that he recorded his swing and blues music in the late 1940s and early 1950s. By the mid-1950s, before the emergence of Ritchie *Valens, he was writing and recording outright rock and roll. "Tin Marín De Do Pingue" gives "Rock Around the Clock" by Bill Haley & the Comets a run for its money. One of his best hits of the period is "Do You Believe in Reincarnation," a doo-wop song complete with Jordanaires-style background vocal harmonies.

Guerrero also included rock in his comedy recordings such as "Elvis Pérez," which was contained within Spanish versions of Elvis Presley hits "Hound Dog," "Don't Be Cruel," and "Heartbreak Hotel." In the 1960s, he wrote and recorded a rock song called "Los Greñudos" (The Messy Haired), backed by his son's teenage band Mark & the Escorts. He also created rock hybrids (part rock/part *norteña*) such as "La Minifalda de Reynalda" (Reynalda's Miniskirt) and "Felipe El Hippie," with Los Hermanos Arellano backing him on the *norteña parts* and Mark & the Escorts on the rock sections. Another important figure in the prerock era is Edmundo Tostado, known as Don Tosti. Don played violin in the El Paso Symphony, upright bass in the big bands in New York, and led a band called The Pachuco Boogie Boys (with Eddie Cano on piano). He accomplished all that before forming his popular Latin band in the mid-1950s, known as Don Tosti and his Orchestra. The recordings by The Pachuco Boogie Boys were often swing or boogie-woogie songs, also employing Caló. Their lead singer was Raúl Díaz, who could scat sing with the best of his Anglo and black counterparts.

In 1958, Pacoima, California's Ritchie Valens (Valenzuela) burst onto the scene as a rock and roller with "Come On Let's Go" and "Donna," which were his compositions, and his rocked-up version of a traditional Mexican **son jarocho* from Veracruz, *"La Bamba." With his tragic early demise, it can never be known what he would have achieved or what direction his music would have taken, but the fact that he created such successful records by the age of seventeen is astounding. Valens influenced many Latino rockers who were to follow, including Chan Romero and Chris Montez. Romero, who grew up in Billings, Montana, came to Los Angeles in the wake of Valens's death. He was invited by Valens's manager, Bob Keane, who had heard Romero's demo and thought of him as Valens's heir apparent. While recording in Los Angeles for Keane's DelFi Records, Romero was invited by Valens's mother to stay at her house, where he became like a *family member in the Valenzuela household. One of the songs Romero recorded in those first sessions was a song he had written called "The Hippy Hippy Shake." Unbeknownst to Romero, the record was also released in England, where it was picked up by an unknown Paul McCartney in Liverpool. He liked it and learned it for his young band, The Beatles. They played the song regularly at their club gigs in Hamburg, Germany, and eventually recorded it on one of their live BBC radio broadcasts. In 1965, "The Hippy Hippy Shake" was recorded by an English band called The Swinging Blue Jeans, who had a number-one record with it on the English charts. The song was revived in 1988 by The Georgia Satellites for the sound track of the movie *Cocktail*, starring Tom Cruise.

Hawthorne, California's Chris Montez (b. Ezekiel Montanez) had met Valens, who had performed at a local dance hall. Fueled by the inspiration he got from Valens, Montez went on to have a hit record with "Let's Dance," which reached number four on the national charts in 1962. The success of "Let's Dance" led to a tour of England with The Beatles, who recorded their first album during that tour. In the mid-1960s Montez had more chart success with mellower songs such as "Call Me" and "The More I See You." Like Romero, Trini *López had to come to Los Angeles to fill a void left by a fallen star. López originally made the trip from Dallas, Texas, to join The Crickets in the wake of Buddy Holly's death. When things weren't moving fast enough for López, who was running out of money, he began to play clubs as a solo artist. An engagement at the famous P.J.'s in Hollywood led to his being discovered by Frank Sinatra. Sinatra signed López to a record deal with his Reprise Records. "Trini López Live at P.J.'s" hit number two nationally and launched López's career. He had several hit singles that reached the national Top 40 in the mid-1960s, the biggest being his version of "If I Had a Hammer," which was number one in twenty-five countries and enjoyed forty-eight weeks on the U.S. Top 40. López has recorded over forty albums in his career.

In the 1960s, East Los Angeles became a hotbed of music. Much like Liverpool in the same era, there were scores, if not hundreds, of bands, numerous venues for teenage dances, and many records being made. Much of this boom was a result of the efforts of two men, Eddie Davis and Billy Cárdenas. Davis was a producer who owned several small record labels, while Cárdenas produced and managed many of the Eastside teenage bands. They worked together and separately to advance the careers of many musicians and singers. Cárdenas's first band was called The Romancers. They recorded two instrumental albums for DelFi Records in 1963, *Do the Slauson* and *Let's Do the Swim*. On these records, The Romancers created the blueprint for what was later to be known as the "Eastside Sound." It featured a tight and funky rhythm section (bass and drums), a "chunka chunka" rhythm guitar, a trebly and poppy Fender Telecaster lead guitar, and a wailing tenor sax. Other features in the original "Eastside Sound" that soon evolved were the baritone sax and Farfisa organ. The standout song on the *Do the Slauson* album was "Slauson Shuffle," written by the band's leader and rhythm guitarist Max Ubállez. Lead guitarist Andy Tesso would influence many East L.A. guitarists of the era. The Romancers went on to record many singles with vocals, including their classic rendition of an Etta James recording, "My Heart Cries." Their version featured some sophisticated and well-executed vocal harmonies. Cárdenas and Davis went on to have three of their Eastside bands achieve national hit records. The Premiers reached number nineteen in 1964 with "Farmer John," a cover of a Don & Dewey R&B recording. This led to several national tours on which they shared the bill with the likes of the Rolling Stones, the Kinks, the Zombies, and the Supremes. The Blendells scored a hit the same year with a cover of an obscure Stevie Wonder song titled "La La La La La." It reached number sixty-two on the national charts, but hit the Top 10 in Los Angeles. They toured with the Dave Clark Five as part of Dick Clark's Caravan of Stars.

In 1965, Cannibal & the Headhunters reached number thirty with their version of a song written by Chris Kenner and Fats Domino called "Land of a Thousand Dances." Lead singer Frankie "Cannibal" García added the "na na na na na" chorus to the song, which had a great deal to do with its success. Riding the momentum of their hit record, Cannibal & the Headhunters toured the United States with The Beatles, including their historic concerts at the Hollywood Bowl and New York's Shea Stadium. Although they did not achieve national status, Thee Midnighters, with their lead singer Little Willie G. (García), were the most popular of the East L.A. bands. Their version of "Land of a Thousand Dances" hit number sixty-seven on the charts, but they never toured nationally. However, they enjoyed several local and regional hits, including their instrumental cruising anthem "Whittier Boulevard." Little Willie G. was a charismatic front man who had a great voice and a cool, smooth stage presence. Although he could belt an up-tempo R&B or rock song, his strong suit was the romantic ballad. Another major star on the Eastside scene was Little Ray (Jiménez). Little Ray was a strong rhythm and blues singer and performer on the level of the best of Motown. He recorded several 45-rpm singles but never had a hit record. Mark Guerrero had a band called Mark & the Escorts, produced and managed by Billy Cárdenas, who recorded two singles for GNP Crescendo Records in 1965, which were reissued by Dionysus Records in 2001 on *Eastside Sound, Volume 2.*

There were other bands and vocal groups who made good records for independent labels such as The Jaguars with the Salas Brothers, The Blue Satins, The Ambertones, Ronnie & the Casuals, The Heartbreakers, The Sisters, The Enchantments, The Village Callers, and The Impalas. Pat and Lolly Vegas (Vásquez), brothers from Fresno, California, came to Los Angeles in the early 1960s. They changed their last name on the advice of an agent to avoid racial discrimination in the nightclubs on the Sunset Strip in Hollywood. Pat, on bass and vocals, and Lolly, on guitar and vocals, recorded *Live at the Haunted House* for Mercury Records. They went on to play on many hit records, including the instrumental classics *Let's Go* by the Routers and *Out of Limits* by the Marketts. The Vegas Brothers became in-demand session players, backing up many artists alongside musicians such as Glen Campbell, Leon Russell, and Dr. John. As songwriters, they wrote a hit for P.J. Proby called "Nicky Hoeky," which led to covers by Aretha Franklin, Bobbi Gentry, and Tom Jones. In the early 1970s, The Vegas Brothers formed Redbone, who had two Top 40 hit records, including "The Witch Queen of New Orleans" and their mega hit "Come and Get Your Love."

In the 1970s, many East L.A. bands with roots in the previous decade emerged with major label record deals. With the raised consciousness brought about by the *Chicano Movement of the late 1960s, bands began to use names that reflected their Latino heritage. *El Chicano, Tierra, Yaqui, Tango, and Macondo are examples of this change. El Chicano, who were known as The VIPs in the 1960s, scored a national hit with a *Latin jazz instrumental called *Viva Tirado.* Written by jazz musician Gerald Wilson, it paid homage to Mexican bullfighter José Ramón Tirado. The record featured the Hammond organ of Bobby Espinoza and the Wes Montgomery–style guitar work of Mickey Lesprón. El Chicano toured the world extensively, with perhaps their most significant highlight being a successful appearance at the legendary Apollo Theater in Harlem, the African American section of New York City. They had a second Top 40 hit in 1973 with a Latin-flavored pop song, "Tell Her She's Lovely." El Chicano released seven albums in the 1970s, six of them on MCA Records.

Manager/producer Art Brambila succeeded in having three of his artists sign with major labels in 1972. Tierra signed with Twentieth Century Records, Yaqui with Hugh Hefner's short-lived Playboy Records, and Mark

Guerrero with Capitol Records as a solo artist. Tierra was formed by Rudy and Steve Salas, the same Salas brothers who had sung with the Jaguars in the 1960s. Tierra's first self-titled album featured the song "Barrio Suite." It included several musical styles, which, along with the lyrics, captured the spirit of life in the *barrio. Yaqui, whose sound was a mixture of Carlos *Santana, Led Zeppelin, and Crosby, Stills, and Nash, were fronted by strong lead singers George Ochoa and Eddie Serrano. Guerrero recorded two singles for Capitol, including his best song and record of the decade, "I'm Brown." After moving to A&M Records the following year as lead singer and songwriter for the band Tango, A&M bought the Capitol masters and re-released most of them, including "I'm Brown," as part of Tango's first album. Tango's style included mainly rock and roll and country rock. Guerrero's main influences at the time were The Beatles, Bob Dylan, and Buffalo Springfield. In 1971, previous to his Capitol and A&M recordings, Guerrero had a single produced by legendary producer Lou Adler on his Ode Record label. Adler had produced hits for the Mamas and the Papas and Carole King. Another band with roots in East L.A., Macondo had a Latin-flavored album out on Atlantic Records. Macondo was led by Max Ubállez, who had been in The Romancers in the 1960s.

Rubén & the Jets, led by Rubén Guevara, recorded two albums for Mercury Records, *For Real* in 1973 and *Con Safos* in 1974. These albums resulted from a meeting between Guevara and the legendary Frank Zappa. Zappa had previously recorded an album called *Cruisin' with Rubén & the Jets* with his band The Mothers of Invention. After hitting it off with Guevara, Zappa suggested that Guevara form a "real" Rubén & the Jets. The resulting albums were recorded in authentic 1950s doo-wop and R&B styles. Rubén & the Jets toured with artists such as Three Dog Night, T Rex, and Frank Zappa.

Another East L.A. artist to surface in the decade was singer/songwriter Hirth Martínez. He was discovered by Bob Dylan, who connected him with Robbie Robertson of The Band. Robertson produced Hirth's first album, *Hirth from Earth* (1975), and The Band's producer, John Simon, produced the second, *Big Bright Street* (1977). These two albums, on the Warner Brothers label, are filled with extraordinary songs written by Hirth. They run the gamut from Jobim-styled *sambas to melodic ballads, blues, and jazz. Two female artists also emerged in the 1970s. Fresno, California's Carmen Moreno, with a voice that rivals Joan *Báez and Linda *Ronstadt, recorded for Epic, Capitol, and Boardwalk Records, both in English and Spanish. Geri González, who had been a member of the Village Callers in the late 1960s in East L.A., sang rhythm and blues and Latin styles with a world-class voice. She was signed to MCA Records and recorded an album that was never released because she was told she did not sound black enough for rhythm and blues.

With the emergence of the punk movement in the late 1970s, Chicano groups represented that genre as well. One of the pioneering bands was The

Plugz, led by Tito Larriva. The Plugz invaded the Hollywood punk nightclub scene and recorded two albums for Fatima Records. The same record label, started by Larriva and two partners, also released a five-song twelve-inch record by an East L.A. band that had later hit the Hollywood punk circuit called The Brat, featuring lead vocalist Teresa Covarrubias. The Brat did not secure a major label deal but was a good band that many believed deserved to do so. Tito Larriva went on to form Los Cruzados, who recorded two albums for Arista Records in the 1980s, and Tito and Tarantula in the 1990s. Tito and Tarantula have several albums to their credit and have toured the world extensively. Los Illegals formed in East L.A. in 1979 and eventually hit the clubs in Hollywood and secured a record deal with A&M records. Led by world-class visual artist Willie Herrón, Los Illegals' first single was a powerful and energetic punk anthem about the trials and tribulations of an illegal alien in Los Angeles, titled "El Lay." In 1983, their album *Internal Exile* was released, which included a Spanish-language version of the same song. The album dealt with issues such as *immigration, street *gangs, poverty, violence, and alienation. Another band from East L.A. to emerge in the early 1980s was *Los Lobos. They had formed in the early 1970s as a band rediscovering their Mexican musical roots. In the late 1970s they picked up their electric instruments and began to play rock and roll alongside their acoustic Mexican music. Their music became a mix of rock and roll, rockabilly, country, Latin, and traditional Mexican music. They played the punk and new wave circuit in Hollywood, which led to their record deal with Slash/Warner Records. As of 2003, they have recorded eight studio albums and released two major compilation sets. Los Lobos' version of "La Bamba," from the movie of the same name, was number one in the nation in 1987. They have headlined all over the world and opened for such legendary rock groups as The Grateful Dead, The Clash, The Eagles, and U2. Los Lobos have won the respect of music critics and fans around the world as a band of quality and integrity. In the 1990s and into the new millennium, Chicano/a musical artists continue to emerge from Southern California, influenced and inspired by those who came before them. These artists have not only created a niche for themselves in the Chicano/a music scene but have contributed a significant sound to mainstream rock music and Latina and Latino popular music.

Further Reading

Guerrero, Lalo, and Sherilyn Meece Mentes. *Lalo, My Life and Music*. Tucson: University of Arizona Press, 2002.

Loza, Steven. *Barrio Rhythm: Mexican American Music in Los Angeles*. Chicago: University of Illinois Press, 1993.

Peña, Manuel. *The Mexican-American Orquesta*. Austin: University of Texas Press, 1999.

Reyes, David, and Tom Waldman. *Land of a Thousand Dances: Chicano Rock 'n' Roll from Southern California*. Albuquerque: University of New Mexico Press, 1998.

Sheridan, Thomas E. *Los Tucsonenses: The Mexican Community in Tucson, 1854–1941*. Tucson: University of Arizona Press, 1986.
http://www.markguerrero.com.

Mark Guerrero

Chicano. In the late 1960s, Mexican American civil rights activists applied the word *Chicano* to their political, advocacy, and protest activities that collectively became known as el Movimiento Chicano (the *Chicano Movement). Proudly, Chicanos proclaimed an Indian-Hispanic heritage of **mestizaje* (biracial hybridity) as a foundation for racial and socioeconomic equality and access to the political process. Many in the movement challenged the previous Mexican American generations for what some saw as a pathological inferiority complex, which included self-hatred and denial of their racial and ethnic reality. The affirmative use of the "Chicano" rubric was a departure from earlier negative usages in the 1920s when it denoted lower-class Mexican immigrants and in 1940s and 1950s slang when it often substituted for Mexicano to distinguish the new generation of immigrants from the people left behind and from the more established Mexican Americans. The evolution of the term to symbolize the realization of a newfound and unique identity contrasts with the attitudes of aspiring middle-class Mexican Americans of the 1930s and 1940s who looked with disdain on their brothers and sisters who did not assimilate to the dominant Anglo American norm by transcending their working-class *mexicanidad* (Mexicanness). Many middle-class Mexican Americans applied the word *Chicano* pejoratively to identify the lower classes.

"Chicano" has survived and adapted to turn-of-the-century attitudes and generational changes, as in its combination form "Chicana/Chicano" to indicate gender inclusiveness and equality. Use of the term occurs most frequently among those circles that have maintained unbroken ties to the Chicano Movement—university students, artists, intellectuals, scholars, grassroots activists, and others. Outside of this environment, however, the term is unevenly applied, and among Mexican immigrants it is often dismissed and sometimes scorned. Nevertheless, once extremely controversial, the use of Chicana/o no longer draws the same heat and polemic that it first did when it became popular among activists in the 1960s.

Much of the opposition to the expression in the 1960s came from prior generations of Mexican Americans, including affluent managers and professionals, who had gained their political and civic experience through exercising a more moderate form of political tactics than the direct, confrontational strategy applied by the young Chicana/o activists. This debate and occasional antagonism rested more on a disapproval of militancy itself than on the word *Chicano*, although many Mexican Americans did remember that it had once been used as a slur against the lower classes. During this era the controversy generated active debate that led to the proposing of elaborate hypotheses to explain the term's root origin. Some thinkers within the movement argued that its etymology derived from the ancient Nahuátl word *mexicano* with the "x" phoneme pronounced as an "sh" sound, the same root for the "sh" in the word "Michigan," for example. Others suggested that it derived from a blend of *mexicano* and the Mexican state of Chihuahua and evolved to represent all Chicanas and Chicanos. Among the versions put forward by detractors to disqualify the term was that it came from "chicas patas," an extremely pejorative reference used to denote new arrivals from México. This variety of viewpoints along with the continuing growth of Latina and Latino populations in the United States explains both the cultural similarities and the differences among Latina/o subgroups and why ethnic labels vary from one to another or even within a particular group. Better understanding of *race, ethnicity, and culture within the vitality of Latina/o popular culture requires an introduction to these linguistic challenges and also to the reality of *mestizaje* with its synthesis of cultural achievement and its potential for innovation and shared community.

Further Reading

Rosales, F. Arturo. *Testimonio: A Documentary History of the Mexican American Struggle for Civil Rights.* Houston, TX: Arte Público Press, 2000.

Tatum, Charles M. *Chicano Popular Culture: Que hable el pueblo.* Tucson: University of Arizona Press, 2001.

F. Arturo Rosales

Chicano, El. *See* El Chicano.

Chicano Art: Resistance and Affirmation, 1965–1985. *See* CARA.

Chicano Hip-Hop Rap. *See* Hip-Hop and Rap.

Chicano Movement Music. Sometimes referred to as "*movimiento* music," "farmworker songs," or "Chicano *nueva* **canción*," music of the *Chicano Movement is composed of a diverse repertoire that draws on Mexican traditional and folk-derived popular music, Latin American protest songs, and North American union and civil rights songs. Performed at rallies and demonstrations as well as in coffee houses and on stage, musical activity—like murals and poetry of the period—formed one of the most important expressive realms in which Chicana/os linked politics with art.

Emerging out of the social and political upheaval of the 1960s, the Chicano Movement was influenced by other social movements of the period, such as the civil rights movement, the antiwar movement, and particularly the farmworker movement, which was located primarily in the heart of California's San Joaquin Valley. The Chicano Movement positioned itself as a cultural nationalist response to the various forms of oppression, exploitation, and racism that constituted the experience of ethnic Mexicans in the United States. Simultaneously, like other social movements of the era, the Chicano Movement found itself bound to a multifaceted cultural renaissance and part of the prevailing countercultural spirit of the 1960s. The social unrest of the 1960s inspired and set the stage for a new flowering of activity in Chicano literature, art, *theater, and music called the *Chicano Renaissance.

Huelga Songs and the Farmworker Movement

The beginnings of Chicano Movement music can be traced to the formation of the United Farm Workers (UFW) labor union in 1965. Demanding just wages and better working conditions, the fledgling union initiated a general strike and later a boycott of table grapes. As the UFW attracted volunteers to its cause in rural central California, including many youth from the urban areas, it also attracted artists, musicians, and actors who sought to help organize through expressive means. Although these artistic efforts overlapped in many ways, they formed the basis for politically charged music that would serve the Chicano Movement in later years. Central to these artistic endeavors were the *huelga* song and the founding of El *Teatro Campesino.

Huelga songs were central to the farmworker movement, particularly on the picket lines and at the Friday night meetings. Dealing with the issues and themes of *la causa*, the farmworker cause, *huelga* songs expressed the need to organize against the abuses of the farm bosses. The *huelga* song repertoire was generally identified by thematic material rather than formal musical genres or styles and was, therefore, written in many forms such as marches, **corridos*, and **rancheras*.

While there were a number of original songs written as *huelga* songs, the majority of the repertoire consisted of adaptations of already available songs from various sources including church, folk, and popular traditions. Some adaptations were basically translations of already existing protest songs. For example, the text of the famous civil rights song "We Shall Overcome" was translated into the *huelga* song "Nosotros venceremos." The practice of adapting already existing songs into protest songs has a long tradition in the history of American political music. In fact, the song "We Shall Overcome" is an adaptation of a song from gospel sources.

The flag of the United Farm Workers became a symbol of the Chicano Movement. *Courtesy of the Edward Escobar Private Collection. Photo by Emmanuel Sánchez Carballo.*

The *corrido* (narrative ballad) was a genre that was heavily employed by composers of *huelga* song. The *corrido*, which highlighted the life or deeds of an individual or the significance of a historical event or place, became important to the *huelga* song repertoire. For example, there are numerous *corridos* written about the two main leaders of the UFW, César *Chávez and Dolores *Huerta, as well as others written about Delano, California—the hub of union activity—and various events in the union's history.

However, the most well known song of the farmworker movement—what some call the anthem of the UFW—has no explicit political lyrics. The folk song "De colores" has been sung at union events probably since the inception of the union itself. Although a folk song in nature, "De colores" emerged not in the U.S. Southwest nor in México but in Spain from the *cursillo* movement of the Spanish Catholic Church in the 1940s. The song quickly made its way to the Americas and was picked up in church by ethnic Mexican Roman Catholics. Depicting a vivid pastoral image, "De colores" resonated with farmworkers and also reflected an aspect of UFW organizing strategies of the time as the union adopted a number of religious symbols as its own.

El Teatro Campesino

One of the most prominent examples of artistic endeavor in labor organizing was the founding of the theater group El Teatro Campesino, the Farmworker Theater. El Teatro Campesino, in the early days of the union and the grape strike, performed highly improvised skits called *actos* that told the story of the living, working, and social conditions of farmworkers. El Teatro Campesino would relocate in 1967 outside the confines of the UFW to continue artistically organizing around farmworker issues but also to address larger issues of *Chicano culture and identity. They would go on to become one of the premiere Chicana/o performance ensembles to emerge from the Chicano Movement.

The primary musical vehicle within El Teatro Campesino was the *huelga* song, with much of the main repertoire having been composed by the founding members of the Teatro: Luis *Valdez, Agustín Lira, and Felipe Cantú. Just as the *acto*, the *huelga* song was performed at first on the picket lines and increasingly at the union's Friday night meetings, marches, and rallies. However, the Teatro is significant, along with other anonymous composers, in establishing the *huelga* song genre. The Teatro produced two recordings of *huelga* songs: "Viva La Causa" (1966) and "¡Huelga en General!" (1974).

Outside the immediate sphere of the UFW, *huelga* song was popular among students and youth, a critical constituency of the movement both on and off campus. Student struggles around the quality of public schools, Chicano studies in the classrooms, and access and support in higher education were major issues within the movement. In fact, the first musical ensembles to emerge within the Chicano Movement were student-based, Conjunto

Aztlán at San Fernando Valley State College (now California State University, Northridge) and La Rondalla Amerindia at San Diego State University. La Rondalla Amerindia recorded the *huelga* song "No nos moverán" on Joan *Báez's *Gracias a la vida* album (1974).

Movimiento Music

Although the farmworker cause was one of the unifying forces within the Chicano Movement in the early years, local struggles and expressions in the cities were fundamentally important as well. Springing up throughout the Southwest, or more appropriately *Aztlán, were theater groups, poetry collectives, and musical groups. A number of musicians and actors who were active with the UFW eventually left the union to begin working within the context of the Chicano Movement, including Daniel *Valdez, who recorded the album *Mestizo* on A&M Records (1974). After the release of this album came a number of self-produced albums by grassroots *movimiento* groups. Here are some of the major groups.

Coming directly out of their participation with El Teatro Campesino, the musical group Flor del Pueblo formed in San Jose, California. Although *huelga* songs were an important part of their repertoire, the group was more interested in protest genres from Latin America, such as *nueva canción* singer Suni Paz and troubadour of the *Cuban Revolution Carlos Puebla. In 1977 they produced their album *Música de Nuestra América.*

Equally in San Diego, California, Los Alacranes Mojados formed in the wake of community struggles. With members coming out of the university-based ensembles, Conjunto Aztlán and La Rondalla Amerindia, Los Alacranes had a solid *huelga* song repertoire. However, they were also interested in the genres of protest song emanating from Latin America and Cuba and wrote a number of popular *movimiento* songs. In 1975, they released *¡Levántate Campesino!* with the Mexican *teatro* group Los Mascarones. In 1979, they released their first album, *Rolas de Aztlán.*

With the same intensity but different influences, *Los Lobos del Este de Los Angeles formed in Los Angeles. Having grown up on the "East L.A." sounds of Thee Midniters and the rock and soul music of the era, these Chicano youth put down their electric guitars to pick up Mexican regional folk instruments, such as the *jarana*, *arpa*, and *guitarrón*, steeping themselves in the challenging sounds of **son jarocho* and *huapango* from the state of Veracruz. Although protest genres like the *huelga* song did not form the basis of their repertoire, these musical gestures toward the music of their parents' and grandparents' generation spoke to the politics of their cultural intervention. They were the "house band" to the 1976 recording *¡Si Se Puede!*, a UFW-inspired album of *huelga* songs. In 1978, they released their own album, *Just Another Band from East L.A.*

As multifaceted as it was, Chicano Movement music's various forms spoke to the many constituencies that made up the movement. At times, the music had an explicitly political message, as in the *huelga* song. At other times, its politics were more based in the open expression of a dormant cultural identity rather than polemical lyrics.

Further Reading

Broyles-González, Yolanda. *El Teatro Campesino: Theater in the Chicano Movement.* Austin: University of Texas Press, 1994.

Eyerman, Ron, and Andrew Jamison. *Music and Social Movements: Mobilizing Traditions in the Twentieth Century.* Cambridge: Cambridge University Press, 1998.

Heisley, Robert Michael. "*Corridistas de la huelga*: Songmaking and Singing in the Lives of Two Individuals." Ph.D. dissertation, University of California, Los Angeles, 1983.

Loza, Steven. *Barrio Rhythm: Mexican American Music in Los Angeles.* Urbana: University of Illinois Press, 1993.

Loza, Steven. "From Veracruz to Los Angeles: The Reinterpretation of the *Son Jarocho.*" *Latin American Music Review* 13.2 (1992): 179–194.

Muñoz, Carlos, Jr. *Youth, Identity, Power: The Chicano Movement.* London: Verso, 1989.

Nalven, Joseph. "Some Notes on Chicano Music as a Pathway to Community Identity." *The New Scholar* 5.1 (1975): 73–93.

Peña, Manuel. *The Mexican American Orquesta: Music, Culture, and the Dialectic of Conflict.* Austin: University of Texas Press, 1999.

Reyes, David, and Tom Waldman. *Land of a Thousand Dances: Chicano Rock'n'Roll from Southern California.* Albuquerque: University of New Mexico Press, 1998.

Rosaldo, Renato, Robert Calvert, and Gustav Seligmann, eds. *Chicano: The Evolution of a People.* Minneapolis, MN: Winston Press, 1973.

Villarino, José "Pepe," ed. *Mexican and Chicano Music.* New York: McGraw Hill, 1999.

Estevan César Azcona

Chicano Mural Movement. The Chicano Mural Movement has been an essential and determinative element in the development of the iconographic *Chicano Movement in the United States as well as a coexisting element for historical identity, civil rights defense, and cultural nationalism. On a national scale muralism has been one of the most dominant and lasting contributions of the Chicano Art Movement. Muralism is related to the artistic mural tradition of Mesoamerican civilizations (Aztecas and Maya), who recorded their history on the walls of their temples and pyramids. Chicano muralism grew significantly during and after the 1960s in urban working-class neighborhoods and Chicana/o *barrios of Los Angeles and Southern California in general and now can be found across the United States. During the 1960s and 1970s, many artists saw in the murals the opportunity to support the emerging Chicano Movement with public images that serve as an affirmation of the historical legacy and cultural vitality as well as protest against such social inequities as poverty, colonialism, racism, housing, and *police violence, to name a few.

From a practical standpoint, successful murals fulfill the need to represent one's culture, history, and social issues, especially when a community is ignored and criminalized by the dominant media. Through the murals, artists engage the media by transforming the public space of city landscape in a medium of broadcasts into what José Limon describes as "political semiotic" or the "politics of art." As a form to visually support and give testament to struggles facing the Chicano community, muralists fulfill their need to create a kind of vernacular art, which is in itself public, majestic, and accessible to the masses. Using both neorealism and surrealism, muralists paint cultural representations that reflect the political and social realities of their community and in most cases their hopes for political change and social justice. Mural production became, during the 1960s and 1970s, part of the effort of Chicanos to reinforce, affirm, and invigorate their cultural identity, history, and heritage and at the same time dispute imposed racism, discrimination, and injustice.

Chicano murals follow the inspirational form of 1930s post–Mexican revolutionary–era painters such as Diego *Rivera, José Clemente Orozco, and David Alfaros Siqueiros, collectively known as Los Tres Grandes (The Three Greats), whose murals are legendary in México and who also had an important trajectory in the United States. Chicano artists developed their own styles, unique and original, and started using their murals to rewrite and express their experiences as Chicanos and Chicanas in the United States. As a coexisting element, the Mural Movement has been indispensable in the formation of a common Chicano art form, capable of bringing together the broad diaspora of barrio citizens in a common goal, regardless of artistic background. As a communal form of art, the Chicano Mural Movement brought together a vast variety of barrio talents, including sign painters, graffiti artists, self-taught artists, and those who hold degrees in arts—all united under the common umbrella of social activism and public art for the masses.

Common mural iconography includes images and symbols of Aztec pre-Columbian landscapes with Mexican and Mexican American epic heroes and heroines (e.g., Che *Guevara, Emiliano *Zapata, César *Chávez, and Dolores *Huerta) as well as social resistance and political activists and elements from nature interpreted through native mythology, all of them configuring a cultural identity, nationalism, and romantic and historic pride in city life and architecture. For example, the collective work of the *Mujeres Muralistas resulted in a wide variety of murals that served to visually empower the Latino community in the Mission district in San Francisco, and for many Latinas/os, one of their most famous Mission barrio murals, *Panamerica* (1974), became a place where Mexican and Central American families would gather to receive a type of cultural affirmation in their historical legacies in the Americas. Most murals are instruments documenting and denouncing barrio life, but their interests have transcended community and ethnic boundaries and become international by incorporating the muralists' concerns for the struggles of other people and communities in Vietnam, Africa, and Latin America.

Murals can be interpreted as educational tools in the dynamic context of the Latino communities. During their evolution, murals became an important instrument to promote the consciousness and power of art in expressing the reality of their community but also to disseminate traditions in a multilingual space. Mural artists function as visual educators who transmit and perpetuate by plastic expression the community's ideology and self-determination. Murals transform art into large-scale public education systems embracing the barrio in a way that is comprehensive and accessible to everyone.

Murals encompass both a political and an aesthetic arrangement crucial for the integration and reinforcement of Chicano ideology and cultural naturalism. Today, Chicano murals still serve as agents of cultural and social change, reflecting the ongoing political, cultural, and spiritual struggles suffered within the Chicano communities around the nation.

Further Reading

Castro, Rafaela G. *Dictionary of Chicano Folklore.* Santa Barbara, CA: ABC-CLIO, 2000.

Karp, Ivan, Steven Lavine, and Rockefeller Foundation. *Exhibiting Cultures: The Poetics and Politics of Museum Display.* Washington, DC: Smithsonian Institution Press, 1991.

Limón, José Eduardo. *Dancing with the Devil: Society and Cultural Poetics in Mexican-American South Texas. New Directions in Anthropological Writing.* Madison: University of Wisconsin Press, 1994.

Maciel, David, Isidro D. Ortiz, and María Herrera-Sobek. *Chicano Renaissance: Contemporary Cultural Trends.* Tucson: University of Arizona Press, 2000.

Sturken, Marita, and Lisa Cartwright. *Practices of Looking: An Introduction to Visual Culture.* New York: Oxford University Press, 2001.

William Calvo

Chicano Power Revival. Arizona's Chicano Power Revival (CPR) is also known as the CPR Orchestra, a Latino ensemble performing their own original musical sound, building upon their diverse interpretation of folk, rock, funk, and jazz genres. The group was formed in 1999 by Raúl Yáñez—the band's leader, who is well known for his versatility ranging from classical to jazz. He plays keyboards, sings vocals, and arranges and composes original music for the group. León Santiago is lead singer and percussionist but also plays guitar and cuatro. George Yáñez plays trumpet and sings background vocals. Xavier Yáñez plays bass and sings vocals, and Emerson Laufey plays drums, cymbals, and other Latin percussion. Peter Green is lead trumpet, does background vocals, and is an arranger. Mike Ozuna plays guitar, while

Jake Gabow plays tenor saxophone and flute, composes, and arranges. Steve McAlister plays trombone, and Luis Hernández plays congas and Latin percussion.

In the Southwest desert area, a cultural region whose predominant "Latin" musical genres are represented by (and do not usually stray far from) the traditional festive dance musics of the native *Chicano population (specifically the *cumbia rhythm and the rustic rural sound of Tex-Mex, Tejano, or Norteño songs), the very fact that a group of such disparate influences and ambitious scope as the CPR Orchestra exists and even prospers is unusual. Afro-Cuban *rumba mixes seamlessly with the familiar ebb and flow of the cumbia and with the angular harmonies of jazz. Adding world beat, some bilingualism and even *hip-hop complements the musical mixture.

In 2002, they delivered their first CD, *Chicano Power Revival CPR Orchestra*, and another CD is due out in 2004, featuring Marisa Ronstadt, niece of music legend Linda *Ronstadt. In March 2004, Yáñez took a bold step forward when he introduced a full orchestra piece featuring a single turntable as the soloist. It has received international reviews as a revolutionary breakthrough in the world of music.

Their music maintains a certain familiar Cuban consistency and feel from an always present clave, *tumbao*, and *montuno* in one form or another. This predilection for Caribbean forms might invite a hasty *salsa labeling on first listen, but the members of CPR Orchestra do not see themselves strictly as a salsa band and admit that their sound and musical interests are eclectic.

Further Reading

http://www.cprorchestra.com.

Peter J. García

Chicano Renaissance. The period of artistic, literary, and political activism known as the Chicano Renaissance flourished in the 1960s and 1970s primarily in the United States, although some of its key figures also received important recognition in Europe. Literary and cultural studies scholars credit the groundbreaking work of playwright Luis *Valdez and El *Teatro Campesino, of Rodolfo "Corky" Gonzáles's *I Am Joaquín* (1968), and of *Alurista's poetry (e.g., *Floricanto en Aztlán*, 1971) and literary activism as helping to initiate the era. These *Chicano-identified writers made important contributions to the common language of cultural pride and political solidarity in the face of ongoing inequities against Mexican-origin people in the United States. Some social historians also emphasize the farmworker organizing work of César *Chávez and the period's local partisan politics in the Southwest with galvanizing an advocacy movement that encouraged the burst of creativity among Mexican Americans. They point for evidence to such activities as the Viva Kennedy voter registration clubs, the founding of

PASO (Political Association of Spanish-Speaking Organizations) in Texas, the organizing in New Mexico of the Alianza Federal de Mercedes (Federal Alliance of Land Grants) by Reies López Tijerina, and the forming of the Crusade for Justice in Denver, Colorado, by Corky Gonzáles. Still other observers and participants in the period's *Chicano Movement underscore the role of student activism for creating a social context of collective energy for the period's renaissance in art and literature. Groups like MAYO (Mexican American Youth Organization) in Texas, UMAS (United Mexican Americans) in Colorado and California, the Brown Berets in Los Angeles, *MEChA (Movimiento Estudiantil Chicano de Aztlán) nationally, *MALDEF (Mexican American Legal Defense and Education Fund), the *National Council of La Raza (NCLR), and others emerged to address urgent social concerns through public pressure, intense advocacy, and focused media attention.

First described as a "Chicano Renaissance" by literary scholar Felipe de Ortego de Gasca in an essay published in 1971, the period like other eras of flourishing creativity (e.g., the American Renaissance of the 1850s and the Harlem Renaissance of the 1920s) was better understood and appreciated in hindsight. During the time itself many participants were writing, reading, performing, and organizing to a large extent separately throughout the country in independent coalitions, and some individuals at first worked in relative isolation. The Chicano Renaissance was noteworthy for the emergence of bilingual English/Spanish publications like the landmark periodicals *Aztlán: International Journal of Chicano Studies Research* (Los Angeles, 1967–still publishing), *El Grito: A Journal of Contemporary Mexican American Thought* (Berkeley, 1967–1974), *Agenda: A Journal of Hispanic Thought* (Washington, D.C., 1970–1979), and many ephemera from other alternative presses throughout the country. As well, the era was marked by gatherings of committed activists at local and regional meetings, demonstrations, national conferences, literary festivals, the painting of murals and installation of art exhibitions, and college and community organizing projects. For example, University of New Mexico students working for radio station KUNM-FM covered the 1966 Tierra Amarilla courthouse raid by Reies López Tijerina's Alianza Federal de Pueblos Libres (Federal Alliance of Free Communities) and were able to relay alternative accounts, albeit to small audiences, to counter the hostile press coverage and demogoguery of some politicians. Eventually New Mexico Governor David Cargo ordered National Guard troops and tanks to arrest Tijerina and his small group of local followers in what was to be one of the earliest state actions against *Chicano Movement free speech activities. Three years later Corky Gonzáles organized a different kind of gathering—the Youth Liberation Conference—in Denver, Colorado, that produced the 1969 *Plan Espiritual de Aztlán* (Spiritual Plan of *Aztlán), which opens with *Alurista's poetic call to collective action of all Mexican Americans in AmericAztlán.

Out of these and myriad other activities and energies sprouted the germi-

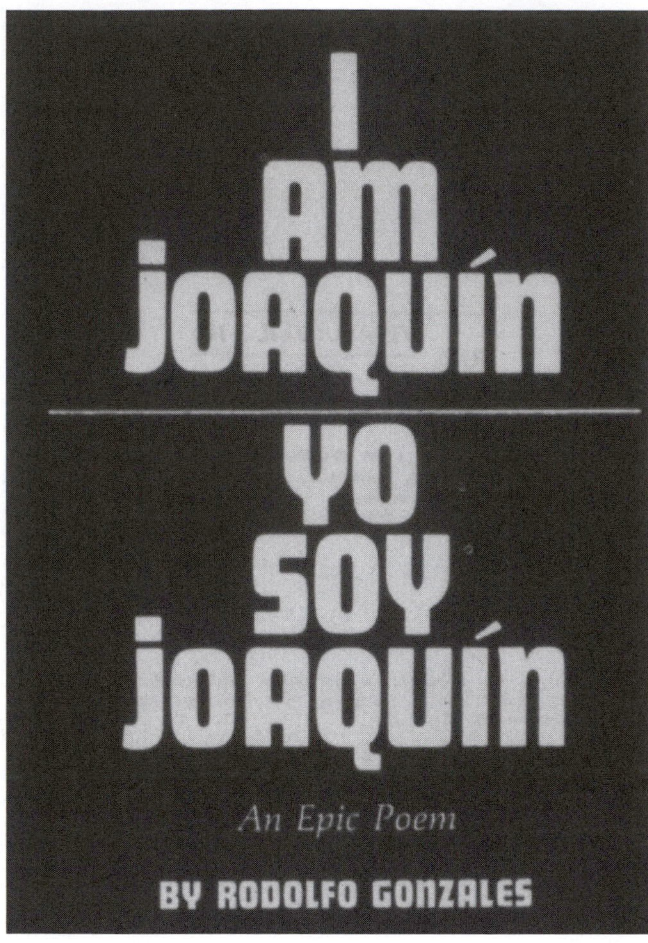

The cover of the now out-of-print first edition of Rodolfo Gonzales' *I Am Joaquín/Yo Soy Joaquín*, one of the foundational works of the Chicano Renaissance movement. *Courtesy of the Cordelia Candelaria Private Collection.*

nal cultural production that converged into the Chicano Renaissance. Some scholars believe that in many ways the period was both influenced and buoyed by the Latin American literary explosion called "the Boom," which came to be associated with the themes and styles of *magic realism. Also occurring in the 1960s the Boom revitalized interest worldwide in the diverse arts and popular cultures of all Latin America, and Chicano literature and art benefited from that international interest. Before long French and German scholars, students, writers, artists, and others began writing about the Chicano Movement in the United States, and European scholars invited El Teatro Campesino, Alurista, and others to perform in their countries. Like novelist Gabriel García Márquez, Colombian recipient of the 1982 Nobel Prize for Literature, and other well-known Latin Americans, most of the Chicano Renaissance writers offered innovative representations of their individual and collective cultural identities through the thematic lenses of conquest, colonialism, and *race and ethnicity in the Americas. Perhaps the era's major legacy was the emergence of an explicitly "Chicano"-identified framework of ethnic and political identity, one that rejected the perceived accommodationism of the previous generation of "Mexican American" and/or "Spanish-speaking" people.

Scholars generally agree that a pivotal transitional link between "Mexican American" and "Chicano" literature—and, hence, of a pre- and post-Renaissance era—is José Antonio Villarreal's important novel *Pocho*, published in 1959, about a young Mexican American trapped in the cultural hyphen between his father's strong Mexican roots and his mother's evolving U.S. American assimilation. *Pocho* functions as a landmark in Latina and Latino literature and popular culture because of its compelling plot and intriguingly developed protagonist and, most importantly, because it was recuperated from oblivion in the 1970s by Chicano studies researchers who were doing the first research and retrievals of historical sources about the Mexican/Mexican American/Chicano experience in order to chronicle the U.S. heritage accurately. In addition to Alurista and Valdez, other important writers associated with the early years of the Chicano Renaissance include attorney activist Oscar Zeta Acosta, author of two of the popular narratives of the period, *The Autobiography of a Brown Buffalo* (1970) and *The Revolt of the Cockroach People* (1973); prolific New Mexican Rudolfo *Anaya who wrote the era's first bestselling and now classic novel, *Bless Me, Última* (1972); journalist and fiction writer Ron *Arias, whose novel *The Road to Tamazunchale* (1975) was acclaimed for its effective use of magic realism; Colorado poet Abelardo "Lalo" Delgado, whose memorable poem of resistance, "stupid america," captures the angst, anger, and activism fueling the Chicano Movement; Texas fiction writer Rolando *Hinojosa Smith, first Chicano recipient of the prestigious Premio *Casa de las Américas literary honor for his novel *Klail City y sus alrededores* (1976; Klail City and Its Surroundings); and Estela *Portillo Trambley, respected feminist playwright (e.g., *The Day of the Swallows*, 1976) and fiction writer (e.g., *Rain of Scorpions and Other Writings*, 1975).

Equally important to the flourishing of the era were three scholar/writers—Tomás Rivera (1935–1984), chancellor of the University of California at Riverside and author of one of the Chicano literary classics, *Y no se lo tragó la tierra* (And the Earth Did Not Swallow Him, 1971), recipient of the first Quinto Sol Literary Prize awarded by *El Grito: A Journal of Contemporary Mexican American Thought* in 1970; Ernesto Galarza (1905–1984), labor sociologist and author of the autobiographical novel *Barrio Boy* (1971) and numerous social scientific studies including *Spiders in the House and Workers in the Field* (1970); and New Mexican–born Sabine Ulibarrí, Spanish-language and literature scholar, poet, essayist, and fiction writer, who published two early volumes of poetry, *Al cielo se sube a pie* (Walking to Heaven) and *Amor y Ecuador* (Love and Ecuador; both in 1966), and the volume of regionalist sketches, *Mi abuela fumaba puros y otros cuentos de Tierra Amarilla* (My Grandmother Smoked Cigars and Other Tierra Amarilla [New Mexico] Tales; 1977). Other writers critical to the vibrant energy of the period were Luis Omar Salinas from Texas, who wrote such striking and inspiring verse collections as *Crazy Gypsy* (1970), *I Go Dreaming Serenades* (1979), and *Prelude to Darkness* (1981), as well as edited the important collection *Entrance: 4 Chicano Poets* (1975); Ricardo Sánchez (1941–1995), another Tejano whose *Canto y grito mi liberación* (I Sing and Shout My Liberation, 1971) was one of the first examples of **pinto* poetry to gain notice and eventually acclaim and who also managed to earn a Ph.D. after release from prison; California journalist and novelist Richard *Vásquez, whose novel *Chicano* (1970) received positive critical review and who succeeded Chicano martyr Rubén Salazar at the *Los Angeles Times*; poet and, later, fiction writer Alma *Villanueva, also from California, whose

Bloodroot (1977) was one of the first chapbooks published by a Chicana; and another Californian, Gary *Soto, one of the first Mexican Americans to be nominated for a Pulitzer Prize (in 1978) and whose mentorship under poet Phillip Levine helped him gain a crossover readership and national publishers at a time when the primary outlet for Chicana/o publishing was in alternative and small presses.

Also contributing to the Chicano Renaissance legacy of an emergent explicitly "Chicano" identity were writers Floyd Salas (*Tattoo the Wicked Cross*, 1967); Raymond Barrio (*The Plum Plum Pickers*, 1969); Sergio Elizondo (*Perros y antiperros* [Dogs and Anti-Dogs], 1972); Nephtalí de León (*5 Plays*, 1972); José Montoya (*El sol y los de abajo* [The Sun and Those Below], 1972); Tino Villanueva (*Hay otro voz poems* [Another Voice], 1972); Raymund Pérez (*The Secret Meaning of Death*, 1972); Richard A. García (*Selected Poetry*, 1973); Raúl Salinas (*Viaje/Trip*, 1973); Rose Mary Roybal (*From La Llorona to Envidia*, 1973); Edmund Villaseñor (*Macho!*, 1973); Juan F. Herrera (*Rebozos of Love* [Shawls of Love], 1974); Silvia Gonzáles (*La chicana piensa* [The Chicana Thinks], 1974); Miguel Méndez (*Peregrinos de Aztlán* [Pilgrims of Aztlán], 1973); Alejandro Morales (*Caras viejas y vino nuevo* [Old Faces and New Wine], 1975); Orlando Romero (*Nambé—Year One*, 1976); Bernice Zamora (*Restless Serpents*, 1976); Aristeo Brito (*El diablo en Texas* [The Devil in Texas], 1976); Angela de Hoyos (*Selecciones* [Selections], 1976); Isabella Ríos (*Victuum*, 1976); Ana *Castillo (*I Close My Eyes*, 1976); Nash Candelaria (*Memories of the Alhambra*, 1977); Inés Tovar (*Con razón corazón* [With Reason, Heart], 1977); Marina Rivera (*Mestiza*, 1977); José Antonio Burciaga (*Cultura*, 1979); Cordelia Candelaria (*Oje de la Cueva/Cave Springs* [selected by Alurista], 1980); Lucha Corpi (*Palabras de Mediodía* [Noon Words], 1980); and other significant voices and viewpoints that produced the brilliant and lasting taproot of contemporary Chicana/o art, literature, aesthetics, cultural criticism, and philosophy.

Further Reading

Candelaria, Cordelia Chávez. *Chicano Poetry: A Critical Introduction*. Westport, CT: Greenwood Press, 1986.

Hernández-Gutiérrez, Manuel de Jesús, and David William Foster, eds. *Literatura chicana, 1965–1995: An Anthology in Spanish, English, and Caló*. New York: Garland, 1997.

Maciel, David R., Isidro D. Ortiz, and María Herrera-Sobek, eds. *Chicano Renaissance: Contemporary Cultural Trends*. Tucson: University of Arizona Press, 2000.

Martínez, Julio A., and Francisco A. Lomelí. *Chicano Literature: A Reference Guide*. Westport, CT: Greenwood Press, 1984.

Ortego Gasca, Felipe de. "The Chicano Renaissance." *Social Casework* 52.5 (May 1971): 295–307.

Cordelia Chávez Candelaria

Chicanos por la Causa. Chicanos por la Causa (Chicanos for the [People's] Cause, CPLC) is a community development corporation established in 1969 in Phoenix, Arizona, and dedicated to building a better future for *Chicano children by providing comprehensive human services to the community. With satellite offices in Tucson and Nogales, Arizona, the mission of CPLC is to build a stronger, healthier community as a lead advocate, coalition builder, and direct service provider. CPLC works to promote positive change and self-sufficiency to enhance the quality of life for the benefit of the clients they serve.

Some of the programs provided by CPLC include community health services; Latinos Unido Contra Sida (Latinos United against Aids), an outreach, behavioral, and substance abuse treatment service for HIV/AIDS patients; Mothers against *Gangs, working to provide alternatives to destructive behavior through constructive activities; Employment and Training Center, providing counseling, career exploration, vocational counseling, on-the-job training, and labor market information; community-based counseling service, providing assistance for stress, depression, chronic mental illness, and marital and health-related issues; housing program, which develops affordable housing in economically distressed neighborhoods, Headstart preschool programs, and alternative high school learning environments; and a domestic violence shelter.

CPLC hosts an educational and informational television show titled *Nuestra Causa Televisión* (Our Cause Television), where issues such as *immigration, education, guns and violence, housing, and health are addressed. The show reaches over 24,000 households monthly.

Further Reading

http://www.cplc.org.

Alma Alvarez-Smith

Children's and Youth Theater. Latina/o children and youth drama (K–12) in the United States derives from a long-standing oral tradition of **cuentos* (storytelling), **dichos* (proverbs that reinforce a moral lesson), **corridos* (ballads), and *secretos y voces* (children's games focusing on playful language). Evolving over centuries, the cultural practices of storytelling, moral sayings, music, and children's games have been interwoven into a Latina/o children and youth performance drama tradition that features elements from indigenous myths, religious tales, and historical events. Evidence indicates that there were children participants in theatrical productions dating to the pre-Columbian era. Pre-Columbian examples include creation stories or legendary characters for children such as *The Moon and the Stars* (Mexican), *El Conejo en la Cara de la Luna* (The Rabbit in the Face of the Moon) (Mexican), *The Golden Flower* (Puerto Rican), *La Cucarachita Martina* (The Little Cockroach, Martina) (Cuban and Puerto Rican), *El Alacran*

(The Scorpion) (Mexican), *El Cucú* (The Cuckoo) (Mexican), *La Muerte* (Death) (Mexican), *The Barking Mouse* (Cuban), *La Llorona* (The Weeping Woman) (Mexican), *Juan Bobo* (Puerto Rican and Dominican), and *Pedro Animal* (Puerto Rican). More and more in the twentieth and twenty-first centuries, these folktales and animal fables are incorporated into theatrical dramatizations for children and youth as a way to valorize and preserve Latina/o ancestry and heritage.

The Spanish colonial (1600–1900) period also shaped children's theater, particularly through the influence of the rich dramatic tradition of religious and secular folk dramas like *Moros y Cristianos* (Moors and Christians), Nativity plays, and *Los Comanches*. The Catholic Church had a long history of using allegorical dramas in the form of **autos sacramentales* to Christianize the Native American populations. During the modern era, the periods of the 1920s through the 1950s, Catholic churches served as agents of socialization into American norms for Latina/o children and youth. Educators and social workers of this period were highly influenced by the recreational theater movement. They sought to teach educational dramatics in the classroom and focused on the influence of mainstream Anglo-American drama on the parochial schools. Latina/o children and youth often performed in productions of *Cinderella*, *La Caperucita Roja* (Little Red Riding Hood), *Tres Cerditos* (The Three Little Pigs), and other traditional European fairytale stories. Also the Spanish-language theater companies flourished during these decades of theatrical activity. Visiting Spanish-speaking companies from México, Spain, and the Caribbean brought Spanish-language theater to the United States, performing in New York City, Florida, Texas, New Mexico, Arizona, and California. Some of the Spanish-language theater companies that performed in New York and Florida were Compañia Española Marita Reid, Compañia de Teatro Bethancourt, and El Nuevo Círculo Dramatico. A few of the Spanish-language theater companies that performed throughout the Southwest were Teatro Aurora, Teatro Zaragoza, Compañia Villalongín, and Compañia Azteca. As children and youth participated in the traveling theater groups, they were also audience members of the community Hispanic theater movement.

In the 1960s and 1970s, many student Latina/o children and youth *teatros* (theaters) formed in social organizations, community centers, public schools, and universities to increase political consciousness, educate children about their culture, and reinforce their ethnic identity. In New York, the Latina/o community theater companies performed plays for Spanish-speaking children and adults from Puerto Rico, Cuba, Spain, Colombia, the Dominican Republic, Venezuela, and Argentina. Three major theater companies that developed during this time in New York and helped define Latina/o plays for young audiences were International Arts Relations (INTAR, 1966), Puerto Rican Traveling Theatre (1966), and Repertorio Español (1968). These theater companies were major forces in developing the talents of young

Latina/os; these companies toured the neighborhoods, offered free-of-charge summer programs, and produced works promoting cultural pride.

In the Southwest, youth/student and children's theater groups that formed during the 1960s and 1970s included La Causa de los Pobres (1965, Denver, Colorado), Teatro Urbano (1968, San Jose, California), the Mexican Bicultural Club: Children's Theater (1969, Pasadena, California), El Teatro de los Niños (1969, Pasadena, California), and Teatro Bilingüe (1972, Kingsville, Texas). Some of the productions consisted of Luis *Valdez's *actos* and skits based on Latina/o folktales and used a variety of improvisational techniques as well as masks, storytelling, juggling, and puppetry. Latina/o children and youth theater companies focused on the social, cultural, and creative development of the child.

In the 1980s and 1990s, new artistic program initiatives launched projects to develop Latina/o audiences and plays, with generous funding from organizations like the Ford Foundation and the Lila Wallace Reader's Digest Fund. Programs that gave more visibility for Latina/o children and youth playwrights were the Kennedy Center's "New Vision/New Voices" play development workshop, "Young Playwrights Lab" at the Los Angeles Theatre Center, the Lila Wallace–Reader's Digest New Works for Young Audiences Program at the Coterie Theatre, and the Mark Taper Forum in Los Angeles. These programs became part of the growth and development in bringing the new voices in Latina/o children and youth dramatic literature to professional mainstage theaters. Some of the Latina/o plays that benefited from these projects include Lisa Loomer's *Bocón* (1989), Josefina López' *Simply Maria or, the American Dream* (1992), José Cruz Gonzáles's *The Highest Heaven* (1996), Magdalia Cruz's *La Gringa* (1998), and Sylvia Gonzáles's *Alicia in Wonder Tierra or, I Can't Eat Goat Head* (1995). Professional children theater companies that have produced works from Latina/o playwrights include, but are not limited to, Child's Play (Tempe, Arizona); Seattle Children's Theatre (Seattle, Washington); Society of the Educational Arts (New York City); and Guadalupe Culture Arts Center–Grupo Animo (San Antonio, Texas).

By the 1990s a new generation of Latina/o playwrights gave more attention to cultural issues and created child characters that embodied a more complex representation of what it is like to grow up Latina/o. The contemporary repertoire of Latina/o plays for children and youth includes *No sacó náda de la escuéla* (He Gained Nothing from School) (1969) by Luis Valdez; *Maggie Magalita* (1987) by Wendy Kesselman; *Farolitos of Christmas* (1995) by Rudolfo *Anaya; *The Drop-out* (1997) by Carlos Morton; *Maricela de la Luz Lights the World* (1998) by José Rivera; *Nerd Lándia* (1999) by Gary *Soto; *Black Butterfly, Jaguar Girl, Piñata Woman, and Other Superhero Girls Like Me* (2000) created by Luis *Alfaro and Lisa Peterson; and *Señora Tortuga*, the unpublished play by Roxanne Schroder-Arce. These titles suggest a small sample of the complex and diverse representations of Latina/o children and youth in the body of contemporary dramatic literature and prove again that drama and theater continue as powerful outlets for expressing creativity, experience, and cultural values.

Further Reading

Reding, Kathy, ed. *Latino Youth in Performance*. Princeton, NJ: Films for the Humanities and Sciences, 1995.

Vigil, Angel. *Teatro! Hispanic Plays for Young People*. Englewood, CO: Libraries Unlimited, 1996.

Cecilia Aragón

Chili. One of the most familiar foods of the Americas associated with Latinas and Latinos is chili—or, in Spanish, *chile*. The familiar food is adapted from the Nahuátl language word *chilli*, used by the Aztecs and other Mesoamerican peoples before 1492 and the arrival of Christopher *Columbus. Referring to a large variety of usually hot peppers indigenous to the hemisphere, chili is best known in the twenty-first century for adding zest and piquancy to the *sabores* (flavors and "tastes" in both sensory and aesthetic senses) of Latina/o ethnic and regional food (*comida*). The place of chili in the history and heritage of Latina/o food and cookery is fundamental, particularly among Mexicans, Mexican Americans, and southwestern Americans, for it was cultivated for use as a prized spice, as a preservative along with salt, and as a basic vegetable group consumed by the native peoples of the Western Hemisphere centuries before the start of European colonialism. The planting, cultivation, and development of chili as a staple in México and the Central American isthmus contributed vital nutritional value to the indigenous diets consisting largely of beans, squash, maize, fish, and meats. For many centuries before the invention and widespread installation of refrigeration, chili functioned as a preservative with salt in the drying of meat and fish.

The varieties of chili products include *jalapeños*, named for Jalapa, México, where their agricultural development reportedly advanced; *poblanos*, named for the colonial Mexican city Puebla; and many derivatives from them. Chili cultivation, preservation, and preparation were highly evolved at the time of the conquest of México in 1521. As a result, many of the most traditional and popular Mexican dishes like *mole* (a thick gravylike sauce), tamales (the corn equivalent of a steamed meat pie or sandwich), and *salsa* (*see* *Food and Cookery) are oftentimes distinguished by their chili flavorings. In general, chilis are used to flavor meats, soups, and a variety of other preparations, including, in the United States, cheese, chutneys, and jellies. *Chiles verdes* (i.e., green chilis) are standard ingredients in *salsa cruda* (raw sauce), a widely popular fresh salsa made of uncooked chopped tomatoes, onions, cilantro (the pungent leaves of the coriander plant), and the green chili of choice, usually *jalapeños* along the U.S.-México border and Anaheim *chiles* in New Mexico and north of Santa Fe. In certain areas, *salsa cruda* is also known as *pico de gallo* (rooster's beak or pecking) and eaten in the

Watercolor still life featuring common Mexican foods: jalapeños, avocados, and tomato. This painting, titled *Aguacate Still Life*, is by artist Manuel Joel. *Private collection of Cordelia Chávez Candelaria. Photo by Emmanuel Sánchez Carballo, Arizona State University.*

manner of chutney and similar accompaniments. One of the ways that the preparation and cooking of chili has been affected by the exchange of food products and cooking methods that occurred when the Spanish and Native American cultures collided and eventually commingled after 1492 is the control or dilution of its hot piquancy caused by the plant's active ingredient, capsaicin. The careful cultivation of seed varieties has produced flavors that range from very mild to medium to very hot. Besides garlic and onion, chili is frequently flavored with *cominos* (cumin), an herb belonging to the carrot family that was imported by the Spanish from its origins in the Mediterranean region and Far East. Nutrition studies have shown that the basic menu of corn, beans, squash, and chili with occasional meat and fish provides a healthy balance of carbohydrates and proteins.

Further Reading

Bayless, Rick. *Mexico One Plate at a Time.* New York: Scribner, 2000.

De'Angell, Alicia Gironella, and Jorge De'Angell. *El gran libro de la cocina mexicana.* Mexico City: Ediciones Larousse, 1980.

Foster, Nelson, and Linda S. Cordell, eds. *Chilies to Chocolate: Food the Americas Gave the World.* Tucson: University of Arizona Press, 1992.

Grant, Rosamund. *Caribbean and African Cookery*. Kingston, Jamaica: Ian Randle Publishers, 1988.

Cordelia Chávez Candelaria

Chocolate, Kid. *See* Kid Chocolate.

Cholo. A term referring to a Latino male youth, usually a *Chicano or Mexican-origin male, *cholo* (or *chola* for a young woman) emerged in the late 1980s as a popular identification among a segment of young Latinos similar to the use of Pachuco by zoot suiters (*see* Zoot Suit) in earlier decades of the twentieth century. Often associated with *gangs and other peer youth group identities in contemporary turn-of-the-century America, the *cholo* style of dress has spread nationally to *fashion and clothing trends beyond Latina/o communities. The baggy shirts, extra large pants dragging low at the hipline, exposed underwear, reverse-billed baseball cap, and long chains for crosses, keys, and other trinkets are dress staples of rap, *hip-hop, and **rock en español* musicians, as well as of skateboard and break dancing youth.

Historically, the term *cholo* was originally based on *race and socioeconomic class. It was applied to peasant mestizos as a pejorative ethnic label to distinguish the rich, the upwardly mobile, and other aspiring members of the Mexican American and other Latina/o middle classes from the working masses. Like **mestizaje* itself, which racial purists and other supremacists disdain as "mongrelization," the *cholo* *stereotype still retains its negative connotations to many people of older generations even though aspects of the *cholo* style have moved across ethnic, racial, and class lines. Popular culture usages of *cholo* appear in the bestselling historical novel **Ramona* (1888) by Helen Hunt Jackson, in the pre-Chicano novel *Pocho* (1959) by José Antonio Villarreal, and in such thematically disparate movies as **El Norte* (1983) and **Mi Familia* (1995).

Cordelia Chávez Candelaria

Chulas Fronteras. The 1976 documentary *Chulas Fronteras* (Beautiful Borders) introduces the audience to the bilingual, music-filled reality of the Texas-México borderlands. From the opening scene of families and vehicles crossing the Rio Grande to the music of Conjunto Tamaulipas to the final scene of Los Pinguinos del Norte (The Northern Penguins) singing the Chicano anthem "México Americano" at a birthday party, *Chulas Fronteras* vividly depicts everyday Tejano (Tex-Mex) culture with care and honesty. Producer Chris Strachwitz, founder of Arhoolie Records, and director Les Blank present a wide array of typical Tejano events and scenes from the Texas-México countryside, accompanied by an impressive sound track of a wide variety of music from the region. The filmmakers sensitively depict important daily events in Tejano society, including barbecues, anniversaries, birthday parties, *family get-togethers, drinking sessions, tamale making, cockfights (*see* Cockfighting), and farm work. The filmmakers include the music and performances of important Texas-Mexican musicians including Los Alegres de Terán (The Happy Ones from Terán), the Jiménez family, Santiago, David, and Flaco *Jiménez, and Narciso Martínez. Unfortunately, with the exception of Lydia Mendoza, female artists are overlooked.

Chula Fronteras was made in the mid-1970s when Mexican Americans were still considered second-class citizens in Texas and segregation still existed. The *film captures the ethnic pride of Tejanos generated, in part, by the popularity of the *Chicano Movement and the successes of the La Raza Unida Party (United Race Party) in the borderlands. Songs in the film deal predominantly with Tejano responses to socioeconomic discrimination and hardship, including songs about migrant farmworkers, the *Texas Rangers ("Los Rinches de Tejas"), race relations ("Un Mojado Sin Licencia" and "Chicano"), and yearning for home in México ("Canción Mixteca"[Mixtec Song]), resistance to oppression ("Corrido de César Chávez"), and other difficulties of Texas Mexican experience. The film's love ballads include "Volver, Volver" (Return, Return), "La Nueva Zenaida" (The New Zenaida), "Mal Hombre" (Bad Man), and "Prenda del Alma" (Soul Garment).

The filmmakers targeted the film to the educational market. They originally distributed it with notes and a cassette tape of the accompanying sound track. The film effectively provides viewers with important and exemplary songs, beautiful scenes of the United States/México borderlands, and informative discussions with musicians and music industry professionals. However, the film fails to address gender issues in the Tex-Mex culture and also the fact that the majority of Tejanos have lived in urban areas since the mid-1970s. Overall, the multilingual, subtitled song texts and discussions with a radio DJ, songwriter/music producer, families, and a farmworker introduce the audience to the difficulties, struggles, and joys of Tejano life. *Chulas Fronteras* was distributed by Flower Films.

Further Reading

Arhoolie Records. www.arhoolie.com/catalog/index.html.

Scruggs, T.M. Film and Video Reviews of *Chulas Fronteras*, *Del Mero Corazón*, *Tex Mex: Music of the Texas Mexican Borderlands*, and *Songs of the Homeland*. *Ethnomusicology* 43.3 (1999): 572–578.

Strachwitz, C., compiler. *Chulas Fronteras/Del Mero Corazon*. El Cerrito, CA: Arhoolie, 1995.

Louis "Pancho" McFarland

Chupacabra. *El Chupacabra* means "the goat sucker" in Spanish and is a popular animal legend that fascinates the popular imagination in the United States, México, and Puerto Rico. Similar to other popular cultural belief phenomena such as the Loch Ness monster and Bigfoot, the Chupacabra is believed to suck the blood from goats, spreading terror and fear among humans. Reports suggest that the creature was first spotted in Puerto Rico in 1994. However, the Chupacabra has since left the island and has most recently been spotted throughout México, South America, and the United States. Named after its sucking of goat blood, the Chupacabra has reportedly attacked and devoured the blood of a wide variety of animals including dogs and sheep. Thus far there have not been any known human victims or fatalities.

Due to the vampirelike manner of killing its prey, the telltale marks on the neck make it easy to tell if the Chupacabra was involved in an animal's death. Animals are found with puncture wounds in their necks and most of their blood removed. Sometimes the victim's organs have disappeared even though the only wounds are small holes in the animal's neck. Similar reports of laserlike cuts on the victim's ears are also common. Although some people say they have seen the Chupacabra's tracks, usually there are no signs of blood or tracks around the dead animals.

The appearance of the Chupacabra is difficult to describe because eyewitness accounts and reported sightings differ. Most say it is either gray or green with a large lizardlike tongue, and some accounts describe it as even having wings. The creature supposedly stands upright like a human, and its height is reported to be anywhere from three to six feet tall. Some witnesses suggest it walks, while others state it flies, and some people have reported it even hops like a kangaroo. Ideas of its origin also vary, and some people believe it may actually be a new hybrid species or a relative to the panther. Others believe it may be a dinosaur or an alien. Another theory suggests that there is a portal to another dimension that stretches from Puerto Rico across to South America, and the Chupacabra has passed through.

It is believed that the Chupacabra might be a goat-sucking, nocturnal alien vampire stranded years ago on earth. If it can fly, it can also evade human detection by possibly burrowing underground. The Chupacabra continues to fascinate the paranormal community and Latinas/os. Chupacabra legends have become as popular as Bigfoot and the Loch Ness monster and are the most recent legendary monsters reported on earth. From the first reported sightings in Puerto Rico, the legend has spread worldwide, especially on television and the Internet. The Chupacabra has been depicted as a fanged bird and a batlike reptile. In Zapata, Texas, along the U.S.-México border the creature is celebrated with an annual festival.

Further Reading

http://www.chron.com/content/chronicle/metropolitan/96/08/10/chupacabra.html.
http://www.elchupacabra.com/whatis.html.
http://www.skepdic.com/chupa.html.

Peter J. García

Cinco de Mayo. Cinco de Mayo, one of the most popular celebrations in the United States, commemorates México's victory over invading French troops at the Battle of Puebla on May 5, 1862. French emperor Napoleon III had declared war on México on the pretense of collecting outstanding foreign debts in response to Mexican President Benito Juárez's had ordered a two-year moratorium on all foreign debt payments. Many historians believe that France's true objective was to expand its colonial presence in the Western Hemisphere and provide assistance to the Confederate Army in the U.S. Civil War. French troops succeeded in taking control of México the following summer, but General Ignacio Zaragoza's decisive 1862 victory at Puebla is believed to have infused the Mexican people with the patriotic fervor needed to inspire the ultimate defeat of the French. For nearly 150 years, Cinco de Mayo has been celebrated in México as a relatively staid event comparable to the observation of Veterans Day or Memorial Day in the United States.

Cinco de Mayo celebrations came to the United States by way of the Mexican immigrant population and the Mexican American community. In the 1960s, California students involved in the *Chicano Movement adopted the *holiday as a symbol of resistance against social oppression. Since the 1980s, Cinco de Mayo has become an immensely popular holiday across the United States, particularly in communities that include large Mexican and Mexican American populations. Major U.S. beer distributors, record companies, and other corporate sponsors have adopted—some say corrupted—the holiday's meaning by promoting commercial festivals awash in Mexican *food, music, and drink. Many Americans, including some Latinos, mistakenly refer to Cinco de Mayo as México's Independence Day. However, *El 16 de Septiembre* (September 16) is the day that Father Hidalgo launched an uprising that sparked the Mexican War of Independence against Spain in 1810.

Further Reading

González, Juan. *Harvest of Empire: A History of Latinos in America.* New York: Viking, 2000.

Meyer, Michael C., William L. Sherman, and Susan M. Deeds. *The Course of Mexican History.* New York: Oxford University Press, 1998.

Viva Cinco de Mayo. http://www.vivacincodemayo.org/history.htm.

Peter J. García

Cinco Puntos Press. Named after the Five Points neighborhood in central El Paso, Texas, this independent publishing house was established in 1985. It specializes in fiction, poetry, nonfiction, and children's books by authors from the U.S.-México border, the American Southwest, and México. It has received the American Book Award for excellence in publishing and has been inducted into the Latino Literary Hall of Fame. Its founders and copublishers are Bobby Bird, a poet and coeditor of *The Late Great Mexican Border* (one of his latest books of poems is *The Price of Doing Business* *in Mexico*, 1998), and Lee Byrd, the author of *My Sister Disappears* (1993). This independent press has published authors such as Rudolfo *Anaya (*Elegy on the Death of César *Chávez*, 2000); Joe Hayes (*La Llorona/The Weeping Woman*, 1998); Paco Ignacio Taibo II (*Frontera Dreams*, 2002; *Just Passing Through*, 2000); Subcomandante Marcos (*The Story of Colors/La Historia de los Colores*, 2003; *Questions & Swords*, 2001), and Benjamín Alire Sánchez (*Grandma Fina and Her Wonderful Umbrellas/La Abuelita Fina y Sus Sombrillas Maravillosas*, 2001).

Further Reading

http://www.cincopuntos.com.

Luis Aldama

Cisneros, Henry (1947–). Henry G. Cisneros, a high-profile figure of the Democratic Party since the 1980s, served the administration of President William Jefferson Clinton in the president's cabinet as secretary of Housing and Urban Development (HUD). Named to the post in 1992, Cisneros was the first Hispanic ever to be nominated for the position, and he was confirmed unanimously by the U.S. Senate and sworn into office by Chief Justice William H. Rehnquist of the U.S. Supreme Court in 1993, serving until 1997. He came to national prominence in 1981 when he was elected the first Hispanic to serve as mayor of San Antonio, Texas, the ninth largest city in the United States, winning by an astonishing 62 percent of the votes cast.

Born June 11, 1947, in a west side Mexican *barrio of San Antonio, Cisneros is the son of Elvira and George Cisneros, whose paternal *family roots extend over fifteen generations in the American Southwest. His maternal grandfather participated in the Mexican Revolution of 1910, which led to his escape to Texas for survival. Young Henry attended parochial schools, which he credits with providing a solid scholastic education and good study habits. An excellent student who skipped ahead a grade, he went to college at Texas Agricultural and Mechanical University and received a Bachelor of Arts and, in 1970, a Master's in urban planning. In 1971 Cisneros moved to Washington, D.C., to pursue graduate studies in public administration at George Washington University, while at the same time working for the National League of Cities as an intern. Cisneros was credited with becoming the youngest White House Fellow in history at the age of twenty-two in 1971. At the culmination of his fellowship, Cisneros decided to pursue another master's degree in public administration at Harvard University before eventually returning to George Washington University to complete his Ph.D. in public administration. With Ph.D. in hand, the future elected politician returned to his hometown in 1974 to teach government and environmental studies at the University of Texas, San Antonio, with affiliate lecturing at Trinity University.

Cisneros began his formal career in public service working as an administrative assistant in the San Antonio city manager's office and shortly thereafter decided to run for a city council seat. Aligning himself with the Good Government League, he won the election, attaining another first as the youngest councilman in the city's history ever to be elected. Cisneros earned a good reputation during his first term on the city council as a bright, progressive, concerned representative, and he was reelected to office in 1977 in a major landslide. That victory set the stage for his 1981 election as the first Mexican American to serve as mayor of his hometown, home of the *Alamo and historically having a large Hispanic population. In the years following, he was reelected three more times with amazing vote majorities: example, 94 percent, 72 percent, and in 1987 with double the number of votes of his closest opponent. Cisneros is credited with leading the effort to revitalize downtown San Antonio during his four mayoral terms. In addition, Cisneros rebuilt the city's economic base, attracted high-tech industries, increased tourism, and created flourishing employment in downtown San Antonio. In 1985, his achievements in his home state and birthplace were recognized by his being honored by his peers when he was elected president of the National League of Cities.

Cisneros's career as an elected political officeholder was seriously affected in 1991 when his wife of twenty-two years, Mary Alice Perez, filed for divorce, and rumors of the mayor's extramarital affairs circulated. The parents of two daughters, Teresa and Mercedes, and a son, John Paul, the couple eventually reconciled. However, the scandal spread on the eve of his nomination to head HUD, and Cisneros immediately became a tabloid fixture of the Clinton administration for having a long-term affair with Linda Medlar, a political fund-raiser in Texas, and for paying her about $200,000 to hide the fact from public disclosure. Medlar sued Cisneros in 1994 for supposedly stopping the payments, and she alleged that Cisneros lied to the Federal Bureau of Investigation (FBI) during his routine background check for his federal cabinet appointment. He continued his cabinet work and public career throughout the scandal, which included the naming of an independent counsel by Attorney General Janet Reno to investigate charges that he had lied to the FBI about the secret payments to Medlar (now known as Linda Jones). In 1998 Jones pled guilty to multiple fraud and obstruction of justice charges and received a three-and-a-half-year sentence to federal prison; significantly, Cisneros was not named in her case since her story was proven to be false in court. The next year, after a four-year intensive investigation, Cisneros reached a plea agreement with the federal prosecutor and pled guilty to a misdemeanor count of lying to the FBI during his 1993 background check for the cabinet post. Punished with a $10,000 fine and public embarrassment, the former mayor of San Antonio did not serve any jail or probation sentence, and the entire legal matter was purged from his record when President Clinton pardoned him in January 2001 at the end of his eight-year presidency.

In 1993, Henry Cisneros joined the Clinton cabinet, becoming the first Latino to be named Secretary of Housing and Urban Development. *Courtesy of* Latino Leaders Magazine.

Despite the personal scandal and its spillover into his political career, respect for the charismatic Cisneros among many in the general public, in business, and in Democratic circles was largely undamaged, although political scientists agree that his promising future in the arena of elective politics was derailed. Before making history in the Clinton administration as the first Hispanic HUD secretary, Cisneros had created a national fixed-income asset management firm known as Cisneros Asset Management Company, which he chaired. Media savvy, Cisneros made frequent use of the media to address issues affecting the state of Texas. He hosted a television show named *Texans* and *Adelante*, a national daily *Spanish-language radio show. Cisneros also served actively on boards and was deputy chairman of the Federal Reserve Bank of Dallas. Other board appointments include serving on the board of the Rockefeller Foundation, chairman of the National Civic League, and chairman of the Advisory Committee on the Construction of San Antonio's Alamo Dome. Throughout the years, Cisneros has received numerous awards and honors. Among the honors received are being named in 1982 as one of the "Ten Outstanding Young Men of America" by the U.S. Jaycees and as Outstanding Mayor a few years later by *City and State Magazine*. In 1991 *VISTA Magazine* gave him its Hispanic Man of the Year award. Cisneros headed the multinational media and television giant Univisíon Communications as president and chief operating officer from 1998 until he resigned in August 2000 about the time of the company's stock market tumble at the start of the latest American recession. Since then he has headed American City Vista, a real estate and construction development firm he established in California where he lives with his family.

Further Reading

"Henry G. Cisneros." http://www.gale.com/free_resources/chh/bio/cisneros_h.htm.

Kanellos, Nicolas, and Cristelia Perez. *Chronology of Hispanic American History: From Pre-Columbian Times to the Present*. Detroit, MI: Gale, 1995.

http://www.roycecarlton.com/pdf/Cisneros-Kit.pdf.

Cordelia Chávez Candelaria and Cristina K. Muñoz

Cisneros, Sandra (1954–). The most famous and successful Mexican American writer, Sandra Cisneros has published in the genres of fiction (both short story and novel), poetry, and essay, and her books have been translated into ten different languages. One of the first Latina writers from the United States to achieve commercial success in her craft, Cisneros is lauded by literary scholars for bringing the viewpoint of Chicana women into the mainstream of feminist literature and contemporary popular fiction. Her first major work, *The House on Mango Street* (1983), won the Before Columbus American Book Award in 1985 and has sold more than two million copies. Her second book, *Woman Hollering Creek and Other Stories* (1991), received the PEN Center Award for Best Fiction in 1992 and has joined *House on Mango Street* as a favorite title on high school and college literature syllabi. Further solidifying her reputation, Cisneros has been awarded such prestigious prizes as a MacArthur Foundation grant and two National Endowment for the Arts fellowships.

Born December 20, 1954, in Chicago, Illinois, Cisneros grew up in the city's South Side in a working-class *family—her father was an upholsterer and her mother a factory worker. She was a middle child and the only girl among six brothers. The family moved to a Puerto Rican neighborhood in Chicago's North Side in 1969, when her parents bought a two-story red house, similar to the one Cisneros describes in *The House on Mango Street*. Her childhood was defined by the family's straddling between American and Mexican cultures because her father frequently uprooted the family for extended visits to México. Strongly Chicana and Mexican-identified, Cisneros describes herself as a feminist and credits her mother for rearing her in a nontraditional manner relative to gender. Issues of feminism, cultural identification, and the influence of a Mexican American family upbringing are all featured prominently in her writings.

Cisneros eventually learned to extrapolate experiences from her childhood and recreate them in her writings. Encouraged by world-renowned poet and sister Chicagoan Gwendolyn Brooks, Cisneros obtained a Bachelor of Arts degree from Loyola University in 1976 and worked on her poetry. She honed her craftsmanship while attending the renowned University of Iowa Writers' Workshop, where she earned a Masters in Fine Arts in 1978. While studying at the Writers' Workshop, Cisneros became conscious that her cultural experiences as a Chicana/Latina and also as a native midwesterner were distinctive, and she decided to focus her writing on these elements and the problems she faced growing up, such as alienation, poverty, and divided cultural loyalties.

Based on poems initially printed in a small distribution chapbook titled *Bad Boys*, Cisneros's first volume of poetry, *My Wicked Wicked Ways*, was published by the highly influential Third Woman Press in 1987 and has since been reprinted (Random House, 1992). Like her later fiction, her poetry creatively integrates personal psychology and geographical space to capture assorted urban life experiences. This weaving of gender, geography, and genre is strikingly developed in *The House on Mango Street* and *Woman Hollering Creek* in which she presents gripping plots about growing up, marital strife, melancholy, and the often frantic effects of borderlands existence and urban life. She also published a book for children, *Pelitos* (1994), and has performed many readings on college campuses, at conferences, and in public schools. Her most recent publication is *Caramelo* (2002), her largest, most sprawling work. Narrated through the eyes of a young girl, *Caramelo* takes place in a variety of settings in México and the United States, as well as in the keen imagination of the sensitive narrator, Celaya, who was named by her mother for the town where Pancho *Villa "met his Waterloo." Praise for the novel has been enthusiastic, high profile, and consistent with the author's extraordinary trajectory.

Further Reading

Authorized Sandra Cisneros Website. http://www.sandracisneros.com/html/about.bio.html.

Elias, Edwardo F. "Chicano Writers: Sandra Cisneros, Second Series." In *Dictionary of Literary Biography*, edited by Francisco A. Lomelí and Carl R. Shirley. Vol. 122. Detroit, MI: Bruccoli Clark Layman Book/Gale Group, 1992.

Tompkins, Cynthia. "American Novelists since World War II: Sandra Cisneros, Fourth Series." In *Dictionary of Literary Biography*, edited by James Giles and Wanda Giles. Vol. 152. Detroit, MI: Bruccoli Clark Layman Book/Gale Group, 1995.

Julie Amparano García

Civdad, La. *See La Civdad.*

Clemente, Roberto (1934–1972). Baseball superstar Roberto Walker Clemente was born in his parents' house in the San Anton *barrio of Carolina, Puerto Rico. He was the youngest of eight children born to Luisa Walker Clemente and Melchor Clemente. His mother was a hardworking laundress who faithfully attended Baptist Church with her children. His father was a foreman on a sugar cane plantation. As black Puerto Ricans, they experienced racism, although not as blatantly in Puerto Rico as later in the United States. Clemente's biographers credit his loving and structured household with instilling the values that helped guide the record-holding athlete throughout his life.

At the age of seventeen, Clemente accomplished the amazing feats of throwing a baseball 400 feet accurately and running a sixty-yard dash in 6.4 seconds. Although his parents wanted him to study engineering, his immense talent and love for softball and baseball led to his "discovery" by Brooklyn Dodgers' scout Al Campanis in 1952 at a tryout camp sponsored by Alex Zorilla's Santurce Crabbers and the Dodgers. On February 1954, Clemente signed a one-year $5,000 contract, with a $10,000 signing bonus, to play in the Dodgers organization. That year he played minor league baseball for the Montreal (Canada) Royals of the International League. In the same year, Branch Rickey, then general manager of the Pittsburgh Pirates, drafted Clemente from the Dodgers for $4,000. In 1955, he began his major league career and was one of only five Puerto Ricans on the team and twenty-nine in the major leagues that year.

Despite his prowess on the diamond, as an immigrant Puerto Rican, Clemente was subjected to racism for both his skin color and culture. Throughout his career, U.S. sportswriters often portrayed him as a hypochondriac and made fun of his English by quoting his speech phonetically. Clemente spoke out against the degrading treatment of Latinos rather than accepting the double standard passively.

Clemente's extraordinary performance contributed to the breakthrough season for Puerto Ricans in the majors in 1961. Not only did Clemente win his first batting title, but Orlando Cepeda, another Puerto Rican, also led the National League (NL) in both home runs and runs batted in. After their stellar seasons, Clemente and Cepeda arrived in together San Juan, Puerto Rico, and were greeted by several thousand fans. During the off-season, Clemente returned to Puerto Rico, where he played with other, mostly black and/or Latino major leaguers in the Puerto Rican Winter League. He played in fifteen winter league seasons and was a player/manager in three others. In 1964 Clemente and Vera Zabala were married in San Fernando Catholic Church in Carolina, Puerto Rico. They had three sons: Roberto Jr., Luis, and Enrique. Roberto Jr. and Luis played minor league baseball before injuries ended their careers.

Closely associated with the Pittsburgh Pirates franchise, Clemente played for the club during his entire career from 1955 to 1972 and earned the all-time Pirates' record for games played, at bats, hits, singles, and total bases. In 1960, the Pirates upset the New York Yankees in the World Series, winning Game Seven on Bill Mazeroski's home run in the bottom of the ninth inning. Clemente was named the NL's Most Valuable Player (MVP) in 1966. In his only other World Series appearance in 1971, he hit safely in all seven games for a cumulative .362 batting average in fourteen World Series games. He played brilliantly in the 1971 World Series, leading the Pirates to a Game Seven victory over the favored Baltimore Orioles and earned the World Series MVP. Playing defense, he was arguably one of the best right fielders of all time. He won twelve Gold Gloves and led the NL in assists five times. He

Roberto Clemente batting during Pittsburgh Pirates versus New York Mets game in 1965. *Courtesy of Photofest.*

was an exceptional hitter who won four NL batting titles and accumulated 3,000 career hits. His all-around skills resulted in his selection to twelve All-Star games.

On December 23, 1972, an earthquake in Managua, Nicaragua, killed over 7,000 people, injured thousands more, and left more than 250,000 homeless. While in Puerto Rico for the winter, Clemente became honorary chairman of the earthquake relief committee. On December 31, 1972, he and four passengers boarded an airplane loaded with relief supplies bound for Managua. Fulfilling an amazing prophecy by seven-year-old Roberto Jr., who begged his father to stay, the plane developed mechanical problems and crashed only two miles off the Puerto Rican coast. There were no survivors. In 1973, Clemente was inducted posthumously into the Baseball Hall of Fame, the first and only player to be inducted without the usual five-year waiting period, which was waived in tribute to his superstar stature, humanitarian goodwill, and untimely death. Honors in his memory include an annual Roberto Clemente Award for public service given to a major league player; the naming of Puerto Rican hospitals and many U.S. schools after him; and a Roberto Clemente Sports City in Puerto Rico, providing sports facilities and training for children. In 1984, the U.S. Post Office issued a Roberto Clemente stamp commemorating what would have been his fiftieth birthday.

Further Reading

Markusen, Bruce. *Roberto Clemente: The Great One.* Champaign, IL: Sports Publishing, 1998.

Clifford Candelaria

Coca, Imogene (1908–2001). Comedienne Imogene Fernández y Coca, of Spanish American descent, was born on November 18, 1908, in Philadelphia, Pennsylvania, to José Fernández y Coca, a vaudeville musician, and Sadie Brady Coca, a dancer. As a child, Imogene Coca demonstrated a talent for both dance and music and began to perform on stage at age nine. She continued to work on stage as a singer and dancer until 1934, when producer Leonard Sillman discovered her comic gift during the production *The New Faces of 1934*. To keep warm, during a break in the production, Coca had borrowed a man's coat. Struck by the ridiculous picture of herself wearing an oversized coat, she improvised a humorous dance. Sillman soon had Coca performing that very dance on stage. Audiences quickly recognized her comedic talent as well, and she worked in the Poconos mountain resorts in Pennsylvania and on Broadway, honing her craft with the likes of Carol Channing, Danny Kaye, and Bill Robinson. Coca achieved national attention in 1949 when she appeared on NBC's *Admiral Broadway Revue*, a musical variety show, which featured Sid Caesar and Mary McCarty in its cast. Shortly thereafter, NBC launched *Your Show of Shows*, a comedic variety show that some consider the precursor of *Saturday Night Live*. In this show, Coca paired with Sid Caesar in some of America's most memorable comedic performances. She won an Emmy for her work in 1951. She was hailed as a "master of pantomime" and continues to be regarded as arguably the finest female comedian of her generation. *Your Show of Shows* lasted only four years, ending in 1954. Coca made occasional returns to television, most notably in guest appearances on *The Carol Burnett Show* and *The Dick Cavett Show* and in reunion specials with Caesar. She also appeared in such *films as *Rabbit Test* (1978) and *National Lampoon's Vacation* (1983). She died on June 2, 2001, in Westport, Connecticut.

Further Reading

http://www.blockbuster.com/bb/person/details/0,7621, BIO-P+13845,00.htm.
http://us.imdb.com/name/nm0168042/bio.

William Orchard

Cockfighting. One of the most controversial pastimes to be classified as a *sport in some contemporary societies, cockfighting is a male-identified practice inherited from the ancient past that is still popular across cultures the world over. It is associated primarily with poorer working-class men at the bottom of the educational attainment ladder, and its multiracial fan base includes significant numbers of Latinos, Filipinos, and African Americans. Some of these passionate fans are documented in the 2003 marathon *film *Cockfighters: The Interviews*, a DVD documentary lasting an amazing eight hours. The film was made by Stephanie Castillo, a filmmaker from Hawaii who grew up in a game-cock breeding family. Castillo states that her goal in researching and producing the documentary was to provide a view of the sport from the perspective of insiders, that is, the "cockers" or breeders, handlers, and spectators who keep the practice alive, even though it has been outlawed by most countries of the world and all but two of the fifty states. The controversy and popularity of her marathon film led Castillo to edit and release a shorter version titled *Cockfighters: The Short Film and the Interviews* (United States, 2003, 115 minutes), which she premiered at the Cinema Paradise Island Independent Film Festival in Honolulu in September 2003. Besides Castillo's documentary, public attention has been focused on cockfighting by the spread of avian flu, which has reached epidemic proportions in Asia. The bird flu has attacked and swept through some breeder farms in the Philippines, leading some cockfighting fans to petition their elected representatives for tougher legislation and policing of imported poultry to prevent further spreading of a disease that they fear could destroy or severely hurt the sport.

Labeled a blood sport, cockfighting consists of human handlers (i.e., cockers) who breed and train poultry, usually roosters, into game fowl that are placed, usually two game cocks at a time, in an elevated enclosed pit ring where they are prodded to fight until one is dead or severely maimed and cannot put up the ferocious contest desired by the fans. The length of cockfights varies from several minutes to over thirty. Sometimes the handlers put more than two cocks into the pit in a ferocious contest called a "battle royal" that ends when only one remains standing over as many as four to eight dead or fatally maimed opponents. To increase the ferocity of the contest, the handlers typically attach sharp objects like spikes or spurs (known as gaffs) made of metal or bone to the legs of the birds before the matches. Both avid fans and casual spectators find the practice entertaining, and most engage in vigorous betting and gambling about all aspects of the cocks, the fighting, and the final bloody outcome.

Archaeologists and cultural historians believe that wild fowl were first domesticated in India for the specific purpose of cockfighting. They find evidence for this in the fact that the ancient historical record lacks any mention of eggs or poultry meat production or cookery as part of the human food chain. Instead, historical accounts record cockfighting as a widespread popular practice in the ancient Orient, particularly in India, China, and Persia. As a result, the standard game-cock appears to be descended from the genus *Gallus gallus*, common name "Indian red jungle fowl," from which all domestic poultry is believed to originate, including the chickens familiar to *food and cooking throughout the world. The record shows that from the Orient the sport traveled in the sixth century B.C. to Greece, where it was rapidly spread by enthusiasts throughout the Mediterranean region. The Romans not only adopted it but helped spread it further during their northern explorations and conquests through Germany, Spain, Great Britain, and eventually, throughout Europe. Harshly condemned by Rome's Christian authorities, cockfighting nevertheless flourished as a popular pastime publicly enjoyed by European and British royalty and the mass male public until the end of the nineteenth century.

With European exploration in the Western Hemisphere after 1492 and Christopher *Columbus's voyages, cockfighting soon took hold in the colonies of North and South America. Massachusetts passed laws against cockfighting in 1836, and Great Britain did so in 1849. It also is not officially recognized as a sport by most Latin American countries despite its secret persistence as an outlawed blood sport. Still popular in parts of México, Puerto Rico, and throughout Haiti, cockfighting continues as a popular if clandestine spectator and wager activity in the United States and Canada.

According to most of the cockers interviewed by Stephanie Castillo, their enjoyment of cockfighting as an amateur pastime derives for the most part from the gambling and wagering associated with the competitions, not from its bloody contests. They point to the multiple opportunities to bet on matches in the context of constantly fluctuating odds and unpredictable outcomes. Others in the film emphasize the financial contribution that cockfighting makes to their local economies as a justification for decriminalizing it. Newspaper accounts from Manila estimate that in the Philippines alone there are approximately 2,000 cockfighting pits that produce jobs and contribute to the nation's revenue base due to its importance for industries like poultry feed, veterinary supplies, gambling, and related peripherals. It remains to be seen if the 2004 bird flu will alter aspects of the sport or lead to its total demise, as feared by several cocker veterans who remember the avian flu epidemic that broke out in the early 1990s.

Further Reading

Dundes, Alan, ed. *The Cockfight: A Casebook*. Madison: University of Wisconsin Press, 1994.

Hawley, Francis Frederick. "Organized Cockfighting: A Deviant Recreational Subculture" [microform]. Ph.D. dissertation, Florida State University, 1982.

Markham, Gervase. *Country Contentments, or, The Husbandman's Recreations* [Early English books, 1641–1700, microform of the 1649 sixth edition]. Ann Arbor, MI: University Microfilms, 1977.

Sarabia Viejo, María Justina. *El juego de gallos en Nueva España*. Sevilla, Spain: Publicaciones de la Escuela de Estudios Hispanoamericanos de Sevilla, 1972.

Scott, George Ryley. *The History of Cockfighting*. London: C. Skilton, 1957.

Wilson, George. *The Commendation of Cockes, and Cock-fighting* [Early English books, 1475–1640, microform of the 1607 edition]. Ann Arbor, MI: University Microfilms, 1957.

Cordelia Chávez Candelaria

Colón, Jesús (1901–1974). Jesús Colón, an integral part of the *nuyorican poet's movement, was born in 1901 in Cayey, Puerto Rico, and moved to New York at the age of sixteen. A writer, reporter, and social activist, Colón was active in political activities that had an effect on both black and white communities. Due to his exposure to abuse and exploitation of lower-class and unskilled workers, his essays often contained his ideas on *race and identification with the working class, which made him a forerunner of the Nuyorican writers, Puerto Rican writers in New York during the 1960s and 1970s, including playwright Miguel *Piñero and poets Miguel *Algarín and Tato Laviera. Colón is the author of a volume of essays in English that reflect on the issues facing the growing population of Puerto Ricans in New York, *Puerto Rican in New York and Other Sketches* (1961), and another collection that was published in 1993, *The Way It Was and Other Sketches*, addressing political consciousness, injustices of capitalistic society, and advocacy for the working-class poor. Colón founded the publishing house Editorial Hispánica (Hispanic Publishers), which features books and information in Spanish, especially in the areas of history, literature, and politics. Colón died in 1974.

Further Reading

Algarín, Miguel, and Bob Holman, eds. *Aloud: Voices from the Nuyorican Poets Café*. New York: Holt, 1994.

Colón, Jesús. *The Way It Was, and Other Writings*. Edited with introduction by Edna Acosta-Belén and Virginia Sánchez Korrol. Houston: Arte Público Press, 1993.

Cordelia Chávez Candelaria

Colón, Miriam (1925–). Miriam Colón, a pioneering *film and stage actress, was born to working-class parents in Ponce, Puerto Rico. She studied drama at the University of Puerto Rico and, with the help of a scholarship to the Erwin Piscator Dramatic Workshop and Technical Institute, she headed to New York to embark on her acting career. She was the first Puerto Rican accepted as a member of the Actors Studio, where she studied under Lee Strasberg and Elia Kazan. A character actor, she has appeared in more than 250 television shows and in numerous films. Some of her film credits include: *Scarface* (1983), *Battle at Bloody Beach* (1961), *The Outsider* (1961), *The Appaloosa* (1966), *Back Roads* (1981), *Sabrina* (1995), and **Lone Star* (1996).

Aside from acting, Colón has spent much of her time advocating for Hispanic performing actors. She was appointed to and served over ten years on

New York's Council on the Arts, served on the Expansion Arts Panel of the National Endowment for the Arts, and has acted as cultural adviser for numerous state and national organizations. Her greatest contribution has been the creation of the Puerto Rican Traveling Theatre, founded in 1966. The *theater is housed in a former fire station in New York and, since its inception, has provided a stage for over fifty plays by playwrights from Chile, Puerto Rico, Spain, Venezuela, Colombia, Brazil, and México. Colón also cofounded the Nuevo Círculo Dramático, a Spanish-language theater in New York.

Miriam Colón in *Alfred Hitchcock Presents* "Strange Miracle." *Courtesy of Photofest.*

Colón has been recognized for her efforts by many organizations such as the National Council of Christians and Jews, *Puerto Rican Legal Defense and Education Fund, and the State University of New York. She received the New York Mayor's Award of Honor for the Arts and Culture and the Athena Award from the New York Commission on the Status of Women. She has also received an honorary degree in letters from Montclair State College in New Jersey.

Further Reading

Kanellos, Nicolás, and Cristelia Pérez. *Chronology of Hispanic-American History: From Pre-Columbian Times to the Present*. Detroit, MI: Gale Research, 1995.

Keller, Gary D. *A Biographical Handbook of Hispanics and United States Film*. Tempe, AZ: Bilingual Press, 1997.

Telgen, Diane, and Jim Kamp, eds. *Latinas! Women of Achievement*. Detroit, MI: Visible Ink Press, 1996.

Alma Alvarez-Smith

Colón, Willie (1950–). Of Puerto Rican descent, William Anthony Colón Roman was born April 28, 1950, in the Bronx, New York. Colón has been a major figure in contemporary Latin urban jazz since the late 1960s and has worked as producer, bandleader, composer, vocalist, and a trombone player. His commitment to Latin music began at an early age. Colón directed the "Latin Jazz All-Stars" during his high school years, and at the age of seventeen he signed on the Fania label where he recorded the hits

"Jazzy" and "I Wish I Had a Watermelon." His 1967 debut album *El Malo* sold 30,000 copies and is considered a classic among *salsa music connoisseurs. He is credited with putting the Afro-Cuban sound into an urban rock and rhythm and blues context that also draws from rhythmic sources across all of the Caribbean and Latin America. In 1974 he began to collaborate with Rubén *Blades and Celia *Cruz. Some of his albums include *The Good, the Bad, the Ugly* (1975), *Siembra* (1978) with Blades and *The Winners* (1987) with Cruz, and in 1995 he recorded a reunion album with Blades called *Tras la tormenta* (Behind the Storm). Colón is committed to social change in the Latino community, ran unsuccessfully for U.S. Congress in 1994, and is involved with a variety of community empowerment projects. Since 1997, Colón has turned his interests toward television and has a recurring role in the Mexican soap opera *Demasiado Corazón.*

Further Reading

Kanellos, Nicolás, ed. *The Hispanic-American Almanac: A Reference Work on Hispanics in the United States*. Detroit, MI: Gale Research, 1993.

http://www.warr.org/colonblades.html.

Robert Chew

Columbus, Christopher (1451–1506). Arguably the most famous explorer in Eurowestern history, Christopher Columbus is also known as Cristoforo Colombo in his native Italian and Cristóbal Colón throughout the Spanish-speaking world. A master navigator and accomplished admiral, he is central to any discussion of Latina and Latino popular culture in the United States because of his landmark role in documented history and also because of his importance as an iconic symbol, especially to the peoples and cultures of the Americas. Both his historical and iconic impacts are so intertwined as to be fundamental features of his continuing legend and legacy. Traditionally celebrated as history's "discoverer" of what to him and other Europeans was a "New World," Columbus's travels and geographical discoveries combined with other scientific and intellectual discoveries of his epoch helped shape and, many historians believe, even accelerate Europe's renaissance period. The consequences of his four transatlantic voyages in 1492–1493, 1493–1496, 1498–1500, and 1502–1504 undisputably opened the sea gates to European exploration, settlement, conquest, development, and exploitation of the peoples and other resources of the Americas.

Columbus and his legacy represent to many thinkers the loss and promise of the Americas to those who were already living in the Western Hemisphere in 1492. In the worldviews of many of the native peoples, they were descended from their homelands' original "first" discoverers, their forebears who had migrated into the Americas in the ancient past from a distant, legendary north. This cultural nativist, indigenist perspective has influenced many Latina/o intellectual, political, and artistic movements, particularly after the revolutions of emancipation from Spain in the nineteenth century. As a result, within Latina/o popular culture Columbus is a complex historical figure of germinal importance as the initiator of the intercultural diversity that constitutes the contemporary Americas and pan-American cultures. For example, whether described as a discovery, an encounter, an invasion, and/or a moment of first transnational East-West contact, Columbus's arrival with shiploads of multilingual, multicultural, and multiracial crewmen began an *immigration process of cosmic proportions. The phenomenal exchange and interanimation of languages, cultures, and *races that occurred thereafter in the Americas and that continues in the present is quintessentially defining of what it is to be an American *of* the Americas, and that *ser* or sense of being is central to Latina/o identities.

Columbus was born in Genoa, Italy, and eventually became a master sailor through advanced study in Portugal, where he developed the dream of finding a western route to India. His visionary worldliness was assured when he received the financial sponsorship to test his explorer's dream from Spain's Catholic monarchs, Ferdinand II and Isabella I. He assembled crews for his famous ships, the *Niña*, the *Pinta*, and the *Santa María*, from throughout Spain, Italy, Portugal, and the Mediterranean including Moors and other Africans. Under his bold, brave, intelligent, visionary, and stubborn leadership, his men managed to survive amazing hardships during the Atlantic crossing, and he managed to prevail over his own distress and their travails and attempted mutiny. He and his surviving crews are credited with being the first documented Europeans to land on Hispaniola, Puerto Rico, and other Caribbean islands known today as the West Indies, and within fifteen years Spaniards had begun exploring North America. Artifactual records discovered long after Columbus set foot in the Indies give evidence of landings in North America by Viking seafarers five centuries before and by Chinese explorers in the early 1400s. However, these prior visits were not documented worldwide, nor is there evidence of extensive exchange and impact comparable to that following 1492.

The 1992 quincentenary commemoration of the first major transnational East-West encounter focused considerable attention on the great advances in scholarly research on Columbus, the nature of the contact, the pre-Columbian civilizations, and scores of related topics. From these many developments in archaeology, anthropology, and historiography emerged major additions and corrections to accumulated knowledge. Critically important to this expansion and shift in understanding have been the incorporation of multiple perspectives from the Americas themselves. Accordingly, the previous received belief in a triumphant "discovery of America" with Columbus in the role of civilized Christian hero bringing great wealth to Spain and Europe and saving the Americas through colonization has been challenged and shown to be partial—that is, both fragmentary and biased.

The advances in scholarship have helped complete and thicken the documentary record through acknowledgment of the damage and destruction wreaked by European conquests, including the horrors of rampant mistreatment and loss of hundreds of thousands of indigenous lives and of the horrific slave trade. The research-based new scholarship also has documented the overlooked contributions of native peoples and the victims of slavery to American civilization and history. No longer viewed solely as a remarkable hero, Columbus at the turn of the century is thus better understood as a deeply flawed and occasionally cruel man with mortal shortcomings. Most scholars still consider him remarkable as a visionary, leader, and navigator, despite his diminishment by the thicker interpretation of the record that lowers him to ground level where robust political debates about him and his iconic status flourish. Those debates were problematized in the late-twentieth-century indigenist political and cultural movements that ascribed centuries of anticolonialist rage and resistance onto the "Admiral of the Ocean Sea," as the Spanish monarchs officially titled him. Cuban, Puerto Rican, Chicano, and other Latin American liberation groups and their supporters vested him with the hegemonic power of the monarchs who sponsored him, the colonists who followed him, and the exploitative slave-owning practices that are still being addressed and have yet to be overcome. Ironically, this historiographical reversal parallels his historical career. What began as a dream full of hope and ambition was followed by the hardships of his four voyages and ultimately by his public humiliation, poverty, and painful death as a bitterly disappointed man.

Many popular culture depictions of Columbus capture these complexities and contradictions, for example, the Cuban *Latin jazz innovator Mario *Bauza's 1994 album *944 Columbus*; the 1992 movie *Christopher Columbus: The Discovery*, starring Academy Award–winning actor Benicio *Del Toro; the counter *Día de la Raza protests called SUBMOLOC or "Columbus" spelled backward; and the naming of the literary prize "Before Columbus American Book Award" to recognize the multicultural plurality of American writing. These and countless other reinterpretations of Columbus reaffirm his historical importance and undiminished iconic centrality to humankind and, therefore, to Latina and Latino popular culture.

Further Reading

Churchill, Ward. *A Little Matter of Genocide: Holocaust and Denial in the Americas, 1492 to the Present*. San Francisco, CA: City Lights Books, 1997.

Goldin, Liliana R., ed. *Identities on the Move: Transnational Processes in North America and the Caribbean Basin*. Austin: University of Texas Press, 1999.

Heat Moon, William Least. *Columbus in the Americas*. Hoboken, NJ: John Wiley, 2002.

Provost, Foster. *Columbus: An Annotated Guide to the Study on His Life and Writings, 1750 to 1988*. Detroit, MI: John Carter Brown Library and Omnigraphics, 1991.

Traboulay, David M. *Columbus and Las Casas: The Conquest and Christianization of America, 1492–1566*. Lanham, MD: University Press of America, 1994.

Cordelia Chávez Candelaria

Comedy. Comedy in the form of double entendre language plays, irony, and social satire with U.S. Latina and Latino culture spans back to pre-Columbian origins with the use of humor within all indigenous cultures in the Americas in both ritualized forms and in everyday popular culture. Humor and comedy, especially in terms of the picaresque literature and drama, were alive and well during the Spanish Conquest of the sixteenth century. History records that during the conquest of México, the Southwest, and Latin America, indigenous peoples would purposely subvert, mock, parody, and slander the Spanish priests and rituals as a way of creating humor among themselves in otherwise somber activities. Some aspects that characterize Latina and Latino comedy are the use of satire, ethnic self-parody, parody of the dominant culture, codeswitching, language plays between Spanish and English, and the fusion of the profane, body functions, sex, and swear words into a self-referential type of catharsis. In the case of contemporary *immigration and the negative ways that Latino immigrants are perceived in the United States, especially Mexicans, there is a subgenre of Mexican and Chicano "jokelore" that makes fun of the border-crossing experience, being labeled a wetback, and being deported.

In more contemporary times, U.S. Latino comedians, most recently with the crossover prime-time comedy hit the *George *López Show*, have had a huge audience among Latinas/os and non-Latinas/os alike. López, although remarkable in having a lead in a prime-time situation comedy show, continues the traditions of other Latino comics that have a strong following in the Latino community and have also crossed over into the mainstream. Some of these figures include Cheech *Marin and his hugely successful role in the film *Up in Smoke* (1978), and later **Born in East L.A.* (1987), and Paul *Rodríguez and his appearances in the *Latin Kings of Comedy*, prime-time late night talk shows, his several commercial release film projects, and his numerous television appearances. Another figure who employs the use of ethnic self-parody, language plays, cultural differences, and mistranslations between Latino cultures and the mainstream culture and who continues to have a great success in comedy shows, film, theater, and appearances on mainstream talk shows is Colombian-born John *Leguizamo, who was raised in the New York Bronx. Another illustrious career was that of the New York–born Puerto Rican and Hungarian Freddie *Prinze, whose groundbreaking television comedy hit *Chico and the Man* (1974–1978), introduced a Chicano character to mainstream television. Interestingly, prior to the civil rights movement of the 1960s and 1970s, which among many issues called for a more just and diverse representation of Latinas/os and other minorities in film and television, one of the most popular television comedies in the history of American television was *I Love Lucy* (1951–1957). The show featured a mixed-race couple played by Lucille Ball and Cuban-born Desi *Arnaz, whose role as the Cuban music bandleader Ricky Ricardo forms part of the classic pantheon of American comedy.

In terms of early comedic figures who had a huge career in film and crossed over from México to Latina and Latino audiences in the United States and the Spanish-speaking Caribbean, there are two Mexican comic film actors whose roles, trajectory, and unique comedic styles continue to be vastly influential in the Latino community because of their working-class personas who poke fun at middle- and upper-class taboos. These include Mario Moreno's recurring character *Cantinflas (1911–1993), with his unique ways of speaking in fragments and innuendoes, and German Valdés's recurring character *Tin Tan (1915–1973), with his characteristic use of Pachuco-style pants, drapes, and feathered fedora. Both also used working-class Caló and *mambo and Cuban dance sequences in their films.

Latino comedy has also had a huge impact on theater and is a driving aspect of fusing humor with social commentary as is seen with the Chicano *Teatro Campesino, the Puerto Rican *Teatro Pregones, and the comedic troupe *Culture Clash*. To illustrate some unique characteristics of fusing humor and pathos to address social issues of oppression, racism, and poverty, Luis *Valdez's *actos* and their use of allegory show how farmworkers can unionize themselves to receive a better wage and health benefits; Valdez, Zarco *Guerrero, and many Chicana/o–Latina/o theater troupes use the *pastorela* to infuse cross-linguistic humor in the traditional story of Jesus and Mary seeking lodging to give birth to Christ. In the case of Guerrero's version, Bethlehem becomes Belén, which is the sacred homeland of the Yaqui (Yoeme) community. The actors' usual Spanglish verbal and visual puns speak to an audience who fluctuates between English and Spanish.

This handbill flyer promotes a performance by Chicano Secret Service comedy ensemble. *Courtesy of the Associated Research Collection, Tempe, Arizona.*

Among prominent women comics, there are several contemporary comedians who not only engage in the acts of cultural, ethnic, and linguistic parody but also challenge sexism and homophobia. The three comedians who have huge followings among the Latina, women's, and the gay, lesbian, and transgender communities, and who are beginning to enjoy some of the support and coverage that male comics receive (although there still is gender inequity among Latino comics, in general), include the Cuban Puerto Rican, Harlem-born Marga Gomez; queer-identified Chicana Monica Palacios; and the classically trained cellist and multimedia stand-up comic María Elena Gaitán. Gomez has appeared on HBO, PBS, Showtime, and Comedy Central and is the writer/performer of six one-person shows that have been produced off-Broadway in New York and has an active national touring schedule in comedy, theater, and academic venues. Palacios also has developed a series of one-woman shows like "Greetings from a Queer Señorita" that tour the country at universities, theaters, and community centers; contributes to

Latina Magazine; and does workshops on Latino theater in Los Angeles high schools. Gaitán has appeared on HBO, and her multimedia shows, "Chola con Cello: A Home Girl in the Philharmonic" and the "Adventures of Connie Chancla" tour throughout the country at a variety of community and university venues.

Comedy and social satire in important avant-garde Latino performance art, also includes two prominent figures: the Mexican-born MacArthur Genius grant recipient Guillermo *Gómez-Peña, whose work on border crossing and U.S.-Mexican border cultures has received significant attention in the United States and on a global level, and the Cuban New York–born Coco *Fusco, whose videotaped performance installation and collaboration *Couple in the Cage* (1992–1994) parodies the "discovery" and "display" of indigenous, African, and non-Western peoples in the history of colonialism. In this performance Fusco and Peña traveled in a cage, as a newly discovered tribe in México, to major museums of anthropology and natural history in the United States, Australia, Great Britain, Argentina, and Spain. They thought the museum attendees would immediately recognize this performance as a farce and satire of how indigenous peoples have been caged and exhibited historically. However, they were amazed by the number of people who believed the spoof was real and lined up to have their pictures taken with the newly discovered "primitive peoples."

Further Reading

Beezley, William H., and Linda A. Curcio-Nagy. *Latin American Popular Culture: An Introduction*. Wilmington, DE: Scholarly Resources, 2000.

Maciel, David, and María Herrera-Sobek, eds. *Culture across the Borders: Mexican Immigration and Popular Culture*. Tucson: University of Arizona Press, 1998.

http://www.sscnet.ucla.edu/chavez/palacios.html.

Arturo J. Aldama

Comic Books. In the world of contemporary U.S. comic books, Latinos are present as writers, artists, and characters. A full appreciation of the representation of Latinos in comic books requires a familiarity not only with the U.S. tradition of comic art but also with that of Latin America, especially México, where comic books have exerted a powerful cultural influence.

The U.S. comic book tradition can be traced to the beginnings of the twentieth century, when it grew out of such genres as the dime novel and detective fiction. Early on, comics were associated with youth cultures and linked with declining literacy and delinquency. Early comic strips exhibited hostile attitudes toward new immigrants and racial others, leading to a call for censoring comic books because of the racial stereotyping and violence depicted in their pages. Frederic Wertham, a psychiatrist who connected comics with delinquency, led the effort for censorship legislation. Comic book publishers eventually adopted a self-regulatory code that resembled the code earlier adopted by the film industry. One of Wertham's books about the toxic effects of comic books, *The Circle of Guilt* (1956), chronicles the life of Frankie Santana, a New York Puerto Rican who was arrested for a gang-related murder.

Although figures like Wertham were concerned about the effects of racial *stereotypes and ethnic slurs, they were often deaf to the comic industry's attempts to address them. For instance, a Senate hearing on the effects of comic books singled out *The Whipping* (1954), a story from an EC Comic that used such derogatory terms as "spick" and "dirty Mexican." The testimony fails to mention that the inflammatory language is used by the villain in the story—a father who so disapproves of his white daughter's relationship with a Mexican American male that he establishes a secret hooded organization that bears a strong resemblance to the Ku Klux Klan. The father and his racist comrades storm into a darkened room to "whip" the daughter's boyfriend but inadvertently beat the daughter to death instead.

Just as they addressed domestic politics, American comics also demonstrated a concern for international politics. President Franklin Roosevelt's Good Neighbor Policy and the heightened suspicions of the early Cold War period provided fodder for story lines that questioned the democratic integrity of Latin American republics. These story lines most often appeared in the superhero comic books that would dominate the post–World War II comic book marketplace.

In response to the civil rights movements of the late 1960s and early 1970s, the comic book industry began to feature racial and ethnic minorities in superhero roles. White Tiger shortly served as Spider-Man's Puerto Rican sidekick, while Firebird, a Chicana superhero, appeared in the Marvel Comic's Incredible Hulk series. Dissatisfied with mainstream comic book attempts to include minor Latino characters, some Latino comic writers and artists began their own series. Judge Garza's *Relampago* (Lightening) (1977) featured the first *Chicano superhero, and Richard Dominguez's *El Gato Negro* (Black Cat) (1993) featured a Chicano social worker who fights crime incognito at night. In 1993, Milestone Comics was founded to increase the diversity of superheroes. Ivan Velez (best known for *Ghost Rider*) authored *Blood Syndicate* for Milestone. Three Latino characters are portrayed in *Blood Syndicate*: Third Rail, who channels electricity; Flashback, who can turn back time three seconds; and Fade, a gay Latino whose body turns incorporeal. The three characters' gang backgrounds were often used to draw attention to urban violence and decay.

Velez's heroes demonstrate a debt to a new brand of superhero that emerged when the *X-Men* debuted in 1975. The X-Men were socially marginalized mutants that were often read as a metaphor for racial minorities in the United States. The X-Men series eventually featured a Latino character, Angelo Espinosa (who later assumed the moniker Spin), in *Generation X* (1994). Superhero comics comprised a large segment of the U.S. comic book market and were largely consumed by young males. Although the superhero subgenre flourishes in Latin America, it does not dominate the market in the same way, and Latin America's comic book readership includes women and men of all ages. México is one of the world's largest consumers and producers of comic books, perhaps only rivaled by Japan. In México, comics are sold in mainstream periodical newsstands and have circulations that exceed many of the nation's newspapers and magazines. Contrary to the United States where comic books have been linked with a decline in literacy, comic book reading has been associated with rising mass literacy in México.

Historietas (little stories), as comics are referred to in México, are graphically illustrated narratives that portray melodramatic stories, often about rags-to-riches transformations. Many incorporate supernatural or underworld elements that recall the atmospherics of film noir. One variation of the *historieta* is the *fotonovela*, a series of photographs that tell a story with the dialogue printed in caption bubbles. In addition to offering a distinct visual language that has influenced Latino comic artists, *fotonovelas* often address social issues of importance to Latino communities. The central figures of these works are typically socially progressive or "modern" women.

The U.S. and Mexican traditions of comic art come together in the work of Gilbert and Jaime Hernandez, whose *Love and Rockets* series has been profoundly influential on the current generation of comic artists and graphic novelists. "Los Hernandez Bros," as they billed themselves on their first issue, started *Love and Rockets* in 1986. Each brother authored distinct strips. Gilbert's took place in the mythical Mexican village of Palomar, while Jaime's were set in post-punk Los Angeles. The comic strips collected in *Love and Rockets* were rendered in black-and-white images at a moment when most artists used color, recalling the black-and-white photography of *fotonovelas*. The stories, like *historietas*, were often melodramatic, engaged social issues, and centered on female characters.

The Hernandez brothers can also be incorporated into a tradition of "alternative comics" in the United States. Alternative comics emerged in the 1980s and 1990s in response to the dominance of superhero comics. These comic books and graphic novels tended to be more visually arresting, possessed sophisticated narratives, and addressed serious topics to adult audiences. The Hernandez brothers have influenced such diverse talents as comic artists Daniel Clowes (*Ghost World*) and Jessica Abel (*ArtBabe* and *La Perdida* [The Lost One]) and fiction writer Junot Díaz. Their ongoing success and artistic innovations will continue to imbue American comic art with a Latino sensibility.

Further Reading

Dorfman, Ariel. *The Empire's Old Clothes*. New York: Random House, 1983.

Dorfman, Ariel, and Armand Mattelart. *How to Read Donald Duck: Imperialist Ideology in the Disney Comic*. Translated by David Kunzle. 1975. New York: International General, 1984.

Hardy, Charles, and Gail F. Stern, eds. *Ethnic Images in the Comics*. Philadelphia, PA: Balch Institute for Ethnic Studies, 1986.

Hinds, Harold, Jr., and Charles Tatum. *Not Just for Children: The Mexican Comic Book in the Late 1960s and 1970s*. Westport, CT: Greenwood Press, 1992.

Nyberg, Amy Kiste. *Seal of Approval: The History of the Comics Code*. Jackson: University of Mississippi Press, 1998.

Rubenstein, Anne. *Bad Language, Naked Ladies, and Other Threats to the Nation: A Political History of Comic Books in Mexico*. Durham, NC: Duke University Press, 1998.

Sabin, Roger. *Comics, Comix, & Graphic Novels: A History of Comic Art*. London: Phaidon, 1996.

Wertham, Frederic. *The Circle of Guilt*. New York: Rinehart, 1956.

Wright, Bradford. *Comic Book Nation: The Transformation of Youth Culture in America*. Baltimore, MD: Johns Hopkins University Press, 2001.

William Orchard

Congressional Hispanic Caucus. The Congressional Hispanic Caucus (CHC) is a coalition of elected U.S. congressional representatives of Hispanic descent. The primary focus of the group is to give voice and promote the causes of Hispanic Americans in the United States and territories from within the legislative process, as well as through public advocacy. In this capacity the CHC represents an important modern example of previous Latina and Latino mutual aid societies and associations (i.e., *mutualistas*). Founded in 1976 during the 94th Congress, the CHC was initiated by Henry B. *González (D–TX), Herman Badillo (D–NY), Eligio "Kika" de la Garza (D–TX), Baltasar Corrada del Río (NP–Puerto Rico), and Edward R. Roybal (D–CA). Roybal served as the group's first chairman. To reinforce their primary goal, the founders sought to work in conjunction with other groups both inside and outside of Congress to fortify the nation's commitment to Hispanic citizens. Further, they wished to expand the Hispanic community's awareness of the workings and intricacies of the American political system.

The CHC is characterized as a legislative service organization of the U.S. House of Representatives and thus is made up solely of members of the U.S. Congress. Members of the CHC are able to further advance the causes of Hispanics by participating directly in one of the CHC's numerous task forces, which range from education and the environment to labor issues and veterans' affairs.

The first Hispanic elected to the U.S. House of Representatives in 1822 was Joseph Marion *Hernández from Florida. Florida, New Mexico, and California were the first states to send Hispanic representatives to Congress, and for decades their numbers were sparse. However, since 1960 more Hispanics have been elected to Congress than in the previous 140 years. This change has come about as a result of major growth in the Hispanic population, among both U.S.-born Hispanics and first- and second-generation immigrants, as well as an increase in the number of progressive grassroots organizations promoting voter registration and voting rights. The increased participation of Hispanics in the voting and electoral process has led to widespread recognition among seasoned politicians and the press of the importance of Latina/Latino voters individually and as a block.

Noteworthy strides were made by several Hispanics from around the United States when they were the first by many accounts to occupy an office in Congress. One of the most notable was Ileana *Ros-Lehtinen, the first *Cuban American and the first Hispanic woman to serve in the U.S. Congress. Elected to Congress in 1989, Ros-Lehtinen, a Republican, represents the state of Florida's eighteenth district. It was during the early 1990s that Hispanic membership within Congress rose substantially. In 1990 Arizona elected Democrat Ed Pastor, a Mexican American from the mining community of Globe, Arizona, as its first Hispanic congressman. In 1992 New Jersey and Illinois elected their first Hispanic representatives, Democrats Robert Menéndez and Luis Gutiérrez, respectively. The membership of the Hispanic Caucus increased to twenty in 1992, making the 103rd Congress the largest and most diverse group in its history with representatives from eight states, Puerto Rico, the Virgin Islands, and Guam.

The Congressional Hispanic Caucus Institute (CHCI), a 501(c)(3) nonprofit, nonpartisan organization, was founded by three Hispanic Caucus members in 1978. The three members—Representatives Edward Roybal, E. "Kika" de la Garza, and Baltasar Corrada—established the CHCI to serve as an educational institute whose outreach programs would serve the Hispanic community nationwide. The primary purpose of this educational organization is to provide leadership development programs to young Hispanics. In addition, CHCI offers access to an array of information regarding scholarships and financial aid opportunities available to Hispanics through a National Directory that offers more than 200,000 resources and a toll-free number (1-800-EXCEL DC). The CHCI considers one of its most important functions to be serving as a provider of its nationally recognized fellowship and internship programs. These CHCI programs provide young Hispanics with exposure to and training about citizenship, civics, and the logistics of the U.S. political system.

From the time of the CHCI's inception in 1978 up until 1984, the board of directors was made up solely of Congressional Hispanic Caucus members. In 1985 the board of directors was expanded to include influential Hispanic businesspersons from the private sector and community leaders from across the country. The diverse backgrounds of the board members allowed them to contribute an array of policy-related knowledge and experience at the local, state, and national levels.

Further Reading

Congressional Hispanic Caucus Institute. http://www.chci.org.
http://www.house.gov/reyes/CHC/.

Cristina K. Muñoz

Conquistador. In 1932, Archibald MacLeish published *Conquistador*, an epic poem about the Spanish conquest of the Aztec civilization. MacLeish relied on Bernál Díaz del Castillo's account of the conquest in *The True History of the Conquest of New Spain* (1908–1916, reprint 1967), based on Díaz's experience as a soldier who marched through México with Hernán Cortés. MacLeish's account avoids the kind of monumental view of the conquest that focuses on major events and heroes, focusing instead on the experiences of the common man. Speaking in the collective "we" and depicting the horrors of colonialism as felt by one of its agents, MacLeish maintains Díaz's vibrant tone. Harriet Monroe, editor of the influential modernist journal *Poetry*, referred to *Conquistador* as "an epic of races rather than heroes." When the poem was published, many misread it as a triumphalist account of the conquest, while others thought that the conquest of México was not an appropriate topic for serious poetry. Most were unanimous in praising the poem's craft, however, particularly its modified use of the terza rima form. The poem was awarded the Pulitzer Prize in 1933.

Further Reading

Donaldson, Scott. *Archibald MacLeish: An American Life*. Boston: Houghton Mifflin, 1992.

William Orchard

Cordero, Angel, Jr. (1942–). One of the top horse racing jockeys of the twentieth century, Angel Cordero, Jr., was ranked third on the all-time list of jockeys when he retired in 1992. To earn that rating, he posted 7,057 lifetime wins and won the Kentucky Derby 3 times (in 1974, 1976, and 1985), the Preakness twice (in 1980 and 1984), and the Belmont once (in 1976). The Thoroughbred Racing Associations, the *Daily Racing Form*, and the National Turf Writers Association voted twice (in 1982 and 1983) to honor Cordero with racing's Eclipse Award for his extraordinary achievements as a jockey and his overall contributions to the *sport as a lifetime supporter and exemplary role model. Another measure of his professional skill and competitiveness is that he won an astonishing four Breeders' Cup thoroughbred races and is still ranked seventh in the Breeders' Cup history of earnings.

Cordero was born into a distinguished family heritage of Caribbean horse racing on November 8, 1942, in Santurce, Puerto Rico. He apprenticed with his father, Angel Cordero Vila, who himself was a respected jockey and horse trainer in Puerto Rico. He also trained and competed with a childhood friend, Juan Manuel "Guengo" Rodríguez, who went on to become a successful and highly touted trainer in Puerto Rican racing. Achieving significant fame in his homeland in the early years of his career, Cordero moved to the United States to test his skills in the international horse racing circuit. His talent was recognized quickly, and he was invited to ride for the prestigious Calumet Farms stables. He secured his stardom after winning the Kentucky Derby, a victory that he soon matched with victories at the Belmont, Preakness, and Breeders' Cups races to further strengthen his professional standing. From 1977 to 1990 his mounts won a record-holding total of over $5 million each year. One of his favorite mounts was the horse that he rode in his second Derby win in 1976, Bold Forbes, the winner that went on to be the Derby's longest-living horse.

Along with the many accomplishments and laurels earned, Cordero and his *family have encountered tragedies as well. A freak accident ended his five-decades-old active career as a jockey in 1992 when a hard fall nearly cost him his life. He worked hard to recover and rehabilitate, and in 1995, against his family's wishes, he decided to saddle up again for the Breeders' Cup race. Living in Greenvale, New York, with his family, Cordero and his three children were struck by tragedy again in 2001 when his wife, Marjorie Clayton Cordero, herself a former jockey, trainer, and aficionado of thoroughbred racing, was killed in a hit-and-run car accident at the age of forty-one. With his characteristic courage and sense of purpose, during his retirement Cordero has embarked on a new career as a jockey trainer and agent, applying his personal strength and tested experience as a rider to the endeavor. He has dedicated his energies to developing the talents of a fellow Puerto Rican, John Velázquez, who immigrated to the mainland to jockey under Cordero's tutoring and agent management. Velázquez has ranked in the top 20 national earnings list consistently and among the top 10 jockeys in the state of New York for a decade. For his lifetime achievements, Cordero was voted into the National Museum of Racing's Hall of Fame in 1988, fulfilling what many view as a remarkable family destiny.

Further Reading

Nack, William. *My Turf: Horses, Boxers, Blood Money and the Sporting Life*. Cambridge, MA: Da Capo Press, 2003.

National Museum of Racing and Hall of Fame. http://hall.racingmuseum.org/jockey.asp?ID=177.

Puerto Rico Profile: Angel Cordero, Jr. 6 July 2001. http://www.puertorico-herald.org/issues/2001/vol5n27/ProfCordero-en.shtml.

Cordelia Chávez Candelaria

Corea, Chick (1941–). The four-decade career of jazz musician Chick Corea is one of the most respected among Latino jazz performers in the United States. As a pianist, arranger, conductor, and promoter, he has helped stretch the limits and boundaries of contemporary jazz and pop/jazz fusion. His innovative ensemble Return to Forever (RTF), formed in 1971, helped transform the sound of jazz with a prefusion softer, *samba-flavored style. Featuring Corea on keyboards, Flora Purim on vocals, her husband *Airto on drums, and reedman Joe Farrell, Corea acknowledges that his idea for the group was inspired by the scientology teachings of L. Ron Hubbard. The Return to Forever group produced two successful albums with the original lineup, and Corea also released several solo piano albums during the same period. Eventually switching to electronic fusion, Corea forged a unique style on the Moog synthesizer and helped spearhead the mid-1970s fusion movement with such experimental albums as *Where Have I Known You Before* (1974) and two Grammy-winning albums, *No Mystery* (1975) and *Romantic Warrior* (1976). The artist's Latino hybridity is revealed in "Spain," the popular song that many regard as his signature theme partly because Corea tributes the art cultures of Spain, Cuba, Brazil, Argentina, and New York and also because Corea wrote the song in 1971 and reharmonized and rearranged it repeatedly over the years.

Armando Anthony Corea, the future musician's given name, was born on June 12, 1941, in Chelsea, north of Boston, Massachusetts. He grew up in a very musical home environment and was encouraged by his jazz trumpeter father to begin studying piano by the age of four. His childhood home was filled with the sounds of musical contemporary giants like Charlie Parker, Dizzy Gillespie, Bud Powell, Lester Young, and Horace Silver, as well as the music of Beethoven and Mozart and other classical staples, whom Corea credits for inspiring his compositional sense. His first significant professional gigs in the early 1960s were playing for Latino bandleaders "Mongo" Santamaría and Willie Bobo, whose Latino musical style persists as a lingering influence on Corea. After that important start, he went on in 1964 to play with trumpeter Blue Mitchell's band. The two-year experience and exposure helped Corea develop his ensemble sense and hone his technique. As a result, another key portal opened for him when he was offered the opportunity to produce some of his original work for the renowned jazz company Blue Note Records. These first hard-bop-influenced recordings appeared in 1966 with "Tones for Joan's Bones." A key turning point in his career occurred in 1968 when Corea joined jazz legend Miles Davis's group. He worked for the trumpeter on his first experiments with fusion and played on some of Davis's most important albums. Jazz specialists acknowledge that Corea's electric piano was perceived at the time as a defining element in the fusion that was part of Davis's new sound.

The 1970s saw Corea leave Davis and his group in an exploratory effort to continue experimenting within acoustic venues. One short-lived step of this exploration was the forming of a new group, called Circle, that included Dave Holland on bass, Barry Altschul on drums, and added Anthony Braxton on sax before it dissolved within a year. Despite its brief life, Circle recorded some valuable albums that contributed to Corea's creative and technical development. The period also saw Corea's increasing fascination and involvement with the religion Scientology, which some observers credit with his greater interest in developing music with broader-than-jazz-enthusiast appeal.

Corea formed three bands that he named Return to Forever. The first of these organized in 1971 and featured Flora Purim as lead vocalist and Airto on percussion. Their influence added a heavy Latin contribution to RTF's fusion. The roster of RTF musicians shifted from this cool Latin sound in the mid-1970s when Corea sought a harder rock rhythm for the group. Continuing to challenge himself and his collaborators further, Corea moved the third and final RTF identity toward classical music themes that included brass, string, and other symphonic motifs. Not as successful as the first two versions, RTF came to its professional end in 1980, after having added some important experimental fusion to the contemporary jazz scene.

After this Corea changed his focus just as he had earlier in his career when groups and collaborations disbanded. He recorded a variety of musical recordings ranging from electronic ensembles, solo piano, and classical music to high-powered acoustic duos. Some of his collaborations included working with artists like Herbie Hancock and Gary Burton. Other Corea projects leading up to the mid-1980 formation of the Elektric Band even included winning several Grammy awards (e.g., for *Leprechaun* [1976, also won two Grammys the same year], *My Spanish Heart* (1976), and *Musicmagic* (1977), the latter for a Return to Forever project with his wife, vocalist Gayle Moran). He also worked with Mad Hatter, Joe Henderson, Freddie Hubbard, Hubert Laws, Chaka Khan, and Nancy Wilson, among many other celebrated musicians.

In 1992, Corea realized a lifelong goal when, in a collaboration with his manager Ron Moss, he formed Stretch Records (now a subsidiary of Concord Records), a label committed to pushing musical boundaries beyond new limits. During the decade Corea focused his time and creative energies on the bands Akoustic and Elektric Band, which were recorded by GRP Records. His collaborators during this period consisted of bassist John Patitucci and drummer Dave Weckl, and the group's virtuoso arrangements of fusion show the complexity and smoothness of mature performers. He also completed a retrospective of five CDs for GRP Records. In the early years of the twenty-first century, Corea continues performing, experimenting, and collaborating with artists like Bobby McFerrin, Gary Burton, and Gonzalo Rubalcaba. Like his famous ensemble Return to Forever, Corea's impact on contemporary music promises to continue stretching beyond the millennium.

Further Reading

Herzig, Monika. "Chick Corea—A Style Analysis." http://www.acmerecords.com/chickpaper.html.

Lyons, Len. *The Great Jazz Pianists*. New York: Da Capo Press, 1983.

Sprague, Peter. *The Jazz Solos of Chick Corea*. Petaluma, CA: Sher Music, 1992.

Clifford Candelaria

Corpi, Lucha (1945–). One of the first Chicana writers to write and publish in Spanish and bilingually in Spanish and English, Lucha Corpi received first-place honors in 1984 in the Tenth Chicano Literary Contest sponsored by the University of California at Irvine for her short story "Shadows on Ebbing Water." Another short story, "Los cristos del alma" (Martyrs of the Soul), earned first place in the *Palabra nueva* (New Word) literary competition the previous year (1983), and Corpi herself has twice been honored by receipt of highly prestigious creative writing National Endowment for the Arts (NEA) fellowships in 1970 and again in 1979–1980.

Corpi was born on April 13, 1945, in Jáltipan, Veracruz, México, a seaside village on the Gulf of Mexico. At the age of nineteen in 1964, she married and emigrated to the United States with her husband during the early years of the *Chicano Movement. They settled in Berkeley, California, but separated after six years. Divorced in 1970, Corpi turned to writing poetry in her native Spanish both as an outlet for her personal emotional stress and as a means of creative expression. That same year she received her first NEA Creative Writing Fellowship for poetry for work that was later included in *Palabras de mediodia* (Noon Words), a collection published in 1980 by Fuego de Aztlán Publications, with a bilingual edition published by Arte Público Press in 2001, demonstrating the lasting quality of her work. *Palabras de mediodia/Noon Words* contains the much-anthologized and critically acclaimed "Marina Poems," a four-poem cycle focusing on *La Malinche (also known as Doña Marina) and the Spanish conquest of México. Corpi's first significant set of poems appeared in 1976 in the anthology *Fireflight: Three Latin American Poets*, published by Oyes. From that early writing to her most recent, the predominant themes of Corpi's short stories, poetry, and novels concern contemporary social issues, particularly focusing on the role and agency of women. She continually challenges the idea that a narrow fate for women is unchanging and inescapable, arguing instead against traditions and conventions that constrain gender circumstances and limit options for human expression.

During the 1970s Corpi attended graduate school at the University of California at Berkeley, and the campus and San Francisco Bay Area became an arena for her active participation in political and civil rights causes. She was one of five founding members of *Aztlán Cultural, an arts service organization that years later would merge with Centro Chicano de Escritores (Chicano Writers Center). She also joined the Comité Popular Educativo de la Raza (Committee for Latina and Latino Education) in nearby Oakland, a grassroots organization of parents, students, and teachers seeking to establish bilingual child care centers and other needed programs in the city's unified school district. Corpi holds a B.A. in comparative literature from the University of California at Berkeley (1975), and a master's degree in world and comparative literature from San Francisco State University (1979). Since 1977 she has been a tenured teacher in the Oakland Public Schools Neighborhood Centers Programs.

Although her first published work was poetry, Corpi started writing prose early in her career, producing the previously noted award-winning short stories. In 1984 she completed her first English-language novel, *Delia's Song*, eventually published by Arte Público Press in 1989, and also her first story in English. The protagonist and fictive events of *Delia's Song* parallel many of the author's own experiences as it captures the personal and transnational struggles of Mexican immigrants, Chicanas and *Chicanos, and other Americans to negotiate life in the late twentieth century.

The last decade of the century saw Corpi multiply honored: in 1990 she was awarded a Creative Arts Fellowship in fiction by the City of Oakland, and she was named poet laureate at Indiana University Northwest in Gary. In 1992 and 1995 Corpi published her first mystery novels, and the first, *Eulogy for a Brown Angel: A Mystery Novel* (1992), won the PEN Oakland Josephine Miles Award and the Multicultural Publishers Exchange Best Book of Fiction prize. Featuring Chicana detective Gloria Damasco, her mysteries incorporate Latina and Latino culture and related social issues as in *Cactus Blood* (1995), a suspense novel about a ritualistic assassin. She has also published books for children, including *Where Fireflies Dance* (1997), an autobiographical work that recounts aspects of the author's childhood in a small Mexican town. She also edited *Mascaras* (Masks), a collection of essays written by fifteen contemporary women authors of diverse American ethnicities (1997).

Further Reading

"Contemporary Authors Online." Gale Group. http://www.galegroup.com.

Curiel, Barbara Brinson. "Chicano Writers: Lucha Corpi, First Series." In *Dictionary of Literary Biography*, edited by Francisco A. Lomelí and Carl R. Shirley. Vol. 82. Detroit, MI: Bruccoli Clark Layman Book/Gale Group, 1989.

Sánchez, Marta Ester. *Contemporary Chicano Poetry: A Critical Approach to an Emerging Literature*. Berkeley: University of California Press, 1985.

BJ Manríquez

Corrido. The Mexican American *corrido* is one of several folkloric expressions that emerged as a truly native musical and literary form throughout greater México. The *corrido* gained a unique status following the 1860s, amid the ongoing and often violent culture clash between Mexican and Anglo Americans along the lower Rio Grande Texas–Mexican border area. The historical function of the Mexican *corrido* has been described as a social barometer of Mexican attitudes toward events affecting their lives. Its contents, poetic organization, musical form, and aesthetic history lead to an alternative interpretation of the nature of violence in Mexican and American societies as seen through the Mexican's sense of history, music, and culture. Today most *corridos* follow a straightforward, simple narrative format providing a date, place, exposition, development, and farewell, or *despedida*. *Corridistas* (*corrido* singers), like their troubadour ancestors, sing about any newsworthy event. Many of the *corridos* from the nineteenth and early twentieth century deal with heroes like revolutionary leaders Pancho *Villa and Emiliano *Zapáta.

Narrative folk ballads of Mexican origin typically have regular metrical features such as rhyming quatrains (abcb) and use traditional imagery. Those of "epic themes" typically refer to conflict—sometimes personal, more often social between men. One important aesthetic feature affecting both structure and style is called *fragmentismo*, the process by which fragments of ballads are torn from their context, leaving much unexplained and producing, at times, abrupt beginnings and endings. Of far greater importance than the limited negative and positive female images is the *corrido*'s larger gender politics and poetics of exclusion and repression.

Further Reading

Montaño, Mary. *Tradiciones nuevomexicanas: Hispano Arts and Culture of New Mexico*. Albuquerque: University of New Mexico Press, 2001.

Peter J. García

Corrido de Gregorio Cortez, El. *See Ballad of Gregorio Cortez, The.*

Cortez, Gregorio. *See Ballad of Gregorio Cortez, The.*

Cota-Cárdenas, Margarita (1941–). Chicana poet Margarita Cota-Cárdenas has made noteworthy contributions to the canon of Chicana/ *Chicano literature with her autobiographical writing focusing on women's issues and the social experience of Mexican Americans in an Anglo-dominant United States. Cota-Cárdenas is known as being one of a small number of Chicana writers relying on Spanish language in her poetry (e.g., *Noches Despertando Inconciencias* [Nights Awakening Unawareness], 1975), as well as for her prevalent use of Spanish-English codeswitching in her fiction (e.g., *Puppet* [1985]). Cofounder of alternative publisher Scorpion Press, she is noted for helping to make the writings of bilingual and bicultural women accessible by gathering together previously published work that had been relegated to a variety of little magazines with small circulation and modest readership.

The oldest of eight children, the future poet was born on November 10, 1941, in Heber, California, where her formative years were spent traveling through California's Imperial Valley. Her parents worked as migrant farmworkers until they eventually became contractors and were able to purchase their own home, thereby ending their *family's migratory existence. Her father, Jesús Cota, originally from Sonora, México, and her mother, Margarita Cárdenas de Cota, who was reared in New Mexico, provided their family with a robust bilingual, bicultural environment that later became a constant inspiration for much of her work. One of her earliest published and frequently reprinted poems, "Nostalgia," published in *Siete Poetas* (Seven Poets, 1978), was inspired by her childhood viewing of a drive-in movie starring the famous Mexican star María *Félix as a nun who heroically rides off alone on horseback into the sunset. Mesmerized by the *film, Cota-Cárdenas begged to become a nun and enroll in the Convent of the Good Shepherd near Mesilla, New Mexico. Her star struck wish was fulfilled, but her obsession lasted only a few weeks when Cota-Cárdenas became weary of the nuns' austere living, grew homesick for her family, and was rescued by her father and returned home.

Passionate about reading and writing since girlhood, Cota-Cárdenas was encouraged (by her teachers and her father) to pursue these interests. Her father gave her a secondhand set of the complete works of Charles Dickens bought at a used bookstore. A star pupil at Orestimba High School in Newman, California, Cota-Cárdenas earned such honors as winning third place in the district's American Legion Essay Contest, being named Outstanding Girl Graduate, and receiving her second American Legion Citizenship Award, first won as an eighth grader. She won a scholarship to study *theater arts at the University of California, Los Angeles, when she graduated from high school in 1959, however, she was pregnant with her first child and declined the award. After the baby was born, she attended Modesto Junior College and later transferred to California State College, Stanislaus, where she earned a Bachelor of Arts in 1966. In 1968 she received a Master of Arts from the University of California, Davis, and twelve years later, in 1980, obtained her Doctor of Philosophy in Spanish literature and language from the University of Arizona.

Cota-Cárdenas discovered the gratification of poetry composition while earning her master's degree. She published her first Spanish-language collection, *Noches Despertando Inconciencias*, in 1975 through Scorpion Press. Cofounded by Cota-Cárdenas and Cuban poet Eliana Rivero, Scorpion Press became a reality through funding from the National Endowment for the Arts to support the work of bilingual and bicultural women. *Noches Despertando* was favorably received and enjoyed reprintings in 1976 and 1977. Its poems are divided in two parts, the first devoted to love and identity and the second section focusing on archetypes, legends, and the examination of self and environment. They are presented through a narrative voice that is at once anguished, compassionate, and ultimately hopeful. Through Scorpion, Cota-Cárdenas and Rivero edited and published several books, including *Siete poetas*, which contained the poem "Nostalgia."

In 1985, after laboring for ten years on the project, Cota-Cárdenas published her first extended fictional title, the novella *Puppet* (1985). *Puppet*'s story is autobiographical in nature and based on a series of real-life events, including the tragic life of a nineteen-year-old Chicano, the Puppet of the title, who is mistakenly killed in the *barrio by *police. Writing the novel to vindicate his death, Petra Leyva, a Spanish professor and protagonist in the novel, becomes the professor of "inconsciencia" who experiences a social and political awakening that leads to the examination of her own life and values. Experimental in form and narration, the novel deviates from linear plot structure and forces readers to piece together a fragmented and frenzied presentation of information.

Publishing another collection of poetry, *Marchitas de mayo* (May Fadings) in 1989, Cota-Cárdenas retired from teaching contemporary Latin American and Chicano literature at Arizona State University in 2003. She currently is working on a book about celebrated Mexican author Carlos Fuentes.

Further Reading

Latino Promotions. http://latinopromo.com/speakers/CotaCardenas.html.

Rebolledo, Diana Tey. "The Bittersweet Nostalgia in the Poetry of Margarita Cota-Cárdenas." *Frontiers: A Journal of Women Studies* (September 1980): 31–35.

Salazar, Carmen. "Chicano Writers, Second Series." In *Dictionary of Literary Biography*, edited by Francisco A. Lomelí and Carl R. Shirley. Vol. 122. Detroit, MI: Bruccoli Clark Layman Book/Gale Group, 1992.

Julie Amparano García

CPLC. *See* Chicanos por la Causa.

CPR Orchestra. *See* Chicano Power Revival.

Cruz, Celia (1924–2003). Known throughout her life as "the Queen of *Salsa," Celia Cruz was born in the humble neighborhood of Santo Suárez in Havana, Cuba. One of fourteen children, Cruz showed her musical talents early in childhood, earning her first pair of shoes by singing for tourists. A featured singer on many school and church programs, her parents nonetheless encouraged her to pursue the more desirable career as a schoolteacher. However, Cruz's success in radio singing contests made her decide to gamble on a career in music, and after studying at the Havana Conservatory, she was performing at various nightclubs and in musical reviews such as *Las Mulatas de Fuego* and *Zum zum ba bae.*

In 1950, Havana's biggest **son* band, La Sonora Matancera, recruited Cruz to replace their lead singer, who had returned to her native Puerto Rico. This group was as famous in Cuba as the Duke Ellington Orchestra was in the United States, and it was Cruz's big musical break with La Sonora Matancera. She traveled extensively throughout Latin America and México and even appeared in a number of *films made in both Cuba and México. Her career with La Sonora spanned fifteen years during which she and the band became known as "Cafe con Leche"(coffee with milk). Some of her best loved songs were recorded during this time period, including "Bemba colora" and "Yerbero moderno." Cruz also created her famous interjection "Azucar!" (sugar) during this time period, inspired by a waiter who asked her if she took sugar with her coffee.

The 1959 revolution created great uncertainty for Cubans, and musicians particularly were not sure of continued employment. In January 1960, La Sonora Matancera began a tour of México, where they would remain until 1962. Cruz became a citizen of the United States in 1961 and continued to perform and record with the group until 1965. Already a star in Cuba, Cruz quickly found steady work at the Hollywood Palladium, where she fell in love with the house band's lead trumpet player, Pedro Knight. The two were married in 1962, and by 1965, Knight had retired from the orchestra to manage his wife's career full-time.

Celia Cruz. *Courtesy of Photofest.*

In 1966, Cruz began collaborating with bandleader Tito *Puente, eventually recording eight albums for Tico records with him. It was becoming clear that the *mambo craze had ended, and both stars went in separate musical directions—although they would collaborate on other projects in the future. Cruz signed with the fledging label Fania Records, eventually teaming up with pianist and bandleader Larry Harlow. An interesting highlight from this period was Cruzs singing role as Gracia Divina in Harlow's salsa operetta *Hommy* (adapted from The Who's rock opera *Tommy*) at Carnegie Hall in 1973.

Cruz's association with Fania Records proved to be perfect timing. During the early 1970s, New York's young Latinos were searching for their roots and sought music that addressed their identity. Fania's founder Johnny *Pacheco envisioned a new style of Latin music—an energetic, danceable style that *barrio youth could relate to their own experience and would serve as an alternative to rock music. Pacheco and Cruz made a concept album called *Celia and Johnny*, which demonstrated Pacheco's innovation in producing updated arrangements of classic tunes. Salsa, as this new style was called, was born, and Cruz quickly became its undisputed queen.

Cruz recorded with Fania All-Stars, the label's house band led by Pacheco, and composed of the label's bandleaders, top sidemen, and vocalists, including Ray Barretto, Willie *Colón, Larry Harlow, Roberto Roena, and Bobby Valentín. These sessions produced the two volumes of *Live at Yankee Stadium*, which also highlighted label mates Héctor Lavoe, Cheo Feliciano, Ismael Miranda, Justo Betancourt, Ismael Quintana, Pete "El Conde"

Rodríguez, Bobby Cruz, and Santos Colón. Clips from their August 1973 and 1975 Yankee Stadium concerts were included in the famous documentary *Salsa* (1976), codirected by Jerry Masucci and Leon Gast, which was instrumental in getting salsa recognized by a crossover audience. Cruz and the group traveled on international tours across England, France, parts of Africa, and all of Latin America, ensuring the spread of salsa music worldwide.

While salsa's flame was diminished somewhat by the *merengue craze in the 1980s, Cruz carved out her niche by collaborating with many different artists both young and old. Director Jonathan Demme recruited her to record "Loco de Amor" (Crazy for Love) with singer David Byrne for his movie *Something Wild* (1986), and she also made anniversary recordings with her first associates, La Sonora Matancera. A special segment of the Grammies in 1987 reunited Cruz with her old friend, Puente, and the two went on to partner on more projects and appeared together in the 1992 film **Mambo Kings*.

Over her lifetime, Cruz collaborated with virtually every significant Latin performer, from Puente and Rubén *Blades to Marc *Anthony and Wyclef Jean. For her achievements, she received more than 100 awards from various countries' institutions, magazines, and newspapers, including honorary doctorates from Yale and the University of Miami. Cruz continued to give vibrant and energetic performances throughout her life and recorded her final album *Regalo de Alma* (Gift of the Soul) only months before succumbing to cancer on July 16, 2003. Her legacy includes seventy albums, twenty of them gold records, and more importantly, the inspiration she has given four generations of musicians and audiences alike.

Further Reading

Clarke, Donald, ed. *Penguin Encyclopedia of Popular Music*. 2nd ed. New York: Penguin Books, 1998.

Roberts, John Storm. *The Latin Tinge: The Impact of Latin American Music on the United States*. 2nd ed. New York: Oxford University Press, 1999.

Hope Munro Smith

Cruz, Ernesto. *See* Gómez Cruz, Ernesto.

Cruz González, José (1957–). Playwright José Cruz González was born in Calexico, California, on March 19, 1957. He has written numerous plays for both adult and young audiences. Many of these plays, including *Marisol's Christmas*, *La Posada*, *Harvest Moon*, *Spirit Dancing*, and *Odysseus Cruz*, have been developed and performed by theater companies across the country. He teaches in the Department of Theatre Arts and Dance at California State University, Los Angeles.

He received a Bachelor of Arts degree in U.S. history with an emphasis in

Chicana/o studies from the University of California at San Diego in 1980. In 1982 he received a Master of Arts in *theater from Arizona State University. He also has a Master of Fine Arts in directing from the University of California at Irvine, which he earned in 1985.

For eleven seasons Cruz González served as the project director of the South Coast Repertory's Hispanic Playwrights' Project. While working at the South Coast Repertory in Costa Mesa, California, he directed productions of *La Posada Mágica* (The Magic Inn) by Octavio Solis, *Man of the Flesh* by Octavio Solis, and *Alicia in Wonder Tierra, or I Can't Eat Goat Head* by Silvia González. In addition, he is one of five playwrights who developed the site-specific *California Scenarios*, which explores the cultural and physical geographies of California. This piece was written in collaboration with Luis *Alfaro, Joann Farías, Anne García-Romero, and Richard Coca. He has also directed productions of *Latins Anonymous* by Diane Rodriguez, Luisa Leschen, Armando Molina, and Rick Najera at the Los Angeles Theatre Center and *My Visits with MGM (My Grandmother Marta)* at Borderlands Theatre and the Bilingual Foundation of the Arts.

In 1995, the HBO New Writers Project selected his play *Calabasas Street* as part of their programming. His play *Mariachi Quixote* was selected by the A.S.K. Theater Projects Common Ground Festival in California. *The Highest Heaven* premiered at Childsplay in Tempe, Arizona, as part of the Kennedy Center's New Visions/New Voices program in 1996 and was later produced through the P.L.A.Y. Program at the Mark Taper Forum in Los Angeles. In 1997, through the Theatre Residency Program for Playwrights sponsored by the National Endowment for the Arts and Theatre Communication Group, Cruz González received a residency at Childsplay in Tempe, Arizona, where in 2000, *Salt & Pepper* was produced and premiered. *Manzi (The Adventures of Young César *Chávez)* premiered at Teatro del Pueblo in Minneapolis, Minnesota, as a touring show in 2001, and in the same year *The Magic Rainforest* premiered at the Kennedy Center in Washington, D.C. Childsplay in Arizona also produced his puppet play *Two Donuts* as a touring show in their 2002–2003 season. In May 2003, Plaza de la Raza at Cal Arts produced his play *Cousin Bell Bottoms*. The Geva Theatre in Rochester, New York, premiered *September Shoes* in June 2003, and his play *Lily Plants a Garden* premiered in February 2004 at the Mark Taper Forum through the Bonderman National Youth Theatre Playwriting Development Workshop and Symposium. From May through June 2003, through the Literature to Life Series in Los Angeles, he produced a one-man show based on Luis *Rodríguez's book *Always Running*.

His plays for young audiences include positive messages about *family, language, culture, and friendship. Through numerous commissions and partnerships with theaters across the country, Cruz González continues to touch the hearts of children and adults of all ages and across cultures.

Further Reading

Cruz González, José. *Calabasas Street*. Woodstock, IL: Dramatic Publishing, 1998.
Cruz González, José. *Salt and Pepper*. Woodstock, IL: Dramatic Publishing, 2002.

Christina Marín

Cuban Americans. The United States and the island of Cuba have had ongoing interaction for centuries. Inhabitants of both regions have relocated back and forth, usually for political or economic reasons, in an open transnational migration. As a result, the descendants of this long lineage of migration have managed to retain ties with each side, and the national politics and policies of each have been closely intertwined. The forms and styles of their popular cultures also are interlocked and reciprocal. Especially in the twentieth century, Cuban immigrants and traveling artists brought island culture forms and practices to the United States. As a result, the music, dance, art, literature, *food, and *sports of the United States were greatly infused with and influenced by Cuban Caribbean features. That transnational exchange, for example, brought the *mambo and the *cha cha cha into American living rooms via the radio and television, and some ethnomusicologists (*see* Ethnomusicology) believe that American jazz may have emerged from the fusion of Afro-Cuban drumming, singing, and jazz intermixed with Afro-American blues in the New Orleans area. Similar enrichments also occurred in American sports where boxing and baseball in particular saw the success of such great athletes as *Kid Gavilán and Minnie *Minoso, respectively. In these and countless other ways, Cuban Americans have left indelible marks on U.S. culture and politics.

Cuban Americans of all ages appear to share a common characteristic regardless of their ideologies or reasons for leaving: They have remained engaged with Cuban politics and retained a desire to return to the homeland. This is partly due to the fact that the United States has been a key escape valve for Cubans fleeing oppressive governments to seek haven in a land of better economic opportunities. Colonized by Spain since the conquest of México in 1521, Spain's colonial grip on Cuba continued until the nineteenth century. Cubans seeking independence were forced into exile as early as 1820, and by the end of the Ten Years' War (1868–1878) refugees to the United States swelled to 7,000 people. Most of these emigrés were professional and upper-class whites who desired emancipation from Spain, but they disagreed on the kind of government that would follow. From the beginning, Cubans have been divided over the extent to which Cuba would depend upon the United States, how race relations would be addressed, whether government should be democratic government or under military rule, and the nature of relations with Spain. From the United States, some political dissidents urged U.S. intervention in favor of independence, while others opposed any U.S. involvement. Many exiles supported Narciso López's clandestine invasions of Cuba between 1848 and 1851. Until the end of the century, debates about the meaning of **cubanidad* (the nature of Cuban identity) consumed Cubans and émigrés alike.

Following the final War of Cuban Independence (1895–1898), the government was tied to the United States politically and economically. The number of people leaving for the United States decreased and consisted mostly of businessmen and members of the upper classes. Many had established business firms in the United States to secure their investments within a more stable economy, especially after the *Dance of the Millions debacle of 1919 when Cuban corporations and individual investors speculated wildly on sugar after World War I, resulting in a 200 percent drop in sugar prices.

The numbers of political refugees swelled again during the early 1930s, particularly during the 1933 revolution that toppled dictator President Gerardo Machado. Since the insurrectionists were leftists and Machado had been supported by the United States until late in the game, most of the escapees chose to flee to Spain or México instead of the United States. Overall between 1900 and 1959, a substantial number of middle-class whites immigrated to the United States, largely for economic purposes. The Cuban economy was not strong enough to employ the emergent professional classes that sought work as teachers, officeworkers, pharmacists, lawyers, doctors, and technicians of all sorts. Between 1952 and 1959, economic immigrants were joined by a vast wave of political exiles fleeing dictator Fulgencio Batista's repression. In those seven years alone, 40,000 Cubans entered the United States.

Not all immigrants to the United States were white and economically self-sustaining, however. Poor blacks also came and worked in the cigar factories in Tampa, Florida, for the same patrons for whom they had worked in Cuba. As Afro-Cubans and former slaves or slave descendants, they suffered triple discrimination in the United States due to the slavery status imposed by their previous employers, their immigrant newcomer status, and the racial prejudice contaminating history and culture in the American South. Left largely to fend for themselves, blacks from the turn of the twentieth century to 1959 survived by forming associations and societies that collected dues and developed their communities by opening their own schools and medical clinics as best they could. Many went back to Cuba after independence, but they usually suffered the most from any economic downturns. In 1912 the Cuban government aided by the United States brutally suppressed the Independent Colored Party. Some black laborers migrated with agricultural work occasionally crossing the Florida Straits. Consequently, less is known of their plight in the United States than other sectors of the migrating Cuban population.

When Fulgencio Batista was overthrown by Fidel *Castro in the *Cuban Revolution and departed Cuba on December 31, 1958, many Cuban Americans were jubilant and left their land of refuge for their native home. But many more—especially conservative supporters of the Batista regime—began an exodus for the United States. They originally thought they would stay only a short time until the United States would rid Cuba of its new leader and government. Nearly half a century later, Castro is still in power, and the Cuban exiles and their Cuban American progeny are firmly situated in Florida and other parts of their new homeland.

From the 1920s to 1960, Cuban traditions brought by emigrés and traveling artists infused Cuban culture and in time affected music, dance, art, and literature in the United States. In sports Cubans have enriched the American scene greatly with such marquee athletes as boxers *Kid Chocolate and Kid Gavilán and baseball players Minnie Minoso and Bert Campaneris. Similarly, the visual arts have been enhanced by painters such as Rene Portocarrera and Wilfredo Lam, while intellectuals like Fernando Ortíz and Lydia Cabrera contributed fresh notions of *latinidad* (Latinness) to the omnipresent question of racial and cultural blending in postslavery societies. Cabrera would immigrate to the United States after 1959, but her reputation preceded her by decades. After four decades of continuous migration and travel, the people and cultures of both the mainland and the island have been greatly invigorated by the robust exchange.

Since 1959, Cuban American culture has weighed more heavily in politics than in previous generations, but arts and entertainment have been enriched as before. Famous musicians such as Celia *Cruz, Tito *Puente, Arturo *Sandoval, Gloria *Estefan, Ricky Martínez, and Paquito D' Rivero have captured the stage. Defecting athletes such as Orlando Hernández, too, have set high marks in baseball. Cuban American literature has been made accessible to the Anglo American public through authors like María Cristina García and Oscar *Hijuelos, thus integrating surrealism into linear Anglo thinking. In media entertainment and politics, the case of Elián *González became a household controversy in the United States and Cuba in 1999 as families of all political and ethnic orientations debated the welfare of the boy **balsero* (raft transported immigrant) whose mother was killed en route and whose father wanted him returned to Cuba. The Cuban American impact on U.S. culture and politics has been powerful and lasting, intimate and subconscious.

Further Reading

Bardach, Ann Louise. *Cuba Confidential: Love and Vengeance in Miami and Havana*. New York: Random House, 2002.

Boone, Margaret S. *Capital Cubans: Refugee Adaptation in Washington, D.C.* New York: AMS Press, 1989.

Gerard, Charley. *Music from Cuba: Mongo Santamaría, Chocolate Armenteros, and Cuban Musicians in the United States*. Westport, CT: Praeger, 2001.

González-Pando, Miguel. *The Cuban Americans*. Westport, CT: Greenwood Press, 1998.

Pérez-Firmat, Gustavo. *Life on the Hyphen: The Cuban-American Way*. Austin: University of Texas Press, 1994.

K. Lynn Stoner

Cuban Revolution. To comprehend the texture of *Cuban American popular cultures, their origins, and their influences requires a review of the historical events known as the Cuban Revolution (January 1, 1959–present). For the island nation of Cuba, it marked the end of more than a half century of unstable, elitist government, international and national corruption rings, and foreign dominance by the United States. For six and a half years, rebels of numerous political orientations had resisted U.S.-supported dictator Fulgencio Batista, staging battles and skirmishes in the cities and rural areas of Cuba. In 1958 Batista lost not only popular support but also the allegiance of the Cuban Armed Forces. On December 31, 1958, Batista's own military mutinied against his regime and advised him to leave the country. The exodus of Batista supporters as well as disillusioned revolutionaries and middle-class and elite entrepreneurs was heavy between 1959 and 1962 and created the first mass wave of Cubans who immigrated to the United States after the revolution. Their departure left control of Cuba's government in the hands of Fidel *Castro, one of the architects of the revolution and eventual single ruler of the new government.

As a result of these watershed events, Cuba and the United States experienced major changes in language, the arts, entertainment, literature, music, *sports, everyday identities, and other vibrant aspects of popular culture. Examples are many from every genre and generation. Gloria *Estefan and the Miami Sound Machine, the Mambo Kings, baseball players, Elián González, and many others have joined Desi *Arnaz and Xavier *Cugat in the pop culture lexicon of the Americas. Throughout the world, the icon of Che *Guevara as guerrilla hero and the literary influence of the *Casa de las Américas have had profound impacts on several generations of young idealists and creative artists.

Fidel Castro and the Twenty-sixth of July Movement, as his revolutionary initiative came to be called, used guile and alliance formation to assume control of the various groups opposing Batista and to take command of the island. He promised democratic government, broad land reform, reduction of extensive property and business holdings by foreign companies, and redistribution of urban and rural properties owned by Cuban nationals. Such massive political and economic changes alarmed Cuban elites and the U.S. government. In the Cold War climate, Castro was perceived as a communist, not a reform nationalist, causing the United States to take immediate action against his revolutionary reorganization of the island culture.

The Republican Dwight D. Eisenhower administration (1952–1960) secretly planned an invasion called Operation Zapata, an action intended to raise an insurrection against the new Cuban leader. The invasion plans continued in 1961 when Democrat John F. Kennedy assumed the presidency and forever associated the Kennedy administration with the failed invasion, which came to be known as the *Bay of Pigs (April 13–19, 1961). The foreign policy fiasco embarrassed the United States and, by solidifying popular

Cuban support behind Castro, ironically produced results opposite of what the original planners had intended. Thus pressured by the Yankee giant to the north, in December 1961, Castro declared himself a Marxist Leninist and began to form a strong alliance with the Soviet Union.

After 1961 Cuba became a trading member of COMECON, the economic union of the Soviet Union and its communist allies, and adopted a state-centered strategy to equalize the distribution of wealth. State farms and agricultural collectives provided work for most of the rural population, although approximately 23 percent of agricultural land remained in the hands of small farmers. Literacy brigades taught the basics of reading and writing in the countryside until rural schools populated the entire island. Health clinics brought fundamental medical treatment to the most remote regions, and what had been the under- or unemployed segment of the population were trained in various trades, eventually bringing employment levels to 100 percent. Wages ranged from 100 to 600 pesos per month. Child care centers allowed women to work and attain positions of responsibility in the workforce and the government. Giving evidence of the broad nature of the revolution, the government began cultural and athletic activities designed to unify the people behind the reforms. A form of revolutionary culture emerged that emphasized public art and participation, including poster art, the Nueva Trova (New Troubador) movement, which was politically conscious music with Latin American folkloric roots, the National Ballet under Alicia Alonso, and the Casa de las Américas, among many others.

Cuban diplomacy and foreign policy centered on instigating nationalist and socialist revolutions around the world. Support ranged from moral support and strategic planning to sending guerrilla cells (Che Guevara, 1966–1967, in Bolivia), fomenting revolutions, and committing troops, medical corps, and teachers to regions in conflict (Angola, 1973–1991, and Nicaragua, 1979–1990). Cuba's aggressive diplomacy was juxtaposed with its professed nonaligned position. In 1980, Castro presided over the Non-Aligned Nations Organization. In response to Castro's efforts to export Cuban-style reforms in other parts of the globe, the United States instituted an economic blockade (called *el bloqueo* by the Cubans) against the tiny nation in 1961, which continues in 2004, despite continual efforts to end it by members of the U.S. Congress.

In the face of the blockade by the United States and its allies, the only way Castro's revolution could flourish was through enormous economic and political support from the Soviet Union, as the Cuban economy was unable to pay for its civil services without it. In 1986 Castro declared the Rectification Process whereby government-perceived corruption was halted, and severe government controls were imposed. With the collapse of the Soviet Union and its greatly reduced trade with and support for Cuba, in 1990 Castro declared a new austerity program that the government called a Special Period in the Time of Peace that presumably is still in place. The Cuban economy declined by 60 percent, creating the first massive unemployment crisis in revolutionary history. To stop corruption and the illegal entrance of U.S. dollars into the population, Castro legalized dollars in 1993, which divided the previously homogeneous population into the wealthy (those who had access to dollars) and the poor (those who did not).

Since 1990 Cuban leaders have determined a new economic course for the nation that allows for controlled international commerce, government taxes, small private entrepreneurship, and a modest entrance into global capitalism. Tourism, exportation of biotechnology, and agricultural production are the fuels of a capitalizing economy. A thriving black market provides much of the essential foodstuffs and luxury items for the population, and the state farms and agricultural collectives are quietly being dismantled in favor of more productive private farms; it appears that the Cuban economy is well on the road to privatization. The political structure has not altered despite Castro's advanced age and poor health. The nation's Soviet-style Marxist structure is still firmly in place, and an egalitarian formal economy with a socialist social service system are struggling to survive *el bloqueo* and Castro's dictatorship. Whatever plans exist for governmental adjustments after his death have not been revealed to Cubans or the rest of the world.

Further Reading

Benjamin, Jules R. *The United States and the Origins of the Cuban Revolution.* Princeton, NJ: Princeton University Press, 1990.

Paterson, Thomas G. *Contesting Castro: The United States and the Triumph of the Cuban Revolution.* New York: Oxford University Press, 1994.

Pérez-Stable, Marifeli. *The Cuban Revolution: Origins, Course and Legacy.* New York: Oxford University Press, 1993.

Sweig, Julia E. *Inside the Cuban Revolution: Fidel Castro and the Urban Underground.* Cambridge, MA: Harvard University Press, 2002.

K. Lynn Stoner

Cubanidad. The meaning of *cubanidad*, or the nature of Cuban identity, has been debated by inhabitants of the island since the arrival of the Spaniards with the first voyages of Christopher *Columbus in 1492. The debate has consumed Cubans and, in the nineteenth and twentieth centuries, has also been a concern to Cuban emigrés and their *Cuban American descendants in the United States. Among the original inhabitants of the island, which is part of the Antilles chain (Cuba, Hispaniola, Jamaica, Puerto Rico), the idea of identity had evolved for the most part into a largely homogeneous culture since the indigenous people were 90 percent Taíno at the time of the Spanish Conquest. Scholars believe that the Guanahatabey and the Ciboney tribes were the original inhabitants of Cuba who came to the island from South America. Both were hunter-gatherers whose social organization and cultural practices reflected their food-gathering methods of survival. With the arrival of the Taíno, who are part of the Arawakan Indian stock, the Cuban population developed a basic form of agriculture and continued hunter-gatherer practices.

Columbus's landing and the subsequent Spanish colonial settlements in the West Indies and Mesoamerica complicated issues of identity as the native peoples and Iberian immigrants began intermingling. As a result, the language forms and religious practices began to evolve into a new sixteenth-century **mestizaje*, or mixture of Indian and immigrant Spanish hybridity. The addition of Africans, who were brought to the "New" World primarily as slaves, further compounded questions of racial, ethnic, linguistic, and cultural identity among the island population. Since the colonial period the dominant political, military, and economic power structure was defined and controlled by the Spaniards, the notion of *cubanidad* was expressed in terms of the imported Caucasian, Roman Catholic, Spanish-speaking, and monarchist identity.

Over the centuries, however, as independence movements emerged in the Western Hemisphere, Cuban identity began to shift its terms to more accurately reflect the composition of its inhabitants, who are to this day a vibrant mixture of native stock, Spanish, African, and multiple combinations of these ethnoracial strands. Historically, the success of the antislavery revolution in neighboring Haiti led by former slave Toussaint L'Ouverture in 1804 spread the idea of liberty's grasp to Cuba. At least since then the nature of *cubanidad* has contained strong elements of political self-expression and autonomy. The poet patriot José Martí (1853–1895) is credited with inspiring Cubans to embrace the totality of their ethnic and racial roots—especially the négritude that historically had been oppressed and marginalized—in their struggle to emancipate their country from Spain. Killed in 1895 at the beginning of the final liberation rebellion against Spanish dominance, Martí the revolutionary martyr has become synonymous with Cuban identity as a passion for political independence, and his poetry provided the verses for the famous Cuban anthem of freedom "Guantánamera," which entered North American popular culture idioms in the 1960s and 1970s.

With the fall of the U.S.-backed Fulgencio Batista regime in 1959, debates about the nature of *cubanidad* were compounded with questions of national loyalty and political exile as thousands of Batista supporters emigrated to the United States in opposition to Fidel *Castro's new government. These arguments continued to rage in subsequent decades through the *Bay of Pigs debacle, the American blockade (*el bloqueo*), the nation's affiliation with the Soviet Union, the missile crisis of 1962, and at the turn of the century, the Elián *González controversy. Thus, it is overly simple to define *cubanidad* in one-dimensional terms, for it combines an island geography and Spanish-language heritage with an evolved mestizo ethnicity that includes North American English-language elements. All of these aspects of Cuban identity infuse the island's popular culture contributions to the Americas, from cigars and sugar to Martí and Desi *Arnaz to Lydia Cabrera, Gloria *Estefan, and a myriad of other imports in the past two and a half centuries.

Further Reading

González-Pando, Miguel. *The Cuban Americans*. Westport, CT: Greenwood Press, 1998.

Pérez-Firmat, Gustavo. *Life on the Hyphen: The Cuban-American Way*. Austin: University of Texas Press, 1994.

Subervi-Vélez, Federico A., et al. "Mass Communication and Hispanics." In *Handbook of Hispanic Cultures in the United States: Sociology*, edited by Nicolás Kanellos and Claudio Esteva-Fabregat. Houston, TX, and Madrid, Spain: Arte Público Press and Instituto de Cooperación IberoAmericana, 1994.

Cordelia Chávez Candelaria

Cucaracha, La. *See La Cucaracha.*

Cuellar, José. *See* Dr. Loco's Rockin' Jalapeño Band.

Cuentos. *Cuentos* can be defined as stories or narratives that may relate to a legend, a folktale, a fable, a tall tale, or a children's story and are prevalent among all Latina/o and Chicana/o populations in the United States. A large collection of *cuentos* has been gathered from New Mexico and the Southwest, many of which are written in Spanish and a few in English. Due to their European origin, several of the folktales collected in New Mexico and southern Colorado deal with characters of royalty such as kings and queens. *Cuentos* featuring God, the devil, and death as the main characters provide children or the reader with religious or moral messages for one's proper behavior. Other *cuentos* deal with situations of bewitchment or enchantment.

Further Reading

Castro, Rafaela G. *Chicano Folklore: A Guide to the Folktales, Traditions, Rituals and Religious Practices of Mexican-Americans*. New York: Oxford University Press, 2001.

Gran Diccionario Enciclopedico Ilustrado. Vol 3. Mexico City: Reader's Digest Mexico, 1979.

Mónica Saldaña

Cugat, Xavier (1900–1990). An award-winning orchestra leader with a legendary career, Xavier Cugat was one of the first bandleaders to introduce Latin American dance music to an American public. Born on January 1, 1900, in Gerona, Spain, Cugat moved with his family to Cuba at the age of four. He studied the violin as a youngster in Havana until he became skilled enough to perform for the Havana Symphony. In 1921, he moved to the United States to work as a cartoonist for the *Los Angeles Times*, but his career was diverted when he met legendary silent *film actor Rudolph

Valentino, who advised him to form a *tango orchestra to expand his musical career into the film industry.

Taking Valentino's advice, Cugat formed an orchestra, and by the 1930s he incorporated American and Latin American lead singers. Cugat did not exclusively employ Cuban music in his orchestra; he fused a variety of Latin American popular musical forms. His orchestra was one of the few to appear on the National Biscuit Company's *Let's Dance* radio series, thereby exposing him to a wider audience in the United States. Cugat and his band experimented with the bongo and Cuban *rumba and in the 1940s adopted the *mambo. He immediately became known as the "King of Rumba." Cugat's popularity crossed over into his appearance in films such as *You Were Never Lovelier* (1942), *Two Girls and a Sailor* (1944), and *Neptune's Daughter* (1949). Although there is debate among *Latin jazz music aficionados as to whether Cugat stayed within a strict definition of Latin rhythms, there is a general recognition of Cugat's crossover appeal and generosity toward younger musicians who were in transition from Cuba to the United States, many who later became music leaders in their own right. These musicians included Desi *Arnaz (who popularized the conga while playing with Cugat), *Machito, Tito *Rodríguez, Charlie Palmieri, and singer Miguelito Valdéz. In 1951 Cugat's orchestra was invited to open the Waldorf Astoria in New York, a major recognition of the popularity of Latin-themed music. On October 27, 1990, Cugat died in Barcelona, Spain.

Cugat's selected discography includes *Xavier Cugat's Favorite Collection of Tangos and Rhumbas* (1936), *The Other Americas* (1938), *New Album of Xavier Cugat's Best Compositions and Other Latin American Favorites* (1941), *Xavier Cugat's Folio* (1942), *Meet Mr. Cugat* (1943), *Xavier Cugat's Favorite Hits* (1943), *Xavier Cugat's Mambo-land* (1953), *Viva Cugat* (1958), and *Continental Hits* (1959, reissued 1984).

Further Reading

Cugat, Xavier. *Rumba Is My Life*. New York: Didier, 1948.

Katz, Ephraim. *The Film Encyclopedia*. 4th ed. New York: HarperResource, 2001.

Larkin, Colin, ed. *The Guinness Encyclopedia of Popular Music*. 4 vols. London: Guinness Publishing, 1992.

Yanow, Scott. *Afro-Cuban Jazz*. San Francisco, CA: Miller Freeman, 2000.

Juanita Heredia

Cultural Centers. The inspiration to create many of the nation's Latina/o cultural centers originated in the 1960s U.S. civil rights movement. The dearth of Latino-oriented arts spaces convinced the founders of the earliest institutions to take an activist approach to preserve and promote Latina/o cultural and artistic expression. The results of this direct advocacy were the emergence of multi-use facilities that offered a variety of cultural and educational programs under one roof. It was a practical approach, given the lack of funding and the history of discrimination aimed at most Latina/o communities. Historically, agencies responsible for disbursing public arts funding had placed little value on the promotion and preservation of Latino culture. Consequently, the growth of Latina/o cultural centers often paralleled the political and economic advancement of Latinas/os. Due to the community's increasing clout, there is hope that there will be an increase in arts funding for Latino-oriented institutions.

The exception to the trend outlined above occurred in Florida, where the establishment of *Cuban American communities was led by Cuba's exiled political and business elites, causing the state's art and culture have been strongly influenced by Latin American and Caribbean immigrants. As a result, the development of Latina/o-oriented arts and cultural institutions in that area has been more specialized than elsewhere in the United States. In Miami, the Latin American Art Museum, the Cuban Masters Collection, and La Rosa Flamenco Theater are all part of the state's Latina/o arts and culture scene. Since the 1990s, the state's Puerto Rican, Central American, and Mexican American communities also have begun to expand their influence on the local arts community.

The nation's oldest and best established multipurpose Latina/o cultural centers are typically located in U.S. cities with the largest Latino populations, including San Antonio, Chicago, San Francisco, New York City, Los Angeles, and Miami. The greatest influence on the development of these institutions has depended upon the ethnic makeup of the local/regional Latino population. For instance, Mexican and Mexican American culture have inspired virtually every aspect of program planning at the Guadalupe Cultural Arts Center in San Antonio, Texas, while Puerto Rican and other Caribbean influences have dominated the event planning and programs offered at El Museo del Barrio (The Neighborhood Museum) in New York City.

While the primary goal of these institutions has been to promote and preserve Latino arts and culture, Latino cultural centers, most of which are not for profit, also have played an important role in articulating the social and political interests of the community. Because arts, culture, and politics often overlap, the lines between these interests blur at Latino cultural centers. For instance, San Diego's Centro Cultural de la Raza has a long tradition of hosting arts and education programs that reflect and promote the principles of the *Chicano Movement. Murals at the organization's facility in Balboa Park feature depictions of the origins and struggles of Mexicans, *Chicanos, and their indigenous ancestors.

The following examples of Latino cultural centers across the country present an overview of the regional and ethnic diversity of these institutions. For example, in Chicago, the Mexican Fine Arts Center Museum is located in the heart of the Pilsen/Little Village community, Chicago's largest Latina/o enclave. It was founded by a group of educators and community leaders with about $900 in personal and public donations. The center's programs include literary and theatrical events, dance productions, concerts, *film and video screenings, permanent and touring art exhibits, and a wide array of arts and educational workshops for children and adults. The center's largest annual events are the *Sor Juana Festival, which celebrates Latina achievements in the United States and Latin America, and the Del Corazón Festival (From the Heart), which features U.S. Latina/o and Latin American writers and performers.

The Segundo Ruiz Belvis Cultural Center, also in Chicago, was founded in 1971 by local activists and community volunteers. Their programs are aimed at providing the city's large Puerto Rican community with cultural, artistic, and educational programs. It was named after Segundo Ruiz Belvis, founder of the Secret Abolitionist Society of Puerto Rico, which helped to end slavery in Puerto Rico in 1872. From its inception, the institution has promoted social justice issues while presenting classes, workshops, and performances in art, music, *theater, and literature, as well as teaching language and leadership skills to the Latino community.

In the case of New York City, El Museo del Barrio, located in East or Spanish Harlem, was created by a group of Puerto Rican parents, educators, artists, and community activists in 1969. It offers art exhibitions, publications, educational activities, festivals, and other special events. The organization's stated mission is to "offer a forum for the unique creative languages of the varied communities of Caribbean and Latin American descent, and to provide positive role models for cultural exchange." Like many other Latino cultural centers in the United States, El Museo was created during the civil rights era. El Museo's first location was in a public school; it later moved to a series of neighborhood storefronts. In 1977, the center relocated to a permanent site in the Heckscher Building on Fifth Avenue. El Museo is a founding member of the Museum Mile Association, which includes some of the city's most distinguished cultural institutions, including the Metropolitan Museum of Art and the Guggenheim Museum. The center has broadened its focus over the years to reflect the growth in Mexican, Central and South American, and Caribbean communities in New York.

In San Francisco, another urban center of diverse Latina/o communities, the Mission Cultural Center for Latino Arts and the Galería de la Raza are both located in the heart of San Francisco's predominantly Latino Mission District. The neighborhood is named for the Spanish colonial–era Mission Dolores. Galería de la Raza was founded in 1970 and focuses on Chicano/Latino art. The Mission Cultural Center was founded by a group of artists and community activists in 1977 to promote arts and culture "that reflect the experiences and traditions of Chicano, Central and South American, and Caribbean people." Both the Galería and the Mission Cultural Center are nonprofit institutions. Each of the organizations offers theater, films, art exhibits, dance and poetry performances, and arts-related educational programs.

Centro Cultural de la Raza in San Diego, California, was founded in 1970. The organization's goal is to "create, promote, and preserve Mexican and Chicano and indigenous art and culture." Annual programming features a multidisciplinary educational component, along with literary presentations, theater, visual arts exhibits, and film and video screenings. The center is housed in a circular building known for its colorful wall-sized murals, 150-seat performance space, a 2,000-square-foot art gallery, and several workshop facilities. Centro Cultural de la Raza is located in Balboa Park in the heart of the local Chicano/Mexican community. The facility is home to Ballet Folklórico en Aztlán, founded in 1967. The dance troupe's instructors teach traditional Mexican folk dances going back to preconquest Aztec culture.

Plaza de la Raza is located in Lincoln Park on the edge of East Los Angeles, the historic center of the Mexican and Chicano community, and is home to the Boathouse Gallery and an outdoor theater. The institution programs include its School of Performing and Visual Arts featuring a curriculum of theater, visual arts, dance, and music (including Mexican *folklórico* dance and *mariachi). In recent years, the school's artists have collaborated with the Los Angeles Philharmonic and the American Ballet Theatre. Instructors have included such prominent artists as Carlos Almaraz, Theresa Chaves, and Lula Washington. Plaza de la Raza sponsors a summer concert series called Con Sabor Latino (With Latin Flavor); El Nuevo L.A. Chicano Arts Series presents works by new and emerging Latino artists in theater, dance, and visual arts; and The Margo Albert Festival of the Arts is a family-oriented festival.

The Guadalupe Cultural Arts Center in San Antonio was founded in 1980. It is a multidisciplinary organization that promotes "Latino/Chicano/Native American" art and culture. The facility is located on San Antonio's west side, home to the city's working-class Mexican and Mexican American neighborhoods. The facility is among the largest Latino cultural arts centers in the nation. The center's major annual events include the San Antonio Cinefestival, Juried Women's Art Exhibit, Tejano Conjunto Festival, and San Antonio Inter-American Bookfair and Literary Festival. The facility is also home to Los Actores de San Antonio and the Guadalupe Dance Company. Classes in creative writing, accordion, and **baile folklórico* are offered.

The stated mission of El Centro de la Raza in Seattle, Washington, is to promote a social justice agenda and to provide low-cost social services, as well as education and arts activities to the city's Latino community. The legendary institution was founded in 1972 after about 300 people staged a sit-in at an abandoned schoolhouse to protest the lack of educational opportunities for Spanish speakers. Angry that public officials had ignored their demands, the protesters occupied the school on October 11, 1972, and remained until the Seattle City Council agreed to lease the building to them for $1 a year. The center now provides a variety of social welfare and educational services, as well as arts programs aimed at low-income Latinos.

Mexic-Arte Museum in Austin, Texas, is one of the largest institutions in the state presenting Mexican, Latino, and Latin American art. The organization first opened its doors in an East Austin warehouse. In 1988 Mexic-Arte moved into an abandoned department store building downtown, where it has remained. Over the years, the facility has focused on art exhibits, educational programs, and an eclectic array of traditional and experimental arts performances. The facility's managers have developed strong ties with arts and cultural organizations in México and nationwide.

An important Latino arts organization in Phoenix, AZ MARS (Movimiento Artístico del Río Salado) played an important role in promoting the arts in Arizona; however, it is now defunct. The Museo Chicano in Phoenix continues to offer exhibits and education outreach. In communities without permanent Latino arts and cultural facilities, organizations such as La Peña in Austin, Texas, and Xicanindio Artes in Mesa, Arizona, have long provided multidisciplinary arts and cultural programming. These organizations, for instance, sponsor art exhibits, Day of the Dead (*Día de los Muertos) activities, and performances in a variety of local spaces.

Further Reading

Association of Hispanic Arts. http://www.latinoarts.org.
Centro Cultural de La Raza. http://www.centroraza.com.
Centro de La Raza. http://www.elcentrodelaraza.com.
Guadalupe Cultural Arts Center. http://www.guadalupeculturalarts.org.
Mexican Fine Arts Center Museum. http://www.mfacmchicago.org.
Mexic-Arte Museum. http://www.main.org/mexic-arte.
Mission Cultural Center for Latino Arts. http://www.missionculturalcenter.org.
Museo del Barrio. http://www.elmuseo.org.
National Association of Latino Arts and Culture. http://www.nalac.org.
Plaza de la Raza. http://www.plazadelaraza.org.
Segundo Ruiz Belvis Cultural Center. http://www.ruizbelvis.org.

James E. García

Cumbia. Cumbia is an internationally popular Afro-Colombian song and dance form that originated in Colombia's eastern Atlantic coastal region, La Costa (the coast). While cumbia music has undergone many changes in instrumentation and rhythmic style, most commercial cumbia performances are characterized by a ubiquitous, short-short-long rhythmic motive played on a scraper (which sounds like shi-ki-CHA-shi-ki-CHA). As a commercial Latin music, cumbia has been popular throughout the Caribbean and Latin America and continues to be important to Spanish-speaking immigrants in the United States.

Colombia is a country of extremely diverse geographical regions. Its territory includes portions of the Andes mountains, the Amazon River basin, and both the Pacific and Atlantic coasts. Regional differences are evident in distinctive music genres, competing economic interests, and great ethnic and cultural diversity. Examples of traditional musics and folk dances that are uniquely characteristic of each region include *porro*, cumbia, and *vallenato* from La Costa, *joropo* from the grassy plains of the east, *currulao* from the Pacific coast, and the *bambuco* from the Andean region. Such diversity has presented a challenge to Colombians wanting to forge a unified national identity.

La Costa, the region where cumbia originates, is situated along the Atlantic coast and shares many cultural similarities with the Caribbean region. This is due in part to its close proximity to the Caribbean and the role of one of its major coastal towns, Cartagena, a major distribution point in Spain's African slave trade. As a result of the Cartagena slave trade, a significant number of Colombians in La Costa are of African decent. Because of the influence of African cultural traditions in La Costa, the Costeño genres of *porro*, cumbia, and *vallenato* are regarded as Afro-Colombian.

By contrast, most of Colombia's elite (who hold most prominent positions of power and wealth) are of European descent. While the mixing of Colombia's people from Amerindian, European, and African cultural and ethnic heritage is sometimes held up as a positive sign of national cohesion, quite often Colombia's elite valued their European cultural heritage above the others. In cumbia's rise to the status of a national "Colombian" music from its regional origins as "Costeño" (from the Atlantic coast region) music, it had to overcome the elite's favoritism toward European-derived musics in Bogotá, Colombia's interior capital. As Costeño music and orchestras migrated to the interior, the elites gave in to the beat and welcomed the sound. The popularity and commercial success of cumbia in international markets was one factor that helped it gain acceptance as a symbol of national identity, even as it retained its Costeño and Afro-Colombian identity.

In the process of becoming popular in urban Colombian and international markets, cumbia underwent significant changes. Costeño music scholar Peter Wade argues that when Costeño music was "modernized in its instrumentation and presentation" to increase its appeal to wider audiences, it became "diluted stylistically." These types of musical changes and Colombians' attitudes toward them are very important because they recur repeatedly in the history of cumbia.

In the traditional cumbia, couples danced around the musicians who were seated in the middle of the dance space. In the choreography, the man and woman do not touch; instead, the man dances around the woman, whose steps are smaller, and the man and woman occasionally pass back to back. Since the *cumbiamba*—the gatherings where cumbia would be danced—were typically held at night, the woman would hold bundles of lighted candles as she danced. Since the dance is purported to symbolize the courting of an indigenous woman by an African man, the choreography suggests the *stereotypes of the Afro-Colombian people as more outgoing and the Amerindians as more "reserved and aloof." Such choreographic elements are characteristic of modern, folkloric performances of cumbia.

There were two traditional types of instrumental ensembles that accompanied the cumbia dance. The first type of ensemble used a *pito*—a clarinetlike instrument, also called a *caña de millo* (cane flute). The *pito* carried the melody and was accompanied by three drummers playing different-sized drums and a fifth person playing shakers. The other type of ensemble used two *gaitas*—long, indigenous flutes. One *gaita* player sounded the melody, and the second harmonized while also playing a shaker. The *gaitas* were accompanied by a group of drummers who played patterns similar to the first ensemble. The traditional cumbias were mainly instrumental accompaniment for the dances, but they could include lyrics sung as a call and response between a soloist and a chorus. Lyrics were in a verse-refrain form where the verses consisted of four phrases, each eight syllables in length.

The *porro*—a slower version of cumbia with singing—was the first Afro-Colombian genre from La Costa to be adapted to suit international middle- and upper-class tastes. Around 1905 to 1910, brass bands in the region's towns began adapting the *porro* by adding introductory sections that used the *cinquillo* (five beat) rhythmic motive of the Cuban *danzón, by translating the traditional drum's accents to the cymbals and bass drum and by adding contrapuntal melodic lines. In spite of these adaptations, *porro* and cumbia remained popular mainly within La Costa.

Around this time, *bambuco*, a music genre from the Andean capital's Spanish mestizo culture, became the first popular Colombian music to achieve favor in international markets. From as early as the 1910s and through the 1940s *bambuco* was recognized abroad as the national Colombian song style. It achieved this success when it was recorded not by the string ensembles typical of its native Andean region but rather by full dance orchestras that included modernized renditions of *bambuco* in their repertoires of internationally popular dance genres, like fox-trots, *boleros, and *tangos.

Successive Colombian popular music genres achieved international marketing success through making similar stylistic changes to instrumentation, melody, and rhythm that helped the regional styles appeal to broader audiences. La Costa's *porro* surpassed *bambuco* in international popularity once its style changed to sound much like the ballroom *rumba that had become popular throughout American and European middle- and upper-class salons.

Porro thus became the first Afro-Colombian style from La Costa to achieve popularity both abroad and at home.

Lucho Bermúdez and his Orquesta del Caribe brought Costeño *porros* to the interior when he was hired to open a new night club in Bogotá around 1944. Although his band returned to Cartagena soon after the performance, Bermúdez stayed on and formed a new orchestra of musicians from the interior. The musicians of his new band, Orquesta de Lucho Bermúdez, were trained in classical music, *bambucos*, and *pasillos*, but Bermúdez led them to perform Costeño musical styles. He is credited with winning acceptance for Afro-Colombian Costeño music in the elite social circles of the country's interior.

In the 1940s and 1950s changes in the style of commercial Costeño music (particularly experiments with different combinations of instruments) inspired record companies to label the new sound as *música tropical* (tropical music). By the 1960s, the name *cumbia* became widely applied to commercial recordings of Costeño music; the change in label in part signified further innovations while simultaneously evoking La Costa's musical past.

By the 1970s cumbia was supplanted in popularity within Colombia by another Costeño music called *vallenato* (which means literally "from the valley"). *Vallenato* was a comparably more folksy or down-home cousin of cumbia coming from the semirural regions of La Costa. Originally *vallenatos* were unaccompanied songs of Spanish origin that evolved to be accompanied by an ensemble consisting of accordion, a drum, and a scraper. It is often speculated that *vallenato*'s rise to mass popularity was due to its sponsorship by the region's drug cartels. By the 1980s, as with other traditional musics making their way to national popularity in Colombia, *vallenato* had itself been modified and modernized to include electric bass, back-up vocals, a battery of Latin percussion, and keyboards. Although *vallenato* has outsold cumbia within Colombia since the 1970s, it was not until the early 1990s that *vallenato* surpassed *música tropical*/cumbia as the Colombian sound in international markets.

Known for its beaches, tropical sun, Caribbean waters, and resorts, La Costa was a popular vacation destination for Colombians from the interior of the country. The growth of La Costa's import-export economy and increasingly cosmopolitan population (thanks in part to *immigration from Europe and the Middle East) further increased the region's influence in the national culture. La Costa's reputation as a vacation spot seems to have influenced associations of its music with fun and good times.

The port cities of Barranquilla and Cartagena in particular imported the latest international popular music records whether from New York, Cuba, or México, and their touristic, entertainment venues hosted music groups from abroad. Colombia's first radio station La Voz de Barranquilla (the voice of Barranquilla) was created in 1929. And the country's first two record companies were also established in La Costa, namely, Discos Fuentes (founded in 1934 in Cartagena) and Discos Tropical (founded in 1945 in Barranquilla).

While the emulation of popular international music styles that were disseminated through the radio stations and record stores of La Costa's ports allowed Colombian genres to become popular on the international scene, Colombian cumbias retained some recognizable differences. In comparison to other commercially successful Latin musics like *salsa and *merengue, cumbia has a thinner rhythmic texture with prominent accents on the downbeats (rather than syncopated); many commercial cumbias have rather simple melodies in short, repeated two-bar phrases that are alternated between the soloist and group or between different instruments; and while improvisation is part of cumbia performances, these solos tend not to be virtuosic.

In the late 1960s through the 1970s, bands playing covers of Costeño music began to appear outside of La Costa in other areas of the country. These bands were generally smaller than the ensembles from La Costa, and they used electric keyboards and guitars and a simplified rhythmic texture. The music industry applied the label "cumbia" to this music, which came to displace *porro* in popularity in some regions of Colombia and became very popular internationally. Some Costeño music fans saw the minimization of the tropical rhythms and instrumentation as a degradation of their music.

The new style was attributed to the appropriation of Costeño music by the profit-driven, modern recording studios that began to consolidate in the interior city of Medellín in the 1950s. The first studio in Medellín, Sonolux, was started in 1949; their first label was "Lyra," and they distributed records for RCA Victor in addition to their own. Discos Fuentes moved their headquarters from Cartagena to Medellín in 1954, and they continue to this day to be one of Colombia's most important record companies. While the Medellín industry dominated recordings of cumbia, in La Costa, groups like Pedro Laza y Sus Pelayeros (Laza and His People from San Pelayo) continued to perform a less commercial style of *porro* in addition to a few cumbias. Laza's group also had some recording success with their more roots-oriented, traditional sound and made several albums for Fuentes.

Changes in cumbia continued to occur as record producers like Antonio Fuentes and recording artists like Los Corraleros (The Poultry Farmers) created new combinations of rhythms and instrumentation. One such experimentation in the early 1960s put a horn section (some of whose players came from Laza's Pelayeros) together with accordions. Another important innovation was the addition of the electric bass. Another band, La Sonora Dinamita (The Dynamite Sound), created by the Discos Fuentes label in 1960, became one of the most popular groups in Latin America and are best known for promoting what is termed "chuco-chuco" (an onomatopoeia for the rhythm) or "raspa" (rasping) cumbia (two pejorative terms for the stripped down, mechanical-sounding versions of tropical rhythms).

Recording artists of the simpler commercial cumbia, like La Sonora Dinamita, Los Corraleros, and Los Graduados (The Graduates), were popular within Colombia but had a greater impact outside the country. Through recordings and live performances, these groups helped spread this simpler form of cumbia to México, Central America, Ecuador, Peru, Bolivia, and Chile. Mexican ensembles recorded covers of Colombian cumbias that became national hits across México. In Andean countries, cumbia became domesticated under the label *chicha* (homemade beer) and was popularized through radio and commercial recordings; other labels and variants of hybrid Andean-cumbia genres include *cumbia andina* (Andean cumbia), *cumbia folk* (folk cumbia), and *tropical andino* (Andean tropical music). Though cumbia initially was favored by middle-class urban youth in the Andes, *chicha* and *cumbia andina* came to be associated with the most dispossessed of the Andes regions' poor urban migrants.

Though cumbia has reached most U.S. consumers through the marketing of their Latin American labels by the mainstream record companies, cumbia has also entered through Tex-Mex and *norteño conjuntos* (northern bands) who perform in the United States and include cumbias in their repertoires. Such performers include *Selena (whose cumbias titled "Baila Esta Cumbia" and "Biti biti bom bom" were two of her biggest hits), Bronco and Los Bukis, and Limite.

Colombian-derived cumbia is also one of the central genres played at *sonidero bailes*—deejay dances—popular among some 300,000 Mexican immigrants in New York and New Jersey. As opposed to the style of cumbia popularized by norteño and *Tejano (Texas-Mexican) bands in the 1980s and 1990s (and frequently heard on *Spanish-language radio throughout the United States), the cumbias preferred at these dances come from recordings made in the Mexican immigrants' hometowns in the states of Puebla, Oaxaca, and Guerrero. The style of cumbia coming from these areas of México emphasizes instruments over voices and favors *vallenato*-style accordion playing. In this cumbia, singers' voices are often electronically distorted and are added to the mix to accentuate the rhythm. Unlike the popular versions played on the radio, these cumbias are significantly longer, lasting over six minutes. This Colombian-derived style of Mexican cumbia music is the primary reason people go to the dances, which are an important focus of Mexican immigrant culture and community life in the United States.

Further Reading

Béhague, Gerard, George List, and Lise Waxer. "Colombia." In *New Grove Dictionary of Music and Musicians*, edited by Stanley Sadie. 2nd ed. New York: Macmillan, 2001.

List, George. "African Influences in the Rhythmic and Metric Organization of Colombian Costeño Folksong and Folk Music." *Latin American Music Review* 1.1 (1980): 6–17.

Ragland, Cathy. "Mexican Deejays and the Transnational Space of Youth Dances in New York and New Jersey." *Ethnomusicology* 47.3 (2003): 338–354.
Wade, Peter. *Music, Race, and Nation: Música Tropical in Colombia*. Chicago: University of Chicago Press, 2000.

Rebecca Sager

Dance of the Millions. Reflecting the remarkable creativity and clever humor of the Cuban people, including Cuban American émigrés to the United States, the Dance of the Millions refers to an economic disaster that occurred in Cuba in 1919 when the price of sugar dropped perilously low. The Dance of the Millions is what the Cubans call the period immediately following World War I when Cuban investors engaged in extraordinarily reckless financial speculation on sugar. The debacle resulted in major investment losses by those who participated and had massive negative impact on Cuban markets and investors in sugar commodities. Suffering tremendous hardship as a consequence of the plummeting economy, the workers and their families were forced to survive through extraordinary efforts and mutual support cooperatives. Like the worldwide depression after the 1929 stock market crash that led to songs, literature, and films about the struggles, the Dance of the Millions entered the Cuban folk language and also gave rise to creative responses in Cuba and Cuban American popular culture that persists to the present on both the island and the U.S. mainland. The very nature of sugar as a sweet foodstuff that is used as a base ingredient for cooking hundreds of dishes underscores the popular cultural importance of the historical event. That sugar is also the key product in the manufacture of such high-earning industry products as rum and other multimillion-dollar fermented beverages further captures the gallows wit of the Cubans in baptizing their country's market plunge with a playful description that also illustrates the people's hardy response to adversity.

Further Reading

Pérez-Stable, Marifeli. *The Cuban Revolution: Origins, Course and Legacy*. New York: Oxford University Press, 1993.

Cordelia Chávez Candelaria

Danza. *Danza* is a term that refers specifically to dances that were danced for religious purposes and, although often misunderstood, are an integral part of Latina/o, Mexican, and Chicana/o popular cultures in the United States. Unlike dances that fall under the more general umbrella of *folklórico*, danzas cannot be altered without jeopardizing the integrity of the danza. The alteration of any aspect of a danza including costuming, choreography, step arrangement, or musical accompaniment could change or nullify the spiritual devotion of a danza in its entirety. Many danzas are composed of simple footwork so as to allow for worship without an overwhelming prerequisite of talent and training. There are some danzas, however, that are to be danced only by special classes of people and therefore may contain intricate footwork, daring physical exploits, or some other extraordinary display for the purpose of divine worship or sacrifice.

The vast majority of danzas have their roots in pre-Cortesian México, although some are inspired directly from Spain. The indigenous civilizations practiced several ceremonial and spiritual dances that were later adjusted so they would show devotion to Catholic subjects. The Spaniards did not hesitate to communicate their own heritage by teaching the Danza of los Cristianos y los Moros (the dance of the Christians and the Moors) that depicts the triumph of Spain's Christian defenders over their longtime Moorish invaders. Due to Spanish pressure to indoctrinate the indigenous population in Christianity, or in some instances to protect them from persecution by the Inquisition, few indigenous dances actually persisted in their pure spiritual form past the Spanish Colonial period. Those that survived did so either because they were practiced in remote geographical areas, such as the Danza del Venado (Deer Dance), or because they had a strong devoted following that was willing and able to maintain and practice the danzas in secrecy. Examples of other famous danzas include Los Negritos (The Little blacks), Los Tastoanes (from the Nahuátl word *tlatoani*, meaning spokespersons or leaders), El Venado (The Deer), Hua Huas, **Matachines* and/or Matlachines of any region, Los Voladores (The Flyers), and the Danzas Aztecas (Aztec Dances).

Danzas Aztecas

Danza Azteca refers to danza that was specifically practiced by the Mexica (Aztecs) and continues to be practiced today throughout the United States and México. The Mexica practiced a very rich set of ceremonial dances for various purposes of devotion. Since their devotion was directed toward pagan gods, the Spaniards required them to either cease dancing or to change their devotion to a Catholic spiritual figure. For those who consented to change the object of their devotion, they were also required to cover more of their bodies with European-style clothes, slow down the tempo of the music and dance, and enrich the music with European instruments such as stringed lutes. Those who wished to maintain the danza in its purest form did so in absolute secrecy, relying most frequently on oral tradition to preserve the knowledge of the sacred dances so as to avoid being caught with physical evidence.

Contemporary practice of Danza Azteca can vary from the aforementioned Christianized style to the warrior and pagan worship styles that are characterized by faster steps, pre-Cortesian costuming, and musical accompaniment that consists of various percussion instruments and flutes. All spiritual Azteca or Conchero dancers dance in spiritual circles, which they enter to the left. Before any dance is executed the dancers will cleanse themselves with the smoke of a purifying incense, most commonly sage. Then the dancers will salute the five directions (the four cardinal directions and the center of the circle, which represents the center of the universe) by blowing a conch shell, sending energy in each direction, and praying to ask permission to dance the sacred dances and to pay respect to the divine entities. A small dance called the firma (signature) or cruz (cross) is done to mark the beginning and end of every dance. The structure of the dance is such that those who are of importance to the circle will dance furthest to the inside of the circle so that the other dancers can follow them. Movements are first executed to the left out of reverence for the spiritual energy of death, which the Mexica believed was always present on a person's left side. Steps and movements are also executed with regard to balance, which represents the concept of duality, and numerology, which corresponds to the Mexica spirituality.

Essential costuming among all Aztec dancers includes a *penacho* (head piece that can be as simple as a bandana with a feather, or a full plume of feathers with intricate artwork around the entire head band) and a *maxtli* (piece that covers the waist and rear and hangs down over the space between the legs) for the men and a *huipil* (simple dress made of one or two long rectangular pieces sewn together) for women. Both men and women wear hollowed-out chachayot nuts around their ankles to create a rhythmic sound when they step. Many costume accessories such as chest plates, wrist bands, leg decorations, face paint, and body paint can vary from circle to circle or from dancer to dancer. Conchero circles differ on whether or not the women may also wear warrior clothing (*maxtlis*, chest plates, and *penachos*). The decoration of the costume elements can be of significance to a person's status in the circle or to the circle itself.

The importance of such stylistic detail can vary from one Aztec dance society to the next, depending upon their philosophical views. These differences also dictate whether or not women are allowed to dance, and if so, where they are allowed to dance. Invariably Aztec dance is executed in a spiritual manner, but there are opposing views on whether or not artistic, lyrical representations of Aztec dance may be used for performance and/or educational purposes. If an Aztec dance is converted into a lyrical, artistic staged performance, many believe that it ceases to be true Aztec dance and is therefore no longer considered danza but rather *folklórico*.

Further Reading

Nájera-Ramírez, Olga. *La Fiesta de los Tastoanes, Critical Encounters in Mexican Festival Performance*. Albuquerque: University of New Mexico Press, 1997.
Stevenson, Robert. *Music in Aztec and Inca Territory*. Berkeley: University of California Press, 1952.

Jimmy Newmoon Royball

Danza Azteca. *See* Danza.

Danzón. The danzón was introduced to Cuba by French exiles fleeing the Haitian slave revolt of 1791. This popular Cuban ballroom dance has its roots in the European contradanza (French country dance) of the eighteenth century and is also related to the Habanera. Today, the danzón's melodies and musical influence can be heard in modern *salsa throughout the United States and the Caribbean.

The first danzón, titled "Las Alturas de Simpson," was most likely performed in 1879 by a black composer, cornettist, and bandleader named Miguel Faílde Pérez (1852–1921). Until around 1916, danzones were typically played outdoors by *orquesta tipicas*, cornet-led brass bands accompanied by clarinets, trombone, tympani, and other percussion. In 1910, José Urfé (1879–1957), an Afro-Cuban composer, clarinetist, and bandleader, introduced elements of the Cuban **son* into the danzón in his original compositions, such as "El Bombín de Barreto." These stylistic changes rendered a more familiar "big band swing" sound that appealed to a broader audience.

Danzones were later performed by *charangas francescas* (French orchestras), which consisted of lead flute and backup violins, accompanied by tympani, which was eventually replaced by timbales in the Americas during the early 1950s. Antonio María Romeau (1876–1955) was an accomplished pianist, composer, and bandleader of French descent. In Cuba, he is credited with having introduced the piano to the *danzonera* via his membership in a popular *orquesta*.

By the 1930s, *orquesta tipicas* were rare in Cuba, yet **charangas* existed in various types and sizes. The danzones, like the *charangas* that played them, became bourgeois and were characterized by popular, light classics not associated with the *sones* of the *septetos* or other Afro-Latin and black street music. In grand European fashion, the danzón's first section is usually a promenade.

Today, the danzón movement has become popular in México, especially in the port city of Veracruz, where couples gather on an almost daily basis to dance with a live orchestra in the town square. Mexico City and Tijuana also boast several danzón halls, drawing members of older generations who keep this complex music and dance tradition alive.

Further Reading

Roberts, John Storm. *The Latin Tinge: The Impact of Latin American Music on the United States*. 2nd ed. New York: Oxford University Press, 1999.

Peter J. García

Dawson, Rosario (1979–). Rosario Dawson, a contemporary television and *film actress, was born on May 9, 1979, in New York City of a mixed racial heritage that includes Puerto Rican, African American, Cuban, Irish, and Native American. Rosario's education includes high school in New York City and a stint at the Lee Strasberg Institute. At age fifteen she made her screen debut in the critically acclaimed and controversial movie about teenage sexual angst in New York City, *Kids* (1995). Her big break came when she starred opposite basketball player Ray Allen (playing the role of Jesus Shuttleworth) in *He Got Game* (1998), Spike Lee's portrayal of the pressures and pleasures of being a high-profile high school basketball star. In the film, Rosario portrays Lala Bonilla, Jesús's girlfriend, who is torn between her concern and love for him and pressures to use his success to her benefit.

Since gaining recognition for her fine performance in *He Got Game*, Dawson has had roles in several films including *Light It Up* (1999), *Josie and the Pussycats* (2001), *King of the Jungle* (2001, also starring and produced by John *Leguizamo), *Men in Black II* (2002), and *The Adventures of Pluto Nash* (2002). She has also appeared on the television series *NYPD Blue* and *100 Centre Street*. Her latest work is in Spike Lee's *25th Hour* (2003).

Further Reading

"Actresses on the Rise." *Ebony* (September 2002): 174.
Bowles, Scott. "Here, There and Everywhere." *USA Today*, January 6, 2003, sec. 4D.
Reyes, Luis, and Peter Rubie. *Hispanics in Hollywood: A Celebration of 100 Years in Film and Television*. Hollywood, CA: Lone Eagle Publishing, 2000.
Seiler, Andy. "The Women Who Dazzle the 'Men in Black.'" *USA Today*, July 10, 2002, sec. 5D.

Louis "Pancho" McFarland

Day of the Dead. *See* Día de los Muertos.

De La Hoya, Oscar (1973–). Well-known boxer, Oscar De La Hoya, was born in 1973 in California to Joel De La Hoya and Cecilia Gonzáles De La Hoya. The second of two sons along with a younger sister, De La Hoya grew up in a working-class neighborhood in East Los Angeles. His father boxed briefly in the United States and his grandfather, Vicente, boxed as an amateur featherweight in Durango, México. With his father's encouragement, De La Hoya started boxing at the Eastside Boxing Club in East Los Angeles at the age of six. Naturally left-handed, he was trained to box out of the conventional right-handed stance. By the age of thirteen he had won

Oscar De La Hoya. *Courtesy of Photofest.*

over 100 amateur bouts and lost only twice. He attended Garfield High School and passed the General Equivalency Diploma test.

In October 1990, De La Hoya's mother died of breast cancer at the age of thirty-nine, having hidden her disease from him because she did not want to distract him from his boxing career. Before she died, De La Hoya promised to win an Olympic Gold Medal for her. In 1992, De La Hoya fulfilled his promise by winning the Gold Medal in the 132-pound weight class at the Summer Olympics in Barcelona, Spain, and acquired the nickname the Golden Boy. Later that year he turned professional, signing a five-year $1 million contract with promoters Robert Mittleman and Steve Nelson. During the prefight introductions of his pro debut in 1992, De La Hoya, in a high-profile show of his binational **mestizaje*, wore a sombrero and carried the flags of México and the United States, one in each hand. In 1994 he won his first professional championship, the World Boxing Organization 130-pound class title. He has also won titles at 135-, 140-, 147-, and 154-pound classes. De La Hoya had a pro record of 31–0 when he suffered his first pro defeat to Felix Trinidad in 1999 amid a controversial majority decision. In 2000, he lost in a split decision to Shane Mosely. Both Trinidad and Mosely were undefeated when they won. In 2002, De La Hoya scored a dramatic eleventh-round technical knockout over Fernando Vargas for another 154-pound title. De La Hoya is one of the most popular and highest paid non-heavyweight boxers ever.

Professionally, De La Hoya has not limited himself solely to boxing but has performed musically as well. In 2000, he released *Oscar De La Hoya*, a Grammy-nominated album of love songs, which he sings primarily in Spanish. He has also been an active humanitarian, as in his establishment of the Oscar De La Hoya Youth Center in Los Angeles, which provides mentoring in academics, athletics, and good citizenship to children and teenagers. In his mother's memory, he has made significant contributions to the Los Angeles White Memorial Medical Center for the prevention of breast cancer. Unlike most practicing boxers, De La Hoya ventured into the business side of boxing in 2002 when he became the first Latino boxer to establish a boxing promotional firm, Golden Boy Promotions LLC.

Further Reading

Kawakami, Tim. *Golden Boy: The Fame, Money, and Mystery of Oscar De La Hoya.* Kansas City, MO: Andrews McMeel, 1999.

Clifford Candelaria

Décima. *Décima* is a principal poetic and song form transplanted to New Spain by Europeans throughout colonial times, where it thrived in the American Southwest in the eighteenth and nineteenth centuries. The text includes a ten-line stanza from which the word *décima*—meaning "ten"—is derived. It refers to the ten verses of the numerous stanzas, and the genre is often referred to in the plural. *Décimas* are usually organized into an introductory quatrain; a line from this quatrain is often repeated at the end of each stanza and again at the end of the series of strophes. The subject matter may be religious, political, or philosophical and uses much metaphor. The basic structural framework of these compositions is an octosyllabic meter and a rhyme scheme consisting of ABBAACCDDC.

The *décima* still serves as the framework for songs and **corridos* in New Mexico and in narrative *corridos* of the U.S.-Mexican border region. According to Américo Paredes, singers of the *décima* on the Texas border use an old-fashioned singing style, and the *décima* is sung for informal occasions without musical accompaniment. It is actually chanted rather than sung. The *décima* is an important part of the Mexican *son jarocho* and *valona* traditions and fundamental in the traditions of Chilean *verso*, Panamanian *mejorana*, Colombian and Venezuelan *corrido*, Cuban and Puerto Rican *punto*, and Argentine and Uruguayan *milonga*, among other genres.

Further Reading

Herrera-Sobek, Maria. "The Discourse of Love and *Despecho*: Representations of Women in the Chicano *Décima*." *Aztlán* 18.1 (1987): 69–82.

Paredes, Américo. "The Décima on the Texas-Mexican Border: Folksong as an Adjunct to Legend." *Journal of the Folklore Institute* 3 (August 1966): 154–167.

Peter J. García

Del Río, Dolores (1905–1983). Dolores Del Río was a *film star diva in México and the United States. She was born Dolores Martínez Asúnsolo López Negrete to a wealthy family in Durango, México, in 1905. The fear of the Mexican Revolution forced the family to move to Mexico City, where Del Río's beauty and social status proved helpful. She met Jaime Del Río, her first husband and a screenwriter, and kept his name. When visiting friends in Hollywood, a director was stunned by her beauty and cast her in the film *Joanna* (1925). One of the first Mexican actresses in Hollywood, Del Río participated in several silent films until the arrival of sound hit the movies, and she was no longer offered roles due to her accent. In 1942 she left Hollywood and went back to México, where El Indio Fernández introduced her to the Mexican public. Back in her country, Del Río became one of the leading faces of the Golden Years of the Mexican Cinema. Remembered for her roles in *María Candelaria* (1943), *Doña Perfecta* (México, 1950), and *La Cucaracha* (México, 1958), where she starred with María *Félix, Del Río was part of the national cultural scene until her death in 1983 due to liver failure. A recipient of the highest honor of the Mexican Academy of Cinema, the Silver Goddess, Del Río appeared in sixty-five films. Other films include *Flaming Star* (1960), where she played the role of Elvis Presley's mother, *Cheyenne Autumn* (1964), *Flor Silvestre* (awarded the 1959 Golden Bear of the Berlin Film Festival), and *The Children of Sánchez* (1978).

Further Reading

Rodríguez-Estrada, Alicia I. "Dolores Del Río and Lupe Velez: Images On and Off the Screen, 1925–1944." In *Writing the Range: Race, Class, and Culture in the Women's West*, edited by Susan Armitage and Elizabeth Jameson. Norman: University of Oklahoma Press, 1997.

Gabriella Sánchez

Del Toro, Benicio (1967–). One of a tiny handful of Latinas and Latinos to be recognized by the Academy of Motion Pictures, actor Benicio Del Toro received an Academy Award for his portrayal of a Mexican detective in **Traffic* (2000). Born February 19, 1967, in Santurce, Puerto Rico, Del Toro came to the United States at the age of thirteen but did not get the bug to act until he auditioned for a campus play during his first year at the University of California, San Diego. To participate in the play, Del Toro had to be a declared drama major student. Del Toro changed his major despite his father's disapproval. His father feared that acting did not have a future—a future that proved otherwise through hard work and interesting characters. With his new career choice, Del Toro moved to New York to study at the Circle in the Square Acting School. During his time studying in New York, he won a scholarship to Stella Adler Acting Conservatory in Los Angeles.

In 1987 Del Toro guest-starred on several television shows: *Miami Vice*, *Private Eye*, and *O'hara*. These guest appearances led to roles in *Big Top Pee-Wee* (1988) and *License to Kill* (1989). His role in the television series *Drug Wars: The Camarena Story* (1990) got the attention of Sean Penn. Penn chose to cast Del Toro for his directorial debut in *The Indian Runner* (1991). Del Toro continued making *films such as *Christopher *Columbus: The Discovery* (1992), *Fearless* (1993), *Money for Nothing* (1993), *Swimming with Sharks* (1994), and *The Usual Suspects* (1995), for which he was awarded the 1996 Independent Spirit Award for Best Supporting Male. He also played Benny Dalmau, in *Basquiat* (1996), which earned him an Independent Spirit Award for Best Supporting Actor in 1997.

In 1995, he made his debut as a director, producer, and screenwriter for

Submission, which was screened at the Venice Film Festival. In 1998 Del Toro costarred with Johnny Depp in *Fear & Loathing in Las Vegas*, based on Hunter S. Thompson's cult novel of the same title. In *Traffic* (2000), directed by Steven Soderbergh, Del Toro joined an all-star cast starring Catherine Zeta-Jones, Michael Douglas, Dennis Quaid, Salma *Hayek, and Javier Rodríguez. Along with an Oscar for Best Supporting Actor, Del Toro won a series of awards for his role in *Traffic* including the Screen Actors Guild award for Outstanding Performance by a Male Actor in a Leading Role. Some of his more memorable films include Guy Ritchie's *Snatch* (2001), Sean Penn's *The Pledge* (2001), a cameo in **Bread and Roses* (2001), and *The Hunted* (2003). Del Toro's recent work includes *Ché *Guevara: A Revolutionary Life* (2004).

Further Reading

Keller, Gary D. *A Biographical Handbook of Hispanics and United States Film.* Tempe, AZ: Bilingual Press, 1997.

Silvia D. Mora

Después del Terremoto. *Después del Terremoto* (After the Earthquake, 1979), a short narrative *film, was written, produced, and directed by famed Chicana independent filmmakers Lourdes Portillo and Nina Serrano and distributed through Film Library, New Jersey. The bilingual film centers on a Nicaraguan woman, Ilena, who flees the 1976 Nicaraguan earthquake and migrates to San Francisco, where she finds work as a maid. The film looks at the daily life decisions of an exiled Central American woman and her relationships with her aunts and grandmother. One of the key scenes of the film involves her anxiously awaited encounter with her boyfriend who has just arrived from Nicaragua as a political exile and victim of torture by the U.S.-backed Somoza regime. Through its interweaving of personal and political narratives with the cataclysmic effect of the earthwake, the film comments on how *gender, culture, *family, and community issues are negotiated by an exiled woman adjusting to a new country. Poignant and sad, the film is also affirming in exploring how Ilena carves her identity as a Latina in the United States against cultural and religious expectations.

Further Reading

Fregoso, Rosa Linda. *The Bronze Screen: Chicana and Chicano Film Culture.* Minneapolis: University of Minnesota Press, 1995.
http://www.lourdesportillo.com/nepantla.html.

Arturo J. Aldama

Día de la Raza. Also known in the United States as Columbus Day, an official federal holiday, Día de la Raza is the more common designation of October 12 throughout Latin America. In literal translation Día de la Raza means "day of the race [or of the people]," but a more correct translation to capture how it is understood by bilingual and Spanish-speaking Latinas and Latinos would be "Day of Community among the Peoples of the Americas." It commemorates the arrival of Christopher *Columbus in the West Indies, an event traditionally known as "the discovery of America and the 'New' World." Since the 1960s and the rise of counterculture movements like the American Indian Movement (AIM) and the *Chicano Movement, many scholars and self-identified mestizo activists and others who express solidarity with indigenous peoples and cultures have challenged the idea of celebrating Columbus Day as a solely positive fact of history. Instead, they advocate invoking the Día de la Raza as a teaching moment for critical commemorative events that explore all aspects of the first European/Native American encounter and succeeding conquests and colonialism, including the genocidal results for the native peoples of the Americas. One variant group protesting an uncritical traditional celebration is called SUBMOLOC, Columbus's name spelled backwards, and they frequently demonstrate at federal buildings and Columbus Day parades to try to raise public awareness. Some Italian Americans who honor Columbus because of his birth in Genoa, Italy, and others argue that his amazing achievement as an explorer, natural scientist, and chronicler merits lasting respect. This debate indicates the lasting impact of *race and ethnicity, diaspora, *immigration, and other culture indicators to American history and personality, including Latina and Latino popular culture.

Further Reading

Churchill, Ward. *A Little Matter of Genocide: Holocaust and Denial in the Americas, 1492 to the Present*. San Francisco, CA: City Lights Books, 1997.

Goldin, Liliana R., ed. *Identities on the Move: Transnational Processes in North America and the Caribbean Basin*. Austin: University of Texas Press, 1999.

Cordelia Chávez Candelaria

Día de los Muertos. Día de los Muertos, or Day of the Dead, is a two-day celebration that coincides with the Catholic Church holy days All Saints' Day (November 1) and All Souls' Day (November 2). The Catholic Church considers All Saints' Day a holy day of obligation requiring mandatory attendance of Mass. It is a ritual time to remember and pray for the souls of deceased *family members and friends, especially for the resurrection of souls in Purgatory and for those who are in limbo and have not yet entered into Heaven. Día de los Muertos dates back to prehistoric times in Mesoamerica when the Aztecs would designate an entire month to celebrate death. The original Aztec celebration was held during the time of Miccailhuitontli, which fell during the end of July and the beginning of August. The festivities dedicated to children and to the dead were then moved by the Catholic Church to coincide with All Saint's Day. The first of November is dedicated to children, while the second of November is dedicated to all relatives. Often compared to Halloween, or All-Hallows Day, both *holidays are referred to as Todos Santos (All Saints) in parts of México and the United States. Mexican celebrations are typically private family affairs consisting of all-night vigils at the *camposanto* (cemetery). In the United States they are often public events such as art exhibits, night processions, cultural events, and school activities.

Traditionally the main activity is a visit to the community cemetery where family members clean the graves and place offerings of flowers, candles, figurines, photographs, and *food for the spirit of the deceased. **Cempasúchil*, the Nahuátl (Aztec) name for the yellow marigold, is also called *flor de muerto* (flower of the dead) because it is the preferred flower for Día de los Muertos Mexican commemorations. Many ritual elements reveal a syncretism of European and indigenous American beliefs and practices. Many Indians believe that the souls of deceased persons visit their relatives annually, which requires the family to prepare the deceased's favorite meal and drink, called an *ofrenda*, as a food offering. Home altars (*altares*) as shrines and memorials to deceased relatives and friends are common among many Latino and *Chicano families. Along with personal memorabilia of the dead, the altar is decorated with flowers, *papel picado* (colorful tissue paper), family photographs, fruits and food offerings like *pan de muerto* (bread of the dead), *calaveras* (skeletons), candy, water, candles, toys, religious icons, alcoholic drinks, cigarettes, and other ritual foods like tamales, empanadas, enchiladas, and other dishes. Candied skeletons, skulls, banners, flags, and papier-mâché skeleton toys can be found in colorful attire imitating all aspects of life and help teach children that death is part of the life cycle. These festive skulls and party-loving skeletons that abound during these celebrations both mock and embrace death and serve to remember the departed as a still vital presence in the lives of their survivors. Día de los Muertos folk traditions and current popular practices and Latina/o hybrids reflect the Mexican view of death.

Skeletons are often used in celebrations of the Día de los Muertos. *Courtesy of the Department of Chicana and Chicano Studies Archive, Arizona State University.*

Further Reading

Castro, Rafaela G. *Chicano Folklore: A Guide to the Folktales, Traditions, Rituals, and Religious Practices of Mexican-Americans.* New York: Oxford University Press, 2001.

Peter J. García

Día de los Niños. *See* Día del Niño.

Día del Niño. Literally translated as Day of the Child, El Día del Niño is also sometimes identified as Día de los Niños, or Children's Day. It has been celebrated in México on April 30 since 1924, and in recent years the special *holiday recognition of children has gained increasing popularity in many parts of the United States, particularly in regions with large Latina and Latino populations. For children in México the festivities often include a day off from school and participation in organized community games, traditional songs, music and dancing, holiday *foods, craft making, and sometimes gifts from parents and teachers. One Phoenix, Arizona, flyer announcing its observation in 2003 described it as a traditional Mexican holiday celebrating children and went on to emphasize that the sponsoring group sought to culturally empower children in its celebration of youth. A Lafayette, Indiana, 2003 announcement of Día del Nino events explained that it is a Hispanic holiday to honor the essence of childhood innocence and playfulness.

In 1924 Mexican President Álvaro Obregón issued a decree declaring April 30 as the official day to honor and celebrate children. His decree followed the League of Nations' Declaration of the Rights of the Child, also adopted in 1924 and sometimes called the Geneva Declaration. Like México, other nations established their own celebrations, including Bolivia, which chose April 12 for its official date, Honduras (September 14), Canada (November 20), Japan (May 5), and Serbia (January 14), to cite a few. Most other countries have followed suit in recognition of the Geneva Declaration that was intended to end the abuse of children worldwide and to ensure their protection. Over thirty years after the League of Nations' Declaration, the United Nations General Assembly officially recommended that all countries institute the observation of a universal Children's Day to encourage worldwide fraternity and understanding among young people and to promote the overall welfare of the world's children. The UN General Assembly passed the Declaration of the Rights of the Child in 1959.

The American adaptation of the holiday includes its use of the common plural form, Día de los Niños, and also includes linkages to the promotion of health, literacy, education, and positive *family values. Communities engage in many of the same recreational activities sponsored in Mexican celebrations, although it is rare for schools to be excused on that day. Regardless of the country, it is customary for parents to be encouraged to participate in observance of Día de los Niños since one of its important aims is to educate parents and the general public about the essential role they play in the healthy physical, mental, and emotional development of their children. In addition to ongoing support from UNICEF, the UN agency dedicated to the rights and health of children, the day has become popular with support from schools, community organizations, and Latina/o cultural groups like REFORMA (National Association to Promote Library and Information Services to Latinos and the Spanish Speaking), which has spearheaded its active recognition and promotion.

Further Reading

"Declaration of the Rights of the Child." http://www.unhchr.ch/html/menu3/b/25.htm.

"National Latino Children's Institute." http://www.nlci.org.

Riggs, Robert E., and Jack C. Plano. *The United Nations: International Organization and World Politics*. Chicago, IL: Dorsey Press, 1988.

Rosa Hamilton

Díaz, Cameron (1972–). *Film actress Cameron Díaz was born on August 30, 1972, in Long Beach, California, to a Cuban father and German English American Indian mother. At twenty-one, she came to the attention of director Chuck Russell, when she auditioned for the female lead in the blockbuster *The Mask* (1994), starring Jim Carrey. With no acting experience (she had been a model), she won the role and received critical and popular acclaim. Díaz has acted in more than a dozen movies since her debut. Her acting credits include the independent art house drama *The Last Supper* (1996), romantic comedies *A Life Less Ordinary* (1997) and the mega-hit *There's Something about Mary* (1998), the satirical *Being John Malkovich* (1999), the voice of Princess Fiona in the animated children's movie *Shrek* (2001), action films such as the film version of the 1970s television series *Charlie's Angels* (2000), and Hollywood dramas *She's the One* (1996), *Any Given Sunday* (1999), and *Vanilla Sky* (2001). Díaz, who is light-skinned and blonde, portrays Anglo women and has not yet taken on a role as a Latina or *Cuban American. Her more recent work includes roles in movies such as *Gangs of New York* (2002, with Leonardo DiCaprio), *The Sweetest Thing* (2002), *Charlie's Angels: Full Throttle* (2003), and *Shrek II* (2004).

Further Reading

Hobson, Louis. "Just One of the Gang." *The Toronto Sun*, December 19, 2002, 79.

"Living Life in Glare of the Spotlight." *The Journal*, September 3, 2002, 14.

Reyes, Luis, and Peter Rubie. *Hispanics in Hollywood: A Celebration of 100 Years in Film and Television*. Hollywood, CA: Lone Eagle Publishing, 2000.

Louis "Pancho" McFarland

Dichos. *Dichos* are poetic sayings or wise proverbs that reflect scores of tried and tested communal knowledge of people. Sometimes called *refranes*, they typically disclose a folk philosophy or the worldview of the person telling them. The most aptly delivered *dichos* require skillful timing, audience awareness, and the appropriate situation. Transmitted orally over generations, *dichos* in the United States are most common among the elderly and recent immigrants who are Spanish-language dominant. Increasingly, however, this verbal art form is being recorded and preserved by folklorists, writers, and others in such works as the *film *The *Milagro Beanfield War* (1988), the book *Barefoot Heart* (1999), and *Las Mujeres Hablan* (1989). Examples are: (1) "Para el gato viejo, raton tierno"—A tender mouse for the old cat, or An old geezer courting a young woman; (2) "De tal palo, tal astilla"—From the stick, a splinter, or A chip off the old block.

Further Reading

Aranda, Charles. *Dichos, Proverbs, and Sayings from the Spanish.* Santa Fe, NM: Sunstone Press, 1977.

Arora, Shirley, L. "Proverbs in Mexican-American Traditions." *Aztlán: International Journal of Chicano Studies Research* 13 (1982): 43–69.

Glazer, Mark. *A Dictionary of Mexican American Proverbs.* Westport, CT: Greenwood Press, 1987.

Peter J. García

Doce Verdades, Las. *See Las Doce Verdades.*

Don Francisco. *See Sábado Gigante.*

Downs, Lila (1967–). Lila Downs, a jazz-influenced balladeer, has become a beloved musician internationally due to her ability to charm Spanish-, English-, Mixtec-, and Zapotec-speaking audiences. Born on September 9, 1967, Downs grew up biculturally in Minnesota and in the Mixtec mountain town of Tlaxiaco, Oaxaca, México. Her father, Allen Downs, was Scottish American, born in Colorado Springs, and served as an art professor with specialties in cinematography and drawing at the University of Minnesota. Downs's mother, a Mixtec born in Oaxaca, México, sang traditional Oaxacan music professionally in Mexico City as a teenager, then lived twenty years moving back and forth between Oaxaca and Minnesota. After her husband's death, she remained in México and opened a car parts business. With the ability to speak both Spanish and English, it was here that Lila first came into contact with the tragic stories of many that had crossed the border illegally to get to the United States. Downs currently studies the Mixtec language with the help of her mother and a linguist who teaches her correct pronunciations and assists her with song transcriptions.

Downs began to sing at the age of five and started formal classical voice lessons at age fourteen at Bellas Artes in Oaxaca, then in Los Angeles. During her high school years in Oaxaca, she studied operatic singing and continued voice lessons at the University of Minnesota, where she earned a bachelor's degree in anthropology. Her specialty was in Oaxacan textiles from the Mixteca Alta mountain region. Seeing that women could create a language of their own through the textiles as historical documents influenced her song writing. After finishing her thesis she returned to her musical interests with a new perspective.

A positive musical influence in her youth was the Grateful Dead (*see* Garcia, Jerry), who encouraged her journey back to her indigenous roots. Especially in México, she says, it is important to find those roots because it helps us compare ourselves to others and be proud of who we are. Other musical influences include Woody Guthrie, Bob Dylan, Thelonious Monk, and John Coltrane. Downs explores the different dimensions of voice and musical styles that dominate the rural areas of México. She is aware of the dynamics of urban, rural, and class interactions and the ways in which the arts constantly go back and forth and feed off one another. This translates into a variety of timbres—sound qualities—that she articulates as she moves from an Afro-mestizo song from the Veracruz coast to a Mixtec or Zapotec song from Oaxaca, and so on. When singing a song from the coast she uses a rounded, edgy timbre associated with African American singers. When singing a Zapotec song, the timbre is very nasal, a style that could easily be heard in outdoor contexts. When singing a popular **ranchera*, she is more sophisticated and urban. Her style has been described as "eclectic" and included among new waves of cross-border Latino musicians that includes others such as *Los Lobos, Los Abandoned, Los Villains, Maria Fatal, and Aztec Underground.

She has been influenced by jazz singers and African American music in general and credits the music of African Americans, so filled with different varieties of expression, and credits it as being integral to her understanding of the voice as an instrument.

Downs's works often arise out of collaborations with husband Paul Cohen, a composer, clown, and multi-instrumentalist she met playing *salsa in a Mexican club. She comes up with a poem (the lyrics), and they cocreate the harmonic and instrumental accompaniments. Some of her poems are based on images from the Mixtec language that are found in the ancient codices like the term for *pulque*, the sacred drink from the *maguey* plant that refers to the dead mother, but also to the white water. Cohen came to México as a circus clown and later decided to study music in Oaxaca, so his perspective on music is light-hearted. Improvisation is an important element of their music, an influence from jazz, and even when the songs are set, they try to be as free as possible in performance.

Her first recording was on cassette, called *En Vivo with Lila Downs y Azulao* (the group), recorded in the club Sol y la Luna in Oaxaca City and in Philadelphia. (*Azulao* is a Portuguese term that translates into something like "blued.") Downs has since recorded three CDs. *La Sandunga*, released in 1997, is principally made up of songs by Oaxacan composers. *Yutu Tata/Arbol de la Vida/Tree of Life*, released in 1999, was inspired by the

Mixtec codices. *La Linea/Border*, released in 2001, was inspired and dedicated to the Mexican migrants who die crossing the border into the United States. Both *Tree of Life* and *Border* came out on the Narada-World label. *La Sandunga* was rereleased in 2003 on the Narada label, but it has been sold at her concerts since it came out in 1997. One unofficial CD titled *Trazos* (consisting mostly of Latin standards) was recorded in 2000 in collaboration with a Mexican modern dance company, Contempodanza. This CD was never released commercially. A new CD was released in the spring of 2004.

Downs and Cohen began to give concerts in the United States beginning in 1998, at first mostly in California with the help of Betto Arcos, then a deejay for KPFK in Los Angeles. Their first important concert was at the 1999 Festival of Sacred Music at the Hollywood Bowl in Los Angeles, where the Dalai Lama called upon the people of the Americas for peace. After that, Downs signed a contract with Narada, a subsidiary of Virgin Recordings. She now tours internationally.

In general Downs's songs reflect on social injustice and identity in contemporary life. She sings the traditional *chilena*, which arrived in Oaxaca with sailors from Peru and Chile, as a tribute to the black roots of Mexican culture. *Chilenas* are popular in Oaxaca right now, in the fiestas (*see* Holidays and Fiestas) so common to Mexican life. Her initial intention was to sing songs that are sacred and typically heard only in their local mountain contexts. But in fact her sources are many and varied and include songs she grew up listening to.

Making her debut *film appearance by singing in the acclaimed film *Frida* (2002), Downs successfully demonstrated her flexibility and talents to a wider audience than ever before. She is featured, very prominently with five song credits, in the *Frida* sound track, including the Oscar-nominated song "Burn It Blue" (written by Julie Taymor and Elliot Goldenthal), which she sang with Brazil's Caetano Veloso at the 75th Annual Academy Awards on March 23, 2003. Her songs have been included in film and television, including PBS's *American Family* and NBC's *Kingpin* and the films **Tortilla Soup* (2002), **Real Women Have Curves* (2002), and *La Casa de los Babys* (2003). She currently resides in New York City.

Further Reading

Campbell, Duncan. *The Guardian*, February 10, 2003. http://www.guardian.co.uk/arts/features/story/0,11710,892488,00.html.

http://www.liladowns.com.

Brenda Romero

Dr. Loco's Rockin' Jalapeño Band. Dr. Loco's Rockin' Jalapeño Band is a Latin fusion rock band with politically motivated lyrics that makes use of popular working-class music forms and is a favored band among the

*Chicano community in California and Texas. In 1989, José Bennie Cuellar (Dr. Loco), an anthropologist and professor at San Francisco State University in California, started a Chicano band called Dr. Loco's Rockin' Jalapeño Band.

Cuellar, born and raised in San Antonio, Texas, exhibited an interest in music when he was five years old, and his uncle taught him how to play the clarinet. In the early 1960s Cuellar joined the air force, where he developed his own musical style performing with bands that played rhythm and blues, *Latin jazz, and rock. After his military duties, he started a group and performed in the Las Vegas music scene before moving to California in 1966, where he played with Dick Place and the Placers. Once in California, Cuellar launched his academic career.

Cuellar studied music at Golden West College and then transferred to Cal State University, Long Beach, where he received a B.A. in anthropology (1969). He then pursued his graduate degrees at the University of California, Los Angeles, where he obtained both his M.A. (1971) and Ph.D. (1977) in anthropology. After graduate work he devoted much time to teaching and research, where he focused on topics relating to Mexican American communities, their concerns, culture, and music, as well as ethnicity and aging. Some of the universities, colleges, and institutions where he has taught are University of Colorado at Boulder, University of California at Santa Barbara, San Diego State University, Stanford University Chicano Research Center, Stanford University Medical School's Geriatric Education Center, Prevention Research Center, and University of California at Berkeley.

After an extended break from music to pursue his academic endeavors, Cuellar was invited to play the saxophone by Louie Pérez and David Hidalgo of *Los Lobos and also by Flaco *Jiménez and Doug Sahm of the Texas Tornadoes. By 1987 Cuellar had developed the image of "Dr. Loco" and gained musical success and popularity in the San Francisco Bay area with bands such as Jazzteca and Contra-Contraband. Finally, in 1989 Cuellar created Dr. Loco's Rockin' Jalapeño Band, a band consisting of nine members, all musicians and academics but not all formally trained in music. Their repertoire consists of Chicano music, oldies, rhythm and blues, boogie, shuffle, *merengue, *cumbia, *salsa, Tex-Mex, and traditional Mexican music including **corridos*, *boleros, and **rancheras*. Their song repertoire is made of originals from the band, for example, "Dance Till I Drop," as well as covers and parodies from American pop favorites with a blend of fragments in English and Spanish, for example, "Me Siento So Bad" (I Feel So Bad, by Chuck Willis) and "Pa' lo que Vale" (For What Its Worth, by Stephen Stills). Their first recording was *Con/Safos* (Don't Mess with This) in 1991 and featured "Linda Cholita," "Cumbia del Sol," and "Framed." Some of the albums have acclaimed recognition nation- and worldwide such as *Movimiento*

Music, which received four stars from the *Austin Chronicle* in 1993, and *Puro Party!*, which was ranked number five in the Japanese newspaper *Tokyo Daily Mainichi Shinbun* in 1995.

Currently Cuellar holds positions as professor in the Raza Studies Department and director of the César E. *Chávez Institute for Public Policy, both at San Francisco State University.

Further Reading

http://www.drloco.com.

Peter J. García

Duran, Roberto (1951–). Roberto Duran, a boxing legend who first fought professionally in 1967 at the age of sixteen, is known by the nickname "Manos de Piedra" (hands of stone) because of his powerful punches and lasting power in the ring. He fought his last match at the age of fifty in 2001. Many prizefighting experts rate him as the best ever lightweight (i.e., maximum 135-pound class), and others rank him as high as the third-greatest boxer pound for pound to compete professionally in the twentieth century. Duran is reputed to have beaten up grown men in street fights as a twelve-year-old living in harsh poverty and forced to defend his mother and siblings. Also part of his "Manos de Piedra" legend is being credited with the knockout (KO) of a horse when he was a young man.

Born on June 16, 1951, in Guarare, Panama, to a Panamanian mother and a father from Arizona of Native American and Mexican descent, Duran and his seven or eight siblings (depending on the biography consulted) grew up in a tough environment. His father abandoned the family when Roberto was a boy, and the future world champion was forced into the streets early. He began gym training in his youth and soon was competing professionally. After winning all of his first twenty-one consecutive professional fights without any significant specialized training, Duran's contract was bought by wealthy landowner Carlos Eleta for the minuscule sum of $300. Eleta hired renowned trainers Ray Arcel and Freddie Brown to apprentice the young boxer, and they refined Duran's relentless offensive hitting style and taught him defensive tactics as well. On June 26, 1972, Duran won his first major world title by winning his thirtieth consecutive match, a thirteen-round KO of World Boxing Association (WBA) lightweight champion Ken Buchanan in New York's Madison Square Garden. That key victory led to his domination of boxing's lightweight division until 1979, when he moved up to the welterweight division (maximum 147 pounds). His only loss in sixty-eight fights was to Esteban DeJesús in a nontitle ten-round decision in 1972, which Duran avenged decisively with knockouts in two subsequent title bouts (1974 and 1978).

One of Duran's most famous and historic matches occurred on June 20, 1980, when he won an enthralling fifteen-round decision over one of the sport's most respected, popular, and famous talents, Sugar Ray Leonard. The win earned Duran the World Boxing Association's welterweight title, which he unfortunately held for less than a year. Six months later in a rematch with Leonard, Duran injured his reputation in a stunningly unexpected manner by quitting in the eighth round with the infamous plea, "No más." His action was ridiculed in the press and despised by thousands of fight fans who expected more from "their" Manos de Piedra. Only Duran's perseverance and longevity in the brutal "sweet science" of his chosen profession enabled him to regain the respect of many sportswriters and fans.

The decade of the 1980s was ambivalent for Duran professionally as he fought many other great fighters and champions with mixed results. Losses to Wilfredo Benitez (January 1982 decision), Marvin Hagler (November 1983 decision), and Thomas Hearns (June 1983 KO 2) were interspersed by impressive KOs of Pipino Cuevas (January 1983 round four) and Davey Moore (June 1983 round eight) for the WBA junior middleweight title. After the Hearns fight Duran took a break from the ring and remained inactive for nearly three years. In 1989, he won his last major title with an exciting twelve-round split decision over a younger, bigger, and highly touted Iran Barkley for the World Boxing Council (WBC) middleweight championship. Forced by financial difficulties to continue fighting, Duran, despite being in his forties, managed to fight entertaining matches with Vinny Pazienza and Héctor Camacho, Sr. Fighting his last bout at age fifty in 2001, Duran is still regarded as one of the most skillful competitors in his field in the twentieth century.

Further Reading

Jones, Ken, and Chris Smith. *Boxing the Champions*. Wilshire, England: Crowood Press, 1990.

Myler, Patrick. *A Century of Boxing Greats*. London: Robson Books, 1999.

O'Brien, Richard. *The Boxing Companion*. New York: Friedman Group, 1991.

Clifford Candelaria

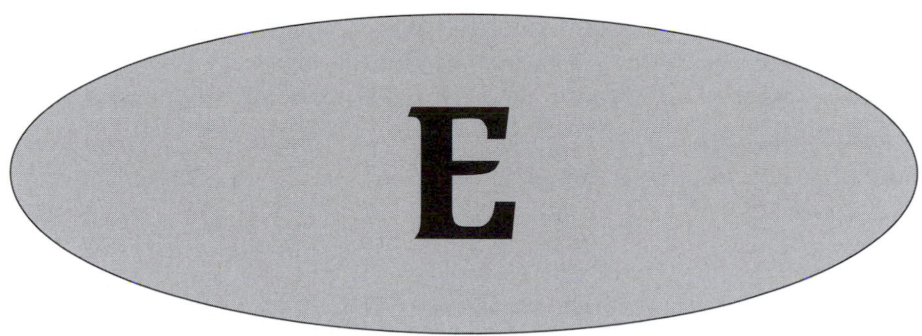

El Chicano. The band El Chicano was originally named The V.I.P.s and formed in East Los Angeles during the late 1960s, at the height of the *Chicano Movement. The El Chicano signature sound mainly consisted of the Hammond B-3 organ, which was played by Bobby Espinosa, the greasy "Wes Montgomery" sounding guitar and improvisation of Mickey Lespron, and the deep groove of the bass playing by Freddie Sánchez, with Latin percussion provided by Andre Baeza on congas and John De Luna on drums.

Their first album, *Viva la Tirada*, had a very free instrumental *Latin jazz feel to it and was recorded by MCA records in 1970. The title track "Viva la Tirada" is a composition by Gerald Wilson, written in honor of Mexican bullfighter José Ramón Tirada. The song became very popular, promoting cultural awareness and pride, especially in Los Angeles, California, and remained at the top of the music charts for thirteen straight weeks. The album's popularity allowed them to tour throughout the country, and in doing so, El Chicano became the first *Chicano group to perform at the legendary Apollo Theater in New York City.

Since their first album, El Chicano has released six other albums with MCA: *Revolution* (1971), *Celebration* (1972), *El Chicano* (1973), *Cinco* (1974), *The Best of Everything* (1975), and *Pyramid* (1976). Some of their hit songs include their rendition of Van Morrison's "Brown-Eyed Girl" in 1972 and "Tell Her She's Lovely" in 1973. In 1976, they also recorded *This Is El Chicano* for Shakey Brooks label, and the CBS recording company released their album titled *You Want Me* in 1982. MCA reissued a greatest hits album titled *Viva! Their Very Best* in 1988 and released another collection of El Chicano songs titled *Chicano Chant* in 1997. The following year,

El Chicano recorded a new album titled *Painting the Moment*, in which they were joined by Steve Salas, who laid both instrumental and voice tracks.

El Chicano has done some work on sound tracks for movies, including, *Donnie Brasco* (1995), *The Latin One* (1988), and *Mi Vida Loca* (1995), and they have signed to do a special on Chicano music for PBS. El Chicano toured across the United States in 2003 and is planning a new album.

Further Reading

Guerrero, Mark. "Chicano: Latin Rock Pioneers." http://www.elchicanomusic.com/home.htm.

George Yáñez

El Mariachi. Set in northern México, the 1992 *film *El Mariachi* tells the story of a struggling guitar-case-carrying *mariachi musician who is mistaken for a mafia hit man. The film's success at the Sundance Film Festival helped reinvigorate critical and creative interest in the promise of low-budget, independent filmmaking. Director Robert Rodríguez, a Texas native, was twenty-three years old when he wrote the script for *El Mariachi*. He produced the film on a budget of $7,000, spending most on actual film purchase and only $600 on special effects equipment, props, and related supplies. Shot in Acuña, México, the hometown of the producer Carlos Gallardo, the film gained the interest of the townspeople who participated as actors at no cost, donated use of their props, and promoted the movie. Acuña's hospital, jail, *police officers, news anchors, and local politicians were all involved in the film. The documentary-style footage filmed with a handheld camera was completed in two weeks. *El Mariachi* was remade as a Hollywood production titled *Desperado* (1995), starring Antonio Banderas and Salma *Hayek. Despite its $7 million budget, the remake did not get the same critical acclaim as *El Mariachi*, which won the 1994 Independent Spirit Award for Best Feature Film. Nominated at the 1993 Sundance Film Festival for the Grand Jury Prize, it won the Audience Award for Best Feature Film and was purchased and distributed by Columbia.

Further Reading

http://www.coastnet.com/~lwr/Fcourt/ElMariachi.htm.
http://www.imdb.com/Tawards?0104815.

Silvia D. Mora

El Norte. Directed by Gregory *Nava and written by Nava and Anna Thomas, *El Norte* (The North, 1983) is a beautiful and harrowing *film telling of the cyclical oppression and violence suffered by Latin American immigrants. The North is a mythical place for Rosa (Zaide Silvia Gutíerrez) and her brother Enrique (David Villalpando), who hear about it in their home in Guatemala. The North is where they must journey to survive the U.S.-backed death squad regimes in Guatemala and the ensuing civil war among the landowners, the military, and the indigenous Maya and student groups.

The pictorial shots Nava shows in early scenes in Guatemala contrast starkly with the border scenes in Tijuana, where Rosa and Enrique wait for an opportunity to cross into the United States. While Nava's film offers a grim reality of *race and class struggle from Guatemala to the inner city of Los Angeles, he also peppers his film with carefully constructed moments of almost surreal or magical beauty. These scenes fill the viewer with a sense of the cultural patterns that Rosa and Enrique negotiate as they make their way into a new, but not necessarily better, world.

El Norte is divided neatly into three segments. The first segment gives the background and history of Rosa and Enrique's plight in Guatemala. The political turmoil that engulfs their family is an all-too-familiar class struggle that they never seem to escape. The second segment depicts the siblings' journey north and is filled with their further struggle to maintain dignity and hope despite their growing realization of the global nature of economic oppression and violence. The third segment focuses on their economic and cultural survival in California.

Nava's film is not a romantic view of the struggle for cultural survival. Ultimately, it is about the restrictions and limits placed on immigrants like Rosa and Enrique who have no other choices. They must adapt, and while we see them learning English and assimilating into other mainstream American customs, we are never allowed to forget their heartbreak over having lost their home and *family. In the final scene, their father's prophetic comments in the first segment of film, where he states that indigenous and campesino peoples are destined to be nothing more than the raw labor, or the "manos de los ricos" [hands of the rich], comes full circle. The film ends with Enrique raising his hands to show he can do manual labor as he jockeys with other Latino immigrants to be picked up as a day laborer.

Distributed by Artisan Entertainment, *El Norte* won the Grand Prix for Feature Films at the World Film Festival in 1984, and it was nominated for an Academy Award for Best Original Screenplay in 1984. In 1996, it was named an "American Classic" by the Library of Congress. The film's cast also includes Ernesto *Gómez Cruz, Miguel Gómez Giron, José Martín Ruano, Stella Quan, and Eraclio Zepeda.

Further Reading

Fregoso, Rosalinda. *The Bronze Screen: Chicana and Chicano Film Culture*. Minneapolis: University of Minnesota Press, 1993.

Cheryl Greene and Arturo J. Aldama

El Nuevo Teatro Pobre de América. *See* Nuevo Teatro Pobre de América, El.

***El Super*.** Directed, written, and produced by León Ichaso and Orlando Jiménez-Leal, *El Super* (1979) is a full-length feature *film that charts the daily travails of a homesick Cuban exile who works as a building superintendent in Manhattan. Missing the tropical warmth of the island, the "super," played by Raymundo Hidalgo-Gato, suffers through a New York winter. He also faces cultural tensions with his teenage daughter (played by Elizabeth *Peña in her breakout film), as she adapts to the more urban life of New York and questions the traditional role of women in Latino families. Some critics argue that this is the first *Cuban American feature film that captures the cultural tensions of surviving in New York.

Further Reading

http://www.hollywood.com/movies/detail/movie/224658.
http://www.ifilm.com/ifilm/product/film_info/0,3699,2329045,00.html.

Arturo J. Aldama

Elizondo, Héctor (1936–). A versatile and talented performing artist, Héctor Elizondo has made a career of portraying nonstereotypical characters in *films that range from comedy to drama. Elizondo was born on December 12, 1936, in West Harlem, New York, to a Basque father, Martín Echevarría Elizondo, and a Puerto Rican mother, Carmen Medina. When promising careers in baseball (scouted by the Pittsburgh Pirates and the New York Giants) and dancing were cut short by a knee injury, Elizondo turned to acting. He found success on Broadway playing such roles as George C. Scott in *Sly Fox* and God in *Steambath*, earning an Obie for the latter in 1971. While still performing on Broadway, Elizondo made his film debut in *The Vixens* (1969).

Elizondo's filmography includes *Landlord* (1970), *Valdez Is Coming* (1971), starring Burt Lancaster, *Born to Win* (1971), *Cuba* (1979), *The Fan* (1981), *Young Doctors in Love* (1982), *Beverly Hills Cop III* (1994), **Tortilla Soup* (2001) with Raquel *Welch, and *The Princess Diaries* (2001) with Julie Andrews. Elizondo has a long-standing friendship with director Garry Marshall, which has resulted in several collaborative efforts with Richard Gere and Julia Roberts, including *American Gigolo* (1980), *Pretty Woman* (1990), and *Runaway Bride* (1999). He received a Golden Globe Award nomination for Best Supporting Actor for his role in *Pretty Woman*.

In addition to his many movies, Elizondo has appeared on television in such series as *Kojak*, *Matlock*, *Hill Street Blues*, *The Rockford Files*, *All in the Family*, and *The Equalizer*. He also directed the television series *Chicago Hope* and *a.k.a. Pablo*.

Further Reading

Keller, Gary D. *A Biographical Handbook of Hispanics and United States Film*. Tempe, AZ: Bilingual Press, 1997.

Unterburger, Amy L., and Jane L. Delgado, eds. *Who's Who among Hispanic Americans 1994–1995*. Detroit, MI: Gale Research, 1994.

Alma Alvarez-Smith

Espada, Martín (1957–). An outspoken advocate for social justice, Martín Espada is an attorney, an educator, an award-winning poet, and the first poet laureate of Northampton, Massachusetts. Like many other bilingual, bicultural writers, Espada writes in English and Spanish to tackle issues of ignorance, poverty, oppression, and the Hispanic condition in the United States. Extrapolating from his Puerto Rican roots, Espada's books of poetry have received critical acclaim, winning the PEN/Revson Award for Poetry, the Before Columbus American Book Award, and the Paterson Poetry Prize and qualifying as a finalist for the National Book Critics Circle Award, among others. Additionally, Espada has won two prestigious fellowships from the National Endowment for the Arts.

Born in Brooklyn, New York, on August 7, 1957, Espada was greatly influenced by the political activism of his father, Frank Espada, a leader in the Puerto Rican community and civil rights movement. Largely autobiographical, Espada's work draws on his father's influence, as well as from his Puerto Rican heritage and work experiences, which range from working as a bar bouncer to a tenant rights lawyer. Shortly after earning a Bachelor of Arts in history from the University of Wisconsin at Madison in 1981 and a Juris Doctorate in 1985 from Northeastern University, Espada published his first book, a collection of political poems called *The Immigrant Iceboy's Bolero* (1982), which featured photography by his father.

The first book to receive wide critical acclaim was Espada's third collection of poetry, *Rebellion Is the Circle of a Lover's Hands* (1990), winning the PEN/Revson Award for Poetry that year. In the collection, Espada chronicles the lives of ordinary people with vivid detail, as well as brutal humor. In 1996 Espada won the American Book Award for another book of poetry, *Imagine the Angels of Bread* (1996), which was also a finalist for the National Book Critics Circle Award. *Imagine the Angels of Bread* brings to light the indignities and suffering faced by immigrants and the working class, including violence in prisons and decaying schools. Other collections of poems include *Alabanza: New and Selected Poems 1982–2002* (2003), *A Mayan Astronomer in Hell's Kitchen: Poems* (2000), *City of Coughing and Dead Radiators* (1993), and *Trumpets from the Islands of Their Eviction* (1987). He also has edited several anthologies including *El Coro: A Chorus of Latino and Latina Poets* (1997) and *Poetry Like Bread: Poets of the Political Imagination* (1994). Currently a professor at the University of Massachusetts at Amherst, Espada teaches Latino poetry, creative writing, Spanish Civil War literature, and the work of Pablo Neruda.

Further Reading

Bedford Introduction to Literature. http://www.bedfordstmartins.com/introduction_literature/poetry/espada.htm.

Martin Espada. http://www.martinespada.com.

"Martin Espada." *Contemporary Authors Online.* Gale Group. http://www.galegroup.com.

Modern American Poetry. http://www.english.uiuc.edu/maps/poets/a_f/espada/espada.htm.

Julie Amparano García

Espinosa, Paul D. (1950–). Recipient of seven Emmy awards and numerous other honors, Paul Espinosa is an independent filmmaker who directs, produces, and writes documentary films and realistic dramas. He is one of the best-known and most recognized contemporary Chicano filmmakers.

His best known award-winning titles include . . . *and the earth did not swallow him* (1996), a dramatic feature he executive produced based on the novel by Tómas *Rivera; *The Hunt for Pancho Villa: American Experience* (1993) and *Ballad of an Unsung Hero* (1984), two documentaries he wrote and produced; and *The Border* (1999), a collaboration among four producer/directors that he executive produced for the Public Broadcasting System. From 1980 to 1990 the *Chicano filmmaker honed his creative skills as director of the KPBS Office of Latino Affairs, a unit he established to focus on Latina/o and U.S.-México border subjects. After that, Espinosa served, until 1994, as executive producer for public affairs and ethnic issues for KPBS-TV in San Diego, California. With his extensive experience writing, directing, producing, and hosting prime-time programming for PBS, Espinosa shifted to independent production in 1997 by founding Espinosa Productions, a company devoted to videos and films documenting all aspects of the *barrios and borderlands of the southwestern United States and northwestern México.

Espinosa was born on August 8, 1950, in Alamosa, Colorado. In 1954, his family moved to New Mexico, where he grew up and attended local schools. After graduation from high school, his good grades and intelligence got him accepted to Ivy League Brown University in Providence, Rhode Island. He earned a bachelor's degree in anthropology from Brown in 1975 and continued graduate studies in modern anthropology at Stanford University, where his focus was television communication and cultural analysis. He wrote his Ph.D. dissertation from copious notes developed from a year of research on the set of *The Lou Grant Show*, where he investigated the elements that contribute to effective television programming based on real-world depictions. After completing an internship in San Diego at PBS affiliate KPBS-TV, Espinosa shifted directions by applying his Stanford Ph.D. not to an academic career in anthropology, but to documentary film projects instead.

Known for conducting painstaking research to ensure the historical and material accuracy of his films, Espinosa's moving work captures the lives of common people and the inside stories of legendary figures. This is seen in his early productions, including *The Trail North* (1983), a documentary narrated by Martin *Sheen that depicts the journey to the United States by one family from México, and *The Lemon Grove Incident* (1986), a docudrama chronicling one of the country's earliest school segregation cases in California. Like them, the 1988 *In the Shadow of the Law*, about four undocumented families living in the United States; *The New Tijuana* (1990), about the politics and economics of the title city; and *Uneasy Neighbors* (1990), about the conflict between San Diego's prosperous homeowners and the constant flow of migrant workers, are powerful documentaries about the dynamic border region. His *Los Mineros: American Experience* (1991) changes geography and cultures to tell a similar story, this time about Arizona's persecuted Mexican American copper miners in their half-century struggle for basic justice.

Espinosa reached farther back in history for two of his longer documentaries, *The U.S.-Mexican War: 1846–1848* (1997), which he produced, and *1492 Revisited* (1992), which he both wrote and produced. These and his other projects were made possible through major funding from public agencies such as the Corporation for Public Broadcasting, the National Endowment for the Humanities, the National Endowment for the Arts, American Playhouse, and the Arizona, California, New Mexico, and Texas state humanities councils, as well as from such private sector sponsors as The John D. and Catherine T. MacArthur Foundation, McDonald's Corporation, and numerous others.

Besides the seven Emmys, Espinosa's projects have also been honored with international recognition in the form of four CINE Golden Eagle awards (México) and Special Jury Awards from the Cairo and Viña del Mar (Chile) Film Festivals. His work has received a national Emmy nomination for News and Documentary Achievement, Best of the Festival Awards from the International Film Festivals of Santa Barbara and Minneapolis, Best Feature prizes from the San Antonio CineFestival and the San Diego Filmmakers Showcase, and top documentary awards from the Houston International Film Festival, the San Francisco Broadcast Industry Conference, the National Latino Film and Video Festival, and the National Educational Film and Video Festival. He and his work have also been recognized with major awards from the American Bar Association, the California Teacher's Association, the California School Board Association, the American Civil Liberties Union, and the National Conference of Christians and Jews.

In addition to film and video production, Espinosa cofounded the California Chicano News Media Association in San Diego, serving as the organization's president from 1983 to 1986; was appointed to the California Council for the Humanities for a term; and was an inaugural member of San Diego's Select Board on Binational Issues. For his lifetime body of work, he was honored by the Mexican government in 1990 with an invitation to take part in "Chicanos 90: Primera Semana de Cine y Video Chicanos" (The First Week of Chicano Cinema and Video), the first ever major Mexican retrospective of Chicano movies. He also served as part of the jury for the Ninth Annual Festival of New Latin American Cinema in Havana, Cuba.

Espinosa and his wife, Marta Sánchez, moved to Tempe, Arizona, in 2004, where he assumed a full professorship in the Department of Chicana and Chicano Studies at Arizona State University, and she joined the faculty of the Department of Languages and Literatures. He plans to continue his filmmaking and is currently working on final production of another film on California.

Further Reading

Dower, Rick. "Paul Espinosa: A Camera in Both Worlds." In *San Diego Online*. http://www.sandiegomag.com/issues/march97. Photographs by Dave Gatley.

Kanellos, Nicolás, ed. "Paul D. Espinosa." In *The Hispanic American Almanac. A Reference Work on Hispanics in the United States*. 3rd ed. Detroit, MI: Gale Group, 2003.

Keller, Gary D., ed. "Paul Espinosa." In *A Biographical Handbook of Hispanics and United States Film*. Tempe, AZ: Bilingual Press, 1997.

Ann Aguirre

Estefan, Gloria (1957–). Gloria Estefan, the internationally renowned Latina singer and humanitarian, began her singing career first with the Miami Sound Machine (originally named the Miami Latin Boys) then as a solo artist. In addition to her award-winning musical contributions, she and her husband, Emilio Estefan, have built Estefan Enterprises to an estimated worth of $200 million. Estefan Enterprises consists of various businesses in industries ranging from restaurants, record production, TV production, talent management, song writing, and soon the production of motion pictures. In addition to their restaurants, cafés, hotels, and nightclubs, the Estefans own Estefan Publishing Company and a $14 million recording studio in Florida named Crescent Moon Studios.

Gloria Fajardo Estefan was born on September 1, 1957, in Havana, Cuba, and at the age of two, she moved with her *family to Miami. In the mid-1970s she was persuaded to join a local music group named the Miami Latin Boys. Estefan became the group's lead singer, performing at restaurants, weddings, and other paying gigs and eventually began a relationship with Emilio Estefan, the band's leader and accordionist. In September 1978, soon after her twenty-first birthday, the two were married, and two years later Gloria gave birth to their son Nayib.

The Miami Latin Boys were renamed the Miami Sound Machine and, later, Gloria Estefan and the Miami Sound Machine. By 1983, the group was well known in South and Central America and had released four successful albums. In 1984 the band crossed over and recorded an English-only album that proved very successful. The album contained a single titled "Conga," which is the only song in history to appear on *Billboard*'s pop, Latin, soul, and dance charts all at the same time.

In 1989, Estefan began her solo career releasing an album titled *Cuts Both Ways*. In March 1990, while on a promotional tour for her album, Estefan's tour bus was struck by a semitrailer, which resulted in severe injuries for Emilio, Nayib, and Gloria. By far, Estefan suffered the worst injuries with a broken back that required surgery to put pins in her spine. A year later, she was back on stage performing and released her album titled *Into the Light*.

Gloria and Emilio Estefan (far right) with members of the Miami Sound Machine. *Courtesy of Photofest.*

In 1994 Estefan took a break from touring and gave birth to her second child, a daughter named Emily.

As part of their business empire, the couple owns Larios, a Cuban restaurant and nightclub that is located in the upscale area of Miami's South Beach strip. They also own Bongo's Cuban Cafe, located at Walt Disney World in Florida. The Cardozo Hotel and Bar on Ocean Drive in Miami also belong to the couple.

The Estefans have been successful in building their personal wealth, but they have never forgotten to give back to their community. In 1997, the Gloria Estefan Foundation was created to support charitable programs for disadvantaged children and to empower young people through education and opportunity. Its mission includes funding annual scholarships for students who need financial assistance so that they may achieve their higher education goals.

Further Reading

http://www.gloriaestefan.com.

Cristina K. Muñoz

Estévez, Emilio (1962–). Actor, director, and screenwriter Emilio Estévez, the son of noted actor Martin *Sheen, is distinguished as being the youngest person to write, direct, and star in a major motion picture. His *film *Wisdom* was released in 1987 when Estévez was twenty-five. Estévez was born on May 12, 1962, in New York City. During his senior year of high school in California, he wrote a play titled *Echoes of an Era* about the life a Vietnam veteran. After graduating, Estévez began his pursuit of an acting career. Unlike his famous father, who acknowledges that he changed his name to Sheen to avoid being typecast in ethnic roles, Estévez kept his father's Spanish surname. Before being cast in feature films, Estévez landed several television roles—for example, in the drama *In the Custody of Strangers* (1982), where he worked opposite his father.

Estévez's feature film debut was in several adaptations of S.E. Hinton's novels, including *Tex* (1982), *The Outsiders* (1983), and later *That was Then . . . This is Now* (1985). During this time, he also played a teen punk rocker in *Repo Man* (1985), a high school jock sitting in Saturday morning detention in *The Breakfast Club* (1985), and a law school student in *St. Elmo's Fire* (1985). Estévez's other credits include *Stakeout* (1987), *Young Guns* (1988), and *Young Guns II* (1990). He then starred in what would become a Disney family/comedy film trilogy, *The Mighty Ducks* (1992, 1994, 1996). In 1996, Estévez produced, directed, and starred in a Vietnam period piece alongside his father, *The War at Home*. Estévez's other credits include made-for-television movies *Western Dollar for the Dead* (1998), *Rated X* (2000), and *Sand* (2001). He wrote, directed, and starred in *Bobby* (2003), a film based on the assassination of Robert Kennedy.

Emilio Estévez in *Young Guns II. Courtesy of Photofest.*

Further Reading

Kanellos, Nicolás, ed. *The Hispanic Almanac: From Columbus to Corporate America*. Detroit, MI: Invisible Ink, 1994.

Kanellos, Nicolás, ed. *The Hispanic-American Almanac: A Reference Work on Hispanics in the United States*. Detroit, MI: Gale Research, 1993.

Parish, James Robert, ed. *The Encyclopedia of Ethnic Groups in Hollywood*. New York: Facts on File, 2003.

Reyes, Luis, and Peter Rubie, eds. *Hispanics in Hollywood: An Encyclopedia of Film and Television*. New York: Garland, 1994.

Tardiff, Joseph C., and L. Mpho Mabunda, eds. *Dictionary of Hispanic Biography*. New York: Gale Research, 1996.

Marisol Silva

Estrada, Erik (1949–). Erik Estrada, a well-known television actor of Puerto Rican descent, was born on March 16, 1949, in New York's Spanish Harlem. His career in acting began with a role as Nicky Cruz, a streetwise youth, in the antidrug *film *The Cross and the Switchblade* (1972). Soon he appeared in minor parts in such other films as *The New Centurions* (1972), *Airport 1975* (1974), and *Midway* (1976). Best known for his role as the highway patrolman Frank "Ponch" Poncharello in the television show *CHiPs*, which ran from 1976 to 1983, he received a Golden Globe nomination for Best Actor in a Dramatic Series in 1980. Estrada was in relative obscurity after *CHiPs* ended until he landed the role of Johnny in the popular *telenovela Dos Mujeres, un Camino* in 1993. Since he did not know Spanish when he took the role, the words had to be spoken to him through a concealed earpiece. Estrada continues to act, playing small roles in feature films and appearing on American television in *The Bold and the Beautiful.* In 1997, his autobiography, *Erik Estrada: My Road from Harlem to Hollywood*, was published by William Morrow.

Further Reading

Estrada, Erik. *Erik Estrada: My Road from Harlem to Hollywood*. New York: William Morrow, 1997.

William Orchard

Ethnicity. *See* Race and Ethnicity.

Ethnomusicology. The ethnographic study of Latina/o music in the United States falls under the academic domain of *ethnomusicology*, the division of musicology that investigates music in its unique cultural context. This anthropological approach to music inquiry includes the study of folk, popular, Eastern art, and other contemporary musics in oral tradition and engages many challenging conceptual issues. These include the origins of music, musical change, musical symbolism and identity, musical universals, the role of music in society, and the biological and psychological basis of music and dance. Although formal investigation is rather recent, serious interest in non-Western music dates back to early European exploratory voyages throughout the world and the philosophical rationale for the study of foreign cultures "that developed" during the Spanish conquest of the Americas. During the Age of Enlightenment, Jean-Jacques Rousseau included samples of European folk, North American Indian, and Chinese music in his *Dictionnaire de musique* (1768), and he also contributed essays to the monumental *Encyclopedia* (1751) compiled under the intellectual leadership of Denis Diderot (1713–1784) and Jean le Rond d'Alembert (1717–1783).

The term *ethnomusicology* was first coined in 1950 by the Dutch scholar Jaap Kunst, replacing the earlier label *comparative musicology* (German *vergleichende Musikwissenschaft*), because comparison was not the foremost feature that distinguished this type of scholarly investigation. Western classical music is not excluded from the research menu, but ethnomusicologists have expressed very little interest in canonical music and academic music making, especially in conservatory and university-based programs. Instead, ethnomusicology as an interdisciplinary field of research is generally the study of music in oral tradition, commercial and popular musics, and in living musical systems. Ethnomusicologists conduct actual field research using a variety of methodologies and approaches, including participant observation, reflexivity, collecting and archiving, restudying older investigations, and exploring innovative and experimental ways of studying music as culture. Ethnomusicologists prefer to study music firsthand rather than reading previous studies, an approach that is scorned and criticized as "armchair investigation." Generally speaking, ethnomusicologists do not rely on written manuscripts or notated scores as the principal means of investigation but instead tend to interact with living musicians and audience members. Music ethnography involves participating in the broader musical life of a community and observing, listening, and collecting field notes and recordings as the primary repository of factually based information gathered and acquired from firsthand accounts, rather than from secondary written sources. This approach serves as the foundation for scholarly investigation.

In the past, most ethnomusicologists studied musical cultures other than their own, but today many native ethnographers study their native communities. In the past, comparative musicologists and early ethnomusicologists transcribed the music they collected and recorded their findings in Western notation, but today ethnographic fieldwork is the epistemological foundation for the field. Ethnomusicology as it is practiced today is indebted to two technical innovations of the late nineteenth century: the invention of the phonograph in 1877 by Thomas Edison and the development of the cents system of pitch measurement in 1885 by the English physicist and phonetician Alexander J. Ellis. The phonograph facilitated fieldwork and offered the possibility of playback from which comparative musicologists transcribed and analyzed music, whereas the cents system divided the octave into 1,200 equal units, enabling scholars to objectively measure non-Western pitch systems and scales.

Comparative Musicology

The United States boasts an incredible musical heritage of assimilation and acculturation from Spain, Portugal, sub-Saharan Africa, México, the Caribbean, and Central and South America, which dates from the sixteenth-century Franciscan missionaries to the newly arrived Caribbean immigrants in New York and Miami. The entire subfield of Latina/o ethnomusicology in the United States awaits more extensive research. Several comparative studies of Aztec and other prehistoric Indian music cultures have been put forth from a variety of disciplines including history, musicology, and anthropology. Most investigations are critical interpretations of ethnocentric sources like the Spanish codices and other Native American visual art forms. Some of the research was completed by comparative musicologists like Robert Stevenson and his research associates. Many of these archeological investigations examine musical instruments, ritual contexts, and iconographic sources of Indian ceremony and dance cycles. Scholars have typically interpreted the roles of musicians, dancers, and musical performances.

One of the biggest problems with historical reconstructions of ancient music cultures lies in the assumption that the past may be reinterpreted or understood based on the empirical evidence from the perspective of the present. We may never know exactly how or what prehistoric musics of the Americas actually sounded like since it was not recorded; nevertheless, musicians and musicologists have made earnest attempts to reconstruct early music cultures based on what is known and what has endured. Likewise, at the time of the conquest, the Aztec Empire was organized into distinct classes and ethnic groups, including Mexica, Tarasco, Tolteca, Huaxteca, Totonaco, Olmeca, Mixteca, Zapoteca, and Mayan. Each group had "its" own language, rituals, and unique musical and dance traditions. In the Southwest, Pueblo, Navajo (Diné), Apache (Ndé), Comanche, Ute, Tohono O'Oodham (Papago, Pima), Yaqui, Seri, and many other indigenous groups contributed to the **mestizaje*.

Musical Folklore

Musical *folklore is an early ethnomusicological model developed by Zoltán Kodály, Béla Bartók, and Constantin Brailoiu in Eastern Europe. In the British Isles, the research carried out by Cecil Sharp and Maud Karples shares with comparative musicology a science paradigm that conceives of music as a collectable, comparable, and ultimately explainable object within an observable and audible phenomenon. In contrast to comparative musicology, musical folklore focuses on the peasants or working class of the scholar's native country or region rather than on universal comparative schemes. In a class of their own are folk song collectors such as Johann Gottfried Herder, who coined the term *Volkslied* (folk song) in eighteenth-century Germany, and Oskar Kilberg in nineteenth-century Poland.

Generations of Mexican, Mexican American, and Anglo American folklorists and folk song collectors worked in the borderlands, including Rubén Cobos, John Donald Robb, Arthur Campa, Aurelio Espinoza, and Cleofas Jaramillo. They were generally motivated by the concern that regional Mexican folk heritage was vanishing. Fieldwork methodology was tainted with romantic nationalism in varying degrees; these scholars were on a quest in search of the natural and the pure. In certain areas, the collection and preservation of folk culture was lucrative to Anglo artists and intellectuals but disastrous to the colonized Mexicans whose culture was now in danger of being gentrified, dispossessed, and exploited. Even today, the political economy of certain states is overly dependent on natural and cultural tourism industries.

Much of the early ethnography devoted to the Southwest is based on the studies of researchers who worked in a newly acquired portion of the United States that was formerly New Spain and Mexican territory. Prior to the ratification of the *Treaty of Guadalupe Hidalgo in 1848, the territory between Texas and California belonged to México. Previous histories suggesting the borderlands were purchased from México on behalf of the United States have been challenged by many Chicana/os, who hold fast to the belief that the land was stolen, or at best taken, using imperial coercion. The oldest Latina/o musical traditions exist in the Southwest borderlands and date back 400 years to the explorations of Spanish conquistadors and colonizers in New Mexico (1598). Arizona was next settled in 1700, Texas in 1716, and California in 1769.

After the conquest, the Spanish missionaries introduced Gregorian music and that of the Toledan rites in the forms of responsories, sequences, parts of the Mass, prayers, praises, religious carols and **villancicos* (Christmas Carols), and other songs based on ecclesiastical monody. Music was an essential part of Spanish colonial life. Missionary music dating back to the California missions includes plainsong, some twenty-four cycles of the Ordinary, individual Mass movements, and settings of the Proper, Psalms, canticles, and hymns. The descendants of many of the original Spanish and Mexican settlers remain in their ancestral homeland, especially in northern New Mexico and south Texas. Scholars, collectors, archivists, and recorders have preserved and maintained some of the oldest Latino musical traditions including **autos sacramentales* such as *Los Moros y Cristianos* (The Moors and Christians) and *Los *Pastores* (The Shepherds).

Other musical genres include ballads such as *romances*, **décimas* (poetic form), and **alabados* (lament) that have been sung in northern New Mexico and south Texas since the early Spanish colonial period of the Southwest. By the early nineteenth century some twenty-one missions established along the California coast boasted a thriving musical life based on the liturgical services of the Catholic Church. Schools, libraries, and missions were built during the sixteenth and seventeenth centuries for the purposes of instructing the Native American population in the Christian faith. The first Franciscan music teacher in the Southwest was probably Cristóbal de Quiñones, who worked in New Mexico between 1598 and 1609.

Most of the American Southwest was under Spanish rule through the early nineteenth century and is culturally bonded with México, Spain, and Latin America. As Mexican immigrants cross the border annually, they continually revitalize the Chicana/o and Mexican musical life of the region. Other uniquely Mexican genres heard in the Southwest include the **corrido* (ballad), *verso* (verse), *indita* (little Indian girl), **canción* (song), and *trovo* (metrical composition or parody), most of which are based on the popular poetic form known as the *copla* (couplet), a verse of four lines with eight syllables or two lines with sixteen syllables as in the ancient romance. The *corrido* and the *décima* were especially prominent during the Mexican Revolution and throughout the late nineteenth century, and many published song texts were distributed and sold as broadsides conveying important news and current information that had an impact on Mexican communities in the United States.

According to the Mexican musicologist Vicente Mendoza, very little *bel canto* (operatic singing) had filtered throughout México at the end of the eighteenth century, but it gradually became the rage, starting with the upper classes and spreading to the whole population. Operatic *romances* (ballad), *cavatinas* (short solo song), and choruses even penetrated the Church to the extent that throughout the country rosaries actually were being sung to Italian aria tunes by European composers like Rossini, Donizetti, and Bellini. However, it took twenty years for Italian opera to really penetrate the whole country; and then in 1850 it transformed into a more sentimental folk song in Silao, Guanajuato, in the compositions of Antonio Zuñiga.

Around 1830, Fernando Calderón and Ignacio Rodríguez Galván created the poetic form that was to become the basis of Mexican song. In México, the *canción *ranchera* emerged from the country's rich folk music tradition with its own melodic peculiarities that included bel canto singing and language preserving in part the romantic song but devoid of the classical music conservatory or erudite procedures and elitist attitudes associated with Italian opera and Western art music. The *ranchera* remained popular in México and the Southwest throughout the twentieth century. It reached a peak in its mass-mediated popularity with José Alfredo *Jiménez, whose career marks a golden age for the genre. Provincial singers and musicians made Mexican songs out of the fashionable European dances of those days including the *polca*, *chotis*, *mazurka*, *valse*, *marcha*, and the like. By 1855 Mexican musical theater was introduced to Spanish *zarzuela* (Spanish comic opera in several acts). *Zarzuela* reached the height of its popularity at the beginning of the last quarter of the twentieth century. By then, musical influences from other Latin American countries had paved the way for later *Latin jazz and other hybrid styles and genres.

The earliest actual sound recordings of Southwest Mexican music were collected by the Anglo regional pioneer Charles Fletcher Lummis (1850–1928), who gathered examples on wax cylinders. His book *The Land of Poco Tiempo* was a repository of New Mexican folk songs published during the late nineteenth century. Another important religious figure during the nineteenth century was a parish priest, Father Juan B. Ralliere, who worked in Tomé, New Mexico, from 1858 to 1911 and is mentioned in local ballads dating to this period. His biography is described in Florence Hawley Ellis's account of his career. Father Ralliere produced a collection of popular religious music titled *Cánticos espirituales*, originally published in Las Vegas, New Mexico, in the nineteenth century and later reprinted in numerous editions. These include musical transcriptions, some in four-part harmonizations.

Latina and Latino Folklorists in the Southwest

The earliest professional and amateur collections of Mexican and Spanish folk and popular musics from the Southwest were documented by several Mexican and Mexican American folklorists, including Vicente T. Mendoza and his wife Virginia, Aurelio M. Espinosa, Juan B. Rael, and Arturo Campa. The numerous collections by Latina scholars rival those produced by Latinos and are no less rigorous or systematic. The folklorists Jovita González, Luisa Espinel, Aurora Lucero-White Lea, Cleofas Jaramillo, and Mela Sedillo worked in the early and mid-twentieth century; and their published works and archival collections provide an invaluable record of musical life in the Mexican American Southwest prior to, during, and after World War II.

The earliest folk songs and popular musics of Texas were collected by J. Frank Dobie and his student Jovita González. Beginning in 1920, Tejano folklorist Américo Paredes devoted his life work to chronicling the Mexican American struggle for justice and equality along the Texas-México border, where violence and conflict between Anglos and Mexicans has a long and bitter history. By recognizing the folk poetry as a literary and musical form, Paredes paved the way for more interdisciplinary readings of song texts, moving beyond the usual poetic analysis of metaphors, rhyme schemes, and comedic and tragic elements. More scholarly attention is needed to address performance styles, genres and subgenre categorizations, cultural poetics, and the ethnoaesthetics of ballads. The melodies of many earlier *corridos* were recorded throughout the twentieth century and are available in archival form. More recent subjects include drug trafficking (**narcocorridos*), September 11, gender conflict, and other current and newsworthy events.

Chicana and Chicano Ethnomusicology: Urban Folk Music to Popular Music

The first *Chicano ethnomusicologist, Manuel Peña, was a student of Américo Paredes at the University of Texas at Austin. Most of Peña's research on *Tejano music examines the Texas-Mexican *conjunto* and Mexican American *orquesta* and important musicians, composers, and singers throughout the twentieth century. Much of his work deals with issues of class, gender, and intercultural conflict, and Peña has trained a number of the next generation of post-Chicana/o ethnomusicologists researching the Southwest borderlands, including Esteban Azcona, Cándida Jáquez, and Peter J. García.

According to ethnomusicologist Helena Simonett, folk music began to draw ethnomusicologists to urban ground—a shift that was kindled by large-scale migration of the people who were regarded as the tradition bearers into the cities. For a long time, folklorists have come to the conclusion that both conservative and innovative forces operate on the traditional cultures that rural immigrants bring with them, acknowledging that the new contexts for social life generate new traditions of their own that are genuinely urban. Of course, folk music in the city does change meanings and continues to be subjected to continuous transformations. In this way, folk music may no longer be viewed as a symbol of the stability and continuity of rural traditions. Scholars have long recognized that tradition is a dynamic cultural invention that is constantly changing as people attempt to maintain older musical styles, dances, and genres while assimilating new and diverse forms of musical and dance entertainment.

Popular music in the United States is perceived as emerging from urban centers and disseminated through sheet music, radio, television, and commercial recordings. It is readily comprehensible to (and perhaps also performable by) a large proportion of the populace, it is used primarily for entertainment, and its appreciation presupposes little or no knowledge of musical theory or (formal) techniques. Since the mid-twentieth century, the categories of popular music, folk music traditions, and art music have been considered to be superficial, due to the similarities and substantial overlap in repertory, especially in Latin America and the Caribbean. In fact, popular music genres in México (and other parts of Latin America and the Caribbean) such as the **son*, the *corrido*, and the *canción ranchera* were often urban renditions of folk genres, whereas the most popular "folk songs" were influenced by nineteenth-century European salon music and opera.

West Coast Latino Music Studies

Ethnomusicologist Steven Loza's *Barrio Rhythm: Mexican American Music in Los Angeles* (1993) attempts to broach history and ethnomusicology in an ambitious work. A native of East Los Angeles, Loza completed his graduate studies at the University of California, Los Angeles (UCLA), where he has taught for several years. Loza's book is the first serious response to Manuel Peña's admonition that "of the three most important areas inhabited by people of Spanish-Mexican descent for as long as three centuries, only California has remained relatively unexplored with respect to the music of this ethnic minority." Loza has also produced some relevant articles; one titled "From Veracruz to Los Angeles: The Reinterpretation of the Son Jarocho" (1992) examines how the genre was diffused, transformed, and appropriated to an urban metropolis by *Los Lobos. Another article, "Contemporary Ethnomusicology in Mexico," provides a very general overview of cultural centers, museums, and academic institutions that sponsor musical research south of the border. Other useful works include a monograph, *Land of a Thousand Dances: Chicano Rock 'n' Roll from Southern California* (1998). The book covers all of the best-known groups including Ritchie *Valens, Carlos *Santana, Thee Midniters, Cannibal and the Headhunters, Tierra, *El Chicano, and lesser-known Chicano punk groups like The Brat, The Illegals, The Undertakers, and the Plugz (now known as Los Cruzados). Likewise, George Lipsitz's *Time Passages* (1990) provides an analysis of Los Lobos as a local Los Angeles band that moved into the American popular music mainstream. Helena Simonett's research on **banda* music in Los Angeles and her earlier research on the social history of Sinaloan band music (1999) and *banda* in southern California have proved invaluable. Simonett's article "Narcocorridos in Nuevo L.A." (2001) is the first investigation of this new subgenre of Mexican balladry. Bostonian journalist Elijah Wald's book on *narcocorridos* also includes an excellent disc recording of many salient contemporary artists including *Los Tigres del Norte and the late Chalino Sánchez.

New Mexican Music, Ritual, and Dance Investigations, and Gender Studies

One of Loza's students is Brenda Romero, a native of New Mexico and currently teaching at the University of Colorado at Boulder. Romero's unpublished Ph.D. dissertation on the **matachines* dance in northern New Mexico (1993) and another ethnographic investigation completed by anthropologist Sylvia Rodríguez (1996) are the two most important studies on this topic in New Mexico to date. Continuing an emphasis on Latino/indigenous interaction, Romero has recently extended her work on the *matachines* to México, and in another article she explores the effects of New Mexico's border status on the gendered musical construction of the *indita* in New Mexico (2002). Today, much music research continues to be completed by folklorists, especially in Texas and New Mexico. Arizona is seriously lacking in ethnomusicology and musical folklore research of Latina/o music cultures.

Literary folklorist Enrique Lamadrid has completed several important studies including a compact disc collection of New Mexican folk and traditional music, several important journal articles, and a book on the Indo-Hispano tradition of Comanchitos in New Mexico. The works of feminist and literary scholar María Herrera-Sobek address the "Mexican Immigrant Experience in Ballad and Song" (1993). She was also first to complete an earlier feminist analysis of the Mexican *corrido* (1990) and of the Chicano/a *décima* in New Mexico using archival materials (1989). Her studies analyze ballad narratives, feminine archetypes, and gender inequality, and champion the traditional agrarian values of hard work, honesty, simplicity, and morality.

Caribbean and Latin American Music in the United States

Since 1900, thousands of people from the Caribbean islands of Cuba, Puerto Rico, Haiti, and the Dominican Republic and from all over Latin America continue to migrate to the urban areas of the United States, where they maintain older folk traditions and invent new popular genres. From these communities many diverse and hybrid Afro-Caribbean and Latin jazz music and dance styles have turned into popular trends and "crazes" for the larger Latina/o communities and have been especially appealing to non-Latin peoples in the United States. The Afro-Cuban *rumba of the 1930s, the Afro-Brazilian *samba of the 1940s and *bossa nova of the 1960s, the Afro-Caribbean *mambo and *cha cha cha in the 1950s, and *salsa in the 1970s have all been integral to the popular music history of the United States. Yet very little research has been conducted on these styles and genres and the artists who promoted and performed them in the United States. According to ethnomusicologist Gerard Béhague, "the Argentine **tango* was introduced to the United States via Broadway in 1913." Early studies of Latina/o music in U.S. cities include two interesting but dated works by Carlota Garfias, *Mexican Folklore Collected in New York City* (1938) and *Puerto Rican Children's Songs in New York* (1958).

More recent works by Latina/o scholars include Steve Loza's ethnomusicological study of Tito *Puente titled *Tito Puente and the Making of Latin Music* (1999); Frances Aparicio's *Listening to Salsa: Gender, Latin Popular Music, and Puerto Rican Cultures* (1998); and Gerard Béhague's edited volume titled *Music and Black Ethnicity: The Caribbean and South America* (1994). Other important works include Peter Manuel's *Caribbean Currents from Rumba to Raggae* (1995); Robin Moore's *Nationalizing Blackness: Afro-Cubanismo and Artistic Revolution in Havana, 1920–1940* (1997); and Lise Waxer's *Situating Salsa: Global Markets and Local Meanings in Latin Popular Music* (2002). To date the most comprehensive and useful study of Caribbean and Latin American music in the United States is John Robert Storm's *The Latin Tinge: The Impact of Latin American Music in the United States* (1999).

Further Reading

Loza, Steve. *Tito Puente: The Making of Latin Music.* Urbana: University of Illinois Press, 1999.

Myers, Helen. "Ethnomusicology." In *Ethnomusicology: An Introduction.* New York: W.W. Norton, 1992.

Peña, Manuel. *Música Tejana: The Cultural Economy of Artistic Transformation.* College Station: Texas A&M Press, 1999.

Romero, Brenda. "Cultural Interaction in the Matachines Dance." In *Musics of Multicultural Americas*, edited by Kip Lornell and Anne Rasmussen. New York: Macmillan, 1997.

Romero, Brenda. "The Indita Genre of New Mexico: Gender and Cultural Identification." In *Changing Chicana Traditions: Continuity and Change*, edited by Olga Nájera-Ramirez and Olga Cantú. Chicago: University of Illinois Press, 2002.

Simonett, Helena. *Banda: Mexican Musical Life across Borders*. Middletown, CT: Wesleyan University Press, 2001.

Peter J. García

Family. In the twenty-first century the Latina/Latino population became the largest ethnic minority group in the United States. That fact led to widespread interest among the general public as well as among policymakers in the characteristics of Latina/o family structures and values, for families and the kinship system of *familia* and *compadrazgo* (i.e., blood relations and extended family ties) generally are considered to form much of the basic core of the human social contract. Thus, as consumers and contributors Latina/o families represent a primary influence on the shape and development of all aspects of popular culture in the United States.

According to the 2000 U.S. Census, the demographic subset of over 32 million Latinas/os comprises over 12 percent of the total population of the United States and constitutes a remarkably diverse subset of numerous nationalities, *races, and ranges of citizenship status. Of this number, 58 percent are of Mexican origin; 10 percent, Puerto Rican; 3 percent, Cuban; and 29 percent, other Hispanic origin. Clearly, then, these groups are marked by very distinct histories and varying circumstances of birth, *immigration, and/or arrival into the United States, all of which often produce starkly different traits and perspectives. Despite these differences, however, these groups nonetheless share a common Spanish heritage, culture, history, and language.

Some of the differences include historical variations from group to group. For instance, the ancestors of today's Mexican Americans (also known as Chicanas and *Chicanos) were conquered as a result of the Mexican War, which concluded with the 1848 *Treaty of Guadalupe Hidalgo and the incorporation of over one-third of the original Mexican land base into the continental United States. Since that watershed event, travel between the United

States and México has been continual across open borders with, for the most part, generally mutual intercultural and transnational benefits. The constant border crossing and immigration into the United States have been of both the legal (i.e., with official documentation) and the illegal (undocumented) varieties, resulting in first- and second-generation Mexican family identities often being defined by the nature of their first arrival. Puerto Ricans, on the other hand, are U.S. citizens by virtue of the island of Puerto Rico existing as a U.S. commonwealth. To a significant degree the migratory path between the island with its over 3.5 million residents and New York City helps to define Puerto Rican and Nuyorican family identities. Also contributing to that identity is the political debate about Puerto Rico's commonwealth status or whether to seek an independent nation status or ratification as the fifty-first state in the Union. Likewise, *Cuban Americans are descendants of a Caribbean island heritage, and they too are marked by unique circumstances. A great many of them and their descendants consider themselves exiles who were forced to migrate into the United States after the *Cuban Revolution and Fidel *Castro deposed U.S.-backed dictator Fulgencio Batista. Because of their political status as refugees, Cuban Americans are seen by many to possess an advantaged position in American society relative to that of other Latina/o immigrants. Other groups—Bolivians, Ecuadorians, Peruvians, Colombians, Chileños, Nicaraguans, Guatemalans, Argentines, and Panamanians—also have divergent histories that have often included countries whose governments have been at war with one another. Many Latinas and Latinos arrive in the United States as undocumented workers, as well as middle-class, educated individuals seeking refuge from deteriorated political and economic circumstances in their home countries.

Stark as these crucial differences among an amazingly diverse Latina/o population are, it is still possible to describe certain shared and distinctive characteristics to the Latina/o *familia*. Based on the 2000 U.S. Census findings, for example, Hispanics are more likely than non-Hispanic whites to be under eighteen years of age, and one in four foreign-born Hispanics (i.e., 25 percent) are naturalized citizens. Seventy-two percent of Hispanics who entered the United States before 1970 obtained citizenship in 2000, while fewer than 7 percent of those immigrating between 1990 and 2000 were citizens. Further, Hispanic households tend to be larger in size than those of non-Hispanic Caucasians (30.6 percent versus 11.89 percent, with five or more persons per household), and more Hispanics of fifteen years of age or older are more likely to be married. Only approximately 40 percent of Hispanics have a high school education, and this statistic also includes Cuban Americans who reflect the general Latina/o population in this as well as other demographic features. Hispanics have higher levels of unemployment, hold more service, operator, and laborer jobs, and less professional and managerial jobs, and as a consequence are more likely than non-Hispanics to live in poverty. Puerto Ricans and Mexicans have higher fertility rates than non-

Hispanic Caucasians, and among younger women, childbearing fertility often results in having children prior to marriage.

Among the more dramatic characteristics of the Latina/o population is the evidence of a growing feminization of poverty, a concept that refers to the deteriorated economic condition of most women, children, and families in single parent female households. For example, although Hispanic children constitute 16.2 percent of the population, they represent over 29 percent of all children in poverty. Many studies have shown that among all ethnic and racial groups, families headed by women suffer lower income levels and thus are much poorer than families in general. Nevertheless, despite this overall trend, whether caused by divorce or separation or nonmarital childbearing, the feminization of poverty generally affects non-Hispanic women more than minority women even though the percentage of unmarried women who head families has increased moderately among Mexican, Cuban, Asian, and American Indian women. Puerto Rican and African American women generally are less likely to be married and more likely to head families on their own and, consequently, are more likely to have children at younger ages and prior to marriage.

Unlike the female head of household profile just described, the traditional patriarchal view of the Latino family is founded on the cultural belief in male superiority and the parallel belief in the inferiority of women. This perspective has its roots in Spanish law and was transmitted to the Americas with colonialism after 1492 and the Christopher *Columbus voyages of exploration and conquest. It also reflects the stereotypical view of the Mexican and Mexican American family that historically has defined sexual roles in families as being male dominant with the husband entitled to unquestioning obedience from his wife. Accordingly, while the female is expected to be loyal to her husband and children, free sexual expression (i.e., promiscuity) is the norm for males. Within this perspective of familism, the patriarchal and authoritarian *familia* is considered more important as an entity for the transmission of social values and economic exchange than are individual members of the family, although the birth of a male child is usually more desirable than a female in this context. In spite of the defining traits of masculine superiority, father dominance, and emphasis on submission to custom and authority, it is generally perceived that Mexican American fathers tend to be more openly affectionate with their children than Mexican fathers.

In the late twentieth century, there were many challenges to the traditional view of the family, and the idea of an unchanging family structure does not hold under close scrutiny either in México, the United States, or among other immigrant Latin Americans. An apt illustration of this evolution may be seen in the popular Mexican *film *Cuando los hijos se van* (When One's Children Leave Home) that was first filmed in 1941, 1957, 1969, and later as a *telenovela* (*Spanish-language television soap opera). The story depicts the struggles of keeping a family together and also portrays the nature of *mexi-*

canidad (Mexicanness). Among the changes in family life and values over time is the loss of the male patriarch's prestige and power within the family. In the original versions the traditional views are challenged vigorously by rebellious children and external social forces, but in the end those views are upheld. In the later films, however, the behavior and values shift. Machismo (or exaggerated masculinity) is depicted as antiquated, and independent women are portrayed as thriving human beings. Other drastic changes in this and other Mexican and Latina/o films reflect the dynamic nature of both *mexicanidad* and *latinidad*, including gender-bending social roles, ethnic and racial tolerance, capitalist ethics, mobile social class, altered views of the church, and migration to the United States. The point to be emphasized is that the idea of a traditional nonchanging Latina/o culture is an illusion, and this is true as well for the basic core family unit.

The *familia* has changed to adapt to changing times and influences, just as have speech and language, music, art, film, *sports, and countless other popular culture forms and practices. Accordingly, Spanish-language *telenovelas* are an important part of entertainment for many Latina/o families. The role they play in the formation of personal and family values varies among socioeconomic and educational levels. Some critics perceive them as propaganda tools to distract their consumers from political consciousness to their poverty and difficult lives. This perspective criticizes the dominant culture imagery typically portrayed that makes certain that no barefoot children or other real-life examples of suffering are shown. Similarly, the gap between rich and poor, politics, terrorism, guerrillas, and drugs or illicit drug use all are ignored or sanitized. These portrayals of Latina/o, usually Mexican, *familias* pervade the television airwaves and impact perceptions with respect to family life and the nature of community.

Sociologists and other social scientists have differed with regard to what happens to Latina/o families after their arrival to the United States. Some believe that as families move from México and other Latin American countries to the United States, women's relationships with men become more equitable, as both genders enter the workforce for economic survival. Others argue that such a view is biased because it begins from the antiquated position that the original Mexican and Latina/o culture is static. Most researchers agree that immigrant families are impacted by a variety of social forces after arriving in the United States, resulting in continual change and adaptation among Latina/o families and culture. This assimilation—that is, the acquisition of language, values, and behavioral patterns of the majority or dominant group—normally leads to the progressive loss of language from one generation to another and in some instances to intermarriage. Inevitably acculturation, which refers to a process of adaptation to one culture when it comes into contact with another, occurs with a resultant exchange and transfer of identity traits between Hispanics and other Americans.

Among the variety of social and cultural forces that have had considerable effect on Latina/o families and culture is military service. Since World War

II especially, serving in the armed forces has been a dominant force in the acculturation of families, and it has led to strong integration into the mainstream of American life through such organizations as the *American G.I. Forum and the League of United Latin American Citizens (*LULAC). More negative forces also have altered family life, notably the marketing and use of illicit drugs, which influences individuals to violate both family and community norms. Experts on social deviance and prison life in the United States report that Hispanics are overrepresented in the prison system and like other inmates have been used for medical and other technoscientific studies that impact issues of privacy and human rights for all. Similarly, extensive studies have shown that the politics and public policy that led to the development of *maquiladoras* (transnational factories) along the Mexican border severely disrupted family life by generally excluding male workers in favor of women who are hired to work for less pay.

Hispanic families have been affected along with millions of others by the pervasive public forces of unchecked materialism, consumerism, media, advertising, and marketing. These unchecked forces are central to the globalization of commerce through political power and media marketing, forces that promote a "me" culture of unchecked narcissism quite contrary to basic family values whether of middle-class Americans or middle-class Latina/o Americans. Combined with the fast-paced world of cyber information and digital technology, these commercial forces create illusions of dialog and community that mask an ideology of unchecked capitalism and consumerism, which in turn promotes widespread conformity and complacency. Embracing capitalist materialism often forces young people especially to devote their lives to consumption and entertainment, devoid of the traditional human ideals of creativity and overcoming the selfishness of infancy. Unsurprisingly in this context, some of the most highly marketed media entertainment icons of the 1990s and twenty-first century have been such corporate constructions as Christina *Aguilera, Ricky *Martin, Jennifer *López, Mariah *Carey, Mario Quintero, and other entertainment stars built to appeal to vast Latina/o global markets.

Future trends that will likely impact the shape and health of Latina/o families are many. Some specialists identify the major challenges facing the Hispanic community and the family to be *globalization and the global economy, immigration, the feminization of poverty, and educational retention. Globalization not only creates economic opportunities but also produces problems that transcend international boundaries related to drug trafficking, crime, and illegal immigration. Immigration also presents special challenges to the general community—including Hispanics—related to a burgeoning population with an ever-increasing diversity of class, race, gender, employment, and other factors that create social stress and conflict. The feminization of poverty causes major stresses on children, women, and family health that are particularly difficult to Hispanic families. Finally, in view of the youthfulness of the Latina/o population, the gap between the educated class and the undereducated and illiterate classes makes educational retention one of the most pressing issues facing the United States in the long term.

In spite of the many challenges facing Latinas/os in the United States indicated in the 2000 census, the instances of successful families are also significantly increasing. Many scholars believe that the survival and vigor of the Latina/o population historically are a result of the effective transmission of a healthy *familia* system over the centuries. As a result, Hispanics are rapidly integrating into politics, business, education, and public service. Some family researchers argue that one of the central issues characterizing successful Latina/o family life in the United States consists of a positive attitude toward life. They note that such a spirit of optimism is an effective counter against becoming embittered by personal tragedy and disappointment and thereby transforms that suffering into personal energy and collective power. Central to this spirit is the philosophy of assuming individual responsibility and not blaming others for their circumstances. Such use of the cultural gifts of intelligence, courage, and *familia* is crucial to fostering the critical consciousness needed to transform the world for the better.

Further Reading

Berg, Charles Ramírez. *Cinema of Solitude: A Critical Study of Mexican Film, 1967–1983*. Austin: University of Texas Press, 1992.

Fox, Geoffrey. *Hispanic Nation: Culture, Politics, and the Construction of Identity*. Tucson: University of Arizona Press, 1996.

Griswold del Castillo, Richard. *La familia: Chicano Families in the Urban Southwest: 1848 to the Present*. Notre Dame, IN: University of Notre Dame Press, 1984.

Montiel, Miguel, and Felipe de Ortego y Gasca. "Chicanos, Community and Change." In *Community Organizing in a Diverse Society*, edited by John Erlich and Felix Rivera. Needham Heights, MA: Allyn and Bacon, 1992.

United States Census Bureau. http://www.census.gov/pubinfo/www/hisphot1.html.

Zambrana, Ruth, ed. *Understanding Latino Families: Scholarship, Policy, and Practice*. Thousand Oaks, CA: Sage, 1995.

Miguel Montiel

Fandango. *Fandango* originally referred to a Spanish dance involving castanets, but since the eighteenth century it has referred to a party or dance. The term was initially used in parts of the southern United States during the early eighteenth century to describe an actual location where dancing and gambling festivities take place. The fandango reached a peak by the 1860s in Texas but eventually declined due to city ordinances prohibiting this form of entertainment. Despite the ban in Texas, fandangos continued throughout the late nineteenth century. U.S. military accounts for the 1850s describe the difference between a **baile* and a fandango, where a *baile* is defined as "a select gathering of invited guests for dancing and general jollification and amusement," whereas "a *fandango* is open and free for all." Elite and aristocratic females did not attend fandangos, and the gentlemen only attended in a "half-way clandestine manner." Some of the early literature on the Gold Rush regions of California mention fandango houses, like those of Texas, especially in communities with large Mexican populations. In Los Angeles a fandango was a public affair that included an assembly of the most disparate and diverse segments of the city's population, where everybody came extravagantly dressed.

Further Reading

Bell, Major Horace. *Reminiscences of a Ranger; or Early Times in Southern California*. Illustrations by James S. Bodrero. Santa Barbara, CA: Wallace Hebberd, 1927.

Peter J. García

Fashion and Clothing. Fashion and clothing are a complex reflection of society. In its most basic form as apparel, clothing is recognized as one of the material essentials for human survival—that is, *food, shelter, and clothing. As fashion, whether haute couture or more ordinary styles for work and recreational activities, clothes also incorporate complex aesthetics from the arts and a variety of pop culture trends. Clothing and the accessories associated with it are among the most important consumer products in human history and, thus, are keenly relevant to Latina and Latino popular cultures in the United States. Highly regulated by both profit-making commerce and social convention, the modes of fashion and clothing are culturally determined by such factors as geography, climate, native textiles, and other material resources, as well as by ethnic customs and individual personal taste. For example, the use of fur in the Arctic regions and grass fibers in tropical island regions historically were dictated primarily by weather and the availability of materials. Since the twentieth-century development of synthetic fabrics and the use of centralized heating and cooling in architecture, fur and grass for the most part have diminished as indispensable for clothing purposes and have increased as aesthetic options of fashion. These changes have resulted in parallel changes in ethnic customs, social trends, and individual taste.

The fashion and clothing of Latinas and Latinos in the United States reflect the diverse customs and values of specific cultural and geographical backgrounds, as well as reflect and contribute to the popular trends of the predominant mass American society. The Latina/Latino vocabulary of fashion consists of numerous recognizable forms of dress that have been documented by and disseminated through the discourses of *history, literature, *film, and other media. Latina/o fashion styles include:

1. The commonplace, functional sleeveless shirt known as a *huipil* (or *güipil*) worn by pre-Columbian natives of the Yucatán and still seen among the Maya;

2. The familiar and popular *rebozo*, or plain shawl covering, of Spain, México, Central and South America, and the Caribbean;
3. The figures of Christopher *Columbus and other European explorers in cape and tricornered seafarer hats romanticized in numerous tableaux;
4. The *conquistadores* (Spanish conquerors) in Roman-style helmets;
5. The woven multicolored shawl covering called a *sarape* and the similar *poncho*, which are commonly used by many indigenous and mestizo people of México and the American Southwest;
6. The simple, usually inexpensive leather shoes, *huaraches*;
7. The silver-studded, usually black equestrian outfit of the *charrería* (traditional Mexican rodeo) known as the *traje de charro*; and
8. The sombrero, the familiar straw or felt hat that first appeared in the fifteenth century and is widely popular in México, in the southwestern United States, and to some extent in Spain.

The garb of the *charrería* for male equestrians, called **charros*, has carried over to other popular entertainment as in the costuming of *mariachi musicians and movie roles like many portrayed by romantic singer actor Pedro Infante. Among certain social groups and villages the *trajes de charro* in black and silver (or sometimes brown and gold) with white shirt and red string tie are occasionally worn as formal dress (like military uniforms and tartan kilts) during times of celebration. Other familiar staples of the *charro* or the original *jinete* (equestrian) and *vaquero* (cowboy) apparel include *botas* (boots), *estribos* (stirrups), sombrero, lariat, and other ranch and rodeo-related items whose names have entered the mainstream American English vocabulary without need for translation. The *appropriation of the *charro* style for crossover to mass commercial pop culture prevails throughout the entire cowboy genre whether literary, in the visual arts, in film and media, or in grassroots pastimes like rodeos and state and county fairs. Striking examples of the mass commercial success of this appropriation include the movie and television hits featuring the legendary Hollywood cowboy swashbucklers Lash LaRue, the Cisco Kid, and Zorro, all clad in the black and silver garb of the antihero borrowed from the *charro*.

Also derived from the equestrian tradition is the fashion associated with the Mexican *revolucionario*, as in the now-iconic pictures of the revolutionaries Emiliano *Zapata and Pancho *Villa with their crisscrossed cartridge belts (*see* History, Chicana/o and Mexican American). The *revolucionario* as freedom fighter was made famous in such films dating as far back as 1914 and *The Life of General Villa*, directed by Raoul Walsh with actual footage of Villa himself, as well as in the 1952 hit *Viva Zapata*, starring Marlon Brando. These and other movie portrayals compared the spirit and courage of Mexican rebels fighting Spanish colonialist tyranny to the freedom-fighting qualities historically ascribed to such North American revolutionary fighters against English tyranny as Nathan Hale and Paul Revere. Persisting into the twenty-first century, the *revolucionario* legend was reinterpreted yet again in the highly hyped, made-for-HBO feature-length movie *And Starring Pancho Villa as Himself* (2003), starring Antonio Banderas.

In stark contrast to the traditional borderlands ranching fashion of the *charro*, *jinete*, and *revolucionario* derivatives is the *zoot suit style associated with the Pachucos (street dudes) of urban *barrios. The masculine zoot suit represents an extreme version of the Western world's conventional three-piece business suit for men appropriated with theatrical verve by marginalized men of color not welcomed to Wall Street and other corridors of majority culture power. Made famous in the 1981 Luis *Valdez movie **Zoot Suit*, parts of the style date as far back as the Harlem Renaissance of the 1920s and 1930s and such jazz-era musicians as Duke Ellington. A detailed description of the outfit and its wearers is memorialized by Ralph Ellison in his classic novel *Invisible Man* (1952). What makes the fashion theatrically ostentatious are such deliberately oversized features as wide-shouldered jackets and baggy draped pants accented with flashy supersized watch chains often drooping below the knee. In one form or another, the zoot suit had a discernible impact on such crossover masculine fashions as those of the film noir private eye, the motion picture mafia dons, the trench-coated G-men, and their spinoffs.

Latina apparel mirrors that of men's in reflecting cultural and geographic backgrounds, even though the Latina/o fashion vocabulary contains fewer recognizable popular styles that have been identified as specifically "Latina." This may be because books and movies tend to focus on the public roles of history, and these traditionally have been performed by men. The indigenous women's clothing of pre-Columbian Mesoamerica was marked by the same functional simplicity still visible in twenty-first-century versions of sleeveless-shirt *huipiles* and tunic-cut *arpillera* blouses, even though the latter have evolved to meet tourist demand for more refined weavings and colorful embroideries than their coarse sackcloth prototypes. Spanish women's styles that arrived in America in the sixteenth century did not differ greatly from that of other European women's dress fashions of the era. The *vestido* or *traje de dama* (lady's outfit) typical of Spanish women and, later, of *criollas* (Caucasian women born in the Americas) disclosed their status as members of the elite class of colonizers. The billowing skirts, refined fabrics, petticoats, corsets, and laces of the *vestidos de dama* also reflected the fact that the wearers of these dresses normally did not engage in independent public activities considered *trabajo de hombre* (men's work) or in extensive menial labor considered *trabajo de criada* (servants' work). Thus, if Latin*o* fashion is linked to horsemanship and public activity, then Latin*a* styles conveyed an opposite emphasis on home-bound domesticity. Arguably the most commonplace vestige of this feminine dress tradition is found in the fancy gowns associated with weddings, first communion, and **quinceañera* rituals.

One well-known accessory of a traditional Spanish and Latina lady's fancy ballgown is the mantilla, a usually lacy silk scarf sometimes worn over an ivory comb to produce a tiara effect. However, like traditional bonnets and hats, the mantilla has diminished in usage as a widespread trend among Latinas in the twenty-first century. Another familiar style associated with Latinas and other working-class women of color is the so-called peasant blouse, a usually white blouse gathered at a round-scooped neckline that can be lowered provocatively off the shoulder. Popularized by the title character in Georges Bizet's opera *Carmen* (1875), the peasant blouse and its variations have been worn by countless female stars from Carmen *Miranda, Rita *Hayworth, and Jane Russell to Rita *Moreno, Natalie Wood, and Jennifer *López. Accordingly, movies and television are prominent purveyors of fashion and clothing styles. The novel of social reform and romance **Ramona* (1884), for example, contributed to the Spanish Fantasy romanticization of nineteenth-century California. The book also inspired a classic love song of the same title and is still commemorated annually in the *Ramona* Outdoor Play staged as community *theater by the people of Hemet and San Jacinto in Riverside County since 1923. The *Ramona* show featuring a cast of hundreds is performed in a natural amphitheater south of Hemet, California; its April and May 2004 performances marked its eighty-first year of production. Serving as a source for the *Californio* fashion adapted to movie versions of the novel, the plain *traje de dama* worn by Ramona's stepmother, Señora Moreno, and her class came to typify hacienda life as a practical yet elegant simplicity. The ensemble is replicated in the travel dress worn by Mexican actor Katy *Jurado in the role of Helen Ramirez in the classic western **High Noon*. The *Ramona* borderlands pastoral style perpetuated in the annual Riverside County Outdoor Play presents the novel's Indian protagonist, Alessandro, and his fellow native workers wearing a straight-cut tunic version of the common *huipil* worn over loose plain trousers.

The fashion of the borderlands pastoral and the urban *barrio combine in the late-twentieth-century style popularized by rap-inspired *hip-hop **cholo* garb. Worn by Chicano/Latino boys and young men, the *cholo* style combines the loose-fitting comfort of the *huipil* with the baggy draping of the Pachucos' zoot suit and features beltless cutoffs or pants falling below the waist to expose underwear and tattoos in a countercultural "¿Y qué?" (So what?) to adult conventions. Widely associated with *gangs and gangsta rap, the *cholo* look appears on countless CD album covers and in movie portrayals of youth such as **American Me*, **La Bamba*, and **Selena*.

In terms of high fashion, except for the Spaniard Cristóbal Balenciaga (1895–1972) and the Dominican Oscar de la Renta (1932–), Latinas and Latinos are more commonly associated with the cheap sweatshop laborers who make the haute couture fashion industry possible than with designer labels and boardwalks. The sweatshop reality of low-paid immigrant labor is depicted in the movies **El Norte* and **Real Women Have Curves*. That fashion and clothing incorporate this socioeconomic reality as well as the aesthetics of art and pop culture further deepens the complexity of clothes and fashion accessories as commodity, commerce, and custom. One Latina writer keenly aware of this fact—Estela *Portillo Trambley—evocatively captures this layered complexity in her classic feminist story "The Paris Gown" (1975). She employs the title's *traje de dama* as a wedding gown to represent the conflicting desires hidden beneath the surface of social customs associated with love, courtship, and sexuality. Taking place in a border zone of Mexican/Chicano culture and psychology, the tale dramatizes the bilingual, bicultural rebellion of its girl protagonist against the constrictions of patriarchal power symbolized by the Paris designer dress. The gown and the girl's rebellion in individualizing how she *nakedly* "wears" it stunningly capture the interlocking issues of gender, sexuality, and ethnicity that define human relations and that also explain the profit-making commerce and social conventions that influence them, as well as fashion and clothing.

Further Reading

Castro, Rafaela G. *Chicano Folklore: A Guide to the Folktales, Traditions, Rituals and Religious Practices of Mexican-Americans*. New York: Oxford University Press, 2001.

Gran Diccionario Enciclopedico Ilustrado. Vols. 9–10. Mexico City: Reader's Digest Mexico, 1979.

Cordelia Chávez Candelaria

Feliciano, José (1945–). Critics and musicians consider singer and acoustic guitarist José Feliciano to be the first major crossover artist who paved the road for younger generations of Latino artists in the United States. Born on September 10, 1945, in Lares, Puerto Rico, Feliciano is one of eleven children born to a longshoreman father and nightclub owner mother. Although he was born blind, he became interested in music at the age of three when he played on a tin cracker can with his uncle. He emigrated with his family at the age of five to New York. Throughout his adolescent years, Feliciano was an active student in the arts, playing everything from the concertina to the accordion and even performing at the Puerto Rican Theatre in New York. He learned as much from records as from his teachers. The rock and roll music of the 1950s had an impact on Feliciano, and he began to sing and play the guitar in coffeehouses in Greenwich Village to assist his family during low economic times. Feliciano actually broke into the music industry by singing in Spanish.

In 1966 when Feliciano performed at Mar del Plata Festival in Argentina, the RCA producers in Buenos Aires recommended that Feliciano record an album of Spanish music, especially the *boleros that he had heard during his childhood. He took classic songs and added the influences of jazz and modern music to create a style of music all his own, a fusion of the traditional Spanish lyrics with modern musical instrumentation. At the age of twenty-

José Feliciano. *Courtesy of Photofest.*

three, Feliciano had already earned two Grammy Awards, including Best New Artist for his 1968 single "Light My Fire," which combined soul, Latin, and folk-rock and reached number four in the pop charts, and recorded several albums in English as well as Spanish. Feliciano has since expanded his talents by taking on acting roles in *film and television, including the film *Fargo* (1996).

Feliciano is well known for three songs in particular: "Light My Fire," which is now a "standard" due to his interpretation; "Che Sera," a mega-success in Europe, Asia, and South America; and "Feliz Navidad," the Christmas song that has now become a worldwide staple of the *holiday season. His artistry was honored in 1996, when he received *Billboard* magazine's Lifetime Achievement Award.

As well, the local government of New York City has paid tribute to Feliciano by renaming Public School 155 in East Harlem, dedicating it as The José Feliciano Performing Arts School.

In May 2001, Feliciano received an honorary Doctor of Humane Letters degree from Sacred Heart University in Fairfield, Connecticut, for his musical as well as humanitarian contributions to the world over the last thirty years. Having recorded over sixty-five albums throughout his life, Feliciano has collaborated with other Latin artists including Gloria *Estefan and Marc *Anthony, earned more than thirty gold records in various countries, and received an Emmy nomination for the television theme of *Chico and the Man* in 1974.

His selected discography includes *The Voice and Guitar of José Feliciano* (1964), *Souled* (1969), *Feliz Navidad* (1970), *Che Sera* (1971), *A Spanish Portrait* (1972), *Sweet Soul Music* (1976), *El latino romántico* (1985), *Gracias, mi gente* (1987), *Latin Street* (1992), and *Señor Bolero* (1998).

Further Reading

Hardy, Phil, and Dave Laing, eds. *Encyclopedia of Rock*. New York: Schirmer, 1988.

Heatley, Michael, ed. *The Ultimate Encyclopedia of Rock*. New York: HarperCollins, 1993.

Slonimsky, Nicolas, ed. *Baker's Biographical Dictionary of Musicians*. 8th ed. New York: Schirmer, 1992.

Stambler, Irwin. *Encyclopedia of Pop, Rock & Soul*. Rev. ed. New York: St. Martin's Press, 1977.

Juanita Heredia

Félix, María (1914–2002). Legendary screen diva María de los Ángeles Félix Guereña starred in forty-seven movies produced in México, France, Argentina, Italy, and Spain. She rose to fame during the Época de Oro del Cine Mexicano (The Golden Age of Mexican Cinema) of the 1930s through the 1950s. Félix was born in Álamos, Sonora, on April 8, 1914; her father, Bernardo Félix, was part Yaqui (Yoeme), and her mother, Josefina Guereña, was of Spanish descent.

Félix debuted in the *film *El Peñón de las Ánimas* (The Rock of the Souls, 1942) with Mexican actor/singer Jorge Negrete. Among her other famous films are *Doña Bárbara* (1943), from which she would take her nickname of La Doña; *La Monja alférez* (The Assistant Nun, 1944); *Enamorada* (Enamored, 1946); *Tizoc* (1956), with Mexican actor/singer Pedro Infante; *La Cucaracha* (The Cockroach, 1959), with Dolores *Del Río; and *Juana Gallo* (Juana Rooster, 1960). Although Félix developed a career in Europe and Latin America, she never wanted to learn English and work in Hollywood. Among the movies produced in Europe are *Mare Nostrum* (1948, Italy-Spain); *Una mujer cualquiera* (Any Woman, 1949, Spain), and *French Can Can* (1954, France-Italy).

The distinctions received by Félix during her career include the *Commandeur dans l'Ordre National des Arts et des Lettres* (Commander in the National Order of Arts and Letters), awarded by the French government in 1996, and three Ariel awards, presented by the Mexican Film Academy. Félix was married four times. Her first husband was Enrique Álvarez, the father of her only child Enrique Álvarez Félix (1934–1996), who also became an actor. Félix also married Agustín Lara (1943), an internationally known Mexican singer and composer; Jorge Negrete (1952), another icon of the Golden Age of Mexican Cinema; and Alex Berger (1956), a French businessman.

Félix inspired works by several artists: Famed Mexican composer Agustín Lara wrote several songs for her, including "María Bonita," and she was also painted by such famous artists as Diego *Rivera and Leonora Carrington. Félix died in Mexico City on April 8, 2002. Her funeral brought an immense sense of national mourning, and tens of thousands of fans came from all over México for the viewing at the Palacio de Bellas Artes (Palace of Fine Arts) to pay their last respects.

Further Reading

Keller, Gary D. *A Biographical Handbook of Hispanics and United States Film.* Tempe, AZ: Bilingual Press, 1997.

Dulce Aldama

Fender, Freddy (1937–). Freddy Fender, singer, songwriter, and actor, has left his footprint on every decade since 1947, when he performed for the first time at the age of ten. His music has spanned a variety of genres, including *Tejano, *conjunto*, country western, rhythm and blues, Cajun funk, rockabilly, and rock and roll, creating a broad audience appeal, which accounts for his continued popularity decade after decade.

Fender was born Baldemar Huerta, on June 4, 1937, in San Benito, Texas. With no formal training, Fender starting singing at a young age and developed his skills and style by watching Tex-Mex musicians perform at neighborhood celebrations and learning blues from black migrant workers he befriended while working in the fields. After dropping out of school at the age of sixteen, he spent the next three years of his life in the marines. Upon his discharge, he found his way back into the world of music and to Hollywood, where he signed on with Imperial Records. He released his first recordings under his given name, but by 1959, he decided to change his name to something that sounded more Anglo, in hopes of attracting a broader audience base. The last name came from the Fender guitar he played, and he chose "Freddy" because it is alliterative and he thought they sounded good together. The combination proved to be very successful.

Freddy Fender. *Courtesy of Photofest.*

The 1960s brought success and devastation for Fender when he released the wildly popular "Wasted Days and Wasted Nights," a national hit that he would rerelease fifteen years later to the joy of a new generation. The song title proved to be prophetic as Fender was convicted that same year for possession of marijuana and sent to Angola State Prison in Louisiana, where he served three years of his five-year sentence. After his release from prison, Fender stayed in Louisiana for a few years, getting acquainted with rhythm and blues and Cajun funk, before returning home to the Rio Grande Valley.

In the 1970s, Fender was persuaded to take his music into the country western arena, where he was welcomed with open arms. He released "Before the Next Teardrop Falls" in 1975 and watched it soar to the top of the country and pop charts, as well as netting him a Grammy nomination. In 1976, he rereleased "Wasted Days and Wasted Nights" and also watched it go to the top of the charts, gaining him another Grammy nomination. Throughout the 1970s, Fender continued to release hits including "Your Cheatin' Heart" in 1976 and a holiday album titled *Merry Christmas—Feliz Navidad* in 1977.

The 1980s brought a new challenge for Fender as he ventured into the world of movies and sound tracks. The Hispanic classic *Short Eyes* (1985) and *She Came to the Valley* (1979) were his stepping-stones into the movies, but by the late 1980s and early 1990s, he had accumulated several roles to his credit, including *The *Milagro Beanfield War* (1989), directed by Robert Redford; *Always Roses* (1991), with Lupe *Ontiveros; *Las Pastores* (1991), with Linda *Ronstadt; and *Who Will Sing* (1992), with Vikki Carr. The versatility of his music is reinforced by the broad spectrum of movies that have featured his music in their sound tracks, including *The Border* (1982), *Rush* (1991), *Son-in-Law* (1993), **Lonestar* (1996), *Slums of Beverly Hills* (1998), and **Price of Glory* (2000).

In addition to acting in movies and producing sound tracks for Hollywood, Fender found time in the 1990s to introduce a new dynamic to his music by teaming up with the Texas Tornadoes, a Tejano group that included Tejano greats Doug Sahm, Flaco *Jiménez, and Augie Meyers. The Tornadoes released three albums before disbanding. In 1999, he and Jiménez teamed up with *Los Lobos and Rick Treviño to produce the album *Los Super Seven*, which earned a Grammy for Best Mexican American Performance.

Fender has continued to make an impression on the music world with every decade, and the new millennium will be no exception. In 2002, Fender's album *La Música de Baldemar Huerta* earned him a Grammy for Best Latin Pop Album. He continues to tour, entertaining a new generation of fans and to the excitement of his longtime fans who have enjoyed his music and followed his career for years. His enduring popularity and success will ensure his continued longevity as a performer.

Further Reading

Keller, Gary D. *A Biographical Handbook of Hispanic and United States Film*. Tempe, AZ: Bilingual Press, 1997.

http://www.freddyfender.com/bio.html.

Alma Alvarez-Smith

Fernández, Evelina (1954–). Evelina Fernández, a Chicana actress, producer, playwright, and screenwriter, was born on April 28, 1954, in Los Angeles, California. Originally a theater actress, Fernández began her professional career playing Della, a principal role in Luis *Valdez's stage production of **Zoot Suit*. She toured with El Teatro de la Esperanza and later joined the Latino Theater Company. Fernández's extensive television credits include *Roseanne, Hill Street Blues, Knots Landing, Judging Amy*, and *City of Angeles*. She appeared as Julie in the 1992 *film **American Me*, for which she received a Desi Award nomination. Her other films include *Downtown* (1989), *Flatliners* (1990), *Postcards from the Edge* (1990), *A Million to Juan* (1994), and *Gabriela* (1999).

Fernández's crowning achievement in film is Sleeping Giant Productions' 2000 project **Luminarias*, directed by José *Valenzuela, University of California–Los Angeles (UCLA) drama professor and Fernández's husband. In Huelva, Spain, at the Ibero-American Awards, Fernández was named best actress for her role as Andrea, the film's protagonist. In addition, she won a Golden Eagle Award for the script, an adaptation of her original stage play. Cheech *Marín, Scott Bakula, Robert Beltrán, Lupe *Ontiveros, and Seidy

López join Fernández in a film that explores issues from domestic violence to interracial dating. The film maintains a comedic undertone as its Chicana characters face the ups and downs of life, love, and self-discovery.

Routledge Press published another of Fernández's plays, *How Else Am I Supposed to Know I'm Still Alive*, in its anthology *Contemporary Plays by Women of Color* (1991). She continues to write screenplays, television episodes, and poetry. In addition, Fernández serves her community through public lectures for both children and adults. Educated at Garfield High School, East L.A. College, and California State University, Los Angeles, she continues to reside in East Los Angeles with her husband and two children.

Further Reading

"Cine." *La Opinión*, November 30, 1999, sec. 2B.

Cole, Melanie. "Film." *Hispanic*, September 30, 1998, 96.

Reyes, Luis, and Peter Rubie. *Hispanic Hollywood*. Hollywood, CA: Lone Eagle Publishing, 2000.

Leonora Anzaldúa Burke

Ferrer, José (1912–1992). José Vincente Ferrer de Otero y Cintrón, a prolific stage and *film actor, was born to Spanish parents in Santurce, Puerto Rico, on January 8, 1912. His parents became naturalized U.S. citizens, and the *family moved to New York City when Ferrer was six years old. Known as a classical stage and film actor, Ferrer was also an accomplished director and producer. He created many memorable characters, from villains to comic figures, and became known for his deep resonant voice. His first major stage role was playing Iago to the celebrated actor and American activist Paul Robeson in *Othello* (1943), which was one of the longest-running Shakespeare productions ever. His film debut, *Joan of Arc* (1948), opposite Ingrid Bergman, earned him his first Oscar nomination for Best Supporting Actor; shortly after he won a Best Actor Oscar for reprising his theatrical lead in the film version of *Cyrano de Bergerac* (1950). His final Oscar nomination was for his portrayal of painter Toulouse-Lautrec in John Huston's *Moulin Rouge* (1952). His debut as a director and producer was with the movie *The Shrike* (1955), which would be the first of a series of films where he would often appear. In 1970 he performed the main character Don Quixote in *The Man of la Mancha* in Puerto Rico, a role that he had played since 1966 in New York.

He was conferred five Tony Awards for Broadway performances, which include two for best acting, *Cyrano de Bergerac* (1947) and *The Shrike* (1952); and three for best director, *The Shrike* (1952), *Stalag 17* (1953), and *The Fourposter* (1952). The musical *Oh, Captain!* (1958), based on the book by Al Morgan and Ferrer, was nominated for musical of the year. Ferrer also earned three Emmy nominations for television performances, and in 1985, President Ronald Reagan awarded him the National Medal of Arts. This was the first time this award was bestowed. He died in Miami on January 26,

1992, after having performed in more than sixty films and dozens of plays and several television credits.

Further Reading

http://www.tonys.org/p/tonys_search JOSE FERRER.
http:www.us.imdb.com/Bio?Ferrer,%20José.

Heidi García

Film. D.W. Griffith's *Ramona: A Story of a White Man's Injustice to the Indian* (1910) ambivalently represents Latinas/os at the dawn of full-length cinema. On one hand, the film indicts the violent Euroamerican displacement of Califorñios and mission Indians, namely, the Luiseño. This is shown through the way the upper-class landowner Califorñio Felipe and Ramona, his half-Luiseño wife, are driven to México. However, the film also creates nostalgia about the Spanish mission days before the 1850s Euroamerican colonization of California, ignoring the brutality, slavery, and genocide against the California native tribes and the mestizos who worked in slavelike conditions for the missions and for the Califorñio landowning families. In *Ramona* the exile of both the Califorñio and the Indian foreshadows decades of U.S. cinema's relegation of Hispanics, mestizos, and Indians to *stereotypical roles, when those roles were so few.

While in the 1920s Italian actor Rudolph Valentino excited a growing public of white female moviegoers as an exotic icon, the "Latin Lover," ongoing antimiscegenation or segregation laws impeded the integration of Latinos in most areas of the United States, a reflection of U.S. attitudes toward Latinos and toward Latin America in the early and mid-twentieth century. Carmen *Miranda's 1940s musical appearances as a sexualized caricature of poor Afro-Brazilians also encouraged acceptance of the U.S. Good Neighbor Policy, which stipulated a Latin American economic dependence on the United States. Bedecked in her trademark fruit-laden hats and outlandish costumes, the Brazilian-born Portuguese Miranda was a spectacle of overflowing body movement and color that clashed with and perhaps resisted the more restrictive sexual norms of the United States. In classic Hollywood, non-Latino actors monopolized the sexualized and stereotypical Latina/o roles. Herbert Biberman's Marxist-influenced **Salt of the Earth* (1954) broke this pattern by featuring a mostly Mexican American cast playing Mexican American roles in the docudrama about a mining strike in the Southwest that illustrates how race, class, and gender intersect in the struggles for social and labor justice.

Enforcing the theme of cultural imperialism, the genre of westerns from the 1930s to the 1970s focused on the virile and moral self-defense of whites against Indian and Mexican attacks. Common images of Mexican bandits and thieves further justified U.S. segregation and pan-American economic subjugation by suggesting that Latinos were racially inferior and thus needed whites to lead and control them. Television in the 1950s was fueled with westerns that idealized white male aggression in opposition to Mexican criminality. Actor John Wayne typified the tall, swaggering, white ideal of the cowboy who is tested but ultimately dominates a celluloid West mostly inhabited by "savage" Indian and immoral Mexican challengers.

Actress Dolores *Del Río started out in Hollywood by playing "Latin Spitfire" and "foreign" roles, but she moved on to make Mexican movies in the 1940s and became an icon of the Época de Oro (Golden Age) of film in México from 1935 to the early 1950s. For immigrant or internally colonized Latina/o populations, films of this era through alternative venues in the United States provided Spanish-language and Latina/o narratives that, while often problematic in terms of gender, race, and class, were familiar and more varied than the limited roles that U.S. cinema offered. For example, while a virgin/whore dichotomy consumed nationalist Mexican images, U.S. film was obsessed with the image of the Mexican woman as whore in relation to the purity of Euroamerican actresses. In the mid-twentieth century, México was the largest producer of films in Latin America; and they were the most widely viewed by Latinas/os in the United States. The U.S. Latina/o viewing audience was in its majority of Mexican origin and lived in the Southwest and in the Midwest. Interestingly, as seen in the films that feature the Mexican Pachuco comedian *Tin Tan, Cuban and Afro-Caribbean music and culture had tremendous influence on Mexican-produced films during that time, aided by the musical contributions from the legendary Afro-Cuban *mambo orchestra leader Dámaso *Peréz Prado.

Contemporary U.S. Latina/o life suffered from invisibility as directors, production companies, acting guilds, and general staffing in the industry continued to exclude Latinas/os in the 1960s and 1970s. Latina/o actors were often faced with the difficult decision of either going without work or taking stereotypical roles. Although urban Latino populations grew in large numbers, the patterns of media exclusion for Latinos continued. The Vietnam War protests, United Farm Workers strikes, and the Chicano student empowerment and anticolonial movements worldwide sparked the *Chicano Movement, which spawned a major challenge for Hollywood to lift the racial, gender, and class barriers that prevented the production of more affirmative representations of Latinas/os in film. A resurgence in Indian and African pride among racially and/or culturally mixed Latinos challenged the Eurocentric focus of Hollywood. Chicano, Puerto Rican, and other Latina/o alternative media practices emerged. Latinas/os organized the National Latino Media Coalition, the Latino Consortium, and the Chicano Cinema Coalition, in addition to Latina/o-themed film festivals such as the International Festival of New Latin American Cinema held in Havana in 1979. Outside of Hollywood, Latina/o producers, actors, and cinema specialists struggled to operate independently and infiltrate mainstream media. Through protests, legal suits, and coordinated meetings, Latinas/os gained some independent space and minor representation in the mainstream.

Although there was increasing conglomeration of media in multinational corporations in the 1980s and the 1990s that clashed with the independent and revolutionary visions articulated by Latino media advocacy in the 1970s, Latino/a film continued to be shown in independent venues and began to be shown on cable access and on PBS in addition to commercial theaters. Luis *Valdez's **Zoot Suit* (1981) challenged stereotypes of Mexican criminality by highlighting the racial injustices of the Zoot Suit Riots and the Sleepy Lagoon Case in 1940s Los Angeles. Edward James *Olmos starred in this first major Chicano-written and Hollywood-produced film. **El Super* (1979), *Short Eyes* (1979), *The *Ballad of Gregorio Cortez* (1983), **El Norte* (1983), *Crossover Dreams* (1985), **La Bamba* (1987), **Born in East L.A.* (1987) and **Stand and Deliver* (1988) offered works directed by Latinos. In the 1990s *Hangin' with the Homeboys* (1999), **American Me* (1992), **Bound by Honor* (1993), **Mambo Kings* (1992), **El Mariachi* (1992), and **Mi Familia/My Family* (1994) introduced Puerto Rican, Dominican, Cuban, Mexican, Chicano, and pan-Latina/o perspectives that began to achieve some economic success.

Women have operated more independently but have not yet achieved the same level of commercial success as directors even in the new millennium. Laura Aguilar, Frances Solomé España, Sandra P. Hagn, Rita González, Sandra Peña, and Lourdes Portillo operate as independent video artists. In terms of actresses, Jennifer *López and Rosie *Pérez gained celebrity status for their roles in films that only sometimes involved narratives that specify their real status as Puerto Rican women. Mexican actress Salma *Hayek crossed over from Mexican to U.S. film with Hollywood successes. López in particular has adapted to the multimedia corporate structure by gaining fame in films such as **Selena* (1997), *Anaconda* (1997), and *Angel Eyes* (2001).

Latina/o film is not dependent solely upon Hollywood because independent films such as Robert Rodríguez's *El Mariachi* or Evelina *Fernández's **Luminarias* (2000) can gain critical acclaim and a sizable audience. Film shown on *Spanish-language television stations make an impact on Latina/o popular culture; Telemundo and Univision dominate the Spanish-language media market with a large influence from Florida-based *Cuban Americans. In addition, cable channels and the Internet allow some Latinos/as to further connect with Latin American sources of film and media. Also, the constant flow of immigrants from Latin America renews the need for Spanish-language programming that is transnational in its offerings; hence films and soap operas from México, Venezuela, and Brazil (dubbed in Spanish) are a mainstay for Latina/o audiences in the United States. In addition, the recent rise of satellite dish programming brings into the United States even more diverse programming from Latin America.

Despite the recent accomplishments of Latinas/os in film, which echo earlier triumphs by actor Anthony *Quinn and Emmy, Grammy, Oscar, and Tony Award winner Rita *Moreno, so the lack of pro-Latina/o executives in the film industry continues, especially for Latinas who face sexism in addition to race and class exclusion and bias. In the case of Ela Troyano's independent film *Latin Boys Go to Hell* (1997), she engages with the issues of gay Latina/o sexuality that are also ignored or demonized by Hollywood or even by successful Latino directors and producers. The United States has far to travel to escape the legacies of segregation and cultural imperialism in the present age. A true critique of the larger imperialistic operations of the United States in Latin America has yet to find a popular screening.

In the new millennium, we are witnessing commercial release films by Latinos and non-Latinos that offer a more complex, rich, and noncriminalized representation of Latina/o subjects, especially gender, and communities. Some of these films include David Ryker's, **La Ciudad* (1999), Ken Loach's **Bread and Roses* (2001), Karyn Kusama's **Girlfight* (2000), and Miguel Arteta's **Star Maps* (1997). Also, Lourdes Portillo's gripping Chicana aesthetic border documentary *Señorita Extraviada* (2001), on the disappearances of women in Ciudad Juaréz, México, was screened on PBS and has achieved wide acclaim in the United States and in México. There is also a "rebirth" of Mexican cinema that is crossing over to the United States with such films as **Amores Perros* (2000), **Y Tu Mamá También* (2001), and *El Crimen de Padre Amaro* (2003), to name a few.

Further Reading

Aguila, Justino, and Carla Meyer. "Latino Actors Celebrate Small Victories against Typecasting." *San Francisco Chronicle*, September 16, 2001, 33.

Anger, Kenneth. *Hollywood Babylon*. New York: Dell, 1983.

Cano-Murillo, Kathy. "Mexican Actress Won't Live by 'Bread' Alone." *The Arizona Republic*, May 31, 2001.

Navarro, Mireya. "Trying to Get Beyond the Role of the Maid: Hispanic Actors Are Seen as Underrepresented, with the Exception of One Part." *New York Times*, May 16, 2002, E1.

Gabriel Estrada and Arturo J. Aldama

Flores, Juan (1943–). Born on September 29, 1943, in Alexandria, Virginia, Juan Flores is an established language scholar and pioneer in the field of Puerto Rican studies and critical cultural studies. Author of numerous books and other scholarly publications, his book *The Insular Vision* (1979) received the internationally prestigious *Casa de las Américas prize for best scholarship in 1980 and another book, *Poetry in East Germany*, received a *Choice* magazine award for best book of the year. He grew up in New York City and attended Queens College, receiving his B.A. in 1965. He continued his studies at Yale University, where in 1970 he earned his Ph.D. in German. From 1968 through 1975 he was an assistant professor in the Department of German Studies at Stanford University. In 1975 he returned to New York to serve as research director of cultural studies at the newly formed Center for Puerto Rican Studies at the City University of New York (CUNY). During the 1980s he taught in the Sociology Department at Queens College, and in 1989 he directed the International Studies Program at City College, where he was promoted to full professor. In 1992 he worked in City College's Department of Latin American and Hispanic Caribbean Studies and in CUNY's Graduate Center, teaching seminars in sociology theory, popular music, and Latino cultural studies. From 1994 to 1997 he served as director of the Center for Puerto Rican Studies at Hunter College and has directed Hunter's Mellon Minority Undergraduate Fellowship Program since 1999. His visiting professorships include appointments at Harvard, Columbia, Princeton, New York University, and Brown.

Besides the books *Poetry in East Germany* and *The Insular Vision*, Flores also wrote *Divided Borders: Essays on Puerto Rican Identity* (1993) and *From Bomba to Hip-Hop: Puerto Rican Culture and Latino Identity* (2000). He translated *Memoirs of Bernardo Vega* (1984) and *Cortijo's Wake* (2003), both by Edgardo Rodríguez Juliá. He also coedited with Jean Franco and George Yudice *On Edge: The Crisis of Contemporary Latin American Culture* (1992). His work continues to appear in journals and newspapers in the United States and Latin America.

Further Reading

Meyer, Nicholas, ed. *The Biographical Dictionary of Hispanic Americans*. New York: Facts on File, 1997.

http://www.news.cornell.edu/Chronicles/4.5.01/Flores_lect.html.

http://www.prdream.com/patria/centro/09_27/bioflores.html.

Heidi García

Folklore. Folklore is often considered the old-fashioned or countrified aspects of the general culture. However, folklore is living culture that is generated, transmitted, and reconstituted among contemporary human beings in all kinds of communities. Because cultural phenomena constantly move between and among communication spheres—from print media to oral storytelling to television and back in a constant cycle of reproduction—folklore can be found in popular culture, mass-mediated culture, and even elite or avant-garde culture.

The three largest Spanish-speaking groups in the United States—Mexican Americans, Puerto Ricans, and *Cuban Americans—have distinctive cultural histories and settlement patterns. For instance, centuries-old Mexican American communities of the Southwest were forcibly annexed to the United States in 1848. The United States claimed Puerto Rico as a protectorate in 1898, and in 1917 declared all Puerto Ricans to be U.S. citizens. However, massive migration from the island to the United States occurred only after World War II. Puerto Ricans settled primarily in New York City and the Northeast. Cubans arrived next as refugees from the 1959 socialist revolution on their island. They settled primarily in Miami and New York. Since the 1980s immigrants from other Latin American countries and mainland México have come to the United States in increasing numbers, settling not only in the large cities but also in towns and rural areas throughout the country. Many of these new immigrants are undocumented when they arrive, and they must struggle to obtain legal status.

Nevertheless, Latinas and Latinos of distinct nationalities share a common Spanish Roman Catholic heritage. In the U.S. Southwest, México, and Central America, this heritage mixed with indigenous traditions to form distinctive new world cultures. In the Caribbean and Brazil the early extermination of indigenous groups and the importation of African slaves resulted in a strong African cultural influence. Sometimes common cultural traditions express Spanish colonial roots; sometimes they represent a later dissemination of ideas from one group to others; and sometimes they express contemporary experiences that Latinas/os of many nationalities share.

The Latino/a ritual calendar starts with the New Year, when families gather to celebrate renewal. Many households customarily play the song "El Año Viejo" (The Old Year) at the stroke of twelve and dance in the new year. This popular song was composed by Venezuelan Crescencio Salcedo and recorded by the Mexican singer Tony Camargo in 1953, and it has become a seasonal tradition. On January 6, the Día de los Reyes Magos (Three Kings Day), many children receive their Christmas presents, not from Santa but from the Three Kings who arrived in Bethlehem to present gifts to the Christ child.

During Holy Week, the week before Easter, Catholics contemplate the last days of Christ, his betrayal, humiliation, death, and resurrection. Many immigrant communities reenact Christ's final days on Holy Thursday or Good Friday. Called La Judea or La Pasión, this street procession sometimes culminates in a simulated crucifixion. In the Southwest, a related tradition of **Penitentes*, or lay religious brotherhoods, arose in isolated communities during the nineteenth century. *Penitentes* perform public and private expressions of atonement. They sponsor processions of penitents bearing heavy crosses or whipping themselves. At the same time the *Penitentes* provide important sources of mutual aid to their members. They built distinctive *moradas*, or meeting halls, for their activities that continue to dot the countryside.

Latino/a festivals celebrating ethnic pride and solidarity often occur during the summer months or in September, when many Latin American countries won independence from Spain. These festivals feature popular music, foods, crafts, and folk dances. Colombians may perform an old-style *cumbia; Puerto Ricans dance the *plena and the African-influenced *bomba; Mexicans may dance any of a number of regional dances, from the *jarabe tapatio* of Guadalajara to the **sones* of Vera Cruz; Nicaraguans dance the baile de marimba. These **bailes folklóricos* represent modern choreographed versions of the social or ritual dances of earlier times. However, social dances, such as the modern cumbia, the *polca norteña*, *salsa, *merengue, and *tango, are equally folk dances, since they embody the expressive styles of distinctive contemporary groups.

Long-standing Latina/Latino communities may also commemorate important community events annually. The Fiesta of Santa Fe, New Mexico, for example, reenacts the "bloodless reconquest" of the Pueblo Indians by Don Diego de Vargas in 1692. The 1992 video documentary *Gathering Up Again: The Fiesta of Santa Fe* shows how this Latina/o tradition both resists Anglo domination and participates in the oppression of its own other, the Native American. While the fiesta purportedly celebrates the union of three cultures—the Spanish, the indigenous, and the Anglo American—it paradoxically demonstrates their continuing segregation and the inequalities and personal injuries such divisions produce. Other southwestern communities perform the **matachines* ritual dance, which reenacts the conquest and conversion of Moctezuma, the sixteenth-century Aztec ruler.

Latina/o immigrant communities often unite around a national festival from their country of origin. For instance, Miami's Nicaraguan community celebrates La Gritería (The Cries) on December 8 in honor of the Patron Saint of Nicaragua, La Purísima Concepción de María. During this festival homeowners and businesses set up and decorate outside altars. Groups of singers walk from one altar to the next, stopping at each to sing traditional **villancicos*, or songs in honor of the virgin. After each performance, a group member shouts, "¿Quién causa tanta alegría?" (Who causes such happiness?), to which the rest respond, "¡La Virgen María!" (The Virgin Mary!). The owner of the altar then dispenses sweets and treats to the singer. Puerto Ricans, on the other hand, hold *parrandas*, or social gatherings, around Christmastime, when they sing *aguinaldos*, or Christmas carols.

The *Virgin of Guadalupe, once the patron saint of México, is now the patron of all Latin America. Many communities venerate this Indian or mestiza virgin on December 12. In communities where Mexicans predominate, devotees often hold a predawn service called *"Las Mañanitas." *Mariachi bands visit the church at 4 A.M. to serenade the Virgin with a version of the Mexican birthday song: "Estas son las mañanitas que cantaba el Rey David. Hoy por ser día de tu santo, te las cantamos a ti. Despierta, mi bien despierta, mira que ya amaneció, ya los pajaritos cantan, la luna ya se metió" (This is the song that King David sang. Today, for your saint's day, we sing it to you. Wake up, my friend, wake up. Look it's already morning. The little birds are already singing. The moon has gone in.). Such rituals demonstrate the loving familiarity the faithful feel toward the miraculous Virgin.

Many communities also perform a children's pageant that reenacts the Virgin's apparition in 1531, shortly after the conquest. Legend has it that the Virgin ordered the Indian shepherd Juan Diego to tell the bishop to build her a church where a temple to the Aztec goddess Tonantzin had stood. She directed him to pick flowers on an ordinarily barren hill and wrap them in

Folklore is often depicted in murals painted on community walls. *Courtesy of artist Leo Tanguma.*

his cloak. When Juan Diego unfurled the cloak, the authorities found the image of the Virgin imprinted on the cloth and built the church. The Virgin of Guadalupe is an extremely popular icon for Latinas/os. Wrapped in a blue cloak decorated with golden stars and surrounded by a golden halo, she can be seen not only in churches and home altars but also in murals, calendars, T-shirts, and body tattoos.

On the nine nights preceding Christmas, many Latina/o communities host Las *Posadas. These partly chanted play processions reenact Joseph and Mary's search for shelter in Bethlehem. Costumed participants travel from house to house requesting entry, while homeowners ceremoniously refuse to let them in. Finally, a host admits the group and rewards them with festival foods. On the final night, Christmas Eve, the performing group reenacts Christ's birth in the manger. A similar tradition from the Southwest is called *Los *Pastores*, the shepherds' play.

Of course, the growing number of Latina/o Protestants do not participate in religious customs involving the worship of saints or the Virgin Mary. They may, however, perform plays from the Protestant tradition, such as *The Everyman Play*, where Satan and Jesus battle for a poor sinner's soul. Protestant churches also possess their own body of hymns and contemporary religious music in Spanish.

Another Latino/a *theater tradition is rooted in the history of Latina/o labor organizing. These theater groups use improvisational techniques to raise public consciousness about community problems such as worker exploitation, *police brutality, domestic violence, and alcohol and drug addiction. The United Farm Workers' Organizing Committee's *El Teatro Campesino, which initially formed in Southern California in the mid-1960s, was one of the earliest and most active of these groups. Latino/a mural art also developed out of earlier social and even revolutionary movements (*see* Chicano Mural Movement). The brilliant murals found in poor and working-class urban *barrios document a history of struggle, contemporary social ills, and ethnic pride. In the late 1980s and 1990s, graffiti writers also began to paint murals using their distinctive graphic style. In large cities like New York and Philadelphia these self-taught artists spray-painted elaborate memorial walls in remembrance of those who had been murdered in *gang wars. Residents' attitudes toward these memorial walls were mixed—were they warnings against or glorifications of gang violence?

Latino/a families celebrate many individual rites of passage, but none has become so popular as the **quinceañera*, or fifteenth birthday. Once a coming-out party for the daughters of society families, the "sweet fifteen" party is now a popular family celebration among all social classes. The young debutante, accompanied by a court of friends, presides at a formal party that includes dancing and a festive meal. In Puerto Rican neighborhoods, one can find small businesses devoted to the production of *capias*, or hand-made party favors for *quinceañeras* and other rites of passage. These favors, assembled from lace, ribbon, manufactured plastic ornaments, paper, wire, and other materials, serve as treasured mementos of important events. Another fixture in Puerto Rican neighborhoods are *casitas*, small one-room wooden houses built in vacant lots or gardens. They serve as retreats for men, who visit and play cards together in these nostalgic invocations of their rural island homes.

Latina/o communities also share a rich tradition of alternate medical beliefs and practices. The humoral theory of medicine, that is, the notion that illnesses and cures can be categorized as hot or cold, forms the basis for many home remedies. According to this theory, a healthy body is warm and moist. A person may become ill either because she/he experiences a dramatic change in temperature, as would occur if one took a cold shower immediately after working up a sweat, or by overconsuming substances categorized as hot or cold. Many Latina/o community members consult *curanderos* (healers), *espiritistas* (spiritual healers), or *santeros* (artisans of religious images) for medical, psychological, and social problems before or in addition to seeking standard medical treatment (*see* Healing Practices, Spirituality, and Religious Beliefs). In the Southwest, the *caso*, or account of a miraculous healing, is so common that folklorists regard it as a specific genre of folk narrative. There is even a strong tradition of parody *casos*, jokes told by some Latinas/os disparaging the beliefs of others. Certain healers achieved widespread and long-lasting fame, becoming the subjects of folk legend. Such was the case of turn-of-the-century south Texan Don Pedro Jaramillo. Rudolfo *Anaya's novelistic account, in *Bless Me, Última* (1972), of a rural New Mexican childhood contains a compelling literary portrait of a Latina *curandera*. Yet urban *salseros* (salsa musicians) also commonly pay tribute to the alternative medicine of *mamis* (mothers), *abuelitas* (grandmothers), and *curanderos*, as is evident in Eddie *Palmieri's 1998 composition "Dueño del Monte" (King of the Mountain).

In Latino communities of Caribbean origin, an individual may visit a *botánica*, a kind of alternative pharmacy that offers both spiritual and herbal supplies. There she may consult a spiritualist, a person who communes with the dead to advise clients on personal or medical problems. Spiritualism is a nineteenth-century religion that continues to have followers in both Anglo-American and Latin American communities. Alternately, a devotee of *santería* may visit a *santero* for advice or ritual cure. *Santería* is an African-derived religion that involves divination, spirit possession, and a strong respect for nature. Practiced in *casas*, or houses, outside the Catholic Church, *santería* has its own priests and rituals. Yet practitioners see no conflict between their Roman Catholic and *santería* beliefs. In colonial-era Cuba, enslaved Africans worshipped their *orishas* (powers or divine emissaries). Yet they disguised this "pagan" religion by associating each *orisha* with a Catholic saint. Thus, Santa Bárbara was identified with Changó, the Yoruba God of fire and thunder. Today, Latinas/os of many nationalities embrace *santería*. The film documentary *The King Does Not Lie: The Initiation of a Shango Priest* (1992) shows how *santería* is a growing, multiracial religion that continues to speak to contemporary human needs.

Latinas/os' common bilingual experience has led to interesting forms of codeswitching, verbal play, and a great wealth of jokes. Spanish language jokes maintain boundaries not only between Latinos and "gringos" but also between Latinos who remain outside the mainstream culture and those who are more assimilated. Joking also reinforces class and gender boundaries, as well as interethnic boundaries among different Latino nationalities. For instance, in Miami, newer Nicaraguan and South American immigrants express hostility toward entrenched Cubans by making them the butts of their jokes. Joking may equally function to express solidarity: Some Guatemalans in southern Delaware use their native Maya tongue only to trade jokes on rare occasions when they encounter others who speak their natal language.

In this television age, one is more likely to find folktales about the idiot-heroes Pedro de Urdemales and Juan Bobo, or the wiley Tío Conejo and Tío

Coyote, in cartoons or in children's books rather than recited orally. These trickster figures demonstrate a blatant disregard for custom and morality but often triumph in the end anyway.

Legends about encounters with the devil, or demonic dogs or pigs, however, continue to be recounted among friends. One of the most popular revenants is *La Llorona, or the weeping woman, who lingers near bodies of water. Legend has it that La Llorona either married a man without her parents' approval or became pregnant by him before marriage. She had one or more children, whom either she, their father, or her own father drowned. Subsequently, the young woman went mad and wandered the countryside weeping for her lost children. She led a dissolute life, died, went to heaven, and was sent back to earth to search for her children. The legend has been dramatized repeatedly on television. Poet and novelist Sandra *Cisneros alludes to it in her short story "Woman Hollering Creek" (1991). Singer Joan *Báez takes up the theme in her 1972 song "La Llorona." Oral transmission has been equally powerful; teens of many ethnicities and regions today relate their own strange encounters with the wailing woman.

Another storytelling tradition, the **corrido*, or ballad, is a narrative song usually performed with the accompaniment of a guitar. Américo Paredes wrote extensively both about the *corrido* and the distinctive new world communities that produced them (1995). Sung in the language of a dominated group, they provided a unique perspective on society and history that was rarely voiced in mainstream U.S. history books or media. For instance, the nineteenth-century *Texas Ranger was romanticized in the Anglo television program *The Lone Ranger*. For Tejanos (Texans of Mexican descent) he was a despised tyrannical figure, the henchman of invading Anglo ranchers. In his influential work *With a Pistol in His Hand* (1958), Paredes pieces together existing legends, *corridos*, and journalistic accounts to tell the story of Gregorio Cortez, an honest farmer who fought the Rangers to protect his land, his family, and his honor (see *Ballad of Gregorio Cortez, The*).

Today, the enemy that the *corrido* hero must elude and overcome is more likely to be a representative of the Immigration and Naturalization Service (INS) border patrol. A recent *corrido*, titled "Superman es ilegal," provides an undocumented immigrant's perspective on the racism inherent in U.S. *immigration regulations. It begins by parodying the Superman jingle—"¿Es un pájaro, es un avión? No hombre, es un mojado" (Is it a bird? Is it a plane? No man, it's a wetback)—and concludes by arguing that Superman should be kicked out of the country just as the Mexican workers are. Undocumented immigrants from El Salvador and Guatemala, who fled the Central American genocide of the 1980s, developed their own distinctive narrative form called the testimonial within the context of the Sanctuary Movement. These narratives conveyed horrific and traumatic experiences that would ordinarily remain unspoken. They were packaged in a language that could stir the conscience of North American citizens and promote the case of those suing for refugee status. Thus, old narrative traditions provide a vehicle for airing new grievances, while new narratives quickly develop formulaic patterns to reflect the shared dimensions of individual experience.

Latina/o folklore is as rich in tradition as it is in creativity, as varied as the communities that produce it. At times Latina/o folklore provides a perspective distinct from that voiced in mainstream popular culture. At others, it enriches the popular culture of the English-speaking as well as the Spanish-speaking United States.

Further Reading

Anaya, Rudolfo. *Bless Me, Última*. Berkeley, CA: TQS Publications, 1972.

Borland, Katherine. "Folklife of Miami's Nicaraguan Communities." 1993. http://www.historical-museum.org/folklife/folknica.htm.

Cisneros, Sandra. *Woman Hollering Creek and Other Stories*. New York: Random House, 1991.

Cooper, Martha, and Joseph Sciorra. *"R.I.P." Memorial Wall Art*. New York: Thomas and Hudson, 1994.

DeBouzek, Jeanette. *Gathering Up Again: The Fiesta of Santa Fé*. VHS. Color. 47 min. Albuquerque, NM: Quotidian Independent Documentary Research, 1992.

García, Juan, ed. *Perspectives in Mexican American Studies I: Readings in Southwestern Folklore, an Anthology*. Tucson: University of Arizona Mexican American Studies and Research Center, 1989.

Gleason, Judith, and Elisa Mereghetti. *The King Does Not Lie: The Initiation of a Shango Priest*. VHS. 50 min. New York: Filmmakers Library, 1992.

Herrera-Sobek, María. "Corridos and Canciones of Mica, Migra, and the Coyotes: A Commentary on Undocumented Immigration." In *Creative Ethnicity: Symbols and Strategies of Contemporary Ethnic Life*, edited by Stephen Stern and John Allan Cicala. Logan: Utah State University Press, 1991.

Paredes, Américo. *With His Pistol in His Hand: A Border Ballad and Its Hero*. Austin: University of Texas Press, 1958.

Schoemaker, George H., ed. *The Emergence of Folklore in Everyday Life: A Fieldguide and Sourcebook*. Bloomington, IN: Trickster Press, 1990.

Katherine Borland

Food and Cookery. Although culinary customs and everyday soul food are often undervalued when national histories are written with their traditional focus on wars and politics, food and cookery constitute an important place in the history and heritage of people and their cultures. Indeed, one of the fundamental traits that unites all people is the universal human search for food and water. This trait applies to Latinas and Latinos in general but especially to the *comida* (food) and *sabores* (flavors and "taste" in both sensory and aesthetic senses) identified with particular Latina/o ethnic and regional populations. Food—its planting, growth, preservation, distribution, trade, commerce policy, and consumption—provides a resilient thread of tradition that binds the present to the distant past of ancestors and forgotten events. Similarly, cookery—the many practical and more artistic activities associated with food preparation and serving—has historically contributed to the definition of cultures, geographical regions, and even of nations. To think of such sacred customs as Passover, the Last Supper, Ramadan, and Lent (*la cuaresma*), as well as of such social customs as toasting when honoring a person or event or of *pasteles de cumpleaños* (birthday cakes) when celebrating anniversaries of any sort, is to recognize how much the core of human ritual and countless other familiar symbols of community and social interaction are food centered.

Thus, because the exchange of food products and cooking methods is so basic and commonplace when nations and cultures collide and commingle, it is impossible to offer a single comprehensive look at Latina and Latino food and cookery. Touched on here are ethnically and regionally based items like, for example, jalapeños from Jalapa, México; *asopao de pollo* (chicken soup) from Puerto Rico, *Cuba libres* (alcoholic beverages) from Havana, and *sopaipillas* (fried pastry) from New Mexico, to name examples from four different national traditions. Popular culture anecdotes are included as well to illustrate the linkage of culinary customs to practices other than solely food gathering, agricultural commerce, and eating, as in the food customs associated with *Dia de los Muertos and **quinceañera* (fifteenth birthday) celebrations. In addition, the critically important Latina/o social practices of at-home hospitality, family bonds, community ties, mutual respect, and other culturally linked activities have been steeped by centuries of time. They have also been field-tested in the laboratories of millions of *comales* (hotplates that date to pre-Columbian times) and *cocinas de castillo* (royal kitchens that were brought over with Spanish royalty, literally "castle kitchens") to produce an amazing **mestizaje*, or hybrid, of blended cuisines drawn from the Americas and Spanish Iberia, both of which had drawn from Asia and Africa through active trade networks and as a result of military and political events.

Accordingly, the history of Latina/o cuisine like that of most foods of the world reveals many twists and turns consisting not solely of one national stock or single melting pot (*olla*) of dishes but rather containing many different *caldos*, *sopas*, and *capirotadas* (broths, soups, and stews or puddings) derived from a vast variety of sources of flora, fauna, and manufactured products. This Latina/o culinary diversity includes basic starches, vegetables, fruits, seafood, and fauna indigenous to the Americas, as well as ingredients imported from Europe, northern and western Africa, and Asia via both the Bering Sea crossing and the European-Chinese contact attributed to Marco Polo. Among the countless indigenous Mesoamerican foods that were introduced to Europe by the Spaniards after the Conquest of México and the colonial empire in the Americas were:

Chocolate. The cacao-based sweet that was introduced by the Aztec ruler Montezuma to the conqueror Hernán Cortés and the Spaniards who translated the sound of *xocoatl* (pronounced sho-ko-ahtul) into the Spanish word *chocolate* that was borrowed intact into English. Served as a hot beverage flavored with cinnamon, vanilla, and sugar, it remained a Spanish secret for decades until its introduction to France, then England, and eventually the rest of Europe.

Jalapeño (pronounced hall-oh-penyo). A piquant pepper native to Jalapa, México, and used as a spice to flavor meats, soups, and a variety of other preparations, including most recently, in the United States, cheese. It is a standard ingredient in *salsa cruda* (raw sauce), a widely popular fresh Mexican condiment made of uncooked chopped tomatoes, onions, jalapeños, and cilantro (the pungent leaves of the coriander plant). In certain areas, *salsa cruda* is also known as *pico de gallo* (rooster's beak or pecking) and eaten in the manner of chutney and similar accompaniments.

Maize. The grain staple of the Americas also known as Indian corn. The Spanish word *maiz* comes from the native Taíno word *mahiz*. Christopher *Columbus and the other early explorers introduced corn to Europe, and it is now spread throughout the planet with the first and second growers of the world being the United States and China. The Indians taught European conquerors and colonists how to grow, harvest, prepare, and store the indigenous grains, which include yellow, blue, and multicolored varieties still eaten and also used for decorative purpose usually in the autumn harvest time. Also used as livestock feed and as packing material in industry, corn is nutritionally inferior to other cereal staples because of its low protein and other nutrient value. Nevertheless, it is used throughout the Americas to make basic doughs (*masa*) for such other staples as *tortillas, the ubiquitous round, thin cakes eaten as bread. Nor can its fermented form as bourbon whiskey be overlooked, given its importance as a liquor commodity and also as a political historical catalyst (as in its employment by the United States to "pacify" the native peoples as well as in the two U.S. antitax events known as the 1794 Whiskey Rebellion and the Whiskey Ring of the 1800s).

Mole. A popular gravylike sauce made of red chili, ground nuts, spices, and enough chocolate to deepen the other flavors without overpowering them. Commonly used as a marinade for chicken and pork on very special occasions, mole is considered the national dish of México by many knowledgeable observers. Traditional mole dishes are simmered from carefully selected ingredients, subtly spiced, and typically cooked in Mexican-made *ollas* (earthenware crock pots).

Tamales. The equivalent of a sandwich or individual meat pie (or English pastry) made of a ground corn flour paste wrapped around a meat, vegetable, or other filling, and cooked inside corn husks. Prepared in México from the earliest antiquity, early Spanish explorers of the sixteenth century wrote about eating them and described several varieties during the Conquest. Tamales made in Gulf Coast regions like the Yucatán are distinguished by their banana leaf wrappers instead of corn, while in Morelia, Jalisco, and elsewhere the paste is made of fresh corn, and the fillings are sweetened with fruits and vanilla. Because good tamales are hard to make and require a time-consuming preparation, one Chicana poet has written that the first assembly-line process began with tamale making in México many centuries before the building of Ford factories in Detroit, Michigan, which are usually credited with the assembly innovation.

Tequila. The distilled liquor made from the fermented juice of the Mexican agave plant and named for the town of Jalisco in the state of Oaxaca, where it originated and continues to be produced. Normally, tequila is unaged and transparently clear, but aged varieties take on an amber or strawish yellow hue. The beverage is another example of *mestizaje* (cultural hybridity) in that it resulted from a process introduced by the Spaniards to a drink already prepared by the native Mesoamericans. One of the most popular drinks of North America at the turn of the millennium is the tequila-based Margarita cocktail, a mix of lime and tequila served over crushed ice in a salt-rimmed glass. The conventional way that Mexicans and other Latin Americans usually drink tequila is neat with a side pinch of salt and a wedge of lime.

Vanilla. Also associated with northern México, where the tropical orchid plants from which they are harvested grow. The Aztecs used the vanilla (pronounced vah-nee-ya in Spanish) bean to flavor their *xocoatl* beverage before the Spaniards arrived, and it became a highly prized commodity in Spain and Europe after 1521. The Mexican variety is sometimes called Bourbon vanilla, and its use among Mexican cooks is a practice that is often treated with ritual respect.

These and numerous other foods and native dishes of the central and southern areas of Mesoamerica have undergone major adaptations and transformation after centuries of multinational, intercultural, and cross-cultural exchange following the Conquest.

Many other food staples of Mesoamerica are more common in northern México where they originated, and although they traveled across the Atlantic, many did not enter the common culinary lexicon of Spain and Europe. These include the meat entrees *adobo* or *carne adobada* (chili marinated meats that are slow roasted) and *barbacoa* (barbecued meats). Another northern native foodstuff is the beverage *pulque*, a Mexican beer characterized by its cloudy white color and sour yeasty taste. *Pulque* is made from the fermented sap (called *agua miel* or honey syrup water) that seeps from the agave (also known as the maguey or century plant), and its composition has been lab tested and shown to be a cheap and important source of nutrients and amino acids. Another liquor made from agave is mescal (sometimes spelled "mezcal"), a distilled beverage that is cheaper but stronger in flavor than tequila. The ubiquitous enchilada (chili-drenched tortilla and cheese dish), whose point of origin is uncertain, is another basic entree of Mexican cookery that has not emigrated beyond the Americas. Made a variety of ways, enchiladas require corn tortillas, cheese, chopped onions, and red or green chili sauce but can be varied with the inclusion of shredded beef, chicken, pork, and other ingredients.

Foods found primarily in the southwestern United States—that is, formerly *northern* México—and the borderlands region of what some scholars identify as "Greater México" feature many mestizo adaptations of ingredients and preparation method. They include:

Burrito. A rolled tortilla filled with beans, meat, or other ingredients to make a handy sandwichlike lunch staple. The word *burrito* means "little donkey," which reflects the common homeliness of the dish as a simple food. In the latter half of the twentieth century, burritos have been marketed aggressively in the United States and have entered the eclectic American cuisine as a rival to hamburgers and hotdogs in public school cafeterias.

Fajitas. The thin strips of sautéed beef that Texas claims as a native dish. Usually eaten with either corn or wheat flour tortillas, fajitas are often accompanied with pinto beans and red and/or green chili.

Monterey Jack cheese. One of only four cheeses noted as having originated in the United States, in this case in the Monterey Bay area of northern California. A usually white, semisoft, smooth cheese resembling cheddar, Monterey Jack is also considered a descendant of the *queso del país* (Mexican country cheese) that was manufactured and sold door to door by Doña Juana Cóta de Boronda before the Gold Rush era of the mid-nineteenth century. Monterey Jack is sometimes flavored with spices, pimientos, and/or jalapeño peppers and also aged into a dry variety that takes on a yellow-gold color and resembles the texture and flavor of well-aged cheddar. Although Doña Juana's contribution to its origin is not credited in its name, her family's adobe home and cheese-making building have been preserved as a historical California site in the Carmel Valley. The inventor of the cheese is disputed, with some culinary researchers attributing its origins to Doña Juana, others to Domingo Pedrazzi of Carmel Valley or to David Jacks, who first began mass-marketing the cheese, and others to the Franciscan missionaries who reportedly brought it to New Spain in the 1700s.

Nachos. The popular recreational and tavern snack consisting of corn chips (*tostadas*) topped with melted cheese, often Monterey Jack or another mild country-style cheese. A staple of American fast-food eateries, nachos are often accompanied by olives and a *salsa cruda* or *pico de gallo* condiment.

Sopaipilla. A deep-fried fritterlike bread that puffs into a pillow appearance. Long associated with New Mexican cooking, *sopaipillas* (pronounced so-pie-peeyas) may have derived from Indian fry bread since their methods of preparation are similar. They are often served with *frijoles de olla* (fresh-cooked beans) and *posole* (hominy stew) or eaten as a dessert with local honey or other sweetener. Because they are trickier to prepare than most Latina/o breads, *sopaipillas* usually are cooked at home or by specialty restaurants.

Taco. A fried corn tortilla filled with beans, meat, or other staple ingredients and usually topped with cheese and a *salsa cruda* or *pico de gallo* condiment for a convenient meal. Because tacos are viewed as an easy dish to pre-

> pare, historians surmise that they might have originated in the rough campfire cooking of vaqueros (cowboys) working the range. A standard of the Taco Bell food chain and megacorporation, tacos rival hamburgers, hotdogs, and burritos in popularity in the United States of the twentieth and twenty-first centuries.

These and many other examples of Mexican foods of the borderlands region of Greater México are now widespread throughout the United States and the central and southern regions of México, and they repeatedly have entered literary popular culture as in the Chicano poet *Alurista's rhyming of the sun, moon, and communion host with the tortilla and fiction writer Sandra *Cisneros's emphasis on food and cookery in her novel *Caramelo* (2002).

The distinctive dishes and cuisine of other Latina/o ethnicities contain some of the same or similar ingredients of Mexican cookery, as well as related methods of preparation. Yet they combine into distinct foods that are identified with their respective places and cultures of origin. For example, beans (frijoles) are a staple of most Latina/o cuisines, but they vary from

Staples in the Latina/o kitchen include beans, rice, corn, and chiles. *Photo by Emmanuel Sánchez Carballo.*

pinto, red, black, and other varieties, and they are served differently in the Caribbean countries. The Cuban *frijoles negros* (black beans) are frequently served as an entrée with steamed white rice and presented with or without meat or fish. One version of black beans and rice is called *moros y cristianos* (Moors and Christians), a name attributed to the indigenous Indians who encountered blacks and whites for the first time after Columbus's arrival. Other favorites of the *Antilles include:

Aguardiente. The liquor originating in Cuba and known more commonly as rum. Its full name is *aguardiente de caña* (literally: sugar cane burning water) and became one of Spain's most profitable Cuban exports during the colonial period. The literal translation of *cañas* is "canes" and refers to the tall, tough cane plant indigenous to the Caribbean islands and coastal areas of Mesoamerica from which sugar is extracted and rum fermented. Eventually *aguardiente* distilleries were built elsewhere in the Antilles including in Puerto Rico and Martinique. A staple agricultural and economic crop of Cuba until the Cold War response to the *Cuban Revolution by the United States, sugar cane farming declined sharply when the United States instituted the trade embargo against Cuba (*see* History, Cuban American). Fibers of the cane plant were traditionally used for textile materials by the indigenous people of the region.

Cuba libres. One of the most popular drinks of North America until the Cuban Revolution, the cocktail originated in Havana and combines the native rum (*aguardiente*) with Coca-Cola and lime on the rocks. The name is as ironic in its satiric humor as the black beans and rice dish known as *moros y cristianos* (Moors and Christians), for it conveys the history of Cuba as a conquered and colonized country in combination with the freedom (*libre* means "free") associated with the United States that Coca-Cola represents.

Asopao de pollo. A chili marinated chicken stew served with plantain dumplings. Usually identified with Puerto Rico, *asopao de pollo* translates roughly as "stewed chicken" and is typically thought of as a special holiday dish eaten, for example, during the *parrandas* (all-night house-to-house visits among friends and relatives) associated with Christmas, Los Tres Reyes Magos (Three Kings Magi Day), and festivities known as Octavitas intended to keep the joy of Christmas alive. Classic versions of the *asopao de pollo* entrée consist of an *adobo* (i.e., dry rubbing of salt, oregano, garlic, black pepper, and turmeric) applied to the chicken pieces and cooked with red pepper, potatoes, white rice, onion, tomato, cilantro, garlic, bay leaf, olive oil, and *bollitas de platano* (little balls, or dumplings, of green plantain).

Ceviche. A marinated seafood staple of the Caribbean rim, the dish is not native to the Americas since one of its key ingredients is lime juice, and limes were first brought to the hemisphere by Spanish and Portuguese settlers in the sixteenth century. Nevertheless, *ceviche* is treated as "native" by Latinos who grew up in water-bound regions. In basic terms, the dish, usually served as an appetizer, marinates fresh fish and shellfish in undiluted lime

> juice that pickles (i.e., cooks and preserves) the raw fish. The result can then be accompanied with salsas (sauces) and salads and served fancy in crystal goblets or simple inside a tortilla to make a seafood taco.

These distinctive Antillean foods and dishes represent only a tiny sampling of the vast cuisine that emerged from the amalgamation of native American with European cookery. They illustrate the distinctive identities of their places and cultures of origin, even as they also demonstrate their portability beyond the Caribbean north, south, and across both oceans.

Besides the indigenous dishes and drinks described, a large part of the Latina/o menu consists of food imported by the Europeans from their native lands. Among the "Old World" foods brought to the Americas by the Spaniards were Andalusian beef, *arroz* (rice), *bolillos* (wheat flour bread rolls), empanadas (turnovers stuffed with sweet fruit, meat, and/or vegetable fillings), olives, olive oil, tapas (small servings of a variety of dishes), wines, and many others. Other European influences that mixed with the cuisines of the Americas include potatoes, pastas, wheat flours, and whiskies, and after the *Treaty of Guadalupe Hidalgo was signed in 1848, many Anglo-American adaptations entered Latina/o cooking, like an amazing range of barbecue varieties, taco salads, enchilada casseroles, "mild, medium, and hot" chili sauces, and "hard and soft" tortilla chips. While cuisines the world over share a great variety of sources, both the breadth and diversity of the seven culinary roots outlined above are especially vast because of the continuous and continuing intermingling contact of East with West and North with South and reciprocal influences.

Further Reading

Bayless, Rick. *Mexico One Plate at a Time*. New York: Scribner, 2000.

De'Angeli, Alicia Gironella, and Jorge De'Angeli. *El gran libro de la cocina mexicana*. Mexico City: Ediciones Larousse, 1980.

Gilbert, Fabiola Cabeza de Baca. *We Fed Them Cactus*. Albuquerque: University of New Mexico Press, 1954.

Grant, Rosamund. *Caribbean and African Cookery*. Kingston, Jamaica: Ian Randle Publishers, 1988.

MacKie, Cristine. *Life and Food in the Caribbean*. Kingston, Jamaica: Ian Randle Publishers, 1995.

Romano, Dora de. *Rice and Beans and Tasty Things: A Puerto Rican Cookbook*. Translated by Jaime Romano. Hato Rey, Puerto Rico: Ramallo Bros., 1986.

Cordelia Chávez Candelaria

Fuentes, Daisy (1966–). A crossover television host, model, and MTV video jockey (VJ), Daisy Fuentes was born in Cuba to a Cuban father and a Spanish mother and spent her early childhood in Havana and Madrid before moving with her family to New Jersey at the age of seven. As a community college student, Fuentes worked as a "weather girl," news anchor, and reporter at a local television station. A demonstration tape sent to

Daisy Fuentes. *Courtesy of Photofest.*

MTV won her a position with *MTV Internacional*, a weekly Spanish-language program she hosted for its full six-year run. The success of *MTV Internacional* led to MTV Latino, a full channel dedicated to Latin music; and Fuentes assumed host and VJ duties for this new venture. From there she moved to the parent MTV channel and became MTV's first Latina VJ and a crossover success. Fuentes became a star hosting shows such as *The Top 20 Video Countdown* and *House of Style* (where she took over for model Cindy Crawford).

Fuentes's growing celebrity and cross-cultural appeal led to further successful forays into television, film, and modeling. Her television credits include roles in *Loving*, *Cybill*, *Dream On*, and *The Larry Sanders Show*. She has served as host of her own CNBC talk show (*Daisy*, part of that channel's *Talk All-Stars*), *America's Funniest Home Videos*, the *ALMA Awards, *Dick Clark's New Year's Rockin' Eve*, and the Miss Universe pageant. In 1996, Fuentes broke into film with a role in the Quentin Tarantino–produced *Curdled*. Her modeling and endorsement work (for Revlon, Pantene, American Express, and Miller Lite, among others) have also contributed to her fame. She has been featured on the cover of the Spanish-language *Cosmopolitan* and *Harper's Bazaar*, as well as *Fitness*, *Shape*, and **Latina*. In 2003, she appeared on the cover of *People*'s first Spanish language swimsuit edition.

Further Reading

"Daisy Fuentes Brief Biography." http://features.yahoo.com/webceleb/daisy.
Daisy Fuentes Official Website. http://www.daisyfuentes.com.

Durrani, Shandana. "Thriving Miss Daisy." *Cigar Aficionado* (November 1997). http://www.cigaraficionado.com/Cigar/Aficionado/people/fk1197.html.

Darren Crovitz

Fusco, Coco (1960–). Coco Fusco is an internationally acclaimed Afro-Cuban interdisciplinary artist and curator born in New York City on June 18, 1960. She earned her Bachelor of Arts degree in literature and society and semiotics from Brown University in 1982. In 1985 she received a Master of Arts degree in modern thought and literature from Stanford University. She is an associate professor in the School of Visual Arts at Columbia University. Her performance work and multimedia art installations have toured North and South America, Europe, South Africa, Australia, New Zealand, Korea, and Japan. She has given lectures in Italy, México, Spain, Canada, England, Sweden, and the United States.

Fusco has written two books, *English Is Broken Here: Notes on Cultural Fusion in the Americas* (1995) and *The Bodies That Were Not Ours and Other Writings* (2001). In addition, she is the editor of *Corpus Delecti: Performance Art of the Americas* (1999). *Stuff*, a play coauthored with Nao Bustamante, also appears in the anthology *Out of the Fringe: Contemporary Latina/Latino Theatre and Performance* (1999), edited by Caridad Svich and María Teresa Marrero. As a performance and border theorist, her articles and essays have been published in periodicals such as *The Village Voice*, *The Nation*, *Los Angeles Times*, *Arts Magazine*, *Journal of Performance Studies*, and **Latina* magazine. Fusco has collaborated with numerous artists including Guillermo *Gómez-Peña (*The Couple in the Cage: A Guatinaui Odyssey*, 1993), Nao Bustamante (*Stuff*, 1996), Ricardo Dominguez (*Dolores from 10 to 10*, 2002), and Sergio De La Torre (*Acceso Negado/Access Denied*, 1998).

As an artist/theorist/educator, her work has been funded by the New York State Council on the Arts, the New York Foundation for the Arts, National Endowment for the Arts, Arts International, the Los Angeles Department of Cultural Affairs, the Franklin Furnace Fund for Performance Art, the Rockefeller Foundation, and Temple University. In 1995 she was awarded the ATHE (Association of Theatre in Higher Education) Research Award for Outstanding Journal Article for her essay titled "The Other History of Cultural Performance," which was published in the spring 1994 issue of *Drama Review*. That same year she received the Critics' Choice Award from the American Educational Studies Association for her book *English Is Broken Here: Notes on Cultural Fusion in the Americas*. In 2000 she received the Tyler School of Art Merit Award for Outstanding Research from Temple University.

Fusco has held artist-in-residencies at the California Institute for the Arts, as well as the University of Illinois, Chicago. She has been a visiting artist at University of Colorado, Boulder, the Kun Kun Cultural Center in San Cristobal de las Casas in Chiapas, México, Otago Polytechnic in Dunedin, New Zealand, the Santa Fe Art Institute in New Mexico, and the Arts Council of Andalusia, Spain. She was a Mellon Fellow at the California Institute for the Arts from September 1994 to May 1995.

In December 2003, Fusco premiered an exhibit she developed with cocurator Brian Wallis titled *Only Skin Deep: Changing Visions of the American Self*. This piece is described as a comprehensive exhibition about *race in American photography and opened at the International Center of Photography in New York City. Another recent performance piece, *The Incredible Disappearing Woman*, is about women, sex, and death in the U.S.-México borderland. This piece was commissioned by the Portland Institute for Contemporary Art and premiered in 2002 at Wesleyan's Center for the Arts.

Fusco's work deals with border and *immigration issues, cultural identity, gender politics, and *globalization. Through both her individual work and her collaborative efforts with other artists, Fusco communicates to a broad audience on issues that many others would rather sweep under the rug. She uncovers cultural injustices and speaks through an artistic megaphone to remind people of the realities of the world in which they live.

Further Reading

Fusco, Coco. *English Is Broken Here: Notes on Cultural Fusion in the Americas*. New York: New York University Press, 1995.

Vercoe, Caroline. "Towards an Ambivalent Gaze: A Reading of Works by Coco Fusco." In *Body Politics and the Fictional Double*, edited by Debra Walker King. Bloomington: Indiana University Press, 2000.

Christina Marín

Galán, Nely (1963–). As an accomplished television producer, Nely Galán has made significant contributions to Latina and Latino popular culture by producing major television programs that target Latina/o audiences and aim to bridge the cultural gap between Latina/o and mainstream television in the United States. Galán was born in Santa Clara, Cuba, and grew up in Teaneck, New Jersey, where her family moved when she was two. Entrusted at age twenty-two with the management of the *Spanish-language television station WNJU-TV, a Telemundo affiliate in New Jersey, Galán earned the distinction of being the youngest television station manager in the United States. Later Galán worked with Time Warner and co-created the production company Tropix, aimed at placing Latina/o faces on American television. Galán helped launch the Fox Latin American Channel, Fox Kids in Latin America, and Fox Sports Américas. In 1998, Galán was named president of entertainment for Telemundo and directed *Sólo en América*, the first Spanish-language sitcom on American television. In 1994 Galán founded gaLAn entertainment, dedicated to producing crossover urban television programming and feature *films. The gaLAn company has produced over 400 episodes of Spanish- and English-language programming aimed at the Latino audience, including a reality television series, *True Love Stories* (2002–), a Spanish-language *Cuban American sitcom, *Los Beltrán* (2000–), and a talk show addressing "taboo" topics like safe sex practices, abortion, and divorce, hosted by a Catholic priest, *Padre Alberto* (1999–).

Further Reading

Kossak, Jennifer. "Hispanic Outlook in Higher Education." *Latino Leaders* 6 (1995): 6.

http://www.galanent.com.
http://www.smc.edu/events/pressreleases/1999/galantalk.htm.

Brenda Rascón

Gangs. One of the most common *stereotypes of Latino youth in contemporary twenty-first-century popular culture is that of gang members. Along with the conventional stereotypes of the Latin lover from the early decades of motion pictures and of the Mexican maid from the closing decades of the twentieth century, the sinister image of the gang member in baggy pants, knotted head scarf, and tattoos has appeared regularly in movies and television programming and contributed to general public perceptions of Latinos. **West Side Story*, both the 1957 Broadway play and the 1961 movie, opened the cinematic door to the gang portrayals when its director/producers set the Shakespearean theme of doomed "Romeo and Juliet" lovers within a Puerto Rican gang context. Since then the role of gang bangers has been cast repeatedly in Latino terms literally from A to Z—for example, **American Me* and **La Bamba* to *Mí Familia* and **Zoot Suit*.

This lopsided negative media portrayal of Hispanics has elicited vigorous challenge from Latina/o advocates and other media watchdogs. The prestigious *National Council of La Raza (NCLR), for example, has released several policy reports calling for fewer stereotypical gang portrayals and more responsible and complete representations of Latinas/os and other minorities. The NCLR report "Don't Blink: Hispanics in Television Entertainment" (1996) calls attention to the paucity of Latina/o television roles and programming, a conclusion that echoes the same charges made twenty years earlier in a highly influential federal government study, *Window Dressing on the Set, an Update* (1977), researched and compiled by the U.S. Commission on Civil Rights. *Window Dressing on the Set* demonstrates the deeply rooted persistence of the twin problems of racial bias and (mis)representation as a source for the widespread negative gang portrayal of Latinos and other young people of color. The civil rights study was based on public hearings regarding the invisibility on television of minorities with particular emphasis on African Americans.

One reason for this critical outcry, besides the obvious concern with stereotypic representation, is that the actual material experience of gangs, their origin, youth participation in them, and related social aspects constitutes an extremely complex sociocultural phenomenon. Despite media fascination with gangs and the many research studies on gang membership, the very definition of the term and the member composition of gangs are the subject of considerable debate among researchers, law enforcement, educators, and others. This is understandable when the word itself historically has been applied to such diverse associations as, for example, the Jesse James gang of the American cowboy frontier, the Ohio gang of corrupt politicians including U.S. President Warren G. Harding in the early twentieth century, the Stern gang of Palestinian terrorists in the 1940s, and the ruling Gang of Four of the People's Republic of China in the 1970s. These varied uses of the term have one important feature in common, criminal actions by groups of participants.

Contemporary sociologists and other experts describe gangs as organizations of mostly young men and boys (1) that inhabit territories (i.e., "turf") with identifiable geographical boundaries, (2) that possess clear-cut top-down lines of leadership and authority, and (3) that provide an acknowledged fellowship and in-group loyalty among the members. Specialists also generally agree that gangs usually are united (4) by ethnic and racial identity, as well as (5) by regulated conventions of dress and appearance including the wearing of similar clothing, tattoos, hairstyles, and related identifiers.

Debates about the definition of gangs concern, for the most part, two primary areas of debate: criminal activity and the participants' admission of gang membership. The first issue relates to whether or not gangs form and boys and young men join the pack to engage in crime or whether the criminal and delinquent activity follows after membership is established as an inevitable result of the collective and unregulated banding of boys, adolescents, and men. Most social workers generally agree that the member's original gang participation is usually motivated by a need to redress dysfunctional family situations, not to commit criminal acts. Others believe that the unbearable domestic situation pushes vulnerable youth to gangs that inevitably lead to criminal acting out, even if such activities are not part of the original intent of individual members. Another view is that crime leaders usually recruit gang members from poverty-stricken, dysfunctional areas because the problem development of future gang prospects makes them especially vulnerable to strong boss manipulation. Regardless of original source or intent, most observers concede that gangs engage in delinquency and crime, usually drug related, as a normal routine.

The second primary issue of debate concerns whether a reliable way of defining gang membership is by a participant's actual admission that he (or she) belongs to a gang. Self-identification as a "gang-banger" is one method employed by certain urban ethnographers to count and track gang size and activity. This view is challenged by other researchers, many law enforcement practitioners, and social workers who argue that the very nature of gang membership requires clandestine, *un*acknowledged involvement, thus making self-identification as a gang member unlikely. Proponents of this view believe that data gathered according to this definition is likely to be incomplete and unreliable. Despite this definitional texture, most research investigators concede that gangs normally are marked by a combination of several of the above traits and that they vary in size and composition from region to region.

Researchers also concede that gang membership is harmful to the well-being, health, and lives of both individual gang members and surrounding communities. Many social scientists believe that the experiential gang reality lies like a vast societal iceberg of severe multifaceted problems beneath the tip of cool gang imagery portrayed in the profit-making entertainment outlets of musical sounds, media screens, and advertising. To the victims of gang crime especially, as well as to public advocates for and observers of the basic needs of dysfunctional families, low educational achievers, and the chronic unemployed, gangs are anything but *hip-hop cool or entertaining show business. Victims and informed advocates know that gangs are seeded and thrive in a troubled habitat of children's and adolescent needs that **cholo* exploitation entertainment moguls overlook or romanticize for profit-making ends. As a result, they help perpetuate the hoods-on-the-hood icons and stereotypes applied to all Latina/o young people.

One segment of gang increase is in the number of women recruits, particularly in the large cities on the East and West Coasts like New York and Los Angeles. For example, the Puerto Rican Latin Queens have been identified in *police and newspaper reports as increasingly active in the New York area. In the Chicana/o context, reports of girls and women getting "jumped in" and "sexed in"—that is, coerced into gang participation—appear in greater and greater numbers and are the subject of recent studies. Despite the increase in female membership, gender politics in gangs follow fundamentalist patriarchal norms with a tyrannical *patrón* (boss) maintaining his power through violent intimidation and the status of girls linked to the turf status of her dominating, profit-making *patrón*. Disturbing recent studies report that the "jumping in" initiation practices for girls may include such violent sexist activities as being beaten by other gang members, as well as being forced to "get sexed in" (i.e., required to have sex with the gang's leaders and, in some instances, all the gang members). The Chicana gang the East Side Norteñas from northern California disagree that *cholas* (young females in gang dress) are dominated by *cholos*, according to sociological fieldwork conducted from 2000 to 2002.

By and large, research studies indicate that gang participation leads to and exacerbates a swamp of societal problems including violent crimes, school dropouts, drug use, high rates of teen pregnancy, sexually transmitted diseases, AIDS, and early mortality. Studies also show that schools (6–12 grade levels) often offer important socializing networks for gang recruitment and other drug-related gang activities, including spray paint vandalism (i.e., "tagging") on one end of the delinquency spectrum to murder at the other extreme. Research investigations point to troubling domestic environments (e.g., broken families marked by poverty, addiction, violence, sexual abuse, filth, and very young unwed parents, usually single mothers unable to provide for their children) as the key sources of gang participation.

In spite of the high media and entertainment profile of Latinos as gang members, available research shows that, when the data are disaggregated by ethnicity, location, and generational time in the United States, proportionately few Latino youths actually participate in street gangs. Available statistics place the level of membership from 2 percent to 9 percent, depending on region and neighborhood. Of course, the figures for gang-related juvenile crime vary according to the definitions that are employed and counting methods applied, but they hover around 2 percent to 5 percent. Latino gangs usually develop along ethnic and racial lines and are typically composed of one dominant ethnicity, for example, all Chicanos, Mexican immigrants, or immigrants from El Salvador. Although some Latino gangs may include one or two Caucasian or African American members along with biracial members, it is expected that all the gang members be Spanish-speaking or at least be acquainted with street Spanish (i.e., Caló). Most Latino gang members are citizens born in the United States, and a great many in the Southwest are indigenous third, fourth, and older generation Latinos, not recent immigrants, despite reports of growing numbers of immigrant Latino gangs, particularly in the largest cities on the coasts. Alienation from family and society appear to be the most significant predictor of future gang affiliation, leading many advocates to push intervention efforts toward this aspect of children's lives and the future of their communities.

Further Reading

Brown, Monica. *Gang Nation: Delinquent Citizens in Puerto Rican, Chicano, and Chicana Narratives*. Minneapolis: University of Minnesota Press, 2002.

Goldstein, Arnold P., and C. Ronald Huff. *The Gang Intervention Handbook*. Champaign, IL: Research Press, 1993.

Hallcom, Francine. "An Urban Ethnography of Latino Street Gangs." http://www.csun.edu/~hcchs006/table.html.

Miranda, Marie "Keta." *Homegirls in the Public Sphere*. Austin: University of Texas Press, 2003.

National Council of La Raza. "Don't Blink: Hispanics in Television Entertainment." NCLR Policy Discussion Paper, Washington, DC, 1996.

National Council of La Raza. *The Mainstreaming of Hate: A Report on Latinos and Harassment, Hate Violence, and Law Enforcement Abuse*. Washington, DC: NCLR Publications, September 1999.

National Council of La Raza. *U.S. Latino Children: A Status Report*. Washington, DC: NCLR Publications, August 2000.

Ramírez Berg, Charles. *Latino Images in Film: Stereotypes, Subversion, & Resistance*. Austin: University of Texas Press, 2002.

U.S. Commission on Civil Rights. 1977. *Window Dressing on the Set, an Update*. Washington, DC: USCCR, 1979.

Cordelia Chávez Candelaria

García, Andy (1956–). Andy García, a major film star, was born Andrés Arturo García-Menéndez on April 12, 1956, in Havana, Cuba. His family moved to Miami, Florida, when he was five. His acting debut came in 1981 when he shot a pilot for the acclaimed television series *Hill Street Blues*. He made his film debut in 1983 in the little-known *Blue Skies Again*. García came to national and international prominence with his performance in the action-drama *The Untouchables* (1987).

García has acted in more than twenty-five films. Included among his many awards and recognitions are a star on Hollywood's Walk of Fame, an Oscar nomination for his role in *The Godfather: Part III* (1991), Golden Eagle Awards in 1991 and 1997, and a 1999 *ALMA Award. He also played the legendary Cuban trumpet player Arturo *Sandoval in the HBO production *For Love or Country: The Arturo Sandoval Story* (2001) and portrayed Spanish poet Federico García Lorca in the 1997 film *The Disappearance of García Lorca*. García has also successfully worked behind the camera as a producer on films such as *The Man from Elysian Fields* (2001), *Just the Ticket* (1999), and *Swing Vote* (1999), and as producer and director of the documentary film of the life and music of Israel "Cachao" López, *Cachao: Como Sur Ritmo No Hay Dos* (Like His Rhythm, There Is No Other, 1993).

García's love for and pride in Cuban culture is evidenced in his film projects as well as his dedication to Cuban music. García has performed, written, and produced songs for the sound tracks of his movies *Steal Big, Steal Little* (1995), *The Birdcage* (1996), *Just the Ticket* (1999), and *For Love or Country*. He has also played with Latin music legends Paquito D'Rivera and Cachao. García helped revive the career of Cachao through producing, mixing, singing, and playing on the albums *Cachao: Master Sessions Vol. I* and *Vol. II* (1994, 1995).

Further Reading

Ebert, Roger. "The Untouchables." *Chicago Sun-Times*, June 3, 1987.

Louis "Pancho" McFarland

García, Hector. *See* American G.I. Forum.

Garcia, Jerry (1942–1995). Jerry Garcia was the lead singer and guitarist for the Grateful Dead and one of the most interesting Latino rock musicians in the United States. He was born on August 1, 1942, as Jerome John García in San Francisco's Mission District. His father José ("Joe") Ramón García, an immigrant from Coruna, Spain, was a jazz clarinetist and dixieland band leader during the 1930s. His mother, Ruth Marie Clifford, met Joe in San Francisco during the early 1930s, and the two were married in 1934.

At the age of five, while on a fly-fishing trip with his father, Garcia witnessed his father drown in the California River after being swept away by the strong current. Just a few months prior his death, Joe and Ruth had invested in a bar located at 400 First Street in downtown San Francisco. After Joe's death, Ruth was forced to manage the "400 Club" alone and sent her son to live with her parents. It was there that Garcia began to develop his skills in music.

As a child, Garcia began to study the piano but was never interested in music theory or learning how to read music notation. Often, Garcia would learn songs entirely by ear and play them back to his instructor, pretending to know how to read the music. Even as a professional musician, Garcia never learned, or even attempted to relearn, how to read or write in Western notation. Both Garcia and his grandmother Tillie were regular listeners of Nashville's Grand Ole Opry, and it was during this time that Garcia claimed to have developed a liking for country music. He was especially fascinated by the blues style mandolin playing and unique vocal style of bluegrass's principal founder, Bill Monroe.

But it was not until the age of fifteen that Garcia began to develop an interest in rock and roll music. After his older brother Clifford, or "Tiff" as he was called, introduced Garcia to rock and roll, he lost interest in piano and opted to learn guitar instead. He pleaded with his mother to buy him an electric guitar, but she reluctantly bought him an accordion instead, thinking that he would be unable to play guitar because he had lost his middle finger in an accident a few years earlier.

Garcia's mother later remarried, and he lived with her again in San Francisco, after living three years in Menlo Park. Garcia devoted most of his time to practicing guitar, learning from recordings by T-Bone Walker and Chuck Berry. After graduating from Balboa High School, Garcia began taking art classes at North Beach Art School and the California School of Fine Arts and became actively involved in the Beat scene.

During the early 1960s, Garcia could often be found in the music clubs around Stanford University or at Dana Morgan's Music Store, where he worked part-time. It was at this music store that Garcia met several of the musicians who would eventually dominate the San Francisco music scene. In 1963, Jerry organized his own "jug band" called Mother McCree's Uptown Jug Champions. This all-acoustic band would play at the same music clubs where Garcia spent most of his time, often playing for the "beatniks" that Garcia had associated himself with. His band played a wide variety of music ranging from country to blues and folk music.

In 1964, shortly after the Beatles' historic appearance on the *Ed Sullivan Show*, Garcia decided to convert his jug band into an electric unit called the Warlocks. Unsatisfied with the change, a couple of the original band members dropped out, leaving room for two new members to join. Ron McKernan, affectionately known as "Pigpen," and Bob Weir remained part of Garcia's new electric band, welcoming Bill Kreutzmann on drums and Phil Lesh on bass. The new music of the Warlocks was heavily influenced by the Beatles and Bob Dylan and reflected the radical thinking of the mid-1960s.

As the band gained popularity in and around the San Francisco area, the members began to experiment with drugs. The U.S. government had established a Veterans' Hospital near Stanford University as a testing site of government-sanctioned experiments with LSD. Many "beatniks" had taken part in these governmental experiments and a number became dependent on LSD. Among them was Robert Hunter, who later became Jerry Garcia's songwriting partner, and Ken Kesey, author of the novels *One Flew Over the Cuckoo's Nest* (1962) and *Sometimes a Great Notion* (1966).

Kesey, who had become very influential in San Francisco's beat scene, had developed his own ideas about LSD experimentation. He rounded up a crew of radical beatniks, rebels, and "intellectual dropouts," known as the Merry Pranksters, to conduct his own group experiments with LSD. The Warlocks had been recruited as the house band for these collective drug experiments known as the "Acid Tests." During these experiments, the band changed its name to The Grateful Dead, and, they too, participated in the Acid Tests, often developing their musical ideas from the hallucinations they experienced while on the drug. The Acid Tests were intended as acts of cultural, spiritual, and psychic revolt, and their importance to the development of The Grateful Dead cannot be overestimated or overlooked.

Within a year, the reputation of The Grateful Dead had spread across the nation and throughout the world. The music of the Grateful Dead had become very popular in the United States and in Europe, and the "Grateful Dead Trip," as the movement was called, was now influencing the same artists that had originally influenced Garcia and his fellow band members. By 1966, artists like Bob Dylan, the Beatles, Jefferson Airplane, Quicksilver Messenger Service, and Janis Joplin were all experimenting with LSD and other drugs to create the revolutionary music of the late 1960s and early 1970s.

A new community of young radical thinkers sprang out of San Francisco's Haight-Ashbury district, the mecca of the Hippie Movement, after The Grateful Dead purchased a house in the area. The area became a youth haven for those who shared similar views, or whose views were influenced by The Grateful Dead. Often, the Dead would stage benefit concerts or free public shows to promote the sense of kinship that came from and fueled their music.

The glory of the Haight-Ashbury district, however, was short-lived. As more people caught wind of the Grateful Dead Trip, the Haight was soon infested with hundreds of runaway students, and the middle-class neighborhood began to face severe health problems, crime, and homelessness. There were so many young people experienced bad trips that at times emergency rooms of local hospitals could not accommodate them all. There were also defective drugs on the streets, rapes and murders, and waves of starry-eyed newcomers who arrived without any means to support themselves, hoping the scene would feed them. By the 1970s, the Hippie Movement had strayed away from its original intent to promote peace and kinship. Drugs, which originally were taken for to induce near-religious hallucinations and to intensify the essence of community and brotherhood, had now become a risky and dangerous business. *Gang violence, prostitution, and homelessness were rampant problems by the turn of the new decade. It was not until 1969 after the Rolling Stones hosted a free concert at the Altamont Speedway that the Dead began to speak out against the corrupted direction their movement was taking.

In 1969, shortly after the Manson Family murders that summer, the Rolling Stones hosted a free concert in which the Hell's Angels were hired as a security force for the concert. That day, the Angels battered numerous people for little or no reason while the Rolling Stones played on stage, and the concert was ended prematurely when an Angel stabbed a black man to death in front of the stage.

In response to that incident, Garcia and the Grateful Dead recorded *Workingman's Dead* (1970), which addressed the issues of violence, drugs, and the changing face of community in both the United States and its counterculture. It was also during that time that Garcia developed a rivalry with Jefferson Airplane. Garcia felt that Jefferson Airplane was "feeling the power of their ability" and using that power to create violence in the streets. Garcia had made a conscious decision to disassociate himself and the band from the violent and aggressive mood that Jefferson Airplane carried on. After *Workingman's Dead*, Garcia and the band released two other recordings: *American Beauty* (1970) and *Grateful Dead* (1971). During the recording of *American Beauty*, Garcia's mother was killed in an automobile accident, and he used his time in the studio as a form of therapy to help him cope with his loss. As a result, *American Beauty* exemplifies his ability to reflect his emotion through his songs.

Guitarist Jerry Garcia of The Grateful Dead smiles as he plays in Highgate, Vermont, in this July 1994 photo. *AP/Wide World Photos.*

During the 1980s and early 1990s, Garcia and the Grateful Dead continued to thrive on the success their earlier music had brought them. During this time, the Grateful Dead had a following of over 110,000 fans who called themselves "Dead Heads." However, it was also during that time that Garcia had developed a dependency on cocaine and heroin, and his health was quickly deteriorating.

On January 18, 1985, Garcia was arrested for possession of illegal drugs in San Francisco. He was reported as having twenty-three packets of "brown and white" substances and was sentenced to a Marin County drug rehabilitation program. After about a year, following Garcia's successful treatment, The Grateful Dead continued touring with Bob Dylan and Tom Petty and the Heartbreakers, during the summer of 1986. After returning from his tour, Garcia fell into a diabetic coma that nearly killed him.

Prior to that moment, Garcia was not aware of any health problems other than the self-inflicted conditions that resulted from his drug addictions. Five days after slipping into a coma, Garcia awoke in a local hospital and was then informed of his diabetic condition. Severe dehydration and fatigue induced the diabetic coma that took its toll on his memory and muscle coordination. After his release from the hospital, Garcia rested and began relearning his skills on guitar with his old friend Merl Saunders. It took Jerry over three months of therapy to regain his abilities on guitar to the point that he could perform again.

Up until 1995, The Grateful Dead continued to tour America. However, the band also continued to witness violence and other illegal activity outside of their performances. The situation became so severe that the band issued an official edict that warned the public of their intent to stop touring if the illegal activity and disturbance of the peace did not stop. In response to this edict, some fans sent death threats to Garcia, one of which was taken very seriously by law enforcement officials.

In mid-July 1995, Garcia checked himself into the Betty Ford Center in Rancho Mirage to completely recuperate from his addiction to heroin and cocaine. He reportedly did this not because of his dependency on the drugs but to be completely sober for his eldest daughter Heather's wedding. After spending a week at home with his family during his fifty-third birthday on August 1, Garcia then checked himself into a Marin County clinic, Serenity Knolls. A few days later, on August 9, 1995, Garcia died in his sleep of a massive heart attack.

Immediately upon hearing of Garcia's death, fans across the world began making makeshift altars in public parks and areas like the Haight and other locations where Garcia had lived and created his music. Even after his death, Garcia has maintained a faithful following that continues to thrive on the legacy he and his band created. Post-1960s music such as rap, techno, and punk has benefited greatly from them.

Through The Grateful Dead, Garcia has been able to influence the minds and attitudes of young people throughout the world for more than thirty years. Having been influenced by major artists of the Beat movement, Garcia and his band members were able to create a musical revolution that in turn influenced the very same artists he had looked to during the Grateful Dead's formative stages. His life, times, and music reflect the very essence of the Hippie Movement, and as a result, he has developed both positive and negative criticisms. He has influenced many aspiring young musicians and artists, and it appears that his legacy will always remain strong in American popular culture and music.

Further Reading

Gilmore, Mikal. *Night Beak: a Shadow History of Rock & Roll.* New York: Doubleday, 1998.

Tharp, Daniel Edward. "Come Hear Uncle John's Band: Religious Behavior in the Wake of the Nineteen-Sixties." Ph.D. dissertation, Arizona State University, Tempe, 1992.

Winnick, Jill. *Jerome John Garcia: Biography of a Legend.* June 1999. http://www.uvm.edu/~jwinnick/growingup.html.

J. Javier Enríquez

Gaspar de Alba, Alicia (1958–). Alicia Gaspar de Alba, born in the border town of El Paso, Texas, in 1958, is a Chicana poet, essayist, fiction writer, and cultural critic. Her work explores borders of space, *race and ethnicity, gender, and sexuality in Chicana/o culture. Her writing draws from the multiple borders of culture and brings issues of *gender and sexuality to the fore. Among Gaspar de Alba's scholarly works are *Chicano Art Inside/Outside the Master's House: Cultural Politics and the *CARA Exhibition* (1998) and *Velvet *Barrios: Popular Culture and Chicana/o Sexualities* (2003). The former study grew out of her award-winning dissertation at the University of New Mexico, where Gaspar de Alba earned a doctorate in American studies in 1994. The dissertation was awarded the Ralph Henry Gabriel Prize for Best Dissertation in American Studies. It examines the cultural, sexual, and representational politics of the "Chicano Art: Resistance and Affirmation" exhibition. The anthology brings together eighteen essays on diverse forms of Chicana/o popular culture. Together both texts contribute to the theorization of Chicano/o aesthetics, especially as they play with and subvert mainstream American renditions of Chicana/o art, literature, and cultural production.

In addition to her scholarly work, she is also noted for her works of fiction. **Sor Juana's Second Dream* (1999) is Gaspar de Alba's first novel, which won Best Historical Fiction from the Latino Literary Hall of Fame in 2000. *The Mystery of Survival and Other Stories* (1993) was her first collection of short stories, which received the Premio Aztlán in 1994. "Beggar on the Cordoba Bridge," a collection of poems in *Three Times a Woman: Chicana Poetry* (1989), was Gaspar de Alba's first compilation of poems. In her stories and poetry, she continually writes of the border terrain that is El Paso and Juárez and of the Córdova Bridge, a central metaphor for the mixing and clash of two cultures and two systems of knowledge.

Gaspar de Alba became an associate professor of Chicana and Chicano Studies at the University of California, Los Angeles (UCLA), in 1994 and received early tenure in 1999. She earned a master's degree in English and creative writing from the University of Texas, El Paso, in 1983, where she also completed a bachelor's degree in English in 1980. Gaspar de Alba has taught at the University of Texas at El Paso, the University of New Mexico, the University of Iowa, and the University of Massachusetts, Boston. Gaspar de Alba is the beneficiary of numerous prizes, grants, and fellowships. She received a Rockefeller Fellowship for Latino/a Cultural Study from the Smithsonian Institution (1999), an Institute of American Cultures Grant (1998–1999), and a UCMexus Research Grant (1998–1999). She was also awarded the Border-Ford/Pellicer-Frost Award for Poetry (1998), the Shirley Collier Prize for Literature (UCLA English Department award, 1998), a Pomona College Minority Scholar-in-Residence Postdoctoral Fellowship (1994–1995), and a Massachusetts Artists Foundation Fellowship award for poetry (1989).

Further Reading

Chávez-Silverman, Susana. "Chicanas in Love: Sandra Cisneros and Alicia Gaspar de Alba 'Giving Back the Wor[l]d.'" In *Reading and Writing the Ambiente: Queer Sexualities in Latino, Latin America, and Spanish Culture*, edited by Susana Chávez-Silverman and Librada Hernández. Madison: University of Wisconsin Press, 2000.

Gaspar de Alba, Alicia. *Chicano Art Inside/Outside the Master's House: Cultural Politics and the CARA Exhibition*. Austin: University of Texas Press, 1998.

Gaspar de Alba, Alicia, and Tomas Ybarra Frausto. *Velvet Barrios: Popular Culture and Chicana/o Sexualities*. New York: Palgrave, 2003.

Miguel A. Segovia

Gavilán, Kid. *See* Kid Gavilán.

Gender. *Gender* is usually described as the ideas about maleness and femaleness that are constructed socially and learned from society, and *sex* as the physical differences that are genetically received. *Sexuality* refers to the acting out of sex and gender as part of the expression of identity. Pertinent to a discussion of gender and Latina and Latino popular culture is the notion of strategic opposition, or that Latina/o manifestations may be viewed as production that explicitly or implicitly stands up against, and stands up to, a dominant Anglo production. Such oppositional force may involve a number of different and overlapping general features relating to where Latinas/os live, the language spoken, social movements and political action, artistic and cultural practices, and related activities. All of these dimensions are crucial to questions of gender and deserve brief summary.

The strategic opposition of life in the *barrio (neighborhood) and other in-group places where Latinas/os reside contrasts with life before the barrio in the country of origin and/or life for better or worse after the barrio, often in adaptation to the Anglo or other dominant majority or sometimes in the person's return to the country of origin. Concerning language, the oppositions are many as in those relating to Standard Spanish (or Castillian), to Mexican Spanish (or other national dialects), and to barrio Spanish, which also involves multiple layers of dialects having to do with class, region, awareness of academic Spanish, and the influence of English. English-language influences permeate Latina/o expression through bilingualism, code-switching, media and entertainment, and the abandonment of Spanish for English for a wide variety of reasons. Another Latina/o oppositional force deals with social movements that may be seen as inevitable and urgent for the defense of ethnic identity/identities (e.g., farmworker and immigrant rights). This oppositional consciousness to artistic and culture forms, themes, genres, or fads also circulates among the people in Latina/o-inflected versions of Anglo culture (e.g., *I Love Lucy* and some Ricky *Martin Top 40 hits), as well as in uniquely Latina/o forms like *mariachi jamborees, the cult of the *Virgin of Guadalupe, and many others.

These oppositional and crucial dimensions of popular cultures reinforce gender roles, sexual identities, and *stereotypes about both. Gender forms thus may be like or continuous with those of the Latin American societies of origin, or they may instead echo patterns characteristic of Anglo society. Most crucially, popular culture expressions may open up spaces for a Latina/o difference and opposition in matters of gender and, concomitantly, sexual desire, masculinity, femininity, transgender identities, and other forms. For example, one cultural phenomenon that exercised an enormous influence in bringing together multiple gender issues in Latina/o society is the life and death of popular music performer, *Selena. In death she quickly became almost a universal cultural icon, most especially for Chicanas/os, but with the release of Gregory *Nava's 1997 narrative film, **Selena*, also for wider crossover audiences. In addition to representing postmodern urban Latino youth culture, Selena—the first woman to succeed individually in the *Tejano/banda music industry—has important gender implications. Among these is her feminist independence in shifting her music away from a solely traditional **ranchera* style, that is, the nostalgic rural songs and music of receding Mexican roots. Also part of her independence from a more rural image was the provocative sexuality of her dress and her creation of a contemporary sexy Latina style in the manner of Madonna.

Urban culture offers one of the most significant juxtapositions between the Mexican roots of many immigrant families who come from nonurban settings and the relentless urban environment of the vast majority of Latinas/os in the United States today. It has been primarily in the urban environment where questions of gender have been staged. Certainly, conventional gender roles, both Hispanic and Anglo, remain dominant. These conventions are represented in such films as Gregory Nava's *My Family* (1995; also released as **Mi Familia*), whose possessive title clearly announces a traditional patriarchal perspective. On the other hand, both Chicana Lourdes Portillo and Nuyorican Miguel Arteta have dealt with urban issues intersected by questions of gender in oppositional ways that creatively challenge the conventions. Also noteworthy is Anglo Allison Anders's highly controversial **Mi Vida Loca* (1993), a film about Chicana homegirls in Los Angeles. One controversy is its presentation of homosocial bonding in positive images (e.g., the women's efforts to make their own lives when they discover they can hardly depend on their men) and also in negative images (e.g., the male *gangs and their mindless violence). Latina/o films like Puerto Rican Miguel Arteta's **Star Maps* (1997) and *Chicano Edward James *Olmos's **American Me* (1992) both present significant queer dimensions, and in Beeban Kidron's *To Wong Foo, Thanks for Everything, Julie Newmar* (1995) Colombian American John *Leguizamo is one of the three male stars who play their roles dressed as women.

Other popular culture figures who can be profitably studied from an urban perspective that intersects gender and Latina/o ethnicity are Chicano performers El Vez, *Cuban American singer Gloria *Estefan, and Nuyorican Jennifer *López, who has recently taken on mass appeal to queer audiences. If the traditional *bolero has often been seen to embody both an over-the-top feminine sentimentality and a queer sensibility, there is also an unquestionable appeal to queer audiences by Puerto Rican singer Ricky Martin's music and performance presence and other musicians of interest to Latina/o communities like Juan Gabriel, Luis *Miguel, Albita, and La Lupe, who show elements of gender transgression in both their lyrics and their performances. Also the Mexican pop and rock singers Gloria Trevi and Alejandra Guzmán are favorite acts in transvestite shows.

Television for the most part presents an uncritical reflection of conventional forms and categories of Latina/o gender and sexuality. Within its vastness, however, a fragmentary gender representation outside traditional patriarchal and heterosexist patterns is beginning to emerge. For example, nontraditional gender roles are evident in Latina/o productions with examples of complicated *familia* (*family) representations, drag performances, transvestism, and variously queer characters as in the TV series *Los Beltrán*, directed by Joe Menéndez et al., **Sabado Gigante*, the HBO series *Six Feet Under*, and others.

Theatrical productions, in addition to a host of conventional dramatic works, include urban Latina/o performers whose work focuses on gender issues. Josefina *López's homosocial play on women garment workers, **Real Women Have Curves: A Comedy* (1996), provides a Chicana example. The numerous major works of Chilean Guillermo *Reyes offer other Latina/o examples of *theater that focuses explicitly on issues of gender and sexual identity. Also participating in this strategic opposition to traditional gender norms are the Cuban American Carmelita Tropicana (Ela Troyano), the Nuyorican Marga Gomez, the Chicano Luis *Alfaro, the Colombian American John Leguizamo, and the transborder Mexican Guillermo *Gómez Peña. The first three are openly queer and have challenged both the North American and the Latin American patriarchal system and provided trenchant revisions of heteronormativity within the framework of Latina/o cultural interests. While Leguizamo does not describe himself as queer, his performances engage in significant deconstructions of Hispanic patriarchalism, and Gómez Peña, while still essentially masculinist, has found ways to include queer concerns in his texts. The videos *Brincando el charco* (1994) by Nuyorican Frances Negrón-Muntaner, a narrative of lesbian identity bridging New York and San Juan, *90 Miles* (2001) by Cuban American Juan Carlos Zaldívar, in which a return visit to Cuba is inflected by his gay identity, and Carmelita Tropicana's 1997 feature film *Latin Boys Go to Hell*, a romp through gay male Latinity, all present noteworthy representations of gay and gender-bending sexualities.

Although institutional literature has been a forum for the examination of both patriarchal and queer gendering, the Chicano John *Rechy's prolific body of fiction is singularly important for its pioneering and sustaining oppositional writing in U.S. American literature. Similarly important is Michael Nava's gay detective, Henry Rios, who provides the only example of gay Latino detective fiction. The poetry and prose of out gay writer Rigoberto *González exemplifies the space for oppositionally gendered self-expression constructed by Latinas/os at the turn of the century. There is a large body of Latina feminist and lesbian writing, notably that of Gloria *Anzaldúa and Cherríe *Moraga. Of more mass popular appeal are works by women writers that evaluate gender roles and stereotypes, such as Michele Serros's chronicles on Chicana identity like the satirical *How to be a Chicana Role Model* (2000) or Sandra Guzmán's *The Latinas Bible* (2002); the latter even includes a chapter on lesbianism.

Graphic art forms include revisionist images of the Virgin of Guadalupe that accommodate her figure to a host of social and political agendas; Yolanda M. *López's images are well known, but equally remarkable is the bold cover art of the first edition of Carla Trujillo's anthology *Chicana Lesbians: The Girls Our Mothers Warned Us About* (1991). Gender identity, along with ethnic identity, is also central in Jessica Abel's comic book *La perdida* (The Lost One, 2001). Alex Donis and his controversial queer images involving homeboys and authority figures in transgressive sexual practice are also pertinent here.

Many scholars have noted that popular culture is an especially suitable forum for the liberated revision and imaging of gender and sexual roles for several reasons. Because of the enormous quantity and wide distribution of popular culture genres, especially in the electronic entertainment media, there is a remarkable appetite for fresh ideas and experimental themes. Its natural appeal to nonestablishment and other interests apart from authorized institutional forms makes popular culture attractive for a constant challenge of conventions. Finally, advertising and other commercial ties have long relied on pushing the gender and sexual envelope of representation as a means of engaging audiences and selling products.

Further Reading

Almaguer, Tomás. "Chicano Men: A Cartography of Homosexual Identity and Behavior." *Différences* 3.2 (1991): 75–100.

González, Ray, ed. *Muy Macho: Latino Men Confront Their Manhood*. New York: Anchor Books Doubleday, 1996.

Quiroga, José. *Tropics of Desire; Interventions from Queer Latin America*. New York: New York University Press, 2000.

Trujillo, Carla, ed. *Chicana Lesbians: The Girls Our Mothers Warned Us About*. Berkeley, CA: Third Woman Press, 1991.

David William Foster

Gestos (Gestures). Gestos (gestures) are a form of communication involving movement of the body, generally a specific body part, such as a handshake but also a posture, attitude, walk, finger position, or stance performed by Latinas and Latinos in the United States. Gesture is an area of Latina and Latino behavior that is seriously understudied and in need of further research. Gestures need to be understood within a specific social and cultural context, as within a particular ethnic group. Both conscious and unconscious gestures are integral nonverbal expressions of culture and forms of communication that must be better understood especially across the Latina/o diaspora and furthermore cross-culturally in the United States. The unconscious gestures within a culture may be so commonplace that they are often not even perceived or just taken for granted by members of a particular community. One familiar example is when Latina/os converse, and use their heads to point in different directions in an effort to indicate a specific geographic direction.

Conjured conscious gestures are used as a sign of mutuality and unity in a given social class or group. These gestures often are used to exclude others from that particular group. An example of this is how *gang or fraternity members have secret codes that are passed on through hand signs as well as specific finger movements. Other gestures convey specific meanings, such as chest beating or muscle flexing to express virility or machismo or shrugging the shoulders to indicate indifference or ignorance. Among Latina/os, as among other culture groups, hand gestures may indicate frustration, anger, concern, or tenderness. Gestures may also signify membership in a given group such as a gang or class, indicating acceptable or appropriate behavior for members of a group.

One of the most familiar gestures in the United States is the *Chicano handshake, with several variations, that has been widely used since the 1960s *Chicano Movement. This handshake begins with the right hand loosely gripping the front sections of the other person's fingers, followed by a traditional handshake, and ending with a slight fist tapping the knuckles of the other person's hand. Sometimes the thumb of the opposite hand is grasped and followed by a traditional handshake. This gesto identifies many Chicanas and Chicanos who share a commitment to Chicanismo and the ideology and political struggles of the Chicano Movement.

Further Reading

Axtell, Roger E. *Gestures: The Do's and Taboos of Body Language around the World*. New York: Wiley, 1991.

West, John O. *Mexican Folklore: Legends, Songs, Festivals, Proverbs, Crafts, Tales of Saints, of Revolutionaries, and More*. Little Rock, AR: August House, 1988.

Armando Quintero, Jr.

Gestures. *See* Gestos (Gestures).

***Girlfight*.** In a breakout role, actress Michelle *Rodríguez plays a Latina teenager from the projects in Brooklyn who becomes an award-winning boxer, challenging both *gender and cultural stereotypes. The first *film for writer/director Karyn Kusama, *Girlfight* (2000) flies in the face of the usual "sports-related" pictures produced by Hollywood. The title of the movie is inappropriate in some ways because the film is about much more than a young woman who takes up boxing.

This film documents how a young Latina who lives in the projects in New York negotiates the pitfalls, social dilemmas, and violence in her life. Diana is not a "girly-girl." She wants to be taken seriously, and she refuses to play into gender *stereotypes. She does not want a man to rescue her—she will fight her own way to the top. While we see her battle with friends at school, her main fight is against the sexism and abuse in her *family. It is clearly problematic that her father sees a need to toughen her up to face the harsh reality of the world, but his only suggestion to Diana is to ask her why she cannot wear a dress once in a while. Her father gives her brother "Tiny" an opportunity to learn to box, and one day while delivering his boxing lesson payment, Diana asks her brother's coach to teach her, too.

Diana pours her anger and frustration with her life in the projects into becoming a boxer. We see her transform, and Kusama contrasts Diana's progress with the other young women at school. During a fitness test in school, Diana outruns and outperforms the others in every category. While her friends barely make it around the track for one mile, she sprints with power. Diana's physical strength is the result of her determination to break the pattern of violence in which she lives.

Kusama's camera shots capture the bleakness of this life. The dinginess of the old boxing gym—with sayings written on yellowed pieces of paper stuck on the walls—is a constant reminder of the way lives become stuck, forgotten, or simply overlooked. In *Girlfight*, Diana's decision to fight—other women and even her boyfriend in a climactic scene at the end—shows a shift between gender relationships and the balance of power. *Girlfight* won the Grand Jury Prize at the Sundance Film Festival. Executive produced by John

Sayles and distributed by Screen Gems, *Girlfight* also stars Jaime Tirelli, Ray Santiago, Paul Caldéron, and Santiago Douglas.

Further Reading

http://www.allmovieportal.com/m/2000_girlfight20.html.

Cheryl Greene

Globalization. Globalization is by definition a worldwide phenomenon. It refers to the widespread practice of corporate outsourcing of business activities. The practice involves the moving of industry factories, operating plants, and related labor operations from among affluent First World nations where the corporation's business headquarters are located to countries outside the original home country. The intent in outsourcing is to find pools of cheap labor and low-cost natural resources for their enterprises. Latinas and Latinos are directly affected by the far-reaching tentacles of globalization in numerous socioeconomic ways, primarily as workers and consumers. As a result, Latina/o popular culture forms have been both transformed and created out of the border crossing reach of corporate outsourcing developments. These transformations are evident in art, food and cookery, language, music, clothing, literature, media and other digital forms, and so on. Examples include the international circulation of such representations of Latina/o everyday experience as the visual artwork of Yolanda *López, the drama of *Teatro Campesino, Caribbean music by Cuban and Puerto Rican artists, and the increased global exchange of food products like *frijoles negros* (black beans), chili, tostadas, and countless others.

Other major consequences at the turn of the century have been the negative environmental and social consequences of multinational outsourcing on people's daily lives, local communities, and basic natural resources. Notable among these impacts is the transformation of the border region between the United States and México, particularly around the areas of the *maquilas*, factories owned by American and other foreign corporations that are usually run by Mexican or other Hispanic locals. Sociologists and policy researchers agree that the lives of the workers, *maquiladoras*, a great many of whom are displaced girls and women, and their communities, often are pushed into chaos as traditional life ways and living styles are replaced by disrupted families, boomtown transience, drug and crime infiltration, and increased violence.

In response to these ill effects a growing grassroots phenomenon has emerged to resist and reverse the local impacts of the global traumas caused by corporate outsourcing. It is a bottom-up activism among deterritorialized and disenfranchised people who increasingly are uniting into mutual aid associations and other cooperatives to provide reciprocal support. Many of these *community-based organizations have been formed by immigrant workers and other refugees in attempts to counter the labor exploitation that compounds their victimization and makes the harms of globalization even worse. One major resistance response over the decades has been the mailing of millions of dollars earned in rich countries by immigrant refugees to their families living in the workers' original poor homelands. The collected billions of earnings sent out of the First World have contributed to bettering the daily lives and also helping to rebuild local economies in the homeland. In this way, the grassroots activists have built a parallel grassroots global action network to combat the overwhelming economic power of highly consuming nations like the United States, Japan, northern Europe, and their allies. Other more formal alliances have sprouted over the years and taken on the status of nongovernmental organizations (NGOs) to address severe problems like the mass murders of hundreds of women in the Juarez/El Paso borderlands. These activists are motivated by concerns with survival in the face of the limitless advantages of rich nations in expropriating resources from their multinational partners among developing nations that include most of Latin America, Africa, and Asia. Many popular culture artists, filmmakers, writers, and researchers have addressed the multifaceted transnational phenomenon of globalization and *appropriation—award-winning filmmakers Estela *Portillo Trambley, Paul *Espinosa, and Alex *Rivera; writers Guillermo *Gómez-Peña and Alfredo *Véa, and **narcocorrido* and *hip-hop music, among many others. The globalized outsourcing of American jobs emerged as a major issue in the 2004 U.S. presidential elections.

Further Reading

Lee, James R. *Exploring the Gaps: Vital Links Between Trade, Environment and Culture*. West Hartford, CT: Kumarian Press, 2000.

Mignolo, Walter. *Local Histories/Global Designs: Coloniality, Subaltern Knowledges and Border Thinking*. Princeton, NJ: Princeton University Press, 2000.

Sassen, Saskia. *Globalization and Its Discontents: Essays on the New Mobility of People and Money*. New York: New York University Press, 1998.

Schoonover, Thomas. *Uncle Sam's [Spanish American] War of 1898 and the Origins of Globalization*. Lexington: University Press of Kentucky, 2003.

Cordelia Chávez Candelaria

Gómez Cruz, Ernesto (1933–). Ernesto Gómez Cruz, a native of Veracruz, México, is an established Mexican actor who began his acting career in the 1960s, first appearing in the Mexican *film *Los Caifanes* (1966). Since that time he has appeared in over 150 films, more than a dozen plays, and a number of *telenovelas* (soap operas). Gómez Cruz had important roles in the following Spanish-language films: *Reed: Insurgent Mexico* (1973); *Peregrina* (1974, about the murder of Felipe Carrillo Puerto, governor of the state of Yucatan); *Canoa* (1975); *Letters from Marusia* (1975); *Recourse to the Method* (1978, based on Alejo Carpentier's novel), and *Sandino* (1990). His success as a Mexican film actor led him to cross over to U.S. films, beginning with his appearance in Gregory *Nava's **El Norte* (1983) as Arturo

Xuncax. In Mexican film director Jorge Fons's film adaptation of Nobel laureate Nagub Mahfouz's novel *Midaq Alley* (1998), Gómez Cruz plays the controversial figure of Don Rutilio—a macho tavern owner sexually attracted to young men. His role in *Herod's Law* (1999) was critically acclaimed, and two years later he appeared as the character Tropillo in Gore Verbinski's *The Mexican* (2001). Recently, Gómez Cruz played the important role of mentor/bishop to the wayward priest in the controversial Mexican film *The Crime of Father Amaro* (2002).

Luis Aldama

Gómez-Peña, Guillermo (1955–). Guillermo Gómez-Peña, a major award-winning performance artist, filmmaker, writer, critic, and border theorist, uses his multimedia installations to address cultural identity issues in the ever-changing process of *globalization. The central focus of Gómez-Peña's work often deals with the politically thought-provoking issues surrounding the Mexican/U.S. border. He explores the cross-cultural existence of Latinos in the United States, as well as the perceptions of Latinos formed by others in the *barrios and borderlands of the world.

In addition to his artistic installations, and performance art pieces, some of which have toured North America, Latin America, Europe, Asia, Australia, and North Africa, Gómez-Peña has written several books since 1994. These publications include *Warrior for Gringostroika* (1994), *The New World Border* (1996), *Mexican Beasts and Living Santos* (1997), *Codex Spangliensis* (2000), and *Dangerous Border Crossers* (2000). He has won numerous awards and fellowships including the Prix de la Parole at the 1989 International Theatre of the Americas in Montreal, Canada, and the New York Bessie Award, also in 1989. In 1993 he was awarded the Viva Los Artistas Award from the Los Angeles Music Center. In 1991, Gómez-Peña received the highly prestigious MacArthur "Genius" Fellowship, a high honor that he held through 1996. His experimental radio performance piece titled *Border Notebooks* won the Corporation for Public Broadcasting's Silver Award in Performance/Spoken Word Category in 1991. In 1996 his video *El Naftazteca: Cyber Aztec for 2000 AD* received first prize at the Cine Festival in San Antonio, Texas. He won this honor again in 1998 for his video *Temple of Confessions*. In 1997 he was awarded the American Book Award for his publication *The New World Border*. In 2000 the Taos Talking Pictures Film Festival honored him with the Cineaste lifetime achievement award. Gómez-Peña participated in the establishment of the Border Arts Workshop in 1984 with David Avalos. It is a binational collective of artists and activists creating performance pieces, murals, and multimedia installations to make comment on the power inequities and cultural frictions and fusions that surround the U.S.-México border, especially the Tijuana and San Diego regions. He has worked as an editor for both *High Performance* magazine and the journal *Drama Review*. In addition, he has often been a guest commentator for National Public Radio (NPR).

Gómez-Peña was born in 1955 and raised in Mexico City until 1978 when he came to the United States. He studied linguistics and literature at the National Autonomous University of Mexico (UNAM), as well as post studio art at the California Institute of the Arts. Gómez-Peña has succeeded in putting the U.S.-México border under a cultural microscope to comment on the issues of culture, politics, and identity. Through art, multilinguality, and humor he attacks cultural *stereotypes and turns a mirror on the dominant cultural paradigm to awaken and motivate a cross-national dialogue. He resides primarily in San Francisco, California.

Further Reading

Bonney, Jo, ed. *Extreme Exposure: An Anthology of Solo Performance Texts from the Twentieth Century*. New York: Theatre Communications Group, 2000.

Gómez-Peña, Guillermo. *Dangerous Border Crossers: The Artist Talks Back*. New York: Routledge, 2000.

Christina Marín

Gonzáles, Henry B. (1916–2000). Representing the heavily Hispanic-populated Twentieth District in San Antonio, Texas, Congressman Henry B. Gonzáles was the first Texan of Mexican descent to be elected to the U.S. Congress. Elected in 1961 and serving until his retirement in 1998, Gonzáles' career spanned four decades of public service during which his voice often was the only elected Latino perspective on Capitol Hill. He is thus a direct descendant of such historic Latina and Latino political leaders of the past as Joseph Marion *Hernández (1793–1857) and Senator Dennis Chávez (1935–1965), as well as a significant part of contemporary America's grassroots politics with its accompanying impact on popular culture. Gonzáles's passion for openness in government, including full disclosure from financial institutions, his populist voice for the disenfranchised, and eloquent voice in support of aid for the poor gave him the reputation of being a friend of labor, the poor, women, and the elderly. Throughout his political career, he was also known as a public servant who placed great value on the responsibility entrusted in him by his constituents.

The future congressman was born in 1916 in San Antonio and was christened Henry Enrique Barbosa Gonzáles, a name that was usually shortened by friends simply to "Henry B." His parents, Leonides Gonzáles and Genevieve Barbosa Gonzáles, emigrated from México to San Antonio at the turn of the century. His father, a former mayor in Mapimi, Durango, greatly influenced Gonzáles's decision to attend the University of Texas. He later transferred to St. Mary's University Law School, where he graduated in 1943. Gonzáles's venture into politics began with a shaky start in 1950 with an unsuccessful campaign for the Texas State House of Representatives. He was supported by the Mexican and black communities but was discouraged from running by Anglo activists who believed that a Mexican could not win. He lost the election by a very narrow margin of 2,000 votes. Undeterred by the setback, he continued in politics and in 1953 captured a seat on the San Antonio City Council, making him the first Mexican American elected to the council. His term was riddled with controversy and conflict over issues including civil liberties and desegregation, and he came to be widely recognized as a competent, albeit controversial, councilman. Significantly, he was the only incumbent from that council to be reelected.

Three years later, Gonzáles challenged a conservative Republican opponent for his district's state senate seat. In a very hard fought campaign he defeated his opponent in 1956 and became the first Mexican American member of the Texas State Senate since statehood was ratified in 1845. Despite encountering heavy opposition throughout his senate tenure, "Henry B." was reelected to the office in 1960. In 1961 with key support from President John F. Kennedy, Gonzáles launched a bid for the open position of U.S. congressman representing Bexar County. His first and subsequent victories to the U.S. Congress were never easy, but his perseverance held for thirty-seven years. He amassed an impressive record of service and is credited by his peers as having lived true to his beliefs on a daily basis and of never forgetting where he came from. Also described by some of his colleagues in Congress as a somewhat eccentric and comic figure, he was known for giving epic-length speeches on the floor of Congress. At the same time, he was held in high regard by fellow elected officials for his uncompromising stand against segregation and for his stewardship of the Banking Committee during the savings and loan scandals of the 1980s. He retired from politics in 1998 due to poor health and passed away on November 28, 2000.

Further Reading

"Bentsen Statement on the Death of Legendary Texas Congressman Henry B. Gonzales." 2000. http://www.house.gov/bentsen/nr_gonzal.htm.

"Congressman Henry Gonzales." *National Housing Institute*. 1998. http://www.nhi.org/online/issues/98/pitcoff.html.

Gómez-Quiñones, Juan. *Chicano Politics: Reality and Promise, 1940–1990*. Albuquerque: University of New Mexico Press, 1990.

Alma Alvarez-Smith

González, Elián (1993–). In the fall of 1999, the United States and Cuba became embroiled in a controversy that will be remembered in history as one of the most complex and costly custody battles in the history of the United States. At the heart of the dispute was young Elián González, who escaped Cuba, lost his mother en route to drowning, and ended up in the United States without his parents. Over the next six months the custody battle, which had the drama, glitz, and politics to rival a Hollywood movie, played out in the courts of law, the Congress of the United States, the media, and the streets of Miami as partisan politics undermined concern for the boy himself.

The story of González unfolded on Thanksgiving Day 1999 when six-year-old González was rescued off the shore of the Florida coast, the miraculous lone survivor of an attempted escape from the dictatorship of Fidel *Castro's

Cuba (*see* Cuban Revolution). With Florida's coast only 144 kilometers (89.5 miles) from Cuba, it is not uncommon to find individuals successfully arriving on the coast of Florida, seeking the freedom and asylum that the United States can provide. In the case of González, the situation became complicated when his mother, Elisabeth Brotons González, along with the other passengers on the boat, perished during the attempt, leaving him at the mercy of opposition groups who wanted to make decisions on his behalf. On one side were his mother's Miami relatives, mostly Republican partisans. On the other were his father in communist Cuba, along with the U.S. government trying to maintain neutrality and be correct in observing international law.

Once in the United States, González was sent to live with relatives in Miami, who wanted to carry out his mother's wish to have him grow up free of Castro's regime. They found aid and support from sympathizers who felt he would have a better life in the United States living with his relatives. González's father, Juan Miguel González, a patriotic communist, having divorced Elisabeth in 1991 and living with his new wife and family happily in Cuba, requested that his son be returned to him. The opposition on all sides of the controversy made their positions known through calls and letters to their representatives in Congress, picket lines, and pleas to the media for support and action. His father, whether by choice or Cuban government dictate, did not travel to the United States to retrieve his son for several months. When he finally arrived, the Miami relatives refused to give up Elián and instead petitioned for a political asylum hearing for the boy. The drama, tears, and impassioned pleas played out in the media on a daily basis, while the nation watched the international tug-of-war.

Eventually, U.S. President Bill Clinton authorized Attorney General Janet Reno to order that the boy be reunited with his father and returned to Cuba. The relatives refused the directive, and on the morning of April 22, 2000, agents of the Immigration and Naturalization Service, under the direction of Reno, stormed the home where González was residing and took him by force. He was reunited with his father and now resides in Cardenas, Cuba, with his new family. In the aftermath, several U.S. lawsuits were filed as a result of the raid and what some consider a "kidnapping" of Elián González.

Further Reading

http://www.CapitalismMagazine.com/Cuba.
http://www.pbs.org/newshour/bb/law/elian.
http://www.vkblaw.com/elian/elianindex.htm.

Alma Alvarez-Smith

Gonzalez, Pancho (1928–1995). Regarded as one of the best tennis players of all time, Ricardo Alonso "Pancho" Gonzalez played most of his career before the *sport reached the popularity it now enjoys. He won his first U.S. Open Championship at Forest Hills in 1948 at the age of twenty when he was ranked seventeenth nationally. Winning the same title the following year, Gonzalez was part of the American team, which beat Australia to hold on to the Davis Cup in 1949. Despite these successes he decided to leave the amateur circuit to join the professional ranks that same year when he was ranked number one in the world at the age of twenty-one. This economic decision forever affected the way his lifetime standings are perceived because it was before the open era that began in 1968 and allowed pros and amateurs to compete against each other. Professional tennis players usually did not attract the press attention given to amateurs who played the prestigious tournaments like Wimbledon, and their statistics are kept separate from the amateur record books. However, some sports experts and cultural historians think that when his lifetime achievements are taken into account, Gonzalez may have been the greatest tennis player of all time. For example, he was ranked sixth in the world in 1969 at the age of forty-one, and in 1972 he won a tournament to make him the oldest male player to record a title in the open era, an accomplishment that is still unmatched, making his 1948–1972 active career span unprecedented for its longevity in world-class tennis.

Gonzalez was born on May 9, 1928, in Los Angeles to a working-class *Chicano *family. Not scholastically inclined, he became a habitual truant, which prevented him from playing in the junior tournaments available to youth in Southern California. As a result he recalls always feeling left out of the affluent tennis mainstream, a fact that he credits with goading him to play harder. He left high school to join the navy, where he was able to continue perfecting his game and move up in the national rankings until his first Forest Hills championship in 1948. Described by tennis experts as a marvelously pure player with an effortless service that delivered thunderbolts, the right-handed athlete claims that he learned his fast-attack style on the West Coast.

When Gonzalez began the professional tour, he competed against the reigning monarch, Jack Kramer, who defeated the rookie in several well-publicized matches. Nevertheless, Gonzalez became a very popular attraction on the tour for both his skill and colorful theatrics, and his name was a recognized draw coveted by promoters. Among the many marquee tennis stars he beat were Kramer, Don Budge, Pancho *Segura, and Frank Sedgman, leading him in 1954 to proclaim himself "Emperor Pancho," which he defended proudly through a decade's challenges of major and minor opponents. During this period, Gonzalez won the U.S. Professional singles title a record eight times, an achievement that helped make him synonymous with tennis during the 1950s and early 1960s. Indeed, some sports commentators argue that if his dominance of tennis from 1951 to 1962 is accorded the performance value it merits, especially alongside his 1948–1972 longevity span, then his twelve-year domination far exceeds the achievements of many other great players (e.g., Jimmy Connors, Bill Tilden, Rod Laver, and others) with shorter winning career spans. Even his old nemesis Kramer rates Gonzalez a better player than such tennis masters as Pete Sampras or Laver, a view echoed by other exceptional players in history including the great Arthur Ashe, who called Gonzalez the only idol he ever had.

Further Reading

Collins, Bud, and Zander Hollander, eds. *Bud Collins' Modern Encyclopedia of Tennis*. Garden City, NY: Dolphin Books, 1980.

Hernandez, David. "Pancho Gonzalez: Greatest Tennis Player of All Time." E-mail article to author, December 17, 2003.

http://www.estadium.ya.com/daviscup/Pancho%20Gonzales.htm.

Clifford Candelaria

Gonzalez, Richard. *See* Gonzalez, Pancho.

González, Rigoberto (1970–). *Chicano poet, novelist, and journalist, Rigoberto González is one of a tiny number of Latinos who serve as nominating and voting members of the influential National Book Critics Circle charged with selecting the annual National Book Award nominees and recipients. González has received favorable notice and numerous awards for his writing. His major honors include the John Guyon Prize for Literary Nonfiction from *The Crab Orchard Review* in 1999, the John Simon Guggenheim Memorial Foundation Fellowship for Poetry in 2000, and the National Poetry Prize from the *Borderlands: Texas Poetry Review* in 1995. The subjects and themes of his imagination are as diverse and inclusive as the multicultural America he employs as a canvas, but much of the focus of his verse is on the bilingual, bicultural interplay of being Latino in an Anglo-dominant society. Also appearing in his fiction is González's representation of the experience of being gay, bisexual, and/or otherwise unconventional in an orthodox, heterosexist universe.

González was born in Bakersfield, California, on July 18, 1970, to immigrant parents from the state of Michoacán, México—Avelina Alcalá of Janamuato and Rigoberto González Carrillo of Zacapu. The firstborn son, he has a younger brother who was also born in Bakersfield. In 1992, he earned a Bachelor of Arts degree from the University of California (UC) at Riverside, then continued his postbaccalaureate studies at the University of California at Davis, where he earned a master's in English in 1994 before pursuing the Master of Fine Arts in creative writing from Arizona State University, awarded in 1997. In 2003, he returned to UC–Riverside to receive the University's Outstanding Young Alumnus Award for his literary achievement.

Nominated for the Pushcart Prize four times for work published in periodicals, González's first collection of poetry, *So Often the Pitcher Goes to Water Until It Breaks* (1999), was selected as one of only five volumes published in the 1999 National Poetry Series. His second collection of poems, *Other Fugitives and Other Strangers* (1999), was a finalist for the 1999 Alice Fay Di Castagnola Award from the Poetry Society of America. Other publications include two poetry chapbooks, *The Night Don Pedro Buried His Best Friend, the Rooster* (1998) and *Skins Preserve Us* (1999), and a children's book, *Soledad Sigh-Sighs* (2003). González first novel, *Crossing Vines*, was published by the University of Oklahoma Press in 2003. A book reviewer for the *El Paso Times* since 2002, he has been appointed to writing residencies in Spain, Brazil, and Costa Rica, as well as the first artist-in-residence at the Ezra Pound House in Sun Valley, Idaho. He is a visiting professor at the New School University in New York and currently lives in Brooklyn. His current projects include a biography of Chicano writer Tomás *Rivera and translations from the Spanish of the body of work by Mexican writer Salvador Novo.

Further Reading

http://www.morpo.com/viewer.php?vol=3&iss=3&disp=167.
http://www.press.uillinois.edu/s99/gonzalez.html.

BJ Manríquez

González, Tony (1976–). Enjoying a successful career in the National Football League (NFL), Tony González plays the position of offensive tight end for the Kansas City Chiefs of the NFL's American Football Conference (AFC). At six feet four and 248 pounds, González, who wears jersey number 88, is a three-time Pro Bowl selection. A first-round pick by the Chiefs in the 1997 NFL draft, González's impressive career statistics have secured him a reputation among coaches and *sports pundits as a top-tier franchise player. In seven NFL seasons he has posted over 425 receptions and gained over 5,200 yards, averaging over 12 yards per carry and totaling over forty-five career touchdowns. The offensive tight end has been ranked consistently as a "must-start" player in the ancillary Fantasy Football online matchups.

Based on this gridiron productivity, in early 2002 his high-profile agent, attorney Tom Condon, advised González to turn down a record seven-year $31.5 million contract with an $8 million signing bonus for the 2002 season. The star thus garnered major media attention for rejecting the most lucrative offer ever presented to a tight end in NFL history. Condon argued that based on his production in his last three seasons his client's pay should be equivalent to the higher-paid wide receiver class of pros. The dispute continued until after the 2002 season started, but González eventually signed a one-year contract for over $3 million. Often described as the NFL's best tight end, he was engaged at the end of the 2003 NFL season in negotiating with the Chiefs an expected long-term contract to resolve their highly publicized differences. The team's disappointing finish and the failure to make it to the 2004 Super Bowl did not cloud the current year's negotiations because overall González had an impressive year.

The future professional star was born in Torrance, California, on February 27, 1976. He attended the University of California at Berkeley, where he twice earned varsity letters as a standout Golden Bear football player, and he graduated in 1998 having played thirty-three games and caught eighty-nine passes for a 1,302 yards total (14.6 average). He also earned a varsity letter in basketball. This significant detail on González's biography as a two-sport starter dates back to his high school years when he was a prep sensation in both football and basketball at Huntington Beach (California) High School. His interest in pursuing a simultaneous basketball career in the National Basketball Association (NBA) led him to play an off-season stint in the NBA's Miami Heat summer league. However, the president and general manager of the Kansas City Chiefs, Carl Peterson, strongly opposes the idea of his playing in both the NBA and NFL, wanting him to focus on the latter. Although it has been a lifetime dream for the Mexican American celebrity, González acknowledges that his quest for NBA playing time may prevent the Chiefs from offering him a long-term, multiyear contract. His stellar performance in the 2003 pro football season did not move him closer to realizing his double sport dream. In 2003, he started in sixteen games (nearly three more than the NFL average for his position) and completed seventy-one receptions (four more than the NFL average) for a season gain of 916 yards, bringing his lifetime total to 5,647. This outstanding performance explains why the Chiefs negotiated hard and successfully to keep him on the roster.

Further Reading

Teicher, Adam. "Minus the Smiles, González Arrives to Sign Chiefs' One-Year Contract." *Kansas City Star*, August 31, 2002.

"Tony Gonzalez." http://www.nfl.com/players/playerpage/12400.

Cordelia Chávez Candelaria

Grito de Lares. A Puerto Rican uprising for emancipation from Spain, the heroic Grito de Lares (Cry of Lares) took place on September 23, 1868, during a period of intense political debate about slavery and its abolition in Puerto Rico. Like the galvanizing symbolism of other famous grassroots events and movements in the Americas from the Boston Tea Party and Underground Railroad to the Grito de Dolores, the Grito de Lares movement captures the spirit and soul of Puerto Rican people and their popular culture. The incident was led by a small group of liberal reformers, abolitionist intellectuals, artists, and other island thinkers promoting independence. Because the revolt was fairly spontaneous and therefore poorly planned, it was quickly suppressed and its leaders muzzled. However, the fact that it occurred at the same time as the ardent struggle for independence in the sister island colony of Cuba intensified the magnitude of the impact of Grito de Lares, for together the two events led Spain to slacken its absolutism and grant several key reforms to Puerto Rico in the next few years. After this, Spain itself instituted its first republican government, forcing Queen Isabella II to abdicate and to pardon all the political prisoners imprisoned in both the colonies and in Spain. These events combined to bring an end to slavery in Puerto Rico, thereby realizing one of the original goals of the Cry. Like the freedom songs of the black civil rights movement and *Chicano Movement, it still inspires democratic sentiment among those familiar with the *Boricúa struggle.

Further Reading

Martínez-Fernández, Luis. *Torn Between Empires: Economy, Society, and Patterns of Political Thought in the Hispanic Caribbean, 1840–1878.* Athens: University of Georgia Press, 1994.

Cordelia Chávez Candelaria

Guajira. The *guajira* is one of the popular music styles of the Cuban working class. Like other Cuban rural music including *rumba, *guajira* was transplanted to urban areas including Havana and Miami during the twentieth century. The instrumentation was a small guitar called the *tres* (twelve-stringed guitar), guitar, and varied percussion. The form of the music is very simple and includes a ten-lined verse—**décima*—from seventeenth-century Spain. The lyrics of *guajira* music usually are about issues of the working people or the *guajiros*.

The *guajira* is similar to the **son montuno* but lacks the faster driving pace and is more delicate. It remains mostly a rural or country-based acoustic music and a national symbol for Cubans and Cuban Americans. The important 1999 documentary on Afro-Cuban music titled the **Buena Vista Social Club* brought some of the old *guajiros* (guajira singers) back into the limelight, including artists such as Compay Segundo, Eliades Ochoa, and Pia Leyva. The most popular *guajira* ever heard is one based on "Guantanamera," the Cuban revolutionary poem written by José Martí. This piece has been redone repeatedly and remains popular today.

Further Reading

Roberts, John Storm. *The Latin Tinge: The Impact of Latin American Music on the United States.* 2nd ed. New York: Oxford University Press, 1999.

George Yáñez

Guerra, Juan Luis (1956–). *Merengue artist Juan Luis Guerra has become an international success by blending merengue, Afro-pop, American jazz, and *salsa with complex vocal harmonies and beautiful yet unique lyrics. His music can be characterized as primarily merengue but far different from the familiar commercial pop sound. Harmonically his music is very complicated, especially by commercial music standards. The percussion of the music lends itself to being very tropical in nature and in sound, evoking the cultural and natural beauty of the Caribbean Islands.

Regarded as an excellent musician, this singer, songwriter, and producer, born in the Dominican Republic in 1956, studied music at the Berklee College of Music in Boston, Massachusetts. While attending school, he realized his musical passions, interests, and admiration were in American jazz. Upon completion of his musical education in the United States, Guerra returned to his native country, where he recorded his first album, *Soplando* (Blowing, 1984). The album was done in Manhattan Transfer-style vocals and was poorly received. Disappointed with the lack of success on his first venture, he turned his attention to the native musical style of his country and focused his musical interests on compositions in Latin American styles including merengue, *bachata*, and salsa. It proved to be a winning solution as evidenced by the success of one of his most popular albums, released in 1989, titled *Ojalá Que Llueve Café* (Hopefully It Will Rain Coffee). In 1990 he released *Bachata Rosa* (Pink Rose) and gave legitimacy to *bachata* dancing, which previously had been considered too sensual or erotic to be performed in public. He followed the *bachata* success with *Areito* in 1992, featuring friend and fellow musician Rubén *Blades in one of the numbers.

Guerra virtually stopped touring and recording for several years so he could focus his time on radio and television programs and his evangelical church. Ending his self-imposed hiatus in 1998, he released a new album titled *Ni es lo mismo ni es egual* (It Is Neither the Same Nor Equal). The album, containing ballads and simple arrangements, features trumpeter Arturo *Sandoval and percussionist Luis Enrique on one track each.

Guerra is also recognized internationally as being the uncle of Amelia Vega, Miss Universe 2003. Representing the Dominican Republic, Vega was crowned in Panama at the fifty-second annual competition, beating out seventy-one other delegates.

Further Reading

Wilson's and Alroys Record Reviews. http://www.warr.org/guerra.html.

George Yáñez and Alma Alvarez-Smith

Guerrero, Lalo (1916–). Legendary musician Eduardo "Lalo" Guerrero is the son of Eduardo and Concepción (Doña Conchita) Guerrero. Born in Tucson, Arizona, and raised in the *Barrio Libre, his father was the head boilermaker in the roundhouse of the Tucson Southern Pacific Railroad. One of seventeen children, Guerrero began his musical career while still in grammar school, learning guitar from his mother at age fourteen. His father contracted amyotrophic lateral sclerosis (Lou Gehrig's disease) and died in 1972; his mother died in 1974. Accompanied by his brother Frank, Guerrero moved to Los Angeles when he was eighteen to follow his dream of becoming a successful recording artist. He recorded exclusively in Spanish for a few years, and his records sold modestly in the Southern California market. His first solo recording debuted in 1948, and his songs soon were aired on *Spanish-language radio in the Los Angeles area, increasing his popularity and performance opportunities.

His musical idols included Rudy Vallee, Al Jolson, Eddie Cantor, and later, Bing Crosby. Imperial Records invited Guerrero to record in English and change his stage name to Don Edwards. Unsuccessful, he returned to his Mexican American audiences during the 1950s and began recording musical parodies like the "Ballad of Pancho López," a parody of the "Ballad of Davy Crockett." Guerrero's version was a hit and sold more than 500,000 copies. During the mid-1950s he performed on the *Tonight Show* hosted by Steve Allen, and later on the *Art Linkletter Show*. Guerrero's musical parody has been criticized because it humorously satirizes *Chicano themes. Several original parodies composed and recorded in the 1950s included "Tacos for Two" and "I Left My Car in San Francisco," parodies of "Tea for Two" and "I Left My Heart in San Francisco," respectively. In the 1960s, Guerrero opened his own nightclub, Lalo's Place, in Los Angeles, which was financed from his recording sales and performances.

Today Guerrero is regarded as a pioneer of Chicana/Chicano music. He began speaking and performing to Chicana/Chicano student organizations on college and university campuses while maintaining a concert circuit of largely Anglo audiences at luxurious restaurants in Los Angeles, Palm Springs, and elsewhere. He has spoken out against negative stereotyping and racism and used his musical performances to protest against American prejudice and discrimination. His song "No Chicanos on TV" is a parody of the Joyce A. Kilmer poem "Trees" and brings attention to the television industry's omission, negative stereotyping, and relegating of Chicanos and Mexicans to minor roles.

Guerrero has received numerous awards for his contributions to America's hybrid mestizo music culture and for his public stands on social issues. The Latino organization Nosotros (meaning "we" or "us") awarded him two Golden Eagle Awards in 1980 and 1989. The Smithsonian Institution recognized him as a "National Folk Treasure" in 1980. In 1991, he was awarded a National Heritage Fellowship by President George H. W. Bush, Sr. He was inducted into the *Tejano Music Hall of Fame in 1992. In 1998, he was presented a Cultural Institute Lifetime Achievement Award by Mexican President Ernesto Zedillo, and the *National Council of La Raza (NCLR) recognized him with an *ALMA Award in 1992.

Further Reading

Reyes, David, and Tom Waldman. *Land of a Thousand Dances: Chicano Rock 'n' Roll from Southern California*. Albuquerque: University of New Mexico Press, 1998.

Tatum, Charles M. *Chicano Popular Culture: Que Hable el Pueblo*. Tucson: University of Arizona Press, 2001.

Peter J. García

Guerrero, Zarco (1952–). Zarco Guerrero, of Mexican, Yaqui, and Juañeno (Native American tribes from Sonora, México, and California, respectively) descent, was born in 1952 in Mesa, Arizona, where he still resides. He is a mask maker, musician and composer, sculptor, *theater director, actor, multimedia artist, and community arts advocate. He has written three plays, *A Song for the Forest People* (1990), *Face to Face in a Frenzy* (1998), and *Qué Pasión! An Extraordinary Easter Story* (2000); the latter is in collaboration with his wife and three children. He is the cofounder of *Xicanindio Artes, Inc., of Arizona, a nonprofit organization, and he currently directs and plays in the band Zúm Zúm Zúm, which performs folk, rock, jazz, and social protest music from Latin America. He has been awarded the Arizona Governor's Arts Award for his artistic contributions to the community; the prestigious 1994 Scottsdale Arts Council's Chairman's Artists Award; an AriZoni award for Costume Design for the masks executed for Arizona State University's production of *Alicia in Wondertierra*, a nationally touring play by Silvia Gonzáles; the National Endowment for the Arts fellowship to study mask making in Japan; and the Arizona Commission on the Arts' Artist Project Grant to pursue his mask carving in México and Indonesia. He has also directed the Phoenix-based Teatro Bravo! pro-

Known for his colorful, characteristic masks, such as the ones shown here, Zarco Guerrero is also a musician and composer, sculptor, theater director, actor, multimedia artist, and community arts advocate. *Courtesy of Zarco Guerrero.*

duction of *Frida*, based on the life of Frida *Kahlo. A genuinely renaissance creative artist, Zarco is widely known as one of Arizona's cultural treasures.

Further Reading

Keller, Gary. *Contemporary Chicana and Chicano Art*. Tempe: Bilingual Press, 2002.

Trino Sandoval and Arturo J. Aldama

Guevara, Che (1928–1967). Ernesto Rafael Guevara de la Serna was an Argentine-born Marxist revolutionary and Cuban guerrilla leader. He came to be known as "Che," an Argentinean Spanish expression meaning "buddy," the name by which his life and career as a revolutionary and associate of Fidel *Castro have been remembered by his followers. An international legend in his own lifetime, Guevara's image on millions of posters and T-shirts has become synonymous with revolution, freedom fighting, and social change. The photograph of Guevara in a black beret taken by photographer Alberto Korda has become one of the century's most recognizable images and has been reproduced on a vast array of merchandise from posters and T-shirts to baseball caps. His commercial popularity is ironic in that Guevara devoted his life to opposing the evils of capitalism as a socioeconomic political system that, as a form of neocolonialism, contributed to mass wretchedness, poverty, and despair. Guevara in fact rejected both capitalism and orthodox communism. The alternative he suggested was in fomenting revolution for social justice, as he had succeeded in doing with Fidel Castro during the *Cuban Revolution as a member of the 26th of July Revolutionary Movement (Movimiento 26 de Julio), which seized power in Cuba in 1959. After the success of the revolution, he became second in command to Castro in the new Cuban government. He eventually went on to support revolutions in other parts of Latin America, notably Bolivia, where he was captured by Bolivian government troops, with assistance from U.S. Green Berets, on October 8, 1967, and executed without a trial the very next day. His killing brought martyrdom and historic fame.

Guevara's road to revolution started off in 1951 with a motorcycle tour of South America from his hometown of Córdoba, Argentina. The grinding poverty and disease he encountered among the country's indigenous tribes during this road trip led him to delve further into Marxist ideology; for while still in his early teens, Guevara had already started reading Marx and Freud but had also developed a love of French poetry, specifically the nineteenth-century poet Baudelaire, who explored the interstices of human misery in his *Fleurs du Ma* (Flowers of Evil, 1857). The diary he kept during this trip with his good friend Alberto Granado has been published as *The Motorcycle Diaries: A Journey around South America* (1968).

Guevara attended a secondary school in Córdoba, the Colegio Naciones Dean Funes, from where he went on to study medicine at the University of Buenos Aires in 1948. Guevara graduated as a doctor in 1953, specializing in dermatology, and was especially interested in working with leprosy patients. It is ironic that Guevara was disqualified from military service due to asthma, from which he had suffered since the age of two, but was later to become one of the century's best-known guerrilla fighters, coping with his illness while hiding from the army in remote jungles. Soon after his graduation from medical school, he went on another trip, this time hitchhiking to Guatemala and arriving there during the socialist Arbenz presidency. There he witnessed the overthrow of the radical socialist government of Jacobo Arbenz by U.S.–supported Castillo Armas and saw the Central Intelligence Agency (CIA) at work as the principal agents of counterrevolution; he was confirmed in his view that revolution could be successful only through armed insurrection. Although he was by this time a committed Marxist, he refused to join the Communist Party, even though this meant losing the chance of government medical appointment, and he was penniless and in rags.

Guevara at this time lived with Hilda Gadea, a Marxist of Indian background who advanced his political education, looked after him, and introduced him to Nico López, one of Fidel Castro's lieutenants. They married and had a daughter, Hildita. Guevara met several followers of Castro who were in exile on this trip, and he joined them when they went on to Mexico City. There he met Castro when the latter arrived after being released from prison in Cuba. Guevara joined Castro's 26th of July Revolutionary Movement, dedicated to the overthrow of the regime of Cuban dictator Fulgencio Batista, who was supported by the United States and corporate dollars.

Under the influence of Castro, writer Alberto Bayo, and the writings of Mao Tse-Tung, Guevara began to form the tenets of his philosophy of guerrilla warfare, but he was yet to actively engage in combat as a soldier. This finally occured in November 1956, when he joined Castro and his brother Raúl and several other insurgents on the cabin cruiser *Granma* to invade Cuba and start the revolution. Batista's forces were waiting for them, however, and only twelve of the young revolutionaries survived. Guevara, who was then the group's physician, placed his knapsack of medical supplies on the ground to pick up a box of ammunition dropped by a fleeing comrade and, in that split second, as he later recalled, was transformed from doctor to combatant. Within months he had risen to the highest rank, that of commandant or major in the revolutionary army. His 1958 march on Santa Clara, where his column derailed an armored train filled with Batista's soldiers and took over the city, was the major victory that spelled the downfall of the Batista regime.

Guevara was appointed governor of the National Bank by Castro and went on to marry for the second time. This time he married Adelaida March de la Torre, with whom he had four children. He was made Minister for Industry in 1961 and became increasingly hostile toward U.S. interests in the Cuban economy. Although initially Guevara advocated closer ties between Cuba and the USSR, he grew increasingly disillusioned with Soviet-style communism (Stalinism) and in February 1965 made a formal break with it, calling for revolutionary action all over the world. At this juncture Castro informally removed Guevara from office, their ideas for the future of Cuba having radically diverged, although they remained close comrades. Guevara went on to the Congo and later, in 1966, to Bolivia, hoping to inspire the peasants there to throw off their shackles, sparking off an incendiary movement that would spread like wildfire across the world, starting off "twenty new Vietnams."

Both rebellions failed, and Guevara was captured by Bolivian troops, with the support of the CIA. Guevara was executed on October 9, 1967, and his body was buried in a secret grave. He was thirty-nine years old. In June 1997, a team of Cuban and Argentinean scientists recovered the skeleton and repatriated it to Cuba, to whose revolution Guevara had dedicated his life. Because of his wild, romantic appearance, his dashing style, his intransigence in refusing to kowtow to any kind of establishment, his contempt for mere reformism, and his dedication to violently decisive action, Guevara became a legend and an idol for the revolutionary youth of the later 1960s and early 1970s. But he was far more than a mere political icon of the 1960s. In Cuba, he is a symbol of hope and faith, viewed as a true renaissance man. As a doctor, teacher, journalist, photographer, banker, minister of industry, skilled negotiator representing Cuba at world summits, as well as a highly talented military commander and guerrilla fighter, Guevara is seen by Cubans as a great man of the twentieth century.

Further Reading

Anderson, Jon Lee. *Che Guevara: A Revolutionary Life*. New York: Grove Press, 1988.

Casteñada, Jorge. G. *Compañero: The Life and Death of Che Guevara*. New York: Vintage Books, 1998.

Stockwell, Norman. "Reclaiming Che's Legacy." *The Capital Times*, October 3, 1997. http://geocities.com/Hollywood/8702/capital.html.

http://www.popsubculture.com/pop/bio_project/ernesto_che_guevara.html.

Shoba S. Rajgopal

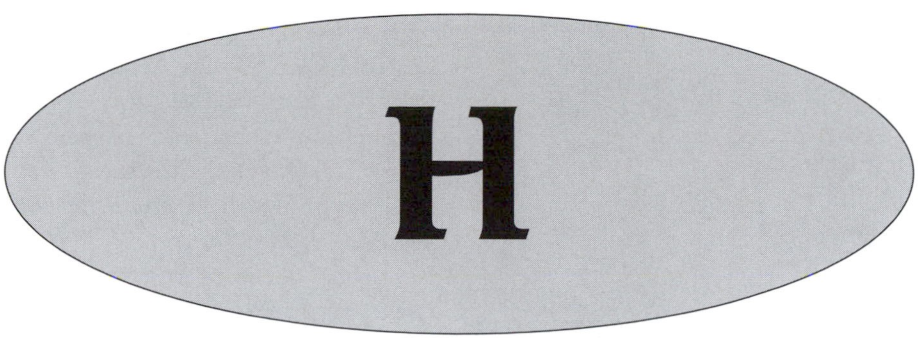

Hayek, Salma (1966–). Actor, model, director, and producer in the United States and México, Salma Hayek was born on September 2, 1966, in Coatzacoalcos, Veracruz, México. Her father, whose parents were Lebanese, was a Mexican opera singer. Hayek's acting career began with her roles in the Mexican soap operas *Nuevo Amanecer* (New Dawn, 1989) and *Teresa* (1989), and during the first season of *Teresa*, Hayek earned México's equivalent to the Emmy, the TV Novela Award, for best actress, and for her role in *Nuevo Amanecer*, she received the TV Novela Award as the best newcomer. Successful in México, Hayek moved to Los Angeles in 1991 in hopes of gaining success in the United States.

During her first year in Los Angeles, Hayek spent her time taking English and acting classes. She studied acting under Stella Adler, who also helped her get her first role in a U.S. *film. Hayek was selected for a role in **Mi vida loca* (My Crazy Life, 1993), by director Allison Anders. Sometime later she appeared on a Spanish-language cable access talk show, and during the airing of one of the shows, director Robert Rodríguez saw her and decided to cast her in his upcoming film *Desperado* (1995). *Desperado*, in which Hayek costarred with Antonio Banderas, became her breakthrough film in the United States, and the success of this film led to additional roles. Rodríguez again cast Hayek in his next film, *From Dusk Till Dawn* (1996).

Hayek's role in *El callejón de los milagros* (aka Midaq Alley, 1995) as Alma earned her a Silver Ariel Award nomination for Best Actress, the equivalent of the Mexican Academy Awards, and four international awards. Hayek's popularity and recognition in the United States increased, and after her role in *Fools Rush In* (1997) with Matthew Perry, her crossover appeal strength-

Salma Hayek, of Lebanese and Mexican roots, has found success as a film actor and as a producer and director. *Courtesy of* Lincoln/Latino Leaders Magazine.

ened even more. Hayek produced and starred in the film *Frida.* (2002), a biopic of famed Mexican feminist painter Frida *Kahlo. Hayek won the 2002 Golden Globe Award for Actress in a Leading Role and an Oscar nomination for her lead role as Kahlo in *Frida*. Hayek's directorial debut was the Showtime feature *The Maldonado Miracle* (2003).

Hayek continues to stay busy with multiple projects in progress. Her production company, Ventanarosa, collaborated with Catch-23 Productions on *Murphy's Law* (2003) based on a story by Hayek's brother Sami. Hayek produced the movie, while her brother directed the romantic comedy. In 2003, Hayek once again teamed up with director Robert Rodríguez and co-star Antonio Banderas in *Once Upon a Time in Mexico*, the sequel to *Desperado* (1995). In her most recent project, *After the Sunset*, due to be released in November 2004, Hayek takes on the role of a retired master thief, opposite Pierce Brosnan.

Further Reading

Smith, Krista. "An Irresistible Force." *Vanity Fair* (February 2003): 120–126, 181–182.

http://www.eonline.com/Facts/People/Bio/0,128,34543,00.html.

http://www.gale.com/free_resources/chh/bio/hayek_s.htm.

http://www.stelladesigns.com/salmahayek/interviews.php.

Silvia D. Mora

Hayworth, Rita (1918–1987). The life story of Rita Hayworth, the legendary screen diva of the 1930s to early 1950s, offers a telling case history for examination of the presence and treatment of Latinas in U.S. mass popular culture. Born Margarita Carmen Cansino on October 17, 1918, in Brooklyn, New York, she was part of a *family of Broadway revue dancers. While dancing in shows with her father in Tijuana, México, the young Cansino was

Rita Hayworth. *Courtesy of Photofest.*

discovered and recruited for the movies by Harry Cohn and Winfield Sheehan, famous Columbia Pictures producers. However, the producers thought that she looked "too Mexican" perhaps because, ironically, her father had darkened her hair and combed it back severely so that she would pass as "more Mexican" for the Tijuana audiences. In keeping with the accepted *race-based Hollywood conventions of the era, which demanded a narrow Anglo-American aesthetic of beauty, she was transformed from a Brooklyn-born vaudeville dancer in Tijuana to a Hollywood screen diva. The Jewish American Cohn completed the transformation by changing her name from Cansino to Hayworth and having her hair dyed copper red.

Her fame as a glamour screen diva reached its pinnacle in the 1940s when she became Columbia Studios' most popular female lead. As Cansino, Columbia type cast her in small parts as an ethnic and exotic female in *Dante's Inferno* (1935), *Human Cargo* (1935), and other B-grade movies. As the whitened Hayworth, the studio cast her in lead roles in such films as *The Shadow* (1937), *Only Angels Have Wings* (1939), *Strawberry Blonde* (1941), and *Blood and Sand* (1941). At the height of her popularity, her likeness as the newly constructed image of the all-American glamour girl even adorned the atomic bomb that was dropped on Hiroshima, giving the notion of "femme fatale" new meaning.

In *Gilda* (1946) and *The Lady from Shanghai* (1948), directed by the legendary Orson Welles, her second husband, she played another femme fatale lead. Her marriages to other high-profile figures include one to jet-setting playboy Prince Aly Khan (1949–1951), during which time she stepped away from the cinema for several years. After her work on *Salome* (1953), her roles became less frequent and the movies themselves more secondary. One of her final appearances on the screen was in the 1972 *Wrath of God*.

After her career faded and the studios replaced her with other aspiring actors treated as female sexual commodities, Cansino/Hayworth disappeared into obscurity. She came into the limelight again in the early 1980s when a reporter working on a tip discovered that the forgotten star, now poor and wasted by alcoholism, was struggling with the early onset of Alzheimer's disease. In another Hollywood irony, the publicity surrounding her battle with Alzheimer's brought national attention to the disease and funding to research its treatment. A revealing example of the sexism toward women in general and Latinas in specific, the story of "Rita Hayworth" offers a template for how patriarchal Hollywood constructs divas and then discards them when their commercial value ends.

Further Reading

Kobal, John. *Rita Hayworth: The Time, the Place and the Woman*. New York: W.W. Norton, 1978.

Leaming, Barbara. *If This Was Happiness: A Biography of Rita Hayworth*. New York: Viking, 1989.

Bill Nerricio

Healing Practices, Spirituality, and Religious Beliefs. Spirituality is central to the lifeways of most Latinas and Latinos. Although this is true for many other cultures, among Latinas/os spirituality is widespread and key to many daily interactions, including health and healing practices. When saying "good-bye," for example, and the response is "hasta luego" (see you later), a frequent reply is "Si Díos quiera" (If God wills it). This belief that the immediate future depends on a supernatural power beyond the individual's control is equally true in health and healing practices where well-being is perceived as an integration of body, mind, and soul. Unlike most contemporary treatments (e.g., those of the American Medical Association) that emphasize chemical and/or surgical treatment for specific ailments, traditional Latina/o healing methods address ailments as part of whole organic systems that comprise spiritual and religious aspects, as well as the physical and somatic elements treated by Western medicine.

Thus, integral to folk healing practices are concerns about ethnic identity, selfhood, worldview, expressions of *family and community values, and reaffirmations of cultural cohesiveness and tradition. Popular healing systems also are commonly interrelated with religious and political goals that affect the entire community. Unlike what is often described for Western medicine with its focus on preventing or curing disease, popular healing systems in ethnic communities are multidimensional because they are embedded in collective social processes by which individuals and their families adapt to their adopted societies. Formal and informal avenues to spirituality occur among Latinas/os, usually through religious practices at established churches and via individual home and family-centered practices often referred to as "popular religion." Latina/o popular religious and spiritual practices serve to sustain hope in the face of illness and problems related to it and also to alleviate anxieties and enhance well-being. These practices also offer spiritual solutions to life's problems and human relations and are the basis for widely utilized, community-based folk healing systems that differ significantly in each of the Latina/o cultures in the United States.

Despite the wide variation in home rituals among Latinas/os, several notable common practices exist. Many Latina/o homes have an altar arranged with figures of saints, offerings of flowers, candles, other sacred objects, and holy water. In the homes of people of Mexican descent there may be photos of deceased relatives on the altar or displayed prominently in a front room, bedroom, or other personal space for prayer. Depending on the belief system of the individual, altars may contain a variety of objects, whether Puerto Rican, Cuban, Mexican, or Dominican in origin. In addition to images and statues of the Catholic saints, images of West African gods and holy figures (usually Yoruban Orishas) along with fruit offerings are often seen on Cuban and Dominican altars. Statues of Native American medicine men healer figures are seen on Puerto Rican altars, and hand-carved folk saints, along with natural objects such as stones and herbal offerings, are found on

Mexican and Chicana/o altars, most commonly used as the sites of daily individual and sporadic family prayers. The sacred figures on the altar have spiritual identities imbued with special meanings for their patron. They may be saints associated with birthdays or baptismal days or images from dreams or visions that may have granted the petitioner's wishes or protected him or her in the past. Women are likely to set up home altars as part of their maternal role of protecting the health and well-being of family members, shielding them from the noxious influences of the neighborhood and the world.

On the social and communal level, most towns in Latin America and the Spanish/Mexican–origin towns in the United States celebrate the birthdays of their patron saints with religious processions in which the image of the saint is carried to the homes of prominent families or officials and communitywide fiestas with music, food, and rides and games for the children. This custom traces to the earliest practices in Mesoamerica and in Spain, and they continue in both. They also continue in less elaborate form in small homogeneous Latina/o communities of the United States, particularly in church congregations with many Latina/o members. Recreating a sense of belonging and of cultural identity, these social customs emphasize integration in communities and, importantly, in a sacred universe.

All ethnic groups regardless of *race or national origin have brought many or all of their main beliefs and healing practices to the United States. Evidence shows that these practices have undergone significant change from generation to generation and in some cases have intensified as a result of the difficult adaptations faced by immigrants in new societal environments that often are economically and psychologically stressful—even hostile—for newcomers. These difficult conditions become even more salient for popular medical practice when we consider that access to health and mental health care services is quite limited for most immigrants and those nonimmigrants who have low or sporadic wages and lack health insurance.

Individual cultural differences are reflected in popular traditional healing practices; however, extensive borrowing and some cross-utilization also take place. Despite variations associated with different Latina/o cultures, there are also a number of broad similarities. For example, there is a widespread belief that the cause of illness and misfortune has a locus external to the individual and may result from mostly spiritual, or spiritual combined with physical, aspects. Similarly, frequent group participation in healing ritual is commonly preferred over individual treatment sessions; thus individuals are most often treated within a family or local community setting. A related view is that both morality and immorality can be the cause of illness and both are factors for healing and recovery. Another important commonality is that the healing process depends largely upon nonverbal and symbolic interactions, together with the common use of herbal pharmacopeias. In these and other ways, traditional healing in Latina/o cultures in the United States is different from the largely individual-centered concepts and chemical-based practices found in standard physical and mental health care.

Three popular ethnomedical systems are found in the United States: *Espiritismo* (Spiritism), *Santería* (Healing with Faith), and *Curanderismo* (Curing with Faith and Homeopathy). Each is associated, respectively, with the three major Latina/o communities of Puerto Ricans, Cubans, and Mexican Americans. Each evolved out of a synthesis of beliefs and practices derived from their separate colonial histories: Spiritism arose from the conjunction of European (French/Spanish) and Afro-Caribbean traditions; Santería, from a combination of folk Catholicism and West African Yoruban traditions; and *Curanderismo*, from a synthesis of folk Catholicism and Mexican indigenous traditions. Spiritualism (a variation of Spiritism with a similar European and folk Catholic background) is also found in México and on the U.S.-México border.

In all of these systems malicious or unaware *ánimas* (spirits/forces) are usually the central cause of physical suffering, emotional distress, or personal problems. Spirits in Spiritism or saints/gods in Santería are the direct cause of suffering as well as sources of healing. In *Curanderismo* and among Mexican Americans the will of God often is invoked as causal, along with a number of other material agents like spoiled food, environmental factors (*aires*), contact with persons wishing harm (consciously or inadvertently, i.e., *mal de ojo, el ojo* [evil eye]), and immoral excesses of sex or greed for money acquisition, deviant behavior, congenital or hereditary characteristics, and witchcraft. Age and general weakness, as well as a "weak character," add to the effect of the agents listed above.

The unifying concept for all these systems is that of harmony and balance. To heal (*sanar* or *curar*) also means "to restore to health," the latter interpreted as harmony within and between individuals and between them and the universe. What is referred to in orthodox Western thought as the physical, social, and existential dimensions of health are integrated as one in Latina/o healing. However, practitioners believe that one phrasing of the "harmony/balance" concept is the theory of balance between hot and cold. For example, foods that are too hot and spicy cause "hot" illness, and "cold" herbal remedies are therefore prescribed by *curanderos/as* (healers). Although extremes in change of climate or contact with heat or cold are believed to cause illness, temperature per se is not what is at risk; rather, hot-cold is a metaphor for excesses in behavior and an ever-present awareness of the danger of imbalance. In all Latina/o healing systems imbalance is a moral issue; thus, in Spiritism, illness-causing (*causa*) spirits are attracted to persons who behave immorally. Those who rebel against social norms, for instance, often are perceived to become ill because they threaten the integrity of the social fabric. Transgressions are sinful because they unbalance the "good" within individuals and generate conflict, which disturbs the social well-being. Santería belief differs in its assumption that, like people, the saints/gods can do both good and evil, and the only way to cope is to ally with and manipulate these powerful beings.

Latina/o healers tend to make few significant distinctions between physical illness, emotional disorders, or social problems relating to crime or business. There is an informal practice of referring complaints assessed as "material" (somatic) to medical doctors, while simultaneously apportioning spiritual aspects of the distress to traditional treatments. All complaints are interpreted as having similar etiologies, and diagnosis proceeds in much the same way, regardless of the type of complaint. Remedies may differ according to the type of complaint; the cause of the distress, such as "bewitchment" or "nervousness," often becomes the label for the distressing condition. Distinctions between somatic and other types of complaints (i.e., psychological or spiritual) are also unsystematic; for example, some of the Spiritist healers in Puerto Rico assert that "nerves are almost always physical" but also maintain that a particular *causa* spirit (sent by a women who desired the client's husband) could cause her "pain and nerve sickness" or that nerves run in the family. The commonality, thus, in the condition labeled "nerves" is that of interpersonal conflict, usually in intimate relationships, which generates excessive emotion, particularly anger.

The processes of diagnosis or identifying the illness in popular healing is quite different from the method in biomedicine or psychotherapy. The clients of healers rarely describe their complaints as the main step in an intake process; rather, the healer is expected to "know" through spiritual means what the client's complaints are. In Santería the diagnostic process is divinatory and is called a *registro*. The *santero* (healer) who specializes in reading the shells (*los caracoles*—modeled after the West African cowrie shells) or palm nuts is known as an *italero*. Sixteen shells, called the "mouthpieces of the Gods," are for sale in any *botánica* (shops that sell remedies, prayers, herbs, candles, and other treatment and ritual objects). Sixteen or twelve (if the diviner is not yet a priest) shells are thrown four times onto a straw mat, and the patterns are interpreted according to the position of the shells. Each letter or pattern "speaks" for one or more Orishas and is interpreted according to a legend or proverb associated with it; this is standardized in the "Table of Ifá" used by the high priests (*babalaos*). The diviner then particularizes the interpretation for a specific client and his/her problem. Not only do healers and priests deal with problems and disordered emotions, but they also prescribe herbal remedies and amulets (*resguardos*) to protect against future harm or to bring about a desired event. It is these latter services, actual manipulations of the future, that are most sought after.

A different type of diagnostic divination is found among Spiritist mediums. First, their personal spirit guides assist them to "see" into the spirit world to identify the spirit causing a client's problems. Then a process of probing takes place in which the healer describes the client's complaints (somatic distress, bad feelings, persistent interpersonal or social problems), and the client confirms or denies them. The *causa* spirit is then called down to possess the body of one of the healers and enjoined to explain its actions. Spirit and client carry on a spirit-dominated discourse in which the social context (usually interpersonal relations) of the client's problems/complaints, including the circumstances and relationships in past lives, is revealed. Much of the remedy (intervention or solution) is symbolically or metaphorically contained within this spirit-client interchange. At the healing table, medium-healers who are not possessed speak to, cajole, and exhort the *causa* spirit to leave the suffering client. The spirit usually expresses the recognition of his/her wrongdoing in molesting the client and agrees to leave once the client forgives it for causing distress. Other remedies, to be carried out at home (prayers, candle lighting, herbs, aromatic baths, ritual cleansing of various kinds), may also be prescribed by the healers, who "receive" this knowledge from their spirit guides.

Both one-on-one consultations and group ritual sessions are held; individuals as clients are most frequent, but couples or sometimes families, and even buildings (i.e., one's home or shop), may be "treated" with a purification process employing incense or other aromatic materials. Again, it might be noted that some aspect of balance is central to healing, whether the etiological belief is in spirits, saints/gods, the devil versus God, natural forces, energies, or vibrations. This focus on other-than-natural forces, which are beyond visible reality and daily life events, significantly differs from medical beliefs about illness.

In Spiritism among Puerto Ricans and other Latinas/os in the United States, the medium-healer is not the agent of intervention but only a vehicle, an instrument to bring about change in the sufferer's condition. Briefly described, the group healing ritual consists of the medium sitting at a table. The session is opened by the recitation of prayers to the Holy Spirit, Jesus (often the "Our Father" and other parts of Catholic liturgy). The mediums then exhort the audience of potential clients to relax by directing them to meditate and to enter the spirit world by seeking visual experience of it. The mediums often become possessed for a brief moment by their main protector-guide spirit who stands behind each medium-healer and presides over the session. The group concentrates on the spirit world, and certain *videncias* (visions) that indicate the relationship of a certain spirit to someone in the audience. That client is then singled out according to a visual description given by the spirit to the medium and summoned to the table (on which sits a vessel of blessed water in which the spirit fluids are captured). The "diagnostic" process described above then takes place.

Healers in each of the Latina/o healing traditions commonly describe themselves as generalists. Women more than men seek the services of *curanderas* frequently for their children's illnesses and for their own problems. The mental health aspects of *Curanderismo* among Mexican Americans in the United States have not been well studied, but conditions generally perceived as physical illnesses—*susto* (fright), *empacho* (blockage in throat, stomach), *bilis* (digestive problems), *caida de la mollera* (fallen fontanel), and *mal de ojo* (evil eye)—have emotional concomitants, while bewitchment and *nervios* (nerves) are directly related to emotional as well as to bodily distress.

Little epidemiological data is available to document the exact extent of utilization of popular healing by Latinas/os in the United States. Nevertheless, many published studies on the varieties of healing and faith-based practices like *Curanderismo*, Spiritism (and its variations), and Santería, report that they flourish as physical and mental health alternatives in specific areas such as Los Angeles, Miami, New York, and the Southwest, as well as other areas with concentrations of Latina/o populations.

Further Reading

Chávez, Leo. "Doctors, Curanderos, and Brujas: Health Care Delivery and Mexican Immigrants in San Diego." *Medical Anthropology Quarterly* 15 (1984): 31–37.

González-Wippler, Migene. *Santería: African Magic in Latin America*. New York: Julian Press, 1973.

Harwood, Alan. *Rx: Spiritist as Needed*. New York: Wiley, 1977.

Kay, Margarita. "Health and Illness in a Mexican-American Barrio." In *Ethnic Medicine in the Southwest*, edited by Eleanor Bauwens et al. with introduction by Edward H. Spicer. Tucson: University of Arizona Press, 1977.

Koss-Chioino, Joan. *Women as Healers, Women as Patients: Mental Health Care and Traditional Healing in Puerto Rico*. Boulder, CO: Westview Press, 1992.

Sandoval, Mercedes C. "Santería as a Mental Health System: An Historical Overview." *Social Science and Medicine* 13B (1979): 137–151.

Trotter, Robert T., and Juan Antonio Chavira. *Curanderismo: Mexican Folk Healing*. Athens: University of Georgia Press, 1981.

Joan Koss-Chioino

Hernández, Joe. *See* Little Joe Hernández y La Familia.

Hernández, Joseph Marion (1793–1857). José Mariano Hernández (also known as Joseph Marion Hernández) was the first Hispanic to serve in the U.S. Congress. Born on August 4, 1793, in St. Augustine, Florida, he was elected to the House of Representatives in 1822 as a delegate from what was then the Spanish-owned and -controlled territory of Florida. His tenure as a congressman was brief, lasting only five months, for reasons not provided in the scanty available biographies. Hernández is important as a predecessor to the expanding numbers of twentieth- and twenty-first-century Latina and Latino public and political servants. As such he predates America's present popular culture domain of media celebrity and public representation of Latina/o issues, but his political and military roles in the nineteenth century were comparable in representing the prominent issues of his era.

Before making his way to Washington, D.C., to serve in Congress, Hernández represented St. Augustine in the Tallahassee Territorial House of

Representatives, where he was elected to serve as its presiding officer. He became known as General Hernández due to his active participation in the U.S. Army as well as for organizing and commanding local militias to fight against the Indians in the Seminole War of 1835. He is credited with leading the 1837 expedition that captured the famous Chief Osceola, which eventually ensured the defeat of the Seminoles in 1842. Prior to his political and military career, Hernández was a plantation owner of lands granted by Spain to colonists who settled in the Spanish colony. He died near Matanzas, Cuba, in 1857.

Further Reading

http://www.dep.state.fl.us/parks/district3/washingtonoaks/info/history.asp.

Cristina K. Muñoz

Herrera, Carolina (1939–). Carolina Herrera, named to the International Best Dressed List from 1971 until 1980, established her unique line of quality clothing designs in 1981. Rivaling the likes of Bill Blass, Armani, and Oscar De la Renta, she gained Fashion Hall of Fame status in 1981, and in 1999 received the Lifetime Achievement in Fashion Award from Fashion Week of the Americas. Her collection has evolved to include a line of bridal dresses, perfumes, men's cologne, a knitwear collection, accessories, and sportswear designed for the younger audience.

Born into a family of privilege, Maria Carolina Josefina Pacanins y Nino began her life in Caracas, Venezuela, in 1939. Her father, Guillermo Pacanins, was an officer for the Venezuelan Air Force before becoming governor of Caracas. Herrera grew up observing glamour, constantly surrounded by people who enjoyed wearing the latest fashion. When Herrera was thirteen years old, her grandmother took her to Paris where she attended a Cristobal Balenciaga fashion show. The construction and simplicity of lines in this couture collection became great inspirations to her when she started designing her own line.

In the late 1960s, Herrera joined one of Venezuela's most prominent families when she married Reinaldo Herrera. She stepped into a luxurious international life and established close friendships with some of the wealthiest, most sought-after people on three continents. Her understanding of the socialite's lifestyle, her exquisite tailoring, and her extraordinary talent have attracted celebrities and royalty to her designs. Over the years, she has graced the silhouettes of notable women such as former First Ladies Jacqueline Kennedy Onassis and Nancy Reagan, actress Kathleen Turner, Marla Maples, Princess Elizabeth of Yugoslavia, and former First Daughter Caroline Kennedy.

She is tremendously proud of the four daughters she has raised, each grown and successful in their respective fields. Herrera now adds the joys of being a grandmother to her list of favorite pastimes.

Further Reading

Tapert, Annette. "Carolina Herrera." *Town and Country Monthly* (1997). http://www.lasmujeres.com/carolinaherrera/designer.shtml.

Telgen, Diane, and Jim Kamp, eds. *Latinas! Women of Achievement.* Detroit, MI: Visible Ink Press, 1996.

Alma Alvarez-Smith

High Noon. Director Fred Zimmerman's 1952 *film *High Noon* has been acclaimed by critics and film historians as one of the greatest Hollywood movies of the century and possibly the best western ever made. Nominated for Best Picture of 1952 and seven other Academy Awards, *High Noon* received four Oscars in the categories of Best Song, Musical Score, Film Editing, and Actor—the second Oscar for Gary Cooper. Much of its acclaim is due to its challenge of the conventional western genre by presenting a morality play with an independent Mexican American businesswoman, the character Helen Ramírez played by Katy *Jurado, at its thematic center, and also to its avoidance of the typical Hollywood motifs of Caucasian cowboy machismo, savage Indians, postcard landscapes, gratuitous violence, and frivolous petticoated women.

Written and filmed during the political persecution of 1950s McCarthyism and the U.S. House of Representatives Un-American Activities Committee hearings, the film may be viewed as the parable of a hero who chooses to be ruled by his individual moral conscience against a town's cowardice. It is often understood to serve specifically as a metaphor for the socialist Hollywood artists (including *High Noon* screenwriter Carl Foreman) and other activists and intellectuals blacklisted by the major studios because of actual or perceived connections to the Communist Party. A low-budget classic, its significance to Latina/o popular culture derives from the Helen Ramírez character being built as the story's only moral and political equivalent to hero Will Kane (Cooper). She alone understands what he does about the town's danger, and she alone takes the only ethical action she can under the circumstances—that is, leave town immediately after advising Kane's bride, Amy, played by Academy Award–winning actor Grace Kelly, on how to express loyalty and courage. Symbolizing Ramírez's centrality to the tale of marginality is the untranslated Spanish dialogue exchanged by her and Kane in the middle of the film. The cultural, political, and aesthetic boldness of that exchange cannot be overstated, particularly in the early 1950s when it was produced. Combined with the script's attention to *race and ethnicity in the form of Helen's statement to Amy Kane that she hates the town and her place as a Mexican woman in it, the movie's use of Spanish is striking. The maturity and sophistication of the plot can be gauged as well by Ramírez's social standing and self-respect despite her relationships at one time or another with the three male principles. Although *High Noon* has been long admired, neither the film's ethnic and gender pluralism nor its concern for registering *mexicanidad* (Mexican identity) received much critical attention until it was noticed favorably by cultural studies and feminist studies scholars in the late twentieth century.

Further Reading

Candelaria, Cordelia. "Social Equity and Film Portrayals of La mujer hispana." In *Chicano Cinema: Research, Reviews, and Resources*, edited by Gary D. Keller. Binghamton, NY: Bilingual Review Press, 1984.

Doane, Mary, Patricia Mellencamp, and Linda Williams, eds. *Re-vision: Essays in Feminist Film Criticism*. Frederick, MD: University Publications of America, 1984.

Limón, José Eduardo. *American Encounters: Greater Mexico, the United States, and the Erotics of Culture*. Boston: Beacon Press, 1998.

Williams, Linda. *Playing the Race Card: Melodramas of Black and White from Uncle Tom to O.J. Simpson*. Princeton, NJ: Princeton University Press, 2001.

Cordelia Chávez Candelaria

Hijuelos, Oscar (1951–). The first Hispanic novelist to win the Pulitzer Prize in fiction, Oscar J. Hijuelos received the esteemed award in 1990 for his bestselling book *The Mambo Kings Play Songs of Love* (1989), which led to his becoming one of the country's most renowned Latino writers. Hijuelos, the son of Cuban immigrants, has won critical and popular praise by turning his *Cuban American heritage into fictional works. By adapting the familiar immigrant themes of hard work and persistence in the face of hardship for his novels, Hijuelos has succeeded in attracting a broad audience in the United States and worldwide. His novels have been translated into twenty-five languages. In addition to the Pulitzer, Hijuelos has received other prestigious awards, such as a National Endowment for the Arts fellowship, a Guggenheim Foundation grant, and the American Academy in Rome Fellowship.

Hijuelos was born in New York City on August 24, 1951, to Cuban-born parents; his father was a hotel worker and his mother a homemaker. Growing up in an area that was alive with the Hispanic culture and pulsating with the *mambo scene, he was so taken with the music that he played in several Latin American bands from his teen years through early adulthood. After graduating from high school, he attended the City College of the City University of New York, obtaining a Bachelor of Arts degree in 1975 and a Master's in English and creative writing in 1976. Hijuelos worked as an advertising media traffic manager for Transportation Display, Inc., in New York City after college but devoted his free time to writing. Some of the short stories he wrote in this period eventually were published in the *Best of Pushcart Press III* anthology in 1978.

Pushcart Press provided Hijuelos his breakthrough as a writer 1978 when his first significant published work, *Columbus Discovering America* (1977), received an outstanding writer citation from Pushcart, and this led to his receiving a number of other scholarships and grants that permitted him the time and means to write his first novel, *Our House in the Last World* (1983). In it, he scrutinizes the life of a Cuban immigrant *family living in America in the 1940s, a fictional canvas that allowed him to examine his own feelings about his Cuban roots, binational heritage, and Americanness. Critics lauded *Our House in the Last World* because it did not follow in the steps of other Cuban books that tended to focus on the political strife in Cuba. Instead, Hijuelos wrote a vibrant immigrant memoir that follows the fate of the Santinio family over several decades, including their *immigration to the United States and the difficulties faced while living in New York's Spanish Harlem. Beyond this, a major theme of *Our House in the Last World* is the issue of Cuban manhood and what it takes to achieve it and at what costs. Extremely well received, the book opened the door to his landing a National Endowment for the Arts fellowship, which allowed him to quit his advertising job and begin writing full-time.

In 1989 Hijuelos published his second novel, *The Mambo Kings Play Songs of Love*, which chronicles the lives of two Cuban brothers, Nestor and César Castillo, who achieve momentary fame before slowly fading into obscurity. The story begins with Nestor and the larger-than-life Mambo King Cesar deciding to leave their native Cuba in the late 1940s and immigrate to New York. Forming an orchestra in Spanish Harlem called the Mambo Kings, the fictional brothers achieve ephemeral fame in the 1950s when they rub shoulders with Desi *Arnaz by appearing on an episode of television's groundbreaking sitcom *I Love Lucy* as Ricky Ricardo's Cuban cousins. With its upbeat broad appeal, *The Mambo Kings Play Songs of Love* was adapted into a commercially successful *film in 1992.

Hijuelos's other novels include *The Fourteen Sisters of Emilio Montez O'Brien* (1993), a narrative that takes a very different approach from its predecessor. Narrated by multiple female viewpoints, the story spans several generations in the life of a Cuban Irish family in Pennsylvania. *The Fourteen Sisters of Emilio Montez O'Brien* was followed by *Mr. Ives' Christmas* (1995), about a man who is trying to piece his life back together after his son's violent murder during the Christmas season. Returning to the immigrant memoir form, Hijuelos's next novel, *Empress of the Splendid Season* (1999), chronicles the trials and tribulations of Lydia España and her family over the course of a half-century. In his sixth novel, *A Simple Habana Melody (From When the World Was Good)* (2002), Hijuelos tells the story of a gifted Cuban composer who returns to the island after being mistaken for a Jew and imprisoned during the Nazi occupation of France.

Celebrated for his important contributions to the literary canon of contemporary American fiction, Hijuelos is noted for his skillful use of a voice that is much like his own: authentically second-generation Cuban American whose ties to the motherland are diminishing year after year. Literary critics credit his writing for its affectionate and respectful tribute to Cuban culture, for his generation's separation from that island past, and for his deft style in intersecting it throughout the U.S. American experience. As a writer, his transnational imagination straddles two ethnic and linguistic cultures in a way that does not abandon or bind either. In addition to writing, Hijuelos teaches at Hofstra University, where he is a professor of English.

Further Reading

Kanellos, Nicolás, ed. *The Hispanic-American Almanac: A Reference Work on Hispanics in the United States*. Detroit, MI: Gale Research, 1993.

Pérez Firmat, Gustavo. "Oscar Hijuelos." In *Modern Latin-American Fiction Writers*. Second Series. Edited by William Luis and Ann González. Vol. 145 of *Dictionary of Literary Biography*. Detroit, MI: Bruccoli Clark Layman Book/Gale Group, 1994.

Ryan, Bryan, ed. *Hispanic Writers*. Detroit, MI: Gale Group, 1991.

Stavans, Ilán. "Oscar Hijuelos, Novelista." *Revista Iberoamericana* 155–156 (April–September 1991): 673–677.

Julie Amparano García

Hinojosa Smith, Rolando (1929–). The first *Chicano author to receive a major international literary award, the Premio *Casa de las Américas in 1976 for his novel *Klail City y sus alrededores* (Klail City and Its Surroundings [1987]), Rolando Hinojosa Smith also received the Premio *Quinto Sol literary award for best novel in 1973 for *Estampas del valle y otras obras* (Sketches of the Valley and Other Works [1994]). His acclaimed fiction was further recognized in 1981 by the Southwest Studies on Latin America award for best writing in the humanities for *Mi querido Rafa* (My Beloved Rafa). Many literary scholars believe that Hinojosa joins the ranks of such eminent regional writers as Mark Twain, Américo Paredes, Frank Dobie, Eudora Welty, and Rudolfo *Anaya with his fictional series The Klail City Death Trip on south Texas life, people, and *Tejano popular culture.

Hinojosa was born on January 21, 1929, in the Lower Rio Grande Valley in Mercedes, Texas, the son of Manuel Guzman and Carrie Effie Smith, a homemaker. His father, a farmer whose ancestors arrived in 1749 in what was then the northern border region of New Spain as part of the José Escandón expedition, fought in the Mexican Revolution against the Porfiriato (*See* History, Chicana/o and Mexican American), while his mother remained with the *family in the United States. Hinojosa was first sent to Mexican schools in Mercedes before being sent later to the segregated public school where all of his classmates were Mexican Americans, many of whom had similar long-standing roots in Texas. He attended an integrated high school, where he published his first pieces in English in the school's annual literary magazine, *Creative Bits*. After graduation from high school, he joined the military in 1946 and served for two years in the army. Later reactivated and assigned to Korea, Hinojosa was sent to the Caribbean as a radio announcer and editor of a Caribbean Army Defense Command newspaper, where he further honed his writing skills.

After discharge from the army, he enrolled at the University of Texas in Austin and graduated with a Bachelor of Arts degree in Spanish in 1954 and began his first teaching job at Brownsville High School. In 1960 Hinojosa began graduate studies in Spanish at New Mexico Highlands University, from which he earned a Master of Arts in 1963. Going on to pursue advanced Spanish-language and literary studies at the University of Illinois, Urbana, he was awarded his Ph.D. in 1969. Since that time he has taught at universities in San Antonio, Kingsville, and Minneapolis and held the Ellen Clayton Garwood Professorship in the English Department at the University of Texas in Austin, 1985–1992, and since 1992 the Mari Sabusawa Michener Chair in the same department. In 1995, he was honored as Outstanding Latino Faculty by the Hispanic caucus of the American Association for Higher Education.

Hinojosa acknowledges that he prefers to compose his works in Spanish, but he serves as his own translator, as in his *Sketches of the Valley and Other Works* translation of *Estampas del valle y otras obras* (1973). Consisting of loosely connected sketches, narratives, monologues, and dialogues, the four-part novel presents a composite picture of *Chicano and Chicana life in the fictitious Belken County town of Klail City, Texas. Stylistically, his fiction employs satire, humor, overlapping plot lines, and multiple individual characterizations of the Chicano people who inhabit Belken County. Avoiding traditional linear plots and generic structures, his novels concentrate on language and the revealing of character elements through the subtleties and psychology of language, including local dialects and Caló. Hinojosa's "Klail City Death Trip Series" consists of eight novels written from the 1970s to the 1990s and begins in part one with Jehu Malacara, a nine-year-old boy who lives with dour relatives after the deaths of his parents. Jehu's life is shown through comic and satiric sketches and narratives of incidents and characters surrounding him. The second part is a collection of incidents about a murder; the third consists of sketches narrated by an omniscient storyteller that reveal the lifestyle of various social groups in Klail City; and the fourth section introduces the series' other main character, Jehu's cousin Rafa Buenrostro, also an orphan, who narrates his experiences and recollection of his life. Hinojosa rewrote *Estampas* in English, publishing it as *The Valley* in 1983. He claims to have set down in fiction the history of the Lower Rio Grande Valley and says his main motivation for writing began with a childhood need to express himself. He takes inspiration from his bicultural background, a knowledge of the history and myths of where he was born, and the relating of official history and the people and popular culture practices that oppose it. Scholars of his corpus of fiction identify approximately 1,000 different characters in his work. Hinojosa has lectured widely throughout the United States, México, Cuba, and Europe. On May 17, 1998, he received the University of Illinois Alumni Achievement Award, the highest award given by the institution's alumni association.

Further Reading

Bruce-Novoa, Juan. *Chicano Authors: Inquiry by Interview*. Austin: University of Texas Press, 1980.

Lee, Joyce Glover. *Rolando Hinojosa and the American Dream*. Denton: University of North Texas Press, 1997.

Saldivar, José David, ed. *The Rolando Hinojosa Reader: Essays Historical and Critical*. Houston, TX: Arte Público Press, 1985.

BJ Manríquez

Hip-Hop and Rap. Latinas/os have been integral to the development of rap music and hip-hop culture since its beginnings in New York's black and Latina/o neighborhoods in the early 1970s. Several Puerto Ricans introduced innovative ideas into each aspect of the culture: rapping or MCing, graffiti writing, breakdancing, and DJing. The style of lyric delivery that today we call rap, characterized by rhythmic speaking over layered combinations of African, disco, Latin, and rock music, began with black rap artists such as Grandmaster Flash and the Furious Five, Afrika Bambaata, and the Cold Crush Brothers; however, it was never solely an African American art form. Puerto Rican MCs such as Prince Whipper Whip, Ruby D, and Robski and June Bug, were among the first young people in New York City to rap, and their presence in hip-hop history is documented in early movies about the culture. When rap music began its ascent into popular music in the mid-1980s, these early Puerto Rican innovators were forgotten and moved to the margins of the music industry and rap music history. Only a few early recordings of Puerto Rican rappers can still be found (*Cold Crush Brothers vs. Fantastic Five Battle*, 1981). Movies such as *Wild Style* (1982), *Style Wars* (1984), *Breakin'* (1984), *Breakin' II* (1984), and *Beat Street* (1984) showcased the new urban cultural movement developing in New York, highlighting breakdancing with rap music providing the sound track and graffiti visually situating viewers in the ghettos and *barrios of New York City and Los Angeles. Among the stars of these movies were the breakdancers from The Rock Steady Crew, a group of Puerto Rican and black breakdancers and graffiti artists created in 1977. The Puerto Rican leaders of Rock Steady gained international fame with the release of these movies. The release of these important movies brought hip-hop culture to the youth masses throughout the United States.

Young Mexican Americans and other Latinas/os began to create their own local brands of hip-hop and rap. By the late 1980s Chicano rappers began to develop their distinctive style of rap music, fusing 1980s break beats with rhythm and blues (R&B) oldies, and the occasional traditional Mexican song, to tell stories of their experiences in Mexican American barrios, utilizing their unique Chicano street vernacular that mixes Spanish, English, Caló, and the black vernacular of the inner city. Kid Frost brought Chicano rap into the national spotlight with his first single, "La Raza," from his album *Hispanic Causing Panic* (1990). From the beginning Frost (*East Side Drama*, 1992) and other early rappers such as ALT (*Another Latin Timebomb*, 1992, and *Stone Cold World*, 1993), Proper Dos (*Mexican Power*, 1992), and A Lighter Shade of Brown (*Brown and Proud*, 1990, and *Hip Hop Locos*, 1992) proudly shouted out their Chicano identities, urging others to develop a sense of pride in their Mexican ancestry. These Los Angeles–based Chicano rappers where aided by the musical production of Chicano producers such as Julio G and Tony G. Along with Ralph M, Julio G and Tony G helped bring rap to Chicano Los Angeles via the *Mix Master Show* on KDAY 1580 AM. Tony G went on to establish G-Spot Studios and help launch the careers of Frost (seven albums to date and several compilation and group appearances), Brownside (*Brownside*, 1992, *EastSide Drama*, 1997, and *The Payback*, 2000), and Slow Pain (*Baby O.G.*, 1995, *The Hit List*, 2000, and *Lil' Don Juan*, 2001).

After the success of these early rappers, other Latinas/os began to emerge on the rap scene. Cuban Mellow Man Ace recorded the gold-selling single "Mentirosa" (Liar) in 1989, and his brother, Sen Dog, helped form the multiethnic group Cypress Hill. Cypress Hill from the Southgate area of Los Angeles released their self-titled debut album in 1991. Since then, they have become one of the best-known rap groups across the globe and have released six studio albums, one live album, and one compilation of their greatest hits remixed in Spanish. Their success has allowed them to develop and nurture new groups and solo projects. Sen Dog helped the Chicano rap group Delinquent Habits (*Delinquent Habits*, 1996, *Here Come the Horns*, 1998, and *Merry Go Round*, 2000) become internationally famous, while B-Real became a founding member of the revolutionary Chicano rap group Psycho Realm (*Psycho Realm*, 1997, and *A War Story, Book 1*, 2000).

By the mid-1990s recorded Chicano rap had moved into other urban areas. Led by Low Profile Records and its roster of Chicano rappers, San Diego boasts the second largest Chicano rap music scene. Lil' Rob (*Crazy Life*, 1997, *Still Smokin'*, 2000, and *The Last Laff*, 2002), Royal T (*Coast to Coast*, 1998), owner of Low Profile Records, Sancho, Proper Dos, and O.G. Spanish Fly (*Back From the Dead*, 2001, and *Higher Than Highland*, 2002) are among the rappers affiliated with Low Profile. Other Chicano rappers from San Diego include Knightowl (*The Knightowl*, 1995, *Wicked West*, 1998, and *Bald Headed Kingpin*, 2001) and Aztec Tribe and Mr. Shadow (*Till I Die*, 1998, and *Pit Bossing*, 2001). The San Francisco Bay Area also has a large Chicano rap music scene led by The Darkroom Family. Sir Dyno (*Interview with a Chicano*, 1996, and *What Have I Become?*, 2000), founder of Darkroom Studios, and Familia rappers including Duke (*Kill Them Slowly*, 2000), Los Traficantes (*Matan Mi Gente* [They Kill My People],

1999), and Oso (*Who Can I Trust?*, 2000) have been prolific since their emergence onto the scene in the mid-1990s. Houston is home to South Park Mexican who has released a total of eight CDs since their debut, *Hustle Town* (1998), and his Dopehouse Records. Chicago is hometown to Los Marijuanos (*Puro Plaito*, 1999) and DJ Payback Garcia (*Aztec Souls*, 2002), and Rip Em Up Productions hails from Albuquerque, New Mexico. Chicano rappers use their art form to comment on important issues in their communities. They rap about love, parties, *gangs and gang violence, *police corruption and abuse, poverty, family, drug use and abuse, the education system, and world politics.

Today, the most widely known Latino rap artists are not Chicanos but Puerto Ricans. In the mid-1990s Fat Joe (*Represent*, 1993, and *Jealous Ones Still Envy*, 2001) became known on the national rap scene along with his crew, The Terror Squad (*The Terror Squad*, 1999). Joe helped launch the career of the bestselling Puerto Rican rapper, Big Pun (*Capital Punishment*, 1998, and *Endangered Species*, 2001). Important Latina/o rappers and DJs include Mexicano 777 (*Entre el bien y el mal* [Between the Good and the Bad], 1998, and *God's Assassin*, 2001), Tony Touch (*Can't Sleep on the Streets*, 1999, and *The Piece Maker*, 2000), the Beatnuts who have recorded eight albums since their debut in 1993, and Funkdoobiest (*Which Doobie UB?*, 1993, and *The Troubleshooters*, 1998). Latinas have also recorded rap CDs, though they have not received the same level of recognition as their male counterparts. Hurricane G (*All Woman*, 1997), Angie Martinez (*Up Close and Personal*, 2001, and *Animal House*, 2002), and JV (*Nayba'hood Queen*, 1994, and *Ladybug*, 2002) have had successful careers as rap artists. Today, dozens of Latinas and Latinos record rap CDs, and thousands more participate in and create hip-hop scenes all across the country. In most U.S. cities, it is common to find Chicanas/Chicanos, Puerto Ricans, and other Latinas and Latinos rapping about their experiences and their communities over complex musical productions that mix Caribbean, Mexican, African, Funk, R&B, and other types of music.

Further Reading

Cross, Brian. *It's Not about a Salary: Rap, Race and Resistance in Los Angeles.* Berkeley: University of California Press, 1994.

Flores, Juan. *From Bomba to Hip Hop: Puerto Rican Culture and Latino Identity.* New York: Columbia University Press, 2000.

McFarland, Louis Pancho. "'Here Is Something You Can't Understand . . . ': Chicano Rap and the Critique of Globalization." In *Decolonial Voices*, edited by Arturo J. Aldama and Naomi Quiñonez. Bloomington: University of Indiana Press, 2001.

http://www.boricua.com.

http://www.brownpride.com.

Louis "Pancho" McFarland

Hispanic Caucus. *See* Congressional Hispanic Caucus.

History, Chicana/o and Mexican American. A fuller understanding of Mexican American popular culture requires a brief review of history, particularly of three important cultural starting points. The first relates to the indigenous pre-Columbian empires of the Culhua-Mexica peoples (Aztecs) and their Mesoamerican predecessors (notably the Mayans, Toltecs, and Olmecs); the second is the imperial dominance of early-fifteenth-century Spain and its consequences; and the third concerns the U.S. expansionism of the nineteenth century and its direct results in forming "Mexican-hyphen-America." These distant but eventually connected points in history contain the seeds of Chicana and *Chicano heritage and resultant popular cultures.

The first historical source comes from the Nahuátl-speaking people known as the Aztecs who ruled the large Mesoamerican empire of today's central and southern México when Christopher *Columbus and later Europeans arrived in the fifteenth and early sixteenth centuries. According to Spanish records, the Aztecs referred to themselves as Culhua-Mexica in an attempt to link themselves with Colhuacán, the site where the most advanced people of Mesoamerica once resided. Some historians believe that "Aztec" stems from the word *Aztlán, an allusion to their original homeland in today's northern México and southwestern United States, as well as to a mythical paradise (like Eden) that was home to their founding gods. Also identified as the Tenochca and the Mexica, the Aztecs used "Tenochca" in naming their largest city and center of their empire, "Tenochtitlán," founded in CE 1325. After independence from Spain in 1821 "Mexica" provided the root for the name given the entire nation.

Scholars attribute the success of the Aztecs in building a lasting state and empire to an advanced system of agriculture, whose high productivity created a rich and populous nation. Featuring complex irrigation networks and reclaimed swamps, they were able to cultivate all available land and expand their empire to over 80,000 square miles (207,200 square kilometer). Closely connected to advancements in agriculture were the highly evolved systems of astronomy and mathematics, which were the foundations for determining the planting seasons, climate, and land and water development. A product of these sciences was the famous "Aztec calendar," which also was used to track religious rites and other ceremonies. Common throughout Mesoamerica and believed to have originated in pre-Mayan cultures, the calendar accurately enumerated a solar year of 365 days and included a sacred year of 260 days, the two cycles producing a third cycle of 52 years.

Another reason for the Aztecs' long-term and widespread domination was the centralized government, which formed alliances with neighboring tribes and conducted flourishing trade networks as far north as present-day Colorado. The Aztecs' dominance occurred through a political order that for the most part was hierarchical and stratified by classes. When the Spaniards led by Hernán Cortés arrived in 1519 approximately 6 million people were under the rule of Tenochtitlán, which alone had over 140,000 inhabitants in an over five-square-mile (thirteen-square-kilometer) metropolis and also held power over 400 smaller states. Critically important to the future of México and later Mexican American culture is that Aztec governance was marked by a hierarchy that integrated politics and theology. The religious and political structure featured leaders at the top of the empire's power structure and a huge labor class of *péones* (serfs, indentured servants, and slaves) at the bottom.

The Culhua-Mexica religion absorbed elements from other Mesoamerican belief systems, primarily the cosmology of the Maya, whose flourishing civilization in the Yucatán region from circa 1000 BCE to CE 1400 is, along with the Toltecs', acknowledged to be the main source of much of Mesoamerica's social evolution. Prominent among their beliefs was that the Earth was the last in a series of supreme creations and that it existed among a number of other cosmological systems, a modern view that indicates a sophisticated understanding of space and planetary motion. The principal Aztec gods were Huítzilopochtli (war), Tonatiúh (sun), Tlaloc (rain), Coátlicúe (earth mother), and Quetzalcóatl (Feathered Serpent). Considered part deity and part human hero (like many demigods in the Judaeo-Christian, Greek, and Roman mythologies), Quetzalcóatl has been interpreted through a European gaze as a messiah figure confused by the emperor Moctecuhzoma (aka Montezuma) in welcoming Cortés as a possible returning Feathered Serpent. Human sacrifice was also practiced as a means of appeasing the gods, a retrograde practice that compares to such Old World human tortures as the stake-burning of non-Christians, pillorying the mentally and physically disabled, and imprisoning the insane, as well as to such twentieth-century tortures as the German gas ovens, the Russian slaughter of millions, the American bombing of Hiroshima and Nagasaki, and other genocidal tortures in Africa, the Middle East, and elsewhere.

At the time that the Spanish explorers appeared in 1519, the drought-plagued but still evolving Aztec Empire and society had begun to disintegrate. The indigenous cultural development experienced a major transformation when the Aztecs' ninth emperor, Moctecuhzoma, whose reign spanned 1502 to 1520, was taken prisoner by the Spaniards and died in custody. Succeeded by Cuitláhuac and Cuauhtémoc, the empire was unable to repel Cortés and his combined forces of Spanish and indigenous allies, including the indispensable *La Malinche. The takeover of Tenochtitlán in 1521 terminated Aztec rule but not the hierarchal pattern of entwined Church and State control of the people and the society's native wealth. Since the same pattern defined the conquering Spanish government and culture, the peoples of Mexico and their descendants share a legacy marked by the merging of religion and politics as a basis of wealth and power.

The second starting point for Chicana/o popular culture can be traced to the imperial expansion of early-fifteenth-century Spain, which began with sponsorship of Columbus's voyages in search of a faster route to the Far East. His arrival in the Western Hemisphere, as yet unknown to most Europeans of his age, was a landmark world event and catapulted the Spain of 1492 and its Catholic monarchs, Isabel and Ferdinand, to a new level of global dominance. For about a century and a half, Spain enjoyed the material harvest of the extraction of "New" (to the Europeans) World resources. Part of that harvest included the costs of colonizing the new lands, controlling the greatly decimated Indians, and expanding into the northern and southern territories beyond Mesoamerica. Like English and French colonialism, the Spaniards were motivated by greed for land and for natural resources to export. Unlike them, Spanish colonizing was pushed as well by an intense desire to spread Christianity, particularly Roman Catholicism. Occurring during the decades of the Holy Inquisition and the Counter Reformation, the imperial expansionism caused terror among many disempowered non-Christians and even among poor Protestants.

Significant to the Mexican American heritage that evolved after 1848 and the signing of the *Treaty of Guadalupe Hidalgo is that, like Mesoamerica's, Spain's cultural roots in Iberia grew out of an environment of combined State and Church political control, thereby carrying on the political trinity of Church, State, and economic wealth that existed in the governmental structure it had toppled. As a result this stratification affected the emergence of **mestizaje* (racial and cultural hybridity) among the populace in such basic practices as language (e.g., Castilian Spanish was viewed as superior), religion (e.g., the *Virgin of Guadalupe as a hybrid of the Christian Virgin Mary and Tonantzin, an Aztec fertility god—mother earth), and racial mixing (e.g., Spaniards born in Spain were viewed as superior, some Spaniards were Caucasian, others were more North African in features). Not surprisingly, 300 years later when a liberation movement stirred and independence from Spain began to take hold in México, the key goals of the revolutionaries focused on separating Church and State rule, gaining equality for indigenous and mixed-race people, and promoting the value of *mexicanidad* (native Mexicanness) to the nation.

Although the seeds for emancipation were sowed much earlier, the battle for freedom from Spain is usually dated back to 1810 and the famous Grito de Dolores (freedom cry from the town of Dolores). Made by Father Hidalgo, the Grito de Dolores exhorted the people to join in rebellion against their maltreatment by the corrupt royalist government, which was in collusion with the Church. This parallel to the U.S. American Revolution provides Mexican Americans a strong underpinning of cultural independence to balance the heritage of State and Church despotism. Agustin de Iturbide, a royalist *criollo* (creole, or full-blood Spaniard born in New Spain), led the brilliant opposition to independence on behalf of the royalist cause and fought against both Hidalgo and fellow liberationist Father José Morelos. Independence from Spain was achieved in 1821, and México replaced Nueva España, but the strength of the previous hierarchy and lingering taste for monarchy led to Iturbide's declaring himself emperor. His brief regime was successfully challenged, and the people of the Mexican federal republic began a century-long effort to end hierarchical rule and install a truly representative democracy.

Symbolically, the green, white, and red colors of the Mexican flag that were adopted by the republic emphasize historical and cultural continuity. The green field signifies independence, the white area represents the purity of the Catholic Church, and the red section refers to the violence of the conquest and the Spanish past, which persists in México's language and elements of culture. The image at the center of the flag shows an eagle (*aguila*) perched atop a cactus (*nopal*) with a serpent (*serpiente*) in its talons and represents a link to the native, pre-European heritage, specifically to the legend that the ancient Mexica ancestors had been guided by the eagle to Anáhuac where Tenochtitlán was founded. Unlike the American Revolution against England, which was bloody on its path to the political empowerment of landowning Caucasian men and passage of a democratic constitution, the bloody Mexican Revolution did not institute a participatory form of governance but maintained the old political, religious, and economic trinity that maintained the stratified society with a tiny number of rich, politically powerful families and a massive peonage numbering in the hundreds of millions. Although the U.S. Constitution did not initially apply to all American men and women, its democratic ideals served as an inspirational magnet for reform in North America and elsewhere, including later Mexican revolutionaries.

Many historians argue that medieval cultures with interlocked Church and State structures resist reform (e.g., the Protestant Reformation whose "protesting" ideas encouraged independence movements, new science, and democratic politics) and tend to perpetuate hierarchical traditions. This was true in Mexican history, for Emperor Iturbide was followed by another tyrant, Antonio López de Santa Anna, who continued the tripartite political order of State, Church, and wealth. Throughout the decades after Mexican independence, many liberal factions tried in vain to institute in their country the example of the younger neighbor to the north, especially that of a secular government. Finally, in 1855 when the full-blood Zapotec, Benito Juarez, a brilliant lawyer from Oaxaca, became president, his administration mounted a serious attempt to separate Church and State and enact other egalitarian reforms. His vision of a modern secular México met vehement opposition, spawned a bloody civil war, and eventually led to foreign intervention by the French with support from other countries who were attracted by México's economic resources and wanted to exploit the country's weakness. Eventually victorious at the legendary Battle of Puebla on *Cinco de

Mayo (May 5) 1867, Juarez is still regarded as a national hero, even though he achieved only partial success in completing the enlightened social reformation he and his liberal followers sought.

Further decades of corruption and abuse of power in the form of the Porfiriato followed Juarez's death (1876–1910). A tyranny established by monarchist General Porfirio Díaz who ruled México for nearly thirty-five years, the Porfiriato was a tight collusion of power based on the familiar trinity of Church, State, and a rich elite class. Díaz is credited with accomplishing major public works like government and military buildings, boulevards, and roads, especially in and surrounding the capital Mexico City, for the convenience of *los ricos* (the ruling elite), as well as providing some education and health improvements. By and large, however, the Porfiriato only greatly deepened poverty among the landless poor and increased the lavish affluence of the rich without developing the country's abundant natural resources into a broad-based infrastructure of prosperity for the majority. The Díaz regime also sold up to 80 percent of the nation's mining interests to foreign investors from the United States, Britain, and other countries, without using the profits for the common good. These failures in conjunction with the hunger and suffering of the masses led directly to the Mexican Revolution of 1910, another bloody civil war with devastating consequences including a string of presidential assassinations and other political murders throughout the country.

The terror and upheaval caused by the violent conflict led to the single largest displacement of Mexicans in the nation's history since the Conquest. Besides the hundreds of thousands displaced internally, tens of thousands of others left for neighboring Central American countries, and nearly a million Mexicans emigrated to the United States. This northward migration was logical since only sixty years before the U.S. Southwest was still northern México and thousands of 1910-era immigrants had family ties in the United States. Besides its demographic impact on the United States, the revolution produced such still celebrated populist revolutionary icons as Emiliano *Zapáta, Pancho *Villa, La Adelita, and the muralists Diego *Rivera, José Clemente Orozco, and David Alfaro Siquéiros, who were adopted as popular culture role models for public art by the *Chicano Movement in the 1960s and 1970s.

In México the revolution finally led to viable constitutional reforms in 1917 (based on Juarez's abandoned 1857 Constitution) and eventually to the forming of the Partido Nacional Revolutionario (PNR—National Revolutionary Party), a movement to unite the country's factions and provide effective secular governance. Promoted by General Plutarco Elías Calles, who was president from 1924 to 1928, the PNR served as the precursor to the current Institutional Revolutionary Party (Partido Revolucionario Institucional [PRI]), which until the election of President Vicente Fox in 2000 would produce most of the nation's presidents in the twentieth century. Despite Calles' well-intentioned Programa de Gobierno ("New Deal"–type government program that included liberal reforms in education, the legal system, land and agriculture, and other areas), his decision to enforce the section of the Constitution of 1917 that called for official sanctions against priests and Church officials who committed crimes created such a public outcry that it provoked a counterreform effort called the Cristiada, a Church-supported bloodbath. Waged by a group self-identified as Cristeros (ultra-Christians), the violence cost some 70,000 lives by the time the crusade ended in 1929.

From the downfall of Díaz's dictatorship, one major issue that dominated the policies of México's political leaders was how to gain effective control of the country's vast mineral resources, which for short-term gain had been sold cheaply to foreign interests. Díaz had followed the colonialist practices of the Spanish motherland by allowing foreign companies to exploit the land and the people and to export México's native wealth to their countries. Another persistent issue was social justice for the masses through the redistribution of land and legal reforms, since Díaz had consolidated enormous tracts to a very few major landowners (*hacendados*). The presidency of Lázaro Cárdenas (1934–1940) was the first to move decisively to address both issues, first, by distributing over 18 million hectares among over a million peasants, and, second, by nationalizing the production of oil. This latter decision almost led to another U.S. invasion, but because of World War II the United States avoided an oil war against México because of the pressure to join forces against Hitler. Cárdenas's administration was also successful in developing other social programs designed to liberalize his nation's pyramidal political, religious, and social structure. Unfortunately, subsequent presidencies returned the country to ultra-right-wing policies that benefited a few at the painful expense of the many. The challenges of the post–Vicente Fox México of the twenty-first century bears the many political scars and the amazing cultural achievements of the nation's remarkable past. Both still deeply affect the lives and culture of U.S. Americans, especially those of Mexican descent, whether first or second generation or others, which date to the earliest Spanish settlements in the sixteenth and seventeenth centuries.

Accordingly, the third point in history with direct bearing on Chicana/o popular cultural practices is the nineteenth-century American expansionism under the policy of Manifest Destiny, which promoted the idea that the United States was destined by God to expand its territory over the entire breadth of North America. Originating in the 1840s, this Anglo-American policy required the securing of both French and Spanish colonies, and its eventual realization explains why some Chicana/o studies scholars identify Mexicans and Mexican Americans as multiply conquered peoples and why the popular slogan "We didn't cross the Border, the Border (double-)crossed us" resonates as a truism among Chicanas/os whose ancestry in the United

States traces to the sixteenth century, before the *Mayflower*'s landing at Plymouth Rock. Along with the 1823 Monroe Doctrine of U.S. foreign policy, which prohibited further foreign colonization or intervention in the Americas, the significance for Latina/o Americans of Manifest Destiny historically has been complicated.

Both principles appear in early U.S. history books as uncomplicated positive achievements for Americans and the United States, but not in the cultural memory and material experience of most Latinas and Latinos and their cultures of origin. This complexity parallels other aspects of American history, like, for instance, that it took 132 years after passage of the U.S. Constitution in 1787 to grant women universal suffrage, nearly 150 years to protect Indian tribal rights, and 178 years to pass the Voting Rights Act that finally guaranteed universal suffrage to African Americans. Similarly, the effects on Mexican Americans of U.S. foreign policy based on the Monroe Doctrine and Manifest Destiny are historically linked to disputes, invasions, wars, and upheaval. Crucial in this history was the case of Texas, originally a sparsely populated frontier province of northern México that the newly independent nation sought to keep under its political control by actively inviting settlers to populate it in the 1820s. México's generous terms for land acquisition and citizenship quickly attracted thousands of Americans, and by the 1830s the Anglo-American immigrants far outnumbered the original *Tejanos (Mexican-origin Texans).

This result differed from the population mix in California, New Mexico, and Arizona, where Mexicans predominated. Assorted legal, economic, and political troubles arose from a variety of causes in Texas, including the attempt by immigrants from the U.S. South to establish slavery in the province contrary to Mexican law, as well as the concurrent U.S. effort to seize Texas under the specious claim that it was part of the Louisiana Purchase agreement. Also troublesome for the native Tejanos with their evolved and stable traditions were the sociocultural differences of language, religion, and everyday customs and practices, for they tended to see the Anglo immigrants as uncultured ruffians lacking social civilities. Due to México's instability as it struggled to build a prosperous democracy out of centuries of colonial rule, the young republic was unable to address the culture clash in Texas except intermittently by military means, which exacerbated the local conflicts and transnational tensions.

Eventually the new Texans revolted and declared independence from México. The famous battle at the *Alamo in 1836 with its legendary cast of participants led to the effective demise of Mexican dominance over Texas, and the new "lone star" nation immediately began its nine-year campaign for annexation to the United States, which was ratified in 1845. Concerned with protecting its northwest provinces, México immediately mobilized its armies in response to the Manifest Destiny–minded policy of the United States. In the United States a small opposition movement against an invasion of México led New England writer Henry David Thoreau to be jailed and the writing of his globally significant essay "Civil Disobedience." To counter dissent President James K. Polk reasserted the Monroe Doctrine, claiming a fear that México was about to sell California to Great Britain as payment for its debt, thereby reinstating a foreign power on the continent. The costly war for all sides began in 1846 and ended in 1848 with the signing of the Treaty of Guadalupe Hidalgo. Among its many landmark results was its addition of approximately 100,000 hyphenated citizens, "Mexican-Americans," to the U.S. population along with six of its largest future states: Arizona, California, Colorado, Nevada, New Mexico, Texas, and Utah.

Another instance of the complicated significance for Latina/o Americans of the Monroe Doctrine and Manifest Destiny was the U.S. military's involvement on the side of antidemocratic conservatives in the Mexican Revolution of 1910. The U.S. Army's pursuit of Pancho *Villa, for example, contributed to solidifying the grassroots hero's legendary status even further among Mexicans and many Mexican Americans, especially in the borderlands. American support for the Mexican repressive ruling class was greatly tied to protection of its oil interests, which would change radically when Cárdenas nationalized the production of oil and established Petróleos Mexicanos (PEMEX) in the 1930s. That decision soured U.S.-México relations for decades afterwards. Other examples of the complicated significance of U.S. foreign policy include the acquisition of Cuba and Puerto Rico as a result of the 1898 Spanish American War and the multiple invasions of Panama, Nicaragua, and El Salvador in support of repressive dictatorships to protect coffee, banana, and other business interests.

The lasting effects of these connected starting points for Mexican Americans and Chicana/o popular culture(s) are too numerous to summarize here. Among the most important because of their fundamental centrality are the ethnic, racial, linguistic, religious, and social forms and patterns observed and practiced every day among Mexican-origin peoples whether newly arrived or seasoned by generations of life in North America. In one way or another most Mexican-origin people and Chicana/o popular culture find a seed, root, or stem in this exciting history and hybrid heritage.

Further Reading

Acuña, Rodolfo. *Occupied America: A History of Chicanos*. 4th ed. New York: Longman, 2000.

Hernández, David. "Vision of the New Mexico of Vicente Fox: A Transition toward Democracy." Unpublished essay, 2001.

Johannsen, Robert W. *To the Halls of the Montezumas: The Mexican War in the American Imagination*. New York: Oxford University Press, 1985.

Kirkwood, Burton. *The History of Mexico*. Westport, CT: Greenwood Press, 2000.

Pastor, Robert, and Jorge Castañeda. *Limits to Friendship: The United States and Mexico*. New York: Knopf, 1988.

Samora, Julian, and Patricia Simon. *A History of the Mexican-American People*. 2nd ed. Notre Dame, IN: University of Notre Dame Press, 1993.
Vásquez, Josefina Zoraida, and Lorenzo Meyer. *The United States and México*. Chicago: University of Chicago Press, 1985.

Cordelia Chávez Candelaria

History, Cuban American. Comprehension of both the familiar aspects and the complex layers of modern Cuba's past and present require knowledge of the events leading up to the revolution that deposed dictator Fulgencio Batista and brought Fidel *Castro to power. Key participants in the events resided abroad as exiles principally in the United States, México, and other Latin American countries, as well as on the island working in every part of society. In the 1950s, political exiles joined a revolutionary underground intent upon overthrowing dictator Fulgencio Batista and, despite Central Intelligence Agency (CIA) infiltration, ran weapons into Cuba to arm the numerous rebel groups that operated independently of one another. The Authentic Party under Prío Socarrás and the Orthodox Party led by Raúl Chibás, opponents in Cuba, sometimes cooperated in drawing up manifestos for government after the ouster of Batista. This and the resident Democratic Revolutionary Party cooperated with the 26th of July Movement led by Castro after Batista ignored earlier agreements to a democratic resolution to his dictatorship. South Florida, as it had been eighty years before, was the launching pad for revolution, and the exiles believed that they were fighting for a free Cuba.

The *Cuban Revolution did not begin as a communist revolution, but it did threaten the properties and elite power of the ruling circles. At the height of the Cold War, such action was by definition communist, especially in the United States. Between 1959 and 1960, the Eisenhower administration attempted to stop Castro's appropriation of U.S. business investments and properties through punishing sanctions and, when all else failed, broke relations with the island. No other American country could survive without U.S. trade. Additionally, Operation Mongoose was under way to assassinate Castro and/or to begin a revolution within the Cuban territory.

Between 1959 and 1962, an unprecedented 250,000 Cubans flooded U.S. *immigration offices, and they were granted asylum by the Cuban Democracy Act passed in 1961 because they were escaping a communist regime. Like their predecessors, they formed belligerent groups intent on overthrowing the enemy government. Cooperating with the CIA, 1,500 exile men formed Brigade 2506 that invaded Cuba in April 1961 to instigate a popular uprising against Castro. The *Bay of Pigs fiasco humiliated the exiles and permanently solidified *Cuban American sentiment against the U.S. Democratic Party they believed had betrayed them. Indeed, anti-Castro Cuban American saboteurs have continued to run independent operations since 1961, if not from Florida, then from other parts of the Americas.

Cubans leaving for the United States after 1959 were as dedicated to overthrowing the incumbent government as former exilic groups had been, and they were as diverse in their political views. They would become, however, the largest and most influential Cuban American population in history due to the four-decades-plus years of Castro's administration and their special status and assistance, which increased their power. The Cuban Democracy Act granted Cubans residency in the United States unless they were criminals, and the U.S. government provided the financing to buy exit visas for people wishing to leave. Cubans could enter without concern for the quotas that limited the number of every other country's immigrants. In the 1960s and 1970s, aid and education programs trained incoming refugees for middle-class professions and helped them obtain jobs. Thus, Cuban Americans, more than any other immigrant group, were prepared to command well-paying jobs and enter politics to press their political views.

Flight from Cuba came in waves that were moderated by Cuban and U.S. government policies. The first exodus (1959–1964) brought over 120,000 Cubans, 14,068 of whom were children sent by their parents on a "Save the Children Program" (commonly called the Peter Pan Project). After 1965, sporadic evacuations occurred more often as the results of Castro's anger with resident dissatisfaction and U.S. publicity of revolutionary failures. By 1979, 800,000 Cubans had become Cuban Americans, a population with a political agenda in search of ways to direct U.S. foreign policy toward Cuba.

While the exiles had a full spectrum of political attitudes, a critical mass claimed the right to speak for all and repressed the voices of dissidents in the United States. Some formed paramilitary groups such as the Omega 7 and

This three-peso bill, used here as background for an invitation to a program at Arizona State University by contemporary Cuban artists, is emblazoned with an image of Che Guevara, one of the most famous figures in modern Cuban history. *Courtesy of the Cordelia Candelaria Private Collection.*

the Alpha 66 that carried out terrorist missions in international and national settings, respectively. Others joined the CIA working as saboteurs and assassins—as in the cases of Che *Guevara's executioner Félix Rodríguez (1967), Chilean Orlando Letelier's murder by Guillermo and Ignacio Novo (1975), and Orlando Bosch's bazooka attack on a Polish freighter in Miami Harbor (1968). The political arm of the right-wing extremists that controlled Cuban American politics was the Cuban American National Foundation (CANF), founded in 1981 and led by Jorge Más Canosa until his death in 1997. Funded by wealthy elites, CANF contributed to state and federal congressional and presidential campaigns in exchange for guarantees that policy toward Cuba would be as hostile as possible. CANF never got the invasion of Cuba it wanted, but it did avert rapprochement and designed policies that tightened the economic embargo.

In April 1980, another wave of immigrants surprised both Castro and then President Jimmy Carter by its size. When a small group of daring malcontents invaded the Peruvian embassy and asked for asylum, Castro intended to humiliate them by offering to let anyone unhappy with the revolution to leave. Carter rose to the occasion by offering the dissatisfied shelter. Cuban Americans amassed a flotilla that picked up people at Mariel Harbor, and by September, 125,000 Cubans were in the United States. For Carter, the political objective succeeded: Castro's "paradise" was revealed as an economic inferno. But he was left with the problem of incorporating 120,000 new arrivals, many of whom were people of color and unskilled laborers. The powerful, upper-class Miami society was not particularly receptive, since they understood the *Marielitos to be economic refugees who in times past had called them *gusanos* (worms) and *escorio* (scum). Moreover, the Marielitos had been born with the revolution and held different values from those of the earlier exilic groups. This combination would dilute the right-wing hold on politics.

By the late 1980s, the Miami political machine was firmly under Cuban American control. In 1989, Lincoln Díaz-Balart, Fidel Castro's cousin, became the first Cuban American member of the U.S. House of Representatives. In that same year, Ileana *Ros-Lehtinen, a child exile, was elected Miami-Dade's Eighteenth District representative. She was the first Hispanic woman to win a seat in Congress. Her campaign manager was Jeb Bush. Certainly Florida politicians and Miami metropolitan leaders had their share of Cuban Americans who made anti-Castro policies the centerpiece of their political agendas. Radio stations were intolerant of Cuban Americans who wished for dialogue with Cuba and an end to hostile diplomacy, and they encouraged violence and fear mongering as means of silencing this opposition. The U.S. government bowed to pressure from the Cuban American community by creating and financing Radio Martí in 1985, which broadcast news with a Cuban American slant into Cuba, and in 1994 TV Martí.

With the collapse of the Soviet Union and the end of aid and trade with the former USSR, the Cuban economy declined by around 60 percent, and the U.S. embargo impeded assistance from other nations. Between 1990 and 1994, life in Cuba was miserable, and people began to fear starvation. Once again pressure to leave swelled, and a spontaneous demonstration broke out in Old Havana on August 5, 1994. Castro said he would not stop anyone wishing to leave the island, so people set out on homemade rafts (*balsas*), thus their name **balseros* (rafters). Many perished at sea, a few made it to land, but the majority were picked up and detained at Guantánamo Bay Naval Base to stem the tide of evacuees. In time, approximately 50,000 detainees were processed and brought to the United States.

Sensing the imminent collapse of the Cuban economy, CANF forced the passage of the second Cuban Democracy Act (1996), sponsored by Representative Robert Torricelli (D–NJ), which prohibited trade by U.S. subsidiaries in third countries with Cuba and blocked U.S. ports to ships that had recently docked in Cuban harbors. President Bill Clinton passed the law as part of a campaign promise but did not enforce it, as it was in violation of international law, but in 1994 in response to the *balsero* incident, he did restrict family remittances to Cuba. In 1996, Clinton also signed the Cuban Liberty and Democratic Solidarity Act, popularly known as the Helms-Burton Bill, designed to strangle the Cuban economy further. Among other things, it forbade money from the International Monetary Fund from going to Cuba, and it pressured Russia to desist from any economic relations with Cuba. Again, the application of the legislation was suspended because it was illegal under international law and alienated the United States' closest allies.

After forty years, Cuban Americans sought their Moses who would part the seas and lead them back to Cuba, their promised land. In November 1999, Elián *González, a six-year-old boy washed ashore in a failed rafting escape, provided the drama that demonstrated the community's power to direct U.S. policy toward Cuba and its heft in determining U.S. domestic elections. By law, González should have been returned to his father in Cuba, but relatives in Miami insisted that he would be subjected to "torture" in a communist country. Massive street demonstrations erupted in Miami's Little Havana, and lawsuits were submitted that caused the federal government to give the case special attention. The Clinton administration met with González's grandmothers and father and determined that the law should be followed and the child should be returned to Cuba to be with his father. As a result, the Cuban American community in south Florida actively campaigned against candidate Democratic Al Gore's presidential bid in 2000 and claim responsibility for his defeat in the contentious and controversial voting in the state of Florida.

In the twenty-first century, the complexity of Cuba's past continues to have lingering effects on the island's people and their kinfolk across the waters on the U.S. mainland. Hovering over both societies and their intermingled lives in the question of leadership succession in Cuba in the face of Fidel Castro's advanced age and deteriorating health. Most Cuban Americans and islanders in one way or another are deeply rooted in the rich soil of this briefly sketched history and the vast treasure that is their shared Cuban heritage—regardless of who runs the government on either side.

Further Reading

Castro, Fidel, and José Ramón Fernández. *Playa Girón*. New York: Pathfinder, 2001.

Eckstein, Susan. *Back from the Future: Cuba under Castro*. Princeton, NJ: Princeton University Press, 1994.

Stubbs, Jean. *Cuba: The Test of Time*. London: Latin American Bureau, 1989.

K. Lynn Stoner

History, Historiography, and Popular Culture. The center of historical knowledge of Latinos must be reconstructed to include and account for the margins of human social experience where they historically have been marginalized from history chronicles written according to dominant culture historiographies. As contemporary critical studies research has repeatedly demonstrated, the very center of the mainstream history of the Americas has been diverse and plural from its beginnings as European and other immigrants commingled with the Native tribal peoples, whose ancestors were themselves immigrants from Asia, in a robust **mestizaje* (interracial and multicultural hybridity) that continues to the present.

This strategic opposition to traditional dominant culture beliefs and perspectives that emphasize one Eurocentric "mainstream" is central as well to Latina/o historians and historiography. Latina/o history refers to research-based narratives of what happened in the past that explicitly or implicitly challenge narrow accounts of history that ignore or underrepresent Latina/o experience, achievement, cultural heritage, and other people of color. Such oppositional dimensions are compatible with and reinforcing of popular culture studies frameworks that underscore grassroots, bottom-up ideas about human expressive forms, practices, and society.

Latina/o historiography, or how historians have interpreted the experiences of Hispanics in the United States, has evolved dramatically in the twentieth and twenty-first centuries. For much of the twentieth century, the American historical profession was dominated by Caucasian males. To the brief extent that these historians wrote about women, Mexicans, Puerto Ricans, *Cuban Americans, and other people of color in the United States, they tended to perceive them as aliens and their diverse pasts as external to their own perspectives and constructions of Americanness, which for the most part was defined as staunchly white. Many historians viewed Mexicans in particular as obstacles that stood in the way of Manifest Destiny and the United States' westward expansion. They generally reflected the racial and gender attitudes of their eras, including beliefs in white racial superiority and negative *stereotypes about American Indians, African American descendants of slaves, and Latinas/os. One example of these usually unstated attitudes was

Frederick Jackson Turner, best known for his frontier thesis of American progress that perceived the U.S. government and people's westward movement as the march of a superior civilization into previously virgin, uncivilized lands. Another esteemed historian of the West, Walter Prescott Webb, echoed this perspective and also contributed to racist stereotyping of Anglos and Mexicans in his famous epic *The Texas Rangers* (1935).

Popular culture forms reflected these historical biases, distortions, and errors about human beings and society. That is, in everyday speech, literature, newspapers, art forms, and storytelling, Caucasians were described as smart, brave, and noble leaders, whereas Mexicans and other people of color were seen as standing in the way of civilization as, by definition, uncivilized aliens outside the center of the white normative culture. Webb's *Texas Rangers* promoted a familiar stereotype about the "natural" cruelty of Mexicans that carried over into nineteenth-century dime novels with swarthy villains wearing Mexican sombreros and guzzling tequila, an image that continued into the twentieth century's movie stereotyping.

Challenges to these and countless similar distortions about Hispanics began to flourish in the mid-twentieth century, as emerging concerns over the civil rights of racial minority groups began to change scholarly thinking and some research approaches to the historiography of America and *all* its constituent parts. Historian Carlos Castañeda's studies on Mexicans in Texas refuted Webb's depiction. Chief among these research-based corrections were George I. Sánchez's pioneering study *Forgotten People* (1940), a history of the dire economic conditions of Mexican Americans in rural New Mexico, and Carey McWilliams's foundational book *North from Mexico* (1949), which provides a broad history of the experiences of ethnic Mexicans living in the southwestern United States from colonial times to 1945 by one of the country's leading social activist reformers. Most crucial to this oppositional historiography, however, was *North from Mexico*'s basic dual themes—that Mexicans' long-standing presence in the Southwest antedated the first British colonies in North America and that, despite this presence, people of Mexican descent had suffered from severe racial discrimination from white people and institutions in the century since the Mexican American War and the 1848 *Treaty of Guadalupe Hidalgo. Despite their pathbreaking vision and ultimately acknowledged merit, these works received little scholarly attention at the time they were published. The prevailing attitude among historian and social scientist descendants of Turner and Webb in the immediate post–World War II period was that while Mexican Americans suffered from discrimination, the basis of their problems were deficiencies in their culture and their inability to assimilate into American society.

A new generation of scholars emerged from the social upheavals of the 1960s to change the biased histories and attitudes commonly abbreviated as "the canon of Western thought." The landmark shift produced profound changes in American life, including scholarly study and university curricula.

In history, this enormous change was identified as "the new social history," and its emergence led to the training of the first significant group of Mexican American and other people of color with advanced degrees in the nation. The changing graduate programs of the 1960s and 1970s brought new practitioners and perspectives to history about Mexican Americans and other Hispanics. Billed as history from the bottom up, the new social historiography focused on the everyday lives of ordinary people rather than the received history of powerful men. Consequently, the experiences of Latinas and Latinos living in the United States became a legitimate topic for scholarly attention, just as a parallel movement occurred in a wide variety of popular culture forms such as *films (**Salt of the Earth* [1954], *I Am Joaquín* [1969], **¡Alambrista!* [1977, rerelease 2002]) and music (the Cuban rhythms of Desi *Arnaz and Xavier *Cugat; the *Chicano **rock en español* of Ritchie *Valens and Carlos *Santana; the bilingual Texas-México borderland varieties documented in **Chulas Fronteras* [Beautiful Borders, 1976]), etc.

Provoked by the inspired rhetoric of the *Chicano Movement, the newly trained Mexican American historians focused on reconstructing their American past from a Chicano perspective. These young scholars refused to assume that Mexican Americans suffered from cultural deficiencies or needed to assimilate into American society to get justice. Instead, by focusing on issues of *race and class, they sought to understand the nature of the conflict that seemed endemic to the relationship between Chicana/os and whites. In short, they concluded that the problem lay not with Chicana/os but with racist attitudes and institutional practices within American society. The work that gave the earliest and the most comprehensive treatment to this approach was Rodolfo Acuña's *Occupied America*, first published in 1972 and since frequently reprinted, which provided a broad overview of Chicano history from the theoretical perspective of internal colonialism. Writing in 1972, Acuña argued that although Mexican Americans live within the boundaries of the United States, they experience the same types of exploitation as colonized people in more traditional colonial settings. The internal colonialism model was an attempt to meld together nationalist ideology, which had been the basis of the Chicano Movement, and Marxist ideology, which many intellectuals had found attractive.

While internal colonialism brought initial theoretical coherence to Chicana/o history, its focus on exploitation and resistance left room for other scholars to explore the inner workings of the Mexican American experience. These works were based on the assumption that the history of the everyday lives of ethnic Mexicans living in the United States was inherently valuable. In the late 1970s and early 1980s, historians such as Mario García and Albert Camarillo wrote community histories; that is, studies of the development of Mexican American communities in cities such as El Paso and Santa Barbara over a long period of time. While these studies did not shy away from looking at conflict, they paid more attention to a community's inner dynamics and the development of community institutions. As community histories provided basic narratives, other Chicana and Chicano historians began addressing topical issues. The 1980s and 1990s saw the proliferation of thematic studies on topics such as politics, labor, and *immigration. The best of these studies, such as David Gutiérrez's *Walls and Mirrors* (1995), went beyond simply addressing the topic to using the analysis of a topic such as immigration to help understand the nature of Chicana/o identity. The 1980s also saw the emergence of Chicana history as a major subfield within Chicano history. In particular, the work on women's and labor history included in such groundbreaking studies as the special issues on Chicanas published by *Frontiers: A Journal of Women Studies* in 1980 and 1990, as well as that of historians Vicki Ruiz (e.g., *Cannery Women, Cannery Lives*, 1987) and Camille Guerín-Gonzáles ("Cycles of Immigration and Repatriation," 1985), addressed a broad array of issues, ranging from dating habits to workforce participation to political involvement, in the lives of Mexican women living in the United States. As a result of these and other Chicana feminist writings, issues of gender and the experiences of women are now an integral part of Chicana/o history.

Further Reading

Acuña. Rodolfo. *Occupied America: A History of Chicanos*. 4th ed. New York: Longman, 2000.

Castañeda, Antonia. "Presidarias y Pobladoras: Spanish-Mexican Women in Frontier California." *Frontiers: A Journal of Women Studies* (co-edited by Cordelia Candelaria and Mary Romero) (January 1990): 8–20.

Guerín-Gonzáles, Camille. "Cycles of Immigration and Repatriation: Mexican Farm Workers in California Industrial Agriculture, 1900–1940." Ph.D. dissertation, University of California, Riverside, 1985.

Gutiérrez, David G. *Walls and Mirrors: Mexican Americans, Mexican Immigrants, and the Politics of Ethnicity*. Berkeley: University of California Press, 1995.

Ruíz, Vicki. *Cannery Women, Cannery Lives: Mexican Women, Unionization, and the California Food Processing Industry, 1930–1950*. Albuquerque: University of New Mexico Press, 1987.

Edward Escobar

History, Puerto Rican. To better comprehend the Puerto Rican contribution to Latina and Latino popular culture requires acquaintance with Puerto Rican history, particularly with the important historical roots of the island's identity that eventually became associated with Nuyorican culture. The first of these primary roots derives from the indigenous heritage that existed prior to the arrival of Christopher *Columbus in what he believed was India. His mistake resulted in the name given to the Caribbean islands: the West Indies (also known as the *Antilles). A second critically important historical root was the imperial Spanish dominance of the Antilles along with the colonial consequences of that rule from 1492 through the nineteenth century when the Spanish-American War ended Spain's hegemony in the region. Accordingly, the U.S. credo of Manifest Destiny and the country's nineteenth-century expansion across North America combine to provide a third crucial underpinning of Puerto Rican history, for both the belief and the transcontinental expansion led to the Monroe Doctrine, which was invoked to acquire Puerto Rico as a U.S. Commonwealth. These separate yet intertwined threads of history and heritage provided the seeds for Puerto Rican and related Nuyorican forms and practices of popular cultures in the twenty-first century.

Over a thousand years before the arrival of the Spaniards and other Europeans, the island known as Boriquén (also spelled Borinquén or Boriken) (*see* Boricúa, Borinqueño) was inhabited by tribal peoples who were hunter-gatherers and who developed the Taíno culture that the Spaniards encountered in the late fifteenth century. These tribes were collectively identified by the Spanish as Arawak Indians who had migrated there from other islands and continents. A clan-based people, the Taíno built small villages and were led by a *cacique* (chief) in what appeared to be tranquil and flourishing low-technology societies. They were occasionally forced to defend themselves from attacks of neighboring Caribbean tribes on islands south and east of them, including what are known today as the Virgin Islands and Vieques Island. With a basic form of agriculture less complex than that of their Mesoamerican neighbors, they nonetheless developed a healthy diet of seafood and *foods such as cassava, sweet potatoes, pineapples, and other tropical crops. Scholars believe that at the end of the fifteenth century when the Spaniards arrived approximately 20,000 to 50,000 Taínos lived on Boriquén.

Many centuries after the first contact between the Spanish and the Taínos, the word and meaning of Boriquén entered the popular culture vocabulary in the Antilles. For example, it is the origin of *"La Borinqueña," the national anthem of Puerto Rico (Himno Nacional de Puerto Rico). In the greater United States many Americans became acquainted with the source of the term *Boricúa* when Puerto Ricans used the term to define themselves and their language and culture. As with other grassroots developments like the African American civil rights movement of the 1950s and 1960s and the *Chicano Movement of the 1960s and 1970s, Boriquén was used by *Nuyorican Poets Café followers and other activists as part of a manifesto of pride in the pre-European indigenous heritage and (re)awakened cultural nationalism. This heightened cultural consciousness led writers like Miguel *Algarín, Miguel *Piñero, Tato Laviera, Judith Ortiz-Cofer, Aurora Levins Morales, and others to celebrate their unity in being Puerto Ricans regardless of the diversity of their places of residence—island or mainland—or primary language. They often sought the symbolic continuity of connecting their twentieth-century identities to the Taíno roots that had been muted or erased during five centuries of colonialism.

The second critically important root of Puerto Rican history began in 1493 when Columbus arrived in the Indies during his second voyage to the "New World" with an armada of seventeen ships and over 1,500 men (sailors, soldiers, priests, farmers, builders, and others). Landing on the island of Guadeloupe, which was ruled by Carib peoples, the Spaniards rescued several Taíno prisoners who had been captured by the Carib and returned them to their home island, Boriquén. That fateful rescue took Columbus to Boriquén on November 19, 1493, where upon anchoring, he claimed the island for his monarchs, Ferdinand II and Isabella I. He immediately renamed the western coast San Juan Bautista in tribute to St. John the Baptist, but he and his men spent little time there on this voyage, choosing to sail west to the larger island he named Hispaniola. Establishing in Hispaniola what was to become the first permanent European settlement in the New World, Columbus's settlers kept themselves busy clearing the land and building fortified villages and virtually ignoring San Juan Bautista for two decades. This neglect radically changed in 1508 when another member of Columbus's expedition, Juan Ponce de León, received permission to explore San Juan Bautista, which was still known as Boriquén to the Taíno.

Ponce de León founded the island's first Spanish town, Caparra, on the northern coast, and it became the site of its first mining and agricultural enterprises. In 1521 Caparra was moved to an islet at the northern end of the harbor, and this portal was renamed Puerto Rico (Rich Port). Over time and through common usage, the port and town grew to be called San Juan, the modern-day capital, and the name Puerto Rico evolved into the name given to the entire island. As in other parts of the Americas, the indigenous people retained their tribal knowledge and names even as they also learned the new knowledge and naming customs of the Spanish conquerors and colonizers. This cross-cultural contact between the recently arrived immigrants and the settled tribal people and the resultant adaptations exemplify the same type of **mestizaje* that occurred elsewhere as "old" and "new" commingled, with each side viewing the other as the "new" and themselves and their own cultures as the "old." One contemporary popular culture effect of this in the twentieth and early twenty-first centuries is the emergence of multiple terms of identity in the popular lexicon to designate Puerto Ricans and other non-Anglo-Americans in the absence of full recognition and acceptance *as Americans* within the hybrid mainstream of U.S. society and culture. Examples include Latina and Latino, Hispanic, and the other ethnic and racial labels of self-identification. Another pop culture by-product of early Spanish dominance and colonization is the commemoration of October 12 as El *Día de la Raza, known as Columbus Day in the United States.

During the first years of Spanish rule, relations with the native Taíno were relatively calm, but the Indians soon objected to their treatment as servants and slaves by their Spanish "protectors," as the European immigrants viewed themselves. The Taíno also resented paying tribute in the form of gold, food, shells, and other native products and also particularly resented the forced instruction in Christianity. Also causing strife and eventually turmoil were the diseases introduced by the Spaniards. The resultant epidemics coupled with maltreatment took a heavy toll by destroying the majority of the Taíno population. The Indians staged a serious revolt in 1511 and enjoyed short-term victories, but their low-tech weapons placed them at a major disadvantage against the better-armed Spaniards, who retained power. As a result of the rebellion and the death of the Taínos from disease, the Spanish began to import Indian slaves from other islands as well as from Africa to fully staff their mining operations. Eventually, however, the decline of gold and other mining production fell off dramatically, and after the 1530s many of the Europeans left Puerto Rico to seek wealth elsewhere. The Spanish sugar cane and ginger plantation owners tended to remain on the island because their African slaves provided ample labor resources for the hard work. Throughout this period, continued raids and attacks by Carib tribes from nearby islands caused the "rich port" colony extreme anxiety as they suffered the pirating of their food, gold, and even slaves. Plundered by alien attackers and disease ravaged, the colony eventually became the target of international piracy as primarily French, British, and Dutch pirates repeatedly landed, pillaged, and burned the coastal villages and also San Germán, Puerto Rico's second settlement after San Juan. This victimization caused the first diaspora out of the island as many colonists left with their Indian, African, and mestizo servants and slaves.

As the Spanish monarchs and their vassals became more experienced as empire builders, they learned the value of Puerto Rico as a Caribbean buffer for the burgeoning growing settlements in Nueva España (New Spain) and Hispaniola. Especially valued as a strategic military outpost was the San Juan harbor, which in effect guarded Spain's entire New World empire. Consequently, in the late sixteenth century San Juan was converted into a military fortress with an impressive governor's palace called La Fortaleza (Fortress) and a massive castle, San Felipe del Morro, at the highest point of the narrow entrance to Puerto Rico's harbor. In addition, a third fort, San Cristóbal, larger and better fortified, was erected on the Atlantic side of the city. By the early seventeenth century, San Juan was circled by an impenetrable stone wall twenty-five feet (eight meters) high and eighteen feet (five meters) thick. Still standing at the dawn of the twenty-first century are two large sections of the wall that once made the city nearly impregnable. Despite these strong defenses, pirates and emissaries of other monarchs continued to besiege Puerto Rico. For instance, Sir Francis Drake attacked San Juan with a large fleet in 1595, and another Englishman, George Clifford, the third earl of Cumberland, actually captured the city but was not able to control it for long because his troops were stricken with disease, and Clifford had to abandon his gains. The city was again taken over by another foreigner in 1625 when Bowdoin Hendrik, a Dutchman, landed and burned the town, but failing to capture the governor, who took refuge in El Morro, Hendrik also was forced to depart.

While San Juan was receiving high-level political and economic consideration and aid from the Spanish rulers, Puerto Rico's rural inhabitants, or *jíbaros*, were overlooked by the class-conscious *españoles* (Spanish immigrants) and *criollos* (those of Spanish descent born in the colonies), who generally considered the rural residents as bumpkins. As a result, the *jíbaros* were forced to fend for themselves and in time cultivated increasingly significant landholdings. In addition, because the viceregal colonial authorities of San Juan typically stayed within the fortified walls of their city, the *jíbaros* found that by engaging in clandestine trade with non-Spanish merchants (e.g., French, British, Danish, and Dutch) they were able to prosper without paying taxes and duties to the authorities or crown. Among the goods they traded were gingerroot, sugar cane, tobacco, cattle, and hides for leather, all of which were highly desired in Europe and in other parts of the North American colonies of England. Remaining loyal to Spain, even if remote and independent from its colonial agents, the *jíbaros* contributed greatly to the island's lasting prosperity as participants in the military forces as well as developers of the region's resources.

The eighteenth century may have produced revolutions of liberation in France and the North American colonies, but such movements did not spread to Spain's empire, partly because the enthroned Bourbon monarchs instituted large-scale economic and administrative reforms that strengthened the mother country's ties to its valued island outpost. The reforms promoted more equitable trade relations between Puerto Rico and Spain through subsidized agricultural production and the integration of the colony's armed forces under a central command system. These changes produced desired financial returns and turned Puerto Rico into a major economic asset for Spain, largely as a result of its expanded commercial agriculture. Fed by fiscal prosperity, the island grew from a population of under 50,000 in 1765 to nearly 200,000 by the year 1800 spread over thirty-four towns. Immigrants from the Canary Islands, Louisiana, and Haiti were also attracted to Puerto Rico and soon contributed important innovations to the island's wealth by introducing more sophisticated methods of crop production. They expanded coffee and sugar cane production, to a large extent by using the labor of thousands of African slaves.

British interest in the island was whetted by stories of the island's commercial successes, as well as by accounts of the *jíbaros'* clandestine trade and buccaneering networks, including being a refuge for runaway slaves, all of which led them to think that Puerto Rico was vulnerable to attack. With his sights on the "rich port" of lore, in 1797 the British general Sir Ralph Abercromby with a small naval force captured Trinidad from Spain. After that victory off the Venezuelan coast, Abercromby pushed on to Puerto Rico, which he attacked as the next weak link in the Iberian chain of imperial fortresses. However, unlike his results in Trinidad, the Englishman was defeated by Puerto Rican armed forces. Apparently, Spain's improved relations with its island outpost returned good military investment when threatened by a formidable adversary. These outgrowths from Spain's imperial colonial roots form a rich and vibrant history of adventures, misadventures, and perseverance that are revealed in the Puerto Rican people, language, popular activities, and beliefs.

Adding to Puerto Rico's vibrant mosaic of history are the distinctive events and developments of the nineteenth century, starting with the French invasion in 1808 of the Iberian Peninsula by Napoleon I, who placed his brother Joseph Bonaparte on the Spanish throne. To show support for their motherland, Spain's colonies in South and Central America refused to pay homage to the Napoleons and asserted their right of governance in the name of their captive Bourbon king, Ferdinand VII, who was imprisoned by the French. Throughout the Spanish Western Hemisphere this pro-Bourbon claim to self-determination evolved in time into revolutionary movements for independence, but not in Puerto Rico. There, the response to the French takeover was decidedly less autonomous, for most of the islanders were comfortable with Spain's strict military and mercantilist policies. The residents of San Juan also were extremely reliant on Spain's administrative and military assistance and willingly continued to observe the new imperial commands, even though they served French designs.

As a result of this pro-imperial temperament, Spanish royalists in other parts of Latin America began to immigrate to Puerto Rico when the revolutionary fervor in their countries progressed to calls for emancipation from Spain. Instead of crossing the Atlantic for safe haven, these monarchists found refuge in Puerto Rico, a more conservative climate. When the French were removed in 1815 and the Bourbon government restored to Spain, Puerto Ricans were rewarded for their loyalty with economic liberties that would ensure their future support for the royal empire. These rewards opened the island's ports to unregulated trade, to the immigration of Roman Catholics regardless of nationality, and to the granting of free land to the new settlers. These immigrants contributed substantially to Puerto Rico's plantation-based economic development, conservative politics and policies, and also to its population, which climbed to nearly 1 million in the late 1800s.

The nineteenth century in Puerto Rican politics witnessed alternating periods of liberal reform and conservative reaction, depending on the mood of the Spanish government across the Atlantic and also on the lasting effects of colonial administrative systems and structures. The periods of relative political freedom (1809–1814 and 1820–1823) and positive reforms included the election of Puerto Ricans as representatives to the Spanish Cortes, or Parliament. One of the liberal changes achieved was the revoking by the Cortes of the absolute power of the island's appointed governor. Oppositely, however, these democratic gains were eventually rescinded during the reactionary pendulum swing back to greater control. These curtailments of freedom and reform in favor of absolutist colonial rule tended to quell opposition and freedom of political and intellectual expression among the populace. For nearly half of the eighteenth century the majority of Puerto Ricans sought the end of military despotic rule, and political ideas favoring independence began to coalesce. Nevertheless, as in other Spanish colonies a contrasting conservative bloc vehemently preferred the status quo, while a smaller group of mostly artists and intellectuals argued for complete independence and a democratic constitutional government.

At the center of this political debate was the issue of slavery and its abolition. When an elected local commission recommended an end to slavery in 1865 (the same year that the U.S. Civil War ended), political conservatives from San Juan to Seville were alarmed enough to pressure the colonial government to arrest the more outspoken and respected liberal reformers. This political persecution backfired and inspired a small group of *independistas*, pro-independence radicals, to lead an uprising on September 23, 1868, now remembered as the heroic *Grito de Lares (Cry of Lares). This movement took place during a period of intense political debate about slavery and its abolishment and was led by a small group of liberal reformers, abolitionist intellectuals, artists, and other island thinkers promoting independence. Because it occurred at the same time as the ardent struggle for independence in Cuba, the impact of the Grito de Lares was magnified, and together the two events led Spain to grant several key reforms to Puerto Rico in the next few years. Shortly thereafter, Spain installed its first republican government, forcing Queen Isabella II to abdicate, pardoned all the political prisoners in both the colonies and in Spain, and ended slavery in Puerto Rico.

The independence movement persisted through the 1880s, and the cry for political autonomy, while yet remaining under Spanish rule, gained momentum. To retain power, the Spanish government tightened its controls even further; however, this only solidified popular support for the reform and independence movement and led to the formation in 1897 of the Autonomy Party in Puerto Rico through cooperation and some collaboration with Spain's Liberal Party. A new autonomous government was formed, which was parliamentary in form but overseen by the governor-general as a representative of the Spanish king. Local legislation, tariffs, taxes, and infrastructure policies were now the responsibility of a two-chamber Parliament. Although these governance realities underscore that Puerto Rico was psychologically and culturally more emancipated than it had ever been in its history, the Spanish-American War of 1898 effectively prevented Puerto Ricans from putting their new reform government into effect.

Clearly, imperial Spanish dominance of Puerto Rico from the era of Ponce de León and throughout its four centuries of colonialism defines Puerto Rican history, heritage, and cultural identity. The Spanish-American War formally ended Spain's hegemony, even though the island's grassroots culture and psychology had been liberated decades before. The conclusion of the war opened the way for U.S. expansionism beyond its borders in an attempt to acquire Cuba, Puerto Rico, the Philippines, and other former colonial possessions of Spain. This third crucially important root source directly involved the United

States in the Caribbean and led to the acquisition of Puerto Rico as an American Commonwealth. At the time, the United States viewed Puerto Rico as a future site for profitable tropical agriculture; nonetheless, its main and immediate reason for seizing the island was to secure a fuel station for its warships. Its location guaranteed a strong U.S. naval presence in the Caribbean and established a strategic pathway to the Isthmus of Panama, where the United States and other nations with commercial ambitions had plans of building a transoceanic canal.

This overview of Puerto Rico's past with emphasis on three important taproots of history summarizes the origins of the island's complex identity of *mestizaje* (ethnic, racial, and cultural hybridity). The island's indigenous heritage, its imperial Spanish dominance and colonization, and the U.S. transnational expansion to annex Puerto Rico as a commonwealth form the separate but interlocking threads of history and heritage that helped produce and also illuminate Puerto Rican and Nuyorican popular cultures in the twenty-first century.

Puerto Ricans, or Puertorriqueños, enjoy an intermingled Spanish, U.S. American, and Afro-Caribbean culture. In comparative measure, the island's social and economic conditions are generally advanced according to Latin American standards, due in part to its ties with the United States. U.S. manufacturing plants and military bases offer a stable economy to the commonwealth, even though the nature of the political relationship had become controversial in the last decades of the twentieth century. Still, the vast majority of Puerto Ricans continue to favor permanent union with the United States. Of this group, a slightly greater number support the current commonwealth status over statehood. In addition, a small but persistent minority advocates independence.

Demographically, the number of persons of Puerto Rican birth or origin who reside in the United States is nearly equal to the size of the island's population. In 1940 only about 70,000 Puerto Ricans lived in the United States; by 1960 the U.S.-based Puerto Rican population had increased to 887,000 (of which 615,000 were born in Puerto Rico and 272,000 in the United States) and had already begun to disperse throughout the country, although the largest group remained in New York City. By the late 1990s the number of Puerto Ricans in the United States had increased nearly fourfold over the 1960 level to more than 3 million, of whom some 1.2 million were born on the island; most were concentrated in New York, New Jersey, Massachusetts, Illinois, Florida, and California. Puerto Ricans throughout North American society occupy leading positions in government, business, education, the arts, *sports, and entertainment.

The enduring consequences of these interconnected historical starting points for Puerto Ricans and their popular culture contributions are too vast to summarize in this brief historical review. Chief among them because of their fundamental centrality to everyday life are the ethnic, racial, linguistic, religious, and social forms and patterns observed and practiced every day among Boricúa-origin peoples whether newly arrived from the island or seasoned by generations of time on the mainland. In one way or another, most Nuyorican and Puerto Rican subjects were seeded, rooted, or stem from this vivid and layered complexity of heritage and history, thereby giving fruit to the popular cultures.

Further Reading

Conrad, James, and John Perivolaris, eds. *The Cultures of the Hispanic Caribbean.* London: Macmillan Caribbean, 2000.

Economist Intelligence Unit. *1998–2002. Country Report: Bahamas, Barbados, Bermuda, British Virgin Islands, Netherlands Antilles, Aruba, Cayman Islands, Turks and Caicos Islands.* London: Economist Intelligence Unit, 2002.

Herrera, Andrea O'Reilly. *The Pearl of the Antilles.* Tempe, AZ: Bilingual Press/Editorial Bilingüe, 2001.

Martínez-Fernández, Luis. *Torn between Empires: Economy, Society, and Patterns of Political Thought in the Hispanic Caribbean, 1840–1878.* Athens: University of Georgia Press, 1994.

"Welcome to Puerto Rico." http://welcome.topuertorico.org/bori.

Cordelia Chávez Candelaria

Holidays and Fiestas. Traditions and festivities that originated in Latin America have long penetrated the United States and are now gaining wider acceptance among non-Latina/os and other ethnic groups. No longer seen as quaint or exotic or as marginalized and repudiated, many Latina/o traditions are better understood today as a result of cultural revivalism, multicultural education, and the changing demographics in the United States. Many holidays and fiestas like *Cinco de Mayo even have become part of the mainstream culture but continue to be misunderstood or seen as just another reason to throw a party. As more and more people continue to migrate, they tend to value and celebrate their own deep-rooted ethnic and ancestral customs and traditions even more than before because they reflect a rich Latina/o social and cultural history and identity as well as diasporic longings and nostalgia over places left behind. Not only are older traditions like *Día de los Muertos (Day of the Dead) being celebrated in new contexts and generating new meanings, but they are also mixing with North American secular influences like Halloween, resulting in a new **mestizaje* (mixing of races) of culture.

Mexican-origin people are known to celebrate what they call Las *Posadas Navideñas every evening from December 16 through December 24. The celebrations are held to commemorate the biblical story of Mary and Joseph's trip from Nazareth to Bethlehem in search of shelter. The word *posada* means lodging, inn, or shelter. Although the *posada* is a religious commemoration, it is also regarded as a social celebration. Every evening a different home in the neighborhood becomes the designated place where people come and *piden posada* (ask for shelter). The home is usually decorated in advance, and there are a variety of traditional holiday *foods served such as tamales, *buñuelos* (fritters), and *pan dulce* (sweet bread) for guests to eat. When the sun sets, some of the people gather outside the home and re-create Mary and Joseph's journey. Half of the guests stay outside the home to ask for shelter, and the other half stay inside to open the doors to the guests. The more elaborate *posadas* include people dressing up and actually acting out the parts of Mary and Joseph. Guests sing Christmas songs together and demonstrate their joy in the season. When the religious portion of the *posada* finishes, the fun begins, and at the end of the *posada*, the guests break a *piñata made of papier-mâché and filled with candy.

Similar to the Mexican *posada*, Puerto Ricans celebrate what they call *Parranda*, also known as *Asalto* (assault) or Trulla (bustle). The main difference is the types of foods served in the homes.

In México and many Hispanic areas of the United States, on December 24 Catholics celebrate the last Mass of the evening, which is called the "Misa de Gallo" (Rooster Mass) or what is also known as Midnight Mass. The Mass is so named because it was a rooster that first witnessed and gave word of the birth of Jesus as the clock struck midnight on December 24.

In most Latin American countries, Catholics also celebrate El Día de los Reyes, the Three Kings Day, on January 6. This celebration commemorates the biblical story of the three kings who gave gifts to Jesus when he was born, and in like manner they also give gifts to all the good boys and girls. In Latin America children receive their gifts on the morning of January 6 as opposed to on Christmas Day. In the evening families and friends gather to cut and eat the *rosca*, a semisweet circular yeast bread that has crystallized fruit on top. Hidden inside the *rosca* are a few miniature dolls representing the baby Jesus. The person who gets the dolls has to give a party on the Feast of Our Lady of Candelaria, which falls on February 2 and is celebrated with figures of *el santo niño* (baby Jesus) among Mexicans, Latina/os, and Chicana/os. Someone else may find a dried fava bean in the dough, and they have to help the party-giver by bringing the drinks. This feast marks the devotion to a small Marian statue found in a cave on the Canary Island called Tenerife in 1400. Believers claim that candles surrounded the Image before being introduced to the island. In time, the Statue was called Our Lady of Candelaria because of the candles. Devotions to this image were introduced to the Americas, Caribbean, and the Phillipines by the Spaniards during colonial times.

Every September 16 Mexicans around the world celebrate México's independence from Spanish rule. Spanish rule of México began in 1521 when Hernán Cortés came to the Americas and proclaimed the new colony as Nueva España, and it was not until September 16, 1810, that Don Miguel Hidalgo (the father of Mexican independence) proclaimed the start of the war for independence, which lasted ten years. The most spectacular celebration takes place in el Zócalo, the main plaza in Mexico City. The Zócalo is located over El Palacio Nacional, or the National Palace, where the president's offices are located. The Zócalo begins to fill up with people on the evening of September 15. When the clock strikes 11 P.M., it is customary for the president to deliver "El Grito," the shout that proclaims México's independence, and he rings the bell that Hidalgo once rang to do the same. The president yells out to the crowd "Viva México," and the crowds shout back "¡Que Viva!" Soon after the Grito, a fireworks display is put on for the crowd. The celebration continues into the wee hours of the morning with people dancing, singing, and eating in the streets.

Similar celebrations are seen in areas of the United States that have a large population of Mexican Americans. One such place is Las Vegas, Nevada, on the weekend closest to the Mexican Independence Day, and many Mexicans travel to Las Vegas specifically to celebrate the holiday. Other towns and cities around the United States, specifically those closest to the Mexican border, celebrate the holiday with rousing celebrations known as Fiestas Patrias, or parties to honor the original homeland.

In the Dominican Republic, February 27 is regarded as independence day, first commemorated in 1844. The holiday is celebrated with what is known as Carnaval, which includes food, dancing, and elaborate parades to commemorate the day. Dominicans in the United States also take part in festivities that honor their independence as well.

El Día de las Madres (Mother's Day) is celebrated on May 10 in Latin America. El Día de las Madres is closely associated with Catholic religious beliefs regarding the Virgin Mary, and it is customary for families to go to church to thank God for the women in their lives. In the United States it is customary to celebrate the mother twice if a family has Mexican roots and U.S. Mother's Day does not fall on May 10.

El Día de la *Virgen de Guadalupe (Day of Our Lady of Guadalupe) is celebrated before the Christmas season officially begins on December 16 with the first *posada*. Mexicans celebrate the festivities of the *Virgin of Guadalupe on December 12. The Virgin is México's patron saint, so it is fitting that her celebration has been one of the most important on the Mexican calendar since 1531. Thousands make pilgrimages to see the Virgin at different churches and temples; the most notable is the pilgrimage to the Basílica de Guadalupe in Mexico City. Believers from around the world travel to what is believed to be the site of her miracle to personally thank the Virgin for favors they have been granted. They regard the Virgin as being a savior among poorer people, and that is why she is so revered and honored. Although the biggest celebration of the Virgin takes place in the Basílica de Guadalupe, she is celebrated on December 12 practically anywhere there is an altar to her.

*Semana Santa (Holy Week), regarded as one of the most important holiday in México, is the final week of Lent and begins on Palm Sunday. In addition to attending mass on Easter Sunday, Latina/os participate in *via cruces* via cruces (stations of the cross), and other ritualized observances.

In New York, Puerto Rican Americans have been celebrating what they have called since 1996 the "National Puerto Rican Day Parade." On May 29, 2003, New York Governor George Pataki proclaimed that the Puerto Rican Parade Week would take place in the Empire State from June 1 to June 8. The National Puerto Rican Day Parade became a successor to the New York Puerto Rican Day Parade that was first celebrated in 1958. "New York has a large population of Puerto Rican Americans (from various regions throughout the island) and there is no better place to have a celebration of this kind. The Puerto Rican community has contributed greatly to the state of New York and the nation as a whole," said Governor Pataki.

In 2000, California was the first state to honor César *Chávez by officially establishing a paid state holiday to commemorate Chávez's life as co-founder of the United Farm Workers Union and to inspire and promote service to the community at large. This holiday is celebrated on March 31 in honor of Chávez's birthday or on the Monday or Friday nearest that day. In Texas and in Colorado, March 31 has been noted as an optional holiday but is not paid as in California. In 2004 Arizona marked March 31 more in recognition than as an official holiday.

December 28 is the celebration of El Día de los Inocentes; the equivalent in the United States is April Fools' Day. As with the Mother's Day celebrations that are sometimes celebrated twice by Latinos in the United States, so is the day of practical jokes.

Carnaval and forms of it are celebrated in numerous Latin American countries and in the United States as well, where it is known as Mardi Gras or Fat Tuesday and is celebrated on a grand scale in New Orleans. Fat Tuesday occurs on the day before the Christian observance of Ash Wednesday, which marks the beginning of Lent. New Orleans has been celebrating this event since the early 1700s when French settlers moved into the area. Parades, parties, and festivals are held on the streets of the French Quarter where people come from all over the United States to take part in the celebration.

In other Latin American areas such as Brazil, people take part in Mardi Gras–like activities, which they call "Carnaval." This celebration also takes place in February but not always during the days proceeding the Lenten season. Brazilians first celebrated this event in the year 1840. Aside from Brazil, other places such as México and Puerto Rico also celebrate Carnaval. In these areas, the celebration is also affiliated with Lent.

*Día de la Raza (Day of Race or, as it is known to many in the United States, Christopher *Columbus Day) is celebrated on October 12. The first recorded celebration of Columbus Day was in 1792. Latinos call October 12 Día de la Raza to mark their collective contributions to the development of the Americas since Columbus first arrived in 1492.

Another holiday that is celebrated widely with parades and other festivities in the United States is *Cinco de Mayo (May 5th), which honors México's victory over the French in the Battle of Puebla (La Batalla de Puebla) in 1862.

Further Reading

Cantú, Norma E. "La Quinceañera: Towards an Ethnographic Analysis of a Life-Cycle Ritual." *Southern Folklore* 56.1 (1999): 73–101.

Castro, Rafaela G. *Chicano Folklore: A Guide to the Folktales, Traditions, Rituals, and Religious Practices of Mexican-Americans.* New York: Oxford University Press, 2001.

DeBouzek, Jeanette, prod. and dir. *Gathering Up Again: The Fiesta of Santa Fé.* New York: Cinema Guild, 1992. Videocassette.

Montaño, Mary. *Tradiciones nuevomexicanas: Hispano Arts and Culture of New Mexico.* Albuquerque: University of New Mexico Press, 2001.

Najera-Ramírez, Olga. "Fiestas Hispánicas: Dimensions of Hispanic Festivals and Celebrations." In *Handbook of Hispanic Cultures in the United States: Anthropology*, edited by Thomas Weaver. Houston: Arte Público Press; Madrid, Spain: Instituto de Cooperación Iberoamericana, 1994, 328–339.

Cristina K. Muñoz

Homies. A pop culture craft that is a popular fad among many Latina and Latino youth, homies are miniature plastic sculptural figures that represent a variety of *barrio people. Artist David Gonzáles is credited with creating the first set that consisted of six figures named 8-Ball, La Raza, Mr. Loco, Sapo, Smiley, and Droopy. They soon were sold as key chain charms, gum machine prizes, and on blister cards. Gonzáles composed biographies for each homie as background to his artwork. For example, he describes Mr. Raza as passionate about his Latino heritage and as possessing degrees in *Chicano Studies and Latin American and Pre-Columbian History, which he uses to promote education and inform his fellow homies about their culture. Mr. Loco's bio describes him as a counselor specializing in proactive work with youth gang members to resolve conflict and violence among rivals.

The homie fad has had its share of controversy because of the perception by some observers, especially within law enforcement, that the figures glorify deviant behavior and *gang membership. Some believe that the representations underscore negative *stereotypes of Mexican young people, while others express appreciation for the artistry and humor of the depictions of barrio experience and people. Despite the negative publicity, the commercial success of homie merchandise has not diminished. According to the http://www.homies.tv Web site, interest has increased and extended beyond the Latina/o community where it originally resided. The Web site reports that purchase orders have been received for the product from every state in the United States, as well as from the Getty Museum in Los Angeles, the Food Network, and countries in Europe, Africa, and South America.

Figures of two pachuco homies and one chola homie (actual size 1½–2⅛" high). *Private collection of Cordelia Chávez Candelaria. Photo taken by Rajeet Chatterjee, Arizona State University.*

Further evidence of the robustness of the fad has been the release of multiple sets of new homie figures, including the Mijos (my sons) series, the Mini Bobble Heads, the Hoodrats, Psycho Clowns, and others. There also have been imitator and spinoff dolls and other products, such as larger-scale figures that bend and a small number of female versions. The word homie derives from "homeboy" and "homegirl" and originally emerged from the ghettos, barrios, and streets to refer to someone from the same barrio (i.e., neighborhood). It is now in general use in colloquial American English, just as the homie product craze appears to have crossed over to wider markets.

Further Reading

Braden, Warren R. *Homies: Peer Mentoring among African-American Males*. Dekalb, IL: Leps Press, 1998.

Cruz, José Miguel, and Nelson Portillo Peña with Rubí Arana, Homies Unidos, and Giovanna Rizzi. *Solidaridad y violencia en las pandillas del gran San Salvador: más allá de la vida loca* (Solidarity and Violence in the Gangs of Greater San Salvador: Beyond the Crazy Life). San Salvador, El Salvador: UCA Editores, 1998.

"Homies Disappearing from a Store Near You." http://www.lapdonline.
http://www.homies.tv/homies.htm.
http://www.homiesunidos.org/.

Cordelia Chávez Candelaria

Huerta, Dolores (1930–). As central to the success of the United Farm Workers (UFW) union as the revered César *Chávez, Dolores Huerta is best known as the union's effective negotiator for three decades from 1966 through the 1980s. Less well known is that Huerta was one of the UFW's original cofounders with Chávez and that before meeting him she was already working as a labor reformer and grassroots organizer in California based on her training with the Community Service Organization (CSO) led by another tireless advocate for the poor, Fred Ross, Sr., who had been trained by the legendary reformer Saul Alinsky. Ross also helped trained Chávez. Huerta helped develop the Union's public relations and outreach efforts, and in the 1980s she established its first radio station, KUFW. During the height of the 2003 California petition campaign to recall its governor, the embattled Governor Gray Davis named Huerta to the University of California Board of Regents, adding another historic first to the list of accomplishments of one of the twentieth century's most significant and influential American leaders.

Although long associated with California, Dolores Fernández Huerta was actually born in Dawson, New Mexico, a tiny coal mining town near the Colorado state line. Dawson was the birthplace of both her parents, Alicia Chávez and Juan Fernández. Huerta's parents divorced when she was a child, and her mother moved to Stockton, California, with her three children. A strong, hardworking woman with high aspirations for herself and her family, Alicia Chávez worked in a variety of food-related jobs as a cannery worker and cook until she had saved enough money to open two hotel businesses catering to fieldworkers. With her remarkable mother as a role model, the future labor leader learned to combine scholastic achievement with hard work as she earned good grades and participated in Girl Scouts until she was eighteen while also working in her mother's businesses. After an unsuccessful first marriage to her high school boyfriend, Huerta divorced and eventually earned an Associate of Arts degree from Stockton's community college. The degree served as a provisional teaching credential, and she began teaching in the early 1950s.

Growing up in the heart of the agribusiness industry and teaching scores of children, including children of migrant farmworkers and food processers, gave Huerta a profound respect for the important role these laborers play in sustaining the First World economy and consumer lifestyle of the people of the United States. The experience also taught her that hard work and good citizenship were not enough to ensure fairness, socioeconomic opportunity, and social justice for these workers and their families. This awareness led her to join the community-based organizing efforts of Fred Ross, Sr., and the CSO in the mid-1950s in hopes of energizing and organizing the farmwork and food-processing communities to press for better wages, improved living conditions, and the enjoyment of the basic civil liberties and civil rights taken for granted by other Americans. While working as a CSO organizer, the future Board of Regent married Ventura Huerta, also a grassroots activist, and they began what became their life's work as community organizers. Chávez also organized for the CSO in another region.

With her solid background in the region and her native talents and intelligence, Huerta was a natural to participate as a leader in the founding of the UFW in the early 1960s. Eventually she and Chávez resigned from secure CSO positions to dedicate their lives to the farmworker cause. She served the union in many roles, most notably as its major contract negotiator, but she served as well as its spokesperson, advocate, and media liaison. As a unionist in the latter half of the twentieth century, she was often the lone woman in an all-male enterprise. History reveals, however, that women and Latinas specifically were active unionists in the early years of the U.S. labor movement dating to the late nineteenth century. Thus, Huerta was part of the feminist reclaiming of agency and leadership in public life associated with the people's movements of the 1960s and 1970s. The appointment of the former teacher to the California Board of Regents in 2003 appeared to many UFW supporters, scholars, and the general public as a fitting capstone to her remarkable public career.

Further Reading

García, Richard. "Dolores Huerta: Woman, Organizer, and Symbol." *California History* 72.1 (Spring 1993): 57–71.

Meier, Matt, Conchita Franco Serri, and Richard García. *Notable Latino Americans: A Biographical Dictionary*. Westport, CT: Greenwood Press, 1997.

Rose, Margaret. "Traditional and Nontraditional Patterns of Female Activism in the United Farm Workers of America, 1962 to 1980." *Frontiers: A Journal of Women Studies* 11.1 (1990): 26–32.

Cordelia Chávez Candelaria

Huerta, Jorge (1942–). Jorge Huerta, a leading authority in *theater and dramatic arts, has been instrumental in the development of contemporary Chicana/*Chicano and Latina/Latino theater in the United States. A professional director and playwright, Huerta is also a Chancellor's Associate Professor of Theater at the University of California at San Diego (UCSD), where he was the first to be appointed the Chancellor's Associate Endowed Chair in Theater in 1994.

Huerta was born to Mexican parents in Los Angeles, where he grew up and later attended college. He obtained his Bachelor of Arts degree in 1964 and Master of Arts in 1966, both in theater from California State College in Los Angeles. In 1974 he received a doctorate in dramatic arts from the University of California at Santa Barbara. Part of his stage development included work in the 1950s as a professional actor on television. Huerta's contributions to Chicana/o and Latina/o theater formally began with his founding of El Teatro de la Esperanza (Theater of Hope) during the early 1970s, a repertory group for which he served as first artistic director. He was also the co-founder and first artistic director of Máscaras Mágicas (Magic Masks) from 1990 to 1992, San Diego's first independent Latino theater company. His work has included extensive directing and speaking on Latina/o theater throughout the United States, Latin America, and Western Europe.

As a scholar Huerta has written and published extensively including publishing the first scholarly book on Chicano drama, *Chicano Theater: Themes and Forms* (1982). His other published scholarship includes *Chicano Drama: Society, Performance and Myth* (2000), as well as editions of three anthologies of Chicano plays: *El Teatro de la Esperanza: An Anthology of Chicano Drama* (1973); *Nuevos Pasos* [New Steps]: *Chicano and Puerto Rican Drama* (1979); and *Necessary Theater: Six Plays about the Chicano Experience* (1989). From 1989 to 1992 at UCSD, Huerta administered one of the first Hispanic American Master of Fine Arts programs in the United States.

Further Reading

Huerta, Jorge. "Chicano Teatro: A Background." *Aztlán* 2.2 (1972): 63–73.

Kanellos, Nicolás, and Jorge Huertas. "Introduction." *Nuevos Pasos: Chicano and Puerto Rican Drama.* 2nd ed. Houston, TX: Arte Público Press, 1989.

Daniel Enríque Pérez

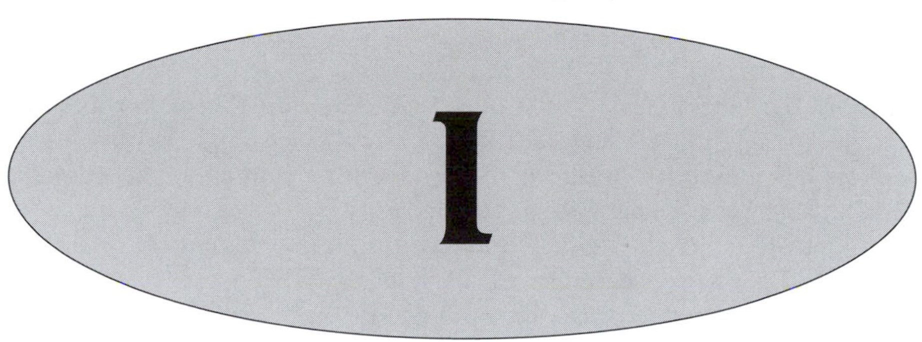

I Like It Like That. Written and directed by Darnell Martin, *I Like It Like That* (1994) won the New York Film Critics Award for Best First Film of 1994. The first feature *film distributed by a major Hollywood production company directed by an Afro-Latina, *I Like It Like That* is set in the Bronx and centers on a Puerto Rican woman, Lisette (Lauren *Vélez), who has to find a job when her husband Chino (Jon Seda) is jailed for stealing. Lisette lands a job as an assistant to a record executive, Stephen (Griffin Dunne), who hires her to establish his credibility in the Latino music world. This film captures the timely questions Lisette faces as a young Puerto Rican mother struggling against the sexism of Chino's jealousy and her new boss's underestimation of her ability to compete in the record industry. Lisette fights to prove them both wrong.

Drawing fine portraits of the economic hardships and social strife of the Bronx's Puerto Rican community, the movie features Lisette's transvestite brother, Alexis (Jesse Borrego), coping with his parents' disapproval of his lifestyle. The film depicts Lisette's chaotic life as a mother, wife, and professional with the strong sense of determination and toughness required to stay out of the welfare system and survive financially. A funny, sexy, and realistic story of female strength of character, the film concludes as Lisette begins to realize her own potential after battling with both her husband's machismo and her Anglo-American boss's *stereotypes. The film's cast also includes Rita *Moreno and Lisa Vidal. *I Like It Like That* is distributed by Columbia TriStar Home Entertainment.

Further Reading

http://www.imdb.com/title/tt0110091.
http://www.suntimes.com/ebert/ebert_reviews/1994/10/945534.html.

http://www.washingtonpost.com/wp-srv/style/longterm/movies/videos/ilikeitlike thatrkempley_a0a494.htm.

Cheryl Greene

Iglesias, Enrique (1975–). Enrique Iglesias, a bestselling Latin pop icon, was born in Madrid, Spain, on May 8, 1975. He is the son of world-famous musical artist Julio *Iglesias. In 1982 he moved to Miami, Florida, to live with his father, and it was during his teenage years that he developed his interest in singing and songwriting. He made his first singing appearance in a school play called *Hello Dolly*. He studied business at Miami University, but he dropped out to concentrate on his singing.

Iglesias started his recording career when he was twenty years old, under the pseudonym of Enrique Martínez, and he then obtained a recording contract with the Mexican company Fonovisa. He achieved success very quickly due to his matinee idol looks and brand of catchy Latin-influenced pop love songs. Iglesias's upbringing in Miami has provided him with cultural influences deriving from Latina/o, European, and American origins. He has written his own songs and also performed those of other songwriters, including Roberto Morales. His debut album, *Enrique Iglesias* (1995), sold a million copies within three months. He followed with four more albums: *Vivir* (1997), *Cosas del Amor* (Things of Love, 1998), *Enrique* (1999), and *Escape* (2001). Iglesias has produced songs in four languages, including Spanish, English, Portuguese, and Italian. In 1996 he was awarded a Grammy for Best Latin Performer. He received awards for being the Best-Selling Male Latino Artist and World's Best-Selling Pop Star at the Monaco Awards in 2002.

Enrique Iglesias. *Courtesy of Photofest.*

Iglesias has also experimented with cinema through his acting performance in the film *Once Upon a Time in Mexico* (dir. Robert Rodríguez, 2003), which is a follow-up to Rodríguez's previous film *Desperado* (1995). Both films focus on the violence and corruption of the drug wars in México. Iglesias plays the part of a *mariachi (a Mexican singer/instrumentalist). Iglesias's music has crossover appeal to mainstream U.S. audiences; for example, the duet between Whitney Houston and Iglesias, "Could I Have This Kiss Forever," was a theme tune at the Olympic Games in Sydney, Australia, in 2000. He also performed at the U.S. Democratic National Convention in August 2001. Following the terrorist attacks on New York and Washington, D.C., on September 11, 2001, Iglesias's song "Hero," from his album *Escape*, became a national anthem of hope and healing for many Americans. He performed "Hero" at the "America: A Tribute to Heroes" benefit, on September 21, 2001, an event designed to commemorate the victims of the attacks. Iglesias continues to write new music and to tour extensively.

Further Reading

http://www.enriqueiglesias.com.

Helen Oakley

Iglesias, Julio (1943–). Julio Iglesias, one of the bestselling popular Spanish singers of all time, was born on September 23, 1943, in Madrid, Spain. His paternal ancestors come from Galicia, and his maternal grandmother was related to Spanish nobility. Iglesias's first ambition was to become a soccer star, and he played as a goalkeeper on the Real Madrid football team. When he was twenty years old, a serious car accident ended his career as an athlete, and he refocused his energy on playing acoustic guitar and writing and singing songs. After training as a lawyer in Spain, he turned his attention to music full time.

His breakthrough came in 1968, when his song "La vida sigue igual" (Life Goes on Just the Same) won the Festival de Benidorm, a Spanish music contest. He subsequently signed a record deal with Columbia Records. His crooning love songs have been compared to the smooth singing style and lush orchestral backgrounds of artists such as Frank Sinatra. He has sold over 200 million records in a diverse number of languages, which in-

Julio Iglesias. *Courtesy of Photofest.*

clude Spanish, French, Italian, German, Japanese, English, and Portuguese. In 1983, the *Guinness World Book of Records* awarded him the Diamond Record Award because he had produced more albums in more languages than any other singer. Iglesias has also experimented with various genres of popular music. His duet with Willie Nelson, "To All the Girls I've Loved Before," was a hit on the country charts in 1984, and in the same year he produced his first English-language album, *1100 Bel Air Place*. In 1988, he produced the rock-influenced album *Non-Stop*. He has also collaborated with Sting and Dolly Parton on the album *Crazy* (1994). In 1997, his album *Tango*, which was nominated for a Grammy Award, extended his singing range to encompass an Argentine genre of music.

Iglesias has had a far-reaching impact on U.S. popular culture and continues to perform and produce popular music. He currently lives in Miami, where a star on the Latin Stars Walk on Miami's 8th Street attests to his success. He also has a star on the Hollywood Walk of Fame. In 1992, the title "Universal Spaniard" was conferred on him in Florida, and in Spain he has been dubbed "Ambassador of Galicia." In 1989 the United Nations Children's Fund (UNICEF) conferred the position of Special Representative in the Performing Arts to him, and he has performed many UNICEF benefit concerts, personal appearances, and other UNICEF projects. On September 8, 1997, he became the first Latin artist to be given the American Society of Composers, Authors, and Publishers (ASCAP) Pied Piper Award for his services to music.

Further Reading

http://www.juliomusic.com/biography.htm.

Helen Oakley

Immigration. Immigration is one of the major sources of and ongoing contributors to Latina and Latino popular culture in the United States because it has provided a substantial part of the population mass—that is, the people, their histories, and cultures. The experiences of immigration and adapting to a historically racially hostile society are reflected in many aspects of cultural, musical, and artistic expression. The struggles of immigrants, notably Mexican border crossers, are reflected in **corridos*, **retablos*, murals, posters, *film, community shrines and altars, *literature, and **dichos*.

Latinas and Latinos migrate to the United States for many reasons such as poverty, lack of employment in the country of origin, political turmoil, repression, unsafe living conditions, and employer demands for cheap labor north of the border. Immigration, especially from México, also results from economic expansion policies instituted by the United States and México to stimulate both economies (e.g., the binational treaty, North American Free Trade Agreement [NAFTA]). Also facilitating migration are *family and other social networks and institutions like churches, which sponsor humanitarian programs to assist immigrants who enter the country for a variety of reasons.

There are several ways Latino immigrants are categorized by the U.S. government. They are classified as either within the country's borders legally or illegally, on a temporary or a permanent basis, or as naturalized U.S. citizens. Legal permanent immigrants may live and work in the United States and eventually can apply for naturalization. Illegal immigrants are those who enter the United States via thresholds other than official border points of entry, and they are variably referred to as illegal aliens, undocumented immigrants, *indocumentados*, and wetbacks or *mojados*. Migration can occur individually and in groups, including entire families. Immigration sometimes occurs through the brokering of a "coyote," or illegal smuggler, who may charge up to several thousand dollars per person to help undocumented immigrants cross over the U.S. international border. Others have taken air flights to their destination without intervention. Part of a thriving black market in human exchange, the Immigration and Naturalization Service (INS) and Border Patrol report that coyotes have replaced drug smugglers as the most dangerous threats to society, manifesting in turf wars where teams of coyotes are fighting and killing other teams of coyotes for the human cargos of individuals who are in search of a better life in the United States.

For the vast majority of Americans, citizenship is an automatic birthright. For immigrants citizenship is conferred through naturalization, an official process that requires that an immigrant be at least eighteen years old, be a legal permanent resident, and must have lived in the United States continuously for five years. Other requirements for citizenship include the ability to speak, read, and write in English, as well as being of good moral character. The term *refugee* is applied to those persons who immigrate from their country of origin because of persecution or well-founded fears of harm based solely on their *race, religion, nationality, membership in a social group, desire for free expression, and related reasons. Refugees are eligible to apply for lawful permanent resident status after one year of continuous legal presence in the United States. After five years of continuous residence as a legal immigrant, refugees may apply for naturalization for U.S. citizenship.

Statistics for undocumented immigrants are never precise because of the hidden underground nature of the population, as well as because of the varying flow of border-crossing traffic. Nevertheless, the best estimates put the overall undocumented immigrant population at approximately 2 to 3 percent of the total U.S. population, or approximately 7 million people based on the 2000 U.S. Census. Almost half of the overall undocumented immigration population is composed of persons who entered the United States legally for business, study, or personal reasons but who then failed to leave after their temporary visas expired. Roughly half of the undocumented immigrant population comes from México, thus making people of Mexican-origin the largest legal and illegal immigrant group in the United States as well as the largest Latina and Latino population subset (about 60

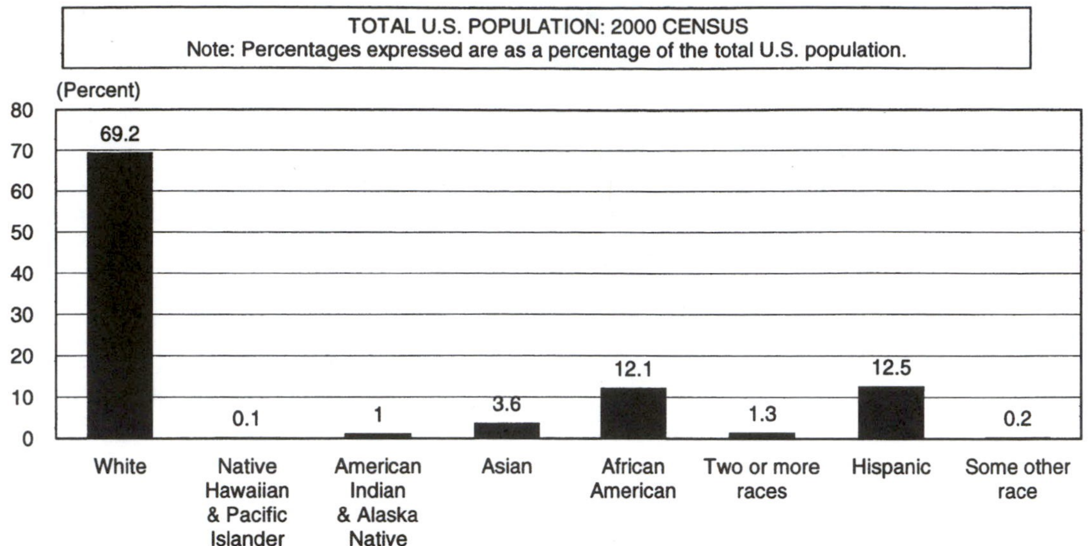

This demographic chart of actual immigration into the United States based on 2000 U.S. Census Bureau statistics refutes some common (mis)perceptions about the Hispanic poluation in the United States. *Chart by Rajeet Chatterjee, Arizona State University.*

percent). Refugee estimates among the Latina/o immigrant population are even harder to specify because of the changing status of immigrants from undocumented to refugee to legal to naturalized classifications. Nevertheless, as the population charts demonstrate, the vast majority of the U.S. population is still Caucasian, despite the demagogic rhetoric of some politicians and right-wing zealots who engage in fear tactics that promote anti-immigrant feelings.

Historically, migration from México was not severely restricted because most Mexican immigrants did not stay within the United States permanently, and migration from México was a fluid back-and-forth phenomenon. After 1910 the Mexican Revolution (*see* History, Chicana/o and Mexican American) led to the most significant wave of Mexican migration north, and best estimates indicate that over a quarter of a million legal immigrants entered the country. Since those early decades of the twentieth century, migration from the southern border has shifted to a constant trickling of immigrants, which increased dramatically after 1942 and the initiation of the *Bracero Program. A contracted worker system, the Bracero Program granted legal temporary status to Mexican laborers on a season-by-season basis to provide workers to satisfy the demands of industry and business for effective and sufficient labor pools. The program ended in the early 1960s by mutual agreement of both the U.S. and Mexican governments.

Another U.S. government policy that led to dramatic increases in Latina and Latino immigration was the passage of the 1965 Immigration Act. This

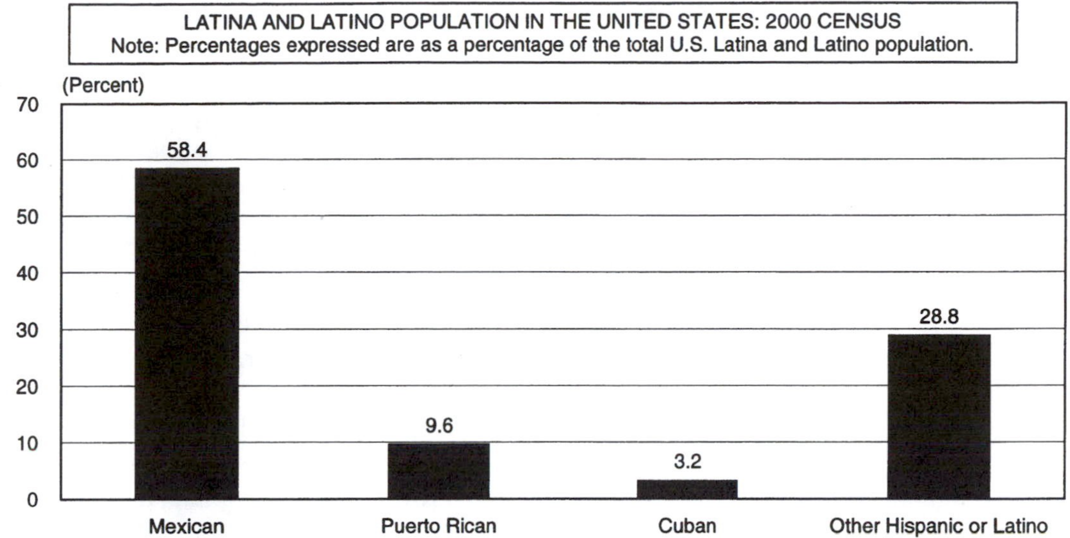

Graph based on U.S. Census Bureau population figures. *Chart by Rajeet Chatterjee, Arizona State University.*

legislation provided opportunities to individuals who previously had been denied immigration rights based solely on ethnicity and race. The act lifted the ban on certain immigrants previously barred from admission and created a system that made it easier for immigrants to enter with their family members. Furthermore, civil and political unrest in Central American countries like El Salvador, Guatemala, and Nicaragua created additional surges in refugee admissions. As a result, the 1960s and early 1970s witnessed a significant number of refugees admitted under special programs outside standard refugee provisions.

The rates of immigration continued to escalate dramatically in the 1980s, even though experts agree that firm numbers are impossible to provide with precision. To address the increase, the U.S. government responded by seeking to reduce the economic lure of jobs, which typically had been the key magnet to immigrants from poor countries with repressive regimes. In 1986 perhaps the most important immigration policy reform of the twentieth century was passed, the Immigration Reform and Control Act (IRCA). The overall objective of IRCA was to decrease the number of undocumented immigrants in the United States by implementing two provisions, Employer Sanctions and Legalization. The Employer Sanctions Provision sought to end the economic lure for immigrants who come to the United States for jobs by punishing employers who knowingly hire undocumented workers. The Legalization Provision was to legalize undocumented immigrants already in the United States, thereby reducing the total number of undocumented individuals. IRCA has greatly influenced Mexican immigration, and the vast majority of the 3 million immigrants who applied for legalization after 1965 were of Mexican origin.

The major immigration policy change in the 1990s was an increased focus on border security, patrol, law enforcement, punishment, and deportation. Funding increased by 300 percent for the purpose of policing the U.S. borders and illegal immigrants, particularly on the southern border. Several policies also were passed that dealt with the welfare and social services utilized by many Latina/o immigrants. For instance, in 1994 California passed arguably the most controversial proposition, Prop 187, also known as the "Save Our State Initiative." Prop 187 addressed illegal immigration costs by prohibiting public education to undocumented immigrant students in school districts and postsecondary institutions. It required school administrators to verify the status of all newly admitted students as well as that of their parents; without verification, they were to be deported. Eventually found to be unconstitutional, this initiative also prohibited all hospital administrators, both public and private, from providing nonemergency health care to the undocumented.

Despite its unconstitutionality, California's Prop 187 set the stage for other anti-immigrant American policies and the rise in welfare reform as a means to decrease illegal and legal immigration at the federal level. In 1996 the Personal Responsibility Act was passed to establish restrictions on legal immigrants from receiving social services, barring legal immigrants from using food stamps and from receiving social security. The act also broadened most restrictions on public benefits for undocumented immigrants from federal, state, and local sources. Also in 1996, Congress increased criminal penalties for immigration-related offenses and enhanced enforcement authority over street-level and border immigration operations. Despite the punitive immigration policies of the 1990s and accompanying public hostility toward immigrants, the new millennium has brought discussions that repeat policies of earlier decades. As of 2004 another temporary worker program, or Bracero Program, is being considered by President George W. Bush and President Vicente Fox of México. The program, which has the support of several governors from southwestern states, would offer temporary workers legal status in the United States for as long as three years, provided they are gainfully employed, follow the rules of the program, and do not break the law. There is sufficient controversy around this proposal to expect that it will be tied up in debate for several years. Policymakers are also debating the merits of another amnesty program that would grant legal status to those who could prove they have lived in the country continuously since 1986.

Cuban immigrants historically have entered the United States as refugees protected by the Cuban Adjustment Act signed into law in 1966 by President Lyndon B. Johnson. The law resulted from the antisocialist and anti–Fidel Castro foreign policy of the United States toward post–Revolution Cuba (*see* History, Cuban American). Providing for accelerated processing of their requests for permanent residency status, the law facilitated quick and smooth transitions for Cuban immigrants arriving in the United States, legally or illegally. Taking advantage of the welcoming legislation, hundreds of thousands of Cuban citizens have migrated to the United States over the past forty years.

Although the Dominican Republic is part of the Caribbean, its inhabitants are not considered U.S citizens like Puerto Ricans, and generally, they do not share the refugee status typically granted to Cuban immigrants. The recent immigration data indicate that Dominicans immigrate legally typically through family petitions and predominantly move to New York and to Florida.

Immigrants from Central America fall under a somewhat different definition of immigrant and refugee status. Although many were granted refugee status in the 1970s and 1980s, more recently Central Americans have been granted Temporary Protective Status. This is an official American government policy, which allows immigrants to reside in the United States on a temporary basis. Under this provision, the attorney general designates Central Americans temporary status when the conditions in their country are unsafe, usually for periods of six to eighteen months, which may be extended depending on the situation.

The INS, also known among Spanish speakers as "La Migra," is the agency previously responsible for immigration policy in the United States. The complex agency had the dual and somewhat contradictory mission of keeping undocumented immigrants out of the country as well as assisting them with their needs. The two main units within the INS—Enforcement and Service—had opposing objectives, which led to serious organizational conflicts. In 2002 the Congress passed the Homeland Security Act, and President George W. Bush signed it into law. The responsibilities of the INS were moved under the supervision of the newly created Department of Homeland Security, and the immediate effect was the separation of its previous functions into the Bureau of Citizenship and Immigration Services (BCIS) and Border and Transportation Security (BTS). The BCIS is charged with implementing service activities such as the processing of immigrant applications and naturalization. The BTS has been given supervision and implementation of enforcement activities. This federal restructuring is intended to produce greater agency efficiency and domestic security. Many scholars believe that another urgent need of immigration policy is for the countries of origin to increase their intervention effectiveness and for the United States to provide official status to the millions of undocumented workers on whom the U.S. economy depends whether through extended work permits, identification cards, amnesty, naturalization, and/or other appropriate action. Such binational action would help lessen victimization of the workers and, eventually, the need for illegal entry.

Further Reading

DeSipio, Louis, and Rodolfo de la Garza. *Making Americans, Remaking Americans.* Boulder, CO: Westview Press, 1998.

Gutiérrez, David. *Walls and Mirrors: Mexican Americans, Mexican Immigrants and the Politics of Ethnicity.* Berkeley: University of California Press, 1995.

Magaña, Lisa. *Straddling the Border: Immigration Policy and the INS.* Austin: University of Texas Press, 2003.

Lisa Magaña

India, La. *See* La India.

Indita. *Indita* literally means "little Indian girl" and is also a term for a ballad form found in New Mexico, Texas, and México that dates from the late eighteenth century. Similar to the **corrido*, it is organized in an eight-syllable verse scheme and sounds similar to Indian chanting and singing. Performed in Hispano and Pueblo villages in New Mexico, *inditas* are performed a capella, sometimes with guitar or drum accompaniment, and may be danced. One type of *indita* treats the subject of *cautivas* (captive women) and deals with captivity and slavery that were commonplace both in the Spanish colonial and the Mexican national periods of the *barrios and borderlands. The Native American influence is heard in the rhythm and changing meters, making the Spanish-language form a truly mestizo (hybrid) musical genre. Usually composed in the first person, *indita* songs narrate significant events that occurred in Hispano and Indian communities.

Further Reading

Campa, Arthur. "The Spanish Folksong in the Southwest." *Albuquerque: University of New Mexico Bulletin, Modern Language Series* 5.1 (1933): 179–223.

Lamadrid, Enrique. "La Indita de San Luis Gonzaga: History, Faith, and Intercultural Relations in the Evolution of a New Mexican Sacred Ballad." In *Ballads and Boundaries: Narrative Singing in an Intercultural Context.* Los Angeles: University of California, 1995.

Mendoza, Vicente T., and Virginia R. Mendoza. *Estudio y clasificación de la música tradicional hispánica de Nuevo México.* Mexico City: Universidad Nacional Autónoma de México, 1986.

Robb, John D. *Hispanic Folk Music of New Mexico and the Southwest: A Self-Portrait of a People.* Norman: University of Oklahoma Press, 1980.

Romero, Brenda. "The Indita Genre of New Mexico: Gender and Cultural Identification." In *Changing Chicana Traditions*, edited by Olga Nájera-Ramirez and Olga Cantú. Chicago: University of Illinois Press, 2002.

Peter J. García

Jacal. A jacal is a type of hut or shack, usually made out of adobe with a straw ceiling and occasionally used among Mexicans in the United States. The Nahuátl word *xacalli* is the root from which the word jacal is derived. The jacal originated in Central México, but in the eighteenth and nineteenth centuries, this custom expanded into Texas and was used throughout the state. The Texas jacal was made out of material found locally, such as mud, clay, adobe, mesquite wood, river grass, cane, stones, and brick rubble. Jacales were one-room structures, typically measuring about twelve-by-twelve feet. The indigenous building materials provided good insulation, and the door and windows were covered with blankets to keep out the cold and the heat.

During the nineteenth century many non-Mexican writers described the jacal as uniquely Mexican, and as with many Mexican customs, the jacal was viewed as a primitive, frail, unsanitary, and immoral structure. Beginning in the 1880s, the use of the jacal became less common due to the changes occurring in the natural environment and life of Texans, and by mid-twentieth century, jacales seemed to have vanished. From the eighteenth to twentieth centuries, records of the jacal have been found in U.S. military reports, newspaper accounts, memoirs, travel narratives, art, and photographs.

Further Reading

Castro, Rafaela G. *Chicano Folklore: A Guide to the Folktales, Traditions, Rituals and Religious Practices of Mexican-Americans.* New York: Oxford University Press, 2001.

Medina, Dennis Glen. "El Jacalito: Images of the Jacal in Texas." November 10, 1995. Master's thesis abstract, University of Texas. http://www.geocities.com/eltejanito/abstract.htm.

Mónica Saldaña

Jalapeños. *See* Chili; Food and Cookery.

Jiménez, Flaco (1939–). Leonardo Jiménez, better known as Flaco Jiménez, was born in San Antonio, Texas, on March 11, 1939, and is a Grammy-winning songwriter, accordionist, and Tex-Mex artist of international fame and popularity. Jiménez learned how to play the accordion by watching his father, Santiago Jiménez, Sr., who is considered one of *conjunto* music's pioneers of the 1930s. As a young boy, Jiménez performed *bajo sexto* with his father's band, debuting on early 1950s single-hit recordings with Los Tecolotes and performing before live audiences. By the age of eighteen, he recorded his first album as a member of the group Los Caporales. Eventually he joined the group Los Caminantes and was given his father's nickname "Flaco" ("skinny" in Spanish). In 1955, they released their first recording for Jaime Wolfe's Rios Records called "Contigo Nomás" (With You No More).

Flaco's musical career took a new direction in the early 1970s when he partnered with Doug Sahm, previously of the Sir Douglas Quintet. He also traveled to New York to play with fellow musicians Bob Dylan and Mac Rebennack. Shortly thereafter, Jiménez began playing for Anglo audiences and traveled around the world with various artists. He rapidly gained international acclaim. Ry Cooder heard Flaco's music and was determined to work with him, and together they recorded *Chicken Skin Music* (1976), *Showtime* (1977), and a sound track for *The Border* (1982).

Flaco won his first Grammy in 1986 for the remake of his father's song "Ay te dejo en San Antonio" (I Will Leave You in San Antonio). He then teamed up with Freddy Fender, Doug Sahm, and Augie Meyers to form the group the Texas Tornadoes and won another Grammy in 1990. In 1996 and 1999 Flaco won his third and fifth Grammies for Best Mexican American Performance. In 1999 he also received a fourth Grammy for Best *Tejano Performance for the record *Said and Done*. Throughout his musical career, Jiménez has received numerous awards including various lifetime achievement and hall of fame awards. In 2003 he was inducted into the International Latin Music Hall of Fame.

In years past, Jiménez has worked with various artists, including Dwight Yoakam, Ry Cooder, Linda *Ronstadt, *Los Lobos, The Mavericks, and Bryan Ferry. He even performed on the Rolling Stones 1994 album *Voodoo Lounge*. In addition to performing on stage, he has appeared on numerous television shows, including *Late Night with David Letterman*, *Austin City Limits*, *Primetime Country*, and *MTV News*. Jiménez mentions that his most memorable career performances are the 1996 Inaugural Ball, Peter Gabriel's WOMAD Festival in Yokohama, Japan, the Montreux Jazz Festival in Montreux, Switzerland, Central Park in New York, and with the San Antonio Symphony Orchestra in 1998.

Further Reading

http://www.flacojimenez.com.

Cristina K. Muñoz

Jiménez, José Alfredo (1926–1973). José Alfredo Jiménez Sandoval was México's most prolific and well-respected composer of vernacular music during the mid-twentieth century and remains a beloved singer among Mexicans and Chicanas/os in the United States. He is best known for his **canciones* **rancheras*, which include "El Rey" (The King), "Ella" (She), "Yo" (I), "Tu y las nubes" (You and the Clouds), "Camino de Guanajuato" (Road to Guanajuato), and dozens more as well as his singing ability. He composed more than 400 songs, of which over 300 have been recorded. He is perhaps less recognized in the United States for his acting, but his music is timeless in and outside of México and the United States.

Born on January 19, 1926, in Dolores Hidalgo, Guanajuato, in a close-knit family, he started singing at an early age and was especially attracted to the songs of Agustín Lara and Maria Cárdenal. By the age of nine or ten he was composing simple children's songs. After the death of his father in 1936, he moved to Mexico City to live with his aunt, Refugio Sandoval. Economic conditions dictated that he leave school, and he pursued a series of menial jobs, the last of which was as a waiter at the la Sirena (The Siren). There, he met the owner's son, who was a guitarist with the trio Los Rebeldes (The Rebels—formed in 1945). Jiménez convinced them to perform his song "Yo" and in 1948 Los Rebeles accompanied him when he sang on radio XEW, Mexico City's most powerful radio station.

His first big break came in 1950 when Andrés Huesca y sus Costeños recorded "Yo," which became a hit. Soon after "Ella," "Cuatro Caminos" (The Four Roads), and others were recorded, and notable singers such as Miguel Aceves Mejía, Lucha Villa, Lola Beltrán, Flor Silvestre, María de Lourdes, and others sought him out for his songs. Early on, he established a relationship with Rubén Fuentes, who arranged his melodies for performance.

In 1951 he performed in his first cinema, a venue that popularized his music via such legends as Pedro Infante and Miguel Aceves Mejía. Jiménez was to star as the "gallant **charro*" (gentleman cowboy) in more than two dozen movies including those based on his own songs, such as *Tu y las nubes* (You and the Clouds, 1955) and *Camino de Guanajuato* (Road to Guanajuato, 1954). His *film work led to further recording contracts, eventually recording more than twenty full disks for RCA and Columbia including several gold records.

His personal life was often complicated by his fast lane living that eventually led to an early death on November 23, 1973, from hepatitis. His songs, however, continue to live through the Mexican *folklore tradition, especially

Famous Mariachi José Alfredo Jiménez. *Photo courtesy of J. Richard Haefer.*

through *mariachi performances. Even more important is his influence on Mexican and Chicana/o identity.

Further Reading

Moreno Rivas, Yolando. *Historia de la música popular mexicana* (History of Mexican Popular Music). Mexico, City: Consejo Nacional para la Cultura y las Artes, 1979.

http://www.geocities.com/Athens/Oracle/7357/jimenez.html.

J. Richard Haefer

Journalism. *See* Newspapers and Periodicals.

Julia, Raúl (1940–1994). Born as Raúl Rafael Carlos Julia y Arcelay on March 9, 1940, to Raúl and his wife Olga in San Juan, Puerto Rico, Julia was a respected figure in *theater and cinema thanks to his Shakespearean and classical stage performances as well as his roles in musicals, *films, and television credits.

In the late 1960s after arriving in New York, he met theater impresario Joseph Papp, who was developing a new concept of New York theater. Papp wanted to converge classical plays, such as Shakespeare, with the community while blending the richness of the country's voices, rhythms, and diverse culture. This great project gave birth to the famous New York Shakespeare Festival, which continues to offer free Shakespeare in Central Park every summer. Julia and Papp developed a very close friendship that Julia viewed as a father and son relationship and that lasted until Papp's death in 1991. Papp, without regarding ethnic inclinations, saw the great talent in Julia and cast him as a lead in Shakespeare's *Titus Andronicus* (1966). Soon after, with Papp's support, Julia became a Broadway star and won four Tony nominations for *Two Gentleman of Verona* (1972), *Where's Charley?* (1975), *The Three Penny Opera* (1977), and *Nine* (1982).

Raúl Julia. *Courtesy of Photofest.*

Julia wanted to access a bigger audience, so he ventured into the film industry, becoming one of the few actors to successfully transition from theater to film. While only doing small parts in his debut films *The Organization* (1971), *Been Down So Long It Looks Like Up to Me* (1971), and *The Panic in Needle Park* starring Al Pacino (1971), he received national acclaim after costarring in **Kiss of the Spider Woman* (1985). Film director Francis Ford Coppola invited Julia to his Zoetrope Studios stock company and cast him in the film *One From the Heart* (1982).

Julia had a special taste for films appealing to the political and social conscience. He starred in the two masterworks *Romero* (1989), based on the life of the archbishop of El Salvador, Oscar Arnulfo Romero, martyred during a church service after fighting for the human rights of the Salvadoran people, and *The Burning Season* (1994), an HBO movie that depicts the life of Chico Mendes, a Brazilian Labor Unionist murdered in 1988. He won a Golden Globe award for best actor in the latter production. Julia starred in the first full-length movie of Puerto Rico, *La Gran Fiesta*—The Great Party (1987). He earned three Golden Globe nominations for *Tempest* (1982), *Kiss of the Spider Woman* (1985), and *Moon Over Parador* (1988). He also acted in movies starring Mel Gibson and Michelle Pfeiffer in *Tequila Sunrise* (1988), Harrison Ford in *Presumed Innocent* (1990), Clint Eastwood, Charlie *Sheen, and Sonia *Braga in *The Rookie* (1990), and Jean Claude Van Damme in *Street Fighter* (1994), his last film.

Among other productions that shaped his uniqueness are the television series **Sesame Street* (1971–1973), the Broadway revival *Man of La Mancha* (1990), and the comedy film *The Addams Family* (1991) and sequel *Addams Family Values* (1993), where he demonstrated that he had skill not only in drama but also in comedy.

Julia's humanitarian sympathy and advocacy for others were evidenced by his seventeen-year tenure as spokesperson for The Hunger Project, a foundation with the mission of eradicating hunger in the world. On October 24, 1994, Julia died of a stroke in Manhasset, Long Island, and he received a state funeral in San Juan, Puerto Rico, to honor his career and accomplishments. After his death the Raúl Julia Ending Hunger Fund was created by The Hunger Project to honor his legacy and commitment.

Further Reading

http://www.puertorico-herald.org/issues/vol4n06/ProfileJulia-en.shtml.
http://www.thegoldenglobes.com/welcome.html?nominee/julia_raul.html.

Arturo J. Aldama

Jurado, Katy (1924–2002). María Cristina Jurado García, a prolific and award winning actress in the United States and México, was born in Guadalajara, México, on January 16, 1924. Her career in acting began in México in 1943 with the film *No Matarás* (You Will Not Kill). She is perhaps best remembered for her role as Gary Cooper's former lover in the classic western **High Noon* (1952). Jurado received a Golden Globe Award for Best Supporting Actress in a Drama for her work in *High Noon*, becoming the first Mexican actress to win that honor. While visiting Los Angeles in 1951 to collect material for a gossip column she was writing, she was cast in *The Bullfighter and the Lady* (1951). Through the 1950s, Jurado continued to be featured in several westerns, which enjoyed great popularity with American audiences. She received an Academy Award nomination for Best Supporting Actress in 1954 for her work in *Broken Lance*. From 1959 to 1964, she was married to American actor Ernest Borgnine.

Her career in the United States became more sporadic after her success in the 1950s. She appeared occasionally on American television, guest starring on such series as *Barretta*, *The Virginian*, and *The Westerner*. In the 1980s, she had a recurring role on the television series *a.k.a. Pablo*, playing Paul *Rodríguez's mother. In 1997, she received a special Ariel Award, México's equivalent of the Academy Award, for career achievement. She was awarded the Ariel on four occasions, three for her acting in Luis Buñuel's *El Bruto* (The Brute, 1952), in *Fe, Esperanza y Caridad* (Faith, Hope, and Charity, 1974), and in Arturo Ripstein's *El Evangelio de las Maravillas* (Divine, 1998), and the fourth one for her lifelong acting career. On July 5, 2002, Jurado suffered a heart attack and died at her home in Cuernavava, México, while making Stephen Frear's *The Hi-Lo Country* (1998) her last acting endeavor. Her long career and acclaim as an actress of enduring merit ensure Jurado's place in Mexican and U.S. cinema history.

Further Reading

Foote, Cheryl. "Katy Jurado: Mexico's Woman of the Western." In *The Hollywood West: Lives of Film Legends Who Shaped It*, edited by Richard W. Etulain and Glenda Riley. Golden, CO: Fulcrum, 2001.

García Riera, Emilio, and Javier González Rubio. *El Cine de Katy Jurado*. Guadalajara, México: Universidad de Guadalajara, 1999.

William Orchard

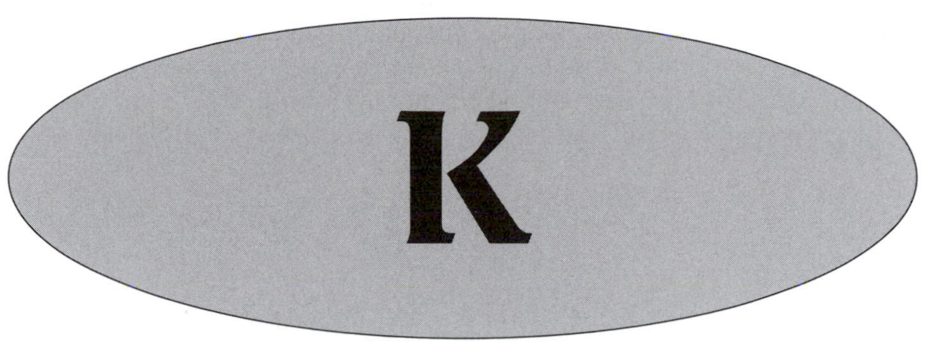

Kahlo, Frida (1907–1954). Frida Kahlo, one of the most celebrated Mexican painters, had a tremendous impact on the genesis of modern feminist art and on Chicana/o, Latina/o, and Latin American artists specifically. Magdalena Carmen Frida Kahlo was born on July 6, 1907, in the Coyoacán *barrio of Mexico City to Matilde Calderón and Guillermo Kahlo, an official government photographer for Porfírio Díaz. In 1922 Kahlo enrolled in the Escuela Nacional Preparatoria, the premier public preparatory school, to study medicine and philosophy in Mexico City. Frida, one of the few female students at the school, had the opportunity to meet Diego *Rivera, who later became her husband, while he was working on a mural.

In an unfortunate incident on September 17, 1925, the bus in which she was riding collided with a streetcar, and Kahlo suffered multiple fractures and was left with chronic pain in her legs and back. During her recovery, Kahlo was confined to bed for several months, and at this time she began to paint self-portraits with the aid of a mirror placed above her bed.

In several of her works, Kahlo illustrates the impact and consequences that this accident had on her life. Her self-portrait *La Columna Rota* (Broken Column, 1944) shows in vivid symbolic force how she perceives her body as fractured or split apart in the chest, with her spinal column in full view, and literally held together by nails and by cotton ties in loose girdle. Kahlo also painted reflects other personal experiences such as her relationship with Rivera, her miscarriages, the articulation of her mestiza identity, her celebration of Mexican popular culture and its use of flowers, colors, fruit, and Nahuátl aesthetics, as well as visual meditations on death and pain, the role of industrialization and technology, the body, and the U.S.-Mexican border.

On August 21, 1929, Kahlo and Diego Rivera were married, and soon after, the couple traveled to various U.S. cities because Rivera had been commissioned to paint murals. In 1939 Rivera and Kahlo agreed to a divorce (although they would remarry in 1940), and Kahlo then traveled to Europe to show her work on invitation from the famous surrealist Andrés Bretón. Kahló and Rivera were prominent figures in the intellectual and cultural life of Mexico City, where she was recognized for her activism and political ideology. (Kahló joined the Communist Party in 1928 when she was just twenty-one).

Frida Kahlo's *Self Portrait with Monkey and Parrot, 1942. Courtesy of Photofest.*

In 1942 Kahlo began teaching at the Mexican art academy La Esmeralda. Initially, she taught at the academy, but due to her worsening health conditions, she eventually had to move her classes back to her blue exterior colonial-style home in the bohemian district of Mexico City, Coyocoán, popularly known as *la Casa Azul* or the Blue House. Kahlo's works were included in numerous exhibitions in several countries, including France and the United States. Her one-woman show took place at the Mexico City Galería de Arte Contemporáneo (Gallery of Contemporary Art) in 1953. Kahló died on July 13, 1954, of a pulmonary embolism.

Among her most notable works are *Las Dos Fridas* (The Two Fridas, 1939); *Autorretrato entre la frontera Mexico-US* (Self-Portrait on the U.S.–Mexico Borderline, 1932); *Hospital Henry Ford* (1932); *Mi nana y yo* (My Nurse and I, 1937); *Autorretrato dedicado a Leon Trotsky* (Self-Portrait Dedicated to Leon Trotsky, 1937); *La flor de la vida* (The Flower of Life, 1944); and *Sin esperanza* (Without Hope, 1945).

Although Frida was extremely well known in Mexican intellectual circles for her activism, willingness to challenge gender and sexual taboos, her support of working-class struggles, and her caustic humor, it was after her death that her self-portraits and her visual language of the racialized and gendered body became such a force within global feminist circles. Her works now are part of the prized collections of the Museum of Modern Art in New York; Fundación Proa, Buenos Aires, Argentina; Montreal Museum of Fine Arts, Canada; National Museum of Women in the Arts, Washington, D.C.; Phoenix Art Museum, and many other landmark museums and collections.

Her complex and empowering life story has been the subject of several important art history biographies, and her life was made into two full-length feature films, the Mexican award-winning *Frida: Naturaleza viva* (Frida: Live Nature, 1983), starring Ofelia Medina and directed by Paul Leduc, and in 2002, the film *Frida*, starring and produced by Mexican actress Salma *Hayek. Her life and work have also been the features of documentaries and a large number of scholarly essays and books that look at, for example, the phenomenon of Frida-mania and *appropriation of her image and most superficial marketing of her life and art are marketed by museums and other cultural institutions in the United States, with Frida handbags, clip-on buttons, postcards, T-shirts, and Frida-inspired jewelry.

Further Reading

Herrera, Hayden. *Frida: A Biography of Frida Kahló*. New York: HarperCollins, 2002.

Kahló, Frida. *The Diary of Frida Kahló: An Intimate Self-Portrait*. New York: Abradale Press, 1998.

Lindauer, Margaret. *Devouring Frida: The Art History and Popular Celebrity of Frida Kahló*. Middletown, CT: Wesleyan University Press, 1999.

Dulce Aldama

Kapp, Joe (1938–). Born in Santa Fe, New Mexico, Joe Kapp came to prominence in the late 1960s as a quarterback for the Minnesota Vikings of the National Football League (NFL), one of the rare Chicanos in the NFL. In high school he was a multisport athlete at William S. Hart High in Newhall, California, excelling at football and basketball. He won a football scholarship to the University of California at Berkeley, where he helped lead the team to the Pacific Athletic Conference title and a top 20 finish in the nation in 1958. Disappointed with his late-round (twelfth) selection by the Washington Redskins in the 1959 NFL draft, Kapp chose instead to emigrate north to play in the Canadian Football League (CFL) for Calgary. Although his rookie CFL season was bumpy, after two knee injury–plagued seasons he was traded to Vancouver, where his great skill and talent once again emerged. He was named the CFL's Most Valuable Player in 1963 and helped lead Vancouver to win the league championship Grey Cup in 1964.

Throughout his public career, Kapp was nicknamed "Injun Joe,"an example of the era's generally accepted blatant racism. Many sportswriters and fans agree that he paved the way for such later Latinos in the NFL as Jim *Plunkett and Pro Football Hall of Famer Anthony Muñoz. In 1967 Kapp finally realized his boyhood dream of playing in the NFL by signing with the Minnesota Vikings. He quarterbacked them to their first ever division title in 1968. The next season he led the team to the Super Bowl, which they lost to the Kansas City Chiefs. Due to a contract dispute with the Vikings, he left the team and signed on with the Boston Patriots in 1970. At this point his football career was abruptly ended because of injuries. Since his retirement from professional sports, Kapp has appeared in movies and also has had success on the lecture circuit as a motivational speaker.

Further Reading

Neft, David, and Richard Cohen. *The Football Encyclopedia*. New York: St. Martin's Press, 1991.

"Pro Football History." *Professional Football Researchers Association*. http://www.footballresearch.com/index.cfm.

Clifford Candelaria

Kid Chocolate (1910–1988). Widely acknowledged as one of the top three to five Latino professional prizefighters of the first half of the twentieth century, Kid Chocolate was also one of New York's most popular entertainers in the 1920s and 1930s. A native of Havana, Cuba, Kid Chocolate's given name at birth on January 6, 1910, was Eligio Sardinias-Montalbo. He later told American reporters that he first started fighting as a newspaper boy when he had to defend his sales territory in Havana. Discovered by a sports page editor after he won an amateur boxing tournament, he trained by watching newsreel films of famous fights. He went on to a glorious amateur career, accumulating twenty-one knockouts in twenty-one bouts. This success led to his becoming a pro and emigrating to the world's boxing capital, New York City, in 1928 at the age of eighteen.

Chocolate rapidly developed a striking reputation as a pro, and his matches soon left the smaller gymnasiums and clubs to be featured in Madison Square Garden. Before long he was a world-ranked featherweight contender, dazzling fans with his quick agility and two-handed punching ability. *Ring Magazine* ranked him number-one contender in 1929. Chocolate fought a total 146 bouts, winning his first title in 1931 as junior lightweight. In 1932 he added New York's world featherweight title to his credits, and he defended it twice because he failed to make weight. Chocolate continued as a prizefighter until 1938, albeit against second-rate competition. Some sportswriters criticized him for not properly training, especially for the big matches, but most recognized him as a gifted artist of the "sweet science," as aficionados call boxing, because of his skill, power, and quickness. He won 131 of his 146 fights, losing only 9 and drawing 6. Inducted into the International Boxing Hall of Fame in 1994, Chocolate returned to Cuba to operate a gym after his retirement. He died on August 8, 1988.

Further Reading

Roberts, James B., and Alexander G. Skutt, eds. *The Boxing Register*. 3rd ed. Ithaca, NY: McBooks Press, 2002.

Cordelia Chávez Candelaria

Kid Gavilán (1926–2003). Recognized as one of the first Latino stars of international boxing, Kid Gavilán's given name was Gerardo Gonzáles, but the Cuban sensation acquired the catchy nickname when he began competing in the United States, and he is listed as such in the record books. He was dubbed "gavilán," the Spanish word for "hawk," because of his speed, quickness, and aggressiveness in the ring. Still remembered by appreciators of the "sweet science" for his celebrated bolo punch, a boxing innovation technique that he perfected, Gavilán claims to have adopted the right-handed wind-up attack as a boy working as a cutter in Cuba's sugar cane fields. Along with *Kid Chocolate, Gavilán helped pave the way for other Latinos in North American *sports. His lifetime statistics as a prizefighter include an International Boxing Commission World Championship title (1951) in the welterweight division. He successfully defended his title belt seven times, as well as compiled a total of 143 ring victories, 30 losses, 27 knockouts, and 7 draws. Amazingly, he himself was not knocked out once during his entire career.

Born in the cane-growing region of Gamaguey, Cuba, on January 6, 1926, Gonzáles made his professional ring debut as a teenager in 1942. Boxing in his homeland and in México, he learned his craft and was encouraged to move north to compete in the more famous and lucrative venues of the United States. He left Havana for New York in 1946 and began to fight his way up the contenders ladder. As a boy he dreamed of boxing in New York's famed Madison Square Garden, and he was able to realize his dream soon after he arrived. Promoted in the press by his nickname, "The Hawk," he faced the major challenge of building his professional career in the United States during the era of the legendary Sugar Ray Robinson (1945–1958), in whose shadow all the non-heavyweights competed.

When Robinson moved into the middleweight class, Gavilán finally fought the title bout that he had long anticipated. In May 1951, he won a decisive unanimous decision against Johnny Bratton to take the first major belt of his career as a professional welterweight competitor. Demonstrating his talent, strength, and dedication, Gavilán proved that he was a worthy successor to Robinson's reign as welterweight by retaining his championship crown for four years. During that period he defended his title seven times, once against Carmen Basilio, who became famous for defeating Robinson in the middleweight division. Gavilán lost his title to Johnny Saxton in a 1954 title fight. Most boxing experts believe the match was unfairly decided against the Cuban champion because of Saxton's ties to the International Boxing Council's (IBC) insider clique, which had become overrun with cronyism and corruption, a chronic situation that has led the U.S. Congress to hold several hearings on boxing over the years in attempts to reform its shady business practices.

After losing his title and with his professional career declining, Gavilán retired from boxing in 1958. He returned to Cuba with hopes of enjoying a comfortable new era with his family, living off the hard-earned money he had made over a fifteen-year span in the ring. The *Cuban Revolution and Fidel *Castro's success in removing dictator Fulgencio Batista from power in 1959 quickly altered his plans, however, and he joined the early exodus of thousands of Cuban exiles to Miami. Still remembered for his pugilistic skill, Gavilán was hired to work in Muhammad Ali's training camp when he first arrived in the United States. When he died at seventy-seven on February 13, 2003, The Hawk was remembered by fans and writers for his amazing stamina, focused competitiveness, mental toughness, and the bolo punch he introduced to the world of prizefighting.

Further Reading

"Kid Gavilán Tribute." http://www.eastsideboxing.com/boxing/Kid%20Gavilan.

"Legends and Lore." http://www.ibhof.com/ibhfcuba1.htm.

Sammons, Jeffrey. *Beyond the Ring: The Role of Boxing in American Society*. Urbana: University of Illinois Press, 1988.

Cordelia Chávez Candelaria

Kiss of the Spider Woman. Directed by Hector Babenco and produced by David Weisman, *Kiss of the Spider Woman* (1985) is an adaptation of

Manuel Puig's novel, which was groundbreaking both in its experimentation with storytelling technique and in its Latino queer focus. The film follows the flourishing friendship and love between macho would-be Marxist, Valentin Arregui (Raúl *Julia), and the flamboyant transvestite, Luis Molina (William Hurt). Both Molina and Valentin share a prison cell in an unidentified, dictator-ruled Latin American country, incarcerated for their "criminal" acts: Molina for cruising men and Valentin for his revolutionary political activities. When first introduced, Valentin openly detests Molina's effeminate manners and proclivity to role-play the raconteur. Molina, though patient with Valentin, is disturbed by his masculine posturing and empty political rhetoric. The time they spend together reveals more similarities than differences. Valentin becomes increasingly engrossed in Molina's maudlin melodrama—his revision of a World War II propaganda film where he spices up a romance between a handsome Nazi counterintelligence chief and an elegant French chanteuse (Sonia *Braga)—and more and more touched by Molina's tender care during his bouts of sickness. As Valentin finds tenderness for Molina, he also comes to realize his own flaws and hypocrisies; he, too, desires to dream of other worlds. Likewise, as Molina falls in love with Valentin, he comes to understand that his forbidden love is not so separate from the concerns of social revolution.

As this intense psychological drama unfolds, the audience witnesses the birth and nourishing of love and the imagination within a brutally violent, oppressive *police state. Witnessed, too, is the power of storytelling not as escape but as a way for two ideologically opposed figures to find common understanding—and as a life-giving force; in the Scheherazade tradition, Molina spins stories for the prison warden to prolong Valentin's life. Director Babenco's juxtaposition of a sepia-tinged, orchestral-filled melodramatic World War II love story with the stark gritty realist documentation of prison emphasizes just such a need for creativity in a bleak world. Finally, the story of Valentin and Molina powerfully asks its audience to read the body, passion, and sexuality in a less rigid male/female tradition. *Kiss of the Spider Woman* was the first independent film to receive Oscar nominations for Best Screenplay, Best Director, and Best Picture, and Hurt's performance won him the Best Actor Oscar in 1985. The film, which was distributed by Sugarloaf Films and rereleased by Strand in 2001, also features José Lewgoy, Milton Goncalves, Miriam Pires, and Nuno Leal Maia. *Kiss of the Spider Woman* has also been adapted and performed on Broadway.

Further Reading

Puig, Manuel. *Kiss of the Spider Woman: and Two Other Plays*. New York: Norton Press, 1994.

http://www.imdb.com/title/tt0089424.

http://www.kissofthespiderwoman.com.

Frederick Luis Aldama

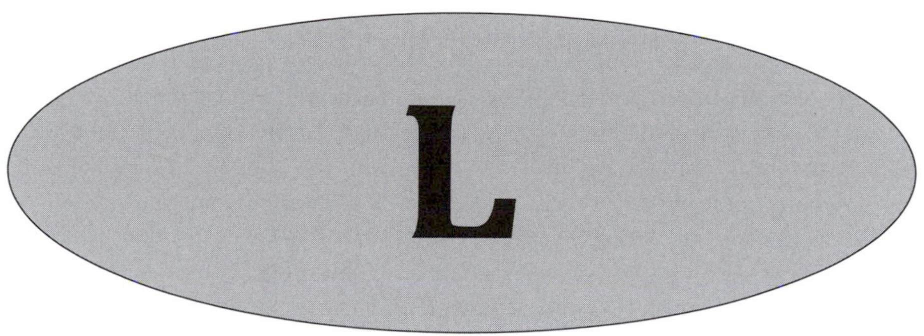

"La Bamba." "La Bamba" is the title of a popular rock and roll song from the 1950s recorded by the late *Chicano singer/songwriter Ritchie *Valens. The song was released in 1958 as part of Valens's three-hit trilogy, which included "Donna" on the flip side and "Come On, Let's Go." It is based on a regional dance and country song form called **son jarocho* from the state of Veracruz. "La Bamba" is regarded as a *mestizo or hybrid musical and dance genre with strong African influences (rhythm, musical instruments, and choreography) unique to the east coast of México. Valens's version mixes *jarocho* music with American rock and roll, producing another **mestizaje*. One of the most popular Mexican songs ever performed, "La Bamba" has been recorded at least 150 times by many artists including Trini *López in 1966, the Plugz in 1979, and *Los Lobos in 1980. **La Bamba* is also the title of a Hollywood movie directed by Luis *Valdez in 1987, about the life and musical career of Ritchie Valens.

Peter J. García

La Bamba. *La Bamba* (1987) is a tragic coming-of-age film based on the life of Ritchie *Valens, a 1950s *Chicano rock and roll singer whose real name was Richard Steve Valenzuela. Valens, who changed his name for crossover marketing purposes, had three top 10 hits: *"La Bamba," "Donna," and "Come On Let's Go." Written and directed by Luis *Valdez and produced by Taylor Hackford, *La Bamba* tells of Valens's rise to fame and the struggles he and his working-class *family experienced in the San Fernando Valley fields.

Valens (Lou Diamond Phillips) is a good kid who worked hard at being a musician and a good son. He is the complete opposite of his envious brother

Bob (Esai *Morales), a biker and drug user who recently got out of jail. Bob cares for his younger brother and tries to help Ritchie with his musical and personal life. Ritchie gets in touch with his Mexican culture when Bob takes him to Tijuana, where he hears a rendition of "La Bamba," the famous **son jarocho* from Veracruz, México. Valens decides to play the traditional folk song to a mainstream American audience. Although he is not fluent in the language, Valens records "La Bamba" in Spanish. In the 1950s, Spanish music was a rarity on mainstream American radio, but the song became a major hit for Valens. *Los Lobos, the East Los Angeles rock band, performed Valens's music on the sound track. Valens's life and career came to an end on February 3, 1959, which singer Don McLean later characterized as "The day the music died." Seventeen-year-old Valens, Buddy Holly, and the Big Bopper all died when their small plane crashed into an Iowa cornfield during a snowstorm. *La Bamba*, which was distributed by New Vision Pictures–Columbia Pictures, was nominated for a Golden Globe award in 1987 for Best Drama. The cast also includes Elizabeth *Peña and Danielle Von Zerneck.

Further Reading

Keller, Gary. *Hispanics and United States Film*. New York: Vantage Press, 1995.

Noriega, Chan. *Chicanos and Film: Representation and Resistance*. Minneapolis: University of Minnesota Press, 1992.

http://www.hollywoodteenmovies.com/LaBamba.html.

Karen Rosales de Wells

"La Borinqueña." The national anthem of Puerto Rico (*himno nacional de Puerto Rico*), "La Borinqueña" was written by Felix Astol Artés (1813–1901) in 1867. The song's massive popularity among the people is reminiscent of other grassroots examples of popular music—such as "Amazing Grace," "We Shall Overcome," "Guantanamera," and "De Colores"—that take on their own special meaning regardless of origin or purpose. The famous writer and political activist Lola Rodriguez de Tió (1843–1924), was moved to adapt the lyrics in 1868 to capture the song's patriotic nostalgia for the indigenous simplicity of the past as a means of inspiring the people of the island to rebel against Spain.

The song was officially adopted as the Commonwealth of Puerto Rico Anthem in 1952. Referring to the indigenous Taíno name of the island originally known as Boriquén (also spelled Borinquén or Boriken), the title pays homage to the tribal peoples who developed the Taíno culture that met Christopher *Columbus and his men in 1492. As such, "La Borinqueña" exemplifies the native Indian and immigrant Spanish linguistic and cultural features of **mestizaje* (hybridity). Columbus is mentioned in one verse as being entranced by the islands magnificent beauty:

Cuando a sus playas llego Colón,
exclamó lleno de admiración:

Oh! Oh! Oh!
(When Columbus arrived at her shores, he exclaimed Oh! Oh! Oh! in admiration.)

The rhymed verses of the song are spoken in the first person, emphasizing a common *puertorriqueño* voice and theme. By singing of the island's natural "blooming flower garden" beauty (e.g., "un jardín florido") and the "magic" of having the "cooing murmurs" and "calm waves" of the sea "at one's feet" ("y dan arrullos/plácidos las olas a sus pies"), the anthem underscores the Caribbean geography as a key source of the collective unity within Puerto Rican popular culture, as well as the inextricable link between a people's common homeland and their political common cause.

Further Reading

Flores, Juan. *From Bomba to Hip-Hop: Puerto Rican Culture and Latino Identity.* New York: Columbia University Press, 2000.
Sánchez Korrol, Virginia. "In Their Own Right: A History of Puerto Ricans in the U.S.A." In *Handbook of Hispanic Cultures in the United States: History*, edited by Francisco Lomelí et al. Houston, Texas, and Madrid, Spain: Arte Público Press & Instituto de Cooperación Iberoamericana, 1993.
"Welcome to Puerto Rico." http://welcome.topuertorico.org/bori.

Cordelia Chávez Candelaria

La Ciudad. Directed by David Riker with a cast of predominantly Latino immigrants who work as day laborers and seamstresses, *La Ciudad* (The City, 1999) is a compilation of four vignettes that relate the various lives of working-class immigrants in New York City. Despite the film's title, the city is not gloriously displayed—it is the backdrop or scene in which Latino and other immigrants struggle for survival. While Riker's vision of the city is more often impersonal, all consuming, bureaucratic, and unforgiving, he shows us how the Latino community recreates the towns and villages of their homeland within New York's grid and builds a complex social network on survival and cultural sustenance for the Latino community. In one scene, a young man from Puebla, México, cannot find the address of his relatives who live within a maze of apartment housing projects. Everything looks the same to him—yet the sound of Latino music from a wedding draws him in, and soon he finds himself talking to a young woman who later turns out to be from his town in México.

Critics have compared Riker's documentary style to the Italian neorealists who depicted the tragedy of real life. He does not offer any solutions, but his film provides a poignant social commentary rarely seen on the big screen. Each story captures how people vacillate between despair and resolve as a particular tragedy unfolds. Riker's camera captures laborers' decision to continue to work despite the death of a coworker, and he reveals a father's disarming charm in a scene about a homeless father and daughter who live in their car. The film focuses on all the ways immigrants fight against an impersonal system that dehumanizes its members. *La Ciudad* is a challenge to viewers to recognize these real-life scenarios and to acknowledge the powerful struggles for perseverance and hope within the Latino immigrant community. It was named the best film about Latin America made outside the region at the Latin American Film Festival in Cuba in 1999. In 2000 it won an Independent Spirit Award for Best Feature Film.

Further Reading

http://movies.yahoo.com/shop?d=hv&id=1800022864&cf=info&intl=us.
http://www.pbs.org/itvs/thecity.

Cheryl Greene

La Cucaracha. A political cartoon strip created by Lalo Alcaraz, *La Cucaracha* began appearing in the alternative newspaper *L.A. Weekly* in 1992. The first strip that Alcaraz completed for the *L.A. Weekly* portrayed, in Alcaraz's words, "a Mexican-American guy who got so mad he turned into a cockroach." The strip presently revolves around Eddie Lopez, a Mexican American editor of the *East Los Times*, and his pet cockroach. The editorial cartoon examines current events relevant to Latinos, deconstructs cultural *stereotypes, and comments on Latino social and cultural politics, with a humor that renders the commentary enjoyable and memorable. *La Cucaracha* is now syndicated by the Universal Press Syndicate and appears daily in newspapers across the United States. The strip has been honored with Southern California Journalism Awards and multiple awards from the L.A. Press Club. Alcaraz is writing a book titled *Roach against the Machine: 10 Years of* La Cucaracha.

Further Reading

http://www.lacucaracha.com.

William Orchard

La India (1969–). *Salsa singer La India emerged as one of the leading artists of the genre in the 1990s, presenting herself as being within the tradition of Afro-Cuban-derived musics, collaborating with such artists as Eddie *Palmieri, Tito *Puente, and Celia *Cruz and bringing that tradition into the twenty-first century by projecting an image of a strong, independent, bicultural American Latina through her performance and songwriting. Linda Belle "La India" Caballero was born in Río Piedras, Puerto Rico, and was raised in the South Bronx, where her family moved when she was a baby. Her early musical training included formal singing lessons at the age of seven, which did not last long. After a brief modeling career, she became part of New York's nascent Latin *hip-hop scene as a teenager, singing backup for the group TKA and working with producer Jellybean Benitez, who had also worked with Madonna. As a member of TKA, India, as she was then known, had a number of Top 10 hits, including "I Can't Get No Sleep," which went to number one on the dance charts.

After one album of English-language house music, 1990's *Breaking Night*, she changed musical directions, a decision she explained by saying, "I felt pressure to follow in Madonna's footsteps, and I didn't want to base my career on sex, so I began to change how I saw myself." This change resulted in a reexamination of her cultural roots, aided by Eddie Palmieri, who happened to hear the singer at the studio of her then-husband "Little" Louie Vega, a well-known disc jockey and producer in his own right. Palmieri wrote and produced her first Spanish-language album, *Llegó La India, via Eddie Palmieri* (La India Arrived, via Eddie Palmieri, 1992), a collection of hard-driving salsa, also featuring *rumba and *merengue.

In 1994, she and Vega released *Yemanya y Ochún* (Yoruba deities, Yemanya rules over seas and lakes and is mother of all, and Ochún is goddess of love, money, and happiness), an album of dance tunes that utilized Santería chants. That same year saw the release of *Dicen Que Soy* (They Say I am), her first album for RMM (Ralph Mercado Management) Records, a label that was a 1990s version of Fania in that almost all of the biggest *salseros* (salsa musicians) worked for the label and that the label guided the sound and direction of the genre. Produced by Sergio George, the dominant arranger and producer in salsa during the decade, the album was much more commercial than her album with Palmieri, mixing romantic and hard salsa with funk-inspired *timba* and including the hit "Vivir Lo Nuestro" (Live Our Own), a duet with Marc *Anthony. In 1996, La India released *Jazzin'*, a collaboration with Tito Puente and the Count Basie Orchestra, produced by Puente and consisting of Latin-flavored big band arrangements of jazz standards, as well as a remix album, *Mega Mix*.

The following year also saw La India representing her varied musical influences on recordings, appearing on her now ex-husband Vega's Masters at Work project, *Nuyorican Soul*, singing disco and her own Grammy-nominated *Sobre el Fuego* (Over the Fire), which featured the self-penned "Voz de la Experiencia" (Voice of Experience), a duet with Celia Cruz, an artist with whom she is often compared. While the two singers are comparable in that they are considered the top female salsa singers of their respective eras, their performance styles bear little similarity. In this regard, she is much closer to another Cuban *salsaera*, La Lupe, a fact highlighted by the inclusion of several songs originally recorded by the latter on her albums, such as "Que te Pedí" (What Did I Ask You) from La India's next album *Sola* (Alone, 1999), which was heralded by *Billboard* magazine as the best salsa record of the year. The greatest hits collection, *India—The Best* (2001), was followed the next year by *Latin Songbird: Mi Alma y Corazón* (Latin Songbird: My Soul and Heart), on which the singer branched out again, including *boleros, *bachata*, and pop songs alongside salsa. Following a now more common practice with Latino artists, La India recorded both salsa and pop versions of the album, *Sedúceme* (Seduce Me), as well a 2003 English-language single, "Seduce Me Now."

La India continues to be regarded, along with Marc Anthony, as one of salsa's top performers, upholding tradition, on the one hand, and breaking it, on the other, working within other styles of music, even combining them at times. In this way, she represents Latina youth culture at the beginning of the twenty-first century: bilingual, bicultural, respectful, and knowledgeable of these commingling cultures and traditions, yet presenting a strong, independent, feminist image, all of which coalesce in her cigar-smoking persona.

Further Reading

Aparicio, Frances. "La Lupe, La India, and Celia: Toward a Feminist Genealogy of Salsa Music." In *Situating Salsa: Global Markets and Local Meaning in Latin Popular Music*, edited by Lise Waxer. New York: Routledge, 2002.

"La India-Salsa." *Music of Puerto Rico*. http://www.musicofpuertorico.com/en/india.html.

Thomson Gale. "La India." http://www.galegroup.com/free_resources/chh/bio/laindia.htm.

Ramón Versage

La Leyenda Negra. One of the most widespread and deep-seated cultural *stereotypes of the modern world after 1492, *La Leyenda Negra*, or Black Legend, grew out of the subsoil of British foreign policy in the sixteenth and seventeenth centuries of flourishing exploration. The gist of the Black Legend accused Spain's monarchs of such extraordinary brutality and tyranny as rulers and protectors of their nation and colonies that they essentially demonized Spain, her allies, and the colonies of New Spain by creating a fervent anti-Spanish and anti–Roman Catholic loathing through much of Great Britain and northern Europe. By tarnishing Spain's rulers and the Spanish *conquistadores* (conquerors) as brutal tyrants, especially in their treatment of the native peoples of the New World and non-Catholics in general, England (and later the United States) believed its (their) own predatory designs of conquest of Spanish lands and resources in North, Central, and South America could be justified. The Black Legend engendered generations of racist attitudes and prejudice against Spain, Spaniards, the Spanish language, and Catholicism and, by extension, against the descendants of colonial México and Latin America. Eventually the racist iconography of *La Leyenda Negra* was projected to Spanish colonials, thereby extending the damaging seeds of Britain's seventeenth-century foreign policy to negative stereotypes of Mexicans, mestizos, Caribbean peoples, and other Latin Americans.

Scholars generally trace the source of *La Leyenda Negra* to two sources: the political envy and xenophobia of European nations, especially Great Britain, toward their Iberian rival in southern Europe, and the writings of enlightened Spanish priests who advocated for humane treatment of the Native peoples of the Americas in the early centuries of Spain's colonial empire.

Over time the political hostility against Spain's conquests and colonial prosperity infiltrated the chronicles and histories of the "New" World written by other Europeans and led to anti-Spanish and, by extension, anti-Hispanic prejudice. Many scholars agree that this attitude infected American historiography and contributed to some of the white supremacist views underlying the U.S. expansionist policies of Manifest Destiny. The second reason concerns the extensive documentation by Spaniards, mostly research scholars in the priesthood, of conquistador violence and abuses inflicted on the native Mesoamerican peoples. Principal among these sources were the reports of Father Bartolomé De Las Casas, who wrote impassioned pleas against the cruel treatment of the Indians by his countrymen to prevent continued mistreatment. Instead of interpreting these reports as humanitarian advocacy and as an example of enlightened thinking among some Spaniards, Spain's covetous rivals chose to focus on the negative, that is, the Black Legend, as a rationale to plunder Spanish ships, lands, and colonists. A Renaissance version of the twentieth- and twenty-first-century tactic of demonizing the foreign opposition, the Black Legend went unchallenged for hundreds of years until the European empires deteriorated and the Americas were forced to address the complex legacy of conquest, colonization, and colonialism.

Further Reading

Gibson, Charles, ed. *The Black Legend: Anti-Spanish Attitudes in the Old World and the New*. New York: Knopf, 1971.

Jiménez, Alfredo, ed. *Handbook of Hispanic Cultures in the United States: History*. Houston, TX: Arte Público Press, 1994.

Maltby, William S. *The Black Legend in England: The Development of Anti-Spanish Sentiment, 1558–1560*. Durham, NC: Duke University Press, 1968.

Powell, Phillip W. *Tree of Hate: Propaganda and Prejudice Affecting United States Relations with the Hispanic World*. New York: Basic Books, 1971.

Cordelia Chávez Candelaria

La Llorona. The legend of La Llorona, or Weeping Woman, is one of the oldest and most widely known folktales among Mexicans and Mexican Americans. According to many scholars, the kernel story dates to the Conquest of México by the Spaniards in 1521. These scholars view the popular legend a mythic version of the important role of *La Malinche in the pivotal events after Christopher *Columbus's four voyages to the Americas. Still flourishing in the *barrios and borderlands where most Chicanas and *Chicanos and immigrant Mexicans now reside, the legend traditionally operates as a parable to teach young people, especially girls, to behave according to strict moral conventions.

The account of La Llorona varies from region to region, but the core plot normally concerns a poor downtrodden peasant woman who abandons or kills her children in retaliation for their father's unfaithfulness to her. For her actions, she is condemned to suffer the eternal punishment of wandering in grief-stricken agony in search of her abandoned or murdered children. Her

*Zarco Guerrero's sculpture of La Llorona. *Courtesy of Zarco Guerrero.*

name comes from the moanful wailing of her cries of grief as she searches endlessly for her children. Many variants describe her as sexually promiscuous, perhaps as revenge for her husband's infidelities. Sometimes used as a *bruja* (witch tale) to coerce obedience from children who are told she might kidnap them to replace her own destroyed babies, La Llorona has been compared to other mythic characters like Medea, Lilith, Pandora, and similar "madwomen" in the attic of patriarchal traditions.

In the late twentieth century many Chicana/o writers and scholars have reexamined her persistence in *folklore and popular culture, and several have concluded that La Llorona represents an important voice of dissent and folk resistance to unjust power. In this view La Llorona's actions, like those of other resisting women (Antigone, Joan of Arc, *Sor Juana, and others), are considered symbolic of the agency of a tyrannized woman who, instead of subjecting her children to live as victims of classist and sexist cruelties, decides her destiny by choosing merciful death for them and eternal suffering for herself. Whether traditional or modern, the Llorona stories persist as cultural instances of unignorable female complexity that have traces in later portraits of Chicana and Latina girlhood like, for instance, those in María Amparo Ruiz de Burton's novel *The Squatter and the Don* (1885), Helen Hunt Jackson's romance **Ramona* (1888), Katherine Anne Porter's 1939 Miranda stories, Frida *Kahló's self-portraits of the artist as a girl and woman beset by an adulterous husband, and the depictions by many contemporary Chicana/o writers and artists including the work of *Alurista, Rudolfo *Anaya, Yolanda M. *López, Estela *Portillo Trambley, Ana *Castillo, Helena *Viramontes, and Zarco *Guerrero.

Further Reading

Anaya, Rudolfo. *The Legend of La Llorona: A Short Novel.* Berkeley, CA: Tonatiuh–Quinto Sol International, 1984.

Pérez, Domino Renee. "Caminando con La Llorona: Traditional and Contemporary Narratives." In *Chicana Traditions: Continuity and Change*, edited by Norma Cantú and Olga Nájera-Ramírez. Urbana: University of Illinois Press, 2002.

Rebolledo, Tey Diana. *Women Singing in the Snow: A Cultural Analysis of Chicana Literature*. Tucson: University of Arizona Press, 1995.

Cordelia Chávez Candelaria

La Malinche (c. 1502–1527). One of the most legendary of the historic figures directly involved in the Conquest of México (1519–1521), La Malinche's given name is believed to have been Malinalli Tenepal, but she is familiar to many by the name, Doña Marina, given her by Spaniard Hernán Cortés at baptism. The native Mesoamericans called her La Malinche, probably as a linguistic ellision of her Náhuatl name and the imposed Spanish name, and she is the only female associated with the Conquest of Tenochtítlán (i.e., modern-day México) whose name has survived on the historical record. Reported to have been a remarkably intelligent woman gifted with natural linguistic abilities, she was given or assigned by her village chief (*cacique*) to serve Cortés and his men and soon distinguished herself as an interpreter.

Little is known of La Malinche's past, but the Spanish record shows her to have been born a Nahua (called "Aztec" by English speakers) in 1502. When she was a child her stepmother gave her away to another coastal tribe, which, in the sexist custom of the times, gave her to Cortés in 1519 along with a group of other young women. Only a teenager when the Spaniards arrived, she spoke her native Náhuatl and other Mesoamerican dialects and quickly learned Spanish. As a result, the scanty record shows that she served Cortés dutifully as an interpreter, guide, and mistress, eventually bearing him two sons. Because of her amazing role at this remarkable crossroads in history, La Malinche was perhaps the first indigenous "American" to confront on a public stage what the twenty-first century recognizes as the gender, cultural, racial, and class issues and problems of **mestizaje*, cultural identity, bilingual consciousness, and transnationality. That she lived through these landmark events as a girl caught in a global conflict between two historic men, Cortés and the Nahua emperor Motecuhzoma, underscores the patriarchal perception of females of any age as chattel and agents of male power.

Some scholars consider La Malinche as the historical source of the *La Llorona legend. Through a traditional male gaze she appears frequently as a traitor and scapegoat (e.g., the Mexican term for "betrayal" is *malinchismo*). Chicana feminists in the late twentieth century, however, have reclaimed La Malinche's biography as that of heroic woman and girl and credited her for a central (if forced) role in the Western Hemisphere's formation. She appears frequently throughout literary and artistic history in the work of muralists Diego *Rivera and David Alfaro Siqueiros, poets Octavio *Paz and Lucha *Corpi, playwrights Estela *Portillo Trambley and Cherríe

*Moraga, to name only a small sample. La Malinche is believed to have died in 1527 at the age of approximately twenty-five.

Further Reading

Candelaria, Cordelia. "La Malinche, Feminist Prototype." In *Chicana Leadership: the Frontiers Reader*. Yolanda Flores Niemann et al., eds. Lincoln: University of Nebraska Press, 2002, 1–14.

Cordelia Chávez Candelaria

La Vida Loca. The phrase La Vida Loca (The Crazy Life) is used to describe the *barrio- *gang life of urban Chicana/os, especially in cities such as Los Angeles, Chicago, and even New York City. La Vida Loca is a lifestyle with a fast-paced, drug-using and -dealing mind-set and revolves around crime and violence. It arose from the Mexican *Pachuco gangs of the 1930s and 1940s and the poverty and alienation that produced them. In East Los Angeles, many Chicana/o teens often turn to this lifestyle as a result of an inferior or defunct school system and/or *family structure, teen pregnancy, poor housing, few opportunities for professional or educational advancement, general apathy and disenfranchisment, and their own bad choices. People that live La Vida Loca often gather on street corners and in parks and flash gang signs, risking violent retaliation. The general mind-set is that they will wind up either dead or in prison, which only further reinforces these potentially dangerous attitudes. Although La Vida Loca is also a romanticized way of life, many that live the wild life desire their lives to be different and less violent.

Popular cultural manifestations of La Vida Loca include *lowriders, T-shirts, and Chicano rap music, especially Kid Frost (*see* hip-hop and rap), literature, and autobiography, especially Luis *Rodríguez. *La Vida Loca* is also the name of a 1992 mural by Carlos "Wiro" Ruiz found in Los Angeles near MacArthur Park. In terms of *film, the issues surrounding La Vida Loca are best represented in Edward James *Olmos's **American Me* (1992), Taylor Hackford's **Bound by Honor* (1993), and the 1993 film **Mi Vida Loca*, written and directed by Allison Anders. Puerto Rican pop singer Ricky *Martin further popularized and, some think, glamorized the expression with the 1999 single "Livin' La Vida Loca" from his self-titled English debut album.

Further Reading

Rodríguez, Joseph. *Gang Life in East L.A.* http://www.zonezero.com/exposiciones/fotografos/rodriguez/default.htm.

Rodríguez, Luis J. *Always Running: La Vida Loca, Gang Days in L.A.* New York: Touchstone Press, 1993.

Armando Quintero, Jr.

Las Doce Verdades. As a folk custom Las Doce Verdades del mundo (The Twelve Truths of the world) is a riddle-and-answer interplay done among Chicana/os in the Southwest. The practice is part of a Christian doctrinal guide and can be performed as a narrated tale, as a recited prayer, or as a proposed adivinanza (riddle). Most of the time, *Las Doce Verdades* occurs in the context of recited answers to a test affecting a person's life, as in the African American "dozens" exchanges. It is also a powerful prayer, sometimes used as an exorcism or superstitious prayer, and has even been described as a popular witches' prayer. The question "Of the twelve truths of the world, tell me one?" is the first to be asked, followed by the respondent's answer. Then a second question is asked: "Tell me two?" The questioning continues in this manner until arriving at the twelfth question. The character asking the questions is usually the devil or a judging person. The answers are religious, pertaining to the life of Jesus Christ, the Catholic Church, and the Bible. Versions of this game have been identified in México, Spain, Portugal, Italy, France, Germany, and South America as well as in the American Southwest states of New Mexico and Texas.

Further Reading

Castro, Rafaela G. *Chicano Folklore: A Guide to the Folktales, Traditions, Rituals and Religious Practices of Mexican Americans.* New York: Oxford University Press, 2001.

Espinosa, Aurelio M. *The Folklore of Spain in the American Southwest: Traditional Spanish Folk Literature in Northern New Mexico and Southern Colorado.* Norman: University of Oklahoma Press, 1985.

Mónica Saldaña

"Las Mañanitas." "Las Mañanitas" (literally the "little [or early] hours of the morning") refers to a host of Mexican songs meant to be sung at *holidays and fiestas (parties) or *serenatas* (serenades). Often sung any time after the middle of the night and into the early morning, these serenades may be for a birthday, for a saint's day, for an anniversary, for Nuestra Señora de Guadalupe (Our Lady of Guadalupe), or for other occasions.

In the United States the music and *letras* (lyrics) of two different *canciones mañanitas* (morning songs) are often mixed together: "Las Mañanitas del Rey David" (The Morning Song of King David), more often in the United States called "Las Mañanitas Mexicanas" (Mexican Morning Song), and "Las Mañanitas Tapatías" (The Guadalajaran Morning Song). There are many additional songs called *mañanitas* in México with a variety of texts, often dedicated to the Virgin. One called "Mañanitas de Jalisco" (The Morning Song of Jalisco) has words very similar to that of "Las Mañanitas Tapatías."

Here is one version of the "combined" *mañanitas*, with the first two verses from the slow, dignified "Las Mañanitas del Rey David" and the rest from the faster "Las Mañanitas Tapatías" (followed by a paraphrased translation). There are, of course, many more verses and different versions of these two songs. While most recordings and the best Mexican *mariachis will perform the song in a fashion similar to the following, if one simply requests "Las Mañanitas," most groups will play only the faster song.

Las Mañanitas

Estas son las mañanitas
Que cantaba el Rey David,
A las muchachas bonitas
Se las cantaba así:

Despierta, mi bien despierta
Mira, que ya amaneció;
Ya los pajaritos cantan,
La luna se metió.

[Música]

Qué linda está la mañana
En que vengo a saludarte
Venimos todos con gusto
Y placer a felicitarte.

El día en que tu naciste
Nacieron todas las flores
En la pila del bautismo
Cantaron los ruiseñores.

The Morning Song

This is the morning song
Once sung by King David,
To all of the pretty ladies;
This is how he sang to them:

Wake up my dear one, wake up
Look it is already dawn;
And the little birds already sing,
The moon has already set.

[Often the faster music is played here as an interlude]
How lovely is the morning
As we come to greet you
We all come with delight
To give you our congratulations.

On the day of your birth
All the flowers were born,
At the baptismal font
The nightingales sang to you.

[second verse]

Ya viene amaneciendo
La luz del día nos dió

Levántate de mañana
Mira que ya amaneció.

[Música]

Quisiera ser un San Juan
Quisiera ser un San Pedro
Y venirte a saludar
Con la música del cielo.

Volaron cuatro palomas,
Por toditas las ciudades,
Hoy por ser día de tu santo
[para cumpleaños y día de santos]
o [Hoy por ser día de las madres]
Te deseamos felicidades.

Con jasmines y flores
Hoy te vengo a saludar
Hoy por ser día de tu santo (de las madres)
Te venimos a cantar.

Already the dawn is coming
And the light of day is shining.
Get up this morning
The sun has already risen.
[Music interlude]

I'd like to be Saint John
I'd like to be Saint Peter
To come and greet you
With the music of the heavens.

Four doves flew
Throughout all the cities,
Today is your birthday
[used for birthday & Saint's day] or [for Mother's day, May 10]
And we wish you happiness.

With jasmine and flowers
Today I come to greet you,
Today because it is your birthday [Mother's day]
We come to sing to you.

Like the familiar "Happy Birthday to You" song, there are many recordings of *mañanitas* by famous Mexican singers. Pedro Infante, Javier Solís, Mariachi Vargas de Tecalitlán, Mariachi México de Pepe Villa, and lesser known groups have recorded the *mañanitas para La Virgen* (songs for Our Lady of Guadalupe), often in *norteño* or **banda* ensembles. The name and concept of *mañanitas* is so ingrained into Mexican and Chicana/o lifeways that hotels, restaurants, and other establishments are often named "Las Mañanitas." In Phoenix, radio station KIFN–AM, calls its morning talk/music show "Las Mañanitas." Many *cancioneros* (song books) usually include one or more versions of "Las Mañanitas," often giving the guitar chords to accompany the melody.

Further Reading

Loeffler, Jack et al. *La Música de los Viejitos: Hispanic Folk Music of the Río Grande del Norte*. Albuquerque: University of New Mexico Press, 1999.

http://ingeb.org/songs/lasmanan.html.

J. Richard Haefer

Las Posadas. *See* Posadas, Las.

Latin American Musical Instruments. Latina/o culture is rich in music that uses various types of musical instruments to express, often without language or words, the passions, emotions, ideals, and stories of diverse groups of people. Many instruments are played in an attempt to imitate sounds heard in nature, while others strive to imitate nonverbal human sounds like the rhythms of the heartbeat and the tones of the human voice. Still other instruments were designed to attempt to echo such natural sounds as sea waves, wind, and rain. Heard in a range of different musical genres and cultural contexts throughout the United States and the Americas, these instruments are categorized according to ethnicity and region of origin, but it is important to emphasize that they are not strictly defined by (or confined to) specific ethnic groups or geographical areas. The following sampling is intended as an introduction to the topic, not as an exhaustive treatment of what is actually a much broader, complex topic.

Mexican American/Chicana/o

The **bajo sexto** is the principal bass instrument of accompaniment in Tex-Mex or *Tejano (*conjunto*) and *norteño* musical styles. A twelve-string guitar originating in Spain, the bajo sexto was introduced in the early twentieth century, around the time when *conjunto* began to establish itself stylistically as a genuine folk or traditional music. Originally, *conjunto* music was an accordion-based style, consisting of a guitar or the bajo sexto along with a *tambora de rancho*, a drum made of goatskin heads, wire rims, and mallets, and reinforced with *henequen* (twine made from agave fiber). The accordion was introduced to Texas-Mexican music around the middle of the nineteenth century by Polish, German, and Czech immigrants who settled near San Antonio in the 1840s. The bajo sexto and *tambora* appear to have been introduced to *conjunto* about the same time and have now become established elements of the grassroots musical style.

The ***guitarrón*** is the acoustic bass guitar found in many types of modern Mexican music such as *mariachi or *trío*. It is significantly different from other bass instruments due to its size and shape, possessing a large body topped by a comparatively short neck. The broad top of the body is usually made from spruce or *tacote*, while the back and sides are of walnut, cedar, or mahogany. The deep sides have a slight V shape, as does the back of the instrument. This results in a high ridged contour that contributes to the *guitarrón*'s unique body shape and deep cavity that helps to produce a unique loud, full, and resonating tone. Despite the large, slightly ungainly size of the instrument, it is very light in weight. The strings are arranged to facilitate playing in octaves, as is the case when the instrument is used in mariachi. Plucking two strings simultaneously in octaves also increases the sound. The short neck is fretless, requiring the performer to *hear* the correct position of the left hand on the strings to produce the appropriate pitches. Due to the high action and stiff tension of the strings, *guitarroneros* (guitarrón players) must develop good muscle tension and dexterity on both hands. *Guitarróneros* learn to use specific scale patterns to move between chord changes, thus providing the harmonic bass to ensembles such as the mariachi. The *guitarrón* replaced the *arpa* (harp) as the bass instrument in mariachi late in the nineteenth century and is sometimes found as the bass in trios as well.

A *huéhuetl* is a large cylindrical shaped, single-headed (membranophone) drum that has three feet and an animal skin surface, and is often inscribed with carving. The instrument is referred to in the Náhuatl language of México and translates as *la voz de los viejos* (the voice of the elders), thereby echoing one of the primal functions of musical instruments, that is, to imitate nonverbal human sounds like the tones of the human voice. After the arrival of *Columbus, the *huéhuetl* was one of the principal instruments used in Aztec dances and rituals. The *huéhuetl* is even considered to be a semideity, along with several other Aztec instruments such as the *teponaztle*, a hollowed-out log with H-shaped slits that create two tongues that are struck with rubber-coated sticks, like a wood block. A pre-Columbian instrument, *huéhuetl*s have been found in archeological sites throughout Mesoamerica.

A ***jarana*** is a small guitar used in *musica jarocha*. It comes in several sizes, with the smallest *jarana* known as the *mosquito* (twenty-one inches long with five strings) and the largest size, known as *jarana tercera* (third jarana), approaching thirty-four inches in length. The *requinto jarocho* is also known as *rejona jabalina* (wild boar, evoked by its sound), or *guitarra de son*, and has four strings that are plucked by a four-inch pick carved from cowhorn. Here again, the *jarana* serves a primal function in its echoing of sounds heard in nature—that is, the wild boar—and mirroring the body shape of a mosquito.

The term ***requinto*** literally refers to a small, higher-pitched version of a *requinto guitarra* (little guitar), and is found throughout Spain, Portugal, and Latin America in various guises, with six to twelve strings. It is used primarily in the *trio romántico* and other small ensembles as the main melodic instrument, while the harmony is provided by one or two *guitarras* (guitars) and often a bass instrument like a *guitarrón* (bass guitar). The requinto often is used to play *serenatas* (serenades) and in *tríos* in restaurants. The body, approximately 20 percent smaller than a normal guitar, usually has a slightly deeper sound box than a guitar and has a cutaway in the lower body that allows the performer to more easily move up the strings to the end of the fretboard. Because of the cutaway some people term this instrument a *guitarra curva*. The neck is fretted all the way to the sound hole on the face of the instrument. Although normally played by plucking the melody, sometimes the strings are played *rasgueado* (scratched), depending upon the type of composition being performed. The center of Mexican *guitarra* and *requinto* manufacturing for more than 200 years is the village of Paracho, Michoacán, but builders such as the Pimentel family of Albuquerque, New Mexico, have gained respected reputations as makers of fine instruments in the United States.

Vihuela refers to a five-string Mexican folk instrument, although details of its regional origin are not known. The term *vihuela* was used during colonial times and referred to a similar string instrument used by the educated and elite aristocracy. The Mexican *vihuela* emerged in Western México and became central to early mariachi ensembles in the nineteenth century. Five-string folk guitars are common throughout central México, but the *vihuela* is most similar to the Spanish guitar. The wood used for the body is a light cedar common in the lowlands of the central and southern regions. The top of the sound box is made of *tacote*, a light-colored, resistant, and malleable regional wood. The *vihuela* is constructed in a round figure-eight shape and is about thirty-one inches in length. Much shorter than a guitar (about forty inches), its width (about twelve inches) is also narrower than a guitar (about fifteen inches). The back of the sound box is similar to the *guitarrón* with a distinct curve that makes the sound box considerably deeper than the guitar (about six inches and four inches deep, respectively). The size of sound boxes varies, and some manufacturers make different sizes according to the varying needs of their customers.

By far, Roberto Morales is the best-known *vihuela* maker in México, and his instruments are analogous to Stradivarius violins. In the United States, Jerry Starr of Albuquerque, New Mexico, produces fine instruments. All five strings are nylon, and the tunings are similar to the five highest-pitched strings of the guitar. The *vihuela* uses a re-entrant tuning; that is, the second string falls a minor sixth from the third string instead of rising a major third. The range of the *vihuela*'s open strings is confined to less than an octave. The neck of the *vihuela* is considerably shorter than the guitar, and the vibrating portion of the *vihuela* string is likewise shorter and does not vibrate as long when plucked. This yields a more percussive sound and gives the *vihuela* a rhythmic and chordal foundation within the mariachi ensemble. The *vihuela* is held in front of the body and is supported by a strap that hangs from the neck pressed against the rib cage. The left hand fingers the chords on the neck while the right hand strikes the strings. Individual strings are never plucked to produce a melody, and the intricate strokes are varied and complex. There is an entire repertoire of strokes used to produce different rhythmic patterns. The rhythmic core of the mariachi consists of the *vihuela*, guitar, and *guitarrón* and must be coordinated and precise. The rhythmic and harmonic patterns must be interlocked with the bass.

Although produced by the human voice, the ***grito*** functions as an instrumental accompaniment. It is a type of shout or sung exclamation, peculiar to particular genres of Iberian American folk and popular musics throughout Latin America, the Caribbean, México, and North America. The characteristic *grito* creates a sense of interactive excitement and provides a festive atmosphere for high-spirited performances of dance and concert musics such as in mariachi; hence the *grito* illustrates the point that the musical voice itself is properly regarded as an instrument in its own right.

Afro-Caribbean and Latin American

Agogó, a Brazilian percussion instrument with origins in West Africa, is important in contemporary American music because it is an essential part of the very popular sound known as "bossa-jazz." The original purpose of the *agogó*, similar to the *batá* drums of Cuba, was to be used in Afro-Brazilian religious ceremonies called *candomble*. The instrument is constructed from a two-note, clapperless double-bell attached to a curved piece of metal and is struck with a stick. Introduced to the United States during the 1970s by Brazilian musicians like *Airto, the *agogó* is heard in such Brazilian rhythms as the *baio* and the *Bossa Nova, which combined with American jazz to create the hybrid form bossa-jazz.

***Batá* drums** are Afro-Cuban, double-headed ritual drums used in the religious practice of *Santería* (Afro-Caribbean spiritual practice), widely practiced among Latinos in the United States, Puerto Rico, and Cuba. Derived from earlier drums of the West African Yoruba tribe, these drums have maintained their original hourglass shape in the Caribbean. *Batá* drums are used in *Santería* (*see* *Healing Practices, Spirituality, and Religious Beliefs) to invoke the *orishas*, or Yoruba gods who preside over the religious ceremony and are believed to be sacred from the moment they are created. *Batá* drums, which have been baptized into the setting of *Santería*, are called *aña*, and may only be played by those who have undergone a special initiation. Unbaptized *batá* drums, called *aberikula*, may be played by anyone. The ritualistic songs played on the *batá* drums are called *toques para los santos*, or beats for the saints, and are played during feasts of initiation, commemoration, weddings, and other such events.

Introduced to the United States in the 1970s by Brazilian musicians, the ***berimbau*** is of Congo-Angolan origin and is classified as a Brazilian percussion instrument. It is made in the shape of a bow and used to accompany the martial art known as *capoira*. A metal string is tied to each end of a long wooden stick, which has an open gourd attached to it. Sound is produced when the metal string is struck with a small stick. The musician can change the pitch by opening or closing the open gourd against his or her chest. Among the more influential musicians to use this instrument was Airto, who combined this and other traditional Brazilian instruments in the evolution of bossa-jazz.

A **bongó** is a small double-headed drum (membranophone) which is played while resting on the seated *bongocero*'s (percussionist's) calves. An integral member of the percussion section in *salsa bands, the bongó's heads are tuned in fourths. Bongos are used in several varieties of Cuban music, including quartets and sextets and in *sones* [*see* **Son*]. In early string-based groups, the bongó is typically played ad lib, while other percussion instruments are played counterpoint to the main rhythms. Basic toque (rhythm) for bongó is called *martillo* (hammer) and sounds as follows: Dicka-docka-dicka-ducka.

Cencerro is the Spanish term for a metal cowbell that is hung around a cow's neck to aid farmers in locating it. During the Colonial period (1533–1825) *cencerros* were used in llama caravans by *llameros* (llama herders), on their journeys to exchange salt for food. Today, in villages like Taraco, located in the Huancavelica highlands of Perú, llama herders continue to use llama caravans to trade with the peasants of the lowlands. A *cencerro* is tied around the neck of the llama that will lead the pack on the journey to the valley below. The purpose of placing a *cencerro* on the lead llama is to ensure that the llamas will follow one another in a single file and keep them from grazing along the way. In other areas of South America, the Quéchua (Indians) of Imbabura and Pichincha from Ecuador celebrate *La Fiesta de San Pedro* (Celebration of Saint Pedro) on June 29. The dancers wear chains of typically twelve *cencerros* tied to their leather capes, ringing as they dance and play side-blown flutes. In another celebration in Spain on February 2, dancers wear *cencerros* mounted on their backs during the *Fiesta de los Diablos* (Celebration of the Devils). The *cencerro* in this regard is used as a musical item pinned to the body of a dancer during celebrations. The *bongoceros* (bongo drum players) and the *timbaleros* (percussionists), Afro-Cuban soldiers who played military drums and later became musicians, turned the cencerro into a musical instrument. These bells can be heard playing in music like salsa, *rumba, and other styles of Cuban music. As the *cencerro* was incorporated into the musical performance, it became modernized and is now manufactured with the care that is reserved for musical instruments and purchased by consumers as a cowbell, supplied with a wooden striker. The *cencerro* as a percussion instrument (idiophone) makes several different tones, depending on where it is struck, and its sound is easy to detect in a salsa band. The *bongocero* plays a small pair of drums between the legs and the *cencerro*, or hand bell entrusted to him, is played during the *Montuno* (chorus section) of an arrangement. In the Cuban rumba music, the *Palito* player (stick player) plays the *cencerro* that is mounted on the drums. The *timbaleros* fix *cencerros* to a pair of tunable metal drums, which are mounted on a stand along with other accessories like woodblocks and a cymbal.

A symbol of South American music culture, the **charango** is an Andean string instrument (chordophone) that is heard around the globe and throughout the United States as one of the principal instruments in Andean ensembles. It is a descendant of the *Vihuela de Mano* (handheld vihuela), or Spanish guitar, introduced to the Americas during the Spanish conquest during the sixteenth century. It comes in three sizes: small, medium, and large. The etymology of the term during colonial times referred to music played on acoustic instruments made of metal by a *charangero* (meaning someone of questionable character and low morals).

Charango tuning varies from region to region. The sound box may be made of an armadillo shell or wood and the neck is fretted. The face includes a bridge and a mouth or sound hole. The strings are attached to the bridge and adjusted with tuning pegs. Armadillo shells have a tendency to warp with age and their resonance is not as good as those made of wood. A distant American cousin to the Spanish guitar, the charango has existed in its modern form since the eighteenth century and was probably constructed small for easy portability. The charango may be strummed with the hand or with a plectrum (pick) and is used as a harmonic and rhythmic accompaniment or plucked as a melodic instrument. Although there are some similarities with the guitar, its rhythmic complexity is more typical of flamenco than classical guitar music.

Clave refers to an offbeat 3/2 or 2/3 rhythmic pattern, which is sustained over two bars and serves as the basis of all Cuban music. As a basic rhythmic foundation, every element and improvisation must conform to the clave pattern. Clave is an African-derived pattern with similar rhythmic patterns heard in other Afro-Latin musics. There seems to be a similar parallel with the two-bar bass patterns in modern black music. The common 3/2 Cuban clave varies in accentuation and likewise with the rhythm being played, while the 2/3 reverse clave, although less common, is used in *guaguancó*.

Claves are twin strikers of resonant wood heard in salsa and in early Cuban music (*see* *Spanish Caribbean Music). Claves players usually sustain the basic clave pattern described above, which is implied rather than stated by modern bands. Many variants of claves exist throughout Latin America and the United States.

Conga drums, also known as Congolese drums, originated in Afro-Cuban cults and typically serve as the predominant percussion instrument in salsa rhythm sections. Arsenio Rodríguez is said to have introduced it to the *conjuntos* (ensembles) and *Machito's Afro-Cubans were the first to use it on New York bandstands. There are several types of congas, including the small *quinto*, the midsized conga, and the large *tumbadora*. Expert percussionists realize the conga's musical capabilities, which include great varieties of timbre (sound or tone). Its acoustic and coloristic possibilities are the result of the various ways the head may be struck or rubbed. When the instrument is raised above the ground it is held in place between the knees of the musician. A conga player is called a *conguero* or *congacero*.

A **cuatro** is a small, ten-stringed guitar which comes in many variations and is played in Spain, Latin America, and the Caribbean. The cuatro is one of the principal instruments in Puerto Rican folk music known as *jibaro* or country music. *Jibaros* reside in the mountains of Puerto Rico and farm the land. Their folk music is the most Hispanic found throughout the Caribbean islands in keeping with the island's history (see History, Puerto Rican). The style is typically string-based and uses traditional Spanish forms like the ten-line **décima* verses and the singing contest known as *trovo*. Though various Puerto Rican salsa singers had used occasional jibaro inflections, Willie *Colón brought the style into salsa by hiring cuatro artist Yomo Toro on the hit *La Murga* for the Christmas album *Asalto Navideño* in 1971.

A **güayo** is an idiophone made of metal, a gourd, or cowhorn scraper and often referred to as a güiro. Among Puerto Ricans, it is constructed from a notched gourd and played with a stick. Poor players produce a steady ratchet-like sound, while skilled ones provide endless, crisp counter-rhythms against the rest of the percussion section. Güiros and other idiophones, like maracas, are typically played by a vocalist. In the Dominican Republic it is

Latina/o music is enhanced by handheld musical instruments that come in a variety of sizes and shapes as in these gourd rattles and clay whistle. *Photo by Emmanuel Sánchez Carballo.*

also called a güira, but it is usually made of metal and played with a metal fork, rendering a harsher sound. The metal güira is rarely heard in salsa.

Maracas are very common percussion instruments that have become a familiar feature of marketing to tourists in México and other parts of Latin America. Made from gourds and containing dry beans or pebbles that make a rattling sound when shaken, maracas provide a rhythmic layer and color for several popular Latina/o styles of music, including salsa, *Latin jazz, *mambo, and *cha cha cha. This instrument is very similar to an infant's rattle and is often seen as a symbol for Latinas/os throughout the Caribbean, México, and Latin and North America. It is a very simple instrument, which was derived from similar rattles of the original Native American inhabitants of the Caribbean Islands, including the Carib Indians.

Timbales are Latin percussion instruments consisting of two small metal drums on a stand, often accompanied by two tuned cowbells, a cymbal, and sometimes other percussion essentials found in many Latina/o musical ensembles in the United States and throughout the Caribbean and Latin America. Descendant of the small military dance and concert band drums, the timbales were originally used only in **charangas* and *orquestas tipicas*, but they gained widespread popularity by the 1940s. Played with sticks, the timbale sounds are created by striking all areas of the drum such as the head, rims, and the sides, and are enhanced by the added cowbell, cymbals, and other optional instruments. One of the standard beats is the *abanico*, which is played on the timbales and consists of a rimshot-roll-rimshot combination. Some of the most famous Latin percussionists in the United States play the timbales, including Tito *Puente and *Sheila E.

The ***tres*** (three) is a stringed instrument fashioned from the Spanish guitar and consists of three double pairs of strings, each tuned with a pitch and an octave. This Cuban instrument is made smaller than the traditional Spanish guitar and differs in the manner the strings are tuned. To play counterpoint to the main melodies performed by a singer, the strings of this guitar are plucked. The typical sound of most Cuban music is produced by the *tres*, along with other plucked instruments. **Guajira* music and the Afro-Cuban *septetos* use the *tres* as the foundation in their music, and it is known as the signature instrument of the Cuban *son*. Arsenio Rodriguez, an excellent player of the *tres*, established this instrument as an essential part of the Cuban *conjunto*. Today the *tres*, with its particular sound, a little shrillish, like the mandolin, is played mainly in traditional orchestras.

The ***tambora*** is often referred to as the *merengue drum because it is essential in performing authentic merengue music. Originating from the Dominican Republic, the tambora is a double-headed drum, which is laid across the performer's lap, where each of the two skins is facing each of the performer's hands. Played with a single drum stick, the player uses his or her other hand on the opposite side of the drum that is not being hit with the drum stick to dampen the sound, creating different tones. Like the other instruments that combine to give Latin American musics their distinctive internationally popular sound, the *tambora* reflects the hybrid **mestizaje* of the culture(s) that produced them.

Further Readings:

Amira, John, and Steven Cornelius. *The Music of Santería: Traditional Rhythms of the Batá Drums*. Crown Point, IN: White Cliffs Media Company, 1992.

Manuel, Peter, Kenneth Bilby, and Michael Largey. *Caribbean Currents: Caribbean Music from Rumba to Reggae*. Philadelphia: Temple University Press, 1995.

Peña, Manuel. *The Texas-Mexican Conjunto: History of a Working Class Music*. Austin: University of Texas Press, 1985.

Roberts, John Storm. *The Latin Tinge: The Impact of Latin American Music on the United States*. 2nd ed. New York: Oxford University Press, 1999.

Rodríguez, Alén, and Olavo de Jesús. *From Afrocuban Music to Salsa*. Berlin: Piranha, 1998.

Sheehy, Daniel. "Popular Mexican Musical Traditions: The *Mariachi* of West Mexico and the *Conjunto Jarocho* of Veracruz." In *Music and Cultures of Latin America*, edited by John Shecter. New York: Shirmer Books, 1999.

Robert Chew, J. Javier Enríquez, Peter J. García,
J. Richard Haefer, Rose Marie Soto, and George Yáñez

Latin American Musicology. *Organology* is the study of musical instruments from every musical tradition in the world, including North and South America and the musical cultures of these regions and the diffusion and distribution from one region to another. It includes the present categories of classical or art music, folk or ethnic music, and Western and non-Western music. Aspects of the study consider (1) inventory, terminology, classification; (2) description of an instrument's construction, shape, sound/musical production, and playing technique; and (3) examination of sociocultural factors and beliefs about an instrument's use, the status of the musicians who play it, and its symbolism and aesthetics. In addition, the field of study takes into consideration the history, origin, and relationship of existent and obsolete instruments, information culled from iconographic sources. Once it is determined which sound-producing objects actually produce music in a particular culture, the fundamental concern of organology is classification.

The objectives and methods of instrument classification for theoreticians and practitioners differ in complementary ways. Practitioners seek to analyze collections of musical instruments to create large categories for virtually all instruments, Western and non-Western, ancient and modern. Their aim is to devise a conceptual tool with practical application. One of the difficulties in trying to categorize instruments based largely on material structure is that many of the instruments do not fit into fixed categories. Theoreticians, on the other hand, tend to take a holistic approach, whereby they consider acoustics, scales, musicians, and performance practice. They try to blend together historical and genetic data with sociocultural factors and beliefs that determine the function of an instrument, with the view toward developing a schematic model for analysis nowadays aided by computers.

Despite the shortcomings of any system of classification, those developed by German theoreticians Erich Moritz von Hornbostel and Curt Sachs in the 1910s have become the most common in contemporary organology. The Hornbostel-Sachs paradigm is based on the assumption that the underlying principle of classification is related to the "vibrating material" itself, or the visible form of the instrument, a concept developed in several civilizations outside the West including ancient China, India, the contemporary Bassari of Senegal, and the Are'are of the Solomon Islands. Nevertheless, although public collections of instruments were established around 1850 in Austria and Germany, the systematic classification, or ethnoclassification, of instruments representative of their native or original homelands was established internationally only in the mid-twentieth century.

Following the earlier classification of instruments by Victor Charles Mahillon at the Musee Instrumental of the Conservatoire Royal du Musique in Brussels into four broad categories, Hornbostel and Sachs in 1914 articulated these categories as (1) chordophones (stringed instruments), (2) aerophones (wind instruments), (3) membranophones (percussion instruments having a skin stretched across a frame), and (4) idiophones (instruments that vibrate themselves to cause sound). They subdivided and ranked the data according to the Dewey decimal system. Notably, categorizing idiophones as distinct from membranophones (as in ancient Indian theory) created a category of instruments of any material in which sound is produced in various ways by rattling, shaking, rubbing, or striking, giving them status as actual musical instruments.

In Latin America and the United States, the task of classification of instruments is highly complex and problematic, due to factors such as the sheer size of the culture area, its layers of indigenous, colonial, and mestizo (mixed race) history, and its highly stratified social organization, which illuminates to a large extent its diverse musical expressions. These musical expressions function as symbols of class, ethnic, and regional identity in both urban and rural contexts. Although an important aspect of the study of Latin American musics and musical instruments examines those in antiquity, the absence of an emic (internal or native) perspective and observational contexts makes this problematic. Two streams of scholarship attempt to deal with this. One is music iconology, the depiction of musical instruments and performance in pottery, wood, codices, and so on. Another is archeomusicology, the study of music through archaeology. Both approaches are speculative and tend to raise questions more than find answers.

Two thousand languages have been spoken since 1492 by Native Central and South Americans. Estimating that about three musical instruments per language group exist, then at least 6,000 instrument names also exist. In addition, Spanish, Portuguese, Africans, and other foreigners who arrived after the Encounter (1492) introduced probably 1,000 more instrument names. Many have disappeared with the disappearance of native cultures, assimilation, and modernization. However, enough remain that there is a need for a classification system and taxonomy with regard to the distribution, symbolism, and use of musical instruments. Karl Gustav Izikowitz made an early attempt to create a bibliography that lists and analyzes all instruments of Native South America, (1970 [1935]). Other such studies have focused specifically on the countries of Argentina, Bolivia, Colombia, Ecuador, Guyana, Perú, and Venezuela.

Two broad types of instrument classification exist in Latin America, namely, indigenous systems based to a large extent on performance context, and ethnomusicological categories developed as extensions of the Hornbostel and Sachs paradigm. The second framework deals with the tangible qualities of instruments and their physical construction, as the following descriptions illustrate.

Idiophones. These include Native American dancers' bells worn on their ankles or used to decorate their costumes (such as the *cencerro* in the Peruvian highlands); *maracas* (gourd shakers); rhythm sticks such as claves; triangles; steel drums; marimbas; the two-note clapperless double metal bell *agogo* in Afro-Brazilian music; and scrapers such as Afro-Caribbean *güayos* or güiros made of metal, gourd, or cowhorn.

Membranophones. These include various hand drums, such as the Afro-Caribbean batá drums, bongos, and congas (with their variants, the small *quinto*, the mid-sized conga, and the large *tumbadora*); as well as ancient ones, for example, the Aztecs' *huehuetl* (upright cylindrical drum) and the Mayans' *tunkul* (slit drum).

Aerophones. The largest and most complex category in the Americas, these consist of various subgroups, such as various Native American flutes (often categorized as edge aerophones, e.g., the *quena* of the Peruvian highlands), trumpet types (or lip-concussion aerophones, e.g., *quepas* of the Peruvian highlands), reed instruments (clarinet and oboe types classed as single and double-reed concussion aerophones, e.g., the Iberian-derived, now indigenized oboe type *chirimia*), panpipes (e.g., the one-part *antaras* of the Quechua or the *siku* pairs of the Aymara), and globular flutes (ocarina).

Chordophones. Stringed instruments derived from Iberian prototypes, these include various types of guitars (e.g., the Mexican and Texas-Mexican *guitarra*, *guitarra de golpe*, *vihuela*, and *bajo sexto*, the small *requinto*, *tres*, and *quatro*, and the large bass *guitarron*), harps, mandolins, and violins.

Electrophones. Electronic sounder instruments are used in contemporary and popular music, such as synthesizers and computer-generated devices.

Corpophones. Body sounders refer to sound produced by body parts, for example, hand claps, fingers snaps, slapping arms or buttocks (exclusive of vocalization).

Notably, two important instruments do not fit comfortably in this classification system. One is the Brazilian *berimbau*, of Congo-Angolan origin and today played by both Brazilian Indians and Afro-Brazilians. This has been classified as a percussion instrument, yet its bow-shaped body attached to an open gourd has a metal string stretched across it, which, when tightened or loosened while struck, produces different pitches. The other is the accordion (both button and keyboard), a Central European import played in various types of urban and semiurban mestizo ensembles throughout Latin America and in Hispanic/Mexican American communities in the United States and Canada (particularly the Texas-Mexican *conjunto*).

Gerard Béhague's argument that performance context is a factor of prime importance particularly in the classification of indigenous Amerindian instruments of Latin America likely worked as a catalyst for subsequent research resulting in holistic types of taxonomies, two of them elaborated below. Additionally, Béhague's observation that certain Indian cultures are "bimusical" (practicing and maintaining to various degrees both the musical styles and contexts of their ancestors and those of their mestizo neighbors) not only suggests but also problematizes a criterion for instrument classification based on the binary of sacred/ritualistic versus secular. (For example, musical instruments used in activities such as shamanistic rituals are considered sacred and thus are separated from those used in secular performance, e.g., batá drums, *antara* panpipes, etc.)

One taxonomy considers distribution and grouping based on symbolism and the iconic qualities of the instruments. The following concepts describe some of the emic (insider or native) characteristics, which are often mutually inclusive.

1. Ideal qualities of sound, for example, the high-pitched whistle of flutes, symbolizing female energy, and the low-pitched buzz in single-reed aerophones, symbolic of the male.
2. Physical duality as iconic of complementarity, for example, male and female pairs of instruments such as those in the *siku* panpipes of the Peruvian and Bolivian Aymara that require two people to play each half of the instrument together.
3. Extramusical power, for example, that attributed to instruments alluding to animals, such as the Quéchua solo panpipe *ayarachi*, which symbolizes the condor; as well as to (super) humans, such as phallic/fertility power of the *kena* flutes of Peru or the *antara* panpipes, often made from human bones during the time of the Incas.

4. The need for communication, for example, demonstrated in the use of the *clarin*, a long, side-blown trumpet type that leads the *minga*, a Peruvian festival that musically enacts communal work.
5. Instruments appropriated from agents of foreign powers, for example, the *chirimia* of Colombia, Ecuador, Guatemala, México, and Perú, a shawm (oboe type) introduced by the Spanish colonists and later indigenized by music makers in the countries mentioned; European-style trumpets and drums introduced by the Portuguese, Spanish, and *criollos* in their colonies as military instruments replacing the indigenous pipe and tabor (flute and drum) ensemble; the late nineteenth- and early-twentieth-century introduction of German-influenced wind and brass band instruments, co-opted by people of newly independent Latin American countries for use in processions and parades during festivals and military rituals; and the now-widespread accordion (*acordeon*), introduced by German immigrants in the early 1900s.

The second taxonomy is concerned with the classification of instruments in Latin America according to three types of distribution:

1. Locations of cultures that use them presently, that is, African-derived membranophones around the coast from Rio de Janeiro (Brazil), stretching north to the Caribbean coast of Colombia, north through Belize, south from Colombia to coastal Ecuador into the Caribbean basin (e.g., the *rum* drum used in the Afro-Brazilian Candomble rituals of the Bahia province in Brazil, batá drums used in the Afro-Caribbean Santería rituals in Cuba), and Spanish- or Portuguese-derived guitar types (mentioned above).
2. Use of instruments by people who did not originally use them but were influenced by the original users in their area, for example, the marimba played by Guatemalan Mayans who learned from Africans.
3. Importation of instruments in popular music, for example, the *charango* in Chile by performers of the political *nueva canción* in the 1960s and 1970s such as Inti Illimani and Chilean rock groups of the 1990s such as Los Javas; the Andean panpipes *zampoñas* first introduced into North American pop music in the late 1960s by Paul Simon and now a staple of the "Pan-Andean sound."

As with the study of popular culture generally, the study of Latin musics has evolved to better account for the many layers and strands of New and Old World influences.

Further Reading

Béhague, Gerard. "Folk and Traditional Music of Latin America: General Prospect and Research Problems." *The World of Music* 24.2 (1982): 3–20.

Caufriez, Anne. "Organology and Traditional Musical Instruments in Museums." In vol. 8 of *The Garland Encyclopedia of World Music*, edited by Timothy Rice, James Porter, and Chris Goertzen. New York: Garland, 1998.

Dournon, Genevieve. "Organology." In *Ethnomusicology: An Introduction*, edited by Helen Myers. New York: W.W. Norton, 1992.

Olsen, Dale A. "The Distribution, Symbolism, and Use of Musical Instruments." In vol. 2 of *The Garland Encyclopedia of World Music*, edited by Timothy Rice, James Porter, and Chris Goertzen. New York: Garland, 1998.

Amelia Maciszewski

Latin Grammy Awards. The 2000 Latin Grammy Awards ceremony was a Latino cultural milestone. Latino music was honored, listeners of Latino music were acknowledged, and numerous Latino entertainers expressed ethnic pride during an internationally telecast program. The inaugural Latin Grammy Awards ceremony was the product of the Latin Academy of Recording Arts and Sciences (LARAS), the first international corporation formed by the National Academy of Recording Arts and Sciences. While seven of the ninety-eight categories within the mainstream Grammy Award ceremony focus on Spanish and Portuguese music, the new Latin Grammys boasted a total of forty categories featuring a range of Latino music. LARAS, relying on linguistic guidelines to determine eligibility for a Latin Grammy, defined "Latin music" as albums with lyrics that are at least 51 percent in Spanish or Portuguese. The CBS telecast of the Latin Grammy Award ceremony marked the first time that an English-language U.S. network featured a bilingual show with musical performances exclusively in Spanish and Portuguese.

The LARAS took up the project of presenting the music of Latin America as one cohesive whole but encountered complications when trying to establish a panethnic award ceremony and valid systems for classifying Latino music. The first year's controversy concerned the lack of recognition of regional Mexican music. In the second year, Cuban-American exile groups protested the presence of Cuban artists at the awards ceremony.

According to the president of LARAS, the mission of the organization is to preserve the identity and vitality of the hundreds of regional forms of Latin music found throughout the world. However, some within the music industry pointed to a lack of inclusiveness in the Latin Grammy Award structure. Fonovisa, the largest independent Latin music label in the United States, boycotted the first annual Latin Grammys to protest what label executives saw as a bias against Mexican regional genres and favoritism to artists signed to Sony's Latin labels. The Fonovisa record label, which specializes in regional Mexican music, was among the first groups to accuse LARAS of being biased against Mexican regional music, a genre closely associated with recently arrived working-class communities. Fonovisa accused LARAS of favoring the pop Latin sound over regional Mexican genres such as **banda*, *conjunto*, *norteño*, and *mariachi. They made their case by pointing to the fact that the telecast did not feature performances by any of the label's popular Mexican regional acts. In addition, they argued that only 5 Fonovisa artists were among the 200 nominees, and all were in the Mexican regional field, none in the major categories such as record, album, singer, or group of the year. A group of Mexican acts on the Fonovisa label protested by returning their Grammys to LARAS. The bands included Los Temerarios, Banda El Recodo, Los Palominos, and *Los Tigres del Norte.

LARAS was prompted to relocate the first Latin Grammy Award ceremony from Miami to Los Angeles due to the *Miami-Dade County Cuba Affidavit*, which prohibits the county from doing business with companies or people with ties to Cuba. The 1996 measure can deny public funds, sites, and permits to cultural events that include Cubans, such as those artists scheduled to participate in the award ceremony. The measure was relaxed by 2001, and the second ceremony was scheduled to remain in Miami. However, the ceremony site was relocated to Los Angeles when talks between Miami city officials and LARAS broke down over exactly where *Cuban American demonstrators could stand in relation to the site of the ceremony. Cuban exile groups insisted on their right to demonstrate across the street from the event. Coordinators of the award show feared that Miami's Cuban exiles would disrupt the event as occurred in the case of the highly publicized demonstration against a 1999 show by the Cuban band Los Van Van. Singer Gloria *Estefan with her husband and influential record producer Emilio Estefan boycotted the ceremony to protest the event's sudden move from Miami to Los Angeles.

The 2001 award ceremony was to be held on September 11 but was canceled due to the terrorist attacks earlier that day. Latin Grammy winners were later announced at a press conference, and fans were able to view the distribution of awards through a live Web cast of the event. The attacks indirectly affected the 2002 ceremony as well, when the entire Cuban contingent of nominees were not granted visas to attend the event, due to stricter travel and *immigration procedures.

The Latin Grammys, like other award shows, has had its share of controversy and continues to be a work in progress, boasting annual increases in viewership, as well as a string of popular celebrity hosts including Gloria *Estefan, Jimmy *Smits, and George *López.

Katynka Martínez

Latin Jazz. Latin jazz is a hybrid musical style using Caribbean and Latin American instruments and rhythmic elements combined with American jazz, rendering what is best known as Latin or Afro-Cuban jazz. Combinations as diverse as an African American gospel or jazz singer fused with Latin percussion and congas renders interesting Latin jazz *conjuntos* and various creative musical possibilities.

As early as the late 1800s Afro-Cuban music began to influence American artists and their music, but jazz took a little longer to change. Initially, the Afro-Cuban tempo and popular rhythms did not mesh well with the classical jazz sound or big band and swing music. With the popularity of bebop came the introduction of newer blends of Afro-Cuban musics. At first the musical style was referred to as Cuban, but as popular interest increased and collaborations resulted, these musical hybrids became identified as the new pop genre called Latin jazz. In 1940 *Machito had already formed an orchestra called the Afro-Cubans. Later his brother-in-law Mario *Bauzá joined the band as a director and suggested using professional jazz players in the horn section. This was the beginning of Afro-Cuban jazz. In 1947 trumpeter Dizzy Gillespie began working with Chano *Pozo. His example was followed by many of the top American jazz artists who also began using Latin and Cuban counterparts, expanding the range of musical possibilities for their ensembles. Friendships and professional relationships were forged between Americans and Cuban artists, and many musical collaborations took hold and evolved. Several of the Americans who worked with Latin artists included Charlie Parker, Flip Phillips, Buddy Rich, Stan Getz, and Benny Goodman, to name a few. The best-known Latin artists who collaborated included Tito *Puente, Mongo Santamaría, Ray Barretto, Paquito D'Rivera, Arturo *Sandoval, and Desi *Arnaz.

It was the musical result of the Afro-Cuban rhythms and Latin musical sound that appealed to the jazz artists, and it created exciting dancing music with an upbeat tempo and high energy. Following the political tensions and economic embargos between the U.S. and Cuban governments, the Latin jazz craze diminished in popularity. New styles like *salsa continued experimenting with jazz, and other instruments like piano and flute transformed the genre. In the late 1970s, artists from Cuba and America began to make efforts to revive Afro-Cuban jazz. Other dance forms and musical styles derived from the original Afro-Cuban jazz, including the **charanga*, *cha cha cha, and the *bossa nova. Latin jazz styles, artists, and ensembles and its social cohesiveness influenced many artists.

Further Reading

Roberts, John Storm. *The Latin Tinge: The Impact of Latin American Music on the United States*. 2nd ed. New York: Oxford University Press, 1999.

Robert Chew

Latin Rhythms. Latin rhythms are simply rhythms that came from a combination of different Latin American countries and the Caribbean Islands but provide a musical foundation for most popular musical forms and dances. The word *rhythm* describes a pattern of sounds and silences that take place in a piece of music and organize the elements of time, beat, meter, and movement. Rhythmic patterns are organized into durations of sound and silence measured by the passing of beats of time. The majority of Latin rhythms heard in *salsa, *merengue, *cumbia, and other popular music come from the Afro-Caribbean cultures of Cuba, Puerto Rico, and the Dominican Republic.

From the seventeenth through the twentieth centuries, the Americas and the Caribbean Islands were colonized by Europeans, resulting in an inextricable blending of *race, language, religion, and music. The rhythms and their spinoffs had and still hold religious value to the people, especially among Afro-Caribbeans. Neighboring Indian tribes including the Taínos and Caribs were the first slaves that were forced to work on the sugar farms and plantations. Under Spanish rule, these tribes were forced to learn Spanish and convert to Christianity. These slaves then gave Christian saints' names to their gods to continue worshiping and avoid religious persecution from the Spanish for maintaining their traditional spiritual practices. One form of Afro-Caribbean spirituality is called Santería, which continues to preserve many religious, ritual, and musical traditions even today. In Santería ceremonies, one can still hear many of the original rhythms of West Africa played on batá drums.

A secular example of the cultural and musical mixture is the **son*. The *son* is a blend of the music of the Spanish and mulatto farmers (*campesinos*) and African slaves. It is believed that the music may have originated toward the end of the ninteenth-century. This music was performed by small ensembles, using various string and percussion instruments. The people of Cuba began to identify this style of music as their own, and it became very popular throughout the island. During the 1920s, the bass guitar and trumpet were added to the instrumentation. The legendary blind *tres* musician Aresenio Rodríguez revolutionized the *son* to include an *escribilla* section. This section is what is now known in modern salsa terms as the improvised *montuno* section of a piece. This revolution later evolved into the *mambo section of a piece and eventually became the dance known as mambo.

The *tumbao* was developed as the bass pattern for the pivotal instrument, the string bass. The *tumbao* pattern motivates the dancers when they hear this music. The *guaguancó* was also later introduced into the *son* style. The *tres* also became one of the most important solo instruments in this style. The most important development during this time was the standardization of the clave rhythm, which is the most important part in Latin music. A clave rhythm is played over two bars and is repeated throughout the whole piece, beginning to end. This rhythm gives the piece the groove and tempo to be followed throughout. Several musical examples of the most-used clave rhythms include the 3/2 *son* clave, 2/3 *son* clave, 3/2 *rumba clave, 2/3 rumba clave, 6/8 clave, and 6/8 clave played in 4/4 triplets.

Further Reading

Malabe, Frank, and Bob Weiner. *Afro-Cuban Rhythms for Drumset: Drummers Collective Series*. Edited by Dan Thress. New York: Warner Brothers, 1994. http://www.formedia.ca/rhythms/origins.html.

George Yáñez

Latin Soul. During the revolutionary period of the late 1960s came a new style of music that combined both *salsa and rhythm and blues (R&B). Latin soul was most popular among East Harlem and Bronx teenagers, who used both English and Spanish lyrics over a music that was somewhat more Latin than black.

Ray Barretto was considered one of the pioneers in Latin soul with his album *Acid* in 1967. This album generously blended *Latin jazz with R&B ingredients. Cuban-born conga player Ramón "Mongo" Santamaría was also equally influential in promoting Latin soul. Santamaría had a remarkable eye and ear for both coming trends and coming musicians. Santamaría made a long line of Latin soul albums for Atlantic and Columbia. The legendary *Machito also jumped on the bandwagon and recorded a Latin soul album titled *Machito Goes to Memphis* (1968). The influence of R&B on Latin music, and vica versa, continued throughout the late 1960s and well into the 1970s.

Further Reading

Roberts, John Storm. *The Latin Tinge: The Impact of Latin American Music on the United States*. 2nd ed. New York: Oxford University Press, 1999.

George Yáñez

Latina and Latino Literature and Popular Culture. Many varied forms of literary expression are fundamental in the everyday lives of people; literature in and of itself is simultaneously an indispensable record, a source, a form, and a practice of popular culture. Both literature's basic medium—language—and its basic method—the tapping of memory and experience through the ancient practice of storytelling—are such common parts of ordinary experience that literature is often underestimated as a vitally important human creation that is indispensable to human survival. In addition, the fictiveness of literature and the "escapist" pleasure it can produce can sometimes cause literature to be mistakenly perceived as lacking the seriousness of such other human activities as commerce, government, or politics. Like food and cookery, religious customs, music, sports, film, and other staples of popular culture, literature is relevant to and interlocked with every other area of human experience and is therefore a fundamental part of Latina and Latino popular culture. For example, the *La Llorona legend that still lives in grassroots Mexican and Mexican American communities has parallels in the ancient Jewish story of Lilith, one of the precursors of the biblical story of Eve, and also in both the Greek tale of Pandora and the classical Greek drama *Medea*. These legends and literary representations of *gender , sexuality, and resisting women echo throughout the human record in Gothic fiction, utopian writing, confessional poetry, *testimonio* (testimony of personal narrative), and other types of literature. The La Llorona example underscores how pop culture refreshes and illuminates a wide range of mutually influencing elements from people's *actual* experience as well as from interrelated symbolic motifs from traditional culture.

In the United States at the start of the twenty-first century, Latina/o literature consists of the genres of poetry, drama, fiction, essay, and similar traditional forms, as well as such other innovative forms of expression as spoken-word performance, *testimonio*, and hybrid multimedia and digital examples. These innovative forms of expression resist categorizing as distinct genres because of the perception among practitioners that the bilingual, bicultural dualities and related multiplicities of Latina/o identity(ies) cannot be contained in unitary, single-voiced generic patterns. Thus, the phrase "Latina and Latino literature and popular culture" refers to literature that is associated with an impressive body of Chicana/o, Puerto Rican, Nuyorican, *Cuban American, Chicanesca, Latinesca, and other mostly Latina/o American writers whose work has gained both critical acclaim and international popularity since the 1960s. Working out of bilingual and, frequently, *multi*lingual language traditions, these writers record their experiences and perceptions in English, Spanish, and various combinations and linguistic registers to narrate and chronicle the history, heritage, and contemporary realities of the ethnic and cultural diversity of the Americas. Collectively, they have inscribed a literary space for previously erased, distorted, and overlooked treatments of Latina/o experience.

Unsurprisingly, the first Mexican American voices to be heard on the literary scene of the United States were so few, so new, and so disparate that at first they were not even read as Mexican American– or Chicana/o-identified writers. For example, María Amparo Ruiz de Burton (1849–1895) is believed to be the first Mexican American to have published fiction in English, but because she published under the pseudonym C. Loyal, her novels *Who Would Have Thought It?* (1872) and *The Squatter and the Don* (1885) were read only as Civil War and California heritage fictions. Only recently has the latter work been recovered by Chicana literary and cultural scholars digging for pre-twentieth-century antecedents. Similarly, Eusebio Chacón (1869–1948) and Fabiola *Cabeza de Baca Gilbert (1898–1990), two New México–born writers, were, until recently, read only as chroniclers of the Southwest or of the Spanish colonial period in the region. Another New Mexican, Fray Angélico Chávez (1910–1999), was long discussed primarily as a religious historian and *family genealogist, while bestselling Texas-born teacher and author Jovita González (1904–1983) was known as a chronicler of her region's *folklore. Another Texas-born writer, the bestselling John *Rechy (1934–), was, for most of his career, largely discussed as part of a vanguard of writers who explicitly depicted homosexuality and gay erotic themes in their work. Not until after the *Chicano Movement of the late 1960s and the *Chicano Renaissance of the 1970s did the writings of these and numerous other early Mexican-origin writers begin to be read within a deeper, distinctively ethnic-identified context.

José Antonio Villareal (1924–) and his landmark novel *Pocho* (1959) are the writer and book generally acknowledged as the transitional text between "Mexican American" and "*Chicano" literature. The son of Mexican parents, Villareal was born in Los Angeles and earned a Bachelor of Arts degree from the University of California at Berkeley in 1950. *Pocho* is important as a literary first; it is both an American bildüngsroman (initiation novel) and also an immigrant novel focusing on the Mexican American experience. What makes it a landmark in Latina/o letters for its time period, besides its well-written style and compelling plot, is Villareal's use of popular culture to tell the story of his protagonist, Richard Rubio, a young Mexican American trapped in the hyphen between his father's strong Mexican roots and his mother's evolving U.S. American assimilation. The title's use of the Mexican Spanish slang *pocho*, a slur used by many Mexican citizens to refer to Mexican Americans (i.e., Chicanas/os), instantly emphasizes the marginalized and deterritorialized Chicano experience as part of the legacy of internal colonialism. From the novel's episodic plot of Richard Rubio as a *picaro* bouncing along a shifting trail of culture clashes (e.g., farmworker union organizing, *Pachucos, *gangs, and interracial dating) through its mosaic of post–World War II newsreel highlights and pop culture vignettes, Villareal echoes a rite of passage angst comparable to that found in J.D. Salinger's *Catcher in the Rye* (1951) and Ralph Ellison's *Invisible Man* (1952). In this way, Villareal contributes a notable character of conflicted ethnic, racial, and national identity to the long line of such liminal figures in American national literature, characters who are rooted to a homeland that refuses to recognize their full humanity.

Despite the relative success of *Pocho*, it was not until the period known as the Chicano Renaissance that Mexican Americans and their activist Chicana/o counterparts made a major collective impact on the U.S. American literary and artistic scene. The Chicano Renaissance flourished in the late 1960s through the 1970s and produced the groundbreaking work of playwright Luis *Valdez and El *Teatro Campesino, of Rodolfo "Corky" Gonzáles in *I Am Joaquín* (1968), and of *Alurista's poetry (e.g., *Floricanto en Aztlán*, 1971) as well as a wide-ranging literary activism that helped initiate and intensify the movement of cultural pride and political solidarity among Mexican-origin people in the United States. The major legacies of the era and its Chicano Movement offshoots include the galvanizing of an advocacy movement that led to an explosion of Chicano-identified creativity and germinal cultural production. Like the Latin American literary "Boom" writers who came to be associated with *magic realism, most of the Chicano Renaissance writers offered innovative representations of their individual and collective cultural identities by offering fresh perspectives on the themes of conquest, colonialism, and *race and ethnicity in the Americas. One of the Chicano Renaissance's most critical achievements was the seeding of an explicitly "Chicano" framework of ethnic and political identity, one that rejected the perceived accommodationism of the previous generation of

"Mexican American" and/or "Spanish-speaking" people. Writers associated with the era sought to capture the dynamic and contradictory fragments of Mexican, Mexican American, and Chicana/o experience as part of one vast present reality—whether material and visible or interior and private as in the spaces of desire, memory, the imaginary, and the ghosts of magical realism. Chicano Renaissance writers incorporated the common beliefs and customs of Mexican Americans in local settings as a way of exposing how their largely hidden everyday lives are affected by and collide with the policies and politics of the dominant culture and government. For political and cultural emphasis, their work also featured a foregrounded reflexivity (i.e., a highly self-conscious use of language and innovative technique to call attention to the craft of fiction-making itself) to underscore the use of literary discourse as a tool for resistance and emancipation (e.g., the *actos* of El Teatro Campesino, the everyman epic hero of *I Am Joaquín*, and the novel *The Road to Tamazunchale* by Ron *Arias).

Despite the Chicano-identified creativity of the Chicano Renaissance, much of the period's remarkable achievements, especially some its most famous titles, reflected narrowly masculine, heterosexual norms of identity and lacked consciously feminist and/or critically gendered and sexually inclusive perspectives. The few Chicanas who published or performed woman-identified material during the period included Estela *Portillo Trambley, Ana *Castillo, Martha P. Cotera, Bernice Zámora, María L. Apodaca, and the San Francisco spoken-word performers Las Cucarachas and Valentina Productions. The 1980s brought a shift away from the traditional male focus, however, as Chicana writers gained voice and visibility in public literary, artistic, and performing venues. In 1980 *Frontiers: A Journal of Women Studies* became the first explicitly feminist publication to publish an explicitly Chicana issue coedited by Cordelia Candelaria, Kathi George, and the *Frontiers* Editorial Collective. It featured contributions by and/or about Estela Portillo Trambley, Tey Diana Rebolledo, Rosaura Sánchez, Maxine Baca Zinn, Margarita Melville, Marta P. Cotera, Linda Williams, Inés Hernández Tovar, Margarita *Cota-Cárdenas, Catherine Loeb, Sylvia Gonzáles, **Salt of the Earth* (1953), *La Chicana: The Mexican-American Woman* (1979), and other now-established figures and titles. The pathbreaking 1980 *Frontiers* issue also included lesbian *testimonios* excerpted from then unpublished manuscript titled *Las Mujeres: Conversations from a Hispanic Community* (1981). The issue enjoyed several printings as it quickly became a cornerstone of women's studies and other reading lists that dared to intersect Chicana/Latina ethnicity with feminist frameworks and inclusive sexualities before they were as widespread in public discourse as in the twenty-first century.

The publication in 1981 of the now-classic collection *This Bridge Called My Back: Writings by Radical Women of Color*, coedited by Cherríe *Moraga and Gloria *Anzaldúa, continued the progressive Chicana agenda and marked an important point in Latina/o literature's intersection with feminism and popular culture, due to its large general audience distribution. The year 1981 also saw the publication of poet Lorna Dee *Cervantes's award-winning first volume *Emplumada* (Plumed) and Gina Valdés's collection *There Are No Madmen Here*. With this energetic beginning, the rest of the decade flourished with Chicana-identified discourses extending and deepening the literary shelf with such forerunner works as the lesbian novel *Faultline* (1982) by Sheila Ortiz Taylor, the personal prose poem *Thirty an' Seen a Lot* (1982) by Evangelina Vigil, and continuing publication by poets Alurista, Luis Omar Salinas, Abelardo "Lalo" Delgado, Ricardo Sánchez, Ana Castillo, Lorna Dee Cervantes, Gary *Soto, and others. Also thriving within the Chicano and growing Chicana Movement was prose fiction by such Chicano Renaissance figures as Rudolfo *Anaya, Portillo Trambley, Rolando *Hinojosa Smith, Richard *Vásquez, José Antonio Villareal, and Nash Candelaria, as well as dramatic work by El Teatro Campesino and spinoff repertory groups like El Teatro de la Esperanza and Su Teatro. New voices that emerged in the 1980s included Alberto *Ríos, Sandra *Cisneros, Cherríe Moraga as playwright and autobiographer, Gloria Anzaldúa, Ana Castillo as fictionist, Jaime Sagel, Helena María *Viramontes, Denise *Chávez, Beverly Silva, Margarita Cota-Cárdenas, and others.

Central to the success of these and other writers were two critical factors: the emergence during the Chicano Renaissance of bilingual presses and the appearance of a Chicana/o literary criticism. Two alternative publishing houses that weathered their formative years and were instrumental to many Chicana/o literary successes are *The Bilingual Review/La Revista Bilingüe*, founded in 1974 by Gary D. Keller, and *The Americas Review* (originally named *Revista Chicano-Riqueña*), founded in 1986 by Nicolas Kanellos. Both continue publishing and have developed into the influential book publishers the Bilingual Review Press and Arte Público Press. The second factor, appearance of a Chicano/o literary criticism, began developing with publication of early critical essays in *El Grito*; in the 1980 *Frontiers* Chicana issue, which included a comprehensive bibliography of works by and about Chicanas; in Kitchen Table/Women of Color Press; and other significant venues. These studies contributed to building a critical vocabulary and interpretive framework for reading, teaching, and writing about Chicana/o literature and the growing body of Chicana/o studies research. In addition, Juan Bruce-Novoa's *Chicano Authors: Inquiry by Interview* (1980) and Ernestina Eger's *Criticism of Chicano Literature* (1982) joined the historical first monograph published on the subject, *Chicano Perspectives in Literature: A Critical and Annotated Bibliography* (1976), edited by Francisco A. Lomelí and Donaldo W. Urioste, and the first book chapter overview of Chicano arts and literature, "Furthering a Rich Tradition" (1977), in Julian Samora and Patricia V. Simon's *Mexican American History*. These titles served as important gateway pioneers for subsequent analyses like *Chicano Theatre: Themes and Forms* (1982) by Jorge Huerta; Bruce-Novoa's *Poetry: A Response to Chaos*

(1982); *Contemporary Chicana Poetry: Critical Approaches to an Emerging Literature* (1985) by Marta Ester Sánchez; *Chicano Poetry, a Critical Introduction* (1986) by Cordelia Candelaria, and so on.

The 1990s and the turn of the century witnessed the continuing surge of both critical and creative literary publishing among Chicanas/os. The surge took place with the important difference of larger audiences and of publication by commercial and other national and international publishers instead of the previously in-group *raza* (race) audiences and alternative presses. These differences occurred for a variety of reasons, including the active advocacy on behalf of Chicana/o studies inclusion by Chicana/o scholars in universities and with publishers, as well as from the growing Mexican and Latina/o population that expanded the readership. In addition, interest from non-Latinos also grew, especially within the commercial business sector, which recognized the future market growth caused by the massive demographic changes occurring in the Americas. Prolific authors like Rudolfo Anaya, Nash Candelaria, Ana Castillo, Sandra Cisneros, Alberto Ríos, Gary Soto, and others were tapped by commercial presses, and their work—both previously published and new material—was printed and distributed on a mass scale. Creative, fresh voices also were published in the decade, such as Alfredo *Vea, author of the brilliant first novel *La Maravilla* (The Marvel, 1993), and Elva Treviño Hart, of the autobiographical novel *Barefoot Heart: Stories of a Migrant Child* (1999). Other established writers (e.g., Cherríe Moraga, Denise Chávez, José Antonio Villareal, Edmund *Villaseñor, and Helena María Viramontes) continue writing and sharing new discoveries and themes in their ongoing concern with literary representation as a means of subverting political bias, corruption, and repression, as well as of celebrating life.

For Puerto Rican and Nuyorican (New York Puerto Rican) writers the literary trajectory parallels some but not all of the Chicana/o experience. They, too, work out of a bilingual language tradition and collectively have inscribed a literary space to account for previously erased or distorted treatments of personal, cultural, and political experience. Originally most of these writers wrote primarily in Spanish, the main language of their island homeland. As migration to the U.S. mainland, for the most part to New York City, increased and the Nuyorican social demographic emerged, various Spanish/English combinations and linguistic registers developed among the people, and these varieties found their way into their chronicles and stories. The first Puerto Rican literary voices to gain prominence unsurprisingly were steeped in the island's long post-Columbian history and established cultural tradition. The first governor of Puerto Rico, Luis Muñoz Marín (1898–1980), was a published poet, and another writer and political activist was Eugenio Hostos (1839–1903), who devoted his life to support the *Boricúa (Borinqueño) movement for self-governance of his homeland in opposition to foreign domination by Spain. Like many Latin American artists and writers before them, Muñoz Marin's and Hostos's public lives as writers were tied to their public roles as activist reformers and/or public officials. Similarly, other writers like the novelist Manuel Zeno Gandía (1855–1930), playwright Alejandro Tapia y Rivera (1826–1882), essayist and poet José Gautier Benítez (1839–1903), and others are examples of the way that political freedom and social justice issues historically defined Puerto Rican creative literature and other popular culture practices. That meshing of politics with poetics continues in the twenty-first century, as illustrated by the celebrated work of the *Nuyorican Poets Café and El *Nuevo Teatro Pobre de América.

To escape political repression and persecution from Puerto Rico's right-wing pro-Spain government, certain Puerto Rican intellectuals and artists, like Eugenio Hostos, who favored independence historically were forced into exile to other parts of Latin America and also to the United States. The Spanish colonial authorities of the island even came to view New York City as a haven for renegade intellectuals and artists seeking asylum. One result of the San Juan–New York axis for intellectual and economic freedom was the expanding of the Puerto Rican creative geography as a context for art and literature. The émigrés added a Borinqueño presence to New York City and the eastern seaboard mainland, and they in turn imbibed the heritage and popular culture practices they encountered in the United States and integrated these elements into their work, thereby contributing to their eventual export back to the island and beyond. One such émigré, self-described "Afroborinqueño" Arturo Alfonso *Schomburg (1874–1938), became active in the island's independence movement and, like Hostos and others, had a major and lasting impact on U.S. education and scholarship. After migrating to New York City in 1891, Schomburg joined other Latina/o exiles in fostering the bilingual, multicultural heritage of the Americas and promoting self-rule throughout Latin America. Schomburg also was involved in the aesthetic and political Harlem Renaissance movement and, to offset the anti-independence persecutions from pro-Spanish authorities, began a lifelong effort to collect and preserve the heritage of the African diaspora and of Puerto Rico/Boricúa. His extensive library and related collections now occupy the world-famous Schomburg Center for Research in Black Culture housed in the New York City Public Library.

Besides the intellectual and political diaspora from Puerto Rico of the late nineteenth and early twentieth centuries, the other major *immigration from the island to the United States occurred after the 1940s as a result of the U.S. government's and commonwealth administration's determination that Puerto Rico was overpopulated. The administration, in conjunction with the U.S. Department of Labor, soon promoted a policy of mass immigration to the United States to alleviate the perceived overpopulation and meet the more immediate, largely unstated problem of an urgent need for workers by American business and industry. Government programs were developed to assist

Puerto Rican émigrés to adapt to the North American environment and to generate job opportunities on the mainland. This mid-twentieth-century diaspora produced a number of writers who wrote about their immigrant experience as displaced islanders and who also began to question the nature and form of their transnational identity, bilinguality, and marginalized culture. Among these immigrants were Puerto Rican poet Julia de Burgos (1914–1953), journalist Bernardo Vega (1885–1973), and writer Jesús *Colón (1901–1974). Writing poems mainly in Spanish, de Burgos lived for over a decade in New York and wrote of the situation of Puerto Ricans in the city (e.g., "Farewell from Welfare Island" and "The Sun in Welfare Island"). Like other Puerto Rican expatriates, Vega and Colón immigrated to New York in search of civil liberties, and both soon penned works about the New York "P.R." experience through their journalistic and personal writings. These early pathbreakers made it possible for the emergence of "Nuyorican" literature in the late decades of the twentieth century.

The robust literary tradition that was rooted on the island continued its own growth and flourishing in the twentieth century, quite apart from New York. Among the island's most respected names of the contemporary period are authors who remained in Puerto Rico and wrote from within that cultural and psychological perspective. These include the fiction writers Rosario Ferré, Pedro Juan Soto, Abelardo Díaz Alfaro, Enrique Laguerre, Emilio Díaz Valcárcel, and José Luis González, as well as experimental playwright René Marqués and poet Luis Palés *Matos, who foregrounded African negritude in the vision and voice of the Americas.

These literary luminaries join the Puerto Rican notables in music, movies, sports, and other venues (e.g., Pablo Casals, Benicio *Del Toro, José *Ferrer, Raúl *Julia, Jennifer *López, Rita *Moreno, Chita *Rivera) whose achievements far exceed the tiny size and modest political power of their island homeland. Along with their predecessors, their work and presence helped influence and spark the creativity of later decades.

The contemporary, post–World War II generation of Puerto Rican and self-identified Nuyorican writers and artists directly challenged some of the most controversial aspects of the Latina/o experience in the United States. These challenges include the majority society's perception of a problematic language barrier for Puertorriqueños despite the fact that their bilingual bicultural history is over 150 years older than the *Mayflower*'s landing in Massachusetts in 1620. Such writers as Piri *Thomas, Pedro Pietri, Miguel *Algarín, Miguel *Piñero, Sandra María Esteves, Martita Morales, and Víctor Hernández Cruz address in their writings the topics of racism, segregation, poverty, and systemic institutional disenfranchisement on the mainland—primarily in New York—as well as the island's poor economic situation. Their poetry and drama frequently express the emotional, political, and cultural impact of expatriate life. Two early examples of this literary generation are the Puerto Rico–based playwright and novelist René

Marqués (pre-Nuyorican) and Roberto Rodríguez Suárez, known as the father of Puerto Rican drama in the United States. Marqués wrote *La carreta* (The Oxcart, 1951) to depict the anguish of the Puerto Rican who abandons his country and immigrates to New York in search of a better life but who, in the end, returns to the island to find personal contentment. Rodríguez Suárez composed plays for the stage and television and founded the first permanent Hispanic *theater in the United States, the Nuevo Círculo Dramático (New Dramatic Circle), an important prelude to the Nuyorican Poets Café, which moved Puerto Rican literature to a new dimension of sophistication and success.

The Nuyorican Poets Café was founded in Manhattan's East Side (or "Losaida," as the lower East Side is called by its Spanish-speaking residents) with the help of the owner, Miguel Algarín, a university professor, writer, and one of the leaders of New York's Puerto Rican literary and political movement. He envisioned it as a venue for emerging Nuyorican artists, writers, audiences, and other supporters of the arts and culture. More closely identified with New York City than with the island, Nuyorican poetry developed to represent the multiple experiences of the many Puerto Rican immigrants to the *barrios and borderlands of New York, especially those who felt alienated from the dominant English-only poetry circles around them. The group formed an alternative literary circle that included Algarín, Américo Casiano, Sandra María Esteves, Felipe Luciano, Tato Laviera, Pedro Pietri, Miguel Piñero, Louis Reyes Rivera, and others who collectively helped shape the future of Nuyorican writing. Their conversations and collaborations led to the compilation of a highly influential anthology of writings, *Nuyorican Poetry: An Anthology of Puerto Rican Words and Feelings* (1975). The book served as the de facto establishment of what became known as the Nuyorican Poets Café and the launching of a Nuyorican-identified aesthetics, politics, and agenda for voicing the Boricúan experience in the Americas.

The next generation of Nuyorican artists that emerged in the 1980s and mid-1990s were exposed to the influential creative work of the original Nuyorican poets and freely moved beyond their pathbreaking originality and that of other literary forebears, whether from the mainland or from the island, even as they made artful use of their contributions. They began incorporating other forms of artistic expression, such as *hip-hop, into their cultural production, soon developing innovative styles of spoken-word performance. Out of this was born the presentation events known as *poetry slams* that have grown in popularity throughout literary and television worlds. Key figures in this important new wave of contemporary Nuyorican writers are Caridad de la Luz, Magda Martínez, Tony Medina, Sandra García Rivera, Héctor Luís Rivera, and Abraham Rodríguez, among others. They have published a number of anthologies, audio albums, and CDs, including *Aloud: Voices from the Nuyorican Poets Café* (1994), winner of a prestigious American Book Award, and *Action: The Nuyorican Poets Café Theater Festival* (1997).

As one of the premier stages for poets, writers, musicians, performance artists, and visual artists, the Café has been recognized for its commitment to providing a multicultural space for the artistic development of diverse members of the community. Fittingly, in 1993 the Nuyorican Poets Café was officially named a living treasure of New York City.

Cuban American writers share some similarities with Chicana/o, Mexican American, Puerto Rican, and Nuyorican literary cultural workers, notably their origin and creativity within bilingual, multicultural, and binational cultural traditions. They, too, have constructed a literary space to chronicle their personal, cultural, and political experience as hyphenated immigrants. As products of the *Antilles, however, Cubans and Puerto Ricans were greatly influenced by the writings of Haitian liberator Toussaint L'Ouverture (c. 1744–1803), a courageous leader who emphasized a Caribbean cultural consciousness as indispensable to overcome the deleterious effects on the people of conquest and colonization by Spanish, French, and English masters. That indigenist viewpoint was slow to develop and did not gain widespread acceptance for over a century until Caribbean and Latin American writers began to write from consciously West Indian identities, including reclaiming and celebrating their marginalized or erased African heritage. Foremost pioneers of this intellectual and literary vanguard were poets Luis Palés Matos of Puerto Rico and Nicolás Guillén of Cuba.

One of the most striking features of Cuban American literary expression is its representation of **cubanidad*, that is, the nature of Cuban identity, which has been debated by Cubans at least since the arrival of the Spaniards in the first *Columbus voyage of 1492. Much of the debate has concerned *race and ethnicity with respect to the island's racial and cultural evolution from its largely homogeneous native Taíno roots at the time of the Spanish Conquest. With the arrival of the Spaniards and subsequent colonizing in the West Indies and Mesoamerica, the identities of both the indigenous peoples and the Iberian immigrants was problematized as a result of their contact and intermingling. By the end of the sixteenth century **mestizaje*, the mixture of Indian and Spanish blood and ethnicity, began to define the language forms and religious practices of the Cuban people. The early presence of African slaves added further complications to the issues of racial, ethnic, and linguistic identity and concerns about the nature of *cubanidad*. Although this early development occurred within a dominant Spanish context, the official language of their island homeland, the late-twentieth and early twenty-first centuries have witnessed a shift to English and bilingual codes among the contemporary generations of Cuban American writers. Also recognized is the importance of the island's indigenous heritage.

The intersection of the islanders' concerns about *cubanidad* and its literature and popular culture perhaps can be illustrated by the work of two important nineteenth-century writers, José *Martí (1853–1895) and Gertrudis

Gómez de Avellaneda (1814–1873), who had powerful impact on their national literature. Many consider Martí to be the father of Caribbean literature. Renowned for his powerful poems on political liberty as a sine qua non for personal and moral freedom, Martí may be best known in the United States as the composer of the verses to the popular song of populist feeling "Guantanamera." His tireless work on behalf of his country's emancipation from Spain, as well as his advocacy for political and economic freedom throughout Latin America, made him a people's hero during his lifetime. That patriotic dedication in support of Cuban independence led to his death on the battlefield and martyrdom at a young age. As an essayist and poet, he is credited for bringing simplicity and transparent lyricism to the poetry of the Americas as a means of bridging the differences of language, race, class, and educational levels in the hemisphere. Martí also emphasized negritude (i.e., blackness as in an Afrocentric aesthetics and imaginary) in language, verse, music, and art.

Gertrudis Gómez de Avellaneda (1814–1873) is recognized for writing the first successful abolitionist narrative in the Americas. Her antislavery novel *Sab* (1841) was published ten years before Harriet Beecher Stowe's famous *Uncle Tom's Cabin* (1852), which often is credited as the hemisphere's first abolitionist novel. She wrote romances as well and threaded them with ideals of civil liberties and justice for workers and women, as in *Two Women* (1842) and *The Flowers' Daughter, or Everyone's Crazy* (1850), a style that anticipated the romance of social reform personified by Helen Hunt Jackson's **Ramona*, a novel translated by Martí. Gómez de Avellaneda lived what was considered an unorthodox life for her epoch. It included her self-expatriation to Spain in search of personal freedom outside the colonialist strictures of her homeland, and she was unapologetic about her unmarried sexuality, even choosing to bear and rear a child as a single parent. For their groundbreaking treatments of liberty as a personal as well as political matter, as well as for their desire to include negritude and justice for workers in discussions of *cubanidad*, Martí and Gómez de Avellaneda are memorialized for their literary and historical importance as modern thinkers, writers, and actors on their nation's stage.

After Cuban independence from Spain and the signing of the Treaty of Paris ending the Spanish-American War of 1898, the United States began its dominant presence on the island, and Cubans engaged in vibrant new forms of literary expression in the twentieth century. *Cubanidad* also encountered new contours and complications as the country saw a marked increase in the influence of American capitalism, culture, and English language on the island, particularly in the capital city of Havana. Among the premier personages in literature in these decades was the folklorist and essayist Fernando Ortíz (1881–1969), who wrote many studies of African elements in Cuban music, social practices, spiritual traditions, and related popular culture (e.g., *La africanía de la música folklórica cubana* [Africana in Cuban Folk Music, 1965, reprinted 2001]; *Los bailes y el teatro de los negros en el folklore de Cuba* [Negro Dance and Theatre in Cuba's Folklore, 1981]; *El huracán su mitología y sus símbolos* [Hurricane Mythology and Symbolism, 1947] and many other ethnographic studies still in print). Another writer who offered a fresh approach to the racial and cultural hybridity of postslavery *cubanidad* was folklorist and fiction writer Lydia Cabrera (1900–1990), whose folkloric interest focused on language as well as *healing practices, spirituality, and religious beliefs (e.g., *Ayapá: Cuentos de jicotea* [Ayapá: Turtle Stories, 1971]; *Cuentos negros de Cuba* [Black Cuban Tales, 1972]; *La medicina popular de Cuba: Médicos de antaño, curanderos, santeros y paleros de hogaño* [Cuba's Folk Medicine: Early Doctors, Healers, and Medicine Men, 1984]) and many other studies and folk-based stories. Nicolás Guillén (1902–1985), another vanguard writer who composed from deep-seated commitment to sociopolitical justice, consistently wove Afro-Cuban traditions and negritude into his lyrical poetry (e.g., *El diario que a diario* [1972; published in English as The Daily Daily, 1989]; *El gran zoo* [The Great Zoo, 1967]; and *Nicolás Guillén: Man-Making Words: Selected Poems* [1973]).

The work of these and other Cuban writers traveled throughout the hemisphere as a result of increased Panamerican transmigration from the 1920s to the 1950s. Cuban tourists, workers, and émigrés helped spread Cuban-origin literature, art, music, dance, foods, and other expressive forms to the United States as well. Everything changed in January 1959 with the success of the *Cuban Revolution in ridding the country of its corrupt dictator, Fulgencio Batista, and the introduction of Fidel *Castro to the world stage. That cataclysmic event compounded the island's obsession with *cubanidad* by adding the difficult issues of diaspora, exile, socialism, communism, and other personal and social conflicts to the question of cultural identity. The revolution divided the Cuban people geographically as well as politically, and many of the post-Batista artists, intellectuals, and writers addressed the diaspora displacements and identity conflicts in their work. They began to acknowledge the new phenomenon of "Cuban Americans" as an effect of *el choque* (the shock) of the revolution, which produced a region in crisis with shifting identities, multiple languages, cultural reconstructions, and the dynamic dialectics of a people and nation in ideological flux.

Specialists of Cuban culture generally agree that the first notable Cuban meriting the label of "exile writer" was Lourdes Casal (1938–1981), a poet and essayist who left her homeland during the revolution and first tackled the problems of diaspora in her writing. She confronted the challenges of self-expression based on cultural values that had been formed in the Cuban homeland in her youth (e.g., *Los fundadores: Alfonso y otros cuentos* [The Founders: Alfonso and Other Stories, 1973] and *Palabras juntan revolución* [Words Gather Revolution, 1981, coauthored with Anani Dzidzienyo and recipient of the prestigious Premio *Casa de las Américas]). Viewed as a portal for examining the paradox and conflict surrounding *cubanidad* as a binational exile identity, Casal's themes are embedded in the tensions and anxiety of a homeland lost to material experience and preserved only in memory (e.g., *El caso Padilla: Literatura y revolución en Cuba* [The Padilla Case: Literature and Revolution in Cuba, 1971]). The other side of the portal of exile encompasses the work of writers who remained on the island or maintained close ties with family and friends there and who simultaneously sought to maintain a space for dialogue with the émigrés. For example, Ruth Behar's *Poemas que vuelven a Cuba* (Poems Returning to Cuba, 1985) and *Puentes a Cuba* (Bridges to Cuba, 1995) engage in conversation with the poems of Lourdes Casal specifically and with other Cuban Americans set on defining a national identity, even if it is fragmented.

Since 1959 Cuban American literature has gained a wider U.S. readership through the works of such writers as Guillermo Cabrera Infante, Reinaldo Arenas, María Cristina García, and Oscar *Hijuelos; playwrights José Triana and Dolores Prida; poets Alejo Carpentier (*Los pasos perdidos* [The Lost Steps], 1983), Mireya Robles, and Nancy Morejón; and many other significant voices (e.g., Belkis Cuza Male, Hilda Perera, Hortensia Ruiz del Viso). Especially in theater and drama, Cuban playwrights and performers have been recognized for successful innovations in theatrical satire. José Triana's *Medea en el espejo* (Medea in the Mirror, 1961) and *La noche de los asesinos* (Night of the Assassins, 1964) have been produced throughout the Americas and Europe. His dramas join the fiction of Guillermo Cabrera Infante in combining entertainment with political parody, as in his *Vista del amanecer en el trópico* (Visions of Dawn in the Tropics, 1974); *Así en la paz como en la guerra* (1960; published in English as *Writes of Passage*, 1993); and *Delito por bailar el chachachá* (Guilty of Dancing the Chachachá, 1995). Similarly celebrated are writings by Reinaldo Arenas, author of *Adiós a mamá: De la Habana a Nueva York* (Goodbye, Mama: From Havana to New York, 1995); *Arturo, la estrella más brillante* (The Brilliant Star Arturo, 1984); and *Color del verano* (The Color of Summer, or, The New Garden of Earthly Delight, 2000). Whether through the literacy brigades established by Castro in Cuba in 1961 or through the Cuban and Cuban American impact on the literature of the Americas, the fact and fiction of *cubanidad* have been powerful and lasting in the modern consciousness.

In the early years of the twenty-first century, the compelling convergence of popular culture and Latina and Latino literature shows promise of continuing impact. The inescapable demographic growth revealed by the 2000 U.S. Census has fueled even keener interest in all aspects of Latina/o life, culture, and creative production. One emergent trend of the 1990s and turn of the century is the appearance of reprintings of writings by Chicana/o, Puerto Rican, and Cuban American titles previously circulated primarily among Hispanics (e.g., the collected works of El Teatro Campesino, of the Nuyorican Poets Café, of José Martí and Lourdes Casal). Another trend is the compilation and publication of numerous collections of Latina/o-themed literature including such titles as *U.S. Latino Literature: An Essay and Annotated Bibliography* (1992), compiled by Marc Zimmerman; *After Aztlán: Latino Poets of the Nineties* (1992), edited by Ray González; *Masterpieces of Latino Literature* (1994), edited by Frank N. Magill; *The Best of the Latino Heritage: A Guide to the Best Juvenile Books about Latino People and Cultures* (1997), by Isabel Schon; *Tropics of Desire: Interventions from Queer Latino America* (2000), by José Quiroga; *Latino Dreams: Transcultural Traffic and the U.S. National Imaginary* (2002), by Paul Allatson; *Latina and Latino Voices in Literature: Lives and Works* (2003), by Frances Ann Day; *Latino Literature in America* (2003), by Bridget Kevane; *Hispanic Literature of the United States: A Comprehensive Reference* (2003), by Nicolás Kanellos; and numerous others. Space limitations prohibit a comprehensive discussion or even listing of the many authors, works, subjects, and themes of this amazing literary production, but it is clearly a vibrant tree with a centuries-old taproot, vigorous branches, and the promise of fertile yield for centuries to come.

Further Reading

Bardach, Ann Louise. *Cuba Confidential: Love and Vengeance in Miami and Havana.* New York: Random House, 2002.

Brogan, Jacqueline V., and Cordelia Candelaria, eds. *Women Poets of the Americas: Toward a Pan-American Gathering.* Notre Dame, IN: University of Notre Dame Press, 1999.

Fowler Calzada, Víctor. "Miradas a la identidad en la literatura de la diáspora" (Snapshots of Identity in Diaspora Literature). *La Habana Elegante, Secunda Epoca* 14 (2001): 43–55.

González-Pando, Miguel. *The Cuban Americans.* Westport, CT: Greenwood Press, 1998.

Pérez-Firmat, Gustavo. *Life on the Hyphen: The Cuban-American Way.* Austin: University of Texas Press, 1994.

Shapiro, Michael J., and Hayward R. Alker, eds. *Challenging Boundaries: Global Flows, Territorial Identities.* Minneapolis: University of Minnesota Press, 1996.

Walter, Roland. *Magical Realism in Contemporary Chicano Fiction: Ron Arias, The Road to Tamazunchale (1975), Orlando Romero, Nambe-Year One (1976), Miguel Mendez M., The Dream of Santa Maria de las Piedras (1989).* Frankfurt am Main: Vervuert Verlag, 1993.

Williams, Raymond L. *The Twentieth-Century Spanish American Novel.* Austin: University of Texas Press, 2003.

Cordelia Chávez Candelaria

Latina Feminism. The foundation of contemporary Latina feminism is a deliberate and collective response to both the surge of feminist consciousness in mainstream society and the civil rights movements of the turbulent and transformative 1960s and 1970s. While civil rights movements were inspired and led by ethnic minorities, Latina feminists recognized that leadership roles were dominantly filled by men who viewed Latinas and other women of color as allies in the social struggle against racism and discrimination but who too often failed to recognize women as social and political equals. Even as they fought alongside Latinos toward the objective of attaining legal rights and cultural recognition, Latina feminists rejected the gender subordination they experienced. As Latinas recognized that the civil rights actions and philosophies of their communities failed to address their rights as women, they turned to the feminist movement but found that the central issues, leadership, and actions of the 1960s and 1970s feminist movement were dominantly directed by and for Anglo women. Latina feminists discovered that the feminist movement indeed attended to gender inequality and sexism, but for the most part, it failed to address the complexity of their experiences as women experiencing not only gender-based discrimination but also racism and, in many cases, discrimination based on socioeconomic status and even *immigration status. Thus, like their Latino allies, Latina feminists refused to allow their racial and ethnic diversity to be obliterated through the concept of the American melting pot, yet they also resisted the privileging of sexism and gender identity as disconnected from race, social class, and sexual orientation that traditionally served, and at times continues to serve, as the foundation of mainstream feminism.

Born of commitment to multiple loyalties—to ethnic and racial communities and to women—Latina feminism consistently attends to the intersections between race, class, ethnicity, sexuality, and gender to deconstruct both monolithic cultural nationalism and mainstream feminism. Two foundational examples are the 1980 "Chicanas in the National Landscape" issue of *Frontiers: A Journal of Women Studies*, the first ever monograph on Latinas published by and for an international distribution journal, and Cherríe *Moraga's and Gloria *Anzaldúa's jointly edited collection *This Bridge Called My Back: Writings by Radical Women of Color* (1981). Anzaldúa's edited collection *Making Face, Making Soul/Haciendo Caras* (1990), a second collection of such testimony in the form of personal narrative, poetry, and essay. In these collections and others, Latina feminists challenge readers to think about the interconnectedness of racism, sexism, and homophobia, not only in contemporary mainstream society but in ethnic communities and movements as well. Through their writing and activism, Latina feminists expand the potential of all social movements striving for human rights. Differentiating feminist issues of the private sphere (consequences of standards of feminine beauty, division of labor within the household) and the sphere of public policy issues like affirmative action and voter education, for example, Latina feminists integrate this distinction into their activism in ways that benefit women as well as Latino communities.

As it is distinct from its counterparts—mainstream feminism and cultural nationalism—Latina feminism is heterogeneous, shifting to accommodate the diversity of Chicana, Puerto Rican, Cuban, and Central and South American feminists living in the United States. Latina feminists are diverse in age, national origin, education, socioeconomic class, language, sexual orientation, among other factors. Also, many Latina feminists do not claim a single nationality or cultural background, writers Sandra Benitez and Aurora Levins Morales stand as representatives of this group. Similarly, a growing population of Latina/os learn English as a first language, and Spanish-speaking Latinos vary in degree and range of bilingualism. Also the Spanish utilized by Latina feminists varies by region and national background and also by the continual innovation of language produced through the intersection of Spanish and English in the English-dominant United States.

In addition to the wide in-group diversity of Latina feminists, the breadth of Latina feminism is enhanced by strong alliances with other feminists, both in the United States and in Latin America to bring attention to women's issues. Using organizations such as the Women of Color Resource Center, the Johns Hopkins University Center for Health and Gender Equity (CHANGE), and the urgently important anti-*femicidio* (femicide) network formed to respond to the mass killings of women along the Juarez-El Paso border (e.g., Operacion Digna/Justice for Our Daughers, Arizona State University West's Border Justice projects, Mexico Solidarity Network, etc.), Latinas have helped bridge cultural differences to promote peace and justice. Because they are committed to the rights and recognition of their cultural communities, Latina feminists are dedicated to social activism, not as abstract or theoretical but grounded in the material circumstances of its advocates.

The heritage of contemporary Latina feminism is steeped with women who were feminists and social activists before contemporary definitions of feminism were formed. Historical forerunners of contemporary Latina activists include María Mercedes Barbudo, a Puerto Rican woman, jailed in 1824 for active resistance against the Spanish colonizers; *las soldaderas*, who fought alongside men in the Mexican Revolution of 1910; Teresa Urrea (1873–1906), an amazing *curandera* (healer) known as La Santa de Cabora whose grassroots popularity led Mexican dictator Porfirio Diaz to deport her to Arizona for treason; and Emma Tenayuca, a famous labor activist and strike leader in Texas in the 1930s. These women exemplified the ideals of feminist activism, and more recently, Dolores *Huerta, Chicana co-organizer of the United Farm Workers, is a civil rights era–example of principle put into grassroots sociopolitical action.

Drawing upon this rich history of community-centered activism, the most pressing issues Latina feminists address are the material conditions of their communities. Having fought for human rights in home nations such as El Salvador, Nicaragua, and Cuba, many Latinas continue to politically mobilize in their U.S. communities. Political marches and public demonstrations continue to be central to Latina feminist activism, as Latina feminists seek to improve conditions including unemployment rates, poverty, inadequate educational systems, poor health care and education, inadequate child care, and underserved reproductive rights. Since feminists are composed both of recent immigrants and long-standing residents of the United States, many also concern themselves with the citizenship and human rights of Latin American immigrants, a concern that also helps solidify international alliances between Latinas and women in Latin American countries. Antonia *Pantoja, founder of the Puerto Rican Association for Community Affairs, was a visionary who worked toward a strong community, especially through leadership development for youth. Important unionizing activity as modeled by women like Huerta and Tenayuca is continued by women like Esperanza Martell, who helped organize the Latin Women's Collective in New York City and who focuses particularly on health issues. As Latinas politically mobilize to bring about positive change, they seek and encourage political empowerment for themselves, for the individuals they interact with, and for the communities to which they belong. Dominantly working class and race conscious, Latina feminists maintain strong connections and commitments to their families, their communities of origin, and Latin American women internationally.

Latina feminism's strong and crucial facet of social activism is complemented by the equally strong and crucial facet of art and scholarship. In practice, social activism inspires Latina creativity and defines much Latina art. Latina

Chicana feminist writers (from left to right) Ana Castillo, Cherríe Moraga, Cordelia Candelaria, and Alicia Gaspar de Alba onstage at the 1987 University of Colorado International Women's Week Conference in Boulder. *Photo by Camille Chávez.*

feminists in the visual arts as well as scholars and writers have felt largely silenced or ignored by Anglo-American feminists and by a broader patriarchal and ethnocentric society. Many Latina feminist writers and artists seek to reclaim voices of U.S. Latina experience that have been omitted from history, community and local political impact, and cultural representation. They use their art to show the inequalities of privilege and power that perpetuate the marginal status of Latinas in the United States. Latina artists often struggle with questions of aesthetics and politics, how to combine agency and creative expression. Thus, the notion of liminality, of being in between worlds, is central to Latina artistic vision. For example, Latina feminists, especially artists, are very conscious of multiple audiences and have sought to negotiate these audiences—white women and men, Latinos and other Latinas—in the linguistic composition of their works, sometimes translating Spanish terms or traditions into English and sometimes demanding that audiences view and interpret according to their unique vantage points, even when it may mean not reaching all audiences fully.

Thematically, Latina feminist artists generate works that express the pain, conflict, and simultaneous richness of their experiences. Many Latina feminist artists represent religion as an ideological and traditional presence, some critiquing the complicity of religion in repressing sexuality and self-definition and others celebrating the power of religious tradition, especially in the figure of the Catholic Virgin. Many also attend to their indigenous heritage in relation to the European heritage that has been socially compelled and privileged. Many also emphasize self-love and love of community, often attuning vision to history and spirituality. They write of women's relationships with each other, valorize the creative and spiritual forces Latinas possess. They honor grandmothers and mothers as role models, storytellers, teachers, and keepers of tradition as well as resistant, powerful women in their own times and ways. They articulate the conflicts of traditional roles of wife and mother and definitions of appropriate and acceptable womanhood and also dismantle limiting *stereotypes such as the marianismo/machismo dichotomy. Marianism refers to the pious belief in and worship of the Virgin Mary. In extreme forms, it becomes mariolatry or idolatry of the Virgin as the perfect exemplar of femininity for girls and women. In every day speech, machismo usually refers to extreme forms of masculinity, male physical superiority, and masculine confidence to extremes of cockiness and arrogance. Among Latinos, particularly Mexicans, the word connotes more complex meanings related to its origins in traditional chivalry and respected sex and gender roles.

Because too often authentic forms of sensuality and sexuality have been distorted, maligned, or inadequately represented in both artistic traditions and alternative outlets, Latina feminists construct their own representations of sexuality and sensuality to capture their own experience. This concern with accurate representations of sexuality has led Latina feminists to link oppressions associated with race and gender to homophobia as well as to the necessity of combatting heterosexism within their cultural communities as well as in society at large. Contemporary Latina artists are also validating the lives of Latina lesbians through artistic representation. Finally, Latina feminist artists are conscious of the interconnectedness of Third World women and bring this consciousness into their creative works, exemplified by Lourdes *Portillo's documentary film, *Señorita Extraviada/Missing Young Woman* (2002), about the over 300 Juarez border murders.

As Latina feminists establish their own artistic traditions through rich innovations in form, style, content, and by enmeshing narrative, poetry, and public performance, as well as giving voice to their own complex sociological positions, other Latinas respond by interpreting Latina productivity in new ways. Additionally, Latina feminist scholars, while still a minority on campuses across the United States, are paving the way for a rising population of feminist-conscious students as they are also helping to reshape curriculum and to foster interdisciplinary bonds between women's studies, Latin American studies, Latina/o studies and related global studies areas. As hosts and presenters of academic conferences, which provide space for dialogue, and as scholars who articulate the force of Latina feminism, Latina academics are also helping mobilize international alliances of idea and activism. Together, Latina artists and scholars have formed their own associations like Mujeres Activas en Letras y Cambio Social (Activist Women in Letters and Social Change) and work to establish productive relationships between professional Latinas and their communities through workshops and other projects. Inclusive and not elitist, Latina feminists do not privilege abstract academic theory over lived experience, political organizing, and artistic production.

Challenges for this generation of Latina feminists include educating young Latinas of the relevance of feminism to their lives, as many Latinas still find themselves in the double bind of feeling torn between mainstream consumerist values or dominant feminism and dissenting communities and identities of race and ethnicity. Latina feminists still must battle the hazards of tokenism, being treated as a representative for what more empowered individuals see as a homogenized community. They must also continue to confront the sustained relegation of their experiences to invisibility or unimportance as well as to avow the necessity and vitality of Latina feminism against the prominent assertion that social transformation has eradicated racism, sexism, heterosexism, and socioeconomic in equality.

Further Reading

Aparicio, Frances R., and Susana Chávez-Silverman. *Tropicalizations: Transcultural Representations of Latinidad*. Hanover, NH: University Press of New England [for] Dartmouth College, 1997.

Candelaria, Cordelia. "Constructing a Chicana-Identified 'Wild Zone' of Critical Theory." In *Feminisms: An Anthology of Literary Theory and Criticism*, edited by Diane P. Herndl. New Brunswick, NJ: Rutgers University Press, 1997.

Sandoval, Chela. "U.S. Third World Feminism: The Theory and Method of Oppositional Consciousness in the Postmodern World." *Genders* 10 (1991): 1–24.

R. Joyce Zamora Lausch and
Cordelia Chávez Candelaria

***Latina* Magazine.** The late 1990s gave rise to an increased number of women's magazines written in English and geared toward Latinas born and raised in the United States. Among these magazines were the now-defunct *Moderna* and *Sí*, as well as *Estilo*, *Latina Style*, and *Latina* magazine. Launched in May 1996 through a joint effort between Essence Communications, publisher of *Essence*, a magazine for African American women, and founder and publisher Christy Haubegger, *Latina* magazine, currently owned by Latina Media Ventures LLC, premiered as a bimonthly magazine. With a mission of striking a balance between the modern and traditional, *Latina* magazine featured actor and singer Jennifer *López in its premier issue and on the cover. With a circulation of 239,000, *Latina* magazine is currently published eleven times a year with a double issue in January. Marketed as a bilingual magazine, *Latina* magazine is written primarily in English with condensed Spanish translations and interspersed uses of Spanglish. *Latina* magazine features articles primarily about fashion, beauty, culture, food, and education, as well as celebrity profiles and interviews. *Latina* was featured on the Adweek Hot List in both 2000 and 2001 and was named Best Magazine by *Advertising Age* in 2000.

Further Reading

http://www.latina.com.

Bernadette Calafell

Latina/os in Film. *See* Film.

Latino Cultural Centers. *See* Cultural Centers.

Latino Visual Arts. An overview of modern and contemporary popular visual art created by U.S.-based *Chicanos, Cubanos, and Puertorriqueños reveals to what extent these Latino constituencies share common ground. Their interconnectedness stems from similar geopolitical and historical circumstances each group has experienced and the preeminent role played by the United States in shaping their respective destinies. They are connected by conquest, colonization, and slavery, as well as by the development of mestizo cultures and societies since the Spaniards arrived in 1492 (*see* **History** entries on Chicanos, Cuban Americans, and Puerto Ricans). This shared history of trauma and turmoil combined with Latina/o material achievement and cultural triumph provided the fertile seedbed for the creative arts and aesthetic production in the Americas.

Example of boom in Latina/o publications in the "Decade of the Hispanics." *Photo by Emmanuel Sánchez Carballo.*

Cuba was first colonized by Spain in 1492. Wars for independence between 1868 and 1898—the latter led by poet and revolutionary José Martí—were met with strong resistance. The United States occupied Cuba from 1898 until 1901, thereafter maintaining effective economic and political control of the island for more than five decades of corrupt dictatorships. Overthrown in 1959 by Fidel *Castro's guerrillas, including the legendary Ernesto "Che" *Guevara, Fulgencio Batista was the last of that group. Subsequently, Cuba declared itself a socialist state, expropriated U.S. businesses, and triggered a complete rift in diplomatic relations with the United States. The year 1961 witnessed the Central Intelligence Agency (CIA)–led *Bay of Pigs invasion aimed at overthrowing Castro. That failed attempt was magnified when Castro declared Cuba a Marxist-Leninist state and aligned his country with the Soviet Union. The ensuing installation of Soviet missiles on the island prompted a naval blockade ordered by President John F. Kennedy. Since the Cuban missile crisis, relations between Cuba and the United States have continued to deteriorate. The George W. Bush administration suspects Cuba of involvement with biological weapons and terrorist activities.

Puerto Rico, too, was once a Spanish colony. *El Grito de Lares (Cry of Lares) of 1868 marked an unsuccessful attempt by a rebel force to proclaim the island a republic, but it heralded profound reforms. Slavery was abolished in 1873, royally decreed autonomy followed in 1897, and autonomous governance began in 1898. That same year, however, the island, a spoil of the Spanish-American War, was ceded by Spain to the United States. In 1917, Puerto Ricans were granted American citizenship by President Woodrow Wilson, although that status did not guarantee their prosperity. The island's U.S.-controlled sugar industry was plagued by poverty and unemployment. Don Pedro Albizu Campos, "Tiger of Liberty," and his Puerto Rican Nationalist Party kindled fervor for independence, insurrections, and even an attempt on the life of U.S. President Harry S. Truman. Albizu Campos would endure periods of incarceration and would die (in 1965) during the course of the thirty-year struggle that would lead first to a referendum of 1952, when Puerto Rico voted for a commonwealth, and second, to a popular plebiscite in 1967 between statehood, commonwealth, and independence. The commonwealth option won again. Today, more than thirty years later, Puerto Ricans on both island and mainland remain divided on the issue of statehood.

Chicanos or Mexican Americans refer to their homeland as *Aztlán, a metaphorical space created wherever Chicana/os happen to reside. Historically, Aztlán is associated with the homeland of the Aztec people. The United States proper and Aztlán are of one piece, the North American continent. In a more conventional sense, Mexican Americans look toward the republic of México as their geographical homeland. México ceded nearly 1 million square miles to the United States in 1848, complying with the Mexican-American War's *Treaty of Guadalupe Hidalgo. Chicana/os did not cross any border. Rather, they were "crossed," so to speak, by the newly mapped border. Put another way, circumstances did not only involve movements of people but a shift as well in the landscape of the American Southwest. Once it was "there," and now it was "here," to borrow a situational characterization from cultural theorist Richard Rodríguez. Muralist Judy Baca sees

Chicana/os like herself living in internal exile. The more than 2,000-mile long U.S.-Mexican border is indeed an "open wound," as writer Gloria *Anzaldúa eloquently put it.

Tellingly, Fidel Castro acknowledged the extensive loss of Mexican territory to the United States in his address of July 26, 1964, in Santiago de Cuba, a speech attended by two young Chicanos, Roberto Rubalcava and Luis *Valdez. Defying a U.S.-imposed travel ban to Cuba, they spent two months there, adopting Castro as their ideological leader. Valdez would later found the *Teatro Campesino (Farm Workers' Theater), arguably the crucible that fomented the cultural front of the Movimiento Chicano (*Chicano Movement).

Since the late 1960s, spurred on by the great momentum of the black civil rights movement, these Latino groups attained greater public visibility in American consciousness. These Latinos strive to retain their respective cultural heritage and identity on the U.S. mainland, even as they proudly identify as bilingual, bicultural Americans. Cubans, Puerto Ricans, and Chicanos residing in the United States generally retain emotional ties to their individual *madres patrias* (homelands). Mindful of the poignant sociopolitical struggles between conquers and conquered in the Americas since at least the late fifteenth century, Latino artists embrace and have a stake in a kindred project: the reclamation of geography, history, and cultural patrimony indelibly inscribed in the collective memories of their cultures.

Visual art practices in the corresponding Latino urban communities vehemently resist cultural and historical erasure, while affirming the uniqueness of the artists' dual identities: *Boricúa (Puerto Rican) American, *Cuban American, and Mexican American. That their visual expressions are "popular" in nature means that the culture group becomes the individual artist's focus of interest. This aesthetic fusion of the one with the many of a given community occurs through the multifaceted/multivalent artistry and process of street murals, including graffiti and sculpted walls—the single-most pervasive popular artform—indoor and outdoor altars and shrines, car culture and its popular magazines, comic books and strips, prints, popular toys, and Web sites. Whatever the medium, certain themes and symbols predominate. Broadly conceived as activist narratives, they express affirmation, celebration, commemoration, declamation, indignation, lamentation, reclamation, and salvation. Couched within those multiple representations are the themes of attachment to homeland; resistance to invasion and annexation of that homeland; negotiation of borderlands; emigration, *immigration, and exile; *family ties and domestic allegories; and political, religious, and social beliefs. Emotional evocations and invocations of memory permeate most themes. This is highly contextualized art stimulated by artistic as well as extra-artistic considerations. Anthropologist Victor Turner's concept of *communitas* is the most significant extra-artistic factor informing these popular artforms, taking into account as it does the complex dynamics of social relationships and the need for areas of communal

An example of twenty-first-century Latina art, this oil painting titled *Smoking Girl* is by Tucson, Arizona, artist Xochitl Gil. From the Associated Research Collection. *Photo by Emmanuel Sánchez Carballo.*

living. Like their creators' visions, the visual artforms demonstrate personal and cultural interconnectedness in various ways.

"Walls with Tongues": Community Murals Voice Collective Sentiments from Indignation to Salvation

At the height of the black civil rights movement, Chicago-based African American muralists William Walker, Eugene Wade Eda, and others executed a mixed-media mural on an abandoned Southside community building. Above the entranceway, they painted the mural's plain title, *The Wall of Truth*. Above the main section, a declaration of affirmation and reclamation appeared printed in bold letters on a makeshift wooden placard:

> We the People of this Community
> Claim this Bldg. in order to Preserve
> What is Ours.

That proactive midwestern stance of 1969 became one of the ideological visions of muralism in marginalized, urban ethnic communities throughout the United States. Such works are overwhelmingly sociopolitical, street-side statements.

A student-rendered mural, *La Causa/Peace, Love and Perfection* (1969–1970), at Merritt College in Oakland, California, featured within its overall composition conjoined images of Guevara, Emiliano *Zapáta (southern chieftain of the Mexican Revolution of 1910 and symbol of land reclamation), and Albizu Campos. The words, *La Causa* (The Cause), allude to the shared problems and aspirations among Cubans, Mexicans, and Puerto Ricans living in their homelands or on U.S. soil and are represented in the painting through three of their most popular and revered icons.

Chicago-based Boricúa American artists José Bermudez, Mario Galán, and Hector Rosario, members of the Puerto Rican Art Association, painted *La Crucifixión de Don Pedro Albizu Campos* (The Crucifixion of Don Pedro Albizu Campos) in 1971 in the city's northside Boricúa community. The thrust of the mural's message is the martyrdom of Puerto Rican nationalists Albizu Campos, Lolita Lebrón, and Rafael Cancel Miranda, whose intense militancy never obtained an independent Puerto Rico. A backdrop to the mural's crucified martyrs, the Nationalist flag of Puerto Rico dresses the entire composition. Likenesses of six Puerto Rican patriots—Ramón E. Betances, Segundo Ruíz Belvis, Mariana Bracetti, Eugenio María de Hostos, Rosendo Matienzo Cintrón, and José de Diego—are at the top of the mural. Luis Muñoz Marín, elected Puerto Rico's first governor in 1948, is portrayed in the guise of Judas Iscariot for having revoked Albizu Campos's pardon of 1947 and returned him to prison. Marín thus betrayed the greater cause of freedom for all Puerto Ricans. The mural's restoration in 1990 attested to its ongoing, galvanizing importance in the neighborhood.

Chicano artist Michael Ríos was invited by Cuba's revolutionary government to visit Cuba in 1975 as part of a Venceremos (We Will Overcome) Brigade to witness the extent of that government's sponsorship of public art, particularly murals and posters. He and other visiting U.S. community muralists returned home persuaded that such a marriage of art and politics could promote people's welfare. Only ten years earlier, Guevara himself had written about the educational and spiritual dimensions of art in the service of revolution. Back from Cuba, Ríos teamed up with fellow Chicano artist Anthony Machado to paint a mural whose title echoed Guevara's own words of declamation and indignation, *Esta Gran Humanidad Ha Dicho ¡Basta!* (This Great Humanity Has Said, Enough!) Created for *People's Murals: Some Events in American History*, a bicentennial exhibition of eight portable murals sponsored in 1976 by San Francisco's Museum of Modern Art, the work was inspired by a poster Ríos had seen during his Cuban visit and by various works of José Clemente Orozco, the celebrated Mexican muralist. Depicting boar-faced soldiers waging battle under conflated U.S. and Nazi flags, the mural is an abbreviated visual allegory of U.S. aggression against all subjugated groups.

César *Chávez, Mexican American leader with Dolores *Huerta of the United Farm Workers (UFW), would attract Luis *Valdez to his cause as thousands others had been Of countless murals associated with the UFW, three examples speak to the centrality of Chávez's mission for Chicanos as a whole and cultural workers in particular; his stewardship of a fair and just labor cause; and his charisma and popularity as a leader. Chicano artist Antonio Bernal's *Untitled* two-section mural of 1968, painted at the Teatro Campesino's headquarters in Del Rey, California, assigns Chávez a prominent place in the composition. Holding the UFW's eagle-emblazoned *huelga* (strike) banner, he is flanked by other culturally and historically symbolic figures: Reies López Tijerina, militant leader of the New Mexican land grants movement, holding the Treaty of Guadalupe Hidalgo; civil rights leaders Malcolm X and Martin Luther King, Jr.; Joaquín Murieta, California "bandit" and folk hero; Emiliano Zapáta; and Pancho *Villa and La Adelita, northern chieftain and *soldadera* (soldier) of the Mexican Revolution, respectively. Their linear alignment and stride suggest marchers demonstrating for a cause, in this instance the right of Mexicans and Mexican

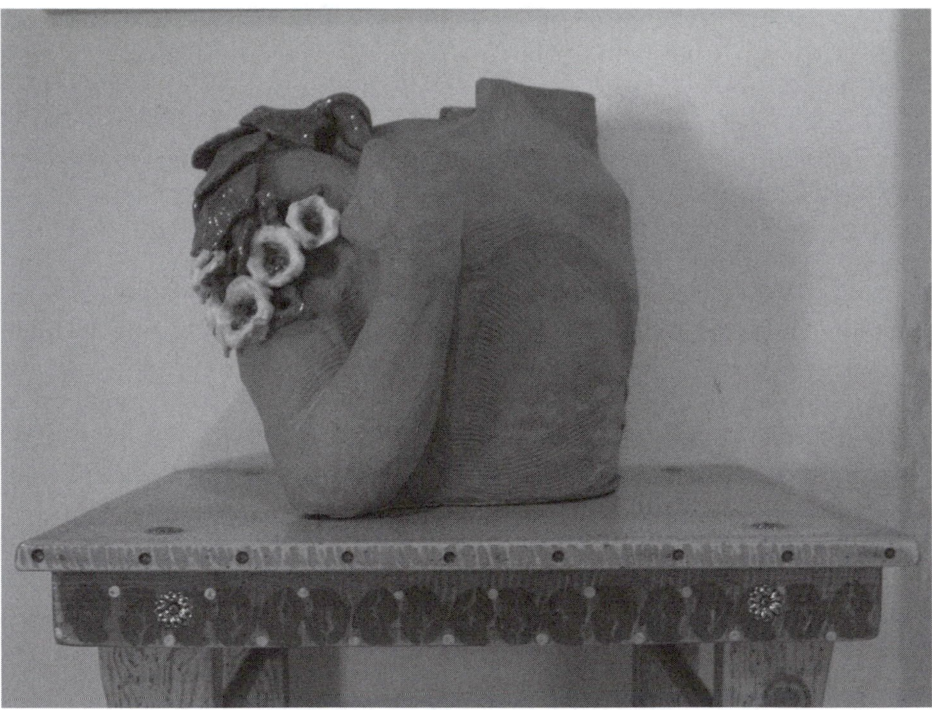

Contemporary terra cotta sculpture, *Torso*, by Santa Fe, New Mexico, artist Pedro Romero. From the Associated Research Collection. *Photo by Emmanuel Sánchez Carballo.*

Americans to landownership and the attendant right to work that land and reap its bounty. Assisted by local youth, José Guerrero, city worker and member of the culturally diverse Chicago Mural group, painted *Sí Se Puede* (Yes, It Can Be Done; 1973) on an alley wall in the heart of Pilsen, Chicago's largest Mexican and Mexican American *barrio. A throng of demonstrators with upraised fists protest in the shadow of the Mexican flag and UFW standard, a red flag with a black eagle in the center, against injustices they must overcome. The printed legend indicates the mural is dedicated to the "great community" that it graces and to the UFW. Chicano social worker–turned-muralist Anastasio Torres formed the Community Cultural Arts Organization in San Antonio, Texas, as a means of steering dropouts back to high school. Between 1978 and 1980, Torres's mural crews transformed Cassiano Homes, a public housing complex, into a vast mural cycle numbering nearly thirty walls. One of these, the *Farmworkers' Mural*, is dominated by *huelga* eagles and an idyllic role model likeness of Chávez.

An artistic collaboration between two artists over some twelve years in four South Bronx neighborhoods inspired free-standing figurative sculptures and sculpto-murals. Boricúa American Rigoberto Torres calls the South Bronx home and his collaborator John Ahearn, a white ethnic academy-trained painter, is a community outsider who was drawn to the barrio by the people and their remarkable ability to overcome suffering. *We Are Family* (1981–1982), *Life on Dawson Street* (1982–1983), and *Back to School* (1985) are three painted walls animated by superimposed colorful plaster cast sculptures of community residents engaged in daily and routine activities and relationships. A paradigm of *communitas*, these sculptured murals, created for and with their participatory audience, display ordinary people assuming extraordinary, almost theatrical roles.

Given that they evolve electronically, murals created collaboratively over the Internet are a new phenomenon. Otherwise, they remain the time-tested work of collectives aspiring to speak for individuals. WebStudio, the Web-driven collaborative art project of Miami-based Cuban American artist Xavier Cortada, affords participants interaction through two Webcams and a live chatroom. During the 1999–2000 academic year, students and teachers from ten Miami high schools teamed up with Cortada to produce ten digital murals—under the serial title *Master-Peace 2000*—each commemorating one of the past millennium's centuries. Utilizing WebStudio, the murals interpreted lessons for humanity drawn from the last 1,000 years. In Cortada's borderless universe, community digital muralism is both national and international in scope.

Chicano and Boricúa American muralists have created many representational and graffiti murals of commemoration, lamentation, and salvation in several major cities, especially Los Angeles and New York. These walls tend to be directed by experienced community muralists in collaboration with *gang members. Designed in 1985 by public artist Daniel Martínez, and painted by members of the Playboys Gang, *Choices* reflects on *La Vida Loca (the crazy, violent life) that a *pandillero* (gang member) has chosen to follow in Los Angeles, leading to his imprisonment depicted on the wall's leftmost scene. An alternative lifestyle promises salvation through faith and religion represented in the commanding, enthroned Christ depicted on the wall's rightmost passage. "Richie," a victim of street violence, is remembered as the focal point in a striking lamentation mural painted in 1992 by New York–based Boricúa American airbrush painter Randall "Dragon" Barquero. Two other Queens neighborhood artists rendered the mural's textual graffiti background. A humble altar with lighted candles accompanies the mural. A memorial wall does not, however, guarantee its depicted subjects a perpetual place in the collective memory because neighborhoods undergo constant change. Similarly, memorialized events may fade from memory and public interest. One example could be the mural of Elián *González's plight documented near his Miami relatives' home. Depicted inside an inner tube—an object often associated with migrant water-crossings—Elián is shown in rough seas on his perilous journey of exile from Cuba to the United States. A Virgin image with huge outstretched hands reaches from heaven, and dolphins accompany and protect the "miracle child," as Elián was popularly known in Miami.

Altars and Shrines: Private and Public Sites of Popular Devotion, Display, and Introspection

While the "Richie" memorial functions as a public altar/shrine, another compelling example is *Hermano, por que?* (Brother, Why?), painted and inscribed in 1973 by David López and the Arizona Mara Gang. Dedicated to one of their own fallen Chicano *carnales*/brothers, the mural in the Maravilla Barrio of Los Angeles is dominated by a tall cruciform grave marker depicted beneath a bold, cursive textual sign interrogating the reader in Spanish: "Hermano, y porque estoy aqui en la tierra? /sin sangrar /sin andar /Hermano, por que?" (Brother, [and] why do I lie buried here? /lifeless and motionless /Brother, why?). A dense bouquet of painted flowers covers the foot of the painted cross. Ultimately blessed by the Vatican itself, this mural moved residents to respond to its pleading and lingering rhetorical question with candles and flowers they placed daily at its base, thus imbuing the mural site with the attributes of an actual altar/shrine.

Conversely, shrines may engender murals. Such was the case in 1992 when a garage door mural was painted by Chicano artist Peter Quesada and neighborhood youth from Montecito Heights, a residential barrio in Lincoln Heights, northeast of downtown Los Angeles. This painting paid homage to another local artist. Beloved creator of year-round community yard *altares* (altars) and *capillas* (shrines) that always displayed the American,

Californian, and Mexican flags, Florencio Morales was fittingly dubbed "el hombre de las banderas" (the man of [the] flags). It was his joy of "living on the hyphen"—to paraphrase *Life on the Hyphen*, a book by Cuban American scholar/writer Gustavo Pérez Firmat—that inspired Morales's Mexican American "baroque" exuberance. The mural in his honor featured Christ as shepherd accompanied by a lamb and a lion. Above them, a *banderole* flanked by doves is inscribed with a loving dedication that echoes Morales's own selfless communal spirit with which he embraced his public. Religious and secular imagery greeted onlookers at the sites of his Christmas and Day of the Dead (*Día de los Muertos) shrines to which invited celebrants added a performative dimension. On September 15, 1991, responding to Morales's handmade advertisement, friends and other congregants assembled in his yard to celebrate Mass and Father Hidalgo's historic Grito de Dolores (Cry of Pains/Independence [from Spain]) as a shared moment of faith and cultural reclamation. A hallmark of Morales's altars and shrines is his penchant for whimsical and macabre elements to startle and entertain the visitor: Florencio himself posing as Count Dracula, a toy pirate, or a scattering of bloody, decapitated heads at Halloween.

Boricúa American *casita* environments, a combination of small one- and two-room wood frame structures provide another example of communal public art. They are reminiscent of building types in Puerto Rico traceable to fifteenth-century Taíno Indian *bohios* (huts)—and what landscape architect Daniel Winterbottom calls "gardens of hope [and] reclamation." These communal Nuyorican (New York–based Boricúa) gardens incorporate diminutive shrines containing statues of Catholic saints, flowers, and candles. Masks like those used on the island during carnival celebrations along with graffiti-style and representational murals commemorating lost family members and scenes of the homeland. Like Morales's shrines, the *casitas* fly both American and Puerto Rican flags, proudly underscoring the conflation of cultures.

In contrast to Morales's mixed messages are the many evocations in hundreds of yard shrines lovingly dedicated to Our Lady of Guadalupe. This icon of icons among devout Catholics as well as secular Latinos is also popular in crafted indoor altars and shrines, a Mexican and Mexican American tradition traceable to the period of colonialism when makeshift altars were sought by itinerant priests for religious ceremonies. Both devout and more secular Chicanos continue to build household altars and shrines as personal expressions of religious, cultural, and/or other personal sentiments. Favorite saints—painted, photographed, and sculpted—rosaries, candles, flowers (real and artificial), photographs of living and deceased loved ones, stones, crystals, cloths, and other material objects adorn and layer the typical home altar or shrine. These lovingly conceived *ofrendas* (offerings), showcased atop all types of stationary and movable furniture, vary in complexity and size but always call attention to themselves as memorial sites of prayer, reflection, and solemnity. The architects of these built environments often share an abiding faith in spiritual healing and the sacred power of artistic continuity and creativity.

Amalia Mesa-Bains, Chicana altar artist and critic–scholar, labels the popular practice of domestic altar building among Mexican Americans as "domesticana." Referring to the makeshift nature of the altars themselves, and to the fact that most of their makers are women, she argues that their conception is informed by a "Chicana rascuache (make-do) sensibility." Other established Chicana/o, Boricúa American, and Cuban American artists have appropriated and expanded upon the domestic art of altar making. New Mexican artist Delilah Montoya's photomural *La Guadalupana* (1998) depicts a large tattooed penitent *pinto* (prison inmate), handcuffed and seen from behind. Its base is a diminutive altar composed largely of Latin American and southwestern motifs: votive candles adorned with Guadalupe, miniature American, Bolivian, Mexican, New Mexican, and Puerto Rican flags, a sarape, and a make-believe serpent. The installation is intended to elicit the viewer's spiritual empathy for the prisoner. The scene of a detained immigrant being frisked by a border agent—his arms akimbo in an allusion to the suffering Christ—is the focal point and a parody of a Tijuana tourist photo backdrop in the now-canonic mixed-media *Donkey Cart Altar* (1985) by California-based Chicano artist David Avalos. The rarely seen back of this "altar" portrays a portrait of Francisco Sánchez, a youngster murdered by the Border Patrol on December 8, 1980. Appealing to an audience's moral introspection, Avalos has substituted upright flashlights—surveillance instruments—for votive candles.

Choosing *La Virgen del Carmen* (Our Lady of Mount Carmel) as the subject of his 1988 altar installation, Boricúa American artist Ángel Suárez Rosado reflects on the *folklore surrounding his icon awakened, clandestine, liberated, and sacred spaces. Painted on the remnants of a boat's bottom with rudder still attached, *Our Lady* holds the talismanic Scapular—one of this saint's attributes—in her right hand, and her son in the crook of her left arm. Votive candles and seashells at the foot of the altar reinforce the artist's ruminations on negotiated space, perhaps through emigration. Cuban American Santería altars are similarly informed by the dynamics of migration, originating in Nigeria. Santería or Orisha worship—a blend of African and Catholic religious practices—evolved in Cuba as a result of the slave trade and arrived in North America through Afro-Caribbean immigration. Juan Boza's Santería altars are a Cuban American response to the baroque exuberance of Morales's altars. Replete with artificial foliage, beads, cloth, dolls, feathers, fruit, shells, and statuettes, *The Beginning and End* (1987) conveys Boza's message that "the spiritual universe [is] essential to well being."

Altars and Shrines on Wheels: *Carruchita*/*Lowrider Art

Chicano artists Jeff Abbey Maldonado and Luis Eligio Tapia change the stage and therefore the style of *ofrendas* to the automobile in *Where Past and Present Meet* (1996) and *Chima Altar II: Bertram's Cruise* (1992). Incorporating the hood and front end of an actual Buick, Maldonado's work is a Day of the Dead *ofrenda*, including a bottle of the deceased's favorite libation. Presided over by an angelic *esqueleto* (skeleton), the tableau fuses the age-old tradition of remembering the dead with automotive technology. Tapia, a New Mexican *santero* (saint maker), constructed his altar entirely of wood. Conceived to resemble arranged furniture, his is a whimsical interpretation of a car cruising along the highway as seen through its interior and windshield. Two dashboard saints overlook a Guadalupana-topped gearshift knob. While a lowrider is deliberately "low 'n slow," subverting the notion of speed usually associated with a car, both altars completely immobilize their subjects with bouncing and rearing hydraulics also undermined. Notably, however, the embellishments consistent with lowriding aesthetics remain a part of the ornately composed and colored installations. Boricúas in New York and San Juan adopted lowriders during the 1970s, usually opting to customize Japanese cars rather than American vehicles. Yet Ramón Guerra, a Boricúa American residing in Boston, airbrushed a painting of the lighthouse in San Juan, Puerto Rico—not unlike *casita* mural subjects—onto the hood of a 1964 Chevy Impala for his American car of choice.

Many lowriders in Mexican American communities are decorated with religious murals depicting Christ, Our Lady of Guadalupe, and even entire shrines. El Santuario de Chimayó (Chimayó Sanctuary) in Chimayó, New Mexico, is splendidly represented in the murals of Chicano artist Randy Martínez, painted on a 1937 Plymouth pickup and a 1979 Cadillac. These *carruchitas* (lowriders) thus are transformed into shrines on wheels.

Comic Books and Strips, Car Culture Magazines, Popular Toys, and Web Sites: Visualizing *Raza* (Mexican American) Humor and Melodrama

Lowrider culture continues to be promoted to a mass readership through its widely circulated magazines. From *Lowrider Magazine* (*LRM*)—which was launched in California's Mexican American barrios in the 1970s and continues thriving to this day on magazine racks virtually everywhere—to its offspring publication *Arte del Varrio* of the late 1970s and 1980s (and its own later iterations as *Lowrider Arte*), Latinos and a broad multiracial public indulge their love affair with the automobile. Lowrider culture, which traces its origins to the 1930s, has grown to international proportions.

During the late 1970s, and again during the late 1990s, graphic artist David Gonzales published a comic strip in *LRM* featuring his **Homies*, iconic barrio personalities, later turned into plastic toy *monitos*—miniature figurines typecast by some as *pandillero*-like—that experienced huge sales numbers in gumball machines and through the Internet. **La Cucaracha* (The Cockroach), a cartoon creation by Eduardo López (aka Lalo Alcaraz), inspired by *Mad Magazine*, became a nationally syndicated comic strip in December 2002. Despite those who regard *Baldo* as *La Cucaracha*'s precedent, Alcaraz argues that his is the first Chicano comic strip to achieve daily status in newspapers. Always one to affirm his culture, Alcaraz began drawing cartoons on fliers to raise money to support the farmworker cause. *Pocho Magazine*, his serialized comic strips, appeared during the early 1990s and sealed his dream to become a cartoonist. Alcaraz finds *Baldo*—featuring the protagonist visiting *bodegas* (taverns) and lowriding—culturally unfocused because the strip was produced by Chicano writers collaborating with a Cuban American artist. He argues that his strip, like *Pocho Magazine* before it, is unequivocally based on Chicano culture. That *La Cucaracha* is written in English should communicate as well to disadvantaged English-only monolinguals.

Highly indignant over the pro-Proposition 187 vote in California, Laura Molina, self-described "Angriest Woman in The World," self-published her comic book/magazine *The Jaguar* in 1996. Today, her failed relationship with David Stevens and the paintings reflecting on that relationship have contributed to and inspired a Web site titled *Naked Dave*, which has spawned a melodramatic field for sparring engagement between the genders. A film documenting this electronic conflict is planned.

Printmaking with a Cause

Nowhere are the activist narratives of affirmation, celebration, commemoration, declamation, indignation, and reclamation better conceived than in printed multiples emerging from the Chicano and Boricúa American movements. Chicana/o artists Ester Hernández and Amado Maurilio Peña, Jr., express their indignation with a sense of humor in *He's Gone Too Far!* (1974) and *Sun Mad* (1982), two silkscreen-colored prints known as serigraphs. Peña's play on a Quaker Oats product spoofs the Nixon administration, while Hernández, angry over the use of toxic defoliants that make farmworkers deathly ill, parodies the Sun Maid trademark as "Sun Mad." In his graphically striking serigraph titled *Taller Boricua* (1974), Jorge Soto Sánchez affirms and commemorates his Puerto Rican patrimony and celebrates and reclaims his ancestral, indigenous history. Boricúa American Marcos Dimas and Cuban American Manuel García invoke the likeness of freedom fighter and political prisoner Lolita Lebrón in a linocut (a print made from a design cut into linoleum) and serigraph from 1971, respectively. Che *Guevara's likeness—borrowed from Cuban photographer Alberto Korda's iconic image of him—reproduced in posters has become so widespread that examples are too numerous to mention. Community muralism and engaged printmaking intersect and share the spirit and energy of *comunitas* in the flourishing projects of Latina/o visual art.

Further Reading

Barnett, Alan W. *Community Murals: The People's Art.* Cranbury, NJ: Associated University Presses, 1984.

Lindsay, Arturo, ed. *Santería Aesthetics in Contemporary Latin American Art.* Washington, DC: Smithsonian Institution Press, 1996.

Mesa-Bains, Amalia, et al. *Ceremony of Memory: New Expressions in Spirituality among Contemporary Hispanic Artists.* Santa Fe, NM: Center for Contemporary Arts of Santa Fe, 1988.

Víctor Alejandro Sorell and Ann Aguirre

League of United Latin American Citizens. *See* LULAC.

Leaños, John Jota (1969–). John Jota Leaños, a performance and graphic artist based in San Francisco, was born on April 14, 1969, in Los Angeles into a Mexican Italian American family. He is also an assistant professor in the Department of Chicana and Chicano Studies at Arizona State University in Tempe and a self-identified cultural worker. He earned a Master of Fine Arts in photography from San Francisco State University in 2000; his installation *Remembering Castration* is a palimpsest of photo and Aztec and Mayan codices that illustrates the need for a contemporary rite of passage and a sense of connection to ancestral homeland. As a transgressing artist-activist, Leaños has campaigned against *globalization and against emerging technologies, which he considers to be the main weapon in the capitalist arsenal of corporate domination, globalization, and means of fighting against activists and progressives. He also endeavors to make visible the active role of Chicana and *Chicano art in the resistance against what he sees as an American-dominated global monoculture both in the United States and the rest of the world.

His work combines contemporary iconography of globalization and technology as well as that of the Latino community—*barrio, border, and *indocumentados* (undocumented immigrants), racial profiling, and the phenomenon of nonstop wireless connectivity for information transfer that continuously brings online more and more sophisticated systems of tracking and surveillance. His work has appeared in edited volumes of Latino art and has been included in the exhibitions at the Whitney Museum of American Art and the Oakland Museum of California. In addition, he has participated in many San Francisco Bay area exhibitions and public art projects.

Two of Leaños's works illustrate his strong sociotechnological concerns. In *The Mission Y2K* (2000) he shows the darker side of technology as it unearths and displaces people: a jet-propelled snow dome filled with Latinos and images of the predominantly Latino Mission neighborhood in San Francisco depicted in flight and without a home; and in *Oppositional Panel*

(1998) he critiques antibilingual education agendas and the controlling of space as forms of neocolonialism that lead to historical amnesia and genocide. He recently curated the exhibit *Digital Mural Project* at San Francisco's Latino Mission District Galería de la Raza (2000) as well as the special exhibition at the Oakland Museum of California titled *Pasajes y Encuentros: Ofrendas for the Days of the Dead* (2001). In the second exhibit, he brought together a variety of Latina/o artists who celebrate the Day of the Dead (*Día de los Muertos) in their use of video, mural, and canvas to connect the dead with the living through humor and revitalized indigenous/Catholic spiritualist imagery—*ánima*—as well as to connect the Latino experience with that of other ethnic minority experiences, such as that of the slave trade Middle Passage. Together with Mónica Praba and René García, Leaños formed the group Los Cybrids: La Raza Techno-Crítica, self-described on their Web site as "three artists exploring cultural and somatic mutations caused by the implosion of advanced information technology." When still performing Los Cybrids employed performance, *burla* (humor), and high-tech art to undermine the uncritical, passive acceptance of information technologies as effective tools. It is with this aim of resistance that Los Cybrids have created and performed works such as *El World Brain Disorder: surveillance.control pendejismo*; *Webopticon: Arquitectura of Control*, *De-educación: Computas in the Classroom*; *High Sweat Tech Shop*, and *Global Warmaquina: The Internet and Its Discontents*. Leaños has been the recipient of the Creative Capital Grant, Walter and Elise Hass Creative Work Fund Grant, and the Murphy-Caddigan Award for Visual Arts.

Further Reading

http://www.cybrids.com/artists.html.

Luis Aldama

Leguizamo, John (1964–). An award-winning Colombian-born with Puerto Rican roots film actor, comedian, performer, director, and off-Broadway actor, Leguizamo came to the United States at age four and grew up in New York. He studied his craft at New York University under the legendary Lee Strasberg. His career began in typical stand-up comic clubs, and in 1986 his big break was on the television show *Miami Vice*. The most influential performance of his career has been *Mambo Mouth*, off Broadway, where he portrayed seven different Latino characters. This performance won him star and writer Obie and Outer Critics Circle Awards. Two years later, Leguizamo came back with another one-man show, *Spic-o-Rama*, earning him a Drama Desk Award and a CaleACE award when it aired on HBO. Leguizamo's work in film, television, and theater demonstrates his artistic and talented ability to show his craft in all three genres. His other theater awards include an Outer Critics Circle award for Outstanding Solo Performance (1988) for *Freak*, and in 1998–1999 he won an Emmy for Outstanding Performance in a Variety or Music Program for *Freak* as well. He has appeared

John Leguizamo. *Courtesy of Photofest.*

in over forty-five films dating to the 1985 *Mixed Blood*. His recent film appearances include *Collateral Damage* (2002), *Moulin Rouge* (2001), and Spike Lee's *Summer of Sam* (1999); other notable performances are seen in *Romeo and Juliet* (1996) and *Carlito's Way*, starring Al Pacino (1993).

Further Reading

http://www.imdb.com/Name?Leguizamo,%20John.
http://www.hollywood.com/celebs/detail/celeb/190190.
http://www.romeoandjuliet.com/players/leguizamo.html.

Elizabeth (Lisa) Flores

Leyenda Negra, La. *See La Leyenda Negra.*

Libraries and Archival Collections. The Smithsonian and the Library of Congress and other repositories have begun to acknowledge the importance of Latinas and Latinos to the cultural future of the United States because of the size and relative youth of the population. In addition, collection professionals generally agree that because the founding heritage of vast regions of the United States was Latino and mestizo, any account of the American past and all attempts to understand the present also must understand the indelible cultural imprint of Latinas/os. Despite the fundamental importance of the founding Latina/o heritage and its continuing impact on contemporary American culture, the Smithsonian and others only relatively recently began to be informed about Latina/o contributions to the history and culture of the nation. They were led to this awareness in part by public demand and also by the pioneering efforts of Latina/o collectors who were among the first professionals in the archival and library fields to take note of the pressing need for improved collecting practices relating to Latinas/os.

Leaders in this effort in the late twentieth century were Chicana and *Chicano scholars, archivists, librarians, and others directly concerned with recovering, documenting, and disseminating the active participation and vibrant contributions of Mexican American and other marginalized groups to the national culture. Chicano and Chicana archivists and librarians in the late 1960s and early 1970s joined efforts to develop a new mission: to capture, collect, and preserve the history of La Raza, the Mexican Americans, or Chicanos, as the *Movimiento* activists and participants called themselves at the time. This mission had a twofold purpose—for the sake of all future archival and library users and for the good of Chicana/o communities, which for the most part were deprived of public records and collections about themselves and their heritage. Working with university deans, library directors, and other education and preservation administrators, the archivists and librarians laid the groundwork for building Chicana/o studies archival and library collections. In the process, they established collection development goals, guidelines, and objectives; approved acquisitions budgets for their departments; purchased archival supplies and preservation materials; and hired Chicano/a library and archives staff and students to assist them in their efforts. This proactive approach resulted in, for example, the Benson Collection at the University of Texas at Austin, the Chicano Research Collection at Arizona State University, the Colección Tloque Nahuaque at the University of California at Santa Barbara, and others.

These academic professionals took their cues about what to collect from the myriad events that comprised the *Chicano Movement in the Southwest: civil rights; bilingual education; labor strikes; the Chicano Moratorium; the Vietnam War; the United Farm Workers movement; the assassinations of John and Robert Kennedy; Chicana issues; and student protests on high school, college, and university campuses. They sought photographs; *family histories and stories; *immigration documents; business and financial records; personal archives and correspondence; diaries and unpublished manuscripts; ephemera; oral histories; and organizations' records. They went into their Chicano communities and brought these unique materials into their archival repositories and libraries, where they were arranged, processed, and cataloged according to modern library and archival standards.

Support for their archival and library collections and programs came from Chicano/a faculty, staff, and most important, the Raza communities. Faculty encouraged students to learn about and study the Chicano civil rights movement by using these materials to write their research papers. Staff members helped archivists and librarians process and arrange the manuscript and photograph collections and made them available for use. Community activists became those important donors who created endowments or opportunities for archivists to acquire notable manuscript collections and additional primary sources that reflected their communities. These shared efforts became part of a sweeping Chicano/a cultural nationalism that linked academia with activists throughout the Southwest in a positive way: Important records were collected and preserved to ensure their availability in the decades ahead. Librarians and archivists have continued to specialize in developing Chicano/a archival collections and have opened their doors for anyone whose research interests are in the field of Chicano/a studies. Electronic databases, Internet Web sites, online exhibits, and subject indices maintained in Chicana/o archives and libraries have enabled historians, educators, and students to research, write, and interpret the Chicano/a experience.

Major Chicana/o archival and library collections in the Southwest include the Chicano Research Collection at ASU's Hayden Library in Tempe; the Mexican American Library Program housed within the UT Benson Latin American Collection in Austin; the Mexican American collection of Stanford University; the UCSB Colección Tloque Nahuaque; the Chicano Studies Library at the University of California, Berkeley; the Chicano Studies Research Library in Los Angeles; and the Southwest Resource Center located within the Zimmerman Library at the University of New Mexico in Albuquerque. Each of these Chicana/o archival, research, and library collections has invaluable quantities of historical documents on state and regional history as well as numerous literature, art, and personal papers to support the research and teaching agendas of faculty, programs, centers, and institutes.

Long before these late-twentieth-century strides forward in library acquisitions and archival collecting, one of the most important Latina and Latino collections was being compiled in Puerto Rico and New York by Arturo Alfonso *Schomburg, who described himself as an "Afroborinqueño" or Puerto Rican of African descent. Equipped with a good education, Schomburg developed an amazing love of books when he was a boy, and his passion was fueled by his anger at the casual remark of a teacher who glibly stated that people of color had no history, no heroes, or any other notable accomplishments. He wrote that this motivated him to embark on a lifelong quest to methodically challenge and correct the mythology about Puerto Ricans, African Americans, and other marginalized peoples of the Americas. Eventually he documented and wrote about the accomplishments of Puerto Rican artist José Campeche, Haitian liberator Toussaint L'Ouverture, and the Afro-Cuban general Antonio Maceo, among many others. As important, he also collected the materials and oral histories needed to record a fuller picture of the African role in the history, life, and culture of the Western Hemisphere. Schomburg's passion led to his cofounding the Negro Society for Historical Research in 1911, an archival institute that published important papers on black history. A leader of the legendary Harlem Renaissance of the 1920s and 1930s, he directed library acquisitions for Fisk University, all along compiling the now world-renowned collection of Africana housed in the New York Public Library. Consisting of thousands of slave narratives, manuscripts, rare books, journals, artwork, and other remnants of African history, his collection was presented to the Library in 1926. As curator of the holdings, renamed the Schomburg Center for Research in Black Culture, he built the collection into an American treasure of over 6 million items, including photographs, films, audio recordings, rare books, and institutional archives. Today the Center's extensive bibliographic records are cataloged on CD-ROM. Also see Casa de las Americas entry.

Further Reading

Driscoll, Barbara A. "Chicana Historiography: A Research Note Regarding Mexican Archival Sources." In *Chicana Voices*, edited by Teresa Cordova. Austin, TX: Center for Mexican American Studies, 1986.

Garcia-Ayvens, Francisco, and Richard F. Chabran, eds. *Biblio-politica: Chicano Perspectives on Library Service in the United States*. Berkeley: Chicano Studies Library Publications Unit, University of California, 1984.

Guerena, Salvador. "Archives and Manuscripts: Historical Antecedents to Contemporary Chicano Collections." *Collection Building* 8.4 (1987): 3–11.

Marín, Christine, and Rose Díaz. *Libraries and Repositories: Collection Development as a Subversive Activity*. Shawnee Mission, KS: Vanguard Systems, 1990. Sound recording.

Christine N. Marín

Like Water for Chocolate. Directed and produced by Alfonso Arau and distributed by Buena Vista Home Entertainment, *Like Water for Chocolate* (1993) is a screen adaptation of Laura Esquivel's 1989 bestselling novel of the same title. Arau's Spanish-language *film achieved enormous commercial success in its crossover to North American audiences. The turn-of-the-century story chronicles a forbidden love between Tita (Lumi Cavazos) and Pedro (Marco Leonardi). Set in northern México near the Texan border, the movie is narrated by Tita's grandniece (Arcelia Ramírez) and based on Tita's old and tattered recipe book.

The plot of the story thickens with the untimely death of Tita's father, which leaves Mama Elena (Regina Torne) alone to rear her three daughters and tend to the ranch, leaving the youngest, Tita, in the kitchen to be tended by a Kickapoo servant, Nacha (Ada Carrasco). As the youngest, Tita is expected to ensure the *family's tradition of caring for their mother until death. Thus, when Pedro comes to ask for Tita's hand in marriage, Mama Elena refuses and instead offers Pedro her eldest daughter, Rosaura (Yareli Arizmendi), since tradition also requires that the eldest marry first. The movie effectively reveals Tita's emotional and erotic life through *food and her cooking, and her dishes become metaphors of her frustrated love for Pedro.

In 1993, *Like Water for Chocolate* was nominated for Best Foreign Language Film by the Golden Globe and the Independent Spirit Awards voters. In 1992 it received several Ariel Awards in México and also was nominated for Spain's Goya Best Spanish Language Foreign Film Award in 1993.

Further Reading

Esquivel, Laura. *Like Water for Chocolate*. New York: Anchor Books, 1989.

Silvia D. Mora

Literature, Puerto Rican. The fact that the first elected governor of Puerto Rico, Luis Muñoz Marín (1898–1980), is remembered as an accomplished poet as well as a politician aptly illustrates how the island's literary history is interwoven with its political past. Like many of the artists and writers who preceded him in the Spanish colony and later in the U.S. Commonwealth, Muñoz began his public life as a poet and continued it as an activist reformer, politician, and government official. Such nineteenth-century forerunners as novelist Manuel Zeno Gandía (1855–1930), playwright Alejandro Tapia y Rivera (1826–1882), essayist and poet José Gautier Benítez (1839–1903), and writer Eugenio María de Hostos y Bonilla (1839–1903) exemplify the championing of political freedom and social justice that still mark Puerto Rican creative literature and other popular culture practices at the dawn of the twenty-first century (e.g., the *Nuyorican Poets Café and *El Nuevo Teatro Pobre de América).

A representative example of the union of Puerto Rican literature and political activism is Eugenio Hostos, whose life and work demonstrate an unwavering resistance to the foreign domination of his homeland and to the *Boricúa Borinqueño movement for self-governance. Hostos was born in 1839 near Mayagüez, Puerto Rico, and was educated in Spain, where he became involved in the movement for Puerto Rican independence from Spain (*see* History, Puerto Rican). One of the most effective early advocates of self-rule for the West Indies, Hostos left Spain in 1869 when its new constitution refused to give autonomy to Puerto Rico and kept it under Spanish control. Like many other Latin American intellectuals and writers, he sought haven in the United States, where he began editing a Cuban independence journal, *La Revolución*, advocating for Cuba's freedom from Spain. After traveling throughout South America and teaching for several years in Chile, he returned to the United States in 1898, continuing his advocacy for Antillean (i.e., West Indies) independence, which was an especially burning issue in Puerto Rico and Cuba. He and other activist writers were disappointed after the 1898 Spanish-American War when the U.S. government rejected a proposal for autonomy, instead establishing U.S. control over the island as a new American territory. As a result, Hostos continued his self-exile by living in another Antillean island, the Dominican Republic, where he played a major role in pushing for substantial educational reforms and the rights of workers and women. He also wrote fifty volumes of prose, including many essays and treatises on social science topics. At his death in exile in Santo Domingo in 1903, he was hailed as a visionary leader and educator throughout Latin America, and today scholars consider him to be one of Latin America's first systematic sociologists and liberation philosophers.

During the late nineteenth century other Latin Americans like Hostos who supported independence movements in their countries immigrated to the United States to escape persecution from the Spanish colonial government. Spanish authorities came to view New York City as one of the places where renegade intellectuals and artists sought asylum to organize against the Spanish empire in favor of independence movements. Although the exile literatures of these émigrés supported the populist ideals of their home cultures and the rights of poor people, most of them were well educated and from affluent families. After the Treaty of Paris ended the Spanish-American War, Cuba gained independence from Spain, and Puerto Rico was designated a commonwealth of the United States. One result of Puerto Rico's new status in the early decades of the twentieth century was the avid recruitment of large numbers of Puerto Rican workers by U.S. corporations to work on the mainland as agricultural contract workers, primarily in the tobacco industry. This period led to a much greater socioeconomic range of Puerto Rican immigrants in the United States, and through their language, heritage, and popular culture practices they added a Borinqueño presence to the mainland, for the most part in New York City and along the eastern seaboard.

One such émigré, Arturo Alfonso *Schomburg (1874–1938), a self-described "Afroborinqueño," a Puerto Rican of African descent, became active in the independence cause and, like Hostos and others, had a major and lasting impact on U.S. education and scholarship. After migrating to New York City in 1891, Schomburg joined other Latina/o exiles in fostering the bilingual, multicultural heritage of the Americas and promoting self-rule throughout Latin America. Involved in the aesthetic and political movement known as the Harlem Renaissance in the United States, he realized after the death of Cuban hero José *Martí in 1895 that obtaining independence from Spain for the Antilles was remote. As a result, he decided to devote himself to collecting and preserving the heritage of the African diaspora, and today the Schomburg Center for Research in Black Culture in New York is considered one of the world's foremost repositories of Africana and African American—including Latina/o—archives, slave narratives, creative literature, and cultural holdings.

In the 1940s the U.S. colonial administrators of Puerto Rico determined that the commonwealth was overpopulated, and in conjunction with the U.S. Department of Labor, they promoted immigration to the United States to alleviate the problem. The government mounted programs to help the émigrés adapt to the new environment and provide job opportunities on the mainland. This twentieth-century diaspora produced writers who addressed their immigrant experience in leaving the island and who were willing to question the terms of their transnational identity, bilinguality, and marginalized culture. Among these were Puerto Rican poet Julia de Burgos (1914–1953) and journalists Bernardo Vega (1885–1965) and Jesús *Colón (1901–1974). A writer celebrated more after her death than during her life's struggle with poverty and alcohol, de Burgos lived for over a decade in New York writing poems, mainly in Spanish. Her verse spoke of the situation of Puerto Ricans in the city, and shortly before her death in 1953, she wrote two poems in English that evocatively capture that plight, "Farewell from Welfare Island" and "The Sun in Welfare Island." Like the other Puerto Rican expatriates, Vega and Colón moved to New York seeking civil liberties. Vega became a journalist and wrote his autobiography, *Memorias* (1977), which literary scholars consider an important personal chronicle of the history of Puerto Ricans in New York. Fellow journalist Colón wrote for newspapers and periodicals and eventually published *A Puerto Rican in New York and Other Sketches* (1961).

The contemporary generation of Puerto Rican and some self-identified Nuyorican writers and artists confronted head-on the most controversial aspects of U.S. Latina/o experience including the majority society's perception of a language barrier for Puertorriqueños despite a bilingual and bicultural ancestry nearly 150 years older than the *Mayflower*'s landing in Massachusetts in 1620. Writers from this era like Piri Thomas, Pedro Pietri, Miguel *Algarín, Miguel *Piñero, Sandra María Esteves, Martita Morales, and Víctor Hernández Cruz tackled the topics of racism, segregation, poverty, and systemic institutional disenfranchisement on the mainland, as well as the poor economic situation on the island. Their poetry and drama frequently express the emotional, political, and cultural impact of expatriate life. One early example of this literary generation is Puerto Rico–based playwright and novelist René Marqués (pre-Nuyorican) who, in 1949, went to New York City with a grant from the Rockefeller Foundation to study playwriting. Based on his U.S. experience, his first major play, *La carreta* (The Oxcart, 1951), portrays the anguish of a Puerto Rican who abandons his country and immigrates to New York in search of a better life but who, in the end, returns to the island in search of personal contentment. Another important figure in the theater during the 1950s and 1960s was Roberto Rodríguez

Suárez, known as the father of Puerto Rican drama in the United States. He wrote plays for the stage and television and founded the Nuevo Círculo Dramático, the first permanent Hispanic theater in the United States.

Moving away from nostalgia for the island toward an embracing of their mainland realities, Miguel Algarín and Miguel Piñero edited an influential anthology in 1975 titled *Nuyorican Poetry* (*see* Nuyorican Poets Café). Their choice of the term "Nuyorican" was a bold statement that accepted the everyday experience of Puerto Ricans in New York City. "Nuyorican" has since become more than a term to express the Puerto Rican situation in the United States; it also captures an in-group popular culture identity, and some Nuyorican artists describe it as a source of mutual protection. In a 1979 poem called "La Carreta Made a U Turn," Tato Laviera, a young Nuyorican poet, rejected the possibility of returning to the island the way Marqués had proposed in his play, in part because Puerto Ricans on the island did not accept those living on the mainland. After constant rejection, the Nuyoricans themselves rejected the prospect of going back as a sentimental idea. This decolonized attitude appears in much of the fiction of the 1990s. For example, in 1994 Esmeralda Santiago published *Cuando era puertorriqueña* (When I Was Puerto Rican), a novel written in fourteen sections that recreates from her autobiographical, unsentimental perspective the three basic stages of Marqués's *La Carreta*. In *Cuando era puertorriqueña*, the main character, lured by childhood memories, is tempted by the romantic illusion of going back to the island. In the end, she forces herself to accept the reality that she cannot go back to a place that no longer has a space for her.

Bilingual, bi-cultural Puerto Rican writers from the mainland face rejection of their work by writers from the island who do not include the New York writers in the island's literary canon. Thus, the Nuyorican production is not well known among many intellectuals in Puerto Rico. One reason for their rejection by the Spanish-dominant island literati is that the mainland authors usually write in English and "Spanglish," a vernacular dialect that combines both Spanish and English. In the ongoing argument about which literary works should be included in any given country's canon, some scholars conclude that language should not be the primary criterion. They prefer to focus on the cultural and political identity the writers assume as they interpret reality in their works. The highly regarded Nuyorican writer Nicholasa Mohr discusses this phenomenon in her essay "Puerto Rican Writers in the United States, Puerto Rican Writers in Puerto Rico: A Separation beyond Language" (1994) and concludes that she and Nuyoricans like her find it difficult to understand, or even relate to, literature from the island. Mohr accepts that even though she is culturally Puerto Rican, she occupies a separate point of view defined by an awareness of geography, gender, and postcolonial genre different from earlier generations. Others who write from this decolonized, postcolonial space include Judith Ortiz-Cofer, Aurora Levins Morales, Rosario

Morales, Abraham Rodríguez, Ed Vega, Rodney Morales, Edward Rivera, Edwin Torres, and Jack Agüeros.

Increasingly, Puerto Rican, Nuyorican, and related Latina/o literatures are appropriately being considered part of the larger body of North American literature. Anthologies such as *Currents from the Dancing River* (1994), *Barrios and Borderlands* (1994), *Growing Up Puerto Rican* (1997), *Iguana Dreams* (1992), and *Boricuas* (1995) offer readers of any nationality an opportunity to know the vitality and diversity of a wide range of popular cultures and historical experiences distinctively Borinquen and, therefore, American.

Further Reading

Acosta-Belén, Edna. "Hemispheric Remappings: Revisiting the Concept of Nuestra América." In *Identities on the Move: Transnational Processes in North America and the Caribbean Basin*, edited by Liliana Goldin. Austin: University of Texas Press, 1999.

Algarín, Miguel, and Miguel Piñero, eds. *Nuyorican Poetry: An Anthology of Puerto Rican Words and Feelings*. New York: William Morrow, 1975.

Epple, Juan Armando. "Hispanic Exile in the United States." In *Handbook of Hispanic Cultures in the United States: Literature and Art*, edited by Francisco Lomelí et al. Houston, TX: Arte Público Press and Instituto de Cooperación Iberoamericana, 1993.

Mohr, Nicholasa. "Puerto Rican Writers in the United States, Puerto Rican Writers in Puerto Rico: A Separation beyond Language." In *Barrios and Borderlands*, edited by Denis Lynn Daly Heyck. New York: Routledge, 1994.

Heidi García and Cordelia Chávez Candelaria

Little Joe Hernández y La Familia. Little Joe y La Familia has been recognized as one of the world's best *Tejano bands since the mid-1970s. La Familia performs a big band swing sound known as *orquesta tipica* or *orquesta tejana*, which combines a musical mixture of blues, **rancheras*, and polkas. A strong advocate for Mexican farmworkers and the Chicana/o working class, the band has recorded several unofficial anthems like "Las Nubes" (The Clouds) and "Margarita," marking Little Joe as more than a popular singer; he is *un hijo del pueblo* (a native son). He is regarded as an organic intellectual and artistic leader advocating on behalf of working-class Tejanos in particular and the larger *Chicano community in general. Little Joe y La Familia was originally named Little Joe and the Latinaires and was formed in Temple, Texas, in 1959. They performed at large commercial dance concerts and venues that attracted record audiences. Today Little Joe continues to perform songs that appeal to the working classes including popular songs like "Cuando Salgo a los Campos" (When I Go Out to the Fields), which speaks to the daily struggles of Mexican Americans.

Little Joe was born José María de León Hernández, the seventh son of thirteen children. His family members were primarily sharecroppers whose roots went back to the Mexican Revolution. Little Joe recalls that he was born in a three-wall garage with a dirt floor that belonged to a *compadre* (godfather) of his father. His family moved two weeks after he was born because of a flood in which he almost drowned. They moved to the African American part of town where Little Joe was first introduced to black culture and gained an appreciation for blues and jazz. His father, Salvador "La Cotorra" Hernández, worked on the railroad and performed music gigs on weekends. Little Joe was exposed to Mexican popular and folk music on the family radio. Little Joe's father was arrested in 1955 for possession of marijuana and sentenced to twenty-eight months in prison, leaving fifteen-year-old Little Joe as head of the family. Most of his family members continued working in the fields, picking crops around Temple.

By age sixteen, Little Joe bought his first guitar and learned the "basics" from his friends and relatives. In 1957, Little Joe joined the Waco musicians' union and began playing with David Coronado and the Latinaires. The group consisted of Coronado on alto saxophone, Little Joe on guitar, Tony Matamoros on tenor saxophone, and Jacinto Moreno on trap-drums. The band was hired often for weekend dances and even opened for Isidro López in Victoria, Texas. The next year the Latinaires came to the attention of Torero, a label from Corpus Christi, and they recorded their first single (45-rpm record), a rock tune titled "Safari," parts 1 and 2. "Safari" became a landmark in Tejano music, as it may well have been the first rock and roll hit recorded by a Tejano group. In 1959, Coronado left the state and handed the direction of the band over to Little Joe, who also fronted the act. The Latinaires started out as a Top 40 cover band, dressed in glitzy tuxedos, with choreography and vocal harmonies typical of the early rock and roll bands of the 1950s. The Latinaires, like many young Mexican American musicians, hoped to crack the rock and roll market and were attracted to giant pop idols like Elvis Presley and African American singers like Chuck Berry, Little Richard, and Fats Domino. Little Joe and the Latinaires did not penetrate the Top 40 market but left their indelible mark on Tejano music nevertheless.

Unable to compete in the Top 40 market, the Latinaires refocused their musical efforts on traditional Tejano music. However, their musical success took time. Little Joe's first hit single was "El Corrido del West" (The Ballad of the West), recorded in San Antonio. In 1964, the Latinaires recorded a long-playing (LP) album, *Por un Amor* (For a Love), with Zarape Records in Dallas. This album and the lead song "Por un Amor" led to grassroots popularity and regional fame. In the mid-1960s, the Latinaires consisted of six instruments including alto and tenor saxophones, trumpet, guitar (played by Little Joe), bass, and drums, with Little Joe's brother Johnny as solo vocalist and second voice in duets.

The Latinaires relocated to California in the early 1970s during the Vietnam War and amid the height of social activism and political protest of the civil rights, women's, and *Chicano Movements. In California, Little Joe was influenced musically by rock, Top 40, jazz, and other styles. On the West Coast, Little Joe rediscovered his Tejano roots, renaming the band José María de León Hernández y La Familia. One of his most important albums recorded was *Para la Gente* (For the People, 1991) on Sony Discos, and it included the popular Mexican song "Las Nubes" (The Clouds), which became an unofficial anthem for Tejano farmworkers with its catchy tune and stark lyrics. However, the polka *ranchera* (a straightforward, unpolished **canción ranchera* in polka tempo) became one of the band's signature tunes, featuring Joe and Johnny singing a simple duet in the traditional *ranchera* style in parallel harmony.

"Las Nubes" opens with an instrumental introduction with two trumpets, trombone, two saxophones, plus a rhythm section of electric guitar, electric bass, Hammond organ, and trap-drums playing a strong *ranchero* (country) flavor. A string ensemble joins the horns, creating a more sophisticated sound that almost undermines the *ranchero* style by fusing a Mexican folk and American popular swing-jazz. In 1965 the Latinaires recorded another LP, *Amor Bonito* (Beautiful Love), for Zarape Records, which gained considerable popularity and gave the band further momentum for the next three years and moved the Latinaires to its second and most successful stage.

In 1967, Little Joe decided to reorganize his *orquesta* and its members, repertoire, and musical standards. The Latinaires performed mostly rock-oriented tunes and simple arrangements of standard *rancheras* and polkas. Their sound was crude and unpolished, and most of the arrangements were improvised and performed "by ear." Little Joe hired Tony "Ham" Guerrero (aka Martínez), an accomplished and seasoned trumpet player and musician who encouraged the band to begin reading charts. Their 1970 recording *Arriba* was quite different from previous ones with a larger ensemble, polished arrangements, and a bigger and better sound; the group's previous "James Brown" image was history. Little Joe renamed the Latinaires "La Familia," and the members grew long hair and became hippies.

Little Joe returned to Texas in the mid-1970s and formed his own Buena Suerte label (Good Luck) and founded Brown Sound studios. According to Manuel Peña, the aesthetic transformation of the Latinaires was complete, including new fashion and hairstyles, name, counterculture lifestyle, and a Chicano ideology. Throughout his career, Joe has scored an impressive list of successes including being the first Tejano artist to be signed by a major label—CBS Discos in 1986. In the same year he became the first Tejano to perform at one of Willie Nelson's Farm Aid concerts. He later released another album, *Timeless* (c. late 1980s), which stayed on the *Billboard* charts for fifty-seven consecutive weeks. Their 25th Silver Anniversary live recording is also noteworthy. For a complete discography, see Little Joe y La Familia's official Web site.

Further Reading

Peña, Manuel. *Música Tejana: The Cultural Economy of Artistic Transformation.* College Station: Texas A&M University Press, 1999.

Peña, Manuel. *The Texas-Mexican Conjunto: History of a Working Class Music.* Austin: University of Texas Press, 1985.

http://www.littlejoemusic.homestead.com.

Peter J. García

Llorona, La. *See* La Llorona.

Lobos, Los. *See* Los Lobos.

Lomas Garza, Carmen (1948–). Carmen Lomas Garza is a highly prolific visual artist whose genre paintings of working-class *Chicano life are seen in a variety of venues and serve to recapture and recenter Chicano subjects and Chicano culture in the American visual landscape. Lomas Garza is distinguished by her willingness to use full color schemes and the entire canvas to depict realistic "snapshots" or scenes of Chicano *families and the daily and ritualized activities of families living together, eating together, and taking care of each other. Her narrative scenes of quotidian life (a Chicana Norman Rockwell) counterpoint the dominant cultural images of Chicano families as *gang-bangers, undocumented border crossers, violent, dysfunctional, and suffering.

Lomas Garza was born in Kingsville, Texas, and at the age of thirteen decided to become a visual artist. She studied art education and studio art (B.S., 1972; M.Ed., 1973; M.A., 1980). Although her training included lithography and oil, and gouache painting influenced her work, she also recognizes her mother and grandmother with providing artistic training and inspiration. She credits the Galería de la Raza of San Francisco, where she served as the administrative assistant and curator (1976–1981), with contributing to her understanding of non-profit arts organizing. Her work has appeared in major exhibitions, including a solo show at the Laguna Gloria Art Museum in Texas. The Mexican Fine Arts Center Museum, the Smithsonian American Art Museum, and the Oakland Museum have collected her work. She is the recipient of two National Endowment for the Arts awards, and she has created bilingual children's books based on her paintings. She has resided in San Francisco since 1976.

Further Reading

Keller, Gary, et al. *Contemporary Chicana and Chicano Art.* Tempe, AZ: Bilingual Review Press, 2002.

Karen Mary Dávalos and Arturo J. Aldama

Lone Star. Written and directed by John Sayles and distributed by Sony Pictures Classics, *Lone Star* (1995) was nominated for an Academy Award for Best Original Screenplay. The film mixes a variety of filmic genres—drama, mystery, romance, and social realism—to make a commentary on ethnic tensions and histories in Texas. This tale of murder is centered in a small border town called Frontera ("the border"). The film opens with two men digging in the desert, when one of them finds human remains. Near the skeleton they also find an old sheriff's badge. Soon the viewer is enmeshed in a complicated tale about a forty-year-old murder, and it seems that somehow everyone in the small town has a connection to both the corpse, the ex-sheriff, and the most likely suspect, his replacement, Sheriff Buddy Deeds (Matthew McConaughey), who has also since passed away. Complicating issues further, the current sheriff of Frontera is Sam Deeds (Chris Cooper), Buddy's son.

Sayles uses long flashback sequences juxtaposed with the current murder investigation to create a multigenerational, multiethnic narrative of life on the border. In *Lone Star*, the history of the people of Frontera—Mexican, black, American Indian, and white—emerges along with the unfolding tale of murder and motive. Sayles's film technique, his crossing back and forth in time, mirrors the crossing of borders that Sam Deeds and the other characters experience, both psychologically as well as physically.

Lone Star explores the way history gets told and how particular places, people, and events shape cultural memory. Throughout the film, many of the characters recount the past to Sam, and these multiple perspectives allow him to discover the "truth" that he sets out to find in the beginning, no matter how painful or personal. Sam rediscovers his teenage love (Elizabeth *Peña), from whom he had been separated by his father. This relationship underscores the ethnic boundaries that extend far beyond the physical space of the border but affect generations who share the violent history of ethnic conflict in the Mexican American West. The cast of *Lone Star* also includes Ron Canada, Miriam *Colón, Clifton James, Kris Kristofferson, and Frances McDormand.

Further Reading

Pérez, Emma. *Decolonial Imaginary: Writing Chicanas into History*. Bloomington: Indiana University Press, 1999.

http://eserver.org/bs/28/sandoval.html.

Cheryl Greene

López, George (1963–). The first successful Latino host of a major English-language morning radio show on MEGA 92.3 in Los Angeles, George López is now a comedian and star of a prime-time sitcom family series called the *George López Show*. Born circa 1963 in Los Angeles, California, López began his professional career as a stand-up comedian after working as an assembly-line worker from 1981 to 1983 in the same airplane parts factory as his grandmother.

George López. *Courtesy of Photofest.*

In 2000, López played a part in the film **Bread and Roses.* Despite his radio and acting commitments, López continued stand-up comedy, and in August 2000, Sandra Bullock went to see him at Brea Improv. She wanted to launch a Latino comedy sitcom, and her wish has come to fruition in the *George López Show*, which debuted in 2002. His sitcom is about a middle-class *Chicano family that lives in a California suburb with an abrasive yet strong grandmother, Benny López, who is based on his real grandmother, who raised him. A third-generation Mexican American, López focuses his show on universal themes of family, love, and growing up in the context of a Latino family. In 2002, López also had a role in **Real Women Have Curves.*

One of López's major comedic influences has been the late Freddie *Prinze; he even hired Prinze's former manager, Ron De Blasio. López also participates in various charitable causes and organizations, including the Stop the Violence program directed at youth violence. His career credits include *Ski Patrol* (1989), *Fatal Instinct* (1993), *Right Here, Right Now* (CD, Oglio Records/Warner Brothers, 2000), *The Original Latin Kings of Comedy* (2002), and *Tortilla Heaven* (2003).

Further Reading

Gomez-Gonzales, Cecilia. *Laughing at Life*. Riverside, CA: The Press-Enterprise, 2002.

Horsburg, Susan, and Cynthia Wang. "Pool Sharp." *People*, October 21, 2001, 129.

Navarro, Mireya. "A Life So Sad He Had to Be Funny." *New York Times*, November 27, 2002, sec. E1.

Sachs, Mark. "The Good, the Bad, the Funny." *Los Angeles Times*, January 12, 2003, 36.

Marisol Silva

López, Jennifer (1970–). Jennifer López is one of the more prominent Latina public figures in music and film. She was born in the Bronx to Puerto Rican parents on July 24, 1970. López, who has become a one-woman force in Hollywood and the recording industry, had her first television exposure as a "fly girl" dancer on the Wayans Brothers' hit television variety show *In Living Color*, which aired from 1990 until 1994. After displaying her danc-

Jennifer López. *Courtesy of Photofest.*

ing talents on the popular Fox comedy, López acted in two television series, *Second Chances* (1993–1994) and *Hotel Malibu* (1994). She played a young Mexican mother in her film debut **Mi Familia/My Family* (1995). López rocketed to super-stardom playing the role of Tejana music star *Selena. The highly successful film **Selena* (1997) opened doors in Hollywood for López, and she went on to work on *Antz* (1998), *Out of Sight* (1998), and *Anaconda* (1997). In less than a decade López has worked on eighteen films, including *U-Turn* (1997), *The Wedding Planner* (2001), *Angel Eyes* (2001), *Enough* (2002), and *Maid in Manhattan* (2003). López was the first Latina to make $1 million per movie and is the first woman to have the top-grossing movie and album in the United States simultaneously.

Her success as an actress has led to other opportunities including a rhythm and blues (R&B) recording career. She released her first compact disc, *On the 6*, in 1999. The album charted as high as number eight on the *Billboard* albums chart and had three songs peak at number one on *Billboard* singles charts. She followed her successful recording debut with the number-one platinum album *J. Lo* (2001) and released a remix album, *J to Tha L-O!* (2002), and *This Is Me . . . Then* (2002). López has expanded her business interests to include a line of clothing, a restaurant, and perfume.

López cites her Puerto Rican Bronx, *hip-hop roots as the keys to her success. *On the 6* pays homage to her working-class roots, as the "6" refers to the subway line she took from the Bronx to Manhattan to audition for jobs and to go out on the weekends. López's restaurant and clothing line also reflect her urban Puerto Rican/Nuyorican upbringing.

Despite the diversity that makes up the Jennifer López multimillion dollar corporation, López has received more publicity from her personal relationships than all her business ventures combined. In 1997, Jennifer married waiter Ojani Noa, and although they were reported to be in love and very happy, the marriage only lasted until 1998. Between 1998 and 2001, López kept company with hiphop mogul Sean Combs, a.k.a. "P. Diddy," "Puffy," and "Puff Daddy." The couple made headline news on a regular basis and split up in the midst of a scandal involving gun shots at a nightclub where Combs, López, and their friends were partying. In 2001, López married dancer Chris Judd and divorced him nine months later. In 2002, López became involved with actor Ben Affleck in a highly publicized relationship. They became the Hollywood couple everyone was watching and were in the news so much that the moniker "Bennifer" was coined. They became engaged and continued to make headline news as Affleck presented López with a six-carat rare pink diamond ring, as well as other very expensive gifts of cars and jewelry. Blaming the high level of publicity, the 2003 wedding plans were scrapped and the couple officially split up in January 2004. Within weeks of breaking up with Affleck, López was linked to singer Marc *Anthony, someone she had previously dated in the 1990s. In June 2004,

Anthony flew to the Dominican Republic and obtained a divorce from Dayanara Torres, his wife of four years, and married López five days later in California. With a track record of multiple short-lived marriages and high profile relationships, the Ladbrokes British bookmakers are offering odds on López at ten-to-one that López will marry more often than Elizabeth Taylor.

Further Reading

Sawyer, D. "Primetime Live J.Lo." ABC Primetime Live (transcript). 13 November 2002.

http://www.jenniferlopez.com.

Louis "Pancho" McFarland and Alma Alvarez-Smith

López, Josefina (1969–). María Josefina López was born on March 19, 1969, in Cerritos, San Luís Potosí, México, and grew up in Los Angeles, California, after her family moved to the Boyle Heights area when she was five. Best known within Chicana feminist circles as a playwright whose plays center on the lives of Chicana/Latina women, López gained a nationwide audience in 2002 with the release of the movie **Real Women Have Curves*, adapted from her play of the same title. Another of her plays, *Simply María, or The American Dream* (1992), received a Media Award from the National Council of Christians and Jews for promoting cultural awareness throughout its sensitive depiction of the U.S. **mestizaje*, the cultural hybridity of Latina/o America. Before going to college, she worked in a garment factory owned by her sister, an experience that she used as background for *Real Women Have Curves*. López earned a Master of Arts in screenwriting from the University of California, Los Angeles.

Cordelia Chávez Candelaria

Playwright Josefina López saw her play *Real Women Have Curves* turned into a movie in 2002. *Photo courtesy of Josefina López.*

Trini López. *Courtesy of Photofest.*

López, Trini (1937–). Best remembered as a Mexican-folknik fusion singer, Trinidad López III was born on May 15, 1937, in the Dallas *barrio known as "Little México." López began playing guitar and singing Mexican songs at the age of eleven at family sing-a-longs. At fifteen he was playing both Mexican and American music at local Dallas clubs, later forming a combo and touring the Southwest. In 1960 he moved to Los Angeles and began appearing regularly at PJ's, a Hollywood club where he met Frank Sinatra, who helped López begin recording on the Reprise label. Don Costa also heard López performing at PJ's and helped him with the production of additional original hits especially suited for jukeboxes. Although the folk group Peter, Paul, and Mary had a Top 10 hit with Pete Seeger's "If I Had a Hammer" in 1962, the version recorded by López was his first major success. López's recorded version went to number two in 1963. He was also responsible for the widespread popularity of *"La Bamba" and a popular version of a traditional Latin American song, "Hojita de Limón," given the English title "Lemon Tree." Most of his music was a fusion of Mexican and Anglo-American musics including "This Land Is Your Land" (to a quasi-habanera beat), "Cielito Lindo" (Beautiful Little Sky), "America," "Volare" (with a funky version of "Chiapanecas" [Young Woman from Chiapas]), and "Granada" as a showpiece set to different rhythms. Three other López songs made the Top 40 including, "Kansas City," "Lemon Tree," and "I'm Comin' Home, Cindy." López appeared in a number of films including *Marriage on the Rocks* (1965), *The Dirty Dozen* (1967), and *The Reluctant Heroes* (1971). John Storm Roberts, in *The Latin Tinge*, notes "a noticeable increase in Latin-derived rhythms used by American urban-folk singers during the 1960s, owing in large measure to López's influence, which continued through the 1970s as the Latinization of soft- or California-rock and the fringes of country music."

Further Reading

Roberts, John Storm. *The Latin Tinge: The Impact of Latin American Music on the United States*. 2nd ed. New York: Oxford University Press, 1999.

Peter J. García

López, Yolanda M. (1942–). A distinguished artist in the *Chicano Art Movement, Yolanda M. López has etched a place in art history with her riveting works of art that give voice to a people by deconstructing cultural images, uniting a conflux of women's unspoken histories and Mexican popular traditions and, honoring working-class experiences. Her most recognizable artwork is a seminal piece titled *Portrait of the Artist as the *Virgin of Guadalupe* (oil pastel on paper, 1978). López depicts herself as an exuberant runner with Guadalupe's mantle of stars billowing over her shoulder. It is a powerful, energetic, and an in-control-of-her-life portrait. *Margaret F. Stewart: Our Lady of Guadalupe* (1978) is an image of the artist's mother, who worked at an industrial sewing machine; in the picture she is creating her own mantle of stars. *Victoria F. Franco: Our Lady of Guadalupe* (1978) depicts López's grandmother calmly skinning a snake. In a culture that holds the Virgin of Guadalupe in highest respect and reverence, *Portrait of the Artist as the Virgin of Guadalupe* met with strong reaction when it was introduced. It continues to illicit deep emotion today, as it challenges common images of women in religion and traditional culture.

López's pen-and-ink drawing *Who's the Illegal Alien, Pilgrim?* (1978), a widely recognized artwork, is based on America's conflict with its immigrant population. Celebrating women taking leadership roles and fighting for economic, social, and political justice, *Woman's Work Is Never Done* (1995) is a series of silkscreen prints recognizing women's intellectual and physical work. López's solo exhibit *Cactus Hearts/Barbed Wire Dreams: Media Myths and Mexicans* (1984) is an interdisciplinary media installation that includes *Things I Never Told My Son about Being a Mexican* and the video *When You Think of Mexico*.

Born near the Mexican–U.S. border, López was raised by her mother and maternal grandparents. Her uncle Miguel encouraged her to paint and nurtured her artistic skill by gifting her with art supplies. López has stated she recognized her calling as an artist through her work in the *Chicano Movement for civil rights. Always interested in politics, she developed a succession of experiences by working for the John F. Kennedy Presidential Campaign while she was in high school in the early 1960s. Participating in the Student Non-Violent Coordinating Committee in the mid-1960s, López transferred to San Francisco State University's art department and became involved with the Third World Strike for Ethnic Studies. After dropping out of college, she cofounded Los Siete de La Raza (The Seven of the Race) in San Francisco's Latino community, the Mission District. Working at Los Siete, she designed flyers, posters, and political buttons and worked with the

This famous 1978 painting by San Francisco–based artist Yolanda M. López, *Portrait of the Artist as the Virgin of Guadalupe*, became one of the most popular Latina posters ever printed. *Courtesy of Yolanda M. López.*

editor of its newspaper *!Basta Ya!*, designing the cover art and graphics. A self-proclaimed artistic provocateur, López has retooled popular icons to signify contemporary struggles for social and political justice.

López earned her Bachelor of Arts in painting and drawing at San Diego State University in 1975. In 1978 she was awarded a Master of Fine Arts in visual arts at the University of California, San Diego. Her work has been exhibited in *CARA (Chicano Art: Resistance and Affirmation), "The Decade Show" at the New Museum of Art, and several exhibits at La Galería de la Raza, San Francisco, California. López was awarded the Chicanos in Arts Award by the National Association for Chicana and Chicano Studies in 1993.

Further Reading

http://www.mills.edu/ART/ARTH137/StacyFinal.html.

Alma Alvarez-Smith

Los Lobos. Los Lobos (The Wolves) is a West Coast–based rock/Tex-Mex fusion band, which formed in East L.A. in 1974 with original members bass player Conrad Lozano, guitarist and accordionist David Hidalgo, drummer Louie Pérez, and vocalist, *bajo sexto* player, family and guitarist César Rosas. They began as a homegrown *Chicano band in the family living room, rehearsing and talking music, and were discovered in 1973 by promoter Fernando Mosqueda. Mosqueda booked their first concert at a Veterans of Foreign Wars hall in Compton, California, and although the various members played in funk, hard and soft, and Beatles-like bands, their first public performance included Mexican music. Their style and image was funk, their repertoire was limited, and none of them spoke Spanish fluently. Despite audience expectations, they succeeded and built up a strong L.A. following. In 1976, Los Lobos released an album titled *Sí Se Puede!* (It Can Be Done) for the United

Farm Workers, followed by *Just Another Band from East L.A.* released in 1978; works that were later released in CD format in 1994 and 2000 respectively. During the next eight years, their Mexican musical repertoire grew to 150 songs, and they began playing concerts in hundreds of venues. They widened horizons yet again, including a mix of *Tejano and original songs. Los Lobos are eclectic in their musical interests, backgrounds, and collective tastes, which include James Brown, Aretha Franklin, the Rolling Stones, the Beatles, Led Zeppelin, Flaco *Jiménez, Clifton Chenier, Ritchie *Valens, Doug Sahm, Albert Collins, and Fairport Convention.

By the late 1970s, Los Lobos had recast themselves as a rock band, drawing more fans and increased record sales. They recorded the sound track for the 1987 movie **La Bamba*, including 1950s hits like "Come On, Let's Go" and "That's My Little Suzie." The sound track featured Marshall Crenshaw, Carlos *Santana, and Stray Cats' Brian Setzer and became a number-one hit, along with the title song. Los Lobos received considerable attention after winning a *Rolling Stone* poll award. The full-length LP *How Will the Wolf Survive* (1984) did well and included the title song. Rosas and Hidalgo sessioned on Ry Cooder's sound track music for *Alamo Bay* (1995), and Hidalgo on Elvis Costello's *King of America* (1986). Los Lobos backed Paul Simon on "All Around the World" on his LP *Graceland* (1986), toured the United Kingdom in early 1987, and recorded the album *By the Light of the Moon* (1987), produced by T-Bone Burnett. In the late 1980s, they recorded *La Pistola y el Corazón* (The Pistol and the Heart, 1988) and another rock album. *La Pistola y el Corazon*, an acoustic album of purely Mexican folk music, covers a range of traditional performing styles of **sones*, *boleros, and **rancheras*. During the 1990s, their two innovative albums included *Kiko* (1992) and *Colossal Head* (1996).

Their success has been due to their musical innovation and refusal to become predictable. Their 1980s hits are folk or country rock songs. Their 1990s hits on *Colossal Head* are punk tunes like "Más y más" (More and More) and also late 1960s blues. They also continue to compose, record, and perform songs that return them to their 1980s folk rock and country rock days.

Further Reading

Reyes, David, and Tom Waldman. *Land of a Thousand Dances: Chicano Rock 'n' Roll from Southern California*. Albuquerque: University of New Mexico Press, 1998.

Tatum, Charles M. *Chicano Popular Culture: Que Hable el Pueblo*. Tucson: University of Arizona Press, 2001.

Peter J. García

Los Pastores. *See Pastores, Los.*

Los Tigres del Norte. Los Tigres del Norte is by far the most popular, prolific, and longest lasting of the modern *norteño* bands (the regional band style of northern México) and is responsible for popularizing *norteño* music internationally. The band has recorded more than 500 songs on fifty-five albums, appeared in more than twenty movies, and sold more than 32 million records. Their songs present the Mexican experience from both the North and South sides of the U.S.-México border.

Living on a ranch in the small town of Rosa Morada, Sinaloa, the Hernández brothers learned Mexican **canciones* (songs) by listening to their maternal grandfather Ascención Angulo singing to them of life on the ranch. Following an accident their father suffered in 1968, Jorge Hernández (accordion and lead singer), at age fourteen the eldest of the brothers, believed that the boys could help support the family by playing music. Together with brothers Raul, Eduardo (accordion and guitar), and Hernán (vocals and bass) and cousin Oscar Lara (drums), they formed a band and called themselves the "Little Tigers." *Norteño* bands had to travel around extensively to make enough money, and after several trips to northern México, the locals dubbed the group Los Tigres del Norte. Some fans claim they were given this name in San Jose, California.

In 1968 while playing for a *diez y seis de septiembre* (the Mexican Independence day of September 16) dance in Mexicali, they were hired to play a gig in San Jose, California. Finding more work there than in México, they decided to stay and eventually became U.S. residents, but they have never lost their *mexicanidad* (Mexicanness). Soon they were given a contract by Arturo Walker to record on his Discos Fama label. Walker mentored them, providing new instruments and music lessons. They recorded on this label until 1980 when they moved to the Fonovisa Records label, receiving nearly a dozen Grammy nominations, a Grammy for Best Album in 1988 for *Gracias America Sin Fronteras* (Thanks America without Borders), a Latin Grammy in 2000, and a Lifetime Achievement Award from *Primo Los Nuestro*.

Los Tigres have toured with the United Service Organizations (USO) in Japan (1999), Germany, and Italy (2000) and have toured in Spain and throughout the United States and Latin America.

Los Tigres is best known for their recordings of **corridos* (story songs) and *polcas* (polkas), though they also play *cumbias, *boleros, *valses* (waltzes), and even an occasional rock song. The *corridos* tell stories of life on both sides of the border, the struggles of Mexicanos (Mexicans), immigrants, politicians, heroes, and outlaws. Los Tigres soon became the spokes group for Mexicans living in the United States (both *Chicanos and illegals) as well as for Mexicans who looked to the United States as a place to better their way of life. Their 1976 song "Vivan los Mojados" (Long Live the Wetbacks) speculates about what would happen to the American crops if all of the immigrants were sent back to México.

More recent and controversial are the **narcocorridos* (drug economy–related songs) that tell of drug smuggling, shootouts between and among the traffickers and the *police, betrayals and executions. An example of the latter would be the 1972 hit "Contrabando y Traición" (Contraband and Betrayal), the story of a Mexican man and a Chicana from Texas who smuggle marijuana from Tijuana to Los Angeles. After selling the marijuana the man tells her he wants to take his share of the money and visit his girlfriend in San Francisco. However, she has fallen in love with him and is unwilling to share him with another woman, so she shoots him in a dark alley in Hollywood and disappears with all of the money.

After the success of "Contrabando," the group began touring, including trips back to México. However, soon *narcocorridos* became quite controversial and were criticized by both the Catholic Church and México's National Action Party. In 1989, they put out *Corridos Prohibidos* (Prohibited Corridos), an entire album about drug smuggling that caused an uproar in México and the U.S. immigrant community. Los Tigres soon tried to distance themselves from this type of song, returning more to cumbias and love songs. Songs such as "Pedro y Pablo," "El otro México" (The Other México), and "Los hijos de Hernández" (The Sons of Hernández) are all philosophical songs dealing with the yearning of Mexicans to return home because of love lost through separation, and were influenced by their producer Enrique Franco, who was hired about 1980. One could trace the history of Mexican migration by studying the texts of Los Tigres songs from the 1970s to the present.

Los Tigres del Norte's historical significance to Chicana/o and Mexican people occurred in 1988 when they became the first *norteño* band of undocumented immigrants to receive a Grammy, which was awarded for Best Regional Mexican American Recording for their album *Gracias America Sin Fronteras* (Thanks America without Borders).

The music style of Los Tigres is based on the older, traditional *norteño* music with a heavy emphasis on the accordion. Although the older style would also include saxophones, string bass, rhythm guitar, *bajo sexto* (harmony guitar), and drum set, Los Tigres have changed the instrumentation to emphasize the amplified sound of late-twentieth-century country and rock. Some credit Arturo Walker with suggesting that they change to amplified, electric instruments. Today they present spectacular audio and visual concerts with various stage sets throughout the United States and México. Often traveling with an entourage of more than a half dozen semitrailers, they have even been honored with a "national" day (June 17) in the United States and have also played at such important locations as the Festival Internacional Cervantino de Guanajuato.

Today four of the original band members still play in the group. When brother Raul left the band, the youngest Hernández, Luis joined. Their friend Lupe Olivo had previously joined the band to play sax.

In 2002 they formed the Los Tigres del Norte Foundation in California to support worthy nonprofit, charitable organizations in an effort to further the appreciation and understanding of Latino music, culture, and history through education and community outreach programs.

Further Reading

Saldivar, José David. *Border Matters: Remapping American Cultural Studies.* Berkeley: University of California Press, 1997.

J. Richard Haefer

Lowriders. Lowriding is a *Chicano pop culture phenomenon that has spread to other Latina/o groups as well as to enthusiasts of other American cultures and also to other nations around the world. Combining the technology and mechanics of the mainstream automobile industry with the urban aesthetics of the *barrios and borderlands, lowriders are vehicles—mostly cars—that have been customized with special features that result in distinctive driving functions and unique exterior appearance. The name "lowrider" did not enter popular usage until the 1960s, and it comes from the most common custom feature, the physical dropping of the car's chassis and fenders to ride lower and closer to the road than standard vehicles. Many lowriders also are outfitted with hydraulic springs that enable the car to hop and lift in often amazing cruising performances.

The visible cosmetics of lowriders—also known familiarly as *carruchitas* (literally meaning "dilapidated little carts")—vary widely, but most share a tendency to preserve a classic retro style that reflects the car's actual vintage year of manufacture. Another artistically common trait is the use of cultural symbols on the painted exterior, such as representations of the *Virgin of Guadalupe, of pre-Columbian images like *Aztlán and mestizo figures, of the United Farmworkers Union and the Mexican flags, César *Chávez references, and countless others, including special lighting panels. An alternative to the elaborately detailed imagery is a paint job that includes a display of intricate lines and geometric designs, often in a complementary or contrasting combination of colors. The interior styles usually reflect the outer theme and frequently include fringe trims, sequin motifs, tufting, polychrome tinted windows and mirrors, and dimmer lights. As the lowriding fad has spread to other cultures and countries (primarily throughout the Americas, Japan, and parts of Europe), the cosmetics and artwork have expanded to accommodate the respective aesthetics of each society.

Most cultural historians place the origins of this extremely popular grassroots practice in the first half of the twentieth century in the U.S. Southwest, principally Southern California, where two native traditions of America intertwined: the historic Mexican/Chicano culture(s) interwoven with North American automobile culture. These observers trace its emergence to Mexican American barrios (i.e., neighborhoods) and the intertwining of ethnicity, economy, and technology led to the repair of used vehicles to save money. The repairs usually were made from a variety of salvaged parts from other cars and junkyards. Lowriding itself—the low and slow cruising to show off the hip

The Chevy Impala is a favorite of lowriders. *Courtesy of William Calvo, Arizona State University.*

coolness of both the vehicle and the driver and his passengers—echoes the traditional custom of public promenade in the evenings and Sundays that was, and often still is, practiced by Spaniards and Latin Americans, and may have been part of pre-Columbian societies as well. One aspect of the promenade that is the *paseo*, or walk, in which unmarried young people stroll around the *zócalo* (central plaza) in a ritual courtship exercise with girls and young women moving in one direction while boys and young men walk in the other, exchanging significant glances. Urban legend reported in *Lowrider Magazine* suggests that cruising simply continues the courtship and *paseo* tradition practiced in what was once all New Spain then México until the *Treaty of Guadalupe Hidalgo turned over the vast Southwest to the United States.

Some popular culture specialists associate the lowriders' emergence with the 1930s' and 1940s' *zoot suit teenage fad and the main street cruising of *pachucos (i.e., Mexican American zoot suiters) in meticulously restored cars lowered for the optimal visibility of both onlookers and dressed up drivers and passengers. The zoot suit, an enormously oversized jacket over baggy pants with pegged legs, often topped with a fedora, was popularized by blacks in Harlem, New York. Young Mexican Americans called them drapes, and often dropped the fancy fedora altogether. The zoot suit craze spread across the country throughout the late 1930s, popularized by movie stars like Clark Gable. Pachuco customizers and other hot rodders of the period tended to prefer looks, style, and aesthetic distinctiveness, just as in their dress fashion. These cars not only looked clean, but they were also a way of showing defiance against the mainstream culture. Young pachucos cruising in these beauties on Whittier Boulevard, the main strip in East Los Angeles, or boulevards throughout the Southwest, had developed their own style of clothing and hair, which caused concern among mainstream society about the refusal of these young people to assimilate.

The post–World War II economy boom led to vehicles that were customized according to interests, whether capacity, size, speed, interior comfort, or appearance. Talented owners and mechanics with a flair for art and creative style began customizing their salvaged vehicles with distinctive features. Downtown city streets from Española, New Mexico, and El Paso, Texas, to Tucson, Arizona, and East Los Angeles, California, served as backdrops for lowriders by the 1950s and 1960s. Most of the cars cruising the barrios were secondhand, and Chevrolets, less expensive and easier to repair, as well as more stylish compared to practical Fords, became the cars of choice.

Lowriders are usually grouped into several categories for the sake of discussion as well as competition. "Bombas" (bombs) or "oldies" are cars from the 1930s or 1940s, and these typically do not have hop hydraulics. "Clas-

Lowriders are just as meticulous about the interior of the car as they are the exterior. *Courtesy of William Calvo, Arizona State University.*

sics" are cars from the 1950s and 1960s, with the Chevy Impala being a favorite. "Trocas" are trucks and minivans and old (usually 1940s and 1950s) pickup trucks.

The biggest change in the lowriding world has been the introduction of hydraulics. With the emergence of technology, lowriders can be coaxed into being raised and lowered through the use of remote control devices, in addition to making the car hop up, down, and sideways. "Hops" is the term used to include a variety of classics that are mechanically modified to enable a hopping activity often referred to as "jumping," "hopping," "dancing," "clowning," and "switching." The average height a car can hop is fifteen to twenty inches, although the record for a car hop is sixty-four inches and the record for a truck hop is seventy-two inches.

Today, the term lowrider is also used to encompass an entire culture that includes the car, the car owner, the subculture, and clubs associated with the style. Although originally linked to pachucos and gangs, today's lowriders (the owners) are so actively engaged in the subculture of car modifications and competitions that they do not have time to be involved with gangs and ganglike activity. The level of involvement in the care and maintenance of the lowriding cars is extensive and often expands to include spouses and family members. In addition, involvement with other individuals with like interests naturally has evolved into clubs and networking groups to share ideas and support.

Lowrider culture continues to be promoted to a mass readership through its widely circulated magazines. From *Lowrider Magazine*, which was launched in California's Mexican American barrios in the 1970s and continues thriving to this day on magazine racks virtually everywhere, to its offspring publication *Arte del Varrio* of the late 1970s and 1980s (and its own later iterations as *Lowrider Arte*), Latinos and a much more inclusive public indulge their love affair with the automobile.

Further Reading

Calvo, William. *Lowriders: Storytellers of the Chicano Experience*. Master's thesis, Arizona State University, 2003.

Padilla, Carmella et al. *Low 'n slow: Lowriding in New Mexico*. Santa Fe: Museum of New Mexico Press, 1999.

Tatum, Charles M. *Chicano Popular Culture: Que Hable el Pueblo*. Tucson: University of Arizona Press, 2001.

Alma Alvarez-Smith and Cordelia Chávez Candelaria

Luis Miguel. *See* Miguel, Luis.

LULAC. The League of United Latin American Citizens (LULAC) is one of the oldest and largest organizations giving voice to Latinos in the United States. Formed through the merger of three Mexican American civic organizations, LULAC became the impetus for the Mexican American Legal Defense and Education Fund (*MALDEF) and the *American G.I. Forum, two resource and advocacy groups who, in addition to LULAC, have made tremendous advances for the Latino community over the years. LULAC operates on the mission of advancing the economic condition, educational attainment, political influence, health, and civil rights of the Latino population in the United States.

In 1927, three organizations with similar principles were in existence in the state of Texas: the Knights of America, the Order of the Sons of America, and the League of Latin American Citizens. Concerned that multiple organizations working toward the same goals would cause possible division and weakness, Ben Garza, leader of the Order of the Sons of America, invited the other two organizations to join forces. It took two long years and much discussion and negotiating, but the three groups eventually came to an agreement and merged into one organization called the League of United Latin American Citizens. Garza was elected the first chairperson of the newly merged group and would later become the first president general of LULAC.

In the 1920s and 1930s, there were other Latino organizations in existence that wanted to claim back the Mexican land that was lost to the United States, while others refused to recognize the authority of the Anglos. Mexican Americans gathering in large numbers were considered suspicious and could risk facing charges of communism. Whereas many Latino organizations linked their members back to México or their indigenous culture, LULAC was modeled after civic organizations in the United States and urged their membership to stop looking back nostalgically at México and claim their rights as U.S. citizens. LULAC professed a philosophy that would be loyal to the constitution and government of the United States, and members would obey the laws of the country. Membership to LULAC was restricted to native-born or naturalized citizens of Latin extraction, having reached eighteen years of age; English was declared the official language of LULAC; the American flag was claimed as the official flag of the organization; and the official song became "America the Beautiful." Many in the Latino community were insulted by LULAC's embracing of the Anglo society and considered LULAC members turncoats (*vendidos*). LULAC, on the other hand, was determined to avoid suspicions of un-American activities so they could be successful in the long term.

Organizing Mexican Americans during this period was difficult and often dangerous work. LULAC members were harassed by Anglos who felt Mexicans should not pursue an education; some were intimidated by the Anglo establishment and hounded out of their jobs for joining the organization. At the same time, the membership restrictions made it difficult to impossible for some people to join, while others were afraid to join an organization that was confronting authority. Despite the challenges, LULAC has survived for the past seventy years and continues to serve the Latino community to ensure future generations enjoy their constitutional rights as citizens of the United States.

Today, LULAC represents Hispanics in the United States, Puerto Rico, and Guam and has expanded its membership to include anyone of Hispanic origin who is a legal resident of the United States or its territorial areas. LULAC continues to fight discrimination, poverty, educational inequalities, *immigration issues, language, and health issues and is influential in national policymaking.

LULAC's national office is in Washington, D.C., and it has councils throughout the United States.

Further Reading

Márquez, Benjamin. *LULAC: The Evolution of a Mexican American Political Organization*. Austin: University of Texas Press, 1993.
http://www.lulac.org.

Alma Alvarez-Smith

Luminarias. Directed by José *Valenzuela and produced by Sal López, this independent film drew financial support from the Latino community. Originally a stage production by Los Angeles's Latino Theater Company, the film premiered in May 2000.

Evelina *Fernández wrote the screenplay and stars in the romantic comedy about four friends from East Los Angeles. The women, Andrea (Fernández), Sofía (Marta DuBois), Irene (Dyana Ortelli), and Lilly (Ángela Moya), meet weekly at Luminarias, a nightclub, where they share in each other's lives. Each of the women faces and overcomes prejudice—often her own—to find love and fulfillment.

The cast of *Luminarias* portrays the Chicana characters with unusual depth and humanity; they are presented as vulnerable, funny, flawed, strong, and successful. In addition, they are professional, mature Chicanas whose friendship provides the support to overcome life's trials and tribulations. *Luminarias* confronts issues of adultery, spousal abuse, racism, classism, cross-cultural dating, identity, and sexuality without losing its sense of humor. *Luminarias* has been compared to the African American film *Waiting to Exhale*. The film, through grassroots support in the Latino community, has received positive attention and a steady audience.

Further Reading

Terry-Azios, Diana. "Film." *Hispanic*, September 30, 1999, 96.
Van Gelder, Lawrence. "Luminarias." *New York Times*, September 6, 2000, sec. E20.
http://www.luminarias.net.

Leonora Anzaldúa Burke